CAREERS AND OPPORTUNITIES AT THE ROMAN CURIA, 1300–1500

EUROPA SACRA

RELIGION, SOCIETY, AND IDENTITY

VOLUME 29

*Editorial Board under the auspices of Monash University*

*General Editor*
Carolyn James, *Monash University*

*Editorial Board*
Megan Cassidy-Welch, *Australian Catholic University*
David Garrioch, *Monash University*
Peter Howard, *Australian Catholic University*
Thomas Izbicki, *Rutgers, The State University of New Jersey*
Constant J. Mews, *Monash University*
M. Michele Mulchahey, *Pontifical Institute of Mediaeval Studies*
Adriano Prosperi, *Scuola Normale di Pisa*

# Careers and Opportunities at the Roman Curia, 1300–1500

*A Socio-Economic History of Papal Administration*

BRIGIDE SCHWARZ

*Translated and Edited by*
WOLFGANG P. MÜLLER

BREPOLS

© 2024, Brepols Publishers n.v., Turnhout, Belgium.

All rights reserved. No part of this publication may
be reproduced, stored in a retrieval system, or
transmitted, in any form or by any means, electronic,
mechanical, photocopying, recording, or otherwise
without the prior permission of the publisher.

D/2024/0095/229
ISBN 978-2-503-59538-2
eISBN 978-2-503-59539-9
DOI 10.1484/M.ES-EB.5.124334
ISSN 2030-3068
eISSN 2406-5838

Printed in the EU on acid-free paper.

# Table of Contents

| | |
|---|---|
| List of Illustrations | 7 |
| List of Translated Essays | 11 |
| Editor's Acknowledgments | 15 |
| Editor's Introduction | 17 |

### Part I
### Ecclesiastical Benefices

| | |
|---|---|
| **Chapter 1. The Roman Curia and the Late Medieval Benefice Market** | 27 |
| **Chapter 2. Patronage and Clientele in the Late Medieval Church. The Example of Nicholas of Cusa** | 49 |
| **Chapter 3. A 'Rope Team' of Clerics from Hanover in the Late Middle Ages** | 67 |
| **Chapter 4. On Nanker, Bishop of Kraków (1320–1326) and Wrocław (1326–1341)** | 83 |
| Nanker's Career until His Appointment as Bishop of Kraków in 1320 | 84 |
| Nanker and Pope John XXII | 88 |
| **Chapter 5. The Vatican Archives and Their Uses for Regional Historians. The Example of Late Medieval Saxony** | 117 |
| The Source Material of the Vatican Archives | 117 |
| Suggestions for the History of Saxony | 120 |
| The 1399 Exemption of the Meissen Bishopric | 141 |

6 TABLE OF CONTENTS

## Part II
### Curial Offices

**Chapter 6. The Venality of Offices. An Institution from the Period of Absolutism and Its Medieval Roots**  157

**Chapter 7. The Roman Curia from the Great Schism to the Reform Councils (1378–1447)**  177

**Chapter 8. On Behalf of the Pope. The Papal *cursores* from 1200 to about 1470**  201

**Chapter 9. Leon Battista Alberti's Career in the Papal Chancery**  223
An Unwelcome Incident in the Papal Chancery, 1432/1433  223
State of Research and Sources  233
Leon Battista Alberti as Secretary of the Regent in the Chancery, Blasius de Molino  237
As Abbreviator  239
As Chancery Scribe (and Papal Household Member)  248
As Reader in the *Audientia litterarum contradictarum*  254
Final Considerations  262

**Chapter 10. Position and Rank of the (Vice-)Chancellor at the Curia**  263
Remarks on the Contribution of Studies in Diplomatic to the Cultural History of Europe  276

**Bibliography**  283

**General Index**  323

# List of Illustrations

## Figures

| | | |
|---|---|---|
| Figure 5.1. | Regional Distribution of Petitions to Pope Eugene IV from the German Empire (1431–1447). | 122 |
| Figure 5.2. | Number of Petitions from the German Empire (Pontifical Years of Eugene IV, 1431–1447). | 134 |
| Figure 5.3. | Distribution of Petitions from East German Bishoprics (Pontifical Years of Eugene IV, 1431–1447). | 134 |
| Figure 5.4. | Petitions from the German Empire for Higher and Lesser Benefices (Pontifical Years of Eugene IV, 1431–1447). | 135 |
| Figure 5.5. | Distribution of Petitions for (New) Provisions from East German Bishoprics (Pontifical Years of Eugene IV, 1431–1447). | 135 |
| Figure 5.6. | Petitions from the German Empire for (New) Provisions, Licenses, and Dispensations (Pontifical Years of Eugene IV, 1431–1447). | 136 |
| Figure 5.7. | Petitions for Licenses and Dispensations from East German Bishoprics (Pontifical Years of Eugene IV, 1431–1447). | 136 |
| Figure 8.1. | The Papal Couriers, *c.* 1306. | 206 |

## Map

| | | |
|---|---|---|
| Map 0.1. | Germany c. 1500. | 13 |

## Tables

| | | |
|---|---|---|
| Table 4.1. | Clerics from Kraków in the Service of Władysław Łokietek. | 103 |
| Table 5.1. | The Benefices of Two Learned Counsellors under Elector Frederick the Gentle. | 125 |
| Table 5.2. | The Bishops of Meissen, *c.* 1300–1476. | 149 |
| Table 10.1(a). | The Apostolic Vice-Chancellor in the Later Middle Ages. His Residence. | 268 |
| Table 10.2. | Synopsis of the Seating at General Councils (Thirteenth Century). | 273 |

| | | |
|---|---|---|
| Table 10.3. | The Chancery in the Ceremonial Handbooks. | 274 |
| Table 10.4. | Table Arrangements at Receptions, *c.* 1378–1415. | 275 |
| Table 10.1(b). | The Apostolic Vice-Chancellor in the Later Middle Ages. His Competencies. | 280 |

Plate 01. Brigide Schwarz. Photo (2012) courtesy of Ernst Haiger.

# List of Translated Essays

### 1

'Römische Kurie und Pfründenmarkt im Spätmittelalter', *Zeitschrift für historische Forschung*, 20 (1993), 129–52. Published with permission of Duncker & Humblot GmbH, Berlin.

### 2

'Patronage und Klientel in der spätmittelalterlichen Kirche', *Quellen und Forschungen aus italienischen Archiven und Bibliotheken*, 68 (1988), 284–310.

### 3

'Eine "Seilschaft" von Klerikern aus Hannover im Spätmittelalter', in *Quellen und Forschungen aus italienischen Archiven und Bibliotheken*, 81 (2001), 256–77.

### 4

'Untersuchungen zur Geschichte Nankers, 1320–1326 Bischof von Krakau, 1326–1341 Bischof von Breslau', in *Scientia Veritatis. Festschrift für Hubert Mordek zum 65. Geburtstag*, ed. by Oliver Münsch and Thomas Zotz (Ostfildern: Thorbecke, 2004), pp. 373–99.

### 5

'Vom Nutzen des vatikanischen Archivmaterials für die Landesgeschichte, dargestellt an sächsischen Beispielen', in *Diplomatische Forschungen in Mitteldeutschland*, ed. by Tom Graber (Leipzig: Universitätsverlag, 2005), pp. 197–235.

### 6

'Ämterkäuflichkeit, eine Institution des Absolutismus und ihre mittelalterlichen Wurzeln', in *Staat und Gesellschaft in Mittelalter und Früher Neuzeit. Gedenkschrift für Joachim Leuschner*, ed. by Katharina Colberg, Hans-Heinrich Nolte, and Herbert Obenaus (Göttingen: Vandenhoeck & Ruprecht, 1983), pp. 176–96.

## LIST OF TRANSLATED ESSAYS

### 7

'Die römische Kurie im Zeitalter des Schismas und der Reformkonzilien', in *Institutionen und Geschichte. Theoretische Aspekte und mittelalterliche Befunde*, ed. by Gert Melville (Cologne: Böhlau, 1992), pp. 231–58.

### 8

'Im Auftrag des Papstes. Die päpstlichen Kursoren von ca. 1200 bis 1470', in *Päpste, Pilger, Pönitentiarie. Festschrift für Ludwig Schmugge zum 65. Geburtstag*, ed. by Andreas Meyer, Constanze Rendtel, and Maria Wittmer-Butsch (Tübingen; Niemeyer, 2004), pp. 49–71. Published with permission of De Gruyter, Berlin.

### 9

'Die Karriere Leon Battista Albertis in der päpstlichen Kanzlei', *Quellen und Forschungen aus italienischen Archiven und Bibliotheken*, 93 (2013), 49–103. Published with permission of De Gruyter, Berlin.

### 10

'Rolle und Rang des (Vize)-Kanzlers an der Kurie', in *Papstgeschichte im digitalen Zeitalter*, ed. by Klaus Herbers and Viktoria Trenkle (Cologne: Böhlau, 2018), pp. 171–90.

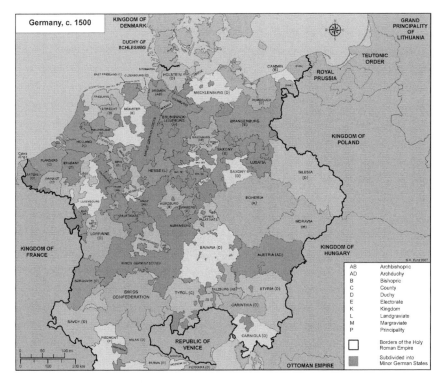

Map 0.1. Germany c. 1500. Original cartography: Joachim Robert Moeschl. Editor and Compiler: Andreas Kunz, IEG Maps, Mainz, 2007. Revised for the updated edition of German History in Documents and Images by Gabriel Moss, 2021. Copyrights: IEG/A. Kunz/GHI/Gabriel Moss. License: CC BY-NC 4.0 International.

# Editor's Acknowledgments

In May 2018, I met Brigide Schwarz at the German Historical Institute in Rome. Well-aware that I was in the presence of one of the leading experts in the history of the late medieval papacy whose work remained almost unknown outside German-speaking circles, I told her about my plan to publish some of her studies on the papal court, or Roman Curia, in English translation. I kept asking if she was willing to send me about a dozen of her favourite essays, until she complied in an email of September 2018. Ten of the twelve titles she suggested to me at the time are included in the present volume. The two I have omitted owe their exclusion to the tight focus of the material assembled here, which concentrates on the Curia as a market-place for lucrative careers and monetary investments between 1300 and 1500.[1]

Shortly thereafter, the project transformed into a testament to her scholarship when Dr Schwarz died from an accident on 13 February 2019. I still remember our first encounter at Bad Homburg near Frankfurt in February 1986, where she spent considerable time walking with me through the local parks, a young student working on his Master's Degree in the company of a German Professor from the University of Hanover (1983–1998). From the start, I was struck by her notable scholarly rigor and massive archival expertise. Just as importantly, though, she brought in the way of a social historian the excitement of reading between the lines to everything.

Proof is found in her 1972 monograph, 'The Organization of Scribal Corporations at the Curia from Their Origins to the Mid-Fifteenth Century' (in German). Despite its unspectacular title, the book provides a groundbreaking analysis of late medieval papal administration from the socio-historical perspective. Previous approaches, marked above all by a sense of moral decadence or anachronistic depiction of the Apostolic Curia as a bureaucratic machine, were replaced in 1972 by a painstaking account of the mechanisms feeding institutional development. As Dr Schwarz was among the earliest to point out, popes and curial officials

---

1 The first, 'Ein "Schülerulk" mit Folgen', concentrates on an episode of local history from Hildesheim which predates the year 1300. The second, of exceptional length and entitled 'Die Exemtion des Bistums Meißen 1399', addresses the supposed papal exemption of Meissen bishopric in 1399. A convenient summary is offered in Essay 5 below, pp. 141–54.

mainly responded to outside demand for their services and sought to gain from it through constant financial and fiscal innovation, usually in competition with one another. Rather than figuring as the monarchical structure of older research, the Curia emerged from her inquiry as an entity calling for description in economic and entrepreneurial terms, an investigation she further pursued in the ten essays translated below.

While preparing the texts for publication, I received invaluable help from Sally Gordon, a Fordham history graduate student and retired Managing Director at BlackRock Inc., whose deep knowledge of modern capital markets gave us much to ponder and compare over the years. She was instrumental in improving the English of the translated essays and alerted me to overly dense passages in need of gentle paraphrasing. I also enjoyed the persistent encouragement of Ernst Haiger (Berlin and Mülheim/ Ruhr), the *Lebensgefährte* of the late Dr Schwarz. I am very grateful to them. In addition, Fordham University generously provided grants from the Academic Pursuits Fund and the Faculty Research Expense Program to cover part of the publication expenses.

# Editor's Introduction

Scholars agree that the rule of Pope Boniface VIII (1294–1303) marked an important turning point in the history of the Western Church. The preceding centuries had witnessed the rise of a papal monarchy. Subsequently, however, the papacy met with repeated challenges, including the move of the papal court from Italy to Avignon (in 1309), as well as the eventual appearance of two and (from 1409) three popes with their respective administrations and areas of 'obedience'.[1] Once this period of the 'Great Schism' ended with the election of Martin V (1417–1431) as the sole remaining pope, a new obstacle to unified governance advanced in the form of 'Conciliarism', which maintained that ultimate authority resided with a General Council of churchmen rather than the pope alone. From the Council of Constance (1414–1418) to that of Basel (1431–1449), ideals of representative church government and 'Reform' competed with papal 'plenitude of power'.[2] Although the latter prevailed again from Nicholas V (1447–1455), victory came at a high price because lay rulers had used the conflict to increase their own control. To secure recognition against the conciliar threat, Pope Eugene IV (1431–1447) had signed numerous 'concordats' with them, abandoning the right of appointment to many ecclesiastical offices for good. The so-called 'territorialization' of churches at the expense of a unified, 'catholic' Church was long underway when the Protestant Reformation began in 1517.[3]

In 1300, Boniface VIII became the first pope to stage a 'jubilee'. In greater numbers than ever before, pilgrims from all over Latin Christendom flocked to Rome to receive his special blessings. As in other years, however, many arrived for mundane rather than devotional purposes. They were in today's language the operators, careerists, and opportunists, who came inspired by the prospect of lucrative deals and employment. The papal court, known as the Roman Curia, offered them something hard to find elsewhere, access to positions that promised regular and life-long pay. In the service of the Church, people could hope to obtain income as absentees, leaving the actual workload to hired substitutes, akin to tenure with permanent leave in modern terms. Late medieval contemporaries

---

1 Rollo-Koster, *Avignon and its Papacy, 1309–1417.*
2 Stump, *The Reforms of the Council of Constance.*
3 Thomson, *Popes and Princes, 1417–1517.*

were well-aware that holders of ecclesiastical benefices and certain curial officials enjoyed privileges of this kind. Roughly four-fifth of the surviving clerical correspondence speak about nothing else.[4]

Between 1300 and 1500, the period under scrutiny in the present volume, the total of applicants for tenured positions increasingly exceeded the available openings, creating market conditions at the Curia which resemble Wall Street nowadays. On occasion, the demand and exchange of benefices and curial offices formed 'bubbles' with impending signs of 'collapse'.[5] Transaction volumes grew feverish to the point where the traded good was reduced to an abstract value and used as an 'asset' for chiefly speculative ends.[6] To be sure, the Roman, or more precisely Apostolic, Curia provided a trading floor that was not very stable, accompanying the pope on travels, from Rome into exile, and even splitting into two or three papal courts during the Great Schism of the Western Church between 1378 and 1415. Its function as a market-place was retained, though, if limited geographically to the respective areas of loyalty, or 'obediences'.[7]

Once again in line with Wall Street, the exchange located at the late medieval Roman Curia was understood as lawful pending judicial proof to the contrary.[8] Benefices and curial offices were 're-packaged' by brokering officials in 'creative' fashion, 'bundled', or 'swapped', in a process that had transactions terminate in a proliferating set of disclaimers, expressed in legalese and anticipating the currently familiar 'small print'.[9] Official standards insisted that the deals were 'canonical', satisfying the rules that church, or canon, law had stipulated. Before long, this implied that lawyers and legal practitioners became indispensable as ecclesiastical administrators and had an edge in securing tenured positions for themselves.[10] Their expertise featured an enormous array of definitions, technical language, and regulations which are indispensable knowledge for historians of the curial market-place. What follows, therefore, is a brief foray into the relevant concepts of 'benefice' and 'office', as well as a summary of the principal tools facilitating their acquisition and management.

---

4 See below, Essay 5, p. 118 n. 3; Zutshi, 'The Papal Chancery', pp. 12–13. By 1400, the Roman Rota functioned as the highest court for litigation over benefices; cf. Salonen, *Papal Justice in the Late Middle Ages.*

5 Discussed above all in Essay 1, pp. 27–48 below. There were strong regional variations; cf. Essay 3, pp. 77-78; Essay 5, pp. 118–19, 132–39; Essay 7, pp. 192–93 below.

6 Especially 'the Italian market seems to have been ... far more capitalized than the German one, so that positions there were traded like monetary assets'; Essay 1 below, p. 30 n. 21.

7 Essay 7 below dwells on the fractured market conditions during the Schism and in the subsequent conciliar period (1378–1447), pp. 177–99; see also Essay 5, pp. 132–33.

8 Contrary to a 'black market'; cf. Essay 1, pp. 34–35 below.

9 Primarily recognizable in the *non obstantibus*-clauses of papal letters; cf. Essay 1 below, pp. 32–34; Essay 4, p. 94 n. 60, p. 97 n. 67.

10 University graduates enjoyed preferment by law; jurists even more so in practice; see Essay 1, p. 31 nn. 24–25; Essay 3, pp. 74–77; Essay 5, pp. 120, 123 nn. 25–26 below.

## Ecclesiastical Benefices and Curial Offices

A consistent law of benefices rapidly took shape with the rise of canonical jurisprudence from the mid-twelfth century onward. While remaining property of the Church all along, benefices were intended for the material sustenance of clerics throughout their lives and could not be sold without incurring the criminal charge of simony. The interested clergy consisted not only of those in the sacred orders of sub-deacon, deacon, priest, and bishop; they also comprised the 'minor ranks' of university students, for instance, and several others who did not fall under the requirement of celibacy.[11] Holders had to be male and unmarried, indicating that sooner or later they were supposed to handle the sacraments or seek priestly ordination. Women were excluded from access, as much as monks and regular clerics vowed to the rule of personal poverty. Support for them had to derive from the collective funds of their religious community.[12]

Adding complexity to the picture, certain regular clergy, like canons, lived in groups under a religious rule but retained the right to individual income, which rendered them eligible for benefices as well. They were members of cathedral or collegiate 'chapters', permitted to hold ecclesiastical positions that could be 'with cure', that is, involving pastoral obligations, or 'without', as in, sinecure.[13] Canons formed guild-like organisations electing their own leaders (provosts or deans, for example) and functionaries (treasurers, etc.), whose charges were usually referred to as 'dignities'. Their benefices figured as 'minor', in opposition to the 'higher' or 'consistorial' ones of prelates.[14] Unless they were monks, bishops also drew personal income from church possessions, tied to their office and known as the *mensa*. Still, the material sustenance of churchmen appointed to bishoprics or the cardinalate was not regulated by the law of benefices.[15]

Curial offices differed in that they were open to the married and laymen, too. Their normative status was not fully framed until after 1300, when a growing number of officials secured life-long tenancy and regular stipends, typically in the form of fees. The Scribes of the Apostolic See famously studied by Brigide Schwarz were among the earliest to transform their position into a fixed one marked by capital letter ('Scribe').[16] They did so by establishing themselves as a corporation or 'college', restricting membership to a maximum, and obtaining from the pope approval of

---

11 Meyer, 'The Law of Benefices'.
12 Below, Essay 3, p. 71.
13 On the distinction between *sine cura* and *cum cura*, see Meyer, 'The Law of Benefices', pp. 378, 387; also Essay 1, p. 28 n. 12 below.
14 Meyer, 'The Law of Benefices' p. 378; cf. below, Essay 1, pp. 28–29.
15 See Essay 4, pp. 88–90 below.
16 Schwarz, *Die Organisation kurialer Schreiberkollegien*; also, Essay 6, pp. 165–67 below.

their statutes and compensation (*taxae*) for scribal services. Many papal administrators, such as the Abbreviators, Couriers or *cursores*, and Proctors eventually followed suit, applying corporate pressure to the pope who had little to gain from their monopolistic intentions.[17] If he was prepared to heed their wishes at all, it was because curial officials acted as his creditors. They acquired their office in the first place by offering him payments or loans, to the effect that they viewed the collection of fees as interest on their initial investment. The pope had to go along in order to maintain his credit with future investors. As the relationship between the two sides evolved, canonists captured it in legal terms by borrowing heavily from the pre-existing law of benefices. One clear difference persisted, however, since offices could be sold without drawing accusations of simony. By 1500, many holders vacated and transferred their offices for money, thus exercising their right as 'vacabilists'.[18]

A host of officials at the Curia served as part of the retinue (or suite) in the residence (*livrée*) of a higher prelate, dignitary, or cardinal.[19] In the present volume, they figure without capitalized initials as scribes, proctors, secretaries, and the like. By contrast, 'curial' officials in the proper sense appear as capitalized Scribes, Proctors, etc. They worked for the pope in 'apostolic' functions permanently assigned to them. Except for the Chamberlain, Vice-Chancellor, and other administrative heads, they tended to turn corporate and were funded by taxes or dues collected from petitioners requesting formal intervention.[20] As mentioned, the acquisition and exchange of curial positions came to be governed by rules taken from the law of benefices, so that the relevant mechanisms can be addressed here in tandem.

## Trading Tools

In canonical terms, benefices could not be bought under any circumstances, whereas curial offices were lawfully purchased in growing numbers as the fifteenth century progressed. All the same, the transfer of either type of position was subject to largely identical norms, building on the premise that holders were eager to pay a lot to obtain possession,

---

17 Meyer, 'The Curia: The Apostolic Chancery', pp. 248–53. On the *cursores*, see also Essay 8 below, pp. 201–22; on the Abbreviators, Essay 9, pp. 239–48.

18 Below, Essay 6, pp. 173–75; Essay 7, pp. 186–90, 198 n. 132. The author's hope to write a 'monograph on the rise of venal positions at the Curia until 1463' (below, Essay 7, p. 187 n. 67) never materialized.

19 For a cardinal's household, 'suite' is the term used in Essay 2, p. 58 n. 55a; also, below, Essay 7, p. 194.

20 Late medieval lists of (scribal) fees have been discussed by Müller, 'The Price of Papal Pardon'; cf. also below, Essay 7, pp. 184–87; Essay 9, pp. 251–53.

keep it at their discretion, and control how it passed on. Traditionally, benefices were conferred by ordinary collators, typically the bishop. From the later 1200s, popes placed an increasing range of benefices under their 'general reservation', beginning with those of clerics dying at the Curia. Other categories were swiftly added.[21] The reserved posts were granted to petitioners by papal 'provision', furnishing recipients with the right to claim their possessory title locally and, if necessary, in court. Successful claimants owed up to one year of income (or annates) from their benefice to the pope for his gracious intervention. Emboldened by demand, the system was complemented by so-called 'expectancies' as a second means of transfer, to the effect that the requesting churchmen obtained from the Apostolic See the right to receive the next available benefice in a specific area. Third among the foremost instruments in need of papal approval was the 'resignation in favour of a third party' which holders used to select their own successor while still alive, or to stage swaps by way of 'permutation'.[22]

Generating annates and other revenue for the papacy, this triad of mandates formed the core of the benefice market with its unique centre at the Roman Curia.[23] It grew in conjunction with the fee income of curial officials, who were responsible for the processing of incoming petitions as well as the drafting and expedition of the pope's responses. In due time, they also started to leave their office with the help of resignations and permutations, organized themselves in the way of benefice-holders into colleges, and monopolized gains by limiting access to their corporation.[24] It is true that canon law contained many stipulations insisting that candidates to an office or benefice were properly qualified, fulfilling, for example, requirements of age, literacy, physical attendance, or priestly rank. Thanks to the doctrine of papal 'plenitude of power', however, the restrictions fuelled market activity of their own at the Curia, which alone could grant dispensations from the general norm, accruing additional fees and forms of apostolic compensation.[25] Some limits proved absolute, it is true, such as the sole admission of unmarried clergy to benefices. But many allowed for exceptions, not least the right to collect full pay without having to serve in person.

---

21 See Essay 1, pp. 29–30 below.

22 Barraclough, *Papal Provisions*; Meyer, 'The Law of Benefices'; and Essay 1, pp. 30–32; Essay 4, pp. 93–97; Essay 6, pp. 167–68 below. Papal letters did not confer possession, only the right to claim it; Essay 1, pp 35–36 nn. 45–48.

23 Annates were payable for apostolic provisions; *servitia* for papal appointments to consistorial benefices; cf. Lunt, *Financial Relations of the Papacy with England*, ii, pp. 169–232, 307–34; also above, n. 11; below, Essay 7, p. 181; Essay 8, p. 210 n. 40.

24 The trend is depicted especially in Essay 6, pp. 169–72; Essay 7, pp. 183–89 below.

25 A survey of the principal dispensations and licenses available from the pope is offered by Salonen and Schmugge, *A Sip from the 'Well of Grace'*; see also Essay 1, p. 43; Essay 6, pp. 170–71; Essay 7, pp. 182–83 below.

## Sources and Approaches

The surviving records of curial administration become continuous with the pontificate of Innocent III (1198–1216). From then on, the 'Vatican Registers' of outgoing papal letters are preserved in hundreds of tomes predating the end of the Middle Ages in 1500. Beginning in the 1300s, they are accompanied by three additional series of correspondence respectively featuring copies of responses and incoming petitions, mainly concerning benefices.[26] Reflecting the fee-generating activity of Apostolic Scribes, Proctors, and their colleagues, serial data soon proliferated. From the fourteenth century, they include among other things fiscal data under the label of 'Income and Expenses' or, later still, that of 'Fees'.[27] Taken together, the late medieval material at both the Vatican and Roman State Archives comprises thousands of volumes counting millions of individual entries. They allude to precedents and effects which manifested themselves, if unevenly, across the whole of Latin Christendom (usually addressed as 'the periphery'), while producing local sources of incalculable quantity as well. How has scholarship dealt with this enormous mass of historical information?

When the Vatican's 'Secret Archives' opened to the public in 1881, various European nations rushed to establish research institutions in Rome.[28] In particular, they planned to explore the vastness of serial holdings from the late Middle Ages. Active to the present day, they devised projects within national parameters. Between 1893 and 1998, for example, the British extended their calendar of registered papal letters relating to Great Britain and Ireland until 1503.[29] The reach of queries and archival units which investigators took on was of even greater consequence. The mere identification of people and places, along with a short reference to the recorded request, was bound to consume less time than the full reproduction of recorded texts, partly attempted by the 'French School of Rome' and again focusing on the pope's registers (to 1378).[30]

Founded in 1888, the 'Prussian Historical Station', renamed 'German Historical Institute' (*Deutsches Historisches Institut*) in 1937, pursued a much more ambitious agenda, not only due to the territorial extent of the Empire at the time, but mainly because the *Repertorium Germanicum* was designed to furnish summaries of each archival item in the Vatican

---

26 Meyer, 'The Curia: The Apostolic Chancery', pp. 239–48, 253–54; Zutshi, 'The Papal Chancery', pp. 16–18.

27 In Latin, *Taxae* and *Introitus et Exitus*; cf. Weiß, 'The Curia: Camera', pp. 222–28; also, Essay 5, p. 117 n. 2, pp. 118–19; Essay 8, p. 211 n. 51 below.

28 Excepting, most notably, Italy and Spain; cf. Boyle, *A Survey of the Vatican Archives*, pp. 14–19.

29 *Calendar of Entries in the Papal Registers*, ed. by Bliss and others.

30 '*Ut per litteras apostolicas*'; accessible through an English interface as well.

mentioning German speakers between 1378 and 1517.[31] Not enough, the demands on collaborators grew as historians widened their scope of interests. The *Repertorium* has continued to expand its questionnaire, enabling complex forms of analysis far beyond the original focus on persons and locations. In the 1960s, social history emerged with questions about the significance of networks for the careers of late medieval churchmen. Brigide Schwarz (1940–2019) embraced the new field from her first stay in Rome of 1966–1968, helping transform the *Repertorium* into an adequate tool for researchers like herself.[32]

## The Author

The task was enormous. For Dr Schwarz, execution hinged above all on the fifth pontificate of the *Repertorium Germanicum* dedicated to Eugene IV (1431–1447), which she managed as chief editor following Hermann Diener's death in 1988. The result appeared in six parts of 3500 pages in 2004, dwarfing the companion volumes of the series for other popes especially in the variety of indices, prepared by Christoph Schöner. Dr Schwarz considered them key to revealing the interconnectedness of recorded persons and places.[33] The enterprise clearly attests to one of the pillars of her expertise, the many years of exposure to archival materials from the Vatican and Rome as member of a working group concerned with pre-modern serial sources. A second pillar consisted of her thorough familiarity with depositories in 'the periphery', showing how papal correspondence linked up with surviving documentation from the local archives, especially in and around Hanover, where Dr Schwarz served as University Professor from 1983 to 1998.[34] It is convenient to note that her studies on the 'rope-teams', or career-building networks, of late medieval clerics, who operated both at home and in the Roman Curia, have recently been assembled into a single book of ten (significantly revised) chapters.[35]

---

31 Reaching far beyond papal letters and indispensable for the type of network analysis undertaken by Dr Schwarz and German scholarship. For instructions on how to use the *Repertorium Germanicum*, see d'Avray, 'Germany and the Papacy'; and p. 23 n. 33 below.

32 A complete list of her scholarly work (until 2004) has appeared in *Kurie und Region*, ed. by Matheus and Rehberg, pp. 451–55; continued until 2020 by Schuchard, 'Brigide Schwarz', pp. 743–46.

33 Cf. *Repertorium Germanicum*, IX, ed. by Diener and others; and the commentary below, Essay 3, pp. 78–79; Essay 5, pp. 118–41.

34 *Die Originale der Papsturkunden*, ed. by Schwarz; to be read in conjunction with the *Regesten*, ed. by Schwarz; see also Essay 3, pp. 79–80.

35 Schwarz, *Alle Wege führen über Rom*, with the author's introduction of 19 January 2019, pp. 13–19, just weeks before her passing. These studies of 'rope teams' are by no means limited to Hanover, summarized in Essay 3, below, pp. 67–81; they also treat Poland in Essay

24    EDITOR'S INTRODUCTION

The third and major component of her scholarship, concerned with the proper interpretation of the 'legalese' and 'small print' in petitions to, and formal responses from, the pope, would certainly merit consolidation into a single and comprehensive publication as well. For the time being, Essay 5 below rests among the translated work of Dr Schwarz to the fullest degree on her expertise in papal diplomatic of the later Middle Ages.[36] In addition, Anglophone readers can readily consult her succinct administrative history of the Roman Curia prior to 1300, published in their language in 2016, as a prelude to the historical developments examined here.[37] Last but not least, there is also an English overview on the fourth and final scholarly focus of Dr Schwarz, summarizing her extensive work on the ties between members of the Roman Curia and students enrolled at the curial university of Rome.[38]

## The Translation

Reflecting the long tradition of German foundational research in the humanities, the prose of Dr Schwarz primarily addresses expert audiences interested in conducting archival research. In the present rendering, some of her technical vocabulary as well as frequent explanations in the form of bullet points have been paraphrased or extended to appeal to a broader English readership. Moreover, paragraphs of short length have often been combined with preceding or subsequent text. Those comparing the two versions side by side will also discover that long phrases have been broken up into shorter ones, either for clarity or in order to accommodate footnotes at the end of a sentence. Their numbering has been retained throughout, even where it appears irregular in the German original (due to belated insertion). Latin and Italian passages have been translated without further indication.

---

4, pp. 83–115; Saxony in Essay 5, pp. 117–54; Berlin, the Lower Rhine, and the Netherlands, cf. Schuchard, 'Brigide Schwarz', pp. 742–43.

36 Especially Essay 5, pp. 141–44; cf. also, Essay 9, pp. 250–52; Essay 10, pp. 276–79 below. David d'Avray is preparing an introduction to the field in English; the collected essays by Zutshi, *The Avignon Popes*, also concentrate on papal diplomatic.

37 Schwarz, 'The Roman Curia (until about 1300)'.

38 Schwarz, 'Who Studied (and Taught) at the University?'.

# Part I

## Ecclesiastical Benefices

CHAPTER 1

# The Roman Curia and the Late Medieval Benefice Market[1]

In the early 1300s, the canons of the choir at the Great Minster of Zurich and its candidates on the waiting list were almost exclusively from families eligible for city council, or from the local nobility.[2] Around 1500, the proportion of children from the town patriciate was even higher — again including a considerable cohort of individuals who were at a very tender age. The Great Minster was used without doubt to provide for younger males. In the intervening period, however, the situation looked quite different. The share of patrician sons had dropped to 8.7 per cent by 1400.[3] The canons originated from more distant areas and had studied at university.[4] Unlike the progeny of the patricians, they also held, or had held, benefices at other churches. The list of aspirants did not contain the names of minors, and several of the clerics at the Great Minster were of lower birth. The reason for their appearance is not difficult to find. They had secured papal provisions to obtain their benefices, which power-brokers from the immediate vicinity had jealously controlled a century earlier.

There is our topic. It deals with the rise and practical effects of papal provisions for benefices and with their late medieval market-place. The spatial and chronological framework of the following analysis is the German Empire, at a time when the papal benefice exchange was of greatest

---

1 This is a slightly modified and annotated version of my presentation at the workshop, 'Problems Concerning the Lesser Churches in the Late Middle Ages', held at the Reichenau in October 1987. I have added more recent publications on the subject by Meyer, *Arme Kleriker auf Pfründensuche*; Meyer, 'Der deutsche Pfründenmarkt'; and Meyer, 'Spätmittelalterliches Benefizialrecht'. The topic was also addressed at the German *Historikertag* in Bochum, 1990, where I gave the keynote lecture; cf. Schwarz, 'Klerikerkarrieren und Pfründenmarkt'; and the resulting volume of papers, in *Bericht über die 38. Versammlung deutscher Historiker*.

2 Fifty eight per cent alone were from families residing in the town of Zurich; Meyer, *Zürich und Rom*, pp. 125, 170.

3 Their share was at fifty-eight per cent in 1320; in 1340, at 29.2 per cent; in 1360, at 20.8 per cent; in 1380, at thirteen per cent; in 1400, at 8.7 per cent; in 1420, at 12.5 per cent; in 1460, at 21.7 per cent; in 1480, at 41.6 per cent; in 1500, at 66.6 per cent; see Meyer, *Zürich und Rom*, p. 170.

4 Although they did not finish as often with an academic degree; Meyer, *Zürich und Rom*, pp. 170–71.

significance for German-speaking applicants.[5] It lasted from the Great Schism (1378–1415) until shortly after the Concordat of Vienna of 1448. My treatment does not concentrate on the great regional differences and delineates the phenomenon only in its contours.[6] I rely above all on material gathered in the *Repertorium Germanicum*.[7] In addition, I draw on my own collections of papal documents preserved in Lower Saxony, and on my research in the Roman Curia.[8]

Those who petitioned at the Roman Curia for an endowed church position had to be familiar with the legal pre-requisites. The same is necessary for modern historians who wish to study the benefice market at the time.[9] The benefices coming to market were always positions at lesser churches or minor prebends at a cathedral. Higher offices (or prelacies) were not traded, because appointments to them followed a different mode.[10] Until 1450, canonries and dignities at cathedral and chapter churches were especially coveted objects.[11] Under certain circumstances, parishes also belonged to that category.[12] Hardly in demand were simple benefices at small

---

5 The main mass of materials in the *Repertorium Germanicum* is concerned with the assignment of benefices. According to the spot checks of Hermann Diener, entries in the papal registers referring to the 'German Empire' (as defined for the *Repertorium Germanicum*) amounted to sixteen per cent until Pius II (d. 1464); under Julius II and Leo X (1503–1520), the same share dropped to five per cent; cf. Diener, 'Materialien aus dem vatikanischen Archiv', p. 394. Due to Diener's untimely death, he was unable to determine the exact occurrence of this change; for preliminary work, see his papers at Rome, German Historical Institute (DHI).

6 On the strong discrepancy between places, see Meyer, 'Der deutsche Pfründenmarkt', pp. 274–75.

7 *Repertorium Germanicum*, I–IX; non-German entries are included in *Die Rota-Manualien des Basler Konzils*, ed. by Gilomen. Following the editorial guidelines of the *Repertorium Germanicum*, Elisa Mongiano (Turin) plans to catalogue the Chancery registers of Felix (V) (1439–1449).

8 *Die Originale der Papsturkunden*, ed. by Schwarz; *Regesten*, ed. by Schwarz.

9 When I refer to 'lesser benefices' here, I use the term in the sense of contemporary canon law for positions that the pope did not grant in his consistory. The classical study of papal provisions is by Barraclough, *Papal Provisions*; also, Baier, *Päpstliche Provisionen*.

10 Higher church offices were filled through election by a corporation of voters or appointment by a superior. Papal confirmation was needed in both cases, unless the pope appointed himself.

11 About the range and variety of benefices there, cf. the volumes of the *Germania Sacra*; and, for the specific example of two Zurich chapters, Meyer, *Zürich und Rom*, pp. 523 ff.

12 In one of several scenarios. The position, say, was endowed so richly that the priest could hire a permanent substitute and live in accordance with his status even when he was far away. This occurred above all in the south-east and north-west of the Empire. The holder of the benefice required papal dispensation from his obligation of residency. Alternatively, pastoral duties were already entrusted to a vicar or *plebanus*, which turned the position into one 'without the care of souls' (a 'sinecure'). Thirdly, it was the petitioner's first benefice, serving him as point of entry into the market-place; for Nicholas Cusanus, see Schwarz, 'Patronage und Klientel', pp. 288–89 (English version below, pp. 51–53). A parish was certainly the maximum goal for those who could not count on close ties to an ordinary collator or at the

villages or those of vicars and sacristans. Their anticipated income normally did not justify the fees payable for provisions and other expenses.[13]

Originally, the assignment of benefices was an important right — and duty — of the ecclesiastical superior, the so-called 'ordinary collator'. This could be the local bishop (primarily for parish churches, but also for specific canonries), or the canons of a chapter church; on the other hand, the rights of lay patronage exercised by a city council, for example, did not equal those of a collator, although they entailed a serious claim to determine the person of the holder.[14] In the High and late Middle Ages, the papacy gained increasing control over the appointment to benefices. In the following, I wish to offer a survey of the pertinent laws in force between 1320 and c. 1520, without discussing their historical origins.[15] The papal conferral of benefices is roughly distinguishable into two types, first, the bestowal of presently vacant positions and, secondly, the grant of future vacancies to be filled by the ordinary collator.

Regarding the first variety, the power to assign vacant benefices could devolve by right to the pope, if the ordinary collator did not act upon it within a fixed time period or was in contravention of other legal rules. Having reserved certain categories of positions to themselves, the popes conferred a great number of benefices under suspension of the ordinary collators' right to appoint. The special reservation of vacancies is of little significance here. By general reservation, though, the papacy assumed exclusive authority over their assignment when they became available 'at the Curia'.[16] This occurred when the previous holder had died there, or when someone resigned his position conditionally 'into the hand of the pope'.[17] Additional scenarios included the translation from one benefice to

---

Curia, and hence had to aim at less attractive benefices. Access to them usually came in the form of affordable papal expectancies for 'poor clerics'.

13 Unsuited for the market were ecclesiastical offices not subject to the law of benefices, such as chaplainries.

14 Fundamentally, all benefices called for collation by the ordinary, whether he was bishop or archdeacon. However, clerical patrons and especially chapter churches often had appropriated this right, whereas lay patrons and sometimes those presented by their parish still depended on investiture by the ordinary. Lay patrons, to be sure, could bypass the latter, if they chose an already ordained candidate; summarized by Kurze, *Pfarrerwahlen im Mittelalter*, pp. 314 ff., 434 ff.

15 Beginning with John XXII (1316–1334), papal provisions started to be granted widely; after 1520, the papacy renounced to the right of nomination in favour of the bishops, insofar as it was still relevant; cf. Meyer, *Zürich und Rom*, p. 7.

16 Linden, *Der Tod des Benefiziaten*; Hilderscheid, 'Die päpstlichen Reservationsrechte'; Hinschius, *System des katholischen Kirchenrechts*, III, pp. 113 ff.

17 Linden, *Der Tod des Benefiziaten*, pp. 117–27; Hilderscheid, 'Die päpstlichen Reservationsrechte', pp. 8–24. Curial clergy enjoyed the important privilege of being able to resign their benefices through papal dispensation in the provinces as well, overriding the rights of local collators; see Meyer, *Zürich und Rom*, p. 97; Weiss, 'Kurie, Konzil und

another, promotion, deprivation, the deposition of the holder by the pope, the impediment of a marriage contract, entry into a monastery, or acceptance of an office that was incompatible with the benefice in question.[18] Lastly, papal control extended to the tenure of curial clergy and their claim to it. Concerning the second type, the popes issued expectancies for benefices in the form of 'expectative letters'. They placed the recipient on a waiting list and ahead of other competitors by the 'right of precedence' (*iure preventionis*).[19] Whenever several papal candidates aimed at one and the same benefice — which was very often the case — there were various possibilities to guarantee preferment. The Curia attempted time and again to create a fair and equitable ranking system.[20]

Across Germany, special papal reservations did not gain in frequency until the fifteenth century.[21] They offered certain persons benefices that would become available in the future, while annulling provisions for generally reserved positions as well as expectancies. This gave recipients the right of precedence for all benefices located in a specific ecclesiastical district and for as long as the grant described in the papal reservation (like a certain amount of income) had not been met in full.[22]

---

Kirchenreform', p. 210 n. 702, p. 251 n. 793. On the prerogatives of curial clergy in general, von Hofmann, *Forschungen zur Geschichte der kurialen Behörden*, I, pp. 287–97.

18 For a brief overview of general reservations for vacancies at the Curia, Meyer, *Zürich und Rom*, p. 42, and the diagram at the end of Meyer's work.

19 Linden, *Der Tod des Benefiziaten*, p. 12; Hinschius, *System des katholischen Kirchenrechts*, III, p. 140. On expectancies, see the contributions of Andreas Meyer, p. 27 n. 1 above; also, Mollat, 'Les graces expectatives'; Tihon, 'Les expectatives *in forma pauperum*'.

20 When the number of papally approved candidates at the top of the waitinglists grew to such levels that local ones fell hopelessly behind, chapter churches abandoned their traditional ranking practices around 1370, after several failed attempts to adapt them. Henceforth, all aspirants for benefices had to secure papal expectancies, including those favoured by the canons of the chapter in question; cf. Meyer, *Zürich und Rom*, p. 119. On various popes seeking to balance their generosity with the demands of fairness, see Meyer, *Arme Kleriker auf Pfründensuche*, pp. 39 ff.

21 The benefice market via the Curia first developed in the French regions, followed by other administratively advanced areas north of the Alps. England abandoned it again before the Schism of 1378, as did France until 1415. In Germany, the exchange peaked in the first half of the fifteenth century. The Italian market, which needs further study, seems to have been differently structured and far more capitalized than the German one, so that positions there were traded like monetary assets.

22 Meyer, 'Das Wiener Konkordat', pp. 137 ff. Special reservation only became important after concordats and conciliar decrees restricted papal activity and pressure from the political leaders increased. Those who gained were, first, high-born favourites of lords, who for some reason could not be provided for from the pool of benefices controlled by their patron; secondly, curial clergy of elevated position who had to add to their portfolio of benefices in order to align it with their promotion to superior rank. For an illustration, see the special reservation for Nicholas Cusanus, pp. 37–41 below; another for Enea Silvio Piccolomini following his elevation to the cardinalate, whose support was expected to come — against

Someone requesting provision with a benefice from his ordinary collator could still petition one from the pope. By expressing doubt about the legal validity of the original request, petitioners could boost their chances against competitors by asking for a 'new provision', which in the form of a confirmation also formed a viable option for those already in possession of a papal provision. Rather than seeking a benefice, it was equally possible to obtain from the papacy the rights of a party through 'surrogation'. This created a claim to a position supposing that neither of two adversaries in litigation over it would win (*si neutri*), casting a glaring light on the intensity of the competition.[23]

In addition, the pope affected the conferral of benefices with another prerogative of his, the right to suspend legal regulations in particular cases. Through dispensation, he furnished individuals with access to positions specifically or in general, whenever there was an impediment like minor age, illegitimate birth, or physical disability. The papacy also dispensed from certain prohibitions or obligations which holders had to face. They were not permitted to accumulate positions, especially those involving pastoral care (*cum cura*). Most benefices required residency or ordination to appropriate clerical rank within a given time span, or they prohibited resignation unless it was unconditional. Papal dispensation paved the way for accumulation, for absence from the location during periods of study or to serve at a princely court, and license to leave the position profitably through resignation to a third party, upon negotiation of a pension, or by exchange, rendering the position for men with ambition the more attractive and marketable.

Lastly, popes intervened by offering certain candidates or groups preferential treatment in the appointment to benefices, although this did not constitute a right that could be claimed in court. Among those enjoying such prerogatives were, first, university students.[24] They obtained expectancies in enormous numbers, graded according to the quality of the benefices and the conditions governing their acquisition.[25] Students

---

vigorous protest — from the German church he had long served as protector; see Brosius, 'Die Pfründen des Enea', pp. 286 ff.

23 This type of provision was only granted to parties who otherwise had to abandon trial. The less frequent *provisio si nulli* was not very likely to prevail from the start; cf. Weiss, 'Kurie, Konzil und Kirchenreform', p. 278 nn. 861 ff. For certain curial clerics such as staff at the Rota and proctors, it constituted the characteristic entry point into the possession of benefices, because they were not confronted with the deterrent aspects of prolonged litigation, which according to my findings in the *Repertorium Germanicum* included the costs of staying at the Curia, the loss of time, and the complexity of the proceedings.

24 Although popes provided them in principle with expectancies, the prospects of poor clerics without benefice gradually worsened from the middle of the fourteenth century; cf. Meyer, *Arme Kleriker auf Pfründensuche*, pp. 53, 57.

25 On the ranking by earlier (that is, preferable) date for certain universities and professors in the higher faculties in competition with other privileged candidates, see Meyer,

32    CHAPTER 1

received dispensations to combine incompatible positions or the total income from accumulated ones. They were freed from canonical obligations of residency or promotion to the holy orders. Secondly, curial clergy counted among those privileged. They included members of the pope's immediate entourage or *familia*, relatives, friends, and individuals under his protection, as well as the respective clienteles of cardinals and other important prelates at the Curia, its officials, and their followers. There were additional people with curial status, too, who nevertheless lived in distant places.[26] An ever-growing range of persons obtained this rank due to specific transactions and in formulations addressing them 'as if they were from the "family" of the pope' and the like.[27] In line with what has been said above about university graduates, papal preferment was subtly graded according to standing in the curial hierarchy. As I will further explore below, the pope granting these prerogatives was of course not bound by his ranking when things became concrete. The third group consisted of princes and nobility. Fourth, the pope extended his prerogatives to people and their followers, whose support he considered beneficiary to the 'common good' of the Church.

The papal favours were granted along with precise rules regarding their substantive and formal execution. They took up large part of the regulations for the Apostolic Chancery, which were only valid during the pontificate of the reigning pope.[28] They were supplemented with administrative norms lacking codification but offering firm guidance for petitioners all the same, known as the 'style of the court' or 'usage of the Roman Curia'.[29] Familiarity with these regulations and customs — or

---

'Spätmittelalterliches Benefizialrecht'. Students had improved chances to obtain better benefices (especially dignities) as well, just as those with an academic degree could count on additional preferment in the issuance of dispensations.

26 It was part of curial practice to furnish preferred persons with offices as a sign of distinction; cf. Schuchard, *Die Deutschen an der päpstlichen Kurie*, p. 28; for the Protonotaries in particular, pp. 94 ff.; the acolytes and subdeacons, pp. 142–43; the *cubicularii* and *referendarii*, pp. 150 ff. On the countless titular abbreviators under Martin V and Eugene IV, see Schwarz, 'Die Abbreviatoren'. Moreover, the pope allowed many curial officials to retain their status after leaving the Curia.

27 As a result, the claim reached far beyond the circle of above-mentioned curial staff whose benefices fell under general papal reservation.

28 The rules in *Regulae cancellariae apostolicae*, ed. (insufficiently) by von Ottenthal, were instrumental for benefices from Urban V (1362–1370) onward; cf. Jackowski, 'Die päpstlichen Kanzleiregeln'.

29 Assembled in manuals for curial employees, but also traceable in the hundreds of thousands of rescripts emanating from administrative practice; cf. Frenz, *Die Kanzlei der Päpste*, pp. 46 ff., 58–59, 79, 121 ff.; also, Segrè, 'I dispacci di Cristoforo da Piacenza', p. 94 and, p. 257, on the custom in the Apostolic Chancery of verifying dispensations and the like which were itemized as 'notwithstanding'.

consultation with those who were expert in them — was vital for everyone in search of a benefice.

The exact wording of papal provisions determined whether a candidate enjoyed good prospects or any, often amounting to a single clause in the text of a granted favour.[30] All could depend on the earliest date of issuance.[31] Also, success might hinge upon simplification of a procedural step.[32] If the written mandate contained a formal mistake, the entire grant risked being null and void, owing to the strict formalism governing litigation over benefices.[33] Under the circumstance, one or multiple petitions to correct the error afforded a remedy.[34] Alternatively, the interested party could request the emendation of specific conditions, as long as the definitive apostolic decision had not been sealed and handed over.[35] Still, successive alterations of an already expedited letter of provision were common in the form of 'reformations' or as 'valid from now on' (*perinde valere*).[36] These improvements and amendments frequently resulted from competitive situations that had just arisen. At other times, though, they were carefully planned to secure — through insertion of additional clauses, for instance — what failed to materialize in the first place.[37] The

---

30 In expectative letters, the clause of preference over all competitors (*anteferri*) was very popular; cf. Meyer, *Zürich und Rom*, p. 88; Weiss, 'Kurie, Konzil und Kirchenreform', p. 195 n. 650.

31 Efforts to create a fair and coherent system of preferment with the help of graded dates (in expectancies, for example, on four successive days, with the earliest being reserved to the best-connected candidates) were compromised because the pope proved non-compliant.

32 Such as permission to omit the reference to 'notwithstanding' impediments, given that imprecision in their wording was the most common cause for expensive and cumbersome emendations, or *reformationes*; see Meyer, *Zürich und Rom*, pp. 23, 91–92.

33 Frequently and despite adherence to complicated rules, the order of the pope or his Vice-Chancellor did not imply that the requested grace was offered in full. Their signatures in the form of a 'so be it as requested' (*fiat ut petitur*), for instance, would not approve both the petition and underlying dispensation, but only the former, while the latter was rejected. Through restrictive interpretation of the mandates and tight adherence to curial usage, the Curia tried to forestall erroneous grants, which could cause a flood of additional petitions and litigation by disadvantaged parties.

34 Claims of provision often did not rest on a single petition but rather on several, one to start with and carrying the decisive date and subsequent corrections of form and content, which might just feature technical details.

35 Concerning the spelling, exact identification of the benefice and the cause of its vacancy, its current value, or the status of 'notwithstanding' impediments. On the difficulty to collect precise data in timely fashion, see Meyer, *Zürich und Rom*, pp. 91–92.

36 They became necessary as competition for the benefice mounted, requiring an earlier date, the extension of a clause, or a new deadline. The correction could be made separately in a papal letter or inserted into the bull based on the original petition (which must survive for us to track the process).

37 This is adequately documented in the reports and letters of proctors; cf. Segrè, 'I dispacci di Cristoforo da Piacenza', p. 33. To obtain the favour, it became important to mobilize powerful supporters, see pp. 38–39 below.

Vice-Chancellor was able to approve various emendations by himself.[38] Unlike the pope, the Chancery was regularly accessible, which made its practices of decision-making more predictable.[39]

Supplications granted and registered at the Curia often did not result in a sealed papal letter (or 'bull'). Andreas Meyer has calculated for the pontificate of Martin V (1417–1431) that the proportion was about ten to one.[40] Petitioners waited with their request for a bull until the underlying petition or petitions were likely to prevail. In case of success, moreover, they were obligated to pay the usual dues, the so-called 'annates' to the Apostolic Chamber and — hard to track in the sources — 'composition' to the Datary for papal dispensations.[41] There were two main options in the preparation of bulls. The longer, more convoluted, and — in relative terms — cheaper version strictly followed the 'style of the court' and was issued by the Chancery. The costlier type, known as the 'secretarial expedition', came from the Apostolic Chamber.[42] In each format, a well-versed person — the petitioner or his proctor — knew of ways to stall or accelerate processing.

These were in sum the curial pre-requisites for acquiring benefices with the pope's help. They determined the trade with them insofar as it was legal and hence alone of interest here.[43] I will not address the late medieval sale

---

38 Frenz, *Die Kanzlei der Päpste*, pp. 95–96.

39 Segrè, 'I dispacci di Cristoforo da Piacenza', pp. 34 ff.

40 Meyer, *Zürich und Rom*, p. 52. Petitions are known to us almost exclusively through the papal registers, which also contain requests that were formally accepted, but in truth rejected at least in part; cf. p. 33 n. 33 above.

41 They were not a novelty from the period of the Schism, unlike the office of the Datary; Frenz, *Die Kanzlei der Päpste*, p. 100. Annates were not collected when benefices were acquired by expectative letter.

42 Frenz, *Die Kanzlei der Päpste*, pp. 132 ff.; Segrè, 'I dispacci di Cristoforo da Piacenza', pp. 36 ff.

43 Meyer, 'Der deutsche Pfründenmarkt', p. 267, has used for benefices an expanded definition of 'market', which like the fairs in the region of Champagne occurred 'neither in a specific place nor at a specific time', but operated 'continuously and everywhere at once', because 'sellers and buyers conducted their business mostly by way of correspondence'. Meyer's quite restrictive understanding does not account for the exceptional significance of the Curia as central to the exchange. He has focused on the relationship between petitioners and collators, with the pope intervening only as super-collator based on his rights of reservation and conferral of expectancies. What is lacking, however, is the papal role in the legitimate trade of benefices with third parties, namely the owners (of positions or of claims to them) and those on the side of demand, an area in which the papacy could offer dispensation to stimulate transactions or grant prerogatives, each of which Meyer has insufficiently noted. Meyer has also failed to consider adequately the special characteristics of the late medieval benefice market. It needs to be distinguished, first, from other ties including non-economic ones between collators and petitioners and, secondly, from the black market, marked by simony and the lack of papal approval (through dispensation) for agreements between collators and recipients, and by the trafficking of positions between third parties without canonical permission to dispose of the office in question, a practice Roland Mousnier has

of spiritual positions for money or material advantages of a different kind, which was always present but branded as 'simony' and unlawful, whether it was undertaken by a collator, patron, or holder. It formed part of a 'black market' for ecclesiastical offices, except where the charge of simony was circumvented through papal dispensation from the canonical prohibition of marketing them or resigning them under condition.[44] Market activity in the sense of an exchange of 'goods' between a buyer and a seller occurred when the pope obtained a portion of the income (or 'annates') associated with the benefice for granting his provision. For a dispensation, he rather collected a negotiable 'composition'. The holders of benefices or rights to them traded them in turn with persons who were interested in these 'assets', although it was the power of the papacy to dispense which rendered them marketable in the first place, gave individuals access to the market, and solicited supply and demand especially through the concession of prerogatives. Benefices were popular as investment items, due to special characteristics like their safe possession from the perspective of the holder (subjective perpetuity), guaranteed linkage between the office and a specific income (objective perpetuity), and other benefits. Benefices were desirable not only because they generated a stipend — as *prebenda* — but importantly also for associated immaterial goods such as relationships, political influence, and rank, quite apart from the spiritual dimension of the position. It is worth noticing, too, that the exchange between buyers and sellers — to be further discussed below — did not unfailingly focus on money and monetary instruments.

From a legal standpoint, the partners in the transaction did not earn anything except a papal rescript. As Ernst Pitz has emphasized, this afforded only a claim to the coveted benefice, a 'right to' the matter. Recipients still had to secure their 'right in it' by gaining possession of it and defending it successfully against challenges. Petitioners had to signal their legal title resulting from a papal provision or expectancy in person or by proctor to the ordinary collator. The pope assigned this task to one (or several) special executors he appointed by name in his mandate of provision.[45] The latter initiated the so-called executorial process at the

---

called the 'trafficking in offices' in connection with secular administration; cf. Schwarz, 'Ämterkäuflichkeit', cols 561–62.

44 A papal dispensation obtained in advance could dispel the suspicion of simony tied to such transactions; its grant was subject to certain conditions.

45 In principle, there was a difference between executorial proceedings based on an expectative letter, on papal provisions with a vacancy (either through reservation or in competition with an appointment made by the ordinary collator), or with positions that had yet to fall vacant. However, these subtleties are not relevant here; for details, see Weiss, 'Kurie, Konzil und Kirchenreform', p. 236 n. 780.

local level.[46] It served to verify, first, the authenticity of the papal bull and, secondly, the factual accuracy of the narrative in the petition for the benefice, the cause of the vacancy, additional (and notwithstanding) positions acquired or pursued by the petitioner, the opposing parties, etc. Thirdly, it examined possible objections from competitors, to make sure that the acquiring petitioner really qualified for the benefice, for example, by having his provision carry the earliest date of conferral. Of course, a candidate showing up on the following day with an earlier date could still invalidate the argument. Fourth, the executor(s) would check the professional and moral suitability of the applicant. When all scrutiny had led to an affirmative outcome, the proceedings were concluded with a mandate that the ordinary collator invest the petitioner symbolically with the benefice.[47] Even afterwards, however, firm possession was not assured, as the act of investiture only implied a 'right to the matter', which often enough had to be defended over long periods against rival supplicants before various courts. A 'right in the matter' was not granted until the presumed holder had kept it unopposed for a year and a day and under strict observance of the canonical norms. Otherwise, different claimants had the opportunity to dispossess him again.[48]

The legal ramifications were obviously rather complicated and demanded constant action by those involved. If someone wished to acquire a benefice on the papal market, he had to show entrepreneurial skills, inventiveness, and vigilance. Mentioned above, the sons of the patriciate at Zurich, who received their position through ordinary conferral, did not have to rely on such qualities. For those taking the papal route, on the other hand, fierce competition was the norm and litigation over benefices commonplace.[49] It was far from certain for an expectancy or provision from the pope to result in actual acquisition of the intended office. According to Andreas Meyer, 71.9 per cent of the expectative letters concerning the Great Minster and the Minster of Our Lady at Zurich between 1320 and 1500 took effect.[50] Simultaneously, some forty per cent of benefices

---

46 Curial clerics were privileged in that they could start executorial trials at the Curia, a right conferred to an ever-increasing number of persons. In the fifteenth century, petitioners sought to have high-ranking officials (especially from the Apostolic Chancery) appointed as executors to launch proceedings there; cf. Weiss, 'Kurie, Konzil und Kirchenreform', pp. 185–86 nn. 585 ff.

47 Whose own powers were expressly suspended on the occasion and whose previous efforts to appoint were voided unless they had created a 'right in the matter'.

48 Papal provisions with a benefice whose holder had acted against canonical norms were not as successful as their frequency in the papal registers suggests; cf. Meyer, *Zürich und Rom*, pp. 101, 113 n. 341. The mere possibility of harassment through similar provisions may have exerted a disciplinary effect, as is shown by the various requests to dispense.

49 For illustrative examples, see Brosius, 'Die Pfründen des Enea'.

50 Meyer, *Zürich und Rom*, pp. 86–87; papal provisions with reserved benefices were instead always successful — for one of the petitioners.

THE ROMAN CURIA AND THE LATE MEDIEVAL BENEFICE MARKET 37

at both churches were conferred after papal intervention.[51] Between 1316 and 1418, that rate stood at eighty per cent.

Individuals seeking a benefice had to collect news about free positions or those believed to become available soon. Information about holders in ill-health or preparing for dangerous trips was certainly helpful, and the papal registers contain many references to people supposed to be dead. For persons in pursuit of a vacancy, it was equally important to learn about its legal status. It was advisable to gather reliable data with speed, because any conferral of papally reserved benefices called for a bull of provision carrying the earliest possible date. Relevant details could be communicated through postal services between the Curia and localities in the provinces, by curial proctors or papal collectors of fees and taxes. Notices concerning competitors and their legal prerogatives were often essential.[52] They were most readily available at the Curia, where word of vacancies arrived the fastest — though not always through particularly trustworthy channels.[53] 'Good connections' were paramount, offering key input as rapidly and exclusively as possible. It was often supplied by lesser servants at the curial offices. Of even greater utility were relationships in the sense of 'social networks', the significance of which has been emphasized by Wolfgang Reinhard.[54] They comprised relatives, compatriots, clients, and patrons, 'friends' not in an emotional sense but in expectation of mutual aid and assistance also from the friends of friends. Among clerics, such ties were forged through membership in the same religious order or monastery, for example, or shared attendance at university.[55] Petitioners for a benefice required these forms of support above all when their request was examined at the Curia.

Insight into the strategies and tactics facilitating acquisition of a benefice is afforded by the endeavours of Nicholas of Cusa (or Cusanus)

---

51 More precisely, 39.5 per cent of the expectative letters and 86.1 per cent for the canonries of the prestigious Great Minster of Zurich between 1316 and 1418; cf. Meyer, *Zürich und Rom*, p. 169. A different figure (of twenty-two per cent) for a shorter period (1417–1431) and without differentiation of the benefices according to type is provided by Weiss, 'Kurie, Konzil und Kirchenreform', pp. 256–57 n. 816. How strongly the market for benefices could affect the composition of clergy in a region is demonstrated by McCurry, '*Utilia Metensia*'.

52 In letters of provision, the petitioner's status in terms of academic degree or curial rank furnished competitors with a first indication of their adversary's prerogatives. It certainly served as a deterrent, if he figured as an eminent prelate at the Curia.

53 Conveyed by visitors, proctors, collectors, or followers of the Roman Curia. If resignations in favour of a third party were not made by curial clerics, they had to be submitted at the papal court, where formal mistakes in a petition could serve as an opportunity for bargaining.

54 Reinhard, *Freunde und Kreaturen*; Schwarz, 'Die römische Kurie' (English translation below, pp. 177–99).

55 Schwarz, 'Die römische Kurie', pp. 248–49 (English translation below, pp. 191–92).

to obtain the provostship in the chapter church of St Martin at Worms.[56] In a letter of 4 August 1439, he asked his friend, the papal *referendarius* and *cubicularius* Petrus de Mera, to approach the pope for provision with the dignity.[57] To improve his chances against competing candidates, Nicholas urged Petrus to request certain conditions like papal assignment of the position in the form of 'motu proprio' and by way of special reservation, which permitted recipients to override the right of local chapters to elect their own provost.[58] Cusanus knew that his prospects in this regard were poor for compelling reasons that he did not fail to mention to the addressee. He also seemed eager to speed up the process of petitioning, for he wrote that the full narrative of the papal mandate could wait until his petition had been approved. The remark implies that he was able to mobilize friends at the Apostolic Chancery — most probably among the secretaries — and expected them to shape the wording of the final papal letter to his greatest benefit.[59] To conclude, Nicholas pressed Petrus to apply 'his usual vigilance and if necessary, the aid of friends'. The text reveals that Nicholas anticipated serious competition.[60] He was familiar with one of his rivals, Heinrich Maesheim of Homberg, a man of considerable standing in the papal Chancery, whose odds were quite favourable simply due to his position and personal presence at the Curia.[61] Nicholas

---

56 Nicholas Cusanus, Enea Silvio Piccolomini, and John of Segovia are noted here as examples, because their benefices have been closely investigated. They also appear in source material located outside the Curia, which sheds light on the way they accumulated and defended their holdings, especially in the form of letters.

57 *Acta Cusana*, ed. by Meuthen and Hallauer, I/2, no. 397. Petrus de Mera was one of four *referendarii* under Eugene IV and especially trusted by the pope; cf. Schuchard, *Die Deutschen an der päpstlichen Kurie*, pp. 152 ff., 190. The letter survives by chance as part of what was once an extensive correspondence.

58 He also needed an express papal declaration that this was a special reservation, whereby the benefice was conferred to none other than Cusanus and while the current holder was still alive.

59 Strictly speaking, the secretaries did not belong to the Chancery, although they were gradually incorporated into it until the end of the Middle Ages; cf. Frenz, *Die Kanzlei der Päpste*, pp. 132 ff. In 1439, they still figured among the pope's immediate entourage and were rather associated with the Apostolic Chamber; see Schuchard, *Die Deutschen an der päpstlichen Kurie*, pp. 82 ff. They also formulated letters more freely, whereas the Chancery had to follow the style of the court.

60 *Acta Cusana*, ed. by Meuthen and Hallauer, I/2, no. 397 line 22: 'Even if it is signed (by the pope) for someone else'. Apart from the competitor mentioned here, there was also the candidate chosen by the chapter of Worms, whose free election was to be annulled explicitly and 'for this one time'.

61 Heinrich held the charge of *abbreviator* from 1429; between 1434 and 1436, he was a *familiaris* of Cardinal Giordano Orsini and subsequently of the pope. He was apparently in personal contact with Walter of Gouda, another *abbreviator* and Nicholas of Cusa's liaison with the Netherlands. Like Cusanus, Heinrich was a papal *nuntius* to the Empire from 1438 to 1439, where the two likely met at the congress of Mainz in March 1439; cf. *Deutsche Reichstagsakten. Ältere Reihe*, XIII–XIV, ed. by Beckmann and Weigel, Index. Both were of

THE ROMAN CURIA AND THE LATE MEDIEVAL BENEFICE MARKET    39

consequently empowered Petrus to resort, if necessary, to the intervention of additional friends he listed by name and with the admonishment to solicit the best possible prerogatives for him.[62] At the same time, Nicholas was aware that he risked pushing Petrus to a point where his various loyalties entered into mutual conflict. As a result, Nicholas assured him that the probability for Heinrich Maesheim to prevail in the provinces was so low that he would lastly agree to cede his claim to the provostship at Worms, undoubtedly in exchange for advantageous treatment elsewhere.

Nicholas of Cusa obviously had friends at the Curia who informed him, conveyed his intentions to the pope, and knew how to obtain the desired provision most effectively and at the lowest cost.[63] He mobilized high-ranking curial officials to speak on his behalf, such as influential cardinals, the foremost papal relative among them, and an all-powerful papal favourite. He cultivated friendships with members of the pope's immediate entourage including *cubicularii* and *referendarii* like Petrus de Mera, who were to steer his petitions toward approval and obstruct the ones of competitors. Nicholas also urged people outside the Curia to intervene.[64] Most decisive, however, was the ability of a petitioner to have the papal provision, once it was granted, successfully executed in the locality so that actual possession of the benefice was achieved and maintained.

---

approximately equal merit, in other words. Heinrich obtained a provision 'motu proprio', dated 29 August 1439 (Vatican, Apostolic Archive, Reg. Suppl. 361, fol. 125$^{vs}$), during the summer break at the Curia and hence well before Cusanus's friends could intervene on his behalf. Heinrich took on the obligation for the papal annates soon thereafter, on 10 September 1439 (Vatican, Apostolic Archive, Annatae 8, fol. 80$^r$), and petitioned on 14 October 1439 for expansion of his dispensation, so that it would cover incompatible benefices as well (Vatican, Apostolic Archive, Reg. Suppl. 363, fols 40$^v$ and 219$^{r-v}$). Still, Cusanus's estimate proved correct, and Heinrich did not obtain the provostship, either.

62 The friends and protectors he had in mind are revealed in the greetings that Petrus was asked to relay at the end of the letter, namely, the two influential Cardinals, Giordano Orsini, a former patron of Cusanus, and Branda da Castiglione; the foremost papal relative in the cardinalate, Francesco Condulmer; the primary papal favourite next to him, Luigi Scarampo; the *magister* at the register of petitions, Christopherus de Sancto Marcello; and very likely the physician and astronomer or astrologer, Paolo dal Pozzo Toscanelli, a close friend of Cusanus.

63 Either 'through the Chamber', as probably in this case, or 'through the Chancery', if not 'through the Correctory' in connection with a petition, with several modifications, or by way of an override (*perinde valere*), and so on.

64 In a proctor's letter to the city council of Dortmund, carrying the date of 2 May 1412 and published by Lindner, 'Beiträge zu dem Leben und den Schriften Dietrichs von Niem', pp. 82–83, there is mention of the *abbreviator* (and secretary) Balduinus of Dijck: 'It is necessary to seek them (i.e. papal mandates for the city) with caution and in secret because of Master Balduinus of Dijck, the counsellor and proctor of the lord of Cologne. Balduinus is a secretary of our Lord Pope and always in his palace along with certain other favourites of his. If they found out that someone wanted a mandate against the lord of Cologne, they would try to prevent it as much as they could'; cited after Schuchard, *Die Deutschen an der päpstlichen Kurie*, p. 186.

40    CHAPTER 1

In order to do so, it was not enough to set the above-mentioned legal processes in motion. The previously cited letter of Cusanus to the *referendarius* Petrus illustrates how the author took care to promote his candidacy for the provostship in and around Worms as well. The benefice in question was in the territories of the Count Palatine, who was likely to exert influence on the assignment and have his own favourite placed in the position. The chapter of the church at Worms, moreover, was poised to name a candidate by exercising its right of election, as Cusanus admitted, and the participants of the Council at Basel would appoint yet another person. Both would stand in his way given that he was a partisan of Pope Eugene IV, who had just been deposed by the Council.[65] The late holder of the provostship, Simon Dorolf from Boppard, on the other hand, had been Nicholas's friend, which could serve as an argument for conferral of the benefice to him.[66] His chances were again boosted by the circumstance that the parish church of Boppard was incorporated into the provostship. The parishioners took an interest in installing their local priest, exerting pressure by threatening to withhold revenues from the parish.[67] Much of the income for the provostship in Worms was generated at Boppard. It consisted of the tithe, which was not of significant value but a reliable source of gain, as Nicholas noted.[68] He knew in detail about the situation at Boppard, having good friends there and excellent ties to the leading

---

65 In the thirty-fourth Session of the Council on 25 June 1439, in *Sanctorum conciliorum nova et amplissima collectio*, ed. by Mansi, XXIX, cols 179 ff.

66 *Acta Cusana*, ed. by Meuthen and Hallauer, I/2, no. 397 n. 5.

67 *Acta Cusana*, ed. by Meuthen and Hallauer, I/2, no. 397 lines 11 and 20. The revenues consisted primarily of the tithes from Boppard. They were divided between the prior and the chapter of St Martin at Worms, because the parish church of Boppard was incorporated into the provostship.

68 *Acta Cusana*, ed. by Meuthen and Hallauer, I/2, no. 397 lines 23–24. The remark can only refer to the relative independence of the provostship from the chapter and to income from the tithe, which was paid rather than collected in kind and sold. If he acquired the benefice, Nicholas was prepared to give up an equivalent one and stop looking for others in the same category; see *Acta Cusana*, ed. by Meuthen and Hallauer, I/2, no. 397 lines 24–25. This was required because his dispensation of 1437 did not permit for his holdings to increase. In the summer of 1437 and while preparing in Rome for his diplomatic mission to Constantinople, he had received from Eugene IV dispensation for up to three incompatible benefices along with significant limitations; *Acta Cusana*, ed. by Meuthen and Hallauer, I/2, no. 303. The approval 'by special grace and in the presence of the pope' indicates the need for papal intervention to justify the departure from Chancery regulations. Various conditions were attached in the bull, see *Acta Cusana*, ed. by Meuthen and Hallauer, I/2, no. 304: First, the three positions could not be parishes; secondly, any third benefice involving pastoral duties had to be exchanged for a compatible one within five years. Otherwise, Nicholas had to give up his first holding (the provostship of Münstermaifeld). He secured a modification of the bull in the Chancery, granted 'by concession' and allowing him, thirdly, to exchange all three positions without restriction; *Acta Cusana*, ed. by Meuthen and Hallauer, I/2, no. 305.

circles in town, who greatly favoured his candidacy.[69] In addition, Cusanus hoped for support from Jacob of Sierck who had been in close contact with him for many years. In May 1439, Jacob had been appointed archbishop of Trier, and although he had no say over the church at Worms, he was the diocesan head and territorial lord of Boppard.[70] Nicholas apparently believed in his prospects of receiving a papal provision with promising conditions and ultimately the benefice, too, because of his strong connections to the Curia and to local leaders at Boppard — as opposed to Worms. Ultimately, though, his efforts were not crowned with success. Heinrich Maesheim, who obtained his papal provision before Cusanus's friends could intervene, also seems to have failed in his bid.[71] The cleric elected by the canons of Worms fared no better, revealing whose local influence was decisive in the end. In 1441, the latter ceded his claim to the chancellor of the Palatinate, who subsequently took possession of the provostship.[72]

The solidarity of friends was again indispensable when it came to preserving a benefice upon acquisition and in case the tenant did not reside in the vicinity because of curial activities or as owner of several positions overly distant from each other. Churchmen who wished to live in accordance with their status as persons 'of merit, or spirit, or birth' absolutely had to accumulate multiple holdings.[73] It was certainly helpful for Nicholas Cusanus that the provostship at Worms — which he called 'most apt for me' — was placed in an area where he had friends able to handle accruing income in his stead. Absentees required a representative to assume their official duties, especially liturgical responsibilities, but also the financial administration, collecting and selling tributes made in kind and transferring the monetary receipts. The loyalty and service of a substitute was most readily guaranteed if he derived advantages of his own from it, by being a client of his far-away patron, for example, or if friends in the locality kept a watchful eye on him. A non-residential owner of

---

69 Another longstanding friend of his was Helwig of Boppard. Nicholas Cusanus was hardly able to conduct these negotiations in person at the time and investigate details. He was highly occupied on diplomatic mission and wrote the letter to Petrus while travelling to the imperial diet at Frankfurt.

70 *Acta Cusana*, ed. by Meuthen and Hallauer, 1/2, no. 397 line 12. Jacob was the ordinary of the incorporated parish in Boppard, but not of the chapter at Worms.

71 The extent to which Heinrich Maesheim (cf. p. 38 n. 61 above), the papally provided candidate, managed to benefit from his claim will remain unclear until the Index to the *Repertorium Germanicum* for Eugene IV is completed.

72 *Acta Cusana*, ed. by Meuthen and Hallauer, 1/2, no. 397; cf. Como, *Das kaiserliche Kollegiatstift St. Martin in Worms*, pp. 29, 31.

73 Esch, 'Das Papsttum unter der Herrschaft der Neapolitaner', p. 770. The minimum was considered to be 200 ducats in 1410, a sum usually out of reach without accumulation of benefices.

benefices had to cultivate friendships and clienteles, maintaining his local network (or 'set') on a continuous basis.[74]

The brokering or concession of benefices in the form of resignations 'in favour of a third party' was a convenient way to promote clients and friends.[75] For the reconstruction of clerical clienteles and circles of friendship, it is therefore useful to trace entire histories of ownership.[76] Failed claims to positions could also be traded by a patron, provided his entourage had better prospects of obtaining them. Such titles were sometimes conferred as a gift or ceded against payment of a lump sum or rent. In fact, the acquisition of provisions for speculative purposes seems to have been frequent.[77] Many petitioners would have run into difficulty, had all benefices they requested been assigned to them.

Clienteles formed 'pools' of benefices, so to speak, which they tried to keep among themselves. Once they — and especially the household, known as *familia* — controlled a position, the patron increasingly treated it as his possession and only circulated it within his entourage. If canon law required it, he acquired benefices by proxy through members of his clientele, be it because he was not allowed to hold them in person, or for the moment, and the like. If clients wished to rearrange their holdings — most typically by exchanging them among fellows — they depended on the patron's approval. Pools of benefices were akin to the monopolistic structures that noble and patrician families from Zurich had used to accommodate their favourites in the early fourteenth century. Reliant on the law of conferral, they had dominated the church chapters in town by providing their own with benefices. Because fifteenth-century patrons did not have the right of collators on their side and lacked any role to this effect according to canonical regulations, they could not maintain acquired positions and obtain new ones except through the papacy and by disciplining their clienteles. To a degree, this approach was lastly acknowledged by the pope. Certain rules of the Apostolic Chancery stipulated, for example, that benefices in the possession of a cardinal's *familia* were not to be reassigned without his consent.[78] Individuals seeking to leave a

---

74 It was apparently because of their neglect of this task that the stature of Enea Silvio Piccolomini and John of Segovia as holders of benefices remained so unremarkable compared to Cusanus; cf. Brosius, 'Die Pfründen des Enea', pp. 307 ff.; Diener, 'Zur Persönlichkeit des Johannes von Segovia', pp. 348 ff., 361 ff.

75 Curial clerics were privileged in this regard.

76 Schwarz, 'Patronage und Klientel', p. 290 (English version below, p. 52).

77 This is the impression one gains from reading about the succession of benefices held by Enea Silvio Piccolomini, or at least his German ones.

78 As a result, they fell under general reservation; cf. Schwarz, 'Die Abbreviatoren', pp. 213 ff.; on this 'cardinal reservation', see also Schwarz, 'Patronage und Klientel', p. 290 n. 20 (English version below, p. 52 n. 20).

clientele were pressured to return holdings they had accumulated through their patron's special intervention.[79]

From the perspective of the churches in the provinces and their clergy, the pope's provision of benefices led to significant structural changes, which have been studied for Zurich and Metz. His intervention deprived oligarchies of locally and regionally powerful families of the possibility to utilize a large part of the economically attractive benefices for accommodation of male offspring and especially for social climbers among them. The holders of benefices through papal provision were at the beginning chiefly of foreign origin, who brought other strangers in their wake. In this way, clerics with a broader horizon and exposure to the wider world were recruited, which must have benefited their churches. In addition, the number of candidates still in their infancy diminished (at least in Germany) among those on the waiting lists. Individuals obtaining clerical benefices through apostolic provision belonged primarily to the privileged petitioners, that is, people with curial status and — above all — university students.

It was often advantageous for a church to count curial clerics among its members, because it helped address at the Curia many requests of the local clergy and laity, for example, by facilitating the grant of various dispensations or indulgences to finance the building of ecclesiastical edifices, or to obtain papal graces marking social distinction like the right to a portable altar, or permission to hear Mass in a domestic chapel and so on.[80] Clerical graduates, whose degree at the time was primarily in canon law, assumed the role of judge delegates or mediators in their newly adopted region, being in great demand due to widespread distrust in the ordinary courts.

In all, it is fair to assume that the superior administrative skills and special familiarity of papally appointed clergy with uniform procedures proved beneficial to their churches. It is perhaps also possible to argue that this allowed ecclesiastical institutions to react with greater flexibility than lay nobility to contemporary economic challenges such as the so-called 'agrarian crisis'.[81] The reduced contingent of churchmen drawn from leading families in the area certainly permitted churches to operate more independently than before. For the individual cleric, provision by the pope implied freedom, mobility, and promotion along with that of relatives. This was particularly true for the large number of academic graduates. Their improved career chances must have been tied to the rapid rise during the

---

79 As noted for John of Segovia when he left the *familia* of Cardinal Juan Cervantes; cf. Diener, 'Zur Persönlichkeit des Johannes von Segovia', pp. 314–15; Schwarz, 'Patronage und Klientel', pp. 302–03 (English version below, pp. 60–61).

80 Cf. the rubric of 'diverse forms' in the papal registers; Frenz, *Die Kanzlei der Päpste*, pp. 77–78. Curial clergy were cooperative in this way, enhancing their own prestige.

81 For the nobility, see Rapp, *L'Église et la vie religieuse en Occident*, pp. 274 ff.

period of matriculated students, newly founded universities, and focus on the *artes* and on canon law.[82] The acquisition of benefices on the papal market not only required, but also allowed for, personal initiative in the pursuit of an education and employment congruent with one's talents. If a position failed to deliver, on the other hand, the mechanism of papally approved resignation and exchange (or permutation) with another offered an easy way out. Simultaneously, at least upstarts seeking a benefice for career purposes had to join a clientele and accept some level of dependency. Once they had advanced to respectability within that circle, which among other things became manifest in the accumulation of holdings, they could use them as flexible assets and exploit, with the assistance of fellow clients, the potential of the market to the fullest.

Ordinary collators and their entourage were on the losing side when faced with the mass-production of papal provisions. Considering themselves as the rightful distributors, they were suddenly at a disadvantage in the fierce competition for benefices. They frequently turned to resistance, which at times assumed dramatic proportions. The abbess and convent of canonesses at Gandersheim, for instance, instigated their servants around 1342 to incapacitate a papally provided cleric by blinding him.[83] Some ignored or undercut apostolic mandates, while others went along. The canons of the Great Minster at Zurich eventually abolished their waiting list after realizing that papal expectancies had repeatedly messed with their rankings through preferment of foreign candidates. Those who had once monopolized the recruitment started to pursue canonries via the papacy as well. Moreover, ordinary collators were not content to address individual attacks on their canonical competency through papal provision. Their representatives proposed complete abolition of the practice at the Reform Councils of Basel and Constance, which also served as gatherings of lobbyists, with suggestions of improvement that were not always

---

82 Meyer, 'Das Wiener Konkordat', p. 116.

83 *Regesten*, ed. by Schwarz, no. 836, between December 1337 and 15 May 1342, a letter from the Great Penitentiary; the provided cleric held an expectancy for a parish to be appointed by the canonesses. Murder occurred as well; cf. *Regesten*, ed. by Schwarz, no. 992 (of 24 April 1371); printed in *Urkundenbuch des Hochstifts Hildesheim*, VI, ed. by Hoogeweg, no. 93. Again, the instigators were nuns from a convent (at Derneburg). Before 1419, the parish priest of Idensen in the diocese of Minden had solicited others to kill his victorious rival at the Curia, a minor cleric; *Repertorium Germanicum*, IV, ed. by Fink and Weiss, nos 947, 2318, 2400, 3722. According to the petitions, the priest was the uncanonical holder of several parishes. The bishop of Minden was also implicated in the murder, because he requested an absolution for it. The examples can be multiplied; cf. Weiss, 'Kurie, Konzil und Kirchenreform', pp. 196–97 nn. 653 ff. Still common in the fourteenth century and especially at the beginning of papal provisions under John XXII, recourse to physical violence diminished later; cf. Caillet, *La papauté d'Avignon*, pp. 395 ff.

disinterested.[84] Their success was limited, however.[85] The concordats of Constance or in this case, the one with the German nation, represented a compromise.[86] The same applied to its later extensions, the agreements from 1441 onward, and that of Vienna, 1448.[87] Each acknowledged the papal right of reservation, albeit with limitations. Voting was restored for elective benefices.[88] All remaining appointments were mechanically divided according to their date of vacancy, so that during the six even months they belonged to the papacy as opposed to the six odd ones. Mentioned above, the universities and the secular lords heavily leaned toward papal provisions, for they were the main beneficiaries.[89]

Because they could not act as ordinary collators, rulers had long supplied their officials with ecclesiastical benefices by way of papal provision.[90] Beginning with the Schism of 1378, they managed to obtain from the Curia prerogatives for an ever-widening circle of people under their protection. They facilitated the acquisition of positions akin to the rights of preferment for curial clerics and university professors.[91] Popes had to cater to them in this regard and by conceding them quotas of the papal power to nominate for benefices, since they needed the princes

---

84 Meyer, 'Das Wiener Konkordat', pp. 108 ff., 128.

85 As decreed in Basel 1436, Session XXIII, 'On Reservations'; in *Conciliorum Oecumenicorum Decreta*, ed. by Alberigo and others, p. 505. Even attendants of the Council were not happy with the decree; it built on the Pragmatic Sanction of Bourges (1438) and was often ignored; Meyer, 'Das Wiener Konkordat', p. 109 n. 2, p. 114 n. 20, pp. 133–34.

86 From the Concordat of Constance, special rules were in place for elective benefices; Meyer, *Zürich und Rom*, p. 44. They were expressly reserved to the ordinary collators, unless they had been in the possession of clergy belonging to the *familia* of a pope or cardinal. The situation was unclear for St Florin, see p. 53 n. 26 below. According to *Acta Cusana*, ed. by Meuthen and Hallauer, I/1, no. 74, the deanery of Liebfrauen was indeed an elective benefice.

87 The original Concordat for the German nation expired on 2 May 1423. Subsequently, reservations were reinstated in line with Chancery rules until 13 April 1425; cf. Schwarz, 'Die Abbreviatoren', p. 216. On the legal status of papal provisions after the concordats of Constance, most recently Meyer, *Zürich und Rom*, p. 45; also, Meyer, 'Das Wiener Konkordat', pp. 123–24; Folz, 'Le Concordat germanique'.

88 The passage concerning principal dignities in the Concordat of Vienna was wrongly interpreted by the Curia — in its own favour, of course; as shown by Meyer, *Zürich und Rom*, pp. 40, 42–43, 49, and especially 108 ff.; Meyer, 'Das Wiener Konkordat', p. 108 n. 4.

89 As a result, they were primarily in search of a compromise; see Meyer, 'Das Wiener Konkordat', pp. 109, 131.

90 Forming for the lords a convenient form of stipend, which is why clerical servants were the predominant type of princely official through the fifteenth century; cf. Moraw, 'Die gelehrten Juristen', p. 81 and elsewhere; the first salaried jurists appeared around that time, p. 118. For laypeople, however, membership in a ruler's council or a contract as legal consultant of an imperial town were maximum career accomplishments; see the literature cited by Schwarz, 'Patronage und Klientel', p. 287 (English translation below, p. 50).

91 Cf. my review of *Repertorium Germanicum*, VI, ed. by Abert and others, in *Historische Zeitschrift*, 242 (1986), 422–24.

46    CHAPTER 1

as allies against the Council.[92] After the Concordat of Vienna (1448), vacancies opening during the 'even' papal months were likely to be filled only by territorial lords, in some areas for years. Starting with Sixtus IV (1471–1484), the papacy left the exercise of nominations with increasing frequency altogether to them, while retaining the fees that were due for the issuance of papal provisions. From that time onward, local leaders claimed — eventually with success — that the benefices they were able to keep within their clientele did not just belong to them by way of patronage. They also considered themselves patrons as defined by church law.[93]

The interplay of competencies in the conferral of benefices between the ordinary collator on the one hand and the territorial lord on the other was of profound consequence for the recruitment of clergy in the chapter churches. Their canonries began to serve (once more) to accommodate younger sons and increasingly people under princely protection, too. Both objectives were facilitated by recourse to the papacy, just as the holders of benefices were well advised to obtain papal dispensation in the form of a 'resignation in favour of a third party', if they wished to keep their position from appropriation at the hands of the collator or ruler. As time went on, the share of foreigners, especially those of curial status and legal training, diminished again among members of the chapter churches. Ordinary collators and princes were content to promote their own followers. Elsewhere, the demand for trained canonists, who had been the main beneficiaries of papal provisions, dropped with the improvement of administrative services in the territories and bishoprics, above all at the judicial courts. Now that (urban) governments and parishes had gained influence over the assignment of ecclesiastical positions as tutors of the sacred sites in their locality, there was unprecedented interest in theologically educated

---

92 The concession of extremely high contingents of papal graces was part of the bargain Eugene IV and Nicholas V had to make after turning against the Council of Basel. The elector of Trier, Jacob of Sierck, for example, had Nicholas V reserve him collation of the provostships in the four most important chapters of his lands; cf. Miller, *Jakob von Sierck*, p. 276. This made it very difficult for the holders of these positions to play a role as independent as Nicholas of Cusa had from 1430 onward. Meyer, 'Das Wiener Konkordat', p. 113 n. 16, prefers to connect conferral of the right of nomination to bishops — not secular rulers — with an earlier papal tradition reaching back into the Avignonese period and aiming at compensation for the almost complete loss of their function as ordinary collators.

93 This is well illustrated in a letter by the archbishop of Trier, Jacob of Sierck, to Cardinal Cusanus (after 11 November 1452), in which Jacob wrote 'that the illustrious Duke of Julich and Berg promised to N. that when the priory of Aachen would become vacant, he should present the son of N., who was still a boy, to the same priory'; *Briefwechsel*, ed. by Koch, I, pp. 84–85. Presentation to the provostship was from 1336 a former imperial prerogative in the possession of the Duke of Jülich (as kindly indicated to me by Professor Meuthen). It was nonetheless an elective benefice, so that the duke could not exercise patronage over it following the Concordat of Vienna in 1448! On the expansion of this right in the late Middle Ages and early modernity, see Weber, *Familienkanonikate und Patronatsbistümer*.

preachers and pastors. In addition, the chapter churches themselves started to turn against non-residential clerics by slowing or stalling the flow of income from benefices as their weapon of choice. Curial clergy responded by refocusing on simple benefices like vicariates and chapels, which until then had been less popular on the papal benefice market.[94]

The papal Curia lost importance in the trade of benefices, not least because non-curial clergy started to obtain benefices more safely and cheaply at home.[95] At the same time, the pursuit of positions through curial channels grew ever more expensive, as the venality of staff positions proliferated and the expedition of papal mandates turned laborious. While the total of petitions aimed at papal authorization plummeted, ordinary collators regained their original function only in a formal sense. The new territorial governments had the final say, and supplicants had to seek their support going forward. The large number of students who previously found accommodation through papally approved expectancies henceforth had to frequent a nearby university.[96] It had to be located close to the benefices they wished to apply for. From there, they had to create and maintain all contacts leading to eventual acquisition in person.[97]

Curial clerics who acquired benefices in the provinces no longer regarded them as fundamental links to their place of origin.[98] Unlike holders of the preceding period, whose principal investment lay in the native region to which they hoped to return, their successors lacked interest in the positions as such and focused only on their monetary yield. For career prospects, they concentrated entirely on the Curia. Benefices also lost in significance as means to reward one's clientele. When the Curia ceased to

---

94 Concerning a group of minor curial clerics (primarily at the apostolic courts), cf. Meyer, 'Das Wiener Konkordat', p. 112 and, especially, pp. 145 ff. Chaplainries, moreover, lacked objective perpetuity and were thus ill-suited.

95 How indispensable it was to have supply and demand converge at the Curia is illustrated by the example of England, where papal expectancies and provisions were not admitted. Beginning around 1400, the figure of the 'chop-church' (a technical term from the sixteenth century) came into existence as a substitute, whose services were primarily needed by English university professors and students. The chop-church existed into the 1800s; cf. Rodes, *Ecclesiastical Administration in Medieval England*, pp. 118–19.

96 Expectancies had been the most important claim for papal candidates, but were hardly requested anymore for lack of utility, as the few remaining positions requiring papal provision were immensely competitive; Meyer, *Zürich und Rom*, p. 172; Meyer, 'Das Wiener Konkordat', pp. 111–12. On the submission of universities and chapters to 'intermediate' territorial control at the expense of the papacy, see also Moraw, 'Aspekte und Dimensionen', pp. 14–15; Moraw, 'Über Typologie, Chronologie und Geographie', pp. 27 ff.

97 Meyer, 'Das Wiener Konkordat', p. 112.

98 Schuchard, *Die Deutschen an der päpstlichen Kurie*, pp. 283 ff., has shown that curial clerics from the Schism through the Age of the Councils (1378–1450) usually considered the Curia as just one, if important, station in their career.

operate as the central marketplace for benefices, the connection between officials there and Western churches everywhere weakened alongside. In similar vein, the supplicants for provisions struggled to obtain approval of their requests from the papal administration.

CHAPTER 2

# Patronage and Clientele in the Late Medieval Church

## *The Example of Nicholas of Cusa*[1]

The person I would like to talk about, Nicholas Krebs, was the son of Henne (or Johannes) Krebs, a merchant.[2] Henne's wife, Katharina (Römer by her maiden-name), came from a family of lay judges in the small town of Bernkastel. Nicholas was born in 1401 in the village of Kues (*Cusa* in Latin) on the Moselle River belonging to the territories of the elector and archbishop of Trier. In recognition of his birthplace, he came to be known as Nicholas of Cusa (or Cusanus). At the age of sixteen, he held the status of *clericus* and began his studies at the University of Heidelberg.[3] As a medieval *clericus*, Nicholas did not have to be a priest, nor was he obliged to join the priesthood, which he did about twenty years afterwards.[4] From 1417, he continued his studies at Padua, which at the time was considered the foremost university in Europe.[5] He obtained his degree as doctor of

---

1  This essay is the footnoted version of a presentation given at the Conference of the Historical Institute of the Adam-Mickiewicz University of Poznań and the Historical Seminar of the University of Hanover on 24 October 1986.

2  The biography by Vansteenberghe, *Le cardinal Nicolas de Cues*, remains fundamental. A brief survey of the most recent research is offered by Meuthen, *Nikolaus von Kues*, which I use to cite evidence in the following. For an accumulative and comprehensive bibliography on the life and works of Cusanus, see *Mitteilungen und Forschungsbeiträge*, 1 (1961), pp. 95–126; vol. 3 (1963), pp. 223–37; vol. 6 (1967), pp. 178–202; vol. 10 (1973), pp. 207–34; vol. 15 (1982), pp. 121–47.

3  Meuthen, *Nikolaus von Kues*, pp. 7–8, 11, 14–15.

4  Meuthen, 'Die Pfründen des Cusanus', pp. 33–34, places his ordinations as deacon and priest between 11 May 1435 and 10 November 1440; *Acta Cusana*, ed. by Meuthen and Hallauer, I/1, no. 236; vol. I/2, no. 438. Because his last dispensation from promotion requirements of 22 June 1428 was valid for seven years, Cusanus unsurprisingly appeared as deacon on 11 May 1435. Unexpectedly, however, he was still a deacon on 21 July 1436 (*Acta Cusana*, ed. by Meuthen and Hallauer, I/1, no. 267), if the indication is correct. After passing the decisive threshold of the diaconate, contemporaries normally did not wait with their ordination to the priesthood longer than the next ember date. Perhaps, he did not find the time to be ordained in his home diocese while at Basel, or he at least pretended not to, given the great political difficulties associated with it (see p. 55, n. 35, p. 56 n. 42 below), and already planned his ordination at the Curia. It would have been impossible for him, I believe, to have left without priestly rank for his trip to Constantinople.

5  Meuthen, *Nikolaus von Kues*, p. 15; on the prestige of Padua as an intellectual centre, see Ascheri, 'Giuristi, umanisti e istituzioni', pp. 59–60. Research in fifteenth-century universities is well underway; cf. Belloni, *Professori giuristi a Padova*.

church (or canon) law there in 1423, along with the permission to teach the subject at any university. Over the next few years, he worked as a professor of canon law at Cologne University and as a juristic consultant. Above all, though, he accepted commissions from his territorial lord, the archbishop of Trier, which among other things took him to Rome on one occasion.

What could a young man of his background hope for, if he had the desire to make a difference in the world? This is apparently what Nicholas Cusanus intended. Had he wished to dedicate himself to scholarship, he would not have abandoned his professorship at Cologne, nor rejected two offers to teach at Leiden University.[6] In short, his background associated him with a middle-class and urban upbringing, a family of means apparently permitting him to embark on his rather expensive course of studies, the skills of a brilliant lawyer, a broad educational horizon, and good connections forged over the course of his academic years.[7] The greatest limit to his chances certainly consisted of his non-noble birth. He was barred from membership (as a canon) in episcopal chapters, for instance.[8]

The principal condition of his career was his status as a cleric. It secured him funding in accordance with his standing, assuming the form of ecclesiastical benefices. Benefices were tied to church offices. They furnished those who held them with permanent income, which churchmen could collect upon dispensation and without having to exercise the associated functions in person. In possession of the highest academic degree, Nicholas Cusanus was privileged by canon law, because he could keep several and better endowed benefices simultaneously.[9] Across Germany, even secular rulers offered juristic positions only to clerics, whose economic support they did not have to guarantee. Contrary to the situation in Italy, lay lawyers struggled to find employment, especially when they originated from among the townspeople.[10]

---

6 Meuthen, *Nikolaus von Kues*, pp. 15, 20, 25, 27. Most law professors behaved like Nicholas, unless they held viable benefices at their place of study; cf. Moraw, 'Die Juristenuniversität in Prag', pp. 473, 478.

7 Meuthen, *Nikolaus von Kues*, pp. 15 ff. On the importance of the ties created as a student, Reinhard, *Freunde und Kreaturen*, pp. 37–38; also, Moraw, 'Zur Sozialgeschichte der deutschen Universitäten', pp. 44–60; and, on Padua as focal point for a new group of imperial and royal jurists around 1430, Moraw, 'Über gelehrte Juristen', pp. 121, 145.

8 At least in the chapter churches he was thinking of, such as those of Trier, Mainz, Cologne, and the like; see Kisky, *Die Domkapitel der geistlichen Kurfürsten*; for Trier in particular, Holbach, *Stiftsgeistlichkeit*; also useful, Fouquet, 'Reichskirche und Adel'.

9 *Regulae cancellariae apostolicae*, ed. by von Ottenthal, p. 194 (§ 33).

10 Moraw, 'Die gelehrten Juristen', p. 81 and elsewhere; the first lawyers to receive a salary were from this time, p. 118. Lay jurists attained the top position of their career when they joined a ruler's council or landed a contract as advisers of an imperial town. Contemporary non-clerical examples of renown were Gregory of Heimburg, Martin Mair, and Laurentius Blumenau. On the learned counselors, cf. Lieberich, 'Die gelehrten Räte'; Boockmann,

While it was difficult to secure provision with a benefice, not to mention a lucrative one, it was even more challenging to hold and maintain it
effectively.[11] As a result, the successful candidate had to rely on networks,
sponsors, and protection, in other words: patronage. Once he had landed
a benefice, moreover, he had to build a clientele to keep it and have it
multiply, which is the main topic of this study. I will not attempt a survey
of all forms of patronage and clientele in the late medieval Church, a goal
out of my reach as scholarship has done very little on the subject. I will
rather restrict myself to the example of Nicholas Cusanus, in order to
illustrate both phenomena so characteristic of clerical career building at
the time.

In practical terms, my approach can conveniently count on considerable source material. The distribution of benefices is well documented
insofar as it concerned the pope, who intervened in nearly all cases,
either because he owned the right of conferral based on general or special
reservation, or acted by way of dispensing candidates from canonical
regulations. Thanks to documentation comprising the petitions directed
to, and approved by, the papacy, it is often possible to identify the
petitioner's protector and determine who held the benefice previously
and successively, which is equally important for the historical analysis.
Regarding the territories of the German Empire, the fifteenth-century data
favour consultation owing to the long-term research project known as the
*Repertorium Germanicum*.[12] In addition, and given his stature as the most
celebrated German churchman of the period, information about Nicholas
of Cusa is systematically gathered in the exhaustive catalogues of the *Acta
Cusana*, which for the moment do not extend beyond the year 1450.[13]

To return to Nicholas of Cusa, he obtained his first benefice in 1425,
a position as parish priest close to where he came from.[14] In an autobio-
graphical note, he was explicit as to who his benefactor was on the occasion. The archbishop of Trier conceded the position to him for his material
support, yielding a steady monetary rent and dues in kind along with the

---

*Laurentius Blumenau*; Moraw, 'Beamtentum und Rat König Ruprechts', p. 59; and especially
Heimpel, *Die Vener von Gmünd*, I, pp. 155, 191 ff. The restricted possibilities of Nicholas's lay
competitors are illustrated in Gregory of Heimburg's biography; Wendehorst, 'Gregor von
Heimburg'.

11 See most recently, Meyer, *Zürich und Rom*.

12 *Repertorium Germanicum*, currently vols I–IV; with an index of persons for vols I–IV; of
places for vols I–III. Outside the series, the *Repertorium Concilii Basiliensis*, ed. by Gilomen,
encompasses data not relating to the Empire as well; it is to appear in 1988.

13 Cf. *Acta Cusana*, ed. by Meuthen and Hallauer, in the Bibliography, p. 282 below.

14 Meuthen, 'Die Pfründen des Cusanus', pp. 16, 22; *Acta Cusana*, ed. by Meuthen and
Hallauer, I/1, p. 7 (no. 21).

church of Altrich.[15] If he was unwilling to be ordained to the priesthood within a year, however, he had to secure papal dispensation.[16] Because he was unable to settle the matter in satisfactory fashion, he lastly resigned the benefice in favour of his brother.[17] He treated his second benefice similarly, a position as member (or canon) of the chapter at St Simeon in Trier, received in 1426 but soon resigned for unknown reasons.[18] In 1428, one Matthias Krebs from Kues — a relative in other words — is mentioned as holder of the canonry. Following his death, the next tenant's name is again that of Nicholas's brother, Johannes. Succeeding the latter at St Simeon and in Johannes's remaining benefices were several individuals (or *familiares*) from Nicholas's 'household', recommended by him after he advanced to the cardinalate.[19]

This shows a feature that was recurrent in connection with clerical clienteles. Benefices that became available for some reason were kept, if possible, within the household.[20] There was nonetheless much fluctuation because benefices frequently had to be abandoned for legal reasons or

---

15 *Acta Cusana*, ed. by Meuthen and Hallauer, I/1, nos 21–22; cf. Meuthen, 'Die Pfründen des Cusanus'. Apparently, the benefice had become vacant by 'free' resignation, so that it could be conferred by its ordinary collator, the local archbishop; otherwise, the right of conferral would have devolved to the pope; cf. *Acta Cusana*, ed. by Meuthen and Hallauer, I/1, no. 30.

16 Cusanus tried requesting permission 'to study in university for ten years or reside at the Roman Curia'; *Acta Cusana*, ed. by Meuthen and Hallauer, I/1, no. 28. This still necessitated his ordination to the subdiaconate within a year; see *Regulae cancellariae apostolicae*, ed. by von Ottenthal, p. 195 (§ 35); and the reform decree by the Council of Constance, in *Conciliorum Oecumenicorum Decreta*, ed. by Alberigo and others, p. 448. Cusanus attempted to delay ordination for a year by asking for rehabilitation and a 'new' papal provision, but the pope did not go along, only granting postponement until the next possible date (i.e. the following ember Saturday); *Acta Cusana*, ed. by Meuthen and Hallauer, I/1, no. 30. The brother applied for the benefice within ten days, given that it was 'vacant due to the non-promotion' of Nicholas; *Acta Cusana*, ed. by Meuthen and Hallauer, I/1, no. 31.

17 Technically, this was not a 'resignation in favour', which would have required approval from the Curia to shun the risk of *simonia iuris*; cf. Gillmann, *Die Resignation der Benefizien*. Papal provision seems to have taken the form of a signed petition rather than a sealed letter; it served to prevent claims by third parties; see *Acta Cusana*, ed. by Meuthen and Hallauer, I/1, nos 31, 68–69. Johannes Krebs of Cusa maintained possession of the benefice until 1450; *Acta Cusana*, ed. by Meuthen and Hallauer, I/2, nos 888–89.

18 *Acta Cusana*, ed. by Meuthen and Hallauer, I/1, no. 30, which mentions it among the disclaimers. He must have obtained this benefice through ordinary collation, too.

19 *Acta Cusana*, ed. by Meuthen and Hallauer, I/1, no. 77, with n. 3; Meuthen, 'Die Pfründen des Cusanus', p. 17; Meuthen, *Die letzten Jahre*, pp. 311–12.

20 As observed by Reinhard, *Freunde und Kreaturen*, p. 73; Meyer, *Zürich und Rom*, pp. 74, 78. On the circulation of benefices within the suite of cardinals, see Paravicini Bagliani, *Cardinali di Curia*, II, pp. 500 ff.; Verger, 'L'entourage du cardinal Pierre de Monteruc', p. 540, although the phenomenon has not been investigated systematically. It is acknowledged in principle in *Regulae cancellariae apostolicae*, ed. by von Ottenthal, p. 215 (§ 119), p. 245 (§ 47), p. 259 (§ 30).

were subject to speculative transactions.[21] Clientele and household were not in opposition to each other. Members of the latter (the *familiares*) belonged to the clientele if they met minimum qualifications. They even played a key role, for patrons could count on them the most. In clerical clienteles, succession was usually reserved to nephews, which is why the expression of 'nepotism' arose.[22] Of course, brothers, cousins, uncles, and more distant relatives also figured among the special persons of trust.

Returning to the phenomenon of benefice transfers within one clientele, it is possible to gain insight into the inner circle and close friendships of a patron by carefully examining who held benefices assigned to a clerical network at earlier and later points in time. The composition, extent, and structure of clienteles is revealed because patrons reserved the most lucrative positions to especially reliable or important clients. Studies of this type are difficult for Nicholas of Cusa and his German contemporaries, since the relevant volumes of the *Repertorium Germanicum* are still without any index of place names.[23]

In applying this method to the fourth benefice obtained by Nicholas, we can identify the holder preceding him and resigning it upon entry into a monastery as the secretary of Otto of Ziegenhain, archbishop of Trier, who for his part acted most likely as the sponsor and perhaps initiator of the transfer.[24] The assumption is further validated when we consider that the archbishop successively intervened as mediator in conflict over the benefice between another client and Nicholas, eventually compensating the latter for his resignation with rental payments made from his own funds as territorial lord.[25] For the previous tenant of Nicholas's fifth benefice, the deanery of a prestigious chapter church, special bonds of trust with the archbishop are also evident.[26] No worries, it is the last benefice transaction I will mention.

---

21 Meyer, *Zürich und Rom*, p. 64, has noted this aspect in the acquisition of benefices by members of the Curia. It would be mistaken and anachronistic, however, to view it as driven by purely economic reasons. Benefices were not sought to resell them for the greatest profit, but to advance one's career by passing them on to clients or patrons; see Schwarz, 'Römische Kurie und Pfründenmarkt' (English version above, pp. 27–48).

22 Cf. the studies of Reinhard, 'Nepotismus. Der Funktionswandel'; Reinhard, 'Papa Pius'; Reinhard, 'Nepotismus'. Also, Esch, 'Das Papsttum unter der Herrschaft der Neapolitaner'.

23 See above, p. 51 n. 12.

24 *Acta Cusana*, ed. by Meuthen and Hallauer, I/1, nos 38–39, 74, and 95; cf. Meuthen, 'Die Pfründen des Cusanus', pp. 19–21. On this benefice, typically providing for the archbishop's collaborators, see *Das Erzbistum Trier*, ed. by Pauly, II, p. 354.

25 *Acta Cusana*, ed. by Meuthen and Hallauer, I/1, no. 39, with n. 1, no. 74 n. 2, and no. 95; Meuthen, 'Die Pfründen des Cusanus', pp. 22–23.

26 The deanery in question was St Florin in Koblenz. In his petition, Nicholas calls himself the archbishop's secretary and commissary, a sure sign that he had the prelate's backing; *Acta Cusana*, ed. by Meuthen and Hallauer, I/1, nos 40–43, 46–47, 74, 79, 285. On the benefice, Diederich, *Das Stift St Florin*, pp. 88 ff.

## CHAPTER 2

In 1427, Nicholas of Cusa was able to derive from his benefices income that was in accordance with his status. Three years afterwards, his employer and patron, Otto of Ziegenhain, died in 1430.[27] What followed was a schism in the archbishopric, which I cannot treat in detail.[28] Nicholas represented the interests of one of the candidates, Ulrich of Manderscheid. He had joined the Manderscheid party because the conflict over archepiscopal succession was not just the result of personal ambition, but also involved dynastic interests of the powerful Manderscheid lordship.[29] In fact, Nicholas of Cusa sided with the Manderscheids from the very start rather than waiting for events to unfold.[30] He opted to do so notwithstanding that, as a jurist, he must have been aware that Ulrich's position was tenuous from a legal perspective.[31] In addition, he had to reckon with repercussions for his own possessions and career in case of defeat and faced modest prospects of gain should Ulrich emerge as the winner. At best, Nicholas could hope for the post of archepiscopal counsellor or chancellor, which did not open access to richer benefices due to his non-noble birth.

To account for his role, it is consequently most plausible to think that he belonged to the clientele of the Manderscheids well before the schism

---

27 Holbach, 'Die Besetzung des Trierer Erzbischofsstuhls', pp. 11–48; on Otto of Ziegenhain, see especially pp. 35 ff.; also, Holbach, '*Disz ist dy ansprache*'. I use the term of 'patron' in the modern sociological sense of 'exercising patronage' and not in the way medieval church lawyers spoke of patronage (*patronatus*) as a legal institution.

28 Laufner, 'Die Manderscheidsche Fehde'. Meuthen, *Das Trierer Schisma*; Meuthen, 'Obödienz- und Absolutionslisten'. There is nothing new in Watanabe, 'The Episcopal Election of 1430'. About the conflict from the perspective of the other electoral princes, cf. Mathies, *Kurfürstenbund und Königtum*, pp. 267 ff. On Manderscheid's rivals, see Fouquet, 'Reichskirche und Adel'; Lager, 'Raban von Helmstadt'; also, Miller, *Jakob von Sierck*; Miller, 'Kurtrier und die Übernahme des Herzogtums Luxemburg'.

29 Neu, *Geschichte und Struktur der Eifelterritorien*, especially pp. 44–49.

30 Together with his colleague at the imperial diet and at the Council of Basel, Hellwig of Boppard, he signed the protocol on the transition of the cathedral canons from the Siercks to the Manderscheid party (*Acta Cusana*, ed. by Meuthen and Hallauer, 1/1, no. 78) and the appeal against the papal provision with the archiepiscopate (*Acta Cusana*, ed. by Meuthen and Hallauer, 1/1, no. 80). Both appear from the beginning as leading counsels and 'administrators' of the Manderscheids, Nicholas, for example, in *Acta Cusana*, ed. by Meuthen and Hallauer, 1/1, no. 94. Meuthen, *Das Trierer Schisma*, p. 81, believes that Nicholas was in Rome with his lord at the end of 1430.

31 Meuthen, *Das Trierer Schisma*, pp. 66–71. Ulrich of Manderscheid was the candidate of a small minority in the chapter. The majority voted for Jakob Sierck, despite massive pressure from the Virneburgs, who sided with the Manderscheids. The pope rejected both when they appealed to him and provided the bishop of Speyer, Rhaban of Helmstatt, with Trier. Several groups in the archepiscopal chapter resisted this transfer until Jakob of Sierck renounced in favour of Ulrich after protracted negotiations. Ulrich was newly and unanimously elected on 10 September 1430. Pope Martin V did not accept the election and sought to impose Rhaban's installment as archbishop of Trier.

at Trier.[32] His father, Henne Krebs, had been in business relations with them, and Nicholas's association with the family is documented in a list of 1435, where his name appears among those banned by the Council of Basel for being followers of Ulrich of Manderscheid.[33] In his own foundation charter for the hospital of Kues, Nicholas stipulated that one vacancy in the house was to be reserved to the head of the Manderscheids and his heirs.[34] He made this provision although his involvement on behalf of the Manderscheids in 1430 had caused him much difficulty and nearly put an end to his career.[35] Moreover, he rarely had dealings with them thereafter, which is why his gesture as hospital founder must be seen as an act of lived reverence (*pietas*), which a current or previous client would have owed his patron out of respect and gratitude for received favours.[36] It is hardly accidental that several of Nicholas's benefices were located in areas controlled by the Manderscheids, and that three brothers from the family were members of the cathedral chapter while Nicholas was active in Cologne.[37]

The Manderscheid faction was an alliance of families from the high nobility, who were related through blood and intermarriage on multiple levels.[38] They exerted control over a widespread clientele of knights, lesser

---

32 Emphasized by Meuthen, *Nikolaus von Kues*, p. 11. One can only speculate about the origins and nature of Nicholas's relationship with the Manderscheids, who had a stronghold around Wittlich.

33 Cf. the lists of absolution and obedience above, p. 54 n. 28.

34 Edited by Marx, *Geschichte des Armen-Hospitals*, p. 59 (§ 6). On his will, most recently Schuchard, *Die Deutschen an der päpstlichen Kurie*, p. 305.

35 Meuthen, *Das Trierer Schisma*, pp. 102 ff., 144 ff., 231 ff., 244 ff. From December 1431, Ulrich of Manderscheid's followers were excommunicated as well. On 18 October 1432, Eugene IV granted the requested aggravation of coercive punishments against them. Although the Council of Basel started new investigations into the case and lifted all sanctions while the proceedings were pending, it lastly ruled against Ulrich (12–14 May 1434), too, followed by the usual mandates of execution and the imperial ban. Given that the injunctions could lead to the loss of benefices, Nicholas risked confiscation of his laboriously accumulated holdings. To prevent it, it was paramount for him to have Ulrich renounce to his claims. On 25 October 1436, Nicholas thus struggled to have his benefices confirmed by Pope Eugene IV; *Acta Cusana*, ed. by Meuthen and Hallauer, 1/1, no. 284.

36 Reinhard, 'Papa Pius', especially pp. 271–72; Reinhard, 'Nepotismus', p. 161.

37 Meuthen, *Nikolaus von Kues*, p. 32; Kisky, *Die Domkapitel der geistlichen Kurfürsten*, p. 61, nos 150 (erroneously assigned to Dietrich, not Johannes), 151, 153.

38 The contours of the group are traceable in contracts and lists of obedience generated during the conflict and discussed by Meuthen, *Das Trierer Schisma*. First, there was the circle of Ulrich's main promoters, noblemen rallying around Count Rudolf of Virneburg. They represented the position of noble canons seeking to reserve the episcopal seat and the canonries of the cathedral to the nobility and striving to defend their autonomy. Among them were Rudolf's sons, the counts of Sponheim, Veldenz, and lesser lords from the Eifel region, with the rest at least keeping away from the opposing candidate. In joining the party, detailed agreements were drawn up to itemize the respective obligations. The Virneburg faction was centered around Koblenz as is evident from later stages of

# CHAPTER 2

nobility (or *ministeriales*), and townspeople with access to financing. The party also included clerics whose benefices were concentrated in key areas of dynastic power. This example shows how the relationship between patrons and clients in the late medieval Church extended to clergy and churches on the one hand and laity on the other, as religious and temporal matters were closely intertwined, not least because secular princes used the law of patronage and their political connections to interfere with appointments to ecclesiastical office, obviously in favour of their own clients.[39]

As mentioned earlier, Nicholas represented Ulrich of Manderscheid at the Council of Basel. Although he could not steer Ulrich's case to a successful conclusion, others might have done worse given that his position was not backed by strong canonical argument. As a result, Ulrich and his partisans were banned.[40] Nicholas avoided losing his benefices by staging a compromise in which the Manderscheids abandoned Ulrich's claim to the archbishopric.[41] The ecclesiastical sanctions were lifted and those banned managed to obtain their rehabilitation.[42]

That Nicholas Cusanus succeeded in having Manderscheid's case treated at length at the Council without ruining his own career was due not only to his expertise in juristic manoeuvring. More than anything, his professional survival depended on close bonds of 'friendship' with important people at the Roman Curia, who already had served him well when he acquired his benefices in the first place. The term of 'friendship' designates in this context social ties that rest on the expectation of deriving

---

the conflict. Participants provided military aid individually or together as well as juristic support. Townspeople and other clients helped with loans and as sureties. There was also a small contingent of clerics and advisers drawn (like Nicholas of Cusa) from the clientele of certain supporters or speculating on advancement. They were important during diplomatic negotiations and in propagandistic efforts. The composition of Manderscheid's entourage is typical of late medieval territorial lords in Germany. The English evidence shows more clearly than continental examples how new relationships of greater flexibility marked the retinue of political leaders; cf. Contamine, *La guerre au Moyen Age*, pp. 275–79, summarizing the scholarship on so-called 'bastard feudalism'. The article by Moraw, 'Über Patrone und Klienten', pp. 1–18, arrived too late for this essay. My thanks to Mr Moraw for leaving me his typescript.

39 To illustrate this, there is the letter written by Archbishop Jacob of Trier (from the Sierck family) to Cardinal Cusanus after 11 November 1452, stating under reference to the provostship of Aachen that 'the illustrious lord, the duke of Jülich and Berg once promised' a certain nobleman 'to present his son, who was still a boy, as candidate for the same provostship'; *Briefwechsel*, ed. by Koch, I, pp. 84–85.

40 Meuthen, *Das Trierer Schisma*, pp. 228 ff.

41 Meuthen, *Das Trierer Schisma*, pp. 249 ff. Ulrich did not really accept the compromise. He fought until the end (d. 1438) for his claim, whereas the Virneburgs pursued a favourable settlement for themselves, pp. 253 ff.

42 Pope Eugene IV confirmed the peace with the Manderscheids on 7 March 1436 and lifted the ecclesiastical sanctions; cf. Meuthen, *Das Trierer Schisma*, p. 252.

benefits from each other (and from the friends of friends). The reciprocal favours were understood in principle as being of equal value according to Wolfgang Reinhard.[43] If contributions of one side greatly exceeded those from the other — thereby turning the relationship into an asymmetrical one — the bond transformed into one between patron and client. Clerical friendships of this kind could be based on shared places of origin, affiliation with the same university or monastery, and the like. Amicable feeling in the sense of modern German usage did not have to be part of such friendships. But they frequently were in the case of Nicholas of Cusa. As a student in Padua, he met with various persons who shared his strong interest in scientific problems and had important functions at the Roman Curia and at the Council of Basel.[44] These worked and intervened on his behalf with others.[45] Nicholas responded by sending them old manuscripts, which his humanist friends craved in particular.[46] In addition, he assisted in the explanation of scientific questions and offered advice and support concerning the union with the Greek Church, aided by his familiarity with the Greek language, which was very exceptional at the time, as was his knowledge of the Greek church fathers.[47]

After denouncing the Council of Basel and joining the pope in 1438, the conciliar party took away his benefices.[48] This was of practical significance because they were mostly located in the lands of the archepiscopal chapter of Trier whose territorial lord, Archbishop Jakob, sided with the Council.[49] Nicholas went on to acquire benefices in the Netherlands, a region that was loyal to Pope Eugene IV.[50] Around the same time, Nicholas started to build his own clientele. His protracted absences during his stay at Basel and on diplomatic mission as well as his accumulation of

---

43  See Reinhard, *Freunde und Kreaturen*, p. 38.

44  There is no study of Nicholas's friends; much documentation can be found in the *Acta Cusana*; cf. Meuthen, *Nikolaus von Kues*, pp. 18–19.

45  Meuthen, *Nikolaus von Kues*, pp. 32–33, for lists of his most important friends at the Curia and, p. 50, in Basel. Friendly intervention during his stay at the Curia in 1425 is likely and proven for 1435; *Acta Cusana*, ed. by Meuthen and Hallauer, I/1, nos 244, 278. The role of friends in attempts to obtain a benefice is plainly visible in *Acta Cusana*, ed. by Meuthen and Hallauer, I/2, no. 397; for their impact on the career of Pope Pius II, see Brosius, 'Die Pfründen des Enea', p. 276 and elsewhere.

46  Meuthen, *Nikolaus von Kues*, pp. 31 ff.; Vansteenberghe, *Le cardinal Nicolas de Cues*, ch. II.

47  Meuthen, *Nikolaus von Kues*, pp. 51–52.

48  Meuthen, 'Die Pfründen des Cusanus', p. 43. Provisions for Nicholas's benefices were already granted in 1438; however, confiscation proceedings continued until 27 January 1440; see *Acta Cusana*, ed. by Meuthen and Hallauer, I/2, nos 347–48.

49  Miller, *Jakob von Sierck*, pp. 115 ff.

50  Beginning in 1438 with one at the dome of Liege. In more sustained fashion after the concordats with the city of 31 October 1441, with Philip of Burgundy for his territories outside the French kingdom (6 November 1441), and for certain areas under his protection and defence (23 April 1442); cf. Schwarz, 'Die Abbreviatoren', pp. 218, 246. On the Dutch benefices, see Meuthen, 'Die Pfründen des Cusanus', pp. 43 ff.

58    CHAPTER 2

outlying benefices beginning in 1438 prompted him to find local people to take care of his official duties.[51] He also needed them to help utilize the economic surplus of his possessions.[52] He had placed his brother in Trier for these purposes.[53] In similar fashion, he mobilized distant relatives for the handling of his Dutch holdings, assisted by clerics he probably met through recommendations from 'friends' among the many members of the Curia with origins in the Netherlands.[54]

Following his appointment as papal diplomat and the status of legate he received later, Nicholas of Cusa was expected to appear with an adequate entourage or 'retinue'.[55] It was known as his 'suite' of clients accompanying him everywhere.[55a] Most of them had the status of *familiares*. Higher curial officials presided over a household (*familia*) of persons who, along with them, were exempt from local jurisdiction and subject to

---

51 For proper appearance and provision, he certainly needed a retinue in accordance with his status; cf. *Acta Cusana*, ed. by Meuthen and Hallauer, I/2, nos 320, 439–40.

52 In a cardinal's household (more below, p. 60 n. 62), proctors on staff regularly had to account for their patron's benefices; Guillemain, *La cour pontificale d'Avignon*, p. 256; Verger, 'L'entourage du cardinal Pierre de Monteruc', p. 524. The duties of a cardinal's chamberlain are clearly outlined in the *Ordinatio pro gubernatione domus reverendissimorum cardinalium* (of 1409–1417), in *Le cérémonial papal*, ed. Dykmans, III, p. 447.

53 Johannes Krebs was canon of St Simeon in Trier to the end of his life, where he had a residence and normally spent his time; *Acta Cusana*, ed. by Meuthen and Hallauer, I/2, no. 560, with n. 6. He took over the parishes of Altrich and Bernkastel and the canonry of St Simeon directly or indirectly from his brother and supported him during stays around Trier. He also served as executor of Nicholas's favourite project, the hospital in Kues; *Acta Cusana*, ed. by Meuthen and Hallauer, I/2, nos 741, 745, and elsewhere. After his brother became cardinal, Johannes obtained additional benefices, although these (at Mainz and Aachen) were not located in a much wider area. Nicholas did not resign the priory of Oldenzaal to Johannes, only providing him with a pension from it; *Repertorium Germanicum*, VI, ed. by Abert and others, no. 2748. Nicholas apparently planned to rely on him as his representative at Brixen, but Johannes died in 1456; cf. Meuthen, 'Nikolaus von Kues in Aachen', p. 18. The younger brother of Jakob of Sierck, Philip, took on similar functions as benefice holder and supervisor of his brother's assets.

54 Under Eugene IV, the share of 'Dutch' curial members grew larger than ever before; Schuchard, *Die Deutschen an der päpstlichen Kurie*, p. 46. Among Nicholas's friends were apparently Heimericus de Campo who taught at Louvain, Gerardus de Randen, Walter of Gouda and, perhaps, Geoffrey Habotey of Bastogne. Others from the Lower Rhine with benefices in the Netherlands can also be assigned to the group, for example, Heinrich Raskop, Nikolaus Baest, Petrus de Mera, and Petrus de Molendino.

55 In the autumn of 1438, he was the last papal legate to go to the imperial diet of Nuremberg; to the Empire late in 1440 (with Juan Carvajal and Jacobus de Oratoribus), 1441 (*Acta Cusana*, ed. by Meuthen and Hallauer, I/2, nos 458–59, 654–68, 687), 1442, and especially 1446 (no. 701); 1448 (no. 762) to the Lower Rhine; 1450 (nos 952–54) on the great legation to Germany, Bohemia, and adjacent territories; 1451 to England, Burgundy, Bohemia; 1455 to England; 1457 to Prussia; cf. Meuthen, *Nikolaus von Kues*, pp. 86–94; Meuthen, 'Nikolaus von Kues auf dem Regensburger Reichstag', pp. 482–83.

55a I use the term 'suite' in the following to avoid associations with feudal law.

## PATRONAGE AND CLIENTELE IN THE LATE MEDIEVAL CHURCH · 59

that of their lord.[56] The demands of proper public display grew with the promotion and elevation of Nicholas to the rank of cardinal in 1448.[57] The new position also enhanced his ability to reward followers as a patron, because the cardinalate brought with it membership in the body (or college) of cardinals that after the pope was the most powerful institution at the Curia.[58] In fact, becoming a cardinal regularly changed the size and composition of a prelate's clientele, according to mechanisms I will outline here in prototypical fashion.

There were many who sought the protection of a new cardinal and especially hoped to become his *familiaris*.[59] They emphasized family ties if they were relatives, friendship with his friends, or reminded him of a shared past in the form of common origins, studies at university, or membership in the same religious order. They offered their services and activated connections or, sociologically speaking, their own 'set' of acquaintances. Frequently, the suite of cardinals comprised persons of high standing such as bishops.[60] If the cardinal was believed to have great

---

56 To my knowledge, this aspect has not yet been examined systematically; cf. Schuchard, *Die Deutschen an der päpstlichen Kurie*, pp. 49 ff. The cardinals at the Council of Constance even maintained that they were not under the jurisdiction of the Apostolic Chamberlain, who was the judge of all members of the Curia; *Acta concilii Constantiensis*, ed. by Finke and others, II, pp. 102–03, 114; III, p. 73.

57 Provisionally already on 16 December 1446 (*Acta Cusana*, ed. by Meuthen and Hallauer, I/2, no. 701), which failed to take effect due to Eugene IV's death; formally on 20 December 1448 and 3 January 1449, see Meuthen, *Nikolaus von Kues*, p. 77.

58 *Acta Cusana*, ed. by Meuthen and Hallauer, I/2, nos 864–65. Following his elevation, Nicholas's relatives, clients, and *familiares* sent a host of petitions referring to the new cardinal; *Acta Cusana*, ed. by Meuthen and Hallauer, I/2, nos 883, 888, 893, 896–901, 910–13, 918–22, 925, 938, 943–48.

59 The status of *familiaris* was formalized through nomination and the issuance of a patent; Paravicini Bagliani, *Cardinali di Curia*, II, pp. 455–59; Schuchard, *Die Deutschen an der päpstlichen Kurie*, pp. 49–50. The chamberlain of the suite kept account of them. Official *familiares* were preferred in the distribution of benefices, a few even more than others. Under John XXII, this concerned certain officials in the suite and relatives; see Teige, 'Beiträge zum päpstlichen Kanzleiwesen', pp. 429–30 (§ 47); subsequently, twelve *familiares* named in the (lost) books of the Chancery, cf. *Regulae cancellariae apostolicae*, ed. by von Ottenthal, p. 210 (§ 104), p. 215 (§ 119), p. 245 (§ 47), p. 259 (§ 30). The *familiares* (or some of them) received part of the *servitia* and *propina* paid to the cardinal; cf. Clergeac, *La Curie et les bénéficiers consistoriaux*, pp. 188–89.

60 Mollat, 'Contribution à l'histoire du Sacré College', has surveyed the courts and clientele of the cardinals. For the thirteenth century, there is the fundamental study of Paravicini Bagliani, *Cardinali di Curia*; for the fourteenth, Guillemain, *La cour pontificale d'Avignon*, pp. 251–76, with map 6 in the Appendix indicating the origin of the *familiares* for 1362 and 1363. For the later Avignonese period until the beginning of the Great Schism, there are several exemplary studies in *Genèse et débuts*, ed. by Favier. They include Guillemain, 'Cardinaux et société curiale'; Rey-Courtel, 'L'entourage d'Anglic Grimoard'; Bresc, 'La génèse du Schisme'; Binz, 'Le népotisme de Clément VII'. See also, Pasztor, 'Funzione politica-culturale', pp. 214 ff.; Rey-Courtel, 'Les clientèles des cardinaux limousins'; Verger,

influence on the pope, rulers and magnates showered him with pensions, promised promotion to his lay relatives and benefices to his clients.[61] Others also tried to win the cardinal's favour in accordance with their means.[62] The cardinal sought to foster these relationships in turn, satisfying expectations as much as he could. A significant clientele in terms of size and composition, and a reputation as someone who acted as guardian of the interests of secular and ecclesiastical leaders undoubtedly increased his standing at the Curia.

The cardinal resided in his own *livrée* in the sense of a jurisdictionally exempt space and maintained his own court in the papal Curia. This required an entourage of *familiares* for purposes of representation. They primarily belonged to the clergy, taking care of household management and the administrative duties awaiting him as member of the church leadership. They also assisted him in his liturgical functions.[63] Others could join the *familia* of a cardinal as well. First, there were the envoys of important nations and powers outside the cardinal's native region, who served as contacts for petitioners from those areas and consisted mostly of secretaries, notaries, and chaplains; secondly, to enhance the cardinal's prestige, both secular and clerical noblemen carried his shield or train, accompanied him in public, waited at his table, or functioned as majordomo presiding over his household and ceremonies. Thirdly, his entourage included *familiares*, who simultaneously held the same status of special trust with different cardinals, governments, rulers, or the pope, or who were top administrators at the Curia. Advice about the adequate appointment of a cardinal's court can be found in a book of ceremonies

---

'L'entourage du cardinal Pierre de Monteruc'; Esch, 'Das Papsttum unter der Herrschaft der Neapolitaner', p. 744, with n. 100.

61 This was most obvious with the relatives of cardinals, important charges, leaders of groups within the cardinalate and heads of dominant clans, such as those from Limoges in the late Avignonese period or the Neapolitans of the Roman observance during the Schism, see Esch, 'Das Papsttum under der Herrschaft der Neapolitaner'.

62 Episodes of petitioners attempting to win the favour of their friends among the cardinals, and especially when they had accepted assignments from them, are numerous in the reports of legates and their fiscal accounts, cf. *Die Rechnungsbücher*, ed. by Schrader, p. 89; the efforts extended to the cardinal's inner circle as well, p. 94; see also and very detailed, Segrè, 'I dispacci di Cristoforo da Piacenza', pp. 63–64, 258, 275–76.

63 As illustrated by Innocent VI's constitution 'Ad honorem' of 1357. It determined who was entitled to the cardinal's uniform (also *livrée*), including all his chaplains and clerical table companions (while only twelve of them could wear the great *livrée*); twenty-five squires in charge of certain functions; additional table companions; those substituting for the cardinal in his benefices; and permanent guests in his suite and their *familiares*. The constitution reveals the manoeuvres with which the *familiares* (and cardinals) tried to increase the (continuously capped) number of those in uniform; printed in Zacour, 'Papal Regulations', pp. 453–55.

PATRONAGE AND CLIENTELE IN THE LATE MEDIEVAL CHURCH 61

from the early fifteenth century.[64] Popes and councils repeatedly sought to limit the number of members in a cardinal's suite, though without enduring success!

The cardinal also had external clients apart from his permanent *familia*.[65] They were either with or without the status of a *familiaris*.[66] It is possible to identify them in a variety of ways, for example, in documentation about the conferral of benefices that were in the possession of a client at one point in time; in petitions to the pope in which the *familiares* always emphasized their corresponding status; and in supplications of cardinals on behalf of members of their clientele or *familia*.[67] Moreover, there is mention of them in rolls (*rotuli*) containing collective requests like those for passports for everyone travelling in a cardinal's suite. They list each traveller sequentially and in accordance with his rank.[68] Laypersons among the clientele are identifiable in the testaments of cardinals as recipients of donations.[69] Acts of filial devotion (or *pietas*) towards a patron can demonstrate association with his clientele and frequently one's hierarchical standing in it, too. If someone was buried next to his patron, he was certainly a significant client and especially trusted.[70]

Legateships offered cardinals an exceptional opportunity in their role as patrons. They improved ties, served to reward clients, and helped win new ones thanks to the 'faculties', or special powers, that cardinals exercised during legatine missions and which normally were reserved to the

---

64 The *Ordinatio pro gubernatione* cited above, p. 58 n. 52; for a paraphrase, see Mollat, 'Contribution à l'histoire du Sacré College', pp. 50 ff.

65 Usually called table companions in the petitions (*familiaris continuus commensalis*), who were part of the suite and received from the cardinal food, clothing, a residence, and his *livrée*.

66 Cf. Verger, 'L'entourage du cardinal Pierre de Monteruc', pp. 523, 526.

67 On the practice of keeping benefices within the clientele, p. 52 n. 20 above. Diener, 'Zur Persönlichkeit', pp. 314–15, observes that patrons exerted much pressure to take benefices from someone leaving the household and preserve them for the *familia*.

68 Most revealing in this context are the registers of *gratiae expectativae* containing at the beginning of each pontificate the *rotuli* of petitions by cardinals, princes, and universities. They are lost for the time from Martin V to Nicholas V (1417–1455) and can be reconstructed only in part; cf. Diener, 'Zur Persönlichkeit des Johannes von Segovia', pp. 299 ff. The studies on the suites of cardinals mentioned above, p. 59 n. 60, are based on such *rotuli*; see also, Hayez, 'Les rotuli presentés au pape Urbain V'; and Verger, 'L'entourage du cardinal Pierre de Monteruc', p. 521.

69 Cf. Paravicini Bagliani, *Cardinali di Curia*, II, pp. 500 ff.; Paravicini Bagliani, *I testamenti dei cardinali*, pp. CXVI ff. Clerics do not appear in a cardinal's testament, unless he failed to provide them with appropriate benefices beforehand.

70 Next to Nicholas of Cusa, his relative, Simon of Wehlen, and his secretary, Giovanni Andrea Bussi, were buried in the Roman church of San Pietro in Vincoli; see Meuthen, *Die letzten Jahre*, pp. 101–02.

pope alone.[71] These included the provision of benefices, eligibility (also known as an 'expectancy') for one of them, or dispensations from the law governing benefices. In addition, they could grant dispensations from marriage impediments and distinctive privileges like the right to private altars and masses, the choice of personal confessors, or graces such as the bestowal of academic degrees.[72] As papal legates, cardinals could expand their area of influence beyond its previous range. Another consequence was that local princes and clerical institutions often benefitted from legateships by using holders as their established intermediaries with the pope.[73]

Following these remarks on the typical cardinal's *familia*, we return to Nicholas of Cusa. We are better informed about his entourage than that of other contemporaries, because it is the only one to have been treated in the scholarly literature, which is not the same as to say that the documentation was particularly rich, rather the opposite.[74] For his entire stay at the papal Curia, forty-eight *familiares* can be associated with him.[75] It is probably a fair estimate that one-third of them served as permanent members of his household, a relatively small number.[76] The endowment of his *livrée* was also quite small according to the inventory of his estate.[77] At the end, he lived in the pope's palace.[78] The large share of clerics among his retinue is notable. They would have accrued lower costs for him because their support came from benefices. Even his stable hands were clerical.[79]

Of course, we come across the usual and essential charges of a cardinal's court, for example, the judge and the majordomo, chaplains, secretaries, and chamberlains. Important functions were recognizably staffed

---

71 Schuchard, *Die Deutschen an der päpstlichen Kurie*, pp. 57–58; McCurry, '*Utilia Metensia*', pp. 313, 317.

72 Ruess, *Die rechtliche Stellung der päpstlichen Legaten*, pp. 122 ff.

73 Paravicini Bagliani, 'Cardinali di Curia', p. 498; Paravicini Bagliani, 'Il personale della Curia romana', p. 402; Schuchard, *Die Deutschen an der päpstlichen Kurie*, pp. 57–58.

74 Meuthen, *Die letzten Jahre*, especially pp. 307–14.

75 Following his elevation, there was a flurry of petitions from relatives, *familiares*, and clients seeking advancement, cf. p. 59 n. 58 above. My collaborator, Joachim Dörrig, has recently discovered six *familiares*, although problems of identification remain until the relevant Indexes to the *Repertorium Germanicum*, are published. Zani, 'Neues zu Predigten', pp. 111–15, 620–21, has spotted one previously unknown chaplain. I am grateful to Mr Dörrig for sharing his data on Nicholas's *familia* with me.

76 See the totals in Schuchard, *Die Deutschen an der päpstlichen Kurie*, p. 51.

77 Mantese, 'Ein notarielles Inventar'. The testament of 6 August 1464 is printed in Marx, *Geschichte des Armen-Hospitals*, pp. 248–53.

78 Meuthen, *Die letzten Jahre*, p. 90.

79 The two *parafrenarii*, Damarus Incus, a cleric from Trier, and Christian Prechen, from Brixen; Meuthen, *Die letzten Jahre*, pp. 309–10. Verger, 'L'entourage du cardinal Pierre de Monteruc', p. 535, shows that the proportion between laypeople and clergy was usually very different.

PATRONAGE AND CLIENTELE IN THE LATE MEDIEVAL CHURCH    63

with blood relations and old acquaintances.[80] Lay relatives, noble, and non-German *familiares* were practically absent.[81] A special place was taken up by Nicholas's partisans who had fled together with him from their territorial lord during his time as bishop of Brixen (beginning in 1451). They were protected by their status and found temporary refuge and work in his *livrée*.[82]

Considering the development of Nicholas's *familia* and the range of benefices circulating among his *familiares*, it is clear that — against the typical standard just mentioned — his extended legateship (from 1451 to 1452) changed remarkably little.[83] The same applies to his elevation to the cardinalate and to the position as prince-bishop of Brixen.[84] Neither the total of household-members nor his sphere of influence increased by much. Due to his notorious lack of funding, Nicholas eventually obtained (in 1463) a double stipend from the cash proceeds of the cardinal's college. He also received financial support from Pope Pius II, in a gesture of old friendship that almost assumed the characteristics of patronage.[85] It deserves mention, moreover, that Nicholas does not seem to have requested the pope's aid, despite being friends with both Nicholas V and Pius II. Among his German compatriots, he was not seen as their cardinal regardless of his legation. They rather turned to the bishop of Augsburg, Cardinal Peter of Schaumburg, who did not even reside at the Curia.[86]

---

80 As auditor, Gebhard Bulach from Rottweil, canon of Brixen and Nicholas's follower there; as secretaries, Giovanni Andrea Bussi (see p. 61 n. 70 above) and Wigand Mengeler from Homberg, associated with Nicholas from the time of Ulrich of Manderscheid and assuming the payment of annates for Nicholas on 16 November 1440 (*Acta Cusana*, ed. by Meuthen and Hallauer, I/2, no. 442); Johannes Stam, also a chaplain, from Trier and Nicholas's scribe from as early as 1445 (*Acta Cusana*, ed. by Meuthen and Hallauer, I/2, no. 620); Dietrich of Xanten as proctor in charge of Nicholas's benefices; as chamberlain, Peter of Erkelenz, certainly the *familiaris* closest to Cusanus; cf. Meuthen, 'Peter von Erkelenz'. On all of them, Meuthen, *Die letzten Jahre*, pp. 148, 307 ff.

81 Of noble origin were Johannes of Raesfeld, Sigismund of Rodestock, Gasparus Blondus, Johannes of Stetenberg, Desiderius of Bistorff, and Petrus Bartholomei de Aleis. There were three Italians and one Portuguese, the rest came from the Empire. Again, the typical proportions in a cardinal's household were very different; Verger, 'L'entourage du cardinal Pierre de Monteruc', p. 531.

82 Including Gebhard Bulach from Rottweil, Konrad Bossinger, and Konrad Zoppot, all three canons from Brixen.

83 On the great legateship, Sullivan, 'Nicholas of Cusa as Reformer', containing little that is new; Koch, *Der deutsche Kardinal in deutschen Landen* (reprinted in Koch, *Kleine Schriften*, I, pp. 495–530). The sources informing about the mission are gathered in Koch, *Nikolaus von Kues und seine Umwelt*, pp. 116 ff.; Wendehorst, 'Zum Itinerar'.

84 The privileges applied to those already belonging to the clientele. They did not notably expand the geographical range from which the clients were recruited, nor the area where their benefices were located.

85 Meuthen, *Die letzten Jahre*, pp. 89, 91.

86 Schuchard, *Die Deutschen an der päpstlichen Kurie*, p. 116.

Alternatively, they relied on Enea Silvio Piccolomini, who later became Pope Pius II.[87] They preferred to approach other 'foreigners' as well.[88]

I cannot address the reasons for Nicholas's weak record as a networker in detail here. It is possible to think of his personality and rigorous ideas as a reformer. Perhaps, he simply lacked the desire for power and the political talent. Furthermore, his failure as bishop of Brixen cost him a lot of money. The absence of influence and his shortage of means must have been mutually aggravating factors. His middle-class origins certainly did not help either. 'Only the Roman Church', he proudly stated in his autobiography of 1449, 'offers the most generous reward to virtue'.[89] The statement was not altogether mistaken, although there were limits to the generosity of the late medieval Church.

He certainly did not neglect his obligations as a patron.[90] The documentation shows him to have frequently intervened in favour of his followers, who remained loyal to him in exemplary fashion.[91] Demonstrations of their *pietas* were as impressive as those of their patron toward his patrons.[92] What was missing in Cusanus, then, was not so much willingness to display the main quality he needed as a patron apart from trustworthiness. He was ready to perform acts of so-called *largitas*, or hands spending appropriately and lavishly. But he did not have the resources.

By offering this admittedly incomplete account, I hope to have conveyed a sense of how patronage and clientele worked in the Church of the late Middle Ages. The current state of research does not permit a more detailed presentation even for those who work on late medieval ecclesiastical history. To begin with, it is the documentary situation that remains deficient in two ways. First, any evaluation of the extant and very

---

87 Brosius, 'Die Pfründen des Enea', p. 288; Schuchard, *Die Deutschen an der päpstlichen Kurie*, pp. 57–58, 203.

88 Brosius, 'Päpstlicher Einfluß', p. 213; Schuchard, *Die Deutschen an der päpstlichen Kurie*, p. 55.

89 *Acta Cusana*, ed. by Meuthen and Hallauer, I/2, no. 849; German translation by Meuthen, *Nikolaus von Kues*, p. 23.

90 For instance, *Repertorium Germanicum*, VI, ed. by Abert and others, p. 447, no. 4467 (petition, 19 July 1453); Meuthen, *Die letzten Jahre*, p. 103; on the benefices Cusanus secured for his relatives and friends, p. 98; he took care of them beyond death by resigning his own benefices to them through dispensation (2 December 1463). They were entitled to a place in his hospital at Kues; Marx, *Geschichte des Armen-Hospitals*, p. 61 (§ 13; cf. §§ 2 and 5).

91 Quite a few clients felt very obligated toward Nicholas of Cusa while he was alive and sometimes thereafter, such as Johannes Stam, Wigand Mengeler, the two rectors of his hospital, Dietrich of Xanten and Peter of Erkelenz, Giovanni Andrea Bussi, and Heinrich Pomert.

92 The Carthusians of Koblenz prayed for him and guarded his intellectual legacy. Some *familiares* were buried next to the cardinal in his title church (above, p. 61 n. 70), or chose his hospital for burial alongside the graves of family and their patron's heart. Giovanni Andrea Bussi composed for him a posthumous laudatory treatise and the inscription on his epitaph in San Pietro in Vincoli; Meuthen, *Die letzten Jahre*, pp. 99–100.

PATRONAGE AND CLIENTELE IN THE LATE MEDIEVAL CHURCH    65

rich serial sources is cumbersome, because their texts are not accessible in modern editions facilitating such inquiries. Secondly, there are the polemical treatises, another type of late medieval sources which church historians have extensively utilized. These works, while informative, are (often with exaggeration) ruthlessly critical. They nonetheless do not bring charges of collusion for the simple reason that the promotion of relatives, clients, and friends was not viewed as odious, but rather as an obligation, just as the virtue of *pietas* was held in high regard.[93] Nepotism itself was not seen as an ill, except when it led to excesses. An additional reason why church historians have paid little attention to the phenomena of patronage and clientele is arguably because the prevailing image of the Church has been one of 'transpersonal administration', as opposed to the interpersonal operations of lay rule in the Middle Ages.[94]

We have noted, on the other hand, that patronage and clientele created personal networks within the Church as well. They were quite comparable to those among the laity, apart from characteristic differences, of course, which included their less localized, if not international composition, greater social and geographical mobility, and focus on one patron.[95] Patronage and clientele were decisive for the appointment to clerical office and ecclesiastical careers, as we have seen. Moreover, the economic function of clienteles was also very significant, in that they guaranteed the transfer of revenue from the benefices to the patron. Especially members of the Roman Curia continued to rely for income largely on their benefices.[96] Clients could be mobilized by their patron for credit, just as he could invoke their obligation of filial devotion, or *pietas*, to come to his aid and serve as surety for his loans from bankers.

Despite the importance of patronage and clientele in the Church, however, it should not be overlooked that both were limited by the transpersonal exercise of ecclesiastical offices mentioned earlier. The priestly hierarchy, after all, expressed itself not only in terms of sacred ordination, but also represented an early form of administrative command structure that in effect did function as such in certain sectors. This can again be illustrated in connection with benefices. Patrons and clients, for instance, could not freely dispose of benefices. As a matter of fact, there were canonical regulations in place concerning the suitability for office, fixed administrative duties, and maximum amounts of revenue. Although dispensation from them was frequently available, it was subject to legal limitations as well. Moreover, if members of the Curia transmitted enormous amounts of

---

93  Reinhard, 'Papa Pius', p. 296; Reinhard, 'Nepotismus', p. 162 n. 10.
94  The formulation is taken from Reinhard, *Freunde und Kreaturen*, p. 52.
95  Reinhard, *Freunde und Kreaturen*, pp. 47 ff., referring to the curial oligarchy around 1600, without need for greater modification during the fifteenth century.
96  Reinhard, *Freunde und Kreaturen*, p. 50.

income from their benefices to Rome, even greater sums arrived there in the form of taxes on benefices, amassed by a web of collectors who were extremely well organized by medieval standards. They gathered ecclesiastical dues from all over Latin Christianity and sent the proceeds to Rome. This occurred without excessive losses — to the amazement and envy of lay rulers.[97]

---

97 The best survey of papal finances remains Bauer, 'Die Epochen der Papstfinanz'; for the period in question here, pp. 471 ff.; reprinted in Bauer, *Gesammelte Aufsätze*, pp. 112–47; also, Lunt, *Financial Relations of the Papacy with England*; Favier, *Les finances pontificales* (reviewed by Esch, in *Göttingische Gelehrte Anzeigen* 221, pp. 133–59). On the collectors in general, see Lunt, *Accounts Rendered by Papal Collectors*, ed. by Graves, pp. 1–30; and, from a socio-historical perspective, Schuchard, *Die päpstlichen Kollektoren*; Schmitz, *Lebens- und Arbeitsweise*.

CHAPTER 3

# A 'Rope Team' of Clerics from Hanover in the Late Middle Ages[*]

Between around 1410 and 1460, across northern Germany and Livonia, we find clerics from Hanover in eminent ecclesiastical positions.[1] In Lübeck, Berthold Rike was provost of the cathedral from 1409 to 1436, Johann Schele served as bishop there between 1420 and 1439, and Volkmar of Anderten was head (or official) of the diocesan court beginning in 1467. The local episcopal chapter included apart from Dietrich Reseler, later bishop of Dorpat (known as Tartu in Estonia today), and Ludolf Quirre who successively advanced to the provostship at the dome of Halberstadt, two additional members staying permanently as canons of Lübeck. In Livonia, a pair of bishops from the Reseler family led the diocese from 1413 to 1441, while Ludolf Grove did the same from 1438 to 1458 in Ösel (modern Saaremaa in Estonia). Dietrich Nagel was provost of the cathedral in Riga, and Ludolf Nagel dean of the bishop's chapter in Ösel. In addition, they were surrounded by ordinary canons from Hanover at Dorpat, Riga, and Ösel. The rest remained in north-western Germany.[2] As mentioned, Ludolf Quirre went to Halberstadt (1454–1463). Arnold of Hesede 'only' obtained canonries at the chapter churches of Minden and Halberstadt. At Hildesheim, he also assumed the function of archdeacon. Hermann Pentel was provost at the cathedral of St Blasii in Brunswick, Johann Ember at St Simon in Goslar. One after the other, Konrad of Sarstedt and Dietrich Schaper became provosts at the nunnery of Lüne near Lüneburg.

How much of this happened by sheer accident? It is unlikely that clerics from Hanover were particularly numerous, pious, or capable. After all, not a single Hanoverian embarked on a major ecclesiastical career prior to 1409. From a wider perspective, Hanover was certainly 'provincial'. It

---

[*] The present article is based on a presentation made at the German Historical Institute in Rome on February 19, 2001. The original format is maintained, the text supplemented with footnotes. I have published studies on all the cited individuals with complete references elsewhere.

[1] Schwarz, 'Alle Wege führen über Rom'; Schwarz, 'Prälaten aus Hannover'; Schwarz, 'Ein Freund italienischer Kaufleute'.

[2] For a detailed assessment of the clerics remaining in north-western Germany, see Schwarz, 'Karrieren von Klerikern aus Hannover'.

could not boast churches of great prestige, as did Hildesheim or Goslar, for example. The most prestigious clerical positions in Hanover were held by priests at parishes and chaplainries under the patronage of the territorial lord, the dukes of Brunswick and Lüneburg, or that of the local town council. Either authority appointed servants of merit to the positions and focused on the aspect of material sustenance. Even the existence of a local (Latin) school was not enough to prepare for more ambitious careers among the clergy.[3] Instead, it was due to the formation of 'rope teams' that the sons of citizens from this middling rural town managed to rise far beyond previous levels. By the time three friends had earned their promotion through the Roman Curia, they went on to help others to advance as well, taking advantage of mechanisms that roughly functioned as follows.

The first to reside at the papal Curia in Rome (before 1392) was Dietrich Reseler.[4] He arrived as the proctor, or legal consultant, of leading men in Lower Saxony. Johann Schele and Berthold Rike soon joined him there. Reseler and Schele quickly gained the support of a compatriot, Dietrich of Nieheim, who also was a distant relative of Schele's. Nieheim played an important role at the Apostolic Chancery and provided the two with notarial positions at the Rota, one of the prestigious papal tribunals. This was a difficult and expensive appointment because it had to be bought. Subsequently, they worked as abbreviators for the head of the Chancery. Owing to Nieheim's intervention, Reseler, Rike, and perhaps Schele obtained next the coveted and venal position of Scribe in the Chancery.[5] Contrary to Nieheim who never attained a university degree in jurisprudence, Reseler, Rike, and Scheler were able to graduate despite their administrative duties with a doctorate in canon law from the elite school of Bologna, an academic accomplishment of greater weight than the German *Habilitation* today.

It was especially helpful that Rike transferred to Bologna, where the powerful Cardinal Cossa ruled over the most important province in the papal territories. Cossa made Rike a member of his household (or *familia*) permitting him to study alongside at the university. In 1407, Reseler joined Rike to concentrate fully on his graduation, despite his administrative responsibilities at the Curia which was in Siena at the time. His move was a tactical one as he sought to distance himself from Pope Gregory XII, whose political fortunes were clearly on the wane. Schele followed Reseler two years afterwards. Nieheim had instructed Reseler and Schele in the art of accumulating claims to benefices and taught them how to secure actual

---

3 Schwarz, 'Die Stiftskirche St. Galli'; Schwarz, 'Alle Wege führen über Rom'.

4 Schwarz, 'Alle Wege führen über Rom'; Schwarz, 'Ein Freund italienischer Kaufleute'; and, Schwarz, 'Prälaten aus Hannover', with Table 1.

5 On these offices, Schuchard, *Die Deutschen an der päpstlichen Kurie*, pp. 96–121.

possession of them in the German Empire far away. Nieheim, Reseler, and Schele exchanged benefices among themselves to improve their odds of acquiring them at churches where they or their friends exerted influence.[6]

In 1410, Cossa became Pope John (XXIII), admitting Rike and Reseler to his circle of consultants. In their new role, they learnt everything about banking there was to know, for Cossa expertly took advantage of rivalries between the Italian banks until he entrusted his finances to the Medici.[7] In 1409 and 1413, the former papal collector for northern Germany and provost of Lübeck, as well as the collector for Livonia and bishop of Dorpat both died.[8] In response, Cossa took care to nominate Rike for the benefice in Lübeck and, using his authority as pope, appointed Reseler as the new bishop of Dorpat. To secure a second transfer route for moneys from the north-east, the one crossing through Silesia, he also conferred to Rike the office of custodian at the cathedral of Breslau (now Polish Wrocław) in 1410.[9]

It took considerable time and effort to transform these nominations into fact. There was conflict with rivals over the offices in Lübeck and Breslau. At Dorpat, the Teutonic Order attempted everything possible to prevent Reseler's installation. The Livonian bishoprics, meanwhile, sought to benefit from the devastating defeat of the Teutonic Knights at Tannenberg in 1410 by favouring a candidate without ties to the Order. Intense diplomatic activity ensued. Friendships and personal networks were mobilized. What helped Rike the most in 1409 was that Reseler and Schele — together with other curial clerics — were already members of the cathedral chapter in Lübeck, a situation that repeated itself in Breslau. Reseler and Schele served as canons at the dome of Dorpat, just as Reseler's family kept trade relations there.

John (XXIII) appointed Rike as collector for northern Germany in 1413 or 1414. Rike was accompanied on his travels through the region by a young accountant of the Medici who had his branch office at Lübeck.[10] His presence was constantly attacked by the Hanse, which rejected banks in principle and did not tolerate them in areas under its political control.[11] Rike again supported the establishment of the Medici in Breslau. In 1415

---

6 See Schwarz, 'Ein Freund italienischer Kaufleute', Table 3.

7 Esch, 'Das Papsttum unter der Herrschaft der Neapolitaner', pp. 772 ff.; de Roover, *The Rise and Decline of the Medici Bank*, pp. 203, 255; von Stromer, *Oberdeutsche Hochfinanz*, pp. 146, 368–69.

8 On the papal collectors, Schuchard, *Die päpstlichen Kollektoren*.

9 Militzer, 'Geldüberweisungen des Deutschen Ordens', pp. 44–45; Esch, 'Überweisungen der Apostolischen Kammer', pp. 295–96.

10 His name was Lodovico de' Baglioni from Perugia; on him, A. Esch, 'Bankiers der Kirche', pp. 347–48; more recently, Fouquet, 'Ein Italiener in Lübeck', pp. 197 ff.; and Schuchard, *Die päpstlichen Kollektoren*, pp. 75–83, with additional literature.

11 See the preceding two notes.

and 1416, he also acted as collector for Poland, Prussia, and Livonia, where he met, besides Reseler, none other than Schele, who worked as legal adviser of the Livonian bishoprics in their fight against the Teutonic Order. Upon his return to the Curia, which from 1414 to 1418 was located at the Council of Constance, Rike represented the case of the Livonians there. When John (XXIII) was deposed in 1415, our three clerics from Hanover suffered a serious setback. Rike returned via Breslau (1417/1418) to Lübeck to concentrate entirely on his role as provost. It was certainly not without Rike's favourable intervention that Johann Schele was elected bishop of Lübeck in 1420. The new pope, Martin V, confirmed the election and appointed Schele his collector for the Nordic kingdoms, Prussia, and Livonia, obliging him to settle his accounts only with the Lübeck representative of the Medici.

Another cleric from Hanover belonging to the same generation, Johann Ember (c. 1365–1423), was much less successful.[12] He spent long years at the Curia and the Council of Constance as legal advocate of the old and prestigious chapter churches in Brunswick. He was unable to complete his studies in canon law. He also struggled to accumulate benefices, with his most valuable holding being a Brunswick parish. Although he won all court proceedings for his clients, the city of Brunswick eventually prevailed against them because of its endurance and superior financial means. The dukes of Brunswick and Lüneburg as patrons of the chapter churches compensated Ember with the provostship of Goslar.

A member of the following generation, Ludolf Grove (c. 1390–1458) was more successful than Ember.[13] He served for many years at the Curia as substitute proctor of the Teutonic Order. Like Ember, he failed to attain a higher academic degree in canon law. Because he was originally employed by the Order to undermine Reseler's elevation to the bishopric of Dorpat, he went to Livonia, where he was given a canonry at the cathedral of Ösel after some time. Soon enough, however, Grove changed sides and joined the party of his bishop who was massively threatened by the Teutonic Knights. His fellow canons elected Grove as their treasurer, and he was sent as emissary of the local bishop and chapter to the Council of Basel (1431–1449). At Basel, he encountered other Hanoverians including Johann Schele, who was among the presidents of the Council and acted as cardinal protector, so to speak, of the Livonian bishoprics in their conflict with the Teutonic Order.

In this contest, Dietrich Nagel (c. 1400–1468/1469), also from Hanover, served as envoy of the high chapter in Riga, after successfully campaigning, along with the bishop of Ösel, against the Order in Rome

---

12 Schwarz, 'Hannoveraner in Braunschweig'.

13 On Grove, cf. Schwarz, 'Alle Wege führen über Rom'; the other two, Schwarz, 'Prälaten aus Hannover'.

from 1429 to 1431. The cathedral chapter of Riga rewarded him with his election to the provostship in 1439. Dietrich Nagel did not hold a degree in church law. He did not have benefices because the cathedral chapter of Riga was composed of monks, Augustinian canons, to be precise, which the Teutonic Order combated vigorously claiming that Riga was a bishopric pertaining to the knights. Simultaneously, Nagel entertained friendships with family in Lübeck and with relatives Reseler had brought in his wake to Livonia. Following Schele's death in 1439, Dietrich Nagel occupied important functions at the Council of Basel, which rapidly lost support from 1441.

Nagel's strong reputation must have contributed to the approval that the Council of Basel gave to Grove's election as bishop of Ösel late in 1439. It was also endorsed by Schele's friends, canons from Lübeck Cathedral who after Rike's death (murdered in 1436), that of Scheler (in 1439), and Grove's departure for his bishopric early in 1440 continued to defend the interests of the Livonian bishops. Attracted by Grove, relatives, compatriots, and friends of his left for Ösel in the same way that some of Reseler's relations had followed him to Dorpat. The Teutonic Order persuaded the Roman Pope, Eugene IV (1431–1447), who had been deposed by the Council of Basel in 1439, to nominate a member of the Order as bishop of Ösel that year. The power struggle between Grove and his episcopal rival lasted until 1457. Thanks to the support of friends, Grove emerged as the winner, but especially because he outlived his opponent. Upon Grove's death in 1458, the stalemate of 1439 resumed, with one candidate from the Order appointed to the bishopric by the pope, and another elected by the cathedral chapter of Ösel.

Ludolf Nagel (c. 1425 to c. 1477), Ludolf Grove's nephew, took up his late uncle's cause of defending Ösel's independence. He was not very well trained for it. He had only studied at Rostock without graduating and lacked all experience in the world abroad. His benefices consisted apart from the deanery of Ösel and his membership in the chapter of the meagre holdings available in Livonia (just as it had been for his uncle). Despite vigorous resistance, Dietrich Nagel had to witness the definitive incorporation of the church of Riga into the Teutonic Order. To preserve at least the memory of what had come before, he wrote a history of the local bishops and archbishops and established a pious bequest as a monument to the provosts of the cathedral. Ludolf Nagel was more fortunate in that he lost his deanery at Riga to a candidate from the Order, but held on to prestigious positions in both Ösel and Reval (now Tallinn in Estonia). The latter two churches managed to maintain their independence.

72    CHAPTER 3

A young relative of both Grove and Rike was Ludolf Quirre (*c.* 1395–1463), the cleric from Hanover we know the most about.[14] It was most probably Rike who sent the pupil from the chapter of St Blasii in Brunswick to study the arts first in Erfurt and then Bologna (1416/1417). Quirre would not complete his studies in canon law until 1436, when he received the degree of doctor at the University of Rostock, where Rike was very influential. It seems that Quirre was also a distant relative of Johann Ember, whose estate he administered after taking over his main benefice in Brunswick in 1422. Quirre was already a canon at Hildesheim and Halberstadt and secretary to the dukes of Brunswick and Lüneburg at the time. His accumulation of benefices followed the rules set by the three Hanoverians of the first generation. Until 1454, he did not hold more than one archdeaconry, albeit an important one, which he owed like his remaining positions in Brunswick to the patronage and protection of the ducal dynasty, the Guelfs. The same applied to his benefice in Hanover. In the early 1440s, he joined the episcopal chapter of Lübeck, perhaps as successor of the murdered Berthold Rike and possibly in ways that resembled the recent admission of one of Dietrich Beseler's nephews there. The leap in Quirre's career path at Halberstadt, where he became provost of the cathedral in 1454, was probably due to the intervention of a fellow student from his days in Bologna who had been made bishop of Halberstadt. Just as in St Blasii, Quirre abided by established patterns when he had relatives accepted in his wake as canons of the chapter in Halberstadt.

The career of Arnold of Hesede (*c.* 1400–1476) resembled that of Quirre who was his friend.[15] He also finished his studies in canon law with a doctorate. His benefices consisted of memberships in the diocesan chapters of Minden, Hildesheim, and Halberstadt, and an archdeaconry of lesser significance. Unlike Ludolf Quirre, however, Hesede remained active as university professor, even officiating as rector of the University in Leipzig at one point. He does not seem to have worked in an official capacity for any of the institutions employing his services as legal consultant or on diplomatic missions.

Volkmar of Anderten (*c.* 1410–1481), a younger relative, accompanied Hesede to Leipzig.[16] His career remained locally bound for a long time, with benefices in Hanover. Because he was born into the circle of affluent families who controlled the town council, he did not depend as much as the others on ecclesiastical income. At the Council of Basel, he worked

---

14 Schwarz, 'Ludolf Quirre'; Schwarz, 'Die Stiftskirche St. Galli'. For supplementary information and literature, see Schwarz, 'Karrieren von Klerikern aus Hannover', p. 251 n. 31, p. 266 n. 57.

15 Schwarz, 'Hannoversche Bürgersöhne'.

16 Schwarz, 'Volkmar von Anderten'.

as accredited proctor in the chancery of the very canons from Lübeck Cathedral we have already encountered as representatives of the Livonian bishoprics. He was a follower of the Council to the end. After its dissolution in 1449, he became a member of the mission the dukes of Lüneburg sent to Rome for negotiations toward a settlement with the new pope, Nicholas V (1447–1455). Volkmar of Anderten stayed in Rome and joined the Proctors of the Rota. He apparently acquired a licentiate in canon law in Italy before being accepted into the cathedral chapter of Lübeck in 1463 and advancing there to the position of general official in 1467.

Another cleric from Hanover, Hermann Pentel (*c.* 1395–1463), failed in his attempt to join the cathedral chapter of Lübeck.[17] He was again unsuccessful in trying to obtain the office of head teacher at the episcopal church in Hildesheim or the superior position of archdeacon, notwithstanding the fact that the ducal family of Lüneburg supported him. Like Ludolf Quirre, Pentel was their secretary and managed to secure for the posts in Lübeck and Hildesheim a papal dispensation (or exceptional permission, see below) from the requirement of noble birth or at least a higher degree in church law, which he lacked. Like Quirre, Pentel was repeatedly at the Curia and the Council of Basel, receiving his accreditation as proctor there. He was a cathedral canon at Minden and held an archdeaconry in the diocese, before moving on to become the principal of the school at St Blasii in Brunswick, all benefices under the patronage of the Guelf dukes. In the end, he proved unable to take possession of the provostship at St Blasii.

The two Hanoverians who successively served as provosts of the Benedictine nunnery at Lüne near Lüneburg, Conrad of Sarstedt (*c.* 1385–1440) and Dietrich Schaper (*c.* 1400–1466), warrant our consideration as well.[18] They were related as uncle and nephew. Both graduated from a German university with basic degrees in the arts and went on to work respectively as town scribes in Hanover and Lüneburg. They seemed to have owed their election to the provostship of Lüne to the town leaders of Lüneburg, who used their supervisory role in the convent to greater effect than the local dukes. While Sarstedt's tenure was a success, that of Schaper was severely disrupted by the so-called 'War of the Lüneburg Prelates'. During the conflict, Schaper held the newly established provostship of Lüneburg for a while. Until the end of his life, Schaper fought for his claim to the provostship of Lüne, a struggle which also derailed the career of his brother, Johann Schaper, who gained a licentiate in canon law from Bologna and became canon at the cathedral of Hildesheim. Eventually, he entered a monastery.

---

17 See p. 70 n. 12 above.
18 Schwarz, 'Zwei Lüner Pröpste'.

74    CHAPTER 3

These events are of general interest because they highlight several late medieval developments. To begin with, the contemporary society of estates did not provide for social climbers. Where advancement occurred, it came about very gradually and over several generations. Opportunities to rise were typically tied to the Church. German churches did not function in this way and were rightly described as 'hospices of the nobility', at least prior to the late Middle Ages. In the fourteenth century, so-called 'learned counsellors' undermined the monopoly of the local nobility. At first, these newcomers consisted of legal advisers to the king. From the turn of the century, they also comprised individuals who worked for territorial lords and towns.

Modern interest in the learned counsellors is multifaceted.[19] Social historians are concerned with the possibilities of advancement for sons from the urban milieu, whereas intellectual historians seek to identify the conditions that led to the proliferation of juristic learning in the German Empire.[20] Much less familiar is the contribution of academically trained advisers to the emergence of banks. Unlike the more developed regions to the south and west, the German territories did not sustain an educated elite among the laity. Intellectuals were always paid from funds generated by ecclesiastical benefices. As a result, the recipients had to be ordained as clerics. Their learned subjects had to correspond so that they studied canon law rather than secular law. From an external point of view, the career of a learned counsellor appeared to be a clerical one. It culminated in leading positions at a chapter church or as bishop.[21] To be sure, not only the individual advanced through the ranks as member of the clergy, but also his entire household (or *familia*). Both Schele and Quirre are useful examples to study this.[22]

How did a learned counsellor embark on his career? According to modern Western theories of constitutional government, recruitment and promotion are known to depend solely on the impersonal standards of merit and performance. In the Middle Ages, on the other hand, it was important to have the right parents, originating at a minimum from the upper urban classes. In addition to birth, academic study was paramount and particularly that of church law at an Italian elite university, which culminated in a higher degree (except for noblemen who did not need it). All those who succeeded among our Hanoverians were in possession of

---

19 The relevant literature is enormous by now, including Moraw, 'Die gelehrten Juristen'; Heinig, 'Gelehrte Juristen'; Männl, 'Die gelehrten Juristen'; the publication of Männl's 1987 dissertation was announced years ago; Koch, *Räte auf deutschen Reichsversammlungen*.
20 Sellert, 'Zur Rezeption des römischen und kanonischen Rechts'.
21 Cf. the fundamental works by Peter Moraw, including his 'Stiftspfründen als Elemente des Bildungswesens'.
22 Schwarz, 'Die Stiftskirche St. Galli'; Schwarz, 'Alle Wege führen über Rom'.

such a qualification. The universities functioned as social systems, creating important networks known today as those of 'old boys'.[23]

An academic degree also afforded preferment in requests for papal claims to a benefice. Benefices are known to be church positions in which the official duties were inseparably linked to rights and income. In the late Middle Ages, the latter two (constituting the benefice strictly speaking) were increasingly viewed as the main component, the service obligation instead as a collateral burden (resembling attitudes that German politicians currently attribute to university professors like me). In imitation of aristocratic behaviour, conceptions of secular office-holding were extended to ecclesiastical appointments. They were viewed as fiefs in the feudal sense, apt to support the tenant in accordance with his social status. For that reason, benefices were called 'church fiefs' in northern Germany — although they were not perceived as such from the canonical point of view. They not only furnished material sustenance, but also provided appropriate markers of standing. At the start, the career-minded would collect vicariates, which ranked below the canonries at a cathedral church, if possible, otherwise at a better endowed collegiate church (a rare occurrence in the north). Successively, the canonries coming into focus were combined with an office at a collegiate or preferably a cathedral church. Most coveted among the administrative positions were those including judicial functions (as archdeacon) plus a higher dignity (like that of a provost, dean, or custodian).

How would a career-minded individual attain one of the coveted benefices, if he was not born into the local nobility? His only chance by and large was the pope who issued legal titles. Equipped with them, recipients could join the fray and fight on site for ownership of the position. Every cleric was able to apply, and his prospects would improve depending on the prerogatives he could muster; or because he was able to gather the most reliable information at greatest speed, for example, about the benefice becoming vacant next; or when he had the proper know-how to navigate his case in the best possible way through the immensely complicated administrative channels of the Curia. Robert Brentano once compared the papal court with Franz Kafka's 'Castle'.[24] Curial clergy were particularly well-placed, and among them especially those working at the Rota, in the Apostolic Chancery, or as personal advisers to the pope. The Curia was an exchange in the strict economic sense where papal

---

23 In general, Moraw, 'Der Lebensweg der Studenten'; Schwinges, 'Europäische Studenten des späten Mittelalters'; Maleczek, 'Deutsche Studenten in Italien'. Social networks, not only before and during university studies but also thereafter, are tracked by Gramsch, 'Erfurter Juristen im Spätmittelalter'.

24 Referring to the late thirteenth century, which from a fifteenth-century perspective appeared well-organized; cf. Brentano, *York Metropolitan Jurisdiction*, p. 164.

mandates were traded, including various grants of rights to ecclesiastical appointment, preferment over competitors, and dispensations circumventing canonical impediments to the acquisition or tenure of church offices. This market was shaped by demand.[25] In order to enforce an apostolic order, however, it was also necessary to rely on local friendships, just as it was important — upon execution — to find representatives defending one's interests and to supervise the substitutes who took on the actual duties. Without exception, the successful among the above-mentioned Hanoverians were collectors of benefices, first among them Schele.

Ecclesiastical positions falling under lay patronage were in principle immune to papal intervention, so that there was no competition over them in the curial market-place. The careers of the provosts of Lüne, who only received appointment from their secular lords are consequently of little interest here compared to those of the other Hanoverians. Apart from curial membership (even in the broader sense), it was advisable to spend extended periods at the Curia, the Councils, and 'congresses' like the imperial diets or princely gatherings. The Curia was central to diplomacy, scholarship, and the arts, the site where information from all over the world circulated in unparalleled fashion, whence networks of patronage reached into every corner of the Church, where opportunities were handed out and money flows converged. Concerning the traffic in news and contacts with the leadership, the Councils of Constance and Basel could temporarily compete to some extent.

Service to a prince was the decisive measure in the career of learned counsellors. Pre-requisites of success were primarily a curial office and association with the papal household or that of a cardinal.[26] A position as diplomatic representative of the Teutonic Order was also helpful. Such assignments generated prerogatives on the benefice market. While the Church was more inclined than others to reward performance, social connections remained of exceptional importance.[27] Relatives played a central role, for clergy not so much in the form of direct progeny, of course, but by way of 'nephews'. Nepotism, or the taking care of family, was not shunned, but considered virtuous if it was pursued with proper

---

25 Cf. the section on 'Benefice Market and Clerical Careers' at the *Historikertag* in Bochum, 1990, with contributions from Arnold Esch, Brigide Schwarz, Andreas Meyer, Erich Meuthen, Hubert Höing, and Dieter Brosius, published in *Quellen und Forschungen aus italienischen Archiven und Bibliotheken*, 71 (1991), 241–339; and separately in *Das Repertorium Germanicum*, ed. by Esch; also, Schwarz, 'Römische Kurie und Pfründenmarkt' (English version above, pp. 27–48).

26 It looks as though advancement via the Curia constituted an older career path than secular service; Gramsch, 'Kurientätigkeit als "Berufsbild" gelehrter Juristen'.

27 The classical study is by Reinhard, *Freunde und Kreaturen*; reprinted in Reinhard, *Ausgewählte Abhandlungen*, pp. 289–310.

judgment.[28] Patronage was nearly as significant.[29] Rike, who had long been in the household of Cossa who eventually became Pope John (XXIII) always saw himself as his client, establishing a perennial memorial cult for him at the dome of Lübeck well after John (XXIII) had been deposed and disgraced. Close relationships also arose from university studies, membership in one of the curial guilds, and the like.

In the present essay, relationships based on shared geographical origin are the principal focus. Nieheim, for example, Schele's compatriot and relative, did not hesitate to promote young clerics from Hanover to the best of his abilities. Without the intervention of fellow Hanoverians, the above-mentioned Livonian careerists would have failed to stand up to the Teutonic Order, too. Simultaneously, the career trajectories outlined here call for greater chronological and spatial differentiation than has been offered thus far. First, it is necessary to distinguish the clerics in Livonia from the Hanoverians staying closer to home; secondly, there were periods in which the ties between northern Germany and the Curia were intense and others when they were fraught or entirely interrupted (during the time of the Councils, for instance, especially that of Basel), or looser (such as after the Concordat of Vienna, 1448).[30]

The successful three Hanoverians of the first generation owed their conspicuous rise not least to an unusual situation, the need of a new antipope to create without delay his own Curia. For support, he relied mainly on his areas of 'observance', which included the German Empire and turned northern Germans suddenly into key intermediaries. It was also coincidental that a compatriot of influence stood ready, contributing to a unique constellation in which careers could advance in almost exemplary fashion. The paths of the Livonians were completely different. Only Grove had curial experience, but lacked a protector at the Curia itself. He probably studied canon law there and in Bologna, but did not graduate. Dietrich Nagel fared similarly. Both had been at the Council of Basel for longer periods, where there was also a university, as mentioned. Ludolf Nagel, the youngest, did not have any international exposure. He was even without an academic degree from Germany. He did not leave Livonia until he was already the dean of a cathedral.

None of the three had significant benefices. Aside from their dignities (with Grove as treasurer, Dietrich Nagel as provost, and Ludolf Nagel as dean), they held the associated positions and — for a while — simple

---

28 Reinhard, 'Papa Pius'.

29 On this 'mechanism', see my attempt in Schwarz, 'Patronage und Klientel' (English version above, pp. 49–66).

30 Cf. the work of Christoph Schöner, p. 78 n. 32, p. 79 n. 36 below; concentrating on a single cathedral chapter, the process is described in Willich, 'Wege zur Pfründe'. The development was by no means uniform across the Latin West, see Tewes, *Die römische Kurie*.

ecclesiastical offices in Livonia. The local cathedral chapters were only in part endowed with actual benefices for secular (rather than regular) clergy. Collegiate churches did not exist. Their original families were of lesser social rank than the three Hanoverians of the first generation. The Livonians apparently did not have relevant networks except their native ones as well as blood relations. Only Grove could claim to have served a territorial lord in the Teutonic Order, which kept advisers in such a state of dependency, however, that the service is hardly comparable to that for other lordships.[31] In sum, to be elected by local cathedral chapters, it seems to have been enough considering the precarious situation in Livonia to possess a certain familiarity with church law and personal ties to leading prelates abroad, for example, in Lübeck, at the Curia, or at the Council.

How about those whose careers unfolded in north-western Germany? Due to the disturbances and eventual break-up of relationships between the region and the Curia, brought about especially by the collapse of the curial benefice exchange, some of the above-mentioned factors shaping advancement were no longer relevant for the Hanoverians of the second and third generations.[32] Higher offices at the papal court were henceforth out of reach, with Volkmar of Anderten only attaining subaltern rank. Curial experience consequently diminished. Instead, the Council of Basel was more significant. The study at universities abroad also became exceptional because it yielded few benefits. Regarding the ownership of benefices, Quirre alone bears comparison with his older compatriots owing to his connections with Rike. Princely service, on the other hand, gained in importance. Unlike earlier, however, it did not involve the acquisition of ecclesiastical offices on the open market, but rather by way of secular patronage, which could be provided by town councils as well. The demands on social origin were heavier than they had been for the first generation. Quirre, Arnold of Hesede, and Volkmar of Anderten were all born into families of good standing and with many ties to the nobility. Lack of success on the part of Pentel seems to have rested not least on his modest background and material means, which did not help elevate his status. The sources, to be sure, are not as rich as for the previous period, given that the curial records have largely been lost.

By way of conclusion, a few words are in order about the original sources and their exploration. The curial registers are most important for this type of research. Specifically, they document petitions for benefices directed to the pope, grants of dispensations and prerogatives, and records of financial transactions made in connection with the papal provisions.

---

31 Nowak, 'Die Rolle der Gelehrten'.

32 The collapse of the curial market between 1438 and 1448 is convincingly documented in Christoph Schöner's *Habilitation*, which I have been allowed to consult on several occasions; cf. Schwarz, 'Das Bistum Verden'.

Luckily, we do not have to work through thousands of thick volumes in the Vatican Archives to gather the pertinent material, because there is the *Repertorium Germanicum*. The project, which currently extends to the year 1477, does not need much introduction here.[33] To remind those less familiar with it, the *Repertorium* captures all references to the German Empire or rather, the German-speaking regions, in the form of a brief biography for each petitioner.[34] The entries feature in standardized format a string of data, including the cleric's status of ordination, his home diocese, apostolic prerogatives conceded on behalf of the benefice in question, its previous holders, rival claimants, and the estimated value of the position. The data also comprise qualifications affording precedence over other papal concessions like academic degrees, membership in the household of an eminent person, or service at the Curia or at a princely court. The material is organized in chronological order offering as a result a summary of the careers of benefice holders, or more precisely, the intended trajectories, given that many of the acquired papal claims could not be enforced on the ground.[35]

The documentation gathered in the *Repertorium* reflects the circumstance that the entries in the original registers are already highly formulaic. The *Repertorium* covers a large territory and an extended period permitting long-term insights. Aided by tens of thousands of succinct biographies, social historians can make manifold observations regarding, for instance, personal networks in the form of patronage and clienteles or a shared native background.[36] However, it remains unstated by the Vatican sources where a petitioner was born. At best, his diocese of origin is mentioned, though not his current place of residence. I discovered the rope team discussed in the present article by chance during my work on Ludolf Quirre's vita, which revealed that he was closely connected to Rike and others. During my investigations, the intense cooperation between Nieheim, Reseler, Schele, and again Rike came to the fore, suggesting that it indicated something beyond their roughly contemporaneous presence at the Curia or the ecclesiastical appointments they all held in northern Germany.

I found proof that the members of our rope team came from Hanover primarily in the local town archive. This shows that the very partial curial documentation needs to be complemented and compared with information from the regions. Unlike the data from the Curia, however,

---

33 Brosius, 'Das Repertorium Germanicum'. For a full list of the published volumes, see *Repertorium Germanicum*, I–IX.

34 Schwarz, 'Petenten, Pfründen und die Kurie'.

35 Meyer, 'Der deutsche Pfründenmarkt'.

36 Christoph Schöner is presently working on a database to facilitate similar inquiries. Its functionality is to be tested in exemplary studies dealing with questions of social history; cf. above, p. 78 n. 32.

## CHAPTER 3

the Hanoverian references are in very hidden places and impossible to detect for the non-expert. On clergy, they provide rather erratic remarks throughout. I had to consult the relevant sources systematically — and they still do not yield much. Towns preserved their records according to rationales of their own, seeking to minimize the rights of clerics even before the Protestant Reformation and various administrative reforms intervened with their selective bias.

Given that the task was difficult enough for Hanover (with excursions to Brunswick and Wolfenbüttel), I could not extend my inquiries to all archives potentially containing biographical material, especially because many of the relevant records from the Middle Ages were destroyed across Lower Saxony in and after the Second World War.[37] I therefore had to rely on the documentation in print, of which there is little for the fifteenth century. In addition, the material chosen for publication adds to the one-sidedness of the archives. Two laudable exceptions alleviate the situation in our case, first, the great compilation of Livonian, Estonian, and Latvian charters (to 1471).[38] It is rounded out, secondly, by the reports of proctors from the Teutonic Order (until 1436).[39] Moreover, there is the recent edition of charters from the Lübeck bishopric (to 1436), which again is instrumental for this analysis.[40] Concerning the sources of curial origin, I was able to draw on my summaries of papal mandates preserved in the states of Bremen and Lower Saxony.[41] They comprise a lot that is not found in the registers of the Curia, as the latter contain only a fraction of the papally approved petitions, which in turn were mostly voided at later points in time.[42]

As a result, it may seem advisable to choose topics of medieval research that are better suited for systematic exploration because of fuller coverage in the surviving sources. This is not to say, however, that one should look — like the proverbial drunkard for his keys — only under the lantern and where the ground is well-lit. Did all roads lead through Rome? The answer was in the affirmative while the curial benefice exchange was booming and papal authorizations undercut local monopolies of appointment to ecclesiastical office. When these market mechanisms stalled, however,

---

37 The Main State Archive of Hanover was destroyed by aerial bombardment in October 1943; following the return of the evacuated records, they were severely damaged by flash floods in February 1946; cf. *Übersicht über die Bestände des Niedersächsischen Staatsarchivs*, I, ed. by Haase and Deeters, p. 7; also, Schwarz, *Regesten*, p. XV.

38 *Liv-, Est- und Kurländisches Urkundenbuch*, ed. by von Bunge and others.

39 *Die Berichte der Generalprokuratoren*, ed. by Forstreuther and Koeppen, II–IV.

40 *Urkundenbuch des Bistums Lübeck*, ed. by Leverkus and others, II–V.

41 *Regesten*, ed. by Schwarz, pp. XIV–XVI; and pp. XII–XIII, on the proportion of registered petitions in the Vatican Archives compared to those kept in Lower Saxony. For a supplement, see Schwarz, 'Ergänzungen und Berichtigungen'.

42 Schwarz, 'Dispense der Kanzlei Eugens IV.', pp. 143–44.

service at the Curia suddenly appeared remote as it ceased to be rewarding. Did rope teams like the one investigated here function everywhere in the same way? Such networks, to be sure, had a very personal dimension and depended much on circumstance. And yet, they were particularly durable when they helped create career opportunities. When this was no longer the case, the patronage of lords closer to home became more important.

CHAPTER 4

# On Nanker, Bishop of Kraków (1320–1326) and Wrocław (1326–1341)[*]

Bishop Nanker has always attracted particular attention in Poland. He has been seen as a passionate defender of 'the Polish Cause' against German expansion. Because he died with a saintly reputation according to late medieval chroniclers, theologians have also been interested in him. There were two attempts to have him canonized. Investigators have relied above all on the contemporary narrative sources, including the catalogue of Kraków bishops in several different recensions and the Silesian 'Chronicle of the Princes of Poland', which originated at the court of Duke Ludwig in Brzeg (Brieg) 'around 1385 and was likely authored by Peter of Bitschen' (or Byczyna).[1] These works have been preferred by historians.[2] The theologians have followed suit.[3] Nanker's popular appeal, on the other hand, has rested less on the mentioned historiographical texts than on the known historiographer and canon of Kraków Cathedral, Jan Długosz.[4] In the second half of the fifteenth century, Długosz revised the local catalogue of bishops.[5] He subsequently incorporated it into his widely read 'Annals of the Polish Kingdom', which he again based on Peter of Byczyna's Chronicle.[6] The archival testimony on Nanker's life has also been examined. The

---

[*] I dedicate this contribution to the history of his native Silesia to Hubert Mordek, in memory of our shared time as fellows of the German Historical Institute in Rome from 1966 to 1967.

[1] 'Chronica principum Poloniae', ed. by Węclewski; cf. Labuda, 'Chronik'. A new edition with translation and commentary is planned by Wojciech Mrozowicz (Wrocław).

[2] Grünhagen, 'König Johann von Böhmen und Bischof Nanker'; Fijałek, 'Przełość Nankera, biskupa krakowskiego'; Silnicki, *Biskup Nanker*; Kozłowska-Budkowa, 'Nanker'; and in other national biographies; Ożóg, *Kultura umysłowa w Krakowie*. Nanker is not mentioned in Kowalski, *Prałaci i kanonicy krakowskiej*, although he was still member of the cathedral chapter in Kraków in the first months of 1320.

[3] Urban, 'De testimoniis'; Gustaw, 'Nanker'.

[4] On him, Labuda, 'Długosz'; Kürbis, 'Johannes Długosz als Geschichtsschreiber'. After studying in Kraków, Bishop Zbigniew Oleśnicki commissioned him to investigate the rights and privileges of Kraków Cathedral for decades. This resulted in his great history placing Kraków at the centre.

[5] 'Katalogi biskupów krakowskich', ed. by Szymański, p. 102 (in the Dominican version of 1436); pp. 187–90 (in that of Jan Długosz, 1451).

[6] *Annales seu Chronicae incliti regni Polonorum*; in twelve books; the first ten (to 1410) were mostly compiled from known sources; the rest is original; cf. Labuda, 'Długosz'. I have

84    CHAPTER 4

documentation appears meagre, though, especially for the time prior to his appointment as bishop of Kraków.[7]

In recent times, the research initiative labelled 'Nationes' has assisted in putting an end to the unfortunate tradition of identifying medieval *nationes* with modern nation states.[8] Since then, it has become easier to deal with someone like Nanker, who previously triggered intense emotions as an historical figure.[9] It is one of the achievements of the 'Nationes'-Project to have shown that intellectuals surrounding the political leadership played a key role in the protracted and far from uniform development of the medieval *nationes*. The present essay seeks to demonstrate that Nanker belonged to a group of academics, most of them high-ranking clerics with Kraków Cathedral as their focal point. Around 1300, they attempted to recreate the kingdom of Poland in its original territorial boundaries, believing that it had been founded around the year 1000.[10] In the following, I concentrate on the Vatican source material for Polish history from about 1300 to 1340 and its interpretation.[11] The papal documentation allows for various new insights in the light of canon law as it was valid at the time. It also enables us to trace the transfer of church benefices from one holder to another and identify who chose whom as executor, guardian, surety, or to deposit payments at the Curia. In this way, important social networks are revealed that otherwise remain hidden.

## Nanker's Career until His Appointment as Bishop of Kraków in 1320

Born around 1280, Nanker was from a noble family in Kamień, located in the Silesian Duchy of Bytom, the eastern part of which belonged to the diocese of Kraków.[12] His father, Imram, was already a follower of

---

consulted *Joannis Dlugossi Annales*, ed. by Turkowska, IX, pp. 94–95; pp. 107–08, on Bishop Gerward's mission; pp. 109–10, on Władysław Łokietek's coronation.

7  I hope to have treated this literature adequately. I am not a specialist of Polish history and do not speak Polish. Professor Jerzy Stzrelczyk (Poznań) kindly read my manuscript critically and improved the spelling, for which I am very grateful.

8  How the reception of this recent research has also transformed Polish scholarship is shown in the study of Gawlas, 'Die spätmittelalterliche Nationenbildung'; Kersken, *Geschichtsschreibung im Europa der 'nationes'*; also, Strelczyk, 'Auf der Suche nach der nationalen Identität'.

9  There is even a new play by Wilhelm Swewczyk and Jan Malicki, *Nanker: dialogi wrocławskie*.

10  Gawlas, 'Die spätmittelalterliche Nationenbildung', pp. 131–37.

11  It is (almost) completely available in print; see *Vetera monumenta Poloniae*, I, ed. by Theiner; *Acta Camerae Apostolicae*, ed. by Ptaśnik; *Analecta Vaticana*, ed. by Ptaśnik; and *Bullarium Poloniae*, ed. by Sułkowska-Kuraś and Kuraś, I.

12  Nanker's date of birth is often set earlier (cf. the literature cited above, p. 83 n. 2), though without convincing reason. If he is mentioned in the important papal letter of 21 December

Władysław Łokietek, one of the Polish princes whose power base was in Kuyavia and Sieradz. Łokietek and his rivals fought with varying success over hereditary succession in several duchies and especially Lesser Poland with Kraków at the centre.[13] Nanker received his education at the cathedral school of Kraków. This is stated in a letter Pope John XXII sent to Nanker on 21 December 1328, permitting him to read Mass according to the Kraków liturgy while being at Wrocław as well, for 'having been nourished in the church of Kraków from your boyhood'.[14] The Curia, to be sure, was not self-informed about facts, but merely copied passages from the petitioner's request for papal intervention into the mandate it issued in response, a mechanism we will discuss in greater detail below. As a result, the reference just quoted had to come from Nanker himself, or from the proctor who acted on his behalf.

Around 1300, Nanker became a full member of the chapter at Kraków Cathedral, as it is suggested by the oldest known document mentioning Nanker on 21 August 1304.[15] At that time, he already appeared as the second of five canons, who are listed according to the length of their tenure. He did not hold any office or dignity.[16] His study of canon law at Bologna toward 1306 is considered the next secure date, although I have my doubts about it.[17] From 1308 to 1315, Nanker is documented repeatedly as archdeacon of Sandomierz.[18] In 1313, he travelled regarding matters affecting the church of Kraków as well as his own business and 'many different affairs throughout the land'. Unfortunately, this is all we hear about it.[19] The next record in chronological order attests to Nanker's presence at a highly important political event, the gathering of estates in

---

1328 as 'already advanced in age' and unable to learn the unfamiliar liturgy of Wrocław Cathedral, this meant according to curial style that he was 'around fifty', which is confirmed by the collector's remark of a decade later, describing Nanker as 'old and to some extent in physical decline'; see *Vetera monumenta Poloniae*, I, ed. by Theiner, p. 395. Nanker served as bishop until his death in 1341, at the comparatively high age of above sixty. In determining the latest possible birthdate for Nanker, moreover, the canonical requirements of ordination are relevant; he was ordained bishop in 1320 and archdeacon in 1308, respectively calling for a minimum age of thirty and twenty-five.

13 Cf. Gawlas, 'Wladyslaw I. Lokietek'.

14 *Bullarium Poloniae*, ed. by Sułkowska-Kuraś and Kuraś, I, no. 1497.

15 *Analecta Vaticana*, ed. by Ptaśnik, pp. 69–71 (no. 111).

16 The document was politically important as part of the proceedings between Archbishop Jakub of Gniezno and Bishop Jan Muskata of Kraków before Bishop Henry of Wrocław.

17 See below, pp. 105–08.

18 *Kodeks dyplomatyczny Małopolski*, ed. by Piekosiński, III, nos 138–40; *Analecta Vaticana*, ed. by Ptaśnik, p. 87 (no. 121, of 1308); p. 99 (no. 124, of 1309). Nanker was nominated judge delegate on 13 December 1311, cf. *Bullarium Poloniae*, ed. by Sułkowska-Kuraś and Kuraś, I, no. 1022; erroneously dated in *Zbiór dokumentów*, I, ed. by Kuraś, no. 17; also, nos 18–19 (of 1313). *Kodeks dyplomatyczny Wiekopolski*, ed. by Piekosiński, II, no. 979, features a charter of 29 December 1315 by Władysław Łokietek.

19 *Zbiór dokumentów*, I, ed. by Kuraś, no. 18.

86    CHAPTER 4

Sulejów from 20–23 June 1318, where the decision was made to ask Pope John XXII for his support of the project of restoring the Polish kingdom. Władysław Łokietek, the 'true heir', was presented as candidate to the throne, and the pope was offered in recompense the continuous payment of Peter's Pence 'within the old confines' of the realm, that is, including Pomerelia, the land around Chelmno, and the Silesian duchies.[20] Nanker is identified on the occasion as chancellor of the Sieradz territory pertaining to the central regions under Łokietek's rule. Unfortunately, Nanker is never mentioned elsewhere in this capacity.[21] He clearly belonged to the entourage of the royal pretender.[22] In the documents issued just a day later, it is not Nanker who figures as chancellor, but 'Master Franciscus', who bore the same title in the church of Kraków. We hear more of him in due course.

Thereafter, Nanker disappears almost entirely from the documentation.[23] We encounter him again at the coronation of Władysław Łokietek in Kraków on 20 January 1320, this time in his new function as dean of the cathedral.[24] He retained that office until he was made bishop. The latter event is plainly noted in contemporary chronicles along with the date of 1320. Długosz has written extensively about the electoral proceedings.[25] After the death of Bishop Jan Muskata on 7 February 1320, the members of the chapter formally convened 'according to custom and at the behest of Władysław, king of Poland'. At the gathering 'and upon notification of those absent', Dean Nanker from the noble house of the Oksza was chosen by the majority 'due to his eminence in virtue and conduct'. The king 'as patron' gave his approval. The election was eventually confirmed by Pope John XXIII (or rather John XXII), whereupon Nanker was consecrated by the archbishop of Gniezno in Lenczyce. The account is mistaken when it claims that papal confirmation was requested and granted. The Vatican sources prove the contrary. Assuming the pope had done so, he would have been entitled to payment of the *servitia*. The accounts of the Apostolic

---

20  Cf. the fundamental study by Maschke, *Der Peterspfennig in Polen*, pp. 93–94; on the rally at Sulejów and its consequences, pp. 120 ff.

21  Nanker's predecessor in this office was Master Franciscus, his successor Zbigniew ze Szczyrzyca, documented from 1321. On Zbigniew, see Kowalski, *Prałaci i kanonicy krakowskiey*, pp. 287–88 (no. 253); Ożóg, *Kultura umysłowa w Krakowie*, p. 162 (no. 98). He was chancellor and later king, cf. Rybicka-Adamska, 'Zbigniew ze Szczyrzyca'.

22  *Kodeks dyplomatyczny katedry krakowskiej*, ed. by Piekosiński, I, nos 119 and 120. Nanker has the title of *dominus* ('lord'), Franciscus that of *magister*. Zbigniew, who was also present, is called 'lord' as well.

23  The exception is discussed below, p. 96.

24  In an undated document from Kraków written after 20 January and before 7 February 1320, Nanker is placed after the bishop *in pontificalibus* as dean of the cathedral; cf. *Kodeks dyplomatyczny Małopolski*, ed. by Piekosiński, III, no. 161.

25  'Katalogi biskupów krakowskich', ed. by Szymański, p. 187; cf. the inscription on the tomb, in Urban, 'De testimoniis', p. 279.

Chamber, which are fully preserved from this period, demonstrate in their silence that the *servitia* were not collected in 1320. Jan Długosz's error can be explained by the need during his time to obtain papal confirmation, which did not yet exist when Nanker was alive. Długosz was intent on presenting Nanker's elevation in conformity with the canonical norms. He did not conceal, however, that the election was completely dominated by Łokietek's party.[26] John XXII might not have consented, if his corroboration had been sought or the losing opposition had appealed to him, which does not seem to have been the case.[27] John XXII for his part did not act at all. We are told subsequently about a possible reason for his restraint.

Jan Długosz could have added that the election took place within the canonical time limit of three months, because on 23 March 1320, Władysław Łokietek addressed Nanker in his entourage as 'bishop elect'.[28] When dealing with the election of a bishop, it is always worthwhile checking which benefices he possessed beforehand and lost automatically upon consecration. Successive holders indicate, moreover, which person had to be reckoned with at the church where the benefice was located. Nanker's deanery at Kraków Cathedral went to Bishop Gerward of Włocławek's relative, Bodzęta de Wreśna. I use from here on the Latin name forms.[29] In September 1319, Nanker was still in possession of St Mary's Parish in Kraków.[30] It was reassigned to Johannes Grotonis, a trusted follower of

---

26 Under Nanker's predecessor, Jan Muskata, the chapter had become very polarized; see Nowakowski, 'Krakowska kapituła katedralna'.

27 This lawyer pope was very serious about the observation of canonical rules, unless superior political considerations persuaded him to adopt a different position. For the territory of the German Empire, this is well illustrated by Suhle, 'Die Besetzung der deutschen Bistümer'.

28 *Vetera monumenta Poloniae*, I, ed. by Theiner, p. 165; also, *Lites ac res gestae*, ed. by Chłopocka, I, pp. 9–10. The document attests to the proctorship that the king assigned at Sandomierz to represent him in the proceedings against the Teutonic Order before the papal delegates. It is doubtful whether Nanker was still dean of the cathedral on 9 March 1320, when he is identified as such in the charter of a Silesian prelate; *Regesten zur schlesischen Geschichte*, ed. by Grünhagen and Wutke, V, no. 4027; knowledge of the changes occurring on 7 February 1320 was probably lacking there. Another charter posing problems was issued on behalf of Władysław Łokietek at Kraków; it is dated 26 June 1300 (!) and was issued by his chancellor, in *Kodeks dyplomatyczny Małopolski*, ed. by Piekosiński, III, p. 157 (unnumbered, apparently because the data are contradictory). Łokietek is cited with the titles he held until 20 January 1320; Nanker is called 'bishop by the grace of God', in the way he always would call himself following his consecration.

29 On Bodzęta z Wrześni, see Kowalski, *Prałaci i kanonicy krakowskiej*, pp. 132–33 (no. 14); Niwiński, 'Bodzęta z Wrześni'; also, pp. 103–04 below (Table 4.1). On 23 March 1320, he is still documented as archdeacon of Kruszwica; cf. *Vetera monumenta Poloniae*, I, ed. by Theiner, p. 254. He is not mentioned as archdeacon of the cathedral until 2 October; *Kodeks dyplomatyczny Małopolski*, ed. by Piekosiński, III, no. 164.

30 See below, p. 96.

88   CHAPTER 4

Bishop Gerward, who was rewarded in this way for his services during Łokietek's coronation.[31]

When did Nanker gain possession of the two benefices? It is generally assumed that he became dean of Kraków Cathedral on 20 August 1319, because on that date Pope John XXII confirmed an exchange between Nanker and Johannes de Verulis, the previous holder of the deanery. It is odd, though, that the transaction was to be executed before Bishop Gerward. We must look more closely at the wording of these and other papal letters.

## Nanker and Pope John XXII

### Nanker's Sojourn at the Curia, 1318–1319

Several months after the assembly at Sulejów, Bishop Gerward of Włocławek travelled to Avignon.[32] He went as an envoy of Władysław Łokietek's party and arrived in December 1318 at the latest, given that his presence there is attested for 12 December.[33] He did not undertake the journey alone, of course. The identity of his unnamed companions can be inferred to some extent. Two canons from Kraków had been summoned in person to Avignon for November or December 1318 to account for their administration of the bishop's property (known as his *mensa*). They had improperly laid their hands on it according to the Curia.[34] Both of

---

31 On Łokietek's coronation below, p. 92. In 1322, Johannes Grotonis appears in a curial source as 'Bishop Gerward's chaplain'; cf. *Acta Camerae Apostolicae*, ed. by Ptaśnik, pp. 79 and 86 (no. 140). At this time, he was again at the Curia, to deposit together with Andreas de Verulis, a curial cleric (discussed below, pp. 111–13), the payments made by the collector, Bishop Gerward. For information about Jan Grotowic, see Kowalski, *Prałaci i kanonicy krakowskiej*, pp. 173–74 (no. 74); Matuszek, 'Jan Grotowicz h. Rawa'; Ożóg, *Kultura umysłowa w Krakowie*, p. 143 (no. 36); and pp. 103–04 below (Table 4.1). Between 1325 and 1327, the annual revenues of the parish church were estimated by the collectors at the exorbitant rate of 133 marks; *Acta Camerae Apostolicae*, ed. by Ptaśnik, p. 113 (no. 139).
32 On Bishop Gerward, cf. Kreidte, *Die Herrschaft der Bischöfe von Pomerellen*, pp. 126 ff. (with additional bibliography); cf. Maschke, *Der Peterspfennig in Polen*, p. 124.
33 *Joannis Dlugossi Annales*, ed. by Turkowska, pp. 107–08; cf. Szczur, 'Dyplomaci Kazimierza'.
34 The date of November/December 1318 is probably implied by the letter sent 'from the Curia' on 20 May 1318; cf. *Analecta Vaticana*, ed. by Ptaśnik, no. 144; *Bullarium Poloniae*, ed. by Sułkowska-Kuraś and Kuraś, I, no. 1076. It set for the accused a peremptory deadline of four months, to be calculated upon receipt of the summons; for the remaining contents, see p. 89 n. 37 below. If the time span needed to deliver the letter and citations to the addressees was about two months, the result is November or December. On the same day, the Apostolic Chancery also issued a correction of its grave mistake in a letter of 3 February 1317 concerning the identity of the collectors of Peter's Pence, in which the bishop of 'Wrocław' rather than 'Wrocławek' is named alongside the archbishop of Gniezno; *Acta Camerae Apostolicae*, ed. by Ptaśnik, pp. 49–51 (no. 53); *Bullarium Poloniae*,

ON NANKER, BISHOP OF KRAKÓW AND WROCŁAW   89

them are already known to us as Johannes Grotonis, Nanker's successor as holder of the parish of St Mary in Kraków, and Master Franciscus, who apparently was Nanker's predecessor in the same benefice.[35]

In the previous ten years and following the capture of Jan Muskata, bishop of Kraków, by Władysław Łokietek despite his promise of free passage, the revenues of the episcopal *mensa* had not been sent to the Apostolic Chamber as required by canonical regulations.[36] Instead, they had been collected and used — certainly with Łokietek's approval, if not upon his instigation — by a couple of laymen and three clerics including Johannes Grotonis and Franciscus 'for their own purposes'.[37] The two belonged to the prince's close circle of churchmen. We know about the third through a different source.[38] He was the great archdeacon of Kraków, Ranboldus.[39] Table 4.1 below shows that he came from Łokietek's

---

ed. by Sułkowska-Kuraś and Kuraś, I, no. 1075 (incorrectly summarized). Such confusion repeatedly occurred at the Apostolic Chancery in connection with territories unknown to curial clerics.

35 On Franciscus, see Kowalski, *Prałaci i kanonicy krakowskiej*, pp. 149–50 (no. 38); Koszłowska-Bukowa, 'Johannes Grotonis'.

36 *Analecta Vaticana*, ed. by Ptaśnik, pp. 112–13 (no. 128), 133; *Joannis Dlugossi Annales*, ed. by Turkowska, p. 185: 'Henceforth and with King Władysław looking the other way or pretending, (the bishop) was held captive by nobles from the house of Topór at his estate in Cunow for a long time, escaping outright captivity while suffering the anguish of exile'.

37 20 May 1318; cf. p. 88 n. 34 above. Pope John XXII ordered the archbishop of Gniezno and the bishop of Wrocławek to take the revenues of the *mensa* at Kraków from unauthorized 'administrators' and their heirs and deliver the money to the Curia. This is confirmed by the well-informed historian of the Kraków church, Jan Długosz, in *Joannis Dlugossi Annales*, ed. by Turkowska, p. 186: 'The revenues of the Kraków bishopric were largely withheld or dispersed'. The two bishops were appointed as collectors of Peter's Pence in Poland a year and a half earlier. One of the 'heirs' mentioned by Długosz we encounter by chance somewhat later. His name was Pacoslaus, son of Spitko, the chatelain of Kraków. On 2 August 1332, Pacoslaus petitioned for a benefice in Wrocław, indicating that he drew a pension of ten marks from the 'episcopal *mensa* in Kraków'; see Samulski, *Untersuchungen*, pp. 66–67 (no. 58); also, *Analecta Vaticana*, ed. by Ptaśnik, p. 286 (no. 267; of 18 October 1330). This invites further inquiry.

38 The mandate of 12 June 1330, which is no longer preserved, instructed the archbishop of Gniezno in the name of the Apostolic Chamber to confiscate from 'Ranboldus, self-appointed administrator of the possessions pertaining to the church of Kraków', the gains of his unwarranted administrative role; cf. *Vetera monumenta Poloniae*, I, ed. by Theiner, p. 321; *Bullarium Poloniae*, ed. by Sułkowska-Kuraś and Kuraś, I, no. 1295. They were to be recuperated by the collectors from the archbishop and the heirs (!) of the late Ranboldus — indicating that they had been alienated. On 12 June 1310, Gentilis, the papal legate, complained that the income from the *mensa* at Kraków had not been paid for two years. At that time, it was Jarostius, the custodian of the cathedral chapter, who had acted as unauthorized administrator; *Analecta Vaticana*, ed. by Ptaśnik, no. 132.

39 Ranboldus died in 1322; cf. Ożóg, 'Reinbold'; Ożóg, *Kultura umysłowa w Krakowie*, p. 160 (no. 72*); Kowalski, *Prałaci i kanonicy krakowskiey*, pp. 254–55 (no. 202); Nowakowski, 'Krakowska kapituła katedralna', pp. 4–5; and pp. 103–04 (Table 4.1) below.

90     CHAPTER 4

immediate clerical entourage, whose members traded important offices and benefices among themselves.

It was certainly one of the main points on the agenda of the duke's envoys to settle the conflict concerning the bishop of Kraków.[40] The following problems had to be solved. First, the poorly treated Bishop Jan Muskata had to be reinstated and obtain adequate satisfaction, unless there was room to broker his resignation and compensation. In this case, it was perhaps also possible to agree on a suitable successor. Next, proper retribution was needed in view of the sacrilegious attack on him as a cleric, a matter Pope John XXII did not take lightly at all. The chosen scapegoats may have been the two laymen whose names are given in Długosz's account. In addition, a settlement had to be reached over the lump sum the Curia would accept in return for the ten years of lost income from the bishop's *mensa* at Kraków. An explanation was needed as to why it was illusory to retrieve the full amount, which had long been spent or firmly allocated elsewhere. The three clerical administrators of the *mensa* had to request papal absolution.

Finally, the dignities in the chapter of Kraków Cathedral had to be placed in the hands of Łokietek's trusted followers in order to put them in charge of the divine services in the church where the duke's royal coronation was to occur. This point was crucial considering the scandal a member of the adversarial Bohemian party in the chapter could cause by turning the ceremony into an unwelcome political demonstration! The dignities in question were in descending rank the dean, the great archdeacon, and the provost of the cathedral.[41] The archdeacon — Ranboldus — was reliable, and the same seemed true for the provost. Ranbold's position was apparently not transferred to someone new, which would have left some trace in the papal registers. The fact that Provost Thomas is mentioned for the first time at the coronation may be the result of gaps in the surviving source material.[42] The most important function, that of the dean, had been held for twelve years by the *magister* Johannes de Verolis, a respected and influential curial cleric from Veroli in the southern Papal States. At the

---

40 On 3 February 1317, Pope John XXII ordered Borislaus, the new archbishop of Gniezno, to reconcile the bishop and Duke Władysław. The mandate was voided, however, when the archbishop died at the Curia before 7 November 1317; cf. *Bullarium Poloniae*, ed. by Sułkowska-Kuraś and Kuraś, I, no. 1065.

41 Kowalski, *Prałaci i kanonicy krakowskiej*, p. 22. Below them were — in no entirely fixed order — the head of the school, the chanter, custodian, and chancellor. The contemporary head of the school was Prince Bolesław of Toszek, provided by Pope John XXII with the archbishopric of Esztergom on 2 October 1321; cf. Kowalski, *Prałaci i kanonicy krakowskiej*, no. 38 (with literature). The chanter cannot be identified with certainty. If it was already the curial cleric, Guilelmus de Sanguineto, in 1320, he did not participate in the coronation ceremony. Chancellor Franciscus was also custodian at the time.

42 Kowalski, *Prałaci i kanonicy krakowskiej*, p. 269 (no. 224). His successor was Zbigniew.

Curia, he served as elder statesman, so to speak.[43] He had little incentive to leave Avignon in order to participate in a ceremony occurring some 2000 kilometres away in Poland, in January, and which the pope was at best prepared to tolerate but not to support openly.[44] To be sure, there was also the vice-dean, but he could not substitute for the dean in ceremonial matters. A solution had to be found.

These agenda items suggest that Bishop Gerward's fellow travellers comprised the cathedral canons from Kraków, Master Franciscus, Johannis Grotonis, and Nanker, and likely also the archdeacon, Ranboldus.[45] The noble bishop was further accompanied by relatives, of course. The pope would provide those who were clerics among them with benefices at their departure from Avignon.[46] The troubles at Kraków did not figure among the points of negotiation Długosz mentioned in connection with Gerward's diplomatic mission. He rather referred to the pope's endorsement of Władysław Łokietek's coronation as king of Poland, the re-acquisition of Pomerelia, and the affirmation of old jurisdictional rights that the bishop of Włocławek asserted against the Teutonic Order. This has often been studied, so that I do not have to treat it here.

In Avignon, the group from Kraków had various trusted friends, ready to host Gerward and his entourage and share their contacts with him. There was, to begin with, Johannes de Verulis, the dean of Kraków Cathedral and cleric at the Apostolic Chamber who had frequently served the Polish party. In addition, Gerward could seek assistance from the so-called 'Poles', like Dominicus, *episcopus Methelinensis*, an auxiliary bishop of Archbishop Jakub of Gniezno from 1308 and already at the Curia for several years.[47] Besides, there was Bartholomeus, a canon from Kraków Cathedral who had worked for many years as proctor of the Polish party

---

43 See pp. 109–11 below.

44 Maschke, *Der Peterspfennig in Polen*, p. 124.

45 Franciscus was back in the company of Władysław Łokietek as early as on 7 July 1319; cf. *Kodeks dyplomatyczny Wiekopolski*, ed. by Piekosiński, II, no. 1010.

46 See p. 93 below.

47 In the biography of this chancellor, serving Władysław Łokietek and entering the Dominican convent at Poznań where he soon assumed a leading position as lecturer and prior, the final phase in Avignon seems to have gone unnoticed; cf. Maleczyński, 'Dominik'. According to his testament, he spent many and extended sojourns at the Curia. Aided by a small staff, he transferred moneys collected in Poland to the Curia; *Acta Camerae Apostolicae*, ed. by Ptaśnik, pp. 79 ff. (no. 96). He was there on 5 November 1319; *Acta Camerae Apostolicae*, ed. by Ptaśnik, no. 64; it is unclear if he had left for Poland on 27 June 1320 (no. 65; also, nos 55, 79, 80, 82, 84, 284, 286). He died as a 'poor bishop' at the Curia before 23 December 1323; cf. *Hierarchia catholica Medii Aevi*, ed. by Eubel, I, p. 337, and II, p. xxx; *Die Ausgaben der apostolischen Kammer unter Johann XXII.*, ed. by Schäfer, pp. 674, 721; *Analecta Vaticana*, ed. by Ptaśnik, pp. 218–19 (nos 153–54); *Bullarium Poloniae*, ed. by Sułkowska-Kuraś and Kuraś, I, nos 1138, 1142–43; *Lettres communes de Jean XXII*, ed. by Mollat, nos 10552, 10782–83.

92    CHAPTER 4

at the Curia.[48] For a while, they were joined by Simon de Marsow, a canon from the dome of Wrocław and member of Archbishop Jakub of Gniezno's household (or *familia*).[49] Gerard was also able to have recourse to individuals from the 'family' of Cardinal Gentilis de Montefiore, who before his death in 1312 had spent a long time in Poland and Hungary.[50] Finally, there were other curial clergy holding benefices at churches in the ecclesiastical province of Gniezno.[51]

Gerward indeed managed to reach an agreement with John XXII. This is evident from the annual transfer of 4000 guilds plus interest to Avignon, which Magister Franciscus undertook over three years beginning at the end of 1320 from income he had accumulated during his time as administrator of the bishop's *mensa* in Kraków.[52] It also can be inferred from the fact that John XXII did not interfere with Władysław Łokietek's coronation project despite protests from King John of Bohemia. When the ceremony took place on 20 January 1320, moreover, Bishop Jan Muskata assisted while Nanker in his function as dean led the procession of canons from Kraków Cathedral.[53]

---

48 According to the narrative in the auxiliary bishop's testament of 12 December 1323, in *Analecta Vaticana*, ed. by Ptaśnik, no. 96, he was from about 1309 at the Curia, faithfully serving under the most adverse circumstances as proctor of the 'Polish' party; cf. Ożóg, *Kultura umysłowa w Krakowie*, no. 7, listing him as canon of Krakow Cathedral for 1324–1329; he is not mentioned in Kowalski, *Prałaci i kanonicy krakowskiej.*

49 *Acta Camerae Apostolicae*, ed. by Ptaśnik, nos 57–59.

50 Several household members with the native names of 'San Genesio' and 'Pontecurvo', Lello de Mevanca, and Robertus de Fonte who joined the *familia* of Cardinal Guilelmus Testa. He had claims to a custodianship in Wrocławek, to a beneficed canonry in Wrocław and in Kruszwica; he was to relinquish them on 7 September 1316; cf. *Bullarium Poloniae*, ed. by Sułkowska-Kuraś and Kuraś, I, no. 1040. In 1318, he exchanged the custodianship of Wrocławek for a cathedral canonry with Simon of Marsow; cf. *Analecta Vaticana*, ed. by Ptaśnik, no. 145. On the legation, see Mollat, 'Gentile da Montefiore', without mention of his mission to Poland.

51 Servants of the Apostolic Chamber held benefices in Poland with special frequency according to Sułkowska-Kuraś and Kuraś, 'La Pologne et la papauté d'Avignon', p. 118 (without evidence). Names of curial clergy with benefices in Wrocław have been compiled by Samulski, *Untersuchungen*, pp. 60 ff.

52 *Acta Camerae Apostolicae*, ed. by Ptaśnik, pp. 75–76 (no. 86), where *magister* Franciscus de Cracovia is said to have acknowledged a debt of 4000 guilds incurred 'for certain reasons' during his administration. The first rate of 500 guilds reached Avignon late in 1320, the next of 250 guilds in 1321. Subsequently, there were larger payments in quick succession, 1500 and 1000 guilds in 1322, and 'the rest' of 1200 guilds in April 1323. 4450 guilds were booked in total. Other sums were slow to arrive; cf. *Acta Camerae Apostolicae*, ed. by Ptaśnik, p. 291 (no. 241). Bishop Gerward must have convinced the pope that he could not ask for more given that the alienated money had long been spent. The annual income of the *mensa* is unknown to us; see p. 89 n. 37 above.

53 Długosz states this explicitly. Seven days earlier, the bishop was found in the duke's entourage. The restored relationship, though, is described in ways that would have appalled John XXII. Jan Muskata is addressed by the duke as 'my chaplain' sitting near him, whereas

Of the agreements about benefices forming part of the diplomatic negotiations we encounter a bare minimum in the papal registers, due only to the circumstance that Bishop Gerward prepared for his return to Poland in August or September 1319 and henceforth had to treat unfinished business in writing. The necessary papal provisions and dispensations are listed among the many concessions made to the person of the bishop and his commissioner, Władysław Łokietek.[54] Four provisions were for canonries combined with reservations for the first benefice becoming vacant. Two of them had to be in Kraków and for two relatives of Bishop Gerward, the already mentioned Bodzęta de Wreśna and Bogufalus de Couale.[55] The remaining two were in Wrocław, one for Mathias de Paluca, a nephew of Gerward's, and Andreas Tinacius de Verulis.[56] The three Polish recipients belonged to Gerward's retinue.[57] Their grants were to strengthen Władysław Łokietek's party at both churches and reward each envoy for his success. As we will see, the fourth and final mandate served yet another purpose.

Three additional letters were concerned with appointments to benefices, which the pope undertook without intermediary because they fell under general papal reservation. They all affected Nanker and call for further discussion. In the first, dated 20 August 1320 and following the narrative of events in the letter, the pope stated to have heard that two clerics, one *magister* Johannes de Verulis, who is further identified as papal notary, and Nanker Ingrami, canon at Kraków Cathedral wished to exchange their respective benefices at the church.[58] The pope granted their request, authorizing Bishop Gerward of Włocławek on his behalf to

---

the bishop referred to himself as 'seated near our elder'; *Kodeks dyplomatyczny katedry krakowskiej*, ed. by Piekosiński, I, nos 121–22.

54 *Bullarium Poloniae*, ed. by Sułkowska-Kuraś and Kuraś, I, nos 1121 ff.

55 *Bullarium Poloniae*, ed. by Sułkowska-Kuraś and Kuraś, I, nos 1131–32; *Analecta Vaticana*, ed. by Ptaśnik, nos 150–51; *Lettres communes de Jean XXII*, ed. by Mollat, nos 10319–20. Bodzęta was permitted to accept beyond his expectancy a dignity as well. Bogufal could only add a canonry. On 28 September 1320, he also obtained a provision with a canonry at Wrocław Cathedral; *Analecta Vaticana*, ed. by Ptaśnik, no. 157; cf. no. 158, under the same date but for another cleric of the same clientele.

56 *Bullarium Poloniae*, ed. by Sułkowska-Kuraś and Kuraś, I, no. 1114; *Vetera monumenta Poloniae*, I, ed. by Theiner, no. 229; *Lettres communes de Jean XXII*, ed. by Mollat, no. 10304 (of 10 September 1319).

57 The presence of all four at the Curia can be inferred from administrative usage at the Apostolic Chancery, which issued letters with certain opening phrases (incipits) only to visiting recipients. They would be given three executors, one of them being, if possible, at the Curia; for the documentation, see p. 93 nn. 55–56 above, p. 95 n. 63 below. On Andreas Tinacius de Verulis, pp. 111–13 below.

58 *Vetera monumenta Poloniae*, I, ed. by Theiner, p. 148 (no. 229); *Lettres communes de Jean XXII*, ed. by Mollat, no. 9983?; *Bullarium Poloniae*, ed. by Sułkowska-Kuraś and Kuraś, I, no. 1113, where the document is wrongly combined with the one following.

execute the order of permutation in this one instance (*hac vice*) and while still residing at the Apostolic See.

It is important to know that under the circumstances the exchange of benefices had to occur in principle at the Curia to avoid suspicions of simony 'by law'.[59] If the transaction was not feasible there, the pope was able to appoint a prelate so as to perform it with apostolic authority in the interested locality (*in partibus*). The above letter concedes, however, that execution might take place at the Curia as well, a stipulation warranting additional comment. For the rest, the convoluted and formulaic language of the letter hardly differs from the usual standard ensuring that the risky business of exchange was safely concluded. The formula referring to 'whatever ecclesiastical benefices Nanker may hold' is perplexing among the numerous clauses the letter introduces as 'notwithstanding' at the end. Against the canonical requirement of having to list each of his holdings expressly, they were to be treated as though they had been named one by one 'because it proves impossible to obtain accurate information about them'. Among the exceptions granted to Nanker's counterpart, it is surprising to read in the light of the subsequent papal mandate that he was dean at the collegiate church of Furnes in the (rich) diocese of Therouanne. Johannes de Verulis' other claims to benefices noted as notwithstanding are not relevant here.[60]

The above mandate was supplemented by a second under the same date. It is again addressed to Bishop Gerward. In the narrative, the contents of the previous letter are reiterated, albeit with adjustments in the presentation of the facts. Accordingly, the initiative to exchange the two canonries between holders had been that of Johannes de Verulis, who 'recently' intimated his wish to the pope. The prior papal reply accommodated this petition and is quoted correspondingly. Next, the pope declared his intent to reward 'the mentioned person of Nanker even further for his merits' regarding the church of Kraków. He instructed the bishop to add upon completing the mentioned exchange of benefices the deanery of the cathedral as well, given that it had fallen vacant because of the peaceful appropriation of the deanery at Furnes by Johannes de Verulis. The pope identified the reason for the general reservation to him by noting that the position at Kraków became vacant at the Curia owing to the translation of the previous holder to another. Concerning the exception clauses, it seems remarkable to me that Nanker was permitted to have his oath as dean initially sworn by a proctor, before having to do it in person 'as soon as he came to the church involved'; secondly, we encounter the already familiar formula of notwithstanding conditions including 'whatever ecclesiastical

---

59 Gillmann, 'Die Resignation der Benefizien'.

60 See the remarks below, pp. 109–11; on claims made 'notwithstanding', p. 97 n. 67 below.

benefices the same Nanker obtains, since there cannot be certainty about them given the geographical distance', and so on.

The text reveals that the second letter was predated. Compared to the situation on 20 August, there had been a change insofar as news of the uncontested acquisition of the deanery at Furnes by Johannes de Verulis must have reached the Curia. In line with the papal decretal known as 'Ex debito' of 1316, he had to give up his previously unmentioned possession of the deanery at Kraków Cathedral unless he obtained papal dispensation.[61] Unfortunately, we do not know when Pope John XXII conferred the benefice at Furnes to Johannes de Verulis (possibly on 27 May 1319), nor whether the transaction had been planned all along as compensation for the deanery in Kraków.[62]

As a result, we have developed a better understanding of the first letter as well. The permutation of benefices was tied to the transfer of the deanery at the cathedral to Nanker. While Johannes de Verulis still held his position as canon of Kraków, he received Nanker's position at Furnes, which must have been better endowed. Johannes obtained additional satisfaction, moreover, according to a letter of 11 September 1319. It provided one Andreas Tinacius de Verulis with a canonry at Wrocław Cathedral.[63] The pope did not know him in person, but trustworthy people had vouched for him and Duke Władysław Łokietek had intervened on his behalf. Andreas was permitted — like Nanker — to submit his oath through a proctor, although he had to renew it once he reached Wrocław. It can be surmised who the persons of trust had been, because Andreas was a close relative of Johannes de Verulis, probably his nephew who resided with him at Avignon and acted on occasion as his representative.[64] Andreas de Verulis belonged to the staff of Johannes as abbreviator and

---

61 'Extravagantes Communes' 1.3.4, in *Corpus iuris canonici*, ed. by Friedberg, II, cols 1240–42. The decretal defined vacancies at the Curia with added precision. They comprised resignations into the pope's hands and promotions or translations by him to another benefice, including lesser ones; cf. Meyer, *Zürich und Rom*, pp. 37–38, 151–54.

62 *Lettres communes de Jean XXII*, ed. by Mollat, no. 9478. The permission for the papal notary Johannes de Serulis (!), dean of Furnes, to collect the full amount of income from his benefices for the duration of his stay at the Curia dates to this day. It was common practice to secure such licenses for benefices requiring residency right away. Johannes de Verulis is documented in connection with the deanery, see *Lettres communes de Jean XXII*, ed. by Mollat, nos 9813 (unnamed), 9865, 9924.

63 *Vetera monumenta Poloniae*, I, ed. by Theiner, no. 244; *Lettres communes de Jean XXII*, ed. by Mollat, no. 10334; *Bullarium Poloniae*, ed. by Sułkowska-Kuraś and Kuraś, I, no. 1133.

64 *Regesten zur schlesischen Geschichte*, ed. by Grünhagen and Wutke, V, nos 3990 and 4051. On 27 June 1320, a notary recorded the protest by the proctor of the Silesian dukes against Peter's Pence at the residence of *magister* Johannes de Verulis and *magister* Andreas de Verulis; printed by Maschke, *Der Peterspfennig in Polen*, pp. 320–23.

protonotary.[65] Władysław Łokietek's support implied that Andreas did not have to wait long for his actual acquisition of a benefice in Wrocław. Andreas became especially known as collector of papal revenues in Poland (from 1326 to 1329).[66]

The third letter is from 11 September 1319. Under this date, we find all the concessions Bishop Gerward received just before departing from Avignon, including his passport. The text presents him as petitioner addressing the pope who recently provided Nanker, parish priest of St Mary's in Kraków, with the deanery of the cathedral there. As soon as Nanker was to accept the benefice — a step he was about to take —, thereby leaving his prior benefice in the parish, Bishop Gerard obtained permission by way of exception to dispose of the benefice, although it fell under general papal reservation for having been vacated at the Curia. The pope granted the request because he wished 'to honour your person and impart grace for the honour exhibited to another'.

Looking at the three letters in conjunction, it is notable that they dealt with a canonically complex and precarious transaction, in which there was a lot at stake for the participants. Curial interests in general and those of the Apostolic Chamber specifically were affected as well. As noted, Władysław Łokietek's party wished to install a new dean of its own at the cathedral in view of the impending coronation. Consequently, Johannes de Verulis had to be given a different benefice rewarding him sufficiently for the loss of the deanery at Kraków. This was more easily and readily said than done. As we have seen, peaceful possession of the deanery at Furnes, which was a collegiate church rather than a cathedral, was not yet attained in August 1319. Johannes de Verulis, who as cleric of the Apostolic Chamber had witnessed hundreds of similar exchanges going nowhere, was certainly not willing to resign the deanery at Kraków into papal hands until every detail had been settled appropriately. Conversely, he had to make sure he received the promised compensation, presupposing that Nanker had real control over the benefice he was about to abandon and was truly relinquishing it. Johannes also needed from the church of Kraków and from the local duke assurances of a smooth transfer, acknowledging its full validity. The same necessity extended to the second component of the transaction, namely, the position earmarked for the nephew of Johannes de Verulis at Wrocław Cathedral.

The whole operation could be undermined by a formal mistake. Supposing, for example, that the canonical exceptions applying to one of the two partners were incorrectly itemized, everything was rendered null

---

65 'Who occupied at the time the first chamber for Johannes de Verulis, the papal notary'; Maschke, *Der Peterspfennig in Polen* pp. 320–23; and below, p. 109 n. 118.

66 *Bullarium Poloniae*, ed. by Sułkowska-Kuraś and Kuraś, I, nos 1290–1307, 1314–16, 1353, 1360, 1399, 1402. On his career, cf. the discussion below, pp. 111–13.

and void.[67] Nanker incurred similar risks. As a matter of fact, his list of special clauses is revealing. To begin with, the pope released him from any obligation to declare his benefices and claims to them in detail, owing to the long distance from Poland to Avignon which prevented their full disclosure. This is surprising. Why should Nanker in Kraków not have had complete information about his cathedral canonry and parish at St Mary's? The formulation is meaningful, though, when we assume that Nanker — just as Andreas de Verulis — was in Avignon at the time. From there it was difficult to know with certainty whether he had obtained another benefice for which he had a claim. Nanker's presence at the Curia can also be inferred from other aspects of the transaction. How else was Bishop Gerward able to know that Nanker was about to accept the deanery of Kraków Cathedral? Why did the bishop take on the parish of St Mary, which Nanker had to vacate in turn, and what made him certain that Nanker had full possession of it? Similarly, Johannes de Verulis must have been willing to initiate the exchange only with a partner who was present. And lastly, the wording of Nanker's provision with the deanery, despite the formulaic nature of the curial style, indicates that the pope had met him in person and respected him.[68]

Presupposing that all parties to the contract were present in Avignon, why was Bishop Gerward commissioned with it? We may owe the answer and the three letters just analysed to mere chance. In the summer of 1319, there was a 'change of guard' at the Apostolic Chamber. The longstanding Chamberlain, Cardinal Arnaud d'Aux had stepped down on 23 July, and the appointment of his successor, Gasbart Laval, did not occur until 18 September.[69] It is possible that Johannes de Verulis was among the candidates, too. At any rate, negotiations about composition monies upon resignation of a benefice 'in favour of a third' (besides the pope and the current holder) and dispensations from the canonical norm could not be concluded definitively without the Apostolic Chamberlain. Collection of the so-called annates called for verification as well. They had to be disbursed for provisions undertaken 'by apostolic authority'.[70] Their proper payment had to be guaranteed regardless of whether they were made at the Curia or not, in the Chamber or not.

---

67 The 'notwithstanding' clauses, forming a constant element of papal letters (at the end of the dispositive part), invalidated rights that were in opposition to the pope's mandate.

68 Cf. above, p. 93. The curial style did not allow for more cordial language.

69 Samaran and Mollat, *La fiscalité pontificale en France*, p. 167.

70 As in the case of bishoprics, it was probably necessary to tax the benefices in question for the first time. This required legal clarification regarding their ownership, which hardly adhered to canonical regulations beforehand. The decretal 'Execrabilis' served to facilitate this process, ordering the revision of appointment practices in Poland and elsewhere; cf. Schmitz, *Lebens- und Arbeitsweise*, pp. 61 ff. 'Execrabilis' stipulated that a holder was obligated to renounce to each of his benefices except the last one, supposing that the

## 98    CHAPTER 4

### *Additional Clues Pointing to a Personal Relationship between Bishop Nanker and Pope John XXII*

Pope John XXII knew and liked Johannes Grotonis, who was often at the Curia and travelled from Bologna to Avignon when he was nominated bishop of Kraków in 1326. Długosz still reported that Grotonis was an acquaintance of the pope and his table companion.[71] Długosz wrote this to explain why the pope favoured the candidacy of Grotonis against the express wishes of Władysław Łokietek. In connection with Nanker, on the other hand, Długosz found no reason to dwell on his relationship with the pope. As we have seen, the pope made him bishop in full compliance with the intentions of the new Polish king.

That John XXII encountered Nanker during his sole visit to Avignon and held him in high regard is evident from other curial documentation. In the bull of 1 October 1326 transferring Nanker from Kraków to Wrocław, the pope explained his decision in favour of the candidate by stating that he deserved so 'owing to your multiple merits of virtue with which the Lord has graced your person and which have been brought to our attention and that of your brethren.'[72] The pope and his cardinals, in other words, had been able to meet the man. When Wrocław and Kraków were taxed for payment of the papal *servitia* for the first time in 1326, their bishops protested against it — with Johannes Grotonis appearing personally.[73]

---

acquisition was lawful. Those who received adequate dispensation could select from their remaining benefices two compatible ones within a month and return the rest to the ordinary. If they missed the deadline, their positions went to the pope and fell under his reservation. Dispensations were granted against payment of a composition, annates were due upon renewed provision with a reserved benefice.

71 'Katalogi biskupów krakowskich', ed. by Szymański, p. 191. The bull of nomination does not say so, *Vetera monumenta Poloniae*, I, ed. by Theiner, pp. 290–91 (no. 369). For his sojourn at Avignon in 1319–1320, see p. 87–88 above; for the one in the spring and fall of 1322, *Acta Camerae Apostolicae*, ed. by Ptaśnik, nos 79, 86. At the time of the provision, Grotonis was not yet at the Curia; on 13 February 1327, he personally deposited the payment of the *servitia* there, cf. *Acta Camerae Apostolicae*, ed. by Ptaśnik, no. 107.

72 *Vetera monumenta Poloniae*, I, ed. by Theiner, nos 368, 372; *Bullarium Poloniae*, ed. by Sułkowska-Kuraś and Kuraś, I, nos 1398, 1400. On the notable absence of a formula emphasizing Nanker's 'knowledge of letters', which the curial style required in nominations, cf. p. 107 below. As always, a specific type of document was issued; see Frenz, *Papsturkunden*, pp. 72–74. There was yet another departure from the norm. Whereas the elevation of Johannes Grotonis was communicated to the Polish king (*Vetera monumenta Poloniae*, I, ed. by Theiner, no. 370), a parallel notification is lacking on account of Nanker's new appointment at Wrocław. Concerning the political significance of these papal mandates, see Schwarz, 'Die Exemtion des Bistums Meißen', p. 322.

73 *Acta Camerae Apostolicae*, ed. by Ptaśnik, no. 109 (of 22 April 1327; for Wrocław). Nanker's nomination was administered by proctors, no. 106 (of 13 February 1327; for Kraków). At the synod of Uniejów in 1326, Nanker had assessed the *mensa* of the bishop of Kraków with 1350 guilds, no. 139.

John XXII considerably lowered the payable amount in either case, for Wrocław from 4000 guilds to 1785 and for Kraków from 3000 to 1394.[74] In Nanker's case, the reduction was explained 'in view of Bishop Nanker's person' and not with his achievements as ruler of the Kraków bishopric, which might have been highlighted as well.[75]

From Nanker's time in Kraków, there seems to be only one testimony revealing something about the personal relationship between the pope and the bishop. In 1325, Nanker complained to John XXII that his cathedral church and diocese were overly exposed to papal provisions and expectancies. He also objected to the tithe exemptions for newly arable land, which the Apostolic Chancery was granting to monasteries in his bishopric limiting his own ability to intervene as bishop. These points of aggravation are conveyed to us in the pope's response. John XXII for his part lauded Nanker for publishing the papal bulls against Louis of Bavaria in Kraków, while also reminding him gently that he could not do anything about the papal provisions because they had already been conceded. He was unable to act otherwise, moreover, because the matter was beyond his reach as pope and under the jurisdiction of the Chancery. There was no acknowledgement that Nanker had to be familiar with such canonistic commonplaces. The pope promised, however, 'to apply adequate remedy here and expedite it as he saw fit'. He called himself fortunate to satisfy the bishop's request at least in one regard by granting him absolution 'on the point of death'.[76] In view of the pope's personality, the letter was formulated with unusual sympathy.

In the spring of 1327, Nanker lamented to John XXII that he had made a poor bargain with his translation. The property belonging to the bishop's *mensa* at Wrocław had largely been alienated, and he occupied a lower rank within the church province of Gniezno during ceremonies. The pope in fact took Nanker's worries seriously by allowing him on September 16 to revoke all alienations his predecessor in the bishopric had permitted.[77] To console him further, Nanker was to enjoy in person

---

74 *Acta Camerae Apostolicae*, ed. Ptaśnik, no. 113 (of 28 April 1328). For Wrocław, implementation was conditional, if the revenues there did not improve. On Nanker's payments, see nos 116, 126. Each time, he had the sums deposited at the Curia by members of his entourage.

75 In the bull of appointment, he is generically addressed as one who 'led (the church of Kraków) laudably'.

76 *Bullarium Poloniae*, ed. by Sułkowska-Kuraś and Kuraś, I, no. 1356 (of 18 December 1325); *Vetera monumenta Poloniae*, I, ed. by Theiner, p. 227 (no. 355). Nanker's absolution *in articulo mortis* has survived, see *Bullarium Poloniae*, ed. by Sułkowska-Kuraś and Kuraś, I, no. 1357. It is unknown whether John XXII offered a remedy, unless it was Nanker's transfer to Wrocław he had in mind.

77 *Bullarium Poloniae*, ed. by Sułkowska-Kuraś and Kuraś, I, no. 1453; *Vetera monumenta Poloniae*, I, ed. by Theiner, no. 390. The revocation is expressed in solemn terms as 'with certain knowledge', etc. It is nonetheless a rescript and thus dependent in content on the

his accustomed ceremonial rights again.[78] He also received apostolic authorization to have one canonry respectively at the cathedral churches of Wrocław and Kraków reserved to relatives or members of his household, explicitly honouring Nanker and his 'friends'.[79] The scant documentation defies attempts to determine who among his relatives benefited from the grant.[80]

In 1328, the immunity of Wrocław Cathedral was physically invaded, household members of the bishop were injured, and several canons were driven away. According to Nanker's presentation of the facts in our immediate sources, the papal letters, the attack was directed against the person of the bishop and the collector by his side. A comparative study is needed to assess whether the measures John XXII imposed in response to Nanker's call for aid exceeded papal intervention elsewhere.[81] But it was uncommon for the pope to extend words of consolation, urging Nanker not to waver in his loyalty to the Holy See.[82]

After two months, another string of papal letters followed to improve the bishop's finances at Wrocław.[83] He was given permission to raise a (moderate) subsidy from the diocesan clergy.[84] To tie his entourage more closely to him, Nanker was also allowed to give six clerics who served in

---

statements of 'fact' the petitioner had provided; cf. Schwarz, 'Die Exemtion des Bistums Meißen', p. 306.

78  *Bullarium Poloniae*, ed. by Sułkowska-Kuraś and Kuraś, I, no. 1452; *Vetera monumenta Poloniae*, I, ed. by Theiner, no. 391.

79  *Bullarium Poloniae*, ed. by Sułkowska-Kuraś and Kuraś, I, no. 1454; *Vetera monumenta Poloniae*, I, ed. by Theiner, no. 389: 'Intending to honour your person and to impart grace for the honour exhibited to others'. The benefices could include offices and dignities other than principal ones.

80  In the local sources, we encounter a brother of Nanker's, Pasco, who was judge in Opole; *Codex diplomaticus Silesiae*, ed. by Grünhagen and Wutke, XVIII, nos 4197, 4263. We do not know if another Pasco, or Paulus Andree, a nephew documented as canon of Kraków Cathedral from 1327 to 1335, owed his position to John XXII's reservation; Kowalski, *Prałaci i kanonicy krakowskiej*, p. 237 (no. 174).

81  Dated 1 October 1328, the papal measures comprised the appointment of the archbishop of Gniezno and the bishop of Olomouc as spiritual judges; an invitation to the Polish, Bohemian, and Hungarian kings to fight the attackers; and relief from the most oppressive taxes; cf. *Bullarium Poloniae*, ed. by Sułkowska-Kuraś and Kuraś, I, nos 1487–89; *Vetera monumenta Poloniae*, I, ed. by Theiner, nos 398, 400–01. The letters against Bolko of Ziębice (nos 417–18, 421) follow the same pattern, citing besides the three kings regional leaders as secular powers as well. It deserves notice that the pope was pragmatic in his protection of the church of Wrocław, not paying attention to political theories attributing it to the 'kingdom of Poland'.

82  *Bullarium Poloniae*, ed. by Sułkowska-Kuraś and Kuraś, I, no. 1490; *Vetera monumenta Poloniae*, I, ed. by Theiner, no. 399.

83  On 21 December 1328; *Bullarium Poloniae*, ed. by Sułkowska-Kuraś and Kuraś, I, nos 1497–1501; *Vetera monumenta Poloniae*, I, ed. by Theiner, nos 405–09.

84  *Bullarium Poloniae*, ed. by Sułkowska-Kuraś and Kuraś, I, no. 1498; *Vetera monumenta Poloniae*, I, ed. by Theiner, no. 406.

his household as table companions license to collect revenue while being absent from their benefices.[85] Moreover, he was authorized to reserve one canonry with benefice each at Wrocław Cathedral and five collegiate churches in the diocese.[86] For the person of the bishop, the pope granted the right to read the hours in the way of the church at Kraków, while keeping him obligated to participate in the local rite when the official liturgy was read at the dome of Wrocław.[87] Nanker was named conservator as well.[88] When Nanker repeated his grievances perhaps as early as in 1328, the pope even proposed to have him translated back to Kraków![89]

Two years later, Nanker lamented in his position as bishop of Wrocław in the same way he had done at Kraków that his activities were severely curtailed by old and continuously arriving new papal provisions and expectancies. What embittered him especially was that his former protector, Władysław Łokietek, took care of his clients through the papacy.[90] This led, according to the pope's rendering, 'to the destruction ... of the church and people of Wrocław'. As a result, the bishop was unable to promote his own household members (*familia*). He remained against his duty without possibility to reward the sons of local nobility generously with benefices at the very churches their ancestors had endowed.[91] John XXII responded

---

85 *Bullarium Poloniae*, ed. by Sułkowska-Kuraś and Kuraś, I, no. 1499; *Vetera monumenta Poloniae*, I, ed. by Theiner, no. 407; for the duration of three years.

86 *Bullarium Poloniae*, ed. by Sułkowska-Kuraś and Kuraś, I, no. 1500; *Vetera monumenta Poloniae*, I, ed. by Theiner, no. 408.

87 *Bullarium Poloniae*, ed. by Sułkowska-Kuraś and Kuraś, I, no. 1497; *Vetera monumenta Poloniae*, I, ed. by Theiner, no. 405. The above reference to Nanker's education in Kraków has been taken from this letter.

88 *Bullarium Poloniae*, ed. by Sułkowska-Kuraś and Kuraś, I, no. 1501; *Vetera monumenta Poloniae*, I, ed. by Theiner, no. 409. The conservators were the archbishop of Gniezno and the bishops of Poznań and Olomouc.

89 *Bullarium Poloniae*, ed. by Sułkowska-Kuraś and Kuraś, I, no. 1515; *Vetera monumenta Poloniae*, I, ed. by Theiner, no. 414. Perhaps there were rumours that Nanker's translation had been revoked, which prompted the Bohemian queen to contact the pope on account of Wrocław for her brother; cf. *Bullarium Poloniae*, ed. by Sułkowska-Kuraś and Kuraś, I, no. 1506.

90 17 October 1330; *Bullarium Poloniae*, ed. by Sułkowska-Kuraś and Kuraś, I, nos 1599, 1600 (with incorrect summary); printed in *Analecta Vaticana*, ed. Ptaśnik, pp. 283 ff. (nos 265–66; wrongly dated). In diplomatic fashion, the error is assigned to the clients' initiative, who are said to have misled the pope by claiming they were 'natives of the lands and kingdom, and members of the Polish king's household'. Nanker was confronted here with the theories of various churchmen at Kraków. For him, though, they were 'foreigners' and 'pretenders concealing the truth'.

91 An examination of the *Bullarium Poloniae* reveals that many expectancies for a canonry were in fact granted upon request by the royal couple, whether at Wrocław Cathedral, the collegiate churches of Głogów, Opole, and others at Wrocław, as well as benefices awaiting conferral through the bishop. This trend continued after Nanker's translation; cf. *Bullarium Poloniae*, ed. by Sułkowska-Kuraś and Kuraś, I, nos 1687, 1694–95, 1712, 1716, 1734, 1803, 1888–89, 1902. A single petition by King John of Bohemia is found, no. 1702. The situation

102    CHAPTER 4

by offering him two privileges, one to the effect that he could use his right of 'ordinary' conferral as bishop to provide for six persons 'with apostolic authority'; secondly, Nanker was empowered to reserve at his discretion a canonry with benefice at Wrocław Cathedral and the collegiate churches of Opole and Głogów.[92]

Nanker's collaboration with collectors proved problematic. It was not only their draconian measures that irritated him.[93] He also resented their claim of papal prerogatives he considered to be those of bishops.[94] Like many other prelates, Nanker sought to bypass the collectors and negotiate directly with the Curia. The pope tolerated it.[95] In general, it seems that John XXII treated Nanker with much patience and generosity (Table 4.1).

---

remained unchanged under King Casimir the Great; the 'Chronica principum Poloniae', ed. by Węclewski, p. 550, laments that Casimir only wanted people 'born in Kraków' at the dome of Wrocław.

92 Just two petitions with papal provisions for members of Nanker's household have been preserved; *Bullarium Poloniae*, ed. by Sułkowska-Kuraś and Kuraś, I, nos 1573 (of 1329), 1766 (of 1335). They contain little detail.

93 Nanker appealed against the 'unduly heavy exaction' of the tithe by the collector. The pope did not address it, but urged the latter to treat Nanker 'more humanely'; *Bullarium Poloniae*, ed. by Sułkowska-Kuraś and Kuraś, I, no. 1489; *Vetera monumenta Poloniae*, I, ed. by Theiner, no. 400 (cf. above, p. 100 n. 81). *Analecta Vaticana*, ed. by Ptaśnik, no. 127 (of 5 August 1329); *Bullarium Poloniae*, ed. by Sulkowska-Kuras and Kuras, I, no. 1541. *Vetera monumenta Poloniae*, I, ed. by Theiner, no. 496 (of 21 October 1335); *Bullarium Poloniae*, ed. by Sułkowska-Kuraś and Kuraś, I, no. 1784. Also, no. 1812; *Vetera monumenta Poloniae*, I, ed. by Theiner, no. 509.

94 *Bullarium Poloniae*, ed. by Sułkowska-Kuraś and Kuraś, I, nos 1550, 1568; *Vetera monumenta Poloniae*, I, ed. by Theiner, nos 426, 429. Nanker confiscated the possessions of Vitus, the former bishop-elect of Wrocław who had died at the Curia, not bothering about the provision of the collector Andreas de Verulis with them. The harsh language in the pope's letters does not express a change in attitude toward Nanker, but mere formula as it was used by the Chancery to defend the rights of the Apostolic Chamber and its officials.

95 This relationship cannot be treated here; cf. *Bullarium Poloniae*, ed. by Sułkowska-Kuraś and Kuraś, I, nos 1532–33, 1550; also, nos 1810–12, 1822.

Table 4.1. Clerics from Kraków in the Service of Władysław Łokietek. AD = Archdeacon; Bp = Bishop; CC = Cathedral Canon; PSMK = Parish of St Mary in Kraków; WL = Władysław Łokietek; GW = Gerward of Wrocławek. **Bold = Offices & Benefices Held**.

| *Name* | Ranboldus, d. 1322 | Master Franciscus de Cracovia, d. 1327 | Nanker Ingrami, d. 1341 | Johannes Grotonis, d. 1347 | Bodzęta de Wreśna, d. 1366 | Zbigniew, d. 1356 |
|---|---|---|---|---|---|---|
| *Academic Study* | ? | Doctorate in Canon Law | ? | Canon Law in Bologna | ? | ? |
| *Patron – Office* | ? – 1306–08, Adversary of Bp Jan Muskata | WL – 1315, **Chancellor of Sieradz**; from 1316, **Chancellor of WL** | WL – 1318, **Chancellor of Sieradz** | WL and GW – 1313–15, **Chancellor of Kuyavia**; 1325, **Chancellor of WL** | GW | WL – 1314, **WL's Notary**; 1321–27, **Chancellor of Sieradz**; 1320–23, **Chancellor of WL** |
| *Position at Kraków Cathedral* | From 1281, **CC**; 1306–22, **Great AD** | From 1295, **CC**; 1295–22, **Chancellor** | From 1304, **CC**; late 1319 or early 1320, **Dean** | 1307–11, **Vice-Chancellor**; from 1309, **CC** | From 1319, **CC**; 1320–48, **Dean** | 1315–20, **Vice-Chancellor**; from 1319, **CC**; 1323–49, **Provost**; 1351–56, **Dean** |

| Other Benefices | 1294/1296, **PSMK**; 1286, 1296–1302, **AD of Sandomierz**; 1304–06, **Provost of Wiślica** | From 1308, **PSMK**; from 1317, **benefices in Gniezno**; from 1325, **in Wrocławek, Sandomierz**; from 1320, **Provost of Wiślica** | 1308–15, **AD of Sandomierz**; until 1319, **PSMK** | 1309–20, **Teacher in Scarbimir**; 1313–21, **Provost of St Nicholas**; 1320–26, **PSMK**; from 1325, **CC of Gniezno, Poznań, Wrocławek** | 1317–19 **AD of Kruszwica**; from 1319, **CC of Gniezno, Poznań, Wrocławek** | 1322, **AD of Zawichost**; 1328, **CC of Wrocławek** |
|---|---|---|---|---|---|---|
| Career Peak | As above | As above | From 1320, **Bp of Kraków**; from 1326, **Bp of Wrocław** | From 1326, **Bp of Kraków** | From 1348, **Bp of Kraków** | As above |

## Appendix I: Bishop Nanker's Supposed Study of Canon Law at Bologna

It was Jan Fijałek who proposed in 1916 that Nanker studied canon law at Bologna around 1306.[96] Since then, nobody has challenged the validity of Fijałek's claim.[97] Fijałek provided the following evidence. In the Bolognese 'Acts of the German Nation', several passages from the year 1306 refer to a physical confrontation between the 'German nation' and 'the Poles'.[98] The conflict was settled in conjunction with a new statute that received approval at a plenary session of the 'nations' at Bologna.[99] Peace was apparently restored with a Mass. It was celebrated at the church of the 'German nation', with an archdeacon 'from Poland' among the participants.[100] The dispute did not end there, however.[101] Between May 1306 and October 1309, 'the nation rested for three years, and study was suspended'.[102] Fijałek maintained that the unnamed archdeacon had been Nanker. Because a statute of the papal legate issued in 1279 prescribed for all archdeacons to have studied canon law, Fijałek postulated the same for Nanker, given that he is documented as an archdeacon (though not until 1308).[103] In support of his thesis, Fijałek further argued that Nanker's colleagues in the rank of archdeacon offer direct proof of study

---

96 Fijałek, 'Przeszłość Nankera', pp. 272–73. Pfotenhauer, 'Schlesier auf der Universität Bologna', did not know about this, but noted that both, Nanker's predecessors in Kraków, Jan Muskata, and his successor in Wrocław, Przecław of Pogorzela, had studied in Bologna.

97 For instance, Silnicki, *Biskup Nanker*, pp. 28–29. Reliant on Silnicki and Urban, *De testimoniis*, Gottschalk, 'Nanker', even calls Nanker a 'good canonist'.

98 *Acta nationis Germanicae*, ed. by Friedländer and Malagola, p. 59b line 4: 'The discord we have with the Poles'. Previously, p. 59a lines 12–13, there is mention of a sack in which possessions were brought to safety; of broken candles, p. 59a lines 16–17. Next, litigation fees are listed, p. 59b lines 5 ff., for advocates, a proctorship, paper, and ink to produce documentation in the trial 'between us and the Poles'; and for the scribal services of a notary, p. 59b lines 16–17.

99 *Acta nationis Germanicae*, ed. by Friedländer and Malagola, p. 59b lines 9 ff.: 'Also for the beadle who called the nation on the day when the statute between us and the Poles was confirmed'. Accounts from the Polish perspective do not exist. Cf. p. 105 n. 101 below.

100 *Acta nationis Germanicae*, ed. by Friedländer and Malagola, p. 59b lines 12–13. The presiders gave thirteen pennies (*solidi*) as offerings.

101 'To remove definitively any opportunity for conflict from the nations of our university', the plenary session of the nation from beyond the Alps passed by majority a resolution on 1 May 1306, according to which the origin and not the place of residence was to decide 'when there was doubt as to the nation students belonged to'; *Acta nationis Germanicae*, ed by Friedländer and Malagola, p. 52, no. 7; cf. no. 8. This is probably the statute referred to in the *Acta*, above p. 105 n. 99. On the complicated constitution of the nation 'beyond the Alps', see Steffen, *Die studentische Autonomie*, pp. 94 ff.

102 *Acta nationis Germanicae*, ed. by Friedländer and Malagola, p. 59 (concerning the year 1309). Only three students enrolled in 1306, cf. p. 58.

103 See the 1279 statute of the legate, Philip of Fermo, in *Antiquissimae constitutiones synodales*, ed. by Hube, ch. 40: 'On archdeacons. They are obliged to study canon law for at least three

106    CHAPTER 4

— although the evidence in question is dubious. Not mentioned explicitly but probably relevant for Fijałek's claim was the circumstance that Nanker issued new diocesan statutes at the beginning of his rule in both Kraków and Wrocław.[104] It was Fijałek who edited the statutes from Kraków — at the same time he presented his thesis.

Several counter-arguments can be made. First of all, there is nothing in Nanker's style of governance in either bishopric to suggest that his legal training exceeded what was commonly expected of an archdeacon and chancellor of a territory.[105] To the contrary, the citizens of Wrocław criticized the less than exemplary style of letters emanating from his chancery.[106] The deficiencies of the same office prompted Nanker's secretary, Arnold of Zwrócona (Protzan), from 1307–1319 archdeacon of Głogów, to compose a formulary in 1332.[107] It was intended to improve the situation by combining solid canonistic knowledge with an elegant style. Arnold dedicated the work together with a long preface to his bishop. It does not mention Nanker's supposed legal expertise with a single word.[108] The curial documentation indicates the same. In passages where it could be anticipated, the papal chancery never employed formulas reserved for academics, including Johannes Grotonis.[109] The same also applied to Przecław of Pogorzela, Nanker's successor as bishop of Wrocław.[110]

---

years'. Also, *Kodeks dyplomatyczny Wiekopolski*, ed. by Piekosiński, I, p. 434: 'Archdeacons shall always be installed from among the canon law experts'.

104 On Krakow, see *Najstarsze statuty synodalne krakowskie*, ed. by Fijałek; for Wrocław, see Sawicki, 'Ze studiów nad konstytucjami'; also, Knossalla, '*Acta synodalia decanatus Bythomiensis*'.

105 Nanker as judge delegate left the proceedings of 1313 to vice officials at Kraków Cathedral. They were without academic training which did not cause any problems; *Zbiór dokumentów*, I, ed. by Kuraś, nos 18–27. His mandates as bishop of Kraków are found in part in *Kodeks dyplomatyczny katedry krakowskiej*, ed. by Piekosiński, I; the rest in *Regesten zur schlesischen Geschichte*, ed. by Grünhagen and Wutke, V, in conjunction with those Nanker issued as bishop of Wrocław.

106 *Das Formelbuch des Domherrn Arnold*, ed. by von Wattenbach, I, p. 272, datable shortly after Nanker's accession in Wrocław: 'No less have we wished and ought to (conceal) it when in the letters of your court, which give form to the others, something (stylistically) reprehensible is found at times'.

107 That Arnold had studied canon law is evident throughout his formulary. It is further confirmed by his employment as the bishop's court judge from 1305 to 1307 and subsequently as diocesan 'auditor of cases'.

108 *Das Formelbuch des Domherrn Arnold*, ed. by von Wattenbach. Additional literature in *Repertorium Fontium*, ed. by Potthast, II, p. 402.

109 *Vetera monumenta Poloniae*, I, ed. by Theiner, pp. 290–91 (no. 369), for Johannes Grotonis; and pp. 437–38 (no. 571), for Przecław of Pogorzela. The educational background is also mentioned at the elevation of the bishop of Chelmno in 1319, who had been a 'minor penitentiary'; pp. 156–57 (no. 246). And again, for the bishop of Pomezania; pp. 158–59 (no. 248).

110 When Nanker died, Pope Benedict XII did not follow the advice of his collector, who fully shared the political position of the group at Kraków supporting the reappointment

In a similar vein, the regional sources assign the title of *magister* to legal scholars like Franciscus and Johannes Grotonis in recognition of their education. Nanker is not named in any other way than as 'lord'.[111]

In addition, the narrative sources and letters present Nanker as a pious man with a modest lifestyle. This did not prevent him from exhibiting noble pride when championing the prerogatives of his churches and especially the one of Kraków.[112] To defend them, he did not shy away from conflict with his old patron, King Władysław Łokietek, and subsequently with King John of Bohemia.[113] Nanker's attitude towards John, his theatrical condemnation and instant excommunication 'from now and forever', which omitted prior admonition as it was required, does not suggest that he was a seasoned church lawyer directing excommunication primarily against those who ignored court orders.[114]

Why of all people would Nanker, who at the time was still relatively young, have been the Polish archdeacon his delegation sent to the powerful and self-assured 'German nation' in Bologna? And why would they have

---

of a 'Pole' to the Wrocław bishopric; see *Vetera monumenta Poloniae*, I, ed. by Theiner, p. 395. Maschke, *Der Peterspfennig in Polen*, pp. 198–99, notes that Galhardus identified the interests of the group at Kraków with those of the Apostolic Chamber. Despite reservation of the bishopric during Nanker's lifetime (*Bullarium Poloniae*, ed. by Sułkowska-Kuraś and Kuraś, I, nos 1791, 1907), the pope accepted the elect of the Wrocław Cathedral chapter by appointing Przecław of Pogorzela who had rushed to the Curia; cf. *Acta Camerae Apostolicae*, ed. by Ptaśnik, no. 198; *Bullarium Poloniae*, ed. by Sułkowska-Kuraś and Kuraś, I, nos 1921 (bull of prefecture), 1923. As with Nanker (p. 98 n. 72 above), the papal mandates of prefecture were not directed at any secular leader. On the person of the collector, Schuchard, *Die päpstlichen Kollektoren*, p. 289.

111 As earlier in 1310, when the legate consulted with two 'Polish legal experts', the Masters Fredericus and Bertholdus (*Analecta Vaticana*, ed. by Ptaśnik, p. 138) and *magister* Christianus, canon at Kraków Cathedral (*Kodeks dyplomatyczny katedry krakowskiej*, ed. by Piekosiński, I, p. 138).

112 Nanker stressed from the beginning of his pontificate that Kraków was placed higher than any other church in the province of Gniezno and repeatedly entered litigation because of it; *Kodeks dyplomatyczny katedry krakowskiej*, ed. by Piekosiński, I, pp. 131, 137. He reclaimed old rights in the Spisz region, pp. 132, 139, 141–42; *Regesten zur schlesischen Geschichte*, ed. by Grünhagen and Wutke, V, no. 4358. His successor continued this policy, *Bullarium Poloniae*, ed. by Sułkowska-Kuraś and Kuraś, I, no. 1920. Perhaps contributing to this was the fact that 'Boleslaus', the archbishop of Esztergom , 'son of Bazmer, duke of Silesia', and brother-in-law of the Hungarian king, who had acquired the prerogatives in question, had been Nanker's colleague at Kraków Cathedral, cf. p. 90 n. 41 above.

113 Disenchantment between Nanker and his previous protector Władysław Łokietek is noticeable soon after his accession to the bishopric. The chronicles report a confrontation with the king who in turn is said to have slapped Nanker in the face. Details are lacking, cf. Grünhagen, 'König Johann von Böhmen', pp. 35 ff. The papal bull (*Vetera monumenta Poloniae*, I, ed. by Theiner, no. 610) allegedly responding to a request by the king to have Nanker removed from Wrocław is nowhere to be found.

114 See Grünhagen, 'König Johann von Böhmen', pp. 80 ff., following the 'Chronica principum Poloniae' and Charles IV's autobiography.

called someone from Sandomierz 'the Polish archdeacon', assuming that he already was archdeacon there? Would it not be more plausible to think of the great archdeacon of Gniezno, Poznan, or Kraków, someone visibly representing the party of Władysław Łokietek? This might have been the above-mentioned great archdeacon of Kraków, Ranboldus. It was not even necessary for him to be a student — he could have been a visitor as well. While on his long sojourn at Avignon, Nanker may have developed the respect for canon law which is expressed in the editorial work on the statutes for either of his bishoprics. Under the lawyer pope John XXII, canonistic studies witnessed a new heyday at the Curia. Neither at the church of Kraków nor in Wrocław was there a lack of trained canonists, including those with a doctoral degree both in the cathedral chapter and among the judges and advocates at the various courts. They would have been able to consult with Nanker as the statutes were put together.[115]

---

115 Impressive lists of jurists are provided by Ożóg, *Kultura umysłowa w Krakowie*, I; and Samulski, *Untersuchungen*. They can easily be augmented.

## Appendix II: On Johannes de Verulis and Other Clerics of the Curia

This section gathers information illustrating the role of curial clergy who held benefices in Kraków or Wrocław and are important for the present study. The effort is especially worthwhile because modern scholarship is riddled with incomprehension and mistaken assumptions about administrative life at the Curia and has struggled to overcome them. Three of the clerics are named by their origin as 'de Verulis', referring to Veroli in the Roman province of Frosinone. A whole string of curial churchmen came from there beginning in the mid-thirteenth century.[116] The full name of the eventual dean of Kraków Cathedral was 'Johannes, the son of Master Petrus de Verulis'.[117] Nothing is known about the earliest stages of his career.[118] First, we are told that he was named cleric of the Apostolic Chamber by Pope Clement V right at the beginning of his pontificate.[119] There were four of these positions. John XXII raised Johannes de Verulis to the rank of papal Protonotary (or *notarius domini pape*), which is the title he carries subsequently in the curial documentation as his highest appointment according to protocol. He retained his function in the Chamber as well.[120] Johannes de Verulis died at the Curia on 12 September 1322.

---

116 The bibliographical references in this Appendix are kept as brief as possible. Unfortunately, the archives of the southern Papal States have not been investigated. The cathedral of Veroli and the important collegiate church of San Erasmo remain without detailed studies. Nicolaus de Verulis is documented for 1288–1306, Petrus de Verulis a generation earlier as Scribe of the Apostolic Chancery between 1263 and 1279; cf. Nüske, 'Untersuchungen', I, nos 213 and 254. Cardinals frequently had officials from this location, too. Later, there was a Chancery Scribe, Johannes 'of the late Percivallus de Verulis', 1343–1364. He first served in the household of Cardinal Petrus Bertrandi the Elder, then in that of his nephew, Petrus Bertrandi the Younger, without showing any connections to Poland.

117 A short biography in Schmidt, *Der Bonifaz-Prozess*, pp. 178–79, with additional evidence. Also, Baix, 'Notes sur les clercs de la chambre apostolique', pp. 25–28; Guillemain, *La court pontificale d'Avignon*, pp. 301–03; Nüske, 'Untersuchungen', II, pp. 293–94 (no. 168); Barbiche, 'Les "scriptores" de la chancellerie apostolique', pp. 139–40. Nüske, Guillemain, and Barbiche assume his identity with the contemporaneous papal Scribe in the Chancery, Johannes de Verulis, documented between 1296 and 1308. Schmidt, *Der Bonifaz-Prozess*, p. 178 n. 249, refutes that supposition through a comparison of their handwriting. For references concerning Poland only, see Kowalski, *Prałaci i kanonicy krakowskiej*, pp. 188–89 (no. 97); Ożóg, *Kultura umysłowa w Krakowie*, I, p. 144 (no. 45), each following *Vetera monumenta Poloniae*, I, ed. by Theiner; and *Bullarium Poloniae*, ed. by Sułkowska-Kuraś and Kuraś, I.

118 Unless he was the Johannes de Verulis who served Johannes Boccamazza, Cardinal of Tusculum (d. 1309), as notary; see Fawtier, 'Introduction', in *Les registres de Boniface VIII*, ed. by Thomas and others, IV, p. xxxv.

119 First documented on 25 October 1306 (1308 in the Polish historiography); *Registrum Clementis papae V*, nos 1151–52.

120 Because his duties as Protonotary were not very burdensome, he could keep both offices simultaneously; cf. Zutshi, 'The Office of Notary in the Papal Chancery'. Cited above, p. 96

110   CHAPTER 4

At the Council of Vienne (1311–1312), the four clerics of the Chamber received an unusual amount of public attention for their role in the commission that had to investigate allegations of heresy against the late Pope Boniface VIII.[121] The importance of their office required them to be constantly present at the Curia.[122] They obtained, as a result, dispensations from the obligation to reside where their benefices were located.[123] That Johannes de Verulis never left the pope's immediate surroundings can be documented in great detail. After his appointment as dean at Kraków, he, his relatives, and fellow officials are cited as the preferred executioners of mandates on behalf of 'Polish' recipients.[124] As we have seen, the Silesian party protested in 1320 against the obstruction of justice in front of his house in Avignon.

When did Johannes de Verulis become dean of Kraków Cathedral? He is explicitly documented as such for the first time on 31 July 1307.[125] Subsequently, he is uninterruptedly associated with this title in the curial sources until 20 August 1311.[126] From 15 September 1317 to 20 August 1319, he appears again, though not always by name.[127] If the papal registers refer to him as (bishop-)elect of Viterbo between 1312 and 1317, this does not imply that he had renounced his deanery in Kraków, but that he is identified only in conjunction with his most prominent title. According to the same principle, he is called before and thereafter dean of Kraków Cathedral. His renunciation of the deanery in favour of Nanker Ingrami

---

n. 65, the passage on his notarial office, which Johannes had entrusted to his nephew, proves that he acted as Protonotary not only in a nominal sense.

121  Schmidt, 'Das *factum Bonifatianum*', pp. 623–33.

122  The clerics of the Chamber were responsible for the administration of the Apostolic Chamber, presided over by the Chamberlain. Together with him, they formed the court of the same office. In consistories and commissions, they were charged with record-keeping and composed important letters, etc. For that reason, they had to hold their notarial rank 'by apostolic authority'; Schwarz, 'The Roman Curia (until about 1300)', pp. 193–94, 213–15. Johannes de Verulis was also a notary 'by imperial authority'; cf. Schmidt, 'Das *factum Bonifatianum*', p. 629.

123  It appears that Johannes de Verulis was not an ordained priest, although the deanship of Kraków Cathedral required it. In his case, the duties associated with the deanery would have clashed with his official obligations at the Curia. The pope often gave members of his inner circle dispensation by word of mouth.

124  Examples dating to 1320 include *Bullarium Poloniae*, ed. by Sułkowska-Kuraś and Kuraś, I, nos 1162 (as executor), 1169 (as executor), 1195.

125  *Registrum Clementis papae V*, nos 1922–23.

126  With the title of cathedral dean in 1307; *Registrum Clementis papae V*, nos 1922–23, 2771; in 1308, nos 3090 (as executor), 3258 (as executor); in 1309, nos 3173 (as executor), 3732, 3761, 3765, 3777, 3957, 3976, 4326, 4380; in 1310, no. 6217; also, no. 7236 (of 20 August 1311).

127  His commissions as executor are mostly missing from *Bullarium Poloniae*, ed. by Sułkowska-Kuraś and Kuraś, I.

was probably not completed before late autumn of 1319.[128] Successively, he is mentioned together with his next highest dignity as canon of St Peter in Rome. During the entire period from 1306 to 1322, he is sometimes referred to as the holder of other positions from his portfolio of benefices.[129] He never features with his canonry in Kraków which he retained after 1319, but on occasion with his curial office as Chamber cleric or as Protonotary. It is open to speculation how Johannes de Verulis managed to obtain the deanery. Most likely, the opportunity arose by way of 'a vacancy of the benefice at the Curia'.[130] Until 1319, the cathedral church of Kraków apparently made no attempt to restore this important office to a member of its own chapter. The local clergy must have been content to have a high official from the Curia as defender of their interests there.[131]

Andreas Tinacius de Verulis was a close relative of Johannes de Verulis, probably a nephew.[132] Andreas started his career as Abbreviator prior

---

128 See above, pp. 93–96.

129 This occurred especially when the area he was supposed to serve as executor or commissioner was unlikely to relate to his deanery at Kraków Cathedral, for example, while he acted as canon at the cathedral of Santiago de Compostela or that of St Peter in Rome. The case was different when Johannes de Verulis obtained a papal provision, assigning to him in accordance with Chancery regulations the title of his new benefice, such as when he was given the benefice and function of treasurer at Liege Cathedral in 1310; *Registrum Clementis papae V*, nos 5367, 6421. His other known holdings were a canonry and benefice at Santa Croce in Veroli, a simple benefice in Capua (1319), and a canonry and benefice at Laudun (1319).

130 For the canonical rules prior to 1316, see Meyer, *Zürich und Rom*, p. 37.

131 The situation differed in Wrocław. Attempts by Pope Boniface VIII to use the deanery there to generate income for curial clerics, first the minor-aged nephew of a cardinal (*Bullarium Poloniae*, ed. by Sułkowska-Kuraś and Kuraś, I, nos 952, 959; *Analecta Vaticana*, ed. by Ptaśnik, no. 127), then, perhaps, the household member of another cardinal, the papal Scribe at the Chancery Johannes Laurentii de Pontecurvo, encountered the bishop's stiff resistance. John XXII called him later a 'persecutor of envoys and officials from the Apostolic See'; *Bullarium Poloniae*, ed. by Sułkowska-Kuraś and Kuraś, I, no. 1172; *Analecta Vaticana*, ed. by Ptaśnik, no. 162. The deanery at the cathedral of Wrocław was probably under general reservation from 1301, due to the death of the previous holder, magister Laurentius de Wratislavia, who is called a 'follower of the Curia'. The efforts of Johannes de Pontecurvo to make good on his claim to it during the conflict over the bishopric of Wrocław were in vain; cf. Samulski, *Untersuchungen*, pp. 60–61 (no. 16), 156.

132 Ożóg, *Kultura umysłowa w Krakowie*, I, p. 140 (no. 4); Kowalski, *Prałaci i kanonicy krakowskiej*, pp. 126–27 (no. 7); Samulski, *Untersuchungen*, p. 157. *Regesten zur schlesischen Geschichte*, ed. by Grünhagen and Wutke, V, no. 3968, interpret the entry in Arnold of Zwrócona's formulary (cf. *Najstarsze statuty synodalne krakowskie*, ed. by Fijałek, pp. 228–30) as mentioning Johannes and Andreas de Verulis and date it to September 1319. The recipient, a canon of Kraków Cathedral, is said to have had a vacant benefice from the dome chapter (of Wrocław) already assigned to his 'brother'. To return the favour, he was expected to use his influence on behalf of the king (Władysław Łokietek). The date cannot be earlier than autumn of 1320. Possibly, the text does not refer to Johannes de Verulis, who hardly was Andreas's brother, but to Matthias Paluca; *Bullarium Poloniae*, ed. by Sułkowska-Kuraś and Kuraś, I, no. 1114; also, above p. 93.

112    CHAPTER 4

to 1320, before obtaining one of the coveted posts as Scribe of the Chancery. He is first documented as such in 1324. As noted, his provision for Wrocław dates to 1319.[133] Soon thereafter, he must have secured a benefice there.[134] An obedience was added in 1325.[135] From 1320, he was occasionally involved in affairs of 'Polish' interest. By 1322, curial sources refer to him as chaplain of Bishop Gerward of Włocławek.[136] He maintained good relations with Johannes Grotonis, another household member of Bishop Gerward. When Johannes de Verulis was promoted to the bishopric of Kraków in 1326, the pope transferred the provostship (and former rectory) of St Mary in Kraków from among Johannes's benefices to Andreas.[137] It figured from then on as his highest dignity.[138] Together with it, he seems to have received the canonry at Kraków Cathedral as well.[139] His first mention in connection with it is of 1327.[140] He kept friendly ties with Bishop Gerward's nephew and successor in Włocławek.[141] His rapport with Nanker, on the other hand, was rather strained.[142]

On 22 June 1325, Andreas de Verulis was sent as collector to Poland together with Petrus de Alvernia.[143] He probably did not arrive there until

---

133 See p. 93 n. 56 above.

134 *Regesten zur schlesischen Geschichte*, ed. by Grünhagen and Wutke, v, no. 3611, dates another entry in Arnold of Zwrócona's formulary, cf. *Codex diplomaticus Silesiae*, v, p. 90 (no. 102), to September 1316. It recounts how Andreas de Verulis and Mathias Paluca, who had been accepted as members of the chapter at Wrocław Cathedral refused to pay the customary admission fees. Cf. p. 111 n. 132 above.

135 *Lettres communes de Jean XXII*, ed. by Mollat, no. 22957; *Bullarium Poloniae*, ed. by Sułkowska-Kuraś and Kuraś, I, no. 1322. On 2 August 1325, he received from the compensation for Vitus, partisan of the Polish party, chanter at the cathedral, and claimant to the Wrocław bishopric, who had just died at the Curia, the latter's obedience in the city and diocese, including a house built of stone.

136 *Die Einnahmen der apostolischen Kammer unter Johann XXII.*, ed. by Göller, p. 57; *Acta Camerae Apostolicae*, ed. by Ptaśnik, no. 81.

137 He went to the Curia for that reason; *Acta Camerae Apostolicae*, ed. by Ptaśnik, no. 107.

138 *Bullarium Poloniae*, ed. by Sułkowska-Kuraś and Kuraś, I, no. 1408; *Lettres communes de Jean XXII*, ed. by Mollat, no. 27739; *Analecta Vaticana*, ed. by Ptaśnik, no. 212. Cf. *Bullarium Poloniae*, ed. by Sułkowska-Kuraś and Kuraś, I, nos 1650, 1744, 1796, 1866.

139 *Bullarium Poloniae*, ed. by Sułkowska-Kuraś and Kuraś, I, no. 1589.

140 *Acta Camerae Apostolicae*, ed. by Ptaśnik, nos 79, 81, 93, 100, 180.

141 In 1324, cf. *Acta Camerae Apostolicae*, ed. by Ptaśnik, no. 93 (with Robertus de Ponte); and 1325, no. 100.

142 Nanker took the canonry at Wrocław Cathedral away from Andreas during his time as collector in Poland; *Bullarium Poloniae*, ed. by Sułkowska-Kuraś and Kuraś, I, no. 1568 (of 17 November 1329).

143 Maschke, *Der Peterspfennig in Polen*, pp. 148 ff.; on the travel equipment (30 July 1325), *Acta Camerae Apostolicae*, ed. by Ptaśnik, nos 102–03. The conferral of the obedience in Wrocław (2 August 1322), in *Bullarium Poloniae*, ed. by Sułkowska-Kuraś and Kuraś, I, no. 1322, was certainly part of the preparations; cf. Schulte, *Die politische Tendenz der 'Chronica principum Poloniae'*, pp. 169–70, with Attachment 3.

the fall and stayed to the end of 1328.[144] Under the date of 11 July 1330, his notary, Jacobus Blasii de Verulis, is documented as a companion.[145] Another one was apparently *magister* Stefanus de Pelagio.[146] In Andreas's absence, Petrus de Verulis, to be discussed below, issued receipts for money transfers from Poland. Andreas returned to Avignon in January 1329.[147] He bought a large house there.[148] He remained a much-consulted liaison officer for the churches under his collectorship. From the Curia, he supervised the safe transfer of moneys from Poland, for instance, on behalf of the bishop of Kraków.[149] Bishop Nanker at Wrocław preferred different channels of payment. On 4 March 1342, Andreas was appointed as archbishop of Trani.[150] He held a canonry at that church from 1319.[151] His most valuable benefice until 1342, the canonry at Wrocław Cathedral went to the envoy of the Bohemian king, Arnošt of Pardubice, who later became archbishop of Prague. Andreas's priory of St Mary in Kraków was given to a curial cleric.[152] Andreas de Verulis died at the Curia before 4 April 1343.

The canonry at Kraków Cathedral which had become vacant due to the death of Johannes de Verulis was conferred to another relative, Petrus Jacobi militis de Verulis, on 12 September 1322.[153] It was reserved to the

---

144 John XXII called him back (for the first time) on 23 December 1327, in a letter that cannot have reached Andreas until March 1328; another recall dates to 1 October 1328.

145 *Acta Camerae Apostolicae*, ed. by Ptaśnik, no. 134.

146 *Die Ausgaben der apostolischen Kammer unter Johannes XXII.*, ed. by Schäfer, p. 460.

147 Maschke, *Der Peterspfennig in Polen*, p. 159; following *Acta Camerae Apostolicae*, ed. by Ptaśnik, no. 144. I can spot him in the Apostolic Chancery from 1329.

148 Jean XXII, *Lettres communes*, ed. by Mollat, no. 64213; in 'the street called Lanzaria' in the parish of St Agricola, along with an exemption from taxation for it.

149 *Acta Camerae Apostolicae*, ed. by Ptaśnik, nos 133, 180. On the technical problems of money transfers, cf. Denzel, 'Kleriker und Kaufleute'.

150 *Bullarium Poloniae*, ed. by Sułkowska-Kuraś and S. Kuraś, II, nos 6, 34.

151 He also held a parish in Fermo diocese (1319) and another in Veroli diocese. He had to abandon both; cf. *Bullarium Poloniae*, ed. by Sułkowska-Kuraś and Kuraś, I, no. 1567. He later occupied a canonry at the cathedral of his native town.

152 The papal Protonotary Bertrandus Bertrandi de Maletanis; *Bullarium Poloniae*, ed. by Sułkowska-Kuraś and Kuraś, II, nos 34, 88, etc.

153 *Analecta Vaticana*, ed. by Ptaśnik, p. 224 (no. 161). The executors of this provision were the Chamber clerics Bindo de Senis and Johannes de Regio, who for his part had been, with Johannes de Verulis and the dean of Gniezno, member of the above-mentioned commission at the Council of Vienne; *Bullarium Poloniae*, ed. by Sułkowska-Kuraś and Kuraś, I, no. 1195. On Petrus Jacobi de Verulis, cf. Kowalski, *Prałaci i kanonicy krakowskiej*, p. 251 (no. 196); Ożóg, *Kultura umysłowa w Krakowie*, I, p. 148 (no. 90); both only with documentation from *Vetera monumenta Poloniae*, I, ed. by Theiner; and *Bullarium Poloniae*, ed. by Sułkowska-Kuraś and Kuraś, I. For additional sources, see *Lettres communes de Jean XXII*, ed. by Mollat, nos 23544, 24418, 24915, 25165–67, 25894, 27115, 27182, 27554, 27739, 28120, 28369, 28564, 29258–59, 30254, 30741–43, 43110, 43757, 44307, 44596–97, 45333, 45645, 45739, 47290, 49646, 49648, 50640, 50978–79, 53851, 56544, 56547, 57102, 58833, 62202; Benoit XII, *Lettres communes*, ed. by Vidal, nos 501, 932, 2131, 2668, 2723, 2734, 3379,

114   CHAPTER 4

pope because the previous holder had been of curial status. Petrus de Verulis is mentioned in the curial sources from 1318.[154] He appears among the Scribes of the Chancery from 1326.[155] He was chamberlain of Cardinal Lucas Fieschi who died in 1336.[156] In 1326, Petrus planned for a longer absence from the Curia.[157] He probably thought to accompany his relative, the collector Andreas de Verulis, to Poland.[158] He likely returned to the Curia soon thereafter, however, because we encounter him subsequently and quite often as executor working for Polish clients.[159] He acquired his most valuable benefices in Hungary.[160] They included the provostship of Titel in the church of Kalocsa which normally figures next to his name.[161] His ecclesiastical holdings in his native region were not very lucrative.[162] He died between 30 April and 16 May 1336 at the Roman Curia, so that his benefices fell under general papal reservation.[163] Cardinal Annibaldo de Ceccano recommended a member of his household for the canonry at Kraków Cathedral.[164] Other parts of Petrus's legacy can be tracked to

---

3440; *Die Einnahmen der apostolischen Kammer unter Johannes XXII.*, ed. by Göller, pp. 37, 213, 256, 263; *Die Einnahmen der apostolischen Kammer unter Benedikt XII.*, ed. by Göller, pp. 56, 108, 244.

154 *Die Einnahmen der apostolischen Kammer unter Johannes XXII.*, ed. by Göller, p. 37.

155 In the college of the Scribes, he held positions of trust in October 1335.

156 *Lettres communes de Jean XXII*, ed. by Mollat, no. 27554. He executed the cardinal's testament upon his death on 31 January 1336; Paravicini Bagliani, *I testamenti dei cardinali*, pp. 99, 456.

157 This implied a 'license to earn income in the absence' from his office as Scribe; *Lettres communes de Jean XXII*, ed. by Mollat, no. 24915 (of 13 April 1326). The favour was granted for free, indicating interest on the part of the Apostolic Chamber. Simultaneously, he was appointed executor along with the canon from Kraków Cathedral, Petrus *miles*, then present at the Curia; *Bullarium Poloniae*, ed. by Sułkowska-Kuraś and Kuraś, I, nos 1376–78.

158 He had a cleric named Petrus de Sancto Laurentio; *Die Einnahmen der apostolischen Kammer unter Benedikt XII.*, ed. by Göller, p. 108.

159 *Bullarium Poloniae*, ed. by Sułkowska-Kuraś and Kuraś, I, nos 1434, 1768.

160 The king of Hungary intervened on his behalf; *Lettres communes de Jean XXII*, ed. by Mollat, no. 27554.

161 John XXII reserved the benefice to him on 3 December 1326, in *Lettres communes de Jean XXII*, ed. by Mollat, no. 27182; on 14 January 1327, King Charles of Hungary supported the decision, no. 27554. Did the king act in such a way to fulfil obligations towards Andreas de Verulis? The provostship appears later in the possession of a papal collector for Poland, Galhardus de Carceribus.

162 *Lettres communes de Jean XXII*, ed. by Mollat, nos 27182, 27554. He listed his canonry and benefice at the cathedral, at the collegiate churches of San Erasmo in Veroli, San Antonio in Pofi, and San Stefano in Frosinone. In Pofi and Frosinone, he had additional income from simple benefices which he could not collect while absent; at the dome of Tropea in Calabria he only held an expectancy. His total proceeds amounted to a mere ten Florentine guilds in 1322.

163 His provostship in Titel and the benefices in Kraków and San Erasmo were reassigned at the Curia.

164 *Bullarium Poloniae*, ed. by Sułkowska-Kuraś and Kuraś, I, no. 1796; Benoit XII, *Lettres communes*, ed. by Vidal, no. 2668 (of 16 May 1336). Andreas de Verulis was among the

a relative and Scribe at the Apostolic Chancery, Leonardus Melioris de Verulis.[165]

---

executors. The earnings of the canonry in Kraków Cathedral, which had fallen vacant at the Curia were received by the collector in 1336; *Vetera monumenta Poloniae*, I, ed. by Theiner, p. 443.

165 Kowalski, *Prałaci i kanonicy krakowskiej*, p. 198 (no. 114); Ożóg, *Kultura umysłowa w Krakowie*, I, p. 145 (no. 52). Leonardus Melioris de Verulis is documented as Scribe of the Chancery between 1323 and 1343. The centre of his holdings was in France, though. After Andreas de Verulis' death, he acquired a provision with a canonry and expectancy of a not yet vacant benefice at Kraków Cathedral on 25 August 1343, a claim that apparently never succeeded.

CHAPTER 5

# The Vatican Archives and Their Uses for Regional Historians

*The Example of Late Medieval Saxony*[*]

At the beginning of this essay, I would like to appeal to the good will of my readers. Given the limited amount of time available to me, my inquiries into the regional history of Saxony have been quite superficial. The one area I have investigated in greater depth deals with a very specific topic, the exemption of the bishopric of Meissen in 1399. It is discussed below in the third section. For the rest, I present general observations, backed by examples I have not pursued in detail.

## The Source Material of the Vatican Archives

Tom Graber has dedicated his contribution to the volume originally containing this essay to an authentic papal charter examined under the microscope as it were, thereby developing important insights into the principles of papal diplomatic.[1] In the following and by relying on a different metaphor, I will look at the vast mass of transmitted papal charters from a bird's eye perspective. I will focus on texts that survive in a derivative format in the registers of the Vatican Archives. To begin with, I must dispel still recurrent assumptions according to which the Vatican Archives preserve all the documentation popes have ever produced. It is true that miles of surviving registers support such impressions, as many thousands of volumes remain from the Middle Ages alone. Yet, there is a lot that never made it into the archives, and countless items previously kept there are no longer extant.

Apart from small remnants, the registers today do not set in until 1198, growing over the centuries in diversity as well as in size.[2] With the passing of time, their contribution to political history diminishes steadily. Texts

---

[*] This is the written version of a lecture I gave at Meissen on 21 October 2000. The text has been slightly revised and supplemented with notes.

[1] Graber, 'Ein Spurium auf Papst Gregor X.'.

[2] The best overview is by Boyle, *A Survey of the Vatican Archives*; for a summary of publications from the Vatican Archives, see Schwarz, 'Klerikerkarrieren und Pfründenmarkt', pp. 243–45 nn. 3–6; updated in Schwarz, 'Nutzungsmöglichkeiten des Repertorium Germanicum', p. 65 n. 2.

that can be classified as papal legislation, mandates, or decrees cover an ever-smaller percentage of the material. Nearly all items entered into the registers consist of petitions submitted by natural, and in small part also juridical, persons from across Christendom. They approached the pope individually and without involvement of the ecclesiastical hierarchy, in hopes of obtaining specific advantages. During the period we focus on, from 1350 to 1475, about eighty per cent of the entries in the Vatican registers are concerned directly or indirectly with so-called benefices, or church positions, from canonries in cathedrals all the way down to those for priests serving at an altar.[3]

When the scope is further restricted to requests originating from the German Empire, which was admittedly an enormous territory at the time, it is noticeable that their share was very tiny until about 1350. Subsequently, it grew in accordance with the ability of regional clergy to apply for benefices or maintain their possession by way of papal letters. For students in particular, there was often no alternative mechanism to secure such positions.[4] In the German southwest and west, this trend started in the second quarter of the fourteenth century.[4a] It spread to the remaining parts of the Empire in the first half of the fifteenth, when roughly sixteen per cent of the curial materials were from there, the historical peak in frequency of contact with Rome.[5] Depending on region, though, the incoming petitions varied considerably in terms of contents and accumulation.[6]

For contemporaries, the Curia was a big market-place, where benefices from the Empire alongside others were traded between suppliers and potential acquisitors. They were not sold by papal administrators![7] Instead, the Curia imposed strict market regulations, which manifested themselves in many letters that sought exemption from them. This function determines adequate consultation of the material insofar as we can only follow its inherent logic rather than our own. The Vatican registers primarily inform about secular clerics, who were eligible to hold benefices, and of course, about the benefices themselves. For laypeople and regular clergy, the archives of the Papal Confessor (or Great Penitentiary) are richer,

---

3 I refer here in particular to Eugene IV (1431–1447), whose pontificate I have edited in *Repertorium Germanicum*, v. The exact numbers have been provided by my collaborator, Christoph Schöner.

4 Cf. Meyer, *Arme Kleriker auf Pfründensuche*.

4a The registers of the thirteenth and fourteenth centuries published by the *École française de Rome* are now available electronically; see *'Ut per litteras apostolicas'*.

5 The estimates are by Diener, 'Materialien aus dem Vatikanischen Archiv', p. 394; cf. Tewes, *Die römische Kurie*, pp. 22–23, 28–29, 55, 78–79.

6 Schwarz, 'Das Repertorium Germanicum'; Meuthen, 'Auskünfte des Repertorium Germanicum'.

7 Schwarz, 'Römische Kurie und Pfründenmarkt' (English version above, pp. 27–48).

though I will not discuss them in the following.[8] Before turning to any evaluations of content (including statistical ones), scholars need to be mindful of three things. First, the registered items were produced by petitioners, so that they always reflect the initiative of an interested party. They were not generated by mechanisms existing *ex officio*. Accordingly, I like to speak of outside demand for curial services. Because it occurred in the Middle Ages and not in our age of integrated information flows, it was up to the petitioners to assemble relevant data concerning the benefice in question. They also had to make sure that the benefice market was accessible to them, a prerequisite not found in equal measure across the regions of the Empire.[9] Secondly, the facts alleged in the documentation depended on input from the petitioners and their representatives at the Curia, such as those regarding the identity of persons (academic degrees, priestly ordination, legitimate birth, and so on), the value of the pursued benefice, if it was vacant, and for what reason.[10] The Curia did not verify these assertions, but rather relied on others competing for the same position to spot mistakes. Thirdly, all registered texts merely constituted legal claims awaiting execution against competitors before the local authorities — a process that often resulted in failure.

Let me add another remark. The Vatican data are highly structured and standardized in accordance with the requirements of church law and curial tradition. Based on this circumstance, the *Repertorium Germanicum* has formalized and systematized its own presentation of the material. The documentation it incorporates is especially suited for the preparation of socio-historical studies backed by statistical evidence. Work is currently underway on an electronic database in which all volumes are integrated to accommodate all kinds of research queries.[11] My subsequent observations, on the other hand, rely on searches in digital and printed texts dating mainly to the period from 1417 to 1447.[12]

---

8 *Repertorium Poenitentiariae Germanicum*, I–V, ed. by Schmugge and others.

9 Cf. Schwarz, 'Norddeutschland und die römische Kurie'.

10 Details in Schwarz, 'Klerikerkarrieren und Pfründenmarkt', pp. 252–53.

11 Compiled by Christoph Schöner as part of his *Habilitation*, 'Elektronische Aufbereitung des Repertorium Germanicum und verwandter Projekte – Methoden und Anwendungsbeispiele'. Some of the illustrations included in the present essay have been taken from Part 3: 'Einzelstudien, I: Reich, Kurie und Basler Konzil: Zur Breitenwirkung des Konflikts im Spiegel der Suppliken'. Mr Schöner has extracted for me from Martin V's and Eugene IV's pontificates (1417–1447) all items relating to East German bishoprics and consolidated them in electronic files. This has been of great help in my research, for which I am very grateful to him. He also generously produced several of the illustrations used here, apart from others (below, Figures 5.1 to 5.7) already at his disposal.

12 *Repertorium Germanicum*, I–IX.

## Suggestions for the History of Saxony

In this section, I briefly introduce research strategies that have been tested for other regions, before offering considerations regarding their suitability for the history of Saxony. To begin with, clergy at specific churches have been profiled, a task which has been undertaken mainly from documentation in the Vatican as well as with material from local archives. Work has focused especially on the composition of collegiate churches, their mechanisms of recruitment, the ties between patron and client and their long-term transformation. As an example, the study by Gerhard Fouquet under the telling title of 'The Cathedral Chapter of Speyer (ca. 1350–1540). Noble Friendships, Princely Patronage, and Papal Clientele', deserves notice in this context.[13] Fouquet has distinguished three types of canons, those from the high aristocracy, from noble families with locally circumscribed interests, and the 'careerists'. Next, there are investigations into the career paths of so-called 'learned counsellors', particularly at the princely courts. They consist of social risers whose origins were regularly more modest than those of their fellow canons, and whose life trajectory was not limited to one region. They appear primarily in the Vatican sources because holders of higher academic degrees enjoyed preferment at the Curia. The learned counsellors have been extensively studied by Peter Moraw and his students.[14] Through increased consultation of the curial documentation, the studies could still gain in precision, as the social networks again important here would come into full view.[15]

In addition, inquiries have concentrated on the functioning of the benefice market, which at the time served as the primary conduit for the social rise of clerics. Its rules clearly rival today's markets in terms of complexity. They have been explored in studies addressing the overall phenomenon by Andreas Meyer and myself.[16] Others have used modern statistical methods including Christoph Schöner, or concentrated on single regions and churches, as Brigitte Hotz has done in exemplary fashion

---

13 Fouquet, *Das Speyrer Domkapitel*.

14 Moraw, 'Die gelehrten Juristen', is fundamental; a published version of the dissertation by Männl, 'Die gelehrten Juristen', was announced years ago; Heinig, 'Gelehrte Juristen'; Koch, *Räte auf deutschen Reichsversammlungen*.

15 See my most recent studies on a clerical 'rope team' from Hanover, Schwarz, 'Eine "Seilschaft" von Klerikern' (English version above, pp. 67–81). The social networks during and after university studies have been tracked by Gramsch, *Erfurter Juristen*, including individual *vitae* on a CD-ROM.

16 Schwarz, 'Römische Kurie und Pfründenmarkt' (English version above, pp. 27–48); Meyer, 'Der deutsche Pfründenmarkt'; reprinted (with identical pagination) in *Das Repertorium Germanicum*, ed. Esch. Gramsch, *Erfurter Juristen*, pp. 282–92, has discussed the different research agendas.

for the cathedral chapter of Constance.[17] Finally, research has been done concerning the character and intensity of relations between certain regions and the Roman Curia over extended periods of time. It may seem odd, but these contacts also provide an important measure of the institutionally advanced state or backwardness of an area, as Erich Meuthen, Christiane Schuchard, and Götz-Rüdiger Tewes have demonstrated.[18]

In turning to the regional history of Saxony, scholars must ask from the start to what extent these recent approaches are applicable to the subject. In fact, important restrictions apply. It is not by accident that the exemplary studies just mentioned have chosen the southwest or west of Germany as their object. I could add other works, as the sources there are generally much richer, including those from the Vatican![19] Figure 5.1 shows the overall regional distribution of petitions submitted to Pope Eugene IV (1431–1447) from the German speaking parts of the Empire. The focus is on requests because they constitute the largest category of sources. Unlike the outgoing letters, moreover, they have the advantage of mirroring the wishes of the petitioners most accurately. In the *Repertorium Germanicum*, the bishopric forms the basic geographical unit in the same way as in the original Vatican material. Since it is cumbersome to display some sixty of them, Figure 5.1 presents them redistributed — roughly, I admit — into fourteen larger areas, which Peter Moraw has identified as major regions in the late medieval German Empire according to their state of development.[20] As you will note, the 'Lands of the Wettin Dynasty and the Middle-Elbe', or in terms of dioceses those of Meissen, Naumburg, Merseburg, and Magdeburg, only supplied three per cent of the petitioners and rank with 'Brandenburg, Mecklenburg, and Pomerania' at the low end of the scale.[20a]

It is true that Eugene IV's pontificate was peculiar in certain aspects to be addressed subsequently, but it is the only one for which we have reliable

---

17 Hotz, *Päpstliche Stellenvergabe am Konstanzer Domkapitel.*

18 Meuthen, 'Reich, Kirche und Kurie'; Schuchard, *Die päpstlichen Kollektoren*, Part I; Tewes, *Die römische Kurie.*

19 A model for all subsequent work was the study by Meyer, *Zürich und Rom*; his approach was refined by Hesse, *St. Mauritius in Zofingen*; Wiggenhauser, *Klerikale Karrieren*; van den Hoven van Genderen, *De Heren van de Kerk*. A regional focus has been presented by Borchardt, 'Die römische Kurie und die Pfründenbesetzung'; and Ulbrich, *Päpstliche Provision.*

20 Most recently, Moraw, 'Brandenburg im späten Mittelalter', p. 89. Of the regions proposed by Moraw, 'Burgundy-Savoy' and 'Lorraine' have been omitted here for being covered only by exception in the *Repertorium Germanicum*; for 'Prussia-Livonia', the collection of data is still incomplete.

20a In numbers, the total of examined petitions is 12331 of which 363 are from the 'Lands of the Wettin Dynasty and the Middle Elbe' (Meissen 105; Naumburg 110, Merseburg 44, Magdeburg 104).

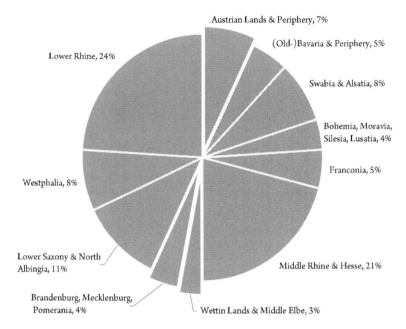

Figure 5.1. Regional Distribution of Petitions to Pope Eugene IV from the German Empire (1431–1447).

statistical data at our disposal.[21] Still, the small percentage of petitions in the Vatican from our region of interest can be confirmed for other popes as well.[22] To round out our knowledge, it is possible to engage in minute examinations of the Vatican material.[23] For the following, I have only 'leafed through' the above-mentioned text files, and my findings remain approximate and preliminary.

For the profiling of clerics, the work of Thomas Willich on the cathedral chapter of Magdeburg is apt to serve as a guide.[24] Apart from the cathedrals, I think that the collegiate chapters of Zeitz, Bautzen,

---

[21] This presupposed the proper definition of standard petitions and filtering of all others, such as multiple requests regarding the same object, those for several objects, or petitions without specific indication of the bishopric in which the coveted object was located; see ch. B ('Datenaufbereitung') in Christoph Schöner's *Habilitation* (as above, p. 109 n. 11). The loss of registered material has not been factored in here (as opposed to Figures 5.2–5.7), because proportions rather than absolute numbers are of significance. In addition, the totals for Utrecht diocese have been included; for the reasons, cf. pp. 132–33 n. 64 below.

[22] See Meuthen, 'Auskünfte des Repertorium Germanicum', for the pontificates of Martin V and Pius II.

[23] I have attempted to show how to do this for the popes of the Great Schism, where the loss of curial documentation is tremendous; cf. Schwarz, 'Ein Freund italienischer Kaufleute'.

[24] Willich, *Wege zur Pfründe*.

and Wurzen would warrant similar inquiries, but not so other churches including Altzelle, which has good coverage in the regional sources. Intuitively, I believe that even the churches I just mentioned as relatively well-documented in the *Repertorium Germanicum* were adversely affected by the tight control the margraves exerted over them. It moved the transfer of benefices to the princely court and university, where we cannot track it any longer. Put differently, many local clerics whose social networks are difficult to discern cannot be spotted in the Vatican sources at all or at best sporadically, as opposed to others who loom disproportionally large.

Research in the careers of the so-called 'learned counsellors' has revealed that they cannot be traced until they attained a certain level of advancement, since clerics from the area did not obtain their first benefices through the Curia. Their names begin to appear from the moment they had to secure legal remedies to protect their possessions, which took the form of papal dispensations from canonical irregularities, permitted tenure of multiple benefices with pastoral duties, personal absence, the lack of required clerical ordinations, the exchange of positions, and so on.[25] This concerned in particular learned counsellors and professors from the two local universities, who often served simultaneously as princely advisers.[26] Entries for their peers from elsewhere occupy entire columns in the *Repertorium Germanicum*. Owing to the strong interference of the territorial lord in church matters, however, competition for the positions, which is very indicative of social networks, was subdued in Saxony compared to the German west.

Given that Eugene IV's pontificate was atypical in several aspects, I have selected the exemplary lives of two benefice holders from the pontificate of Nicholas V (1447–1454) for an examination of their petitions to the pope.[27] Both functioned as learned counsellors under the elector Frederick the Gentle. Their respective curriculum also offers an introduction to the presentation of data in the *Repertorium Germanicum*.[28] You can find the noble Chancellor Georg of Haugwitz (d. 1463) in the right column

---

25 Schwarz, 'Klerikerkarrieren und Pfründenmarkt', p. 252.

26 Moraw, 'Improvisation und Ausgleich'.

27 *Repertorium Germanicum*, VI, ed. by Abert and others, nos 1827 and 1407. The data of his and the following pontificates have long been available in print (cf. p. 119 n. 12 above), facilitating verification by the reader. Despite the publication date of 1985, volume VI still represents the state of research for volumes II–IV. Because the main interest at the time was on names, the entries are for the most part extremely abbreviated, especially regarding the legal information. The indices of volume VI reflect the first stage in the development of mechanically compiled data; cf. Höing, 'Die Erschließung des Repertorium Germanicum'; reprinted in *Das Repertorium Germanicum*, ed. by Esch.

28 The layout of the entries features in bold type the name of the petitioner (identical with the beneficiary in outgoing letters), followed by all correspondence concerning him in chronological order. The individual documents are separated from one another by dashes, whereas the different elements within each document are only distinguished by commas,

124    CHAPTER 5

of Table 5.1 below. His accumulation of benefices was at its peak under Pope Nicholas V. His *vita* in volumes V and VI of the *Repertorium* fully corresponds to the anticipated pattern. In the left column, there is the entry of the secretary, Heinrich Engelhard of Salza (d. 1451). Of urban descent, he was alongside Haugwitz one of the elector's longstanding administrators by 1447 and sent by him on important diplomatic missions. If Engelhard had been from another part of the Empire, his life (in *Repertorium Germanicum*, V) would feature a significant number of references because of his modest income from benefices between his joining of the elector's administration in 1433 and the break-up of relations between the elector and Pope Eugene IV around 1441. Not so with Engelhard, though, whose trajectory resembled in this regard that of other non-noble members in the chancery of the Wettin family.[28a]

Heinrich Engelhard, the secretary, was among the elector's envoys to Eugene IV.[29] Engelhard appeared in Rome as early as February 1447.[30] After the pope died on 23 February, a new delegation, again including Engelhard, had to be sent upon elevation of Eugene's successor.[31] The first three transactions in Engelhard's vita involve expectancies for benefices

---

even when they carry varying dates. For information about the different forms of papal favours, see especially Weiss, *Kurie und Ortskirche*.

28a This is not true of the careers of those who did not stay in Saxony, such as Chancellor Heinrich Leubing from Nordhausen; cf. Gramsch, *Erfurter Juristen*, pp. 378–79 and elsewhere (with no. 361, for his vita).

29 For information from the regional sources, Goldfriedrich, 'Die Geschäftsbücher der kursächsischen Kanzlei', p. 128; following him, Streich, *Zwischen Reiseherrschaft und Residenzbildung*, p. 592, who refers to Engelhard in misleading fashion as 'chancellor' rather than 'head scribe', p. 198. Important new biographical information is found in Gramsch, *Erfurter Juristen*, no. 154. Accordingly, Engelhard was born around 1410. He finished his studies in Leipzig and Erfurt with a bachelor degree in canon law. Between 1435 and 1439, he is repeatedly documented at the Council of Basel where he incorporated in 1439. From then on, he is attested as canon of Meissen Cathedral. In 1443, he went to Pope Felix (V) as the elector's emissary, who conferred Engelhard a profitable position at the Curia (as Scribe in the Chancery). Until 1448, he was repeatedly on diplomatic missions as secretary in the Empire and abroad. At an unknown point in time, perhaps in 1448, he joined the confraternity of the Anima in Rome. On the chancellors of the Wettin dynasty, see also Vogtherr, 'Die Kanzler der Wettiner'.

30 *Repertorium Germanicum*, V, ed. by Diener and others, no. 2743 (of 5 February 1447). Calling himself secretary and speaker of the duke, he requested a dispensation to hold the parish of Eisfeld in the bishopric of Würzburg alongside two benefices with pastoral duties for life. The value of the position is not mentioned, nor whether he had concrete chances to obtain it. The entry disproves the assertion in scholarship on Saxony that the duke was late in shifting his allegiance from the Council of Basel to the Roman pope; for example, Zieschang, 'Die Anfänge eines landesherrlichen Kirchenregiments', pp. 30 ff. On the parish of St Nicholas in Eisfeld (a possession of the Wettin from 1374, part of the rural chapter of Coburg), see Wendehorst, *Das Würzburger Landkapitel Coburg*, pp. 21–23; kindly brought to my attention by Karl Borchardt, Rothenburg on the Tauber.

31 Nicholas V, elected on 6 March 1447, crowned on 19 March 1447.

Table 5.1. The Benefices of Two Learned Counsellors under Elector Frederick the Gentle.

| 1827 | 1407 |
|---|---|
| **Henricus Engelhardi** secr. FREDERICI DUCIS SAXONIE: motu pr. de gr. expect. s. d. 14. iun. 47 de 2 can. s. e. p. in prov. Magdeburg., Trever., Magunt., Bremen. et Colon. elig. 21. nov. 47 S 421 175ʳ – bac. in decr.: exten. gr. expect. de can. s. e. p. eccl. Nuemburg. ac eccl. b. Marie *Erfforden.* Magunt. dioc. ad dign. 3. mai. 48 V 387 328ᵛ– 330ʳ - 1. b. mart. 49 T 7 14ᵛ – suppl. d. duce[:] de declaratione, quod gr. expect. pro BERTOLDO INSTITORIS et JOHANNI ECHTEN et JOHANNI DE RODENBERG ei n. preiudicent 20. febr. 50 S 440 189ᵛˢˢ – et **Paulus Munczmeister**: suppl, eodem de prov. HENRICI de capel. s. c. b. Marie Magdalene in castro Misnen. (14 m. arg.) vac. p. res. PAULI c. pensione 30 sexagenarum grossorum 75 fl. Renen. 20. febr. 50 S 440 190ᵛˢˢ – de nova prov. de can. et preb. eccl. ss. Justi et Clementis *Bebracen.* Magunt. dioc. (4 m. arg.), quos vac. p. o. FRIDERICI DANIEL acc. 24. mart. 50 S 442 113ᵛˢ – de nova prov. de capel. b. Marie Magdalene in cur. episc. castri civit. Misnen. (8 m. arg.). quam vac. p. res. PAULI MUNCZMEISTER in manibus JOHANNIS EP. MISNEN. acc. 9. apr. 50 S 442 185ʳ. | **Georgius de Hug(e)wicz** can. Nuemburg. de mil. gen. prothonot. FREDERICI DUCIS SAXONIE: motu pr. de prepos. eccl. ss. Petri et Pauli *Ciczen.* Nuemburg. dioc. c. can. et preb. annexis (32 m. arg.) vac. p. o. HILDEBRANDI DE GUSENICZ necnon de disp. eam obtin. unac. prepos. *Haynen.* al. eccl. s. Georgii in *Czilow* Misnen. dioc. (10) 11. apr. 50 S 442 297ᵛˢ, L 460 296ʳ–298ʳ – motu pr. de decan. eccl. Misnen. (20 m. arg.) vac. p. prom. GASPARIS ad eccl. Misnen. necnon de disp. eam retin. unac. prepos. eccl. ss. Petri et Pauli *Cziczen.* Nuemburg. dioc. 9. iun. 51 S 452 282ʳˢ, L 467 169ᵛ–171ʳ – 1. b. ian. 52 T 7 156ᵛ+157ᵛ – ann. decan. eccl. Misnen. (47 fl. auri de cam.) 13. ian. 52 IE 421 9ʳ – ann. prepos. eccl. ss. Petri et Pauli *Ciczen.* c. annexis Nuemburg, dioc. p. manus HERMANNI LUTHKUS (60 fl. auri de cam.) 27. ian. 52 IE 421 10ᵛ. |

that had yet to become vacant. On 21 November 1447, he requested the supplementary concession of certain conditions for his expectancy of a canonry in a collegiate church in the provinces of Magdeburg, Trier, Mainz, Bremen, and Cologne.[32] The claim had been issued to him under

---

32 Vatican, Apostolic Archive, Reg. Suppl. 421, fol. 175ʳ. According to established practice, the concession was very extensive. The same form of expectancy and date, however, was successively conferred to more than 600 petitioners, thereby greatly diminishing the value of the favour; cf. the Index of 'Other Dating Clauses', in *Repertorium Germanicum*, VI/2, ed. by Reimann, p. 552. On the dating of expectancies under Nicholas V, especially the preferential

126 CHAPTER 5

the fictitious and preferential date of 14 June 1447 and looked promising. To obtain the special conditions, Engelhard referred to his appointment in the elector's chancery. He secured a form known as *motu proprio*, which put him ahead of other recipients of the same expectancy.[33]

On 3 May 1448, Engelhard asked for an extension of his earlier (undated) expectancy for a canonry with benefice at the dome of Naumburg and at the collegiate church of St Mary in Erfurt, so that he would be permitted to accept a dignity, or office of leadership, in one of the two when it became available.[34] On this occasion, he also mentions his academic degree as bachelor of canon law.[35] Under the date of 20 February 1450, the pope granted a (backdated) petition by Engelhard's patron, the elector, asking him to declare that the expectancies of other candidates would not create any disadvantage for Engelhard.[36] The elector had requested the same expectancy and date for other clients of his, obviously diminishing their individual prospects. In the extant papal registers, none of these petitions can be found, which again offers an indication of the many sources that have been lost.[37] Based on an expectancy that is not identified in the summary of the *Repertorium Germanicum* but may have been the one of November 1447, Engelhard had accepted a canonry and benefice at the collegiate church of Bibra with an estimated annual income of four pounds, not a particularly lucrative asset. It had become vacant though the death of Friedrich Daniel. To solidify his acquisition by legal means, Engelhard asked the pope on 24 March 1450 to issue him a new provision with it.

Two supplications were concerned with a benefice the pope was authorized to reassign.[38] His intervention was needed to counter suspicions of simony, because the position had become available through conditional

---

date of 14 June 1447 and the purpose of a *motu proprio* in that context, cf. Meyer, 'Das Wiener Konkordat', pp. 136–38, with n. 86, on the rolls (*rotuli*) of bundled petitions from the court of Saxony in Vatican, Apostolic Archive, Reg. Suppl. 427, fols 167ʳ–75ʳ.

33 On this form from the Chancery, see *Regesten*, ed. by Schwarz, pp. XVII, XIX; Frenz, 'Motu proprio'.

34 For the dignities at the 'dome' of Erfurt, cf. Pilvousek, *Die Prälaten des Kollegiatstiftes St. Marien*.

35 The petition is not preserved except for the bull in response to it in Vatican, Apostolic Archive, Reg. Vat. 387, fol. 328ᵛ, which also includes the date when it was granted. The bull was probably read in the pertinent office (*bullarium*) in March 1449 (Vatican, Apostolic Archive, Taxae 7, fol. 14ᵛ), implying that the expedition took ten months between the grant and its consignment to the proctor.

36 Vatican, Apostolic Archive, Reg. Suppl. 440, fols 189ᵛ–90ᵛ. His competitors were Berthold Institoris (below, p. 128 n. 44); Johann of Echte (cf. his vita in Gramsch, *Erfurter Juristen*, no. 141), and Johann Rodenberg who is not to be found, at least under that name, in *Repertorium Germanicum*, VI.

37 The names mentioned are Georg Gundolt, Konrad Franken, and Heinrich Tetenborn.

38 Vatican, Apostolic Archive, Reg. Suppl. 440, fols 190ᵛ–91ᵛ; Reg. Suppl. 442, fol. 185ʳ.

resignation upon payment of a pension.[39] It consisted of a chaplainry without pastoral duties at St Magdalen in the castle of Meissen, which was assessed at a value of fourteen marks.[40] The stipulated amount was supposed to be thirty *grossi* or seventy-five Rhenish guilds. The request came from the previous holder, Paul Münzmeister, and the beneficiary of his resignation.[41] Once again, it was the elector who threw his weight behind the petition. It was granted on 20 February 1450 with the above-mentioned concession of the same date. The elector's intervention was likely prompted no so much by the need to overcome papal scruples as to show that the exchange had princely approval. A few months later, the same transfer was presented very differently to the pope. This time, the benefice was described as located 'within the castle of Meissen' and estimated at only eight marks of worth. To account for the vacancy, reference was made to Paul Münzmeister's resignation, which is further described as having been made into the hands of the competent bishop, Johann (Hoffmann) of Meissen, that is, without any conditions attached. Engelhard then asked for a new provision with it, which was issued on 9 April 1450. Was the original request for a dispensation abandoned in view of the high expenses and to remove any hint of simony from the transaction? Or was the pension payment recalculated as debt weighing on the income of the benefice and explaining the reduction of the annual revenues from fourteen to eight marks? It is anachronistic to think that the Curia stumbled over the divergent narratives. As observed previously, it did not check the veracity of contents and left the task of spotting infractions of the canon law to those competing for the benefice, a mechanism predicated on the existence of open competition to function smoothly.

Since Henrich Engelhardt died soon thereafter, before 20 May 1451, we can examine the composition of his benefice portfolio and those who hoped to gain from it. The parish of Eisfeld in Würzburg diocese, which he already held under Eugene IV, was in the possession of Friedrich of Bibra at the time of Engelhard's death.[42] This was against canonical regulations, as one applicant who was a well-informed curial cleric objected in his

---

39 On the resignation and permutation of benefices, see Meyer, *Zürich und Rom*, pp. 151–57.

40 Because it was easier to find a substitute, such a sinecure was certainly preferable to a benefice 'with cure (of souls)', for which Engelhard was already in possession of a dispensation.

41 Not found elsewhere in *Repertorium Germanicum*, v–vi.

42 The spelling of the location is inconsistent, here 'Eißfelt'; 'Hezvelt' in *Repertorium Germanicum*, vi, ed. by Abert and others, no. 526. The value is assessed at twelve marks. Apart from the canonry and benefice at Meissen Cathedral which he held, perhaps not uncontested, from 1439, Eisfeld was the only benefice he had in firm possession for some time. On the parish of St Nicholas in Eisfeld, see p. 124 n. 30 above.

128    CHAPTER 5

own petition for it.[43] Friedrich of Bibra was the son of Bartholomeus of Bibra, Duke Wilhelm's marshal who had to take care of his followers in Franconia at the time. Engelhard probably failed to acquire the canonry with benefice at St Mary in Erfurt, as he still struggled to obtain it when he died.[44] The same is true of the chaplainry at the castle of Meissen. We are now informed that it was tied to a canonry and benefice at the cathedral, just as there is mention of a canonry and benefice at the collegiate church of Bibra, again assessed at four marks.[45] The competition was fierce. The first two benefices were claimed by a curial cleric, Otto Greffe, priest from the diocese of Mainz.[46] They were pursued as well by a chaplain, Paulus Mundel from the circle around the elector Frederick the Gentle.[47] In addition, a nephew of Kaspar Schönberg, adviser to the elector, by the name of Dietrich Schönberg petitioned for them.[48] All three benefices, with those from Meissen counted separately, were also the target of a cleric from Bremen diocese, Johannes Pinnenberch.[49] In sum, it seems that the secretary Engelhard was never quite assured of the benefices he had acquired by title.[50] They were not adequately endowed to support a lifestyle that would have been in accordance with his status.

---

43 Bertholdus Herwici de Cruceborg, a cleric from the diocese of Mainz; *Repertorium Germanicum*, VI, ed. by Abert and others, no. 526. He was a Notary at the Roman Rota and hence perfectly positioned to notice and pursue vacancies; cf. Schwarz, 'Eine "Seilschaft" von Klerikern', p. 268 (English version above, p. 75).

44 *Repertorium Germanicum*, VI, ed. by Abert and others, no. 527; with Bertholdus Institoris de Satzungen, who renounced to his claim to the benefice on 21 May 1453. He was one of the rivals Engelhard had opposed in his petition of 21 November 1447. Bertholdus also had become a Notary of the Rota since then.

45 Which can be inferred from the assessment of fourteen marks in *Repertorium Germanicum*, VI, ed. by Abert and others, no. 3373, which was given to the chapel alone in the petition.

46 *Repertorium Germanicum*, VI, ed. by Abert and others, no. 4673 (of 21 May), requesting the chaplainry (at fifteen marks) in addition to the canonry and benefice. The petitioner, who was a member of the household of Cardinal Juan Carvajal (of Sant'Angelo), had insufficient information about the chaplainry, stating that it was located 'in the city or bishopric of Meissen'.

47 *Repertorium Germanicum*, VI, ed. by Abert and others, no. 4731 (of 15 August 1451). Mundel had accepted the position he described as a canonry and benefice together with the chapel of St Mary (!) and taxable at eighteen marks by way of an expectancy, seeking to be newly provided with it.

48 *Repertorium Germanicum*, VI, ed. by Abert and others, no. 5440 (of 2 June 1452); he asked for a provision *si neutri* with the chaplainry, valued at twenty marks this time and under litigation with Johannes Pinnenberch (next note below). Earlier, von Schönberg had requested provision with the benefice, apparently delaying the transaction.

49 *Repertorium Germanicum*, VI, ed. by Abert and others, no. 3373 (20 May 1451). Pinnenberch also secured a bull for it that it took a year to expedite. He still litigated for the benefice on 2 June 1452 (no. 5440). On 2 February 1453, he ceded his claim to Dietrich of Schönberg; cf. Gramsch, *Erfurter Juristen*, no. 154.

50 Nearly all his requests are found in the registers of petitions, not in those for outgoing letters. The payment of annates, due for direct papal provisions and not for expectancies, is not

THE VATICAN ARCHIVES AND THEIR USES FOR REGIONAL HISTORIANS    129

While equally brief, the list of benefices for Georg of Haugwitz indicates something very different.[51] As recommended, he declared from the outset his noble birth and function as protonotary of the elector. At the time of his first recorded petition, he was already a canon of Naumburg Cathedral, seeking in addition a provision (once more in the form of a *motu proprio*) with the provostship at the collegiate church of Zeitz, as well as the associated canonry and benefice worth a considerable thirty-two marks. These had been vacated through the death of Hildebrand de Gusenicz.[52] A provostship constituted a principal dignity and conveyed great prestige. It was against church law to hold it together with the provostship of Grossenhain (valued at ten marks), which was also a benefice with pastoral obligations and hence 'incompatible'. Haugwitz thus asked for the necessary dispensation, which was granted on 11 April 1450.[53] Subsequently, he petitioned for a provision by *motu proprio* with the deanery of Meissen Cathedral (assessed at 20 marks). It had become vacant due to the appointment of its previous holder, Kaspar of Schönberg, as bishop of Meissen. Since Haugwitz wished to keep the provostship in Zeitz, he applied simultaneously for the required dispensation, which was issued to him on 9 April 1451.[54]

Both provostships were principal dignities which, according to papal interpretation of the Concordat of Vienna (1448) and unlike other church positions, were subject to elections and remained under the pope's right of provision.[55] The visit to the Curia was necessary under all circumstances, however, because the applicant intended to hold two mutually incompatible benefices at once, calling for a dispensation. In the second case, the need for it (resulting from accumulation of the deanery at Meissen Cathedral and the provostship of Zeitz) was equally acknowledged by the Concordat of 1448 because the new benefice, vaguely described as 'vacant

---

recorded for Engelhard, either. They would be mere titles, to be sure, rather than proving veritable possession of a benefice.

51  For biographical information, Streich, *Zwischen Reiseherrschaft und Residenzbildung*, p. 591. His vita in *Repertorium Germanicum*, v, ed. by Diener and others, no. 2059, comprises a favourable sentence (of 26 August 1441) in litigation over a canonry and major benefice at Naumburg Cathedral, along with a dispensation to keep the provostship of Grossenhain next to a second benefice with pastoral duties; to obtain the latter, he mentioned his origin, academic degree as bachelor of canon law, and office as chancellor.

52  He is documented in 1435 as provost of Zeitz and holder of the associated canonry at Naumburg Cathedral; see *Repertorium Germanicum*, v, ed. by Diener and others, nos 7295, 7922.

53  Vatican, Apostolic Archive, Reg. Suppl. 442, fols 297ᵛ–98ʳ; Reg. Lat. 460, fols 296ʳ–98ʳ.

54  Vatican, Apostolic Archive, Reg. Suppl. 452, fol. 282ʳ⁻ᵛ; Reg. Lat. 467, fols 169ᵛ–71ʳ, with a marginal note probably referring to the pertinent bulls, which would have been expedited in January 1452.

55  For principal dignities, the Curia insisted on the (faulty) wording of the Concordat in its registers; Meyer, *Zürich und Rom*, p. 49; Meyer, 'Das Wiener Konkordat'.

by promotion', was reserved to the papacy after its previous holder, Kaspar, obtained the bishopric by provision.

It is worth noticing that nobody else petitioned to the pope for the two positions, not even one of the curial clerics we have encountered in Engelhard's case, participating for speculative purposes in the benefice market and not shying away from litigation. In other places, there would have been an authentic rush for offices of this kind. Its absence here suggests that the question of succession was settled beforehand.[56] Once the Curia had been mobilized, on the other hand, fees needed to be disbursed, as specified in the remaining entries in the *Repertorium Germanicum*. The so-called annates for the deanery at the cathedral amounted to forty-seven ducats. They were paid on 13 January 1452. For the proctorship with its attachments, sixty ducats were due and deposited by Hermann Lutkehus, a curial official.[57] Lutkehus undertook the transfer on 27 January 1452.[58]

This is what can be gleaned from the meagre entries in the older volumes of the *Repertorium Germanicum*. The recent ones offer much more.[59] In addition, I have consulted the Vatican sources for the bishops of Meissen, proceeding diachronically from around 1300 to 1470 rather than limiting myself to a single pontificate. From 1342, they belong for the most part to the group of learned counsellors.[60] The first column of Table 5.2 below contains the name, social origin, and the end of the episcopate in question, usually due to death. The second includes the qualifications

---

56 The entry for Kaspar of Schönberg (see below) states that he was provided by the pope with the bishopric of Meissen the very day this petition was granted (9 June 1451). The election by the chapter was invalidated due to special reservation during the lifetime of Kaspar's predecessor and although the bishop elect received confirmation. It was common practice to reassign benefices someone held prior to his provision with a bishopric under the same date.

57 Lutkehus was a curial abbreviator and scribe, successively rising to the higher charge of 'cleric' at the Lateran register. In *Repertorium Germanicum*, VI, ed. by Abert and others, no. 2200, his entry covers two columns and a half! The focus of his portfolio of benefices and claims was in the northwest of the Empire. He repeatedly deposited payments of annates on behalf of German churchmen.

58 This transaction left more than the petition (Vatican, Apostolic Archive, Reg. Suppl. 452, fol. 282$^{r-v}$), outgoing bull (Vatican, Apostolic Archive, Reg. Lat. 467, fols 169$^v$–71$^r$), and reading of the two bulls (for the provision and the dispensation) in the *Bullaria* (Vatican, Apostolic Archive, Taxae 7, fols 156$^v$ and 157$^v$); the link is close between the latter and pertinent entries in the account books of the Apostolic Chamber (Vatican, Apostolic Archive, Introitus et Exitus 421, fols 9$^r$ and 10$^v$). Such bulls were not handed over until the annates had been paid or someone had offered sufficient surety for them. Unfortunately, account-books for the so-called compositions have not survived. They were payable for dispensations and must have been much higher than the annates.

59 Cf. Schwarz, 'Ein Freund italienischer Kaufleute'.

60 A study parallel to this one I have recently attempted for the bishopric of Verden; cf. Schwarz, 'Das Bistum Verden'. However, the investigation of circumstances leading to the elevation of bishops there (in the same period as here for Meissen) occupies far more space (Part I).

for office, especially membership in the cathedral chapter of Meissen and service to the prince. This column must be read in conjunction with the fifth, which informs about political protectors. For the first column, I have relied above all on the secondary literature, which is especially informative here.[61] Generally speaking, Meissen was a modest bishopric, unattractive to outsiders as well as to high nobility from the region. From about 1370 to 1411, the pull of the Bohemian Crown was notable and clearly impacted local aristocrats. The sole candidate of the Wettin dynasty at the time, Dietrich Lamberti of Goch, did not prevail at the Curia. The seventh column lists attempts of the margrave of Meissen to reduce Bohemian influence by pressuring office holders or through other counteractive measures. Unlike in other bishoprics, the Bohemian candidates did not hail from a much wider area than those backed by the margrave (Table 5.2).

The third and fourth columns were most interesting to me because the pertinent literature is beset with erroneous assertions about Saxony and other areas. It states that the pope constantly interfered in perfectly fine local arrangements, where cathedral chapters chose the best-suited person from their midst who was successively ordained by the competent archbishop, in our case, the one of Magdeburg. The fifth columns shows that this did not happen — if ever — in the two centuries under our scrutiny. To begin with, it is important to keep in mind that Urban V made all bishoprics subject to papal appointment (by so-called general reservation) in 1362/1363, to prevent the ruin of churches through partisanship and rivalling princes. He used his right sparingly, as fiscal considerations remained of secondary significance. The free election of bishops was restored by the Council of Constance in 1418, although nobody resorted to it in Meissen until 1463. The Bohemian candidates only obtained the bishopric through papal provision, translation (from a different diocese), or by special reservation. The margraves instead always had their favourites stage an election, leaving room for doubt about the freedom to vote. From 1370, moreover, papal provision was also pursued by the margraves to improve their chances of installing a preferred candidate. However, the pope and the Luxemburg dynasty ruling in Bohemia simply maintained closer ties until 1411. The request for provision was regularly combined with that of permission to be consecrated by an archbishop of choice. And yet, the archbishop of Magdeburg was hardly diminished in his rights, as the asterisk in the fourth column indicates.

The sixth column shows the expenses at the Curia for provisions, etc. The fees owed for higher benefices, the so-called *servitia*, were only paid

---

61 See von Brunn, genannt von Kaufungen, 'Das Domkapitel von Meißen'; Rittenbach and Seifert, *Geschichte der Bischöfe von Meißen*; Rogge, 'Zum Verhältnis von Bischof und Domkapitel'. Without scholarly claim is Machatschek, *Geschichte der Bischöfe des Hochstifts Meißen*.

132    CHAPTER 5

by those who obtained the position through the pope, just as the annates were collected for lesser benefices. The bishops of Meissen did not start payment of the *servitia* until 1392, when the amount was assessed for the first time and the annual income of the bishop's estate (or *mensa*) was estimated at 500 guilds going forward. The fee varied between 323.5 and 346 guilds, tending to increase. The real costs were exponentially higher, especially when someone had to find supporters at the Curia in the first place, which occurred in 1411. For comparison, 1463 is also of interest here for indicating the connections to banking networks, which were all but lacking in 1411. I have addressed legal questions about the elevation of bishops in my essay on the exemption of the Meissen bishopric, so that the preceding brief commentary on Table 5.2 may suffice in the present context.[62]

To turn to the history of the benefice market, the three east German bishoprics of Meissen, Merseburg, and Naumburg are likely to yield only a small portion of transactions in the Vatican sources overall. They contain little on lesser ecclesiastical positions and thus scant information about the lower rungs on the career ladder. Surprisingly new insights are afforded by examining the exchange of benefices insofar as it took place at the Curia. It depended on several variables which I have partly discussed above. The period when the market was in fullest swing coincided with the pontificates of Martin V (1417–1431) and Eugene IV (1431–1447). It ended quickly after Eugene IV turned against the Council of Basel (1431– 1449).[63] The conflict intensified from 1436, culminating in the pope's deposition by the Council in 1439 and mutual denials of legitimacy. If it is true that the Curia was then the most important exchange for benefices in the German Empire, it follows that the demand for curial intervention in association with benefices by way of provisions, dispensations, etc. must have been hurt significantly when conflict erupted between the Council and Eugene IV. This was in fact the case.

Figure 5.2 features all petitions from the Empire during the various phases of Eugene IV's pontificate, encompassing not only those concerned with benefices, which made up about eighty per cent of the total.[64] At

---

62 See p. 141 n. 88 below.

63 The Council was convened to work (like the better-known one at Constance, 1414–1418) on Church reform, which for many participants meant especially the reduction of papal prerogatives; see Helmrath, *Das Basler Konzil*, pp. 333–34.

64 Concerning Figures 5.2 to 5.7, it deserves notice that the losses among different registers are very uneven. Sometimes a quarter of the original volumes is missing, while elsewhere a year is completely preserved. As a result, absolute numbers, drawn from the surviving material, would have generated heavily distorted impressions, inappropriate for an analysis of the benefice market. To counter this, the total of annual entries for each pontifical year was calculated based on the extant registers and then divided by their number, thereby producing an average value. It was further multiplied by the (known) quantity of perished

the beginning, the number of requests was — as always — high, though perhaps somewhat diminished by the pope's hostile attitude towards the Council of Basel.[65] The relationship normalized in the years from 1432 to 1434, when the Council increased its activities. They peaked between 1435 and 1437, when many participants arrived in Basel and information about benefices circulated with an intensity never witnessed before. The Council had become a hub for the trade in church positions, although the Curia remained the place where authorizations had to be obtained. The contacts between Basel and the Curia were so close that arising needs could be met without delay. Another reason for the growth in demand had to do with the deliberations at the Council about the abolition of papal rights of reservation, sparking fears that the market was ready to collapse and prompting many to 'buy' quickly just to make sure.[66] From the beginning of the so-called neutrality of the German Empire in 1438, the volume of transactions dwindled rapidly.[67] It approached zero in the immediate wake of the Acceptation of Mainz in 1439.[68] A moderate recovery occurred toward the end of the pontificate, when preparations got underway for the Concordat of Vienna, which was concluded with the Empire in 1448.[69]

Figure 5.3 indicates that the general trend for the Empire roughly applied to east Germany as well, always keeping in mind the small totals of cases there. Figure 5.4 shows the demand for benefices across the Empire, separated into higher and lesser ones. Unlike elsewhere, the quantities are expressed in index numbers (= 100 on average) because they highlight small variations better than absolute ones.

---

volumes in a second step and then added (by extrapolation) to the sum from the still available material, leading to 'consolidated' counts in Figures 5.2–5.7. In addition, Utrecht was after Liege (only partly covered in the *Repertorium Germanicum*) the bishopric with the most and richest benefices in the Empire. It had to adjust to the church policies of the hegemonial power of Burgundy, which were completely different from those of the rest of the Empire. Both Utrecht and Liege were excluded, given that the statistical weight of their region (see the share of petitions in Figure 5.1 above) would have misrepresented the situation elsewhere; cf. Schwarz, 'Die Abbreviatoren', pp. 218, 247 (no. 3).

65 Since a new pope was not bound by the mandates of his predecessor, it was helpful to obtain confirmation from him. Many petitioners also viewed concomitant changes in the composition of the Curia as an opportunity. That each pontificate began with the re-issuance of expectancies (as the old ones were no longer valid) is reflected only to a limited extent in the registers; Meyer, *Arme Kleriker auf Pfründensuche*, p. 55.

66 On 24 March 1436, the Council of Basel abolished general reservations by the pope except those conceded by written law; cf. Schwarz, 'Die Abbreviatoren', p. 213 n. 67. Papal expectancies followed on 24 January 1438, see p. 217.

67 17 March, 1438; *Deutsche Reichstagsakten. Ältere Reihe*, ed. by Beckmann and Weigel, XIII, no. 130; a German translation alongside the text has appeared in *Quellen zur Verfassungsgeschichte*, ed. and trans. by Weinrich, pp. 480–85 (no. 123).

68 26 March 1439; *Deutsche Reichstagsakten. Ältere Reihe*, ed. by Beckmann and Weigel, XIV, no. 56.

69 Meyer, 'Das Wiener Konkordat'.

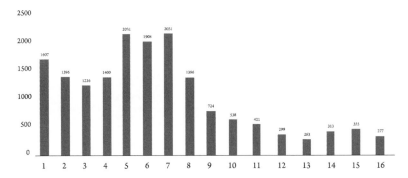

Figure 5.2. Number of Petitions from the German Empire (Pontifical Years of Eugene IV, 1431–1447).

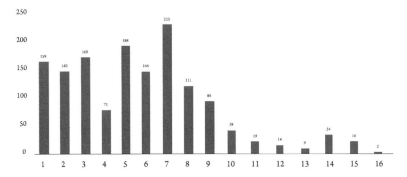

Figure 5.3. Distribution of Petitions from East German Bishoprics (Pontifical Years of Eugene IV, 1431–1447).

It is evident from Figure 5.4 that younger individuals or those farther removed from the Curia were introduced to and took advantage of the benefice market through the Council of Basel. At the same time, petitioners for higher positions standing in closer association with the princely courts were clearly better informed. They reacted more swiftly and decisively to the impending political changes in the Empire such as the neutrality of 1438, the Acceptation of Mainz and, from 1441 onwards, Eugene IV's invitation to sign separate concordats with the territorial princes.[70]

In Figure 5.5, the demand for benefices in the east German areas is not distinguished into higher and lesser benefices. Its sluggish start and

---

70 For details, see the chapter on 'Reich, Kirche und Basler Konzil' in Christoph Schöner's *Habilitation*, cited p. 117 n. 11 above.

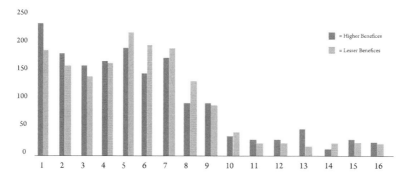

Figure 5.4. Petitions from the German Empire for Higher and Lesser Benefices (Pontifical Years of Eugene IV, 1431–1447).

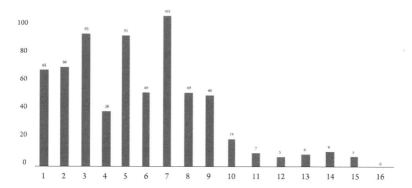

Figure 5.5. Distribution of Petitions for (New) Provisions from East German Bishoprics (Pontifical Years of Eugene IV, 1431–1447).

peak of 1437 varied significantly from that for the Empire as a whole. If we separately consider the requests for dispensations and licenses, which for the most part consisted of indulgences, confessional privileges, permissions for portable altars, the celebration of mass during interdicts, etc., a somewhat different picture emerges according to Figure 5.6. Although petitions for them diminished from as early as 1439, the subsequent period is not without momentary highs.

As shown in Figure 5.7 above, this can be interpreted for both the Empire and east Germany as a sign that petitioners willingly or by necessity postponed their wish to acquire a spiritual favour owing to the disturbed relationship between the Council and Eugene IV, or awaited the outcome, as these papal graces often were not so necessary or even urgent. Those who felt they had to obtain them right then and there, on the other

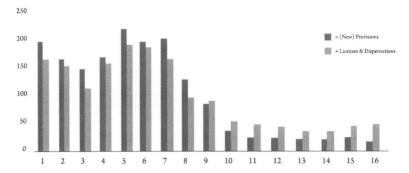

Figure 5.6. Petitions from the German Empire for (New) Provisions, Licenses, and Dispensations (Pontifical Years of Eugene IV, 1431–1447).

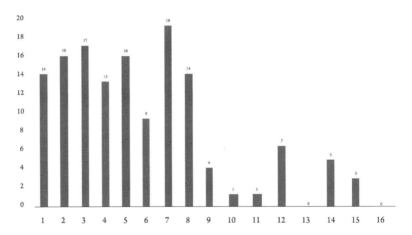

Figure 5.7. Petitions for Licenses and Dispensations from East German Bishoprics (Pontifical Years of Eugene IV, 1431–1447).

hand, preferred to go directly to the pope rather than visiting Basel, which provided the same services. The competency of the Council in this regard met with little acceptance, like the benefice market which instead migrated from the Curia to the regions. Given the low numbers, certain peaks in Figure 5.7 are the result of mere chance, such as when a couple of clerics from Meissen assumed subaltern positions at the Curia in the 1440s.[71]

---

71 I have counted five of these lesser officials or members of a cardinal's household. A few students from Bologna or Florence where the Curia was located at the time must probably be added. Among the well-established petitioners from Saxony were the learned counsellors, Georg of Haugwitz (above, p. 129 n. 51), Heinrich Leubing of Nordhausen (p. 124 n. 28a),

THE VATICAN ARCHIVES AND THEIR USES FOR REGIONAL HISTORIANS    137

In conclusion, it is possible to say that the benefice market was very sensitive to crises — just like a real market! Concerning another point raised previously, what about studies on the variety and intensity of long-term relations between the Curia and specific regions? To find out whether my assessment is correct and the scarcity of information about Saxony in the Vatican sources was effectively the result of tight church control by the territorial ruler, I have implemented a different test, which everyone can check because the sixth volume of the *Repertorium Germanicum* for the pontificate of Nicholas V (1447–1455) has long been available — contrary to the one for Eugene IV. It is known that German princes were busy soliciting papal favours around the time of the Concordat of Vienna (17 February 1448), so as to increase the supervision of churches across their territory.[72] I have tracked all references to the dukes of Saxony in the Indices, from Frederick the Gentle to Duke William and finally Sigismund, that is, every single petition in which they in person, or through clients invoking their lord, successfully turned to the pope as unsuccessful requests were typically not registered.[73] To facilitate consultation, the number of each entry in volume VI of the *Repertorium Germanicum* is subsequently added in brackets.

The two brothers of the Wettin family came to terms with Eugene IV during the last weeks of his life and were amply rewarded for it.[74] The elector Frederick the Gentle was especially involved in the crafting of the Concordat and secured far-reaching concessions.[75] The dying pope ratified and confirmed all appointments to church office in the duchy made contrary to papal prerogatives before 5 February. Eugene's successor, Nicholas V approved in addition the exemption from certain Chancery

---

and Heinrich Stoube of Goch (cf. Gramsch, *Erfurter Juristen*, no. 614), who may have speculated on a turn of events as well.

72  Pleyer, *Die Politik Nikolaus' V.*, pp. 2–20. Supplementary to the princely treaties (see p. 137 n. 74 below), individual bishops signed collateral ones, though not the one from Meissen.

73  This makes it necessary to look in the 'Index of Places' under *Saxonia, Fredericus, Wilhelmus*, and *Sigismundus* with all their derivative and garbled spellings, to place them in chronological order, and arrange them systematically in tables, a proven way to proceed. The tables are not reproduced in this essay.

74  See the reconstruction of events by Helmrath, *Das Basler Konzil*, pp. 317 ff. An important step were the supposedly preliminary princely concordats of 5 and 7 February 1447, printed in *Raccolta di concordati*, ed. by Mercati, pp. 168–77. The Concordat of Vienna can be conveniently consulted in *Quellen zur Verfassungsgeschichte*, ed. and trans. by Weinrich, pp. 498–507 (no. 127). On the Viennese negotiations, Stieber, *Pope Eugenius*, pp. 304–22; Neal, 'The Papacy and the Nations', p. 153. On the legal validity and binding character for the Empire, Raab, 'Aschaffenburg und das Wiener Konkordat'; Angermeier, *Die Reichsreform 1410–1555*, pp. 107–13. On its reception, see also Meyer, 'Das Wiener Konkordat'.

75  Duke William declared his adherence to the pope through Margrave Albrecht Achilles of Hohenzollern as early as on 12 December 1446. Surprisingly, there seems to be no study focusing specifically on the elector's (as opposed to the margrave's) contribution to the negotiations for the Concordat; cf. Hennig, *Die Kirchenpolitik der älteren Hohenzollern*.

138    CHAPTER 5

regulations on 28 March 1447.[76] To settle unresolved issues and officially declare the elector's change of allegiance, a solemn delegation was sent to Rome to signal his obedience, arriving there in November 1447. On the occasion, other favours were obtained for the duke, his entourage, and the envoys.

The most significant concession to the elector was the reservation of the right of nomination to fifty benefices at collegiate churches in the bishoprics of Meissen, Naumburg, and Merseburg.[77] They included particularly those of Zeitz and Wurzen, which we have already identified as paramount in terms of demand.[78] For the duke, the accommodation of his brother Sigismund, who could not establish himself as bishop of Würzburg, was probably important as well (no. 5174). For the rest, Frederick was basically content to request spiritual privileges for his wife and on his own behalf in the form of letters of confession (no. 1301) and for some of the churches receiving special support from him. They included the chapter of Altenburg (nos 126, 4335), the chapel of Corpus Christi at Garsitz in Naumburg diocese, and the Chapel of St Dorothea at Cossebaude (nos 126, 921–22). Large part of the concessions went to his envoys, comprising Count Matthias Schlick — the brother of Kaspar Schlick, chancellor of King Frederick III (no. 4222) — and his entourage, and the dean of Meissen Cathedral and counsellor of the elector, Kaspar of

---

76 Vatican, Apostolic Archive, Reg. Vat. 386, fol. 18[r–v], with the confirmation by Nicholas V (on 4 December 1447) of Eugene IV's bull granting the electoral princes (on 5 February 1447) extensive favours as long as they acknowledged him rather than his rival, Felix (V), in a solemn declaration as the true pope; Reg. Vat. 386, fols 18[v]–19[r], confirming the bull of 7 February 1447, in which Eugene IV validated all appointments to benefices made after the 'Declaration of Neutrality' by the Empire (see p. 133 n. 67 above); and Reg. Vat. 386, fols 17[v]–18[r], with Nicholas V's own mandate (of 28 March 1447) regarding the cancellation of Chancery regulations contrary to the agreement with the electoral princes; the summary in *Repertorium Germanicum*, vi, ed. by Abert and others, no. 1301, is unclear; cf. the original in Dresden, Sächsisches Hauptstaatsarchiv, OU 7009. Also, OU 7047, the original of *Repertorium Germanicum*, vi, ed. by Abert and others, no. 1563, with the papal letter of 23 April 1348. Incidentally, in the charter at Dresden, Sächsisches Hauptstaatsarchiv, OU 6942 (of 1447), the Wettin family is not granted 'by the Curia the right to tax the clergy', as maintained by Helbig, *Der wettinische Ständestaat*, p. 366; and repeated by Rogge, *Zum Verhältnis von Bischof und Domkapitel*, p. 200 n. 101.

77 Nominations grew out of the papal right of reservation. Recipients were entitled to name the candidate for a benefice, whereupon the case was treated like an expectancy. The grant also called for payment of the usual fees (annates). It is very likely that the above-mentioned provisions for Georg of Haugwitz, which were marked, as noted, by a conspicuous lack of competitors, resulted from nominations by the elector.

78 *Repertorium Germanicum*, vi, ed. by Abert and others, no. 4335; under 'Misnen.'; Bautzen is not listed explicitly.

Schönberg (no. 655).[79] Also among them were the elector's chancellor and provost of Naumburg Cathedral, Johann of Magdeburg, two secretaries, Henrich Engelhard of Salza and Christian Reichenbach of Saalfeld, and a notary, Johann Bulkenhagen (no. 2652).[80] The privileges they obtained consisted of expectancies within a large catch-area as discussed above for Engelhard, indulgences permitting the use of portable altars, free choice of a confessor, and the like.

From 1448, the relationship between the elector Frederick the Gentle and the Curia was restored to normalcy, so to speak, in the same way it had always been for Duke William. Petitions from the two concentrated first on the preferential treatment of expectancies (nos 627, 784, 1388, 2072 for Frederick; nos 1256, 1350, 2023 for Duke William), suggesting stiff competition among the applicants; secondly, on dispensations (nos 1407, 2054, 2100, 2435 for Frederick; nos 946, 3056, 3389 for Duke William); and third, on indulgences (nos 1073, 3976).[81] The pope also needed to be consulted when it came to modifications in church organization (no. 1301 and more often). Completely different was finally the 'Penance', which John of Capistrano helped negotiate between the hostile brothers (no. 5887).[82]

Accordingly, it is again suggested that during the pontificate of Nicholas V, Saxony hardly participated in the benefice market, contrary to other regions where princely servants were very busy petitioning and 1447 offered the best opportunity for them to do so. As few as they were, the requests for church positions investigated here were due altogether to constraints created by papal prerogatives such as the right to dispense. At least in terms of canon law, those who did not ask in a timely manner and properly for exceptional privileges risked losing their ecclesiastical holdings.

Ducal petitions of the subsequent years reveal that at Naumburg Cathedral, if not elsewhere, nominations continued to be submitted by others than the elector. They are verifiable in sources both in- and outside the Vatican. Concerning our question about the princely control

---

79 *Repertorium Germanicum*, VI, ed. by Abert and others, nos 655, 4222. He was later bishop of Meissen and uncle of the provost of Meissen Cathedral, Dietrich of Schönberg; cf. above, p. 128 n. 48.

80 For Heinrich Engelhard, see p. 124 n. 29 above. The final two names are absent from Streich, *Zwischen Reiseherrschaft und Residenzbildung*; on Christian Reichenbach of Saalfeld, cf. Gramsch, *Erfurter Juristen*, no. 476.

81 The request for the hospital chapel of St Georg outside Leipzig was probably solicited by the city taking advantage of the chance to do so. The elector could easily comply without incurring expenses. The parish of Ebersdorf was always sponsored by the Wettin family, cf. *Repertorium Germanicum*, V–VI.

82 14 June 1453. About John of Capistrano's visit to the Wettin rulers in 1452, see Werner, 'Johannes Kapistran in Jena'.

140    CHAPTER 5

of churches in the territory, it turns out that the already considerable supervision of cathedral chapters prior to 1447 was successively extended to additional collegiate churches. Saxon clerics increasingly had to rely on the benefice market abroad, if they wished to avoid dependency on their elector's favour.[83]

In the Vatican material from 1417 to 1447, I have noted the following for the diocese of Meissen. It would be worthwhile examining the data in greater depth. First, there were clerics from Meissen who looked for benefices with pastoral duties in areas (also) inhabited by Slavic populations. At hand in the literal sense were petitions for positions in Bohemia, Moravia, and Silesia.[84] Some reached as far afield as Carinthia.[85] Moreover,

---

83 While looking for references to the Wettin in *Repertorium Germanicum*, VI, ed. by Abert and others, I also came across the name and function of persons from Duke William's entourage like the counsellor Heinrich Scheitler (no. 2023), the secretary Christian Hugonis (no. 946), the scribes Johann Portigal (no. 3389) and Johann Herzberg (no. 3056), and the marshal Bartholomeus of Bibra and his relatives (nos 402, 1256, 1350).

84 Heinrich Swartze from Bautzen, a cleric from Meissen diocese, requested a benefice in the bishopric of Prague along with dispensation from the 'defect of idiom'; *Repertorium Germanicum*, V, ed. by Diener and others, col. 1307; the same for Johann Kule, col. 1792; and Johann Görlitz, col. 1938. Two officials in the Apostolic Palace, Johann Schak de Schuneberg and Nikolaus Haberlant, both from Meissen diocese and supporting themselves by carrying sand and 'stones with animals' applied for benefices in Prague and Olomouc, cols 2330 and 2903.

85 *Repertorium Germanicum*, IV, ed. by Fink and Weiss, is unfortunately very incomplete because the relevant areas were non-German-speaking, a deficit partly mended by several studies of Sabine Weiss (especially p. 124 n. 28 above) on benefices in the diocese of Salzburg. Dr Weiss not only re-examined the entries in the Vatican registers but also consulted all the regional documentation. Andreas Colonus, a priest from Meissen bishopric, petitioned for the parish of St Maria Gail and the filial church of St Jakob in Villach in the diocese of Aquileia (col. 79). This required Slavic language proficiency as shown in the request of a competitor (col. 3642). The circumstances were more complex with Jakob Baruth of Bautzen (d. 1422). He was a curial proctor at the Roman Rota and represented parties from Salzburg at the Council of Constance. Apart from benefices at the collegiate church of Bautzen, he pursued others in Wrocław, Prague, Olomouc, and — more importantly in this context — the parish of St Marin near Windisch-Gräz in Aquileia diocese (cols 1500–01). He continued to maintain relations with Meissen Cathedral, where he paid fees to Bishop Rudolf in 1420 (col. 3307). Johann Mos, a cleric from Meissen, was a school master and then town scribe of Wolfsberg in Carinthia and participated in battles around Villach. Because he was implicated in a criminal case, we are comparatively well-informed about him (col. 2171). Johann Seuberlich from Bautzen sought among other positions the parish of St Leonhard in Feldbach, diocese of Salzburg, and benefices near Bautzen (cols 2417–18). Mathias Puntel, a cleric from Meissen, petitioned for the church of St Mary at Irdning, diocese of Salzburg (col. 2764). Nikolaus Ones, a priest from Meissen, asked for the parish of St Petri ob Judenburg in the same diocese (col. 2961). Henrich Richardi from Bautzen, a cleric from Meissen, wanted a benefice in Trent while holding another at Deutsch-Brod in Prague diocese (col. 1260; *Repertorium Germanicum*, V, ed. by Diener and others, no. 3040). Under Eugene IV, I found apart from Heinrich Richardi only Nikolaus Rad, a priest from Meissen applying for the parish of Egg in Gail valley, diocese of Aquileia, no. 7227; and Johann Hartning seeking a parish at Neustadt in Salzburg diocese

the new bishop of Trent, Alexander of Masowia (1423–1444), might have attracted speakers of Slavic languages.[86] Clergy from Lusatia were apparently recommended for being bilingual, or they were confident in their ability to learn another Slavic idiom. Benefices including the care of souls required active and passive command of the parishioners' language. Secondly, many entries refer to attacks by the Hussites, though probably for a reason different than expected. Feel free to discover!

## The 1399 Exemption of the Meissen Bishopric

Not long ago, I concentrated on a single episode by treating the (supposed) exemption of the late medieval bishopric of Meissen in detail. The summaries in the *Repertorium Germanicum* are insufficient for such inquiries, making it necessary to consult the original papal registers. For the present essay, I have paid additional attention to the material preserved in Saxony, not only to overcome the bias in the Vatican sources, but also to show that the local documentation is equally one-sided. For reasons of space, I limit myself here to a rough summary of my previous study in the pre-history and afterlife of the exemption, especially concerning the antecedents.[87] For further information and the citation of specific evidence, I refer to my recently published article on the subject.[88]

On 12 December 1399, Pope Boniface IX exempted the cathedral and bishopric of Meissen and subjected it directly to the Apostolic See. He did so by way of a charter, which exists in an original in the archive of the recipient but merely as a belated notice in the Vatican.[89] From the late Middle Ages, Saxon historiography has considered the document

---

(no. 4736). Clerics from other areas petitioning in the Slavic regions of Styria, Carinthia, and Carniola alongside Meissen included Johann Eckard, a cleric from Mainz (*Repertorium Germanicum*, IV, ed. by Fink and Weiss, col. 1830); Nikolaus of Elstraw from Augsburg (cols 2870–71); and Hartungus Molitoris de Cappel junior (see Gramsch, *Erfurter Juristen*, no. 409). They must have had connections through employment at court or the Curia. There is reason to doubt that they possessed the necessary language skills. Whether these applications amounted to a trend to emigrate or reflected the constraints of war with the Hussites which particularly affected Lusatia may be investigated by regional historians.

86 Cf. Strnad, '*In grossem Irsail*'.

87 Omitted from this account are also the papal exemptions, which the Wettin dynasty secured to exclude the jurisdiction of conservators and delegate judges, apart from that of the archbishop and the native legate as ordinaries.

88 Schwarz, 'Die Exemtion des Bistums Meißen'. Legal and diplomatic questions are extensively discussed there.

89 *Codex diplomaticus Saxoniae regiae*, ed. by Gersdorf, II/2, pp. 284–85 (no. 751). All other references to regional and curial sources can be found in my article, cited above, p. 141 n. 88.

142    CHAPTER 5

as a 'constitution' confirming the autonomy of Meissen.[90] From Johann Tylich, author of the third recension of the Chronicle of the Meissen Dukes written in 1420, it has served as a source of pride in the region.[91] It still does so in the most recent studies of Streich (1988) and Rogge (1996).[92] But is it really a Magna Charta of sorts? Was it intended as such from the perspectives of the petitioner, Margrave William Monoculus, and Pope Boniface IX who granted it? As cause for the issuance of the exceptional privilege (conceded earlier in the Empire only to the bishoprics of Bamberg and Kamień), the Saxon literature has unanimously identified the special favour the margrave enjoyed in the eyes of the pope, citing particularly the beginning of the bull, which speaks in terms of merit of 'the feeling of sincere devotion the beloved son and nobleman shows towards us and the Roman Church'. This interpretation falls into the most immediate trap readers of papal charters must be wary of, by ignoring the stereotypical form, sanctioned by centuries of tradition and fixed to the last component in its precise meaning by thousands of judicial sentences.[93] The opening (or arenga) with the initial words of 'Sincere devotionis affectus' is conventional, unlike the alternative of 'Eximie devotionis sinceritas' at the beginning of the parallel charter.[94] The former merely represented routine language, and neither is proof of special relations between the Wettin and this pope in 1399.[95] Apparently, other evidence cannot be supplied.[96]

All previous interpreters have failed to evade the second trap awaiting those who read the document unaware of the pervasiveness of church

---

90 Oddly, it appears that there was no scholarly legal analysis of the status of Meissen written outside Saxony before Willoweit, 'Die Entstehung exemter Bistümer', pp. 244–53. Among the Saxon contributions, the only one of weight is by Becker, 'Ein Beitrag zur Geschichte'.

91 *Vindemiae litterariae*, II, ed. by Schannat, especially pp. 74, 77; cited after Marquis, *Meißnische Geschichtsschreibung*, p. 166.

92 Streich, 'Die Bistümer Merseburg, Naumburg, Meißen', must be consulted with caution due to many mistakes; Rogge, *Zum Verhältnis von Bischof und Domkapitel*. Both essays do not rely on the Vatican material; their findings are further and negatively impacted by an inadequate knowledge of canon law.

93 See also the treatment by Graber, 'Ein Spurium auf Papst Gregor X.'

94 *Codex diplomaticus Saxoniae regiae*, ed. by Gersdorf, II/2, pp. 285–86 (no. 752); Vatican, Apostolic Archive, Reg. Lat. 82, fol. 176$^{r-v}$; and accordingly, *Repertorium Germanicum*, II, ed. by Tellenbach and Diener, col. 375, with a privilege for the margrave carrying the same date and granting him the right to confer benefices at Meissen Cathedral.

95 'Sincere devotionis affectus' was from the mid-thirteenth century the incipit of many different concessions. Together with 'Eximiae devotionis sinceritas', it was frequently used by the papal Chancery for royal addressees in the 1300s. Both arengas were employed to conform with courtesy requirements.

96 The literature offers only speculation; for example, Rittenbach and Seifert, *Geschichte der Bischöfe von Meißen*, p. 274.

law.[97] The papal mandate begins as usual by recounting the petitioner's request. Following him, the church of Meissen, located with all its rights and possessions in the margrave's territory, was from its foundation free and exempt and directly placed under the Apostolic See. However, and at the initiative of several Roman popes, Meissen was later subjected by metropolitan right to the archbishop of Magdeburg and finally under the legateship of the respective archbishop of Prague. This had occurred at the petitioner's displeasure and to the great detriment and curtailment of the freedom of the church of Meissen. As a result, the margrave asked for renewal of the exemption 'from all lordship and power of the archbishops of Magdeburg and Prague' and for restitution 'of the original status' which he characterized as honourable.

His request is succeeded in the dispositive part by the mandate of the pope, who by no means granted the margrave's wishes in full. He only offered partial exemption, which encompassed the precisely circumscribed jurisdiction of the Magdeburg Archbishop as metropolitan and that of the archbishop of Prague as native legate within the boundaries of his legateship defined in 1365.[98] Their rights of ordination and other liturgical and ceremonial prerogatives of great weight in the Middle Ages remained untouched. The exemption of 1399 responded to the request of a papal favour or privilege, as it is already indicated by the incipit and again by the wording and format of the document. We are therefore not confronted with a definitive decision of the pope at the end of judicial proceedings, say, between Magdeburg and Prague about Meissen and its legal status of dependency, which could not be made outside court. For privileges, on the other hand, duration was normally limited to the pontificate of the granting prelate. The formula promising 'perpetual remembrance of the matter' did not protect against expiration, contrary to what occurred after a legal verdict.

The privilege went against canonical standards in multiple ways. The pope and the margrave acted as though the old imperial bishopric of Meissen was a collegiate church under princely patronage along the lines of Altenburg, for example, which obtained papal exemption through Duke William the Younger in 1412.[99] For this reason, Pope Boniface IX

---

97 Still indispensable are Hinschius, *Das Kirchenrecht der Katholiken*; and Sägmüller, *Lehrbuch des katholischen Kirchenrechts*.

98 For the period prior to the exemption, especially the bull of 1365, I must refer here, and again for the history of the early modern reception, to the long version of my study (p. 141 n. 88 above); Saxon historiography has interpreted the bull of 1365 throughout and wrongly as a mandate of subjection to the archbishop of Prague as metropolitan and the expansion of Prague into a larger church province.

99 On the constitution of the collegiate church of Altenburg and its exemption, cf. Streich, *Zwischen Reiseherrschaft und Residenzbildung*, pp. 91–93. In the Vatican sources (not used by Streich), the relevant documentation preserves only the permission for the provost of

144   CHAPTER 5

circumvented the Apostolic Chancery as guardian of the legal tradition and simply had his letter expedited by the Chamber, a solution he embraced repeatedly.

And finally, why did the pope concede such an extensive privilege to a lesser imperial prince from the periphery, who as the youngest had to share his inheritance with two brothers? People at the Curia did not know where Meissen was and had little investment in it.[100] The first reason for the grant may have been that Pope Boniface IX was not uncontested as pope, for he ruled during the period of the Great Schism from 1378 to 1417, when two — and from 1409 three — popes competed for recognition in Western Christendom. Unprecedented in the history of the papacy, Boniface depended on the German Empire. He needed the support of the German princes and above all that of King Wenzel. In 1399, the king interceded with the pope on behalf of the Wettin Margrave, prompted by interests the pope would not understand until later.[101] In addition, the pope was in financial straits and ready to offer unusual favours against lavish pay. Because he was not familiar with the situation in the north, moreover, he was probably less troubled by a grant that was contrary to the law of the imperial church.[102] And lastly, he had made sure to reduce the intended effect of full exemption to a great extent by restricting the privilege to the jurisdictional sphere.

I have already mentioned the temporal limitation of such privileges. In the present case, the margrave was particularly unfortunate. Because Boniface IX was faced with internal pressures, he annulled all comparable privileges he had granted in a Chancery rule of 1402. There is yet another matter to be considered about the supposed Magna Charta of Meissen. As noted above, the recipient of the favour — in this case the church of Meissen — had to prove to everyone involved and before a papally appointed executor, who for his part had to implement the mandate in the locality, that the facts contained in the charter and briefly reported above

---

Altenburg as directly dependent from Rome to use the papal insignia and offer the blessings of a bishop (14 February 1414); cf. *Repertorium Germanicum*, III, ed. by Kühne, col. 112. The consecration of the 'dome' of Altenburg was performed by the bishop of Merseburg, chancellor of the prince. The grant was not comprehensive, of course. Otherwise, the elector's petition to Pope Sixtus IV of 1480 for total exemption of the church and its subjects from the archbishop of Magdeburg would not have made sense. This calls for renewed examination.

100 No list of bishoprics maintained by the Roman church in the form of a *provinciale* notes the special status of Meissen, by the way.

101 Wenzel relied on the Wettin because he was acutely threatened in his position as Roman king; *Deutsche Reichstagsakten, Ältere Reihe*, ed. by Weizsäcker, III.

102 See Weber, *Familienkanonikate und Patronatsbistümer*.

corresponded point by point to the truth.[103] This would turn into a big problem.

By 1402, the Wettin Margrave found himself empty-handed again. He approached the successor of Boniface IX, Innocent VII, to have the privilege renewed, claiming that Meissen had always been exempt after all. The bull of 1399 had not been an exemption properly speaking and did not fall under the revocation of 1402. It instead provided confirmation of a primordial condition. The new pope agreed to this understanding of the mandate without verifying the legality of its assertions. At the same time, he did not repeat the restrictions on the exemption in the text of 1399, which disappeared behind the formulaic 'et cetera et cetera'.[104] The resulting shift in emphasis toward the 'original autonomy' of Meissen provoked the intervention of the archbishop of Magdeburg, who had not been the target of the bull of 1399. It had been chiefly directed against the archbishop of Prague and Bohemian expansion into Lusatia and beyond. In 1399, the Wettin Margrave may even have regretted that the prelate from Magdeburg was placed at a disadvantage as well.

The consequences became visible for the first time in 1411, when the next bishop of Meissen took office. After a long hiatus, he was again a protégé of the Wettin family and acted as if his position was exempt along the lines of Bamberg and Kamień and without informing the archbishop of Magdeburg. In 1414, the bishop of Meissen challenged his invitation to the Council of Constance (until 1418) by the archbishop as the metropolitan head. Conflict ensued in the form of litigation at the Curia and by way of a feud.[105] In 1418, the Council of Constance deprived the conflict of its rationale in favour of Magdeburg by declaring all papal exemptions from the period of the Schism null and void. When the archbishop explained the legal situation to the Meissen party, however, both the margrave and bishop did not give in and kept invoking their alleged privilege after 1418 as well. For the most part, their subjects did not object.

It was not until 1429 that a cleric from Meissen appealed to the archbishop of Magdeburg as his metropolitan superior, and the second round of conflict began between Magdeburg and the cathedral chapter

---

103 Through the loss of the Vatican documentation, it is unknown who was appointed executor. There seems to be no evidence of it in the regional sources.

104 *Codex diplomaticus Saxoniae regiae*, ed. by Gersdorf, II/2, pp. 322–23 (no. 783).

105 The metropolitan denied the claim Margrave William had used to secure the exemption in the first place, to the effect that Meissen 'was free and exempt from its original foundation' and immediate, objecting that it was 'false'. The archbishop maintained for his part that the margrave had wrongly obtained the privilege. It had clearly been received 'surreptitiously' and lacked any legal basis, which he was able to prove with 'the most manifest documentation'; *Codex diplomaticus Saxoniae regiae*, ed. by Gersdorf, II/2, pp. 394–95 (no. 854). For papal sources from the pontificate of Martin V, see *Acta Martini V. pontificis*, ed. by Eršil, I–III.

of Meissen (backed, of course, by the Wettin family). The contest lasted for several years and went through various proceedings at the Curia. The reconstruction of this litigation, which has only reached us in fragments, again requires detailed knowledge of Romano-canonical procedure and the structure of the Curia. Notably and as usual without exception, the Saxon historiography has mistaken a single procedural step, that is, the preliminary absolution of the bishop of Meissen by a delegate judge in the first instance on 13 November 1431 for final determination of the whole matter. And yet, the maxim of 'Rome has spoken, the case is closed' would not have applied, unless three identical sentences had been passed in three instances at the Curia — while still allowing for subsequent revision!

Entering the second round, the Wettin party repeated its request for renewal of their coveted 'privilege of exemption' on 4 December 1429. The papal response, however, was more cautious than before, ordering only that 'it be done and committed'. The pope, in other words, did not grant anything except that a commissary investigated the affair. Instantly, the inquiry stalled over the very point raising difficulties earlier, namely, the assertion of the Meissen party that its church enjoyed 'original autonomy'. A year later, on 23 December 1430, the Wettin submitted another remarkable petition asking to have the 'public fame and repute' or general belief (on their part) in the existence of the original exemption be accepted as proof instead of written arguments. They requested that an executor 'can and must proceed with the renewal of this exemption in everything and altogether and as though he had legitimate knowledge about the aforementioned first exemption by way of authentic letters and other sufficient documentation'. Furthermore, they urged 'not to be held to prove this first exemption in any way other than by repute and the aforementioned fame, whence the same repute and fame would suffice as stated to prove the aforementioned prior exemption everywhere'. The pope answered in this case with the words 'so be it for five years', postponing the legally necessary rejection for political reasons, as he relied on the Wettin family in the war against the Hussites. His response made it very clear that the Wettin privilege constituted a favour and not a legal right or even good, long-standing custom, for how could he have imposed a temporal limit on his decision otherwise!

The Wettin persisted nonetheless in treating Meissen as though it was exempt, which by then had become general and firm consensus across the territory. Simultaneously, recognition of the same viewpoint outside Saxony was not achieved as readily. It was most easily asserted among those who benefitted from Meissen, say, in the form of tax income. From 1422, we find the province of Magdeburg in the description of areas assigned to papal tax collectors expressly mentioned alongside Meissen, despite its being part of the former in canonical terms.[106] In formal invitations to imperial diets during the war with the Hussites, the situation was similar. On the other hand, it was evidently impossible to convince the archbishop of Magdeburg, who for political reasons remained silent in the decisive phases of the conflict. Until the Age of the Reformation, the return of Meissen to the metropolitan province was an item each archbishop of Magdeburg had to confirm upon his election by oath.[107]

To gauge the position of the Curia regarding the exemption of Meissen, we basically have a reliable measure in the formulary of papal charters to be issued whenever the pope was involved in the elevation of a new bishop. Since Meissen claimed to be exempt, each episcopal appointment (as shown below in the fourth column of Table 5.2) was in fact performed with papal approval, which according to the Concordat of Vienna (1448) would have been unnecessary. The charters of nomination from 1399 to 1555 presuppose an exemption in only three cases, one of 1411 on occasion of the first elevation after 1399 and before cancellation of the privilege in 1418, then in 1451 and 1463. I do not know what prompted the second and third instances. Perhaps, they rested on partial information from the Meissen party and lack of protest from the adversary.

In 1451, the provincial synod of Magdeburg led by the cardinal legate, Nicolaus Cusanus, was faced with problems. It was beyond doubt that the bishop of Meissen had to obey the pope's emissary, but was the bishop able to follow the synodal decrees without compromising his fundamental position? He resolved the quandary diplomatically in external negotiations with the legate, which did not address the status of Meissen. Internally, he simply eliminated the passage referring to it.[108] As late as 1468, the margrave took care to obtain confirmation of the bull of 1399.[109] From then on, the papal charters of nomination were again properly formulated, perhaps because the Curia started to pay greater attention and read the wording of the privilege of exemption, or because they had realized in Meissen how little was lost by formally giving in to the Magdeburg side. After all, the rights of archbishops were hardly substantial anywhere in the second half of the fifteenth century.

---

106 For documentation, see Schuchard, *Die päpstlichen Kollektoren*, pp. 291–93, 297, also discussing the collectors, who belonged without exception to the higher clergy of the region.
107 Willich, *Wege zur Pfründe*.
108 *Codex diplomaticus Saxoniae regiae*, ed. by Gersdorf, II/3, pp. 102–03 (no. 1008); for a better summary, see *Acta Cusana*, ed. by Meuthen and Hallauer, I/2, no. 2045. On Dietrich Bocksdorf, the author of the text, Schwarz, 'Klerikerkarrieren und Pfründenmarkt', Anhang, no. 1.
109 *Repertorium Germanicum*, IX, ed. by Höing and others, col. 1204. An outgoing letter is not preserved. Probably for this reason, the two charters, no. 751 and 783 (above, pp. 141 n. 89, 145 n. 104), were recopied on 26 October 1467, this time at the elector's request; *Codex diplomaticus Saxoniae regiae*, ed. by Gersdorf, II/3, p. 176 (no. 1097).

The concession of the exemption for Meissen in 1399 was not unique. Others tried as well to exploit the weakness of the Curia during the Great Schism and attain their objectives in ecclesiastical politics, such as the bishop of Passau in 1415. His case, though, remained a short-lived episode because the archbishop of Salzburg put up successful resistance at the Curia. The two exemptions led to extremely different outcomes, moreover. The one obtained by Meissen furnished a precious building block in the construction of territorial church governance by the dukes in Saxony. Conversely, the cancellation of the exemption for Passau in 1423 exposed the church to unending rivalry between Bavaria and Austria.

Table 5.2. The Bishops of Meissen, *c.* 1300–1476.

| Bishop: Name, Origin, End in Office | Study; Highest Benefice at Meissen; Princely Service | Election; Special or General Reservation | Provision or Confirmation; *Notification of Abp. of Magdeburg | Protector; Political Status; Investiture | Payment of *servitia* to Apostolic Chamber; Claimed Expense | Ordination; Other Notes Especially on Official Functions |
|---|---|---|---|---|---|---|
| Wittego of Colditz, imperial ministerial in Thuringia; related to his predecessor; d. 07/26/1342 | - Dean of cathedral, from 1311 | Election, before 04/05/1312 (documented as elect) | - | ? | - | Ordination unknown; first mention of local *officialis* |
| Johann of Eisenberg; ministerial in Meissen; d. 01/04/1370 | - Prior of cathedral; chancellor of margrave | Election, 1342 | - | Margraves | - | Ordination unknown; remains secretary of margrave as bishop! 1365, Meissen under legatine jurisdiction of Prague |

| Bishop: Name, Origin, End in Office | Study; Highest Benefice at Meissen; Princely Service | Election; Special or General Reservation | Provision or Confirmation; *Notification of Abp. of Magdeburg | Protector; Political Status; Investiture | Payment of servitia to Apostolic Chamber; Claimed Expense | Ordination; Other Notes Especially on Official Functions |
|---|---|---|---|---|---|---|
| Dietrich of Schönberg; ministerial in Meissen; d. autumn 1370 | Bachelor of canon law; archdeacon of Nisan | Election; annulled despite special reservation | Provision, 05/29/1370; * | Emperor Charles IV? | - | Ordination at the Curia before 07/13/1370; died on his return from there |
| Konrad of Kirchberg; noble from Thuringia; d. 05/26/1375 | 1345–1348 study in Bologna; prior of Bautzen and (claimed) Meissen Cathedral; protonotary of the Wettin | Election; annulled despite special reservation | Provision, 11/13/1370; * | Margraves; patronage | -; cf. p. 141 n. 89 above, no. 607 | Ordination by pope before 03/11/1371; papal collector in 1372 |

| Bishop: Name, Origin, End in Office | Study; Highest Benefice at Meissen; Princely Service | Election; Special or General Reservation | Provision or Confirmation; *Notification of Abp. of Magdeburg | Protector; Political Status; Investiture | Payment of *servitia* to Apostolic Chamber; Claimed Expense | Ordination; Other Notes Especially on Official Functions |
|---|---|---|---|---|---|---|
| Johann of Jenzenstein; Bohemian nobility; 03/19/1379, transfer to Prague | Bachelor of canon law and theology; prior of Wetzlar | Special reservation | Provision, 07/04/1375; * | Emperor Charles IV | - | Ordained by uncle, the abp. of Prague, vacant from 1379 after he was made cardinal by Urban VI |
| Nikolaus 'Ziegenbock'; Dominican from Naumburg citizenry; d. 02/11/1392 | Titular bp. of Chersones, 1366; 1374/1375 auxiliary bp. in Naumburg; 1377–1379 (claimed) bp. of Lübeck; papal collector and diplomat from 1370 | Reservation due to translation | Translation, 04/19/1379; *? | King Wenzel | - | 03/19/1379, promise to cathedral chapter; 07/31/1384, promise of fidelity to margrave; still papal collector |

| Bishop: Name, Origin, End in Office | Study; Highest Benefice at Meissen; Princely Service | Election; Special or General Reservation | Provision or Confirmation; *Notification of Abp. of Magdeburg | Protector; Political Status; Investiture | Payment of *servitia* to Apostolic Chamber; Claimed Expense | Ordination; Other Notes Especially on Official Functions |
|---|---|---|---|---|---|---|
| Dietrich Lamberti of Goch; patrician from Erfurt | Licentiate in law; prior of Bautzen | Election before 06/06/1392 despite general reservation, annulled | - | Margraves | - | The cathedral chapter still defended his rights, 02/07/1393; see Gramsch (p. 120 n. 15 above, no. 218); later custodian of Naumburg Cathedral |
| Johann of Kittlitz; noble from Meissen/ Bohemia; resigned to pope, 12/02/1398; d. 02/20/1408 | From July 1382 bp. of Lebus | - | Translation, 11/01/1392; *? | King Wenzel; investiture by him, 07/04/1393 | First assessment; amount unknown; sureties and payments 1392–1398 (cathedral canons of Wrocław and Prague) | Promise of fidelity to margrave, 03/04/1393; after resignation supported from ducal domain and residing at Bautzen |

| Bishop: Name, Origin, End in Office | Study; Highest Benefice at Meissen; Princely Service | Election; Special or General Reservation | Provision or Confirmation; *Notification of Abp. of Magdeburg | Protector; Political Status; Investiture | Payment of *servitia* to Apostolic Chamber; Claimed Expense | Ordination; Other Notes Especially on Official Functions |
| --- | --- | --- | --- | --- | --- | --- |
| Thimo of Colditz; noble from Meissen/ Bohemia; nephew of predecessor; d. 12/26/1410 | Prior of a nunnery; *relator* of King Wenzel, 1378–1383 | General reservation due to resignation | Provision; 12/02/1398; *? | King Wenzel; investiture? | 333.5 guilds; surety and payments, 1398–1406, also for his predecessor by H. Dwerg and Meissen clerics | Age dispensation; ordination?; promise of fidelity to margrave, 02/23/1399; 'Exemption' 12/12/1399; King Wenzel's envoy to the Council of Pisa, 1409 |
| Rudolf of Planitz; knightly nobility from Meissen; d. 05/23/1427 | Bachelor in canon law; canon and from 1407 prior at Naumburg Cathedral | Election, 01/09/1411; annulled despite general reservation | Provision, 03/11/1411 | Margraves; investiture, 05/4/1415 by King Sigismund in Constance | 323.5 (!) guilds; surety and payments by Meissen clerics; expenses 2800 guilds | Pentecost 1411; sumptuous ordination as exempt bishop in Naumburg |

| Bishop: Name, Origin, End in Office | Study; Highest Benefice at Meissen; Princely Service | Election; Special or General Reservation | Provision or Confirmation; *Notification of Abp. of Magdeburg | Protector; Political Status; Investiture | Payment of *servitia* to Apostolic Chamber; Claimed Expense | Ordination; Other Notes Especially on Official Functions |
|---|---|---|---|---|---|---|
| Johann Hoffmann; from Schweinitz citizenry; d. 04/12/1451 | Master of theology; prior of Grossenhain | Election, 06/06/1427, annulled despite general reservation | Provision, 09/10/1427; * | Dukes; investiture, 05/18/1428 by King Sigismund | 333.5 guilds; surety and payments 1327 by the Medici | Ordination?; repeatedly at the Council of Basel |
| Kaspar of Schönberg; from the Saxon knighthood; d. 05/31/1463 | Master of arts; cathedral dean; councillor of elector Frederick the Gentle | Election, 04/30/1451; annulled despite special reservation | Provision, 06/09/1451 | Dukes; investiture 09/1451 by King Frederick III | 333.5 guilds; surety and payments by the Medici, 1451/1452 | Ordination at the Curia, 07/1451; oath on the conditions of election repeated on his return |
| Dietrich of Schönberg; from the Saxon knighthood; brother of predecessor; d. 04/12/1476 | Master in the arts; cathedral prior | Election, 06/13/1463 | Confirmation, 08/18/1463 | Dukes; investiture, 07/02/1464 by King Frederick III | 346 guilds; surety and payments e.g. by the Medici; expenses 1200 guilds | Ordination? before 12/13/1463; in August 1463, a homonymous cousin, his successor as prior, was at the Curia |

# PART II

## Curial Offices

CHAPTER 6

# The Venality of Offices

*An Institution from the Period of Absolutism and Its Medieval Roots*[*]

In administrative histories of the premodern states in Europe, there is frequent reference to the sale of offices as a pervasive phenomenon. The practice was common in territories with weak tendencies toward Absolutism like Poland and parliamentary England, where lesser judicial positions were sold until 1820, the posts of officers in the army until 1871, and canonries in churches through public auction as late as 1898.[1] It also occurred in highly absolutist regimes such as the Papal States (including the ecclesiastical branch of government, or Curia), which sold specific positions until 1898.[2] The same applied to France, where traces persist today.[3] Also, in the lands of the Spanish Crown.[4] Insofar as these territories had colonies, they exported the institution as well.[5] Meanwhile, the sale of offices was just as vibrant in the Italian city states with their oligarchical constitutions.[6] Or across German towns, where Hamburg, for example, did not abolish the mechanism until 1810.[7] The office trade was certainly not limited to premodern Europe and its offshoots overseas. It was also found in other civilizations like that of the Ottoman Empire or ancient China.[8]

In examining the trade in offices across different states and times, some doubt arises as to whether the term does not fuse overly disparate things instead of explaining them. Consider only the multiple forms of exchange we encounter in medieval and modern England. First and 'oscillating

---

[*] The text (with added footnotes) is based on my inaugural lecture of *Habilitation* at the University of Hanover on 19 June 1979. In the early stages of preparation, I received considerable support from Professor Joachim Leuschner (d. 12 April 1978).

1 Swart, 'Sale of Offices', pp. 45 ff., especially p. 66. For bibliography on individual territories, see the next notes below.

2 Feine, *Kirchliche Rechtsgeschichte*, I, p. 646.

3 Reinhard, 'Staatsmacht als Kreditproblem', p. 290 n. 3.

4 Swart, 'Sale of Offices', pp. 19 ff.

5 Swart, 'Sale of Offices', pp. 41 ff.; Reinhard, 'Staatsmacht als Kreditproblem', p. 290.

6 For Venedig, see Mousnier, 'Le trafic des offices à Venise' (reprinted in Mousnier, *La plume, la faucille et le marteau*, pp. 387–401); for Milan, Chabod, 'Stipendi nominali', pp. 271 ff.; for Rome, Rodocanachi, *Les institutions communales de Rome sous la papauté*, pp. 202–03.

7 Swart, 'Sale of Offices', p. 91.

8 Reinhard, 'Staatsmacht als Kreditproblem', p. 292. On the sale of offices in late Antiquity, cf. Liebs, 'Ämterkauf und Ämterpatronage'; Schuller, 'Ämterkauf im römischen Reich'.

between legality and corruption', there was the sale of offices at the hand of courtiers who appropriated the conferral as their right.[9] Addressed in the original sources as 'sales', moreover, but in fact equivalent to leasing or mortgaging, incumbents treated their offices as freehold property and included them as such in their bequests — without the king's permission or participation.[10] Also, the sale of military posts resulted from compensating the prior owner for his expenses as a warring entrepreneur. In opposition to offices treated as freehold, however, possession was tied to the actual exercise of functions. In either case, the king did not participate.[11] In addition, the acquisition of seats in Parliament occurred through the buying of votes, which the literature has associated with the sale of offices as well.[12] And lastly, there were, in England, if more so in the centralized states, various other forms of office trade, which went as far as to constitute an institutionalized and legalized sale by the crown.

As a result, we must be aware that, terminologically speaking, rather different phenomena are categorized under the same label. They call for careful differentiation, if we wish for an adequate treatment of the medieval roots of a specific variety of trade, namely, the sale of offices in the age of early modern Absolutism. In the following, I will take France as my example, where the venality of offices was most advanced and has also been investigated most thoroughly.[13] I will outline the typical forms without tracing the historical development or peculiarities of specific positions and areas. During the time of the Ancient Regime until 1789, the venality of offices encompassed terminologically the legal and institutionalized sale of public offices by the French crown.[14] At a price determined by the king, the interested party purchased a 'letter of provision' concerning a vacant position along with orders directed at fellow officials to accept the buyer as a colleague and swear him in.[15] If a position was currently unavailable, it was possible to acquire an 'expectancy' or claim to the next vacancy. In this way, the purchaser obtained effective control of the office, which was usually for life, despite a standard phrase in the letter cautioning 'insofar as it pleases us as the king'. The holder could borrow against it, rent it out,

---

9 Reinhard, 'Staatsmacht als Kreditproblem', p. 291. Concerning the frequently fluent relationship between corruption and the sale of offices, cf. also Schuller, 'Probleme historischer Korruptionsforschung'.

10 Swart, 'Sale of Offices', p. 91.

11 Reinhard, 'Staatsmacht als Kreditproblem', p. 303.

12 Swart, 'Sale of Offices', p. 64.

13 Lucas, *Étude sur la venalité*; Pagès, 'La venalité des offices'; Göhring, *Die Ämterkäuflichkeit im Ancien Régime*; Mousnier, *La vénalité des offices*. Cf. Böse, 'Die Ämterkäuflichkeit'.

14 Reinhard, 'Staatsmacht als Kreditproblem', p. 294. Mousnier, *La vénalité des offices*, does not provide a clear definition of venality, a weakness of this great book.

15 On the system of venality in France, see Mousnier, *La vénalité des offices*, pp. 8 ff.; Böse, 'Die Ämterkäuflichkeit', pp. 86 ff.

or put a mortgage on it, always requiring royal permission that he did not have to administer the office in person. The favour was routinely granted. He was also entitled to resell the office or bequeath it by observing the legally appropriate mechanism known as 'resignation in favour of a third'.[16] The formula meant that the current holder renounced (or resigned) his office before the king to another person presented as the successor. The king was obliged to accept the exchange because it belonged to the original sales conditions.

The king consequently lost much of his disposition over the office when it was sold, with two exceptions. The first applied when the office holder died within (initially) twenty or (later) forty days after the purchase.[17] The second called for the tenant's removal from office because of official misconduct, which had to be backed up by a judicial sentence.[18] If an official obtained a position that, due to a ban on accumulation, he was not permitted to hold together with a different one, he was still able to exchange it by way of permutation. But there was yet another option forming a prerequisite for the functioning of the entire system. It was possible to receive from the king an exceptional permission through dispensation from the prohibition of accumulation to buy and keep the additional office as well. With the help of dispensations, a whole array of obstacles could be overcome including, for instance, regulations stipulating mandatory residency where the office was located, age requirements and professional qualifications, or the need to exercise the office in person.[19]

As mentioned, the king was rarely able to intervene with offices from the moment he had sold them. On the other hand, he had various ways to create new offices for sale and did so with increasing frequency. He could establish guilds or boards of officials, assign to them (often fictitious) tasks, incomes, or privileges, and bring them wholesale to market.[20] Alternatively, he could transform offices from non-venal into venal ones, or add positions to guilds that were already in existence, attracting the angered

---

16 *Resignatio in favorem tertii*. The most important theoretician of venality in the early modern period has dedicated an entire book to this legal construct; see Loyseau, *Cinq livres du droict des offices*, pp. 422 ff.

17 The forty-day clause was introduced by Francis I. (r. 1515–1547); Mousnier, *La vénalité des offices*, pp. 44 ff.

18 The treatment of Kubler, 'L'origine de la perpétuité', has concentrated on the normative texts; Autrand, 'Offices et officiers royaux', has examined the court records of the *Parlement* of Paris, where the prohibition of removal took hold from the late fourteenth century, pp. 328 ff.

19 Mousnier, *La vénalité des offices*, p. 28 and elsewhere. It was also possible to be dispensed from swearing not to have paid anything for the conferral of an office, p. 66.

20 The technical term was 'college of officials'. About the first attempt to establish such a college, see p. 168 below. That the collegiality of offices was necessary to attract buyers has not always been understood; for example, by Mousnier, *La vénalité des offices*, p. 83. Cf. p. 174 below.

protest of officials whose share of income was about to be diminished.[21] He could also upgrade the status of officials with privileges, in a move that increased the price of the position and compelled holders to pay the difference.[22] These privileges often served to bestow personal or inheritable nobility and generally provided immunity from taxes and the courts. Fixed salaries constituted the smallest portion of revenue for the officials. They relied primarily on fees for their administrative intervention.[23] They used them to justify many surcharges and acts of extortion — and had to, if they wanted to make good on their initial investment in the position.

This rough sketch may suffice to show that the venality of offices was about the legalized and institutionalized sale of the right to make (limited) use of public positions. The ruler kept the revenues officials collected and administered, as well as the material means of operation.[24] The authority invested in the office was exercised only through delegation and the assigned functions had to be fulfilled in accordance with office regulations. From the financial point of view, the buyer had acquired a (rudimentary) form of annuity or perpetual pension that was based on the revenues of his office.[25] Those subjected to his administration carried the burden of this credit mechanism. Through the sale of offices, the crown was able to involve circles in the financing of his policies who otherwise were exempted from his taxation. It was of grave consequence that the officials acted by and large as creditors of the kingdom.

Regarding the state of research in the sale of offices, mention must be made of groundbreaking work that has focused on Aragon,[26] Castile,[27] Sicily,[28] Venice,[29] and Milan.[30] The topic is rather well explored for the

---

21 Mousnier, *La vénalité des offices*, p. 31; Kubler, 'L'origine de la perpétuité', p. 101 and elsewhere.

22 Mousnier, *La vénalité des offices*, pp. 8, 48; Loyseau, *Cinq livres du droict des offices*, p. 413.

23 On the relationship between salaries, fees, and tips (none of which changed for centuries), cf. Chabod, 'Stipendi nominali'; and, Guenée, *Tribunaux et gens de justice*, pp. 182–83.

24 'Sachliche Betriebsmittel' according to the concept of Weber, *Wirtschaft und Gesellschaft*, ed. by Winckelmann, p. 566.

25 Reinhard, 'Staatsmacht als Kreditproblem', p. 307; citing Bauer, 'Die Epochen der Papstfinanz', p. 486 (reprinted in Bauer, *Gesammelte Aufsätze*, p. 134); and Bauer, 'Mittelalterliche Staatsfinanz', p. 108. Only the original sale resembled an annuity, given that the positions were transferable and did not return to the source of emission until the actual holder died. In the meantime, sales rather constituted the leasing of certain fees.

26 Küchler, 'Ämterkäuflichkeit in den Ländern der Krone Aragons'.

27 Domínguez Ortiz, 'La venta de cargos y oficios públicos en Castilla'; Fraga Iribarne and Beneyto Pérez, 'La enajenación de oficios públicos', pp. 421 ff.; Tomás y Valiente, 'Origen bajo medieval de la patrimonialización y la enajenación de oficios públicos', also separately.

28 Sciuti Russi, 'Aspetti della venalità degli uffici in Sicilia'.

29 Cf. above, p. 157 n. 6.

30 Cf. above, p. 157 n. 6.

THE VENALITY OF OFFICES    161

papal court or Curia (though not the Papal States).[31] The most is known about the venality of offices in France, above all because of the studies by Roland Mousnier and his students. Their investigations were sparked by the great debate between Mousnier and Boris Porchnev concerning the economic, social, and constitutional effect of venality on French Absolutism, which I cannot address in the present context.[32] More recent inquiries into the venality of offices concentrate on the phenomenon in countries that have not yet been adequately covered or deal with a certain region under socio-historical aspects. After the accumulation of additional findings, it will be necessary to proceed to the systematic and comparative analysis of early modern Europe as a whole.[33]

It is my impression that the foundations from which venality arose have hardly been explored. After all, the phenomenon was not introduced at a certain point during the early modern period and subsequently adopted by other states as a feasible solution for various credit shortfalls; it developed instead quite gradually. Contemporary theorists were inclined to trace it back to early medieval times.[34] They did not recognize the basic differences between the sale of offices as the older sources presented it and the practice of their own era after 1500. Apart from their tendency to assign responsibility for every important institution to Charlemagne, they acted on the desire to attribute the earliest possible origin to it. Modern historians have again treated the sale of offices as a single matter from the early Middle Ages to Absolutism and without distinguishing between several phases.[35] This is primarily due to the terminology of the high medieval sources, which refers without differentiation to 'sale' or

---

31 See von Hofmann, *Forschungen zur Geschichte der kurialen Behörden*. For the studies by Bauer, see p. 160 n. 25 above. The treatment by Göller, 'Hadrian VI. und der Ämterkauf an der päpstlichen Kurie', does not add significantly to von Hofmann's work. On the current state of research, Schimmelpfennig, 'Der Ämterkauf an der römischen Kurie'; and Reinhard, 'Ämterhandel in Rom'. For later centuries, see the studies of Georg Lutz, including 'Zur Papstfinanz von Klemens IX. bis Alexander VIII.' I have outlined a research agenda for the period until Pius II (1458–1464); see Schwarz, 'Die Ämterkäuflichkeit an der Römischen Kurie'.

32 Beginning with Porschnew, *Die Volksaufstände in Frankreich*. For a description of the debate, see Salmon, 'Venality of Office and Popular Sedition'.

33 For this reason, the Department of History at the Free University of Berlin has established a research focus on 'Soziale Mobilität im frühmodernen Staat: Bürgertum und Ämterwesen'; cf. *Ämterkäuflichkeit. Aspekte sozialer Mobilität*, ed. by Malettke; and the volume cited above, p. 158 n. 13.

34 Mousnier, *La vénalité des offices*, pp. 14. Differently, Loyseau, *Cinq livres du droit des offices*, pp. 397 ff., who places the beginnings of venality in 1467 and distinguishes it sharply from the leasing of offices.

35 Similarly, Lucas, *Étude sur la venalité*; Pagès, 'La venalité des offices'; Swart, 'Sale of Offices'; also, Mousnier, *La vénalité des offices*, despite certain efforts to differentiate.

*venditio* whenever offices were not conferred without payment.[36] To avoid such fusion or confusion, I will not refer to the venality of offices in my following treatment of the high medieval period from around 1000 to 1250, but restrict my use of the term to the early modern phenomenon.

The expression of *venditio* in connection with offices is common in medieval sources, although it mostly occurs as a polemical term in theoretical and literary works. It is difficult to capture its concrete meaning from case to case, given that the original texts are largely silent about the intentions of sponsors and recipients, as well as about legal implications or payments. One of the reasons for this is that the legality of such transactions was always doubtful.[37] Church lawyers had to reckon with a papal letter that was incorporated into Gratian's *Decretum* around 1140.[38] It stated that it was simony, and heretical, to sell offices that had been created for the administration and safeguard of ecclesiastical property. This also applied when they could only be held by laypersons. Canonistic interpretations of this decree proved important for the *venditio* of offices going forward.

The first step was to specify that the sale of an office was simony if it 'contained or was tied to a spiritual element'.[39] The canonist Tancred (c. 1215) associated this spiritual element with all offices involving the exercise of church jurisdiction and declared their sale under any circumstance as simony. He identified another reason for the illicit nature of such transactions. They entailed an undue risk of burdening the subjects.[40] Hostiensis (d. 1271) extended this understanding to the secular sphere. To confer lay offices with jurisdiction against money was also simony for him, 'because all power is from God and hence spiritual in nature'.[41] As we will see, his view was to exert great influence, although Hostiensis dissociated himself from it in a later work, in which he no longer presented the trade in purely secular offices as simony. He rather viewed it as illicit (owing to the prohibitions of Roman Law) and as a grave sin, for 'the sale of jurisdiction or income deriving from it' constituted 'illicit gain' or usury according to the economic ethics of the time.[42]

After moving back and forth between a sales ban and the acceptance of practical realities that were apparently non-compliant, the interpreters of

---

36 Loyseau, *Cinq livres du droict des offices*, pp. 399–400, explains it by arguing that 'the sale and the lease consist of the same legal rules'.

37 For the following, see especially Lefebvre, 'Les juristes du Moyen Âge'.

38 C.1 q.3 c. 8, in *Corpus iuris canonici*, ed. by Friedberg, I, cols 413–14.

39 Lefebvre, 'Les juristes du Moyen Âge', p. 279.

40 Lefebvre, 'Les juristes du Moyen Âge', p. 280.

41 *Summa domini Henrici cardinalis Hostiensis* (completed in 1253), in X 5.4 no. 1, fol. 234[rb].

42 *Henrici de Segusio commentaria* (completed in 1271), in X 5.3.4 s.v. *Praeterea*, II, fol. 27[va]. Thomas de Aquino, *De regimine Judaeorum*, ed. by Mathis, pp. 100–01, did not consider the sale of offices a sin, but observed that it could lead to oppression of the subjects and invite sin by being a usurious pact.

Roman Law quickly embraced the same distinctions.[43] They concluded with Hostiensis that the purchase of secular offices with jurisdiction amounted to simony.[44] Baldus (1327–1400) considered not only jurisdiction but also the power of command (*imperium*) as God-given. Like Tancred before him, he went on to justify the prohibition to sell positions of this kind with the danger that buyers, in their desire to derive as much profit as possible from them, might oppress the population and harm the common good.[45] In offices without jurisdiction, lawyers found the sale acceptable, provided it was conducted in public. If this went against the regulations of Roman Law, they thought of the ruler's right to dispense as an adequate remedy.[46] Successive limitations stipulated that the office could only be sold by the competent secular superior, who had to be sure that the candidate assumed the position with the intent to serve the common good.[47] This state of the discussion turned into a firm component of all polemical and theoretical writing in the later Middle Ages.[48]

The medieval jurists whose opinions about the sale of offices I have briefly summarized were exposed to the high medieval variety of *venditio* which I will address next.[49] I will remain in France as the example that is already familiar to us. The king there could only confer offices in areas he controlled either because of certain crown rights, or *regalia*, or as lord of his own domain. He could basically bestow them in the form of a lease or as a mortgage.[50] If he gave them away as benefices, there was worry that he would lose control over them, which was less likely to occur with leases

---

43 Lefebvre, 'Les juristes du Moyen Âge', pp. 275 ff.

44 Cf. above, p. 162 n. 41. On the post-glossators, Lefebvre, 'Les juristes du Moyen Âge', p. 282.

45 Baldus de Ubaldis, in *Baldi Perusini tomus primus*, in Dig. 1.14.3, fol. 50ᵛ (no. 6).

46 Cinus de Pistoia, in *Cyni Pistoriensis commentaria*, in Cod. 9.26, p. 558a (no. 3).

47 Lefebvre, 'Les juristes du Moyen Âge', pp. 284–85.

48 The prohibition to sell the office of judge persisted in principle through the early modern period; Mousnier, *La vénalité des offices*, p. 65 and elsewhere, although the charge of simony was rarely raised any longer. It nonetheless weighed on the debate about venality, as is shown by de Luca, *Tractatus de officiis vacabilibus*, who dedicated a whole chapter to the topic, pp. 11 ff. In the fourteenth and fifteenth centuries, simony increasingly turned (along with usury) into a concept devoid of concrete meaning; see Bauer, 'Die Epochen der Papstfinanz', pp. 498 ff. (reprinted in Bauer, *Gesammelte Aufsätze*, p. 143 ff.); Bauer, 'Der Wucherbegriff der *Reformatio Sigismundi*', pp. 111–13. De Luca, *Tractatus de officiis vacabilibus*, p. 10, was also the first to identify with precision the economic dimension of late medieval venality as 'the anticipated receipt of future gain', and not just as selling 'the substance of the matter'.

49 The distinction between high and late medieval varieties goes back to Küchler, 'Ämterkäuflichkeit in den Ländern der Krone Aragons', pp. 325, 328; cf. Schwarz, 'Ämterkäuflichkeit', cols 561–62.

50 Mousnier, *La vénalité des offices*, pp. 14 ff.; Kubler, 'L'origine de la perpétuité', pp. 44–45, 77 ff.; Hollister and Baldwin, 'The Rise of Administrative Kingship', pp. 893 ff.; Guenée, *Tribunaux et gens de justice*, pp. 135 ff. Apart from distribution through benefices, if not leases or mortgages, there was the increasingly preferred conferral *en garde*. Differences between the latter two forms were smaller than one would expect, however, because kings obliged

164    CHAPTER 6

that were regularly short-term. There was not yet the possibility of having official workloads administered by state employees in the modern sense of the word. The tenant of, say, the position of provost — the office leased most frequently — acquired in his district all royal rights, public and feudal, as well as revenues resulting from taxes, tributes, and duties.[51] He leased or mortgaged 'the office as such', not just the means of subsistence it generated.[52] The tenant assumed official obligations in his district comprehensively, in adjudication, taxation, and especially military tasks.[53] In the exercise of his duties, he was bound by royal mandates and local custom. Professional qualifications were unnecessary, and he was tied to the king in personal loyalty.[54] For the duration of the contract, the king was quite unable to hold his representative accountable or dismiss him. The latter was even free to sublease his office to someone else without permission from the king.[55] As a result, an ingenious lessee was well-positioned to profit considerably from the office by squeezing his subjects, as the lawyers had rightly suspected. To be sure, the leasing and particularly mortgaging of offices always risked their permanent alienation from the crown.[56] Due to this potential appropriation, their sale was severely criticized from the end of the thirteenth century.[57] At that time, the concept of inalienable crown rights became fully established.[58] A new understanding of the office started to spread.[59] The change came along with others that deserve our special attention, if we wish to uncover the roots of more recent sales mechanisms.

Let us leave the High Middle Ages now and turn to the late medieval period, which for the present topic coincides with the years from around 1250 to 1530. In the later Middle Ages, certain territories witnessed

---

officials in various ways to contribute financially, asking for lost, mandatory, and other forms of credit; see below, p. 167 n. 73.

51  Hollister and Baldwin, 'The Rise of Administrative Kingship', pp. 893 ff.

52  Scheyhing, *Amtsgewalt und Bannleihe*, p. 291.

53  Hollister and Baldwin, 'The Rise of Administrative Kingship', p. 893; cf. Mousnier, *La vénalité des offices*, p. 15; and Kubler, 'L'origine de la perpétuité', pp. 43–44.

54  Autrand, 'Offices et officiers royaux', pp. 335–36, has noted that in proceedings against officials before the *Parlement* of Paris, faithfulness was treated as the decisive factor until 1388, professional competency thereafter. Close observance of the regulations was henceforth also demanded from those leasing an office.

55  Mousnier, *La vénalité des offices*, pp. 14, 17.

56  Küchler, 'Ämterkäuflichkeit in den Ländern der Krone Aragons', p. 324.

57  Olivier-Martin, 'La nomination aux offices royaux', p. 490.

58  Riesenberg, *Inalienability of Sovereignty*; Strandberg, *Zur Frage des Veräußerungsverbotes*.

59  On this complex development, see especially Autrand, 'Offices et officiers royaux', pp. 295 ff. The notion of public office originated for the most part in church law; cf. Strandberg, *Zur Frage des Veräußerungsverbotes*, pp. 60–61. The practical effects were notable everywhere around 1400; Demurger, 'Guerre civile et changement du personnel administratif', pp. 218 ff.

developments that did not move significantly beyond the sale of offices in its earlier manifestations. England soon formed the classical example of what was locally called 'brokage', the provision of offices by royal administrators and favourites against high payment. The property rights of the office holder were very pronounced. His dismissal was only possible after proper reimbursement of the expenses.[60] Different notions of public office did not come to the fore. The situation across northern, central, and eastern Europe resembled that of England.[61] In the south and west of continental Europe, on the other hand, we find a very distinct form of trade in offices, which at first did not involve the crown. Governments there sought to build central bureaucracies for their entire territory, in which functions were to be performed according to specific responsibilities and competencies. The contours of an appellate structure developed in the judiciary and some control over the exercise of official duties.[62] At the same time, the notion of public office made steady advances following its formulation in the schools of Roman and church law.[62a] In France, the concept fully prevailed by the early 1400s.[63]

In the same territories, we encounter from the middle of the fourteenth century, seldom at the beginning, the mechanisms we have already noted in connection with the venality of offices in early modernity, such as the resignation in favour of a third party or dispensation at the hands of the ruler from obligations to administer in person or reside in a location. The trend initially affected lesser positions in central and local administrations, specifically among scribes who were attached to an office or court, among bailiffs, and forest guards. Their income largely consisted of fees. They were always organized as a 'college', or guild, which may look at first like a curious coincidence.[64]

I would like to explain it by using an example from among the non-spiritual offices of the Roman Curia.[65] There were roughly one-hundred Scribes at the papal Chancery. From Innocent III (1198–1216), they alone had permission to furnish clean copies of the pope's letters and owed him

---

60 Swart, 'Sale of Offices', pp. 47 ff.

61 In addition to Swart, 'Sale of Offices', pp. 68–70, on the Netherlands, and pp. 89 ff., on the Empire, see the literature cited by Reinhard, 'Staatsmacht als Kreditproblem', p. 291 nn. 9–11.

62 Autrand, 'Offices et officiers royaux', pp. 332 ff.; Kubler, 'L'origine de la perpétuité', pp. 43 ff., 125 ff.

62a Cf. above, p. 164 n. 59; and García Marín, El oficio público en Castilla.

63 Autrand, 'Offices et officiers royaux', p. 338.

64 First noted for France by Olivier-Martin, 'La nomination aux offices royaux', pp. 487 ff.; cf. Mousnier, La vénalité des offices, pp. 8 ff.; Kubler, 'L'origine de la perpétuité', pp. 52 ff. For Venice, Mousnier, 'Le trafic des offices', pp. 389 ff.

65 For a detailed discussion of the evidence presented in the following, see Schwarz, Die Organisation kurialer Schreiberkollegien, pp. 25–73.

loyalty that was not in the way of state employees. They were paid per item by the recipient and treated their revenues as a monopoly. They organized themselves — just as other trades did — in the form of a guild, defending their collective business interests and suppressing competition. Like other guilds, they pursued two additional goals. They sought the greatest possible autonomy for their corporation, especially regarding the internal control of their own affairs. This aimed at securing ordinary disciplinary and supervisory authority for their leaders and the numerical limitation of participants to ensure that each colleague received 'nourishment according to his status'. The 'nourishment' was to be distributed as evenly as possible across the board, which called for the implementation of safeguarding mechanisms. On a regular basis, the college of Scribes collected all fees in one account before sharing them with members, including those who were sick or absent.

It is interesting to see how the Curia dealt with the new phenomenon in legal terms. It turns out that the norms for church benefices were simply transferred. The move was facilitated by superficial resemblances. The law of benefices regulated the spiritual offices of the Church. The benefice gave material support to the office and sustenance to the holder. The office and the benefice were inseparable.[66] For our Scribes, it was plausible to adopt rules governing the assignment of benefices in collegiate churches (a cathedral chapter, for instance). Formal parallels between the organization of Scribes and chapters comprised the fixed number of members as well as the sharing, administration, and regular distribution of revenues. The application of norms created for the law of (spiritual) benefices to non-spiritual offices occurred very gradually.[67] It began with provisions for the scribal positions. From the first third of the fourteenth century onward, the pope issued 'expectancies' for the next available vacancy in the guild. In the following decades, he started to accept resignations 'in favour of a third party' and offered dispensation from official requirements such as the need to exercise the function 'in person'. It is possible to recognize here the same terms that characterized venality in early modern France, indicating how they originated in the canonical law of benefices as we will see in greater detail below. Scribal positions increasingly assumed the character of benefices, as the pope used dispensations from actual administrative duties to incorporate purely nominal members for material support into the guild. The example shows that the collegiate organization of offices on the one hand, and the application of church law to them on the other, enabled the pope to improve his financial situation (by way of saving in salaries).

---

66 Sägmüller, *Lehrbuch des katholischen Kirchenrechts*, pp. 210–11.
67 Schwarz, *Die Organisation kurialer Schreiberkollegien*, pp. 167 ff.

THE VENALITY OF OFFICES　167

In France, offices that — just as with the pope and his Scribes — could be requested from the king were called 'attainable'.[68] They were very popular in the fourteenth century despite their lowly status. The promise of a regular cash flow, again supervised by collegiate boards, the prospect of a lifelong income, and the associated privileges of a royal servant, above all immunity, were held in high esteem.[69] The king granted these subaltern charges 'out of grace' through 'expectancies' or letters of provision, that is, without any fixed reward in return.[70] In the absence of special merits or a recommendation from high places, though, it was always advisable to encourage the king's favour with an appropriate 'gift'.[71] Apart from the conferral of offices, the king was also needed for dispensations and the acceptance of resignations on someone's behalf, which figured as royal graces as well. Again, presents certainly improved the chance of petitions to succeed.

The possibilities of exchange, resale, and leasing generated a lively trade in offices with third parties, which obeyed the laws of the market. The king, however, was not participating, whether as buyer or seller. Mousnier defined these transactions as the 'trafficking' of offices to distinguish them clearly from the venality of public positions in the subsequent period of Absolutism.[72] The former prevailed in France, the Iberian kingdoms, and at the papal Curia in the fourteenth century, while remaining dominant through the fifteenth century in other territories (like Venice).

A new stage in the development toward early modern venality was reached when the ruler began to intervene in the market around 1400. Once he regained control of an office through a vacancy, he would only re-distribute it against payment. This rarely happened due to the widespread resignation in favour of another party. Amounts depended on the current trade value and thus assumed the character of a sales price. The transaction grew out of the prior practice of presenting either (as in France or the Curia) a gift to the ruler, or (as in France and Aragon) a previously agreed and instantly forfeited loan.[73] If the size of both the gift and the loan

---

68　'Offices impétrables'; Autrand, 'Offices et officiers royaux', pp. 313 ff. The distinction between 'elective' and 'attainable' office originated in church law.

69　Autrand, 'Offices et officiers royaux', pp. 297 ff.; Olivier-Martin, 'La nomination aux offices royaux', pp. 498 ff.

70　Autrand, 'Offices et officiers royaux', pp. 316 ff.; Mousnier, *La vénalité des offices*, p. 390; García Marín, *El oficio público en Castilla*, pp. 24 ff.

71　The Latin equivalent, *propina*, still means 'tip' in modern Spanish. Such 'gifts' were likely to leave no trace in the documentation; cf. Schwarz, *Die Organisation kurialer Schreiberkollegien*, pp. 177 ff.

72　Mousnier, 'Le trafic des offices', p. 387.

73　Mousnier, *La vénalité des offices*, p. 63; Schwarz, *Die Organisation kurialer Schreiberkollegien*, pp. 177 ff.; Küchler, 'Ämterkäuflichkeit in den Ländern der Krone Aragons', pp. 328 ff.; in addition to lost loans demanded at the time of conferral, rulers often pressed office holders

168 CHAPTER 6

depended on market estimates, they reflected the profit which holders could expect to derive from the office. Conferral henceforth involved a contract between the ruler and his employee. Arising from customary arrangements enabling the trade among third parties in the first place, the right of resignation in favour of a third party was obviously included in the deal. The payment going along with it took on the character of a fee that the ruler collected as compensation for his loss in future sales. The rate was based on the market price (around ten per cent at the papal Curia).[74]

When the venality of offices was fully established, the crown benefitted from older arrangements to secure large quantities of credit by taking rigorous advantage of its administrative supremacy and ability to dispense. At the start, the conditions were favourable.[75] The revenues were long term, and much of the interest was collected from subjects in the form of fees. To perpetuate the flow of income, guilds of officials had to be created or reorganized for sale; they had to be brought wholesale to market. In 1463, the first of them was established in a single manoeuvre, with the papal Curia again taking the lead. It was set up with the explicit purpose of generating funds for a crusade to reconquer Constantinople from the Ottomans.[76] The heavy expenses of foreign policy also prompted France (because of Louis XII's involvement in Italy from 1494) to resort to the systematic sale of offices.[77] Venice followed suit in 1510 (after the defeat at Agnadello).[78]

We have observed when and where the incipient forms of early modern venality arose and how they evolved. I have also hinted at the causes of their proliferation, which I will now discuss at greater length. It is important to note how little research has been done in this regard. It has become clear that the terminology and individual institutions of venality originated in the law of church benefices. In addition, large part of the new understanding of offices derived from ecclesiastical law as well.[79] It proved to be fundamental for the sale of public positions as a permanent set of fixed rights and obligations, which was endowed with specific types of income. Benefices formed the permanent connection (in objective

---

for credit, which they were not always quick to pay back, p. 333. For source material, see also Schwarz, 'Die Ämterkäuflichkeit an der Römischen Kurie', p. 456 n. 23.

74 See von Hofmann, *Forschungen zur Geschichte der kurialen Behörden* I, p. 179, and elsewhere; Mousnier, *La vénalité des offices*, p. 44.

75 Reinhard, 'Staatsmacht als Kreditproblem', pp. 312–13.

76 On this foundation, the college of Abbreviators, whose positions were for resale (*vacabiles*), see von Hofmann, *Forschungen zur Geschichte der kurialen Behörden* I, pp. 109 ff.; Frenz, 'Die Gründung des Abbreviatorenkollegs'; Schwarz, 'Die Abbreviatoren unter Eugen IV.', pp. 38–40.

77 Cf. Böse, 'Die Ämterkäuflichkeit', p. 94

78 Mousnier, 'Le trafic des offices', pp. 393 ff.

79 See p. 164 n. 59, p. 165 n. 62 above.

perpetuity) between a specific income and an office.[80] Because the income was property of the church and especially because it could not be separated from the spiritual duties, any sales attempt amounted to the crime of simony, in accordance with theories that had been formulated during the Investiture Contest around 1100 to prevent the alienation of ecclesiastical possessions.[81] Benefices were conferred (in subjective perpetuity) for life. Holders could not be stripped of them unless they committed serious infractions of church law. These had to be verified in judicial proceedings leading to the formal denial of tenure.[82]

The holder had usufruct of his office without being able to dispose of it at his own discretion. That right remained with the clerical superior also known as the ordinary sponsor (or 'collator'). He 'provided' the clergy under him with benefices and watched over the proper exercise of functions and clerical conduct. If a beneficed cleric wished to leave his station for some reason, he could renounce to his office. The proper sponsor, or collator, could use his power to dispense for a temporary release from obligations such as residency to facilitate, for example, university studies.[83] Having originated as a defence against lay encroachment, the close tie between benefice and office had loosened by the thirteenth century. In the view of many contemporaries, the benefice had become the principal component, while the office was considered an extra burden. Under the influence of Germanic notions of ownership, entitlement to the benefice strengthened as well.[84] The already familiar resignation in favour of another, that is, the binding appointment of a successor, typically a relative, until twenty days prior to the tenant's death, began to apply to benefices from the late 1200s.[85]

At that time, the law of benefices was also and decisively transformed by the theory of papal 'plenitude of power'.[86] The change in doctrine was threefold. First, the pope as bishop of the universal Church was entitled to exercise the rights of a bishop in each diocese. He could, say, provide benefices in any bishopric whatsoever or reserve the appointment of the next beneficiary. Secondly, the pope as lord over all ecclesiastical property

---

80 Sägmüller, *Lehrbuch des katholischen Kirchenrechts*, p. 211.

81 Heintschel, *The Medieval Concept of an Ecclesiastical Office*, pp. 9–10, 38–39.

82 Sägmüller, *Lehrbuch des katholischen Kirchenrechts*, p. 211.

83 Gillmann, 'Die Resignation der Benefizien', I, especially pp. 523 ff.

84 See Jedin, 'Kann der Papst Simonie begehen?', pp. 271–72.

85 Gillmann, 'Die Resignation der Benefizien', I, pp. 687 ff. Closely related were two additional forms of conditional resignation, that is, permutation and the resignation under reservation of a pension.

86 For a good summary of *plenitudo potestatis*, see Plöchl, *Geschichte des Kirchenrechts*, II, pp. 72 ff.; also, Hinschius, *Das Kirchenrecht der Katholiken und Protestanten*, III, pp. 115 ff. (§ 144). On the fiscal dimensions of this theory, Bauer, 'Die Epochen der Papstfinanz', pp. 469 ff. (reprinted in Bauer, *Gesammelte Aufsätze*, pp. 121 ff.).

and hence all ecclesiastical offices was uniquely empowered to institute and abolish them. And third, he could dispense from nearly every regulation of the canon law due to the plenitude of his power. The combination of both, the law of benefices and the doctrine of papal plenitude of power supplied the foundations, much admired by contemporary rulers, of the systematic control and taxation of church offices by the pope. Those seeking a benefice made sure to visit the Roman Curia to secure the most effective, that is, papal, title or provision for it. The Curia became the destination of everyone eager to obtain additional benefices, or wishing to resign one (against payment of a pension or for the sake of a better position), because only the pope could dispense from the canonical prohibitions.[87] In this way, the benefice trade at the Curia began to flourish, to the known and great dismay of Martin Luther, among others.[88]

How precisely did the reception of church regulations and above all the legal doctrine of benefices prepare the ground for the sale of offices? Under the influence of church law, the notions of office also changed, as mentioned, in the lay sphere.[89] In the belief that jurisdiction originated in God and was spiritual, the position of judges was treated in France as a spiritual one.[90] It became permanent, and holders were appointed for life. They could not be dismissed upon co-optation into the judges' guild and did not have to follow royal orders in the exercise of their duties. This development was not restricted to judges, but extended to all positions with elements of jurisdiction.[91] Toward the end of the fourteenth century, the concept of public offices as permanently instituted (according to Max Weber's administrative and sociological principle of 'perennial' status) and tied to a fixed set of functions had been established.[92] Not until this assimilation of public and church office was achieved, it became possible to view and treat the income of holders analogous to that from benefices.[93] This in turn formed an important pre-requisite of early modern venality.

In addition, the understanding of the ruler's function transformed under the impact of church law, too. The lord claimed for his territory the

---

87 Gillmann, 'Die Resignation der Benefizien', I, pp. 698–99.
88 On the fiscal exploitation of the benefice trade around 1400, see Esch, 'Simonie-Geschäft in Rom', pp. 443 ff.
89 Cf. above, p. 168 n. 79.
90 About the reception of this formulation by Hostiensis, p. 163 n. 44 above.
91 Autrand, 'Offices et officiers royaux', p. 289.
92 See p. 165 n. 63 above.
93 Ullmann, *Principles of Government*, pp. 57 ff.; also, Ourliac, 'Souverainité et lois fondamentales', pp. 29 ff. Loyseau, *Cinq livres du droict des offices*, p. 412 (§ 22), also compared the sovereign power of the French king over offices with papal plenitude, 'possessing above the law all authority over benefices'.

same plenitude of power as the pope.[94] In connection with offices, he attributed to himself full territorial control over taxation and administrative matters. All positions resting on fees payable by the subjects fell under his omnipotence.[95] He could freely and 'by royal grace' create such offices.[96] Owing to his 'gracious generosity', he had to accept limitations regarding the material support of his officials.[97] The fee revenue had to ensure a level of sustenance in line with their social status.[98] Simultaneously, the number of positions could grow through the introduction of new payments or their increase.

This theory gained explosive political force when rulers extended the analogy with papal plenitude of power. Parallel to the pope in view of the bishops, the king treated leading nobility as 'ordinary' collators, whose conferral of offices he could pre-empt with the help of provisions, expectancies, and reservations. The right to create such positions he withheld from them definitively.[99] In France, the king justified his intervention with an original royal right to bestow all offices, which had partially fallen into the hands of great feudal lords by way of longstanding custom or prescription.[100] As a result, those pursuing a fee-based position in a feudal lordship often turned immediately to the king. Their move weakened the claim of local applicants to the point where they approached the royal court themselves, requesting out of caution the provision or confirmation of their appointment in the provinces.[101] When it came to the infringement of rules concerning the appointment to offices, the decision about it reverted to the king. In the law of benefices, this was called the right

---

94 On conceptions of rule under the French kings, Kienast, *Deutschland und Frankreich*, II, pp. 394 ff.; for Castile, García Marín, *El oficio público en Castilla*, pp. 137 ff.

95 Mousnier, 'Le trafic des offices', pp. 390–91.

96 Like the citizens of Venice, the French nobility, but also the urban elites, considered and pursued offices as a source of revenue appropriate to their status. Among the nobles, this tradition reached back to the feudal era. Cf. Mousnier, 'Le trafic des offices', pp. 390–91; for France, see Stocker, 'Office as Maintenance'.

97 García Marín, *El oficio público en Castilla*, p. 32; Autrand, 'Offices et officiers royaux', pp. 317 ff.

98 García Marín, *El oficio público en Castilla*, p. 31; Schwarz, *Die Organisation kurialer Schreiberkollegien*, pp. 39–52.

99 García Marín, *El oficio público en Castilla*, pp. 137 ff. The sources also present the standpoint that apart from the ruler's right to nominate in the last instance, he was entitled to so do in general. For France, see Olivier-Martin, 'La nomination aux offices royaux', pp. 490 ff.; Kubler, 'L'origine de la perpétuité', pp. 112, 151 ff. The difference was made clear in newly conquered areas, where it was easier for the crown to impose itself.

100 This theory is found in Castile; cf. García Marín, *El oficio público en Castilla*, p. 138; and in the Papal States; see de Luca, *Tractatus de officiis vacabilibus*, p. 5. Exercise of the custom rested for de Luca on the ruler's concession.

101 García Marín, *El oficio público en Castilla*, pp. 491–92; Guenée, *Tribunaux et gens de justice*, p. 169.

172    CHAPTER 6

of devolution.[102] By appropriating another prerogative of the pope who alone could accept renunciations and especially resignations in favour of a third party (presupposing dispensation from legal regulations), lay rulers claimed the right to confer offices 'for once' and by way of devolution.[103] They consequently adopted the whole doctrine of papal dispensatory power.[104]

However, not all norms of ecclesiastical law were channelled instantly and without resistance into the regulations governing appointment to offices in the lay sphere. Very close to the standards for benefices were certainly those for non-spiritual positions at the Roman Curia. In France, there was on the one hand the traditional personal relationship between the king and his servants.[105] On the other, the conception of an absolute ruler in Roman law ('what pleases the prince has the force of law') also worked against the principle of life-long tenure and the impossibility of removal.[106] It was characteristic of French notions to have offices (in parallel with the lord's demise in feudal law) become automatically vacant at the time of the king's death. It was therefore inescapable for holders to require formal confirmation by his successor.[107] Appointments were valid only 'at the pleasure of the prince', an expression that, as we have seen, recurred formulaically in his letters of provision.[108]

With support from the highest French lay courts, the *Parlements*, the guilds opposed the king's pretentions to dismiss officials at his own discretion and especially based on what he considered to be administrative misconduct.[109] The most effective instrument they could use was the law of the church and its concept of office, which was employed against the

---

102 On the right of devolution, Hinschius, *Das Kirchenrecht der Katholiken und Protestanten*, III, p. 167 (§ 148a). For its use by rulers, see Olivier-Martin, 'La nomination aux offices royaux', p. 493; García Marín, *El oficio público en Castilla*, p. 137. Another adaptation of the law of benefices were the reservations, including the general reservation of 1321, as well as the expectancies which were omnipresent. The king often accommodated the wishes of feudal lords to have their office converted into a royal one; cf. Mousnier, *La vénalité des offices*, p. 24.

103 Mousnier, *La vénalité des offices*, pp. 44–45; Guenée, *Tribunaux et gens de justice*, p. 169; Kubler, 'L'origine de la perpétuité', pp. 114, 130 n. 24; Olivier-Martin, 'La nomination aux offices royaux', pp. 498–99.

104 As is evident from the inclusion of disclaimers (*non obstat*) in letters of nomination, whereby the king expressly suspended valid rules that normally would have opposed acquisition of the office by the nominee; cf. Olivier-Martin, 'La nomination aux offices royaux', p. 496; Kubler, 'L'origine de la perpétuité', p. 144. In other cases, he explicitly dispensed from the norms, see p. 159 n. 18 above.

105 Mousnier, *La vénalité des offices*, pp. 25–26; Kubler, 'L'origine de la perpétuité', p. 144.

106 'Quod principi placuit legis habet vigorem'; cf. Kienast, *Deutschland und Frankreich*, II, p. 414.

107 Mousnier, *La vénalité des offices*, pp. 25–26; Kubler, 'L'origine de la perpétuité', p. 282.

108 Mousnier, *La vénalité des offices*, p. 8 and elsewhere; Kubler, 'L'origine de la perpétuité', pp. 197 ff.

109 Autrand, 'Offices et officiers royaux', pp. 324 ff.

ruler as well.[110] After protracted disputes, the king gave in by conceding in principle the impossibility to remove state employees in an ordinance of 1467.[111] In practice, however, he frequently went against it. Only venality helped attain permanent tenure for the officials.

Since the middle of the fifteenth century, rulers embraced the new concepts of public and royal office to raise additional funds, first in concealed fashion and then ever more openly. They did so primarily because of the discrepancy between their economic needs and their political leverage. Their expenses had increased enormously, while there was no room to raise the ordinary income without prior consent from the estates of clergy, nobility, and towns, or against resistance from the 'nations' within the Church.[112] Some of the revenues had even diminished significantly. In France, for instance, the Hundred Years War had ruined the royal finances. Among the expenses, the largest portion of the budget went into the expansion of central administration and the wars with Burgundy and in Italy.[113] At the Roman Curia, income was strained by the Great Schism, followed by the Reform Councils and papal agreements with various lay nations in the form of concordats. Costs had gone up dramatically owing to the reconquest and consolidation of the Papal State, hegemonial Italian politics, and the demands of public display placed on the Renaissance papacy.[114] In Castile, civil war had strongly reduced royal wealth. The conquest of Muslim territory and the growth of central government added to the deficit.[115]

An increase in revenues was only possible by taking advantage of royal prerogatives, including the elevation to noble rank, academic promotions, and legal mandates.[116] For the pope, dispensations were also an important source of gain along with indulgences.[117] Aside from these lucrative rights,

---

110 Loyseau, *Cinq livres du droict des offices*, p. 413 and elsewhere, justified the rejection of deposition for state employees or their automatic suspension at the ruler's death with church rules; also, Kubler, 'L'origine de la perpétuité', pp. 146–47; and especially Autrand, 'Offices et officiers royaux', p. 330 and elsewhere.

111 *Ordonnances des rois de France*, XVII, pp. 25–26; also, in *Recueil général des anciennes lois françaises*, ed. by Jourdan and others, IX, pp. 541 ff.; for historical precedents, see Kubler, 'L'origine de la perpétuité', pp. 157 ff.

112 Reinhard, 'Staatsmacht als Kreditproblem', p. 304. On the profound effects of the conciliar decrees during the reform period, Bauer, 'Die Epochen der Papstfinanz', pp. 475 ff. (reprinted in Bauer, *Gesammelte Aufsätze*, pp. 126 ff.).

113 Reinhard, 'Staatsmacht als Kreditproblem', p. 307.

114 Cf. p. 173 n. 112 above; and Reinhard, 'Staatsmacht als Kreditproblem', p. 307, with n. 92.

115 García Marín, *El oficio público en Castilla*, p. 144. Konetzke, 'Territoriale Grundherrschaft und Landesherrschaft'.

116 Reinhard, 'Staatsmacht als Kreditproblem', pp. 310–11.

117 Income from dispensations, indulgences, compositions, and the sale of offices was administered by the Datary. The revenues were considered tied to the dispensatory powers of the pope and lumped together under the technical term of *spiritualia*. The exact amount

174    CHAPTER 6

popes and lay rulers controlled the sale of offices, which rested on their authority over them and their sovereign power to dispense. At the Roman Curia, income from this source amounted by the end of the fifteenth century to roughly thirty per cent of all revenues.[118] In France, the share was similar in the early 1500s.[119] It continued to grow in both cases.

Supply obviously presupposed adequate demand. On the part of the buyers, there were various motivations contributing to the development and expansion of early modern venality. They can be identified as follows. Some of the offices were very expensive. They were not affordable unless families pooled their financial resources and took out big loans.[120] Interest in these positions was undoubtedly great and predicated on the significant presence of a monetary economy in western and southern Europe. Little is currently known about the economic and social situation of the buyers. Only detailed socio-historical inquiries can shed further light on it.[121] Those who purchased an office not seldom left their familiar local and social settings in pursuit of upward mobility. Horizontal and vertical moves in terms of status formed a precondition for the sales mechanism and promoted it.

The acquisition of an office satisfied not only the quest for regular income and other material benefits, but also afforded social rank and the privileges going with it, certainly one of the main causes rendering the positions attractive. Express statements about the motivation of buyers are unlikely to emerge from more detailed research, with sources being reticent about the subject because it was problematic for contemporaries. Another pre-requisite for the development and spread of early modern venality was the existence of mechanisms that secured purchasers the unrestricted advantages of ownership once it had been obtained. This was the function of the guilds formed by officials. As I hope to have shown in connection with the papal Scribes, they were indispensable for the collection, management, and redistribution of fees as well as the safeguarding of corporate interests against the ruler.[122] As a result, new categories of offices

---

depended on the intervention of church leaders and varied greatly; cf. Partner, 'The "Budget" of the Roman Church'.

118 Partner, 'The "Budget" of the Roman Church', p. 269.

119 Mousnier, *La vénalité des offices*, p. 67.

120 For a nice case, Reinhard, 'Ämterhandel in Rom', pp. 58–59.

121 Reinhard, '*Staatsmacht und Staatsgewalt*', pp. 313–14; this is the particular focus of the research project mentioned above, p. 161 n. 33.

122 This aspect has hardly been noted in scholarship; but see von Hofmann, *Forschungen zur Geschichte der kurialen Behörden*, I, pp. 109 ff.

including those of purely fictitious character always assumed the form of colleges.[123]

In this context, the new understanding officials were increasingly able to impose on their relationship with the ruler was also relevant. Due to the practice of trading offices with third parties and especially based on early forms of sale, buyers grew ever more convinced that the benefits of their position constituted interest on the capital they had invested in the first place. Progressively, this interpretation led them to viewing their lord in a different light, whereby they as owners of the position appeared as partners in a sales contract. The jurists of the fifteenth and sixteenth centuries reinforced that view. It was widespread opinion that an unwelcome official could not be removed even when the king returned the original payment for the position, because just as with an actual sales contract, dissolution was always contingent on the consent of both parties.[124] By contrast, the crown insisted, at least in the wording of its documents, that the transaction figured as a loan and the two sides as creditor and debtor. Ultimately, though, royal employers had to accept the constantly advancing adversarial notion, if they wished to foster demand for their offices in the future. Venality hence cemented the impossibility to remove state employees.

The institutionalized and legalized sale of public offices by the ruler is a characteristic institution of early modern Europe. As in other cultures, their monetized conferral and trade also existed in the European Middle Ages. I hope to have demonstrated where they differed and how the early modern practice could not have developed without the institutions or the theological and juristic doctrines of the medieval period.

---

123 Beginning with Julius II (1503–1513), the Curia started to offer guild memberships that constituted pure loans; von Hofmann, *Forschungen zur Geschichte der kurialen Behörden*, I, pp. 159 ff.

124 De Luca, *Tractatus de officiis vacabilibus*, p. 20, distinguished in response to the question of whether the ruler could dismiss an official through reimbursement and against his will by denying it for higher offices because of the existence of a reciprocal contract; for lower positions, he permitted removal under three conditions. If there was just cause, the reimbursement reflected market value, and the employee was compensated in his social status as well, p. 34 (§ 34). On the dissolution of offices that were for sale, see pp. 37 ff. (§ 14). Loyseau, *Cinq livres du droict des offices*, pp. 411 (§ 17), 413 (§ 24), and elsewhere, spoke of a contract in good faith requiring mutual consent for cancellation.

CHAPTER 7

# The Roman Curia from the Great Schism
# to the Reform Councils (1378–1447)

Briefly put, there is a nexus between the 'origins' and 'existence' of an institution on the one hand, and its 'crisis' and 'reform' on the other.[1] It is understood as the typical trajectory of institutional history to have a phase of relative stability followed by a crisis, which contemporaries addressed or sought to overcome with the help of reform.[2] In the volume originally including the present essay, Bernhard Schimmelpfennig has treated the papacy and the Curia of the High Middle Ages. He concluded that the papacy was 'without doubt and in various aspects an institution'. And yet, he was hesitant to define it as 'altogether institutionalized'.[3] He applied his statement to the high medieval period, which he extended to the beginning of the Avignonese period (in 1309). The time of the papacy in Avignon (from 1309 to 1378) witnessed institutional consolidation as well as further institutionalization, especially from the perspective of the Curia.[4]

The successive era of papal history starting with the Great Schism of 1378 is commonly viewed by scholarship as a time of crisis.[5] It can certainly be understood as an age of reform, although not in the sense of a reform occurring in fact. There were instead reform demands, proposals, and debates, taking such hold of contemporaries that it is not far-fetched to speak (with Francis Rapp) of a fifteenth-century obsession.[6] In these calls for change, the papacy and the Curia figured as primary targets. Given the colloquial use of the term, there is a stronger manifestation of crisis in a schism on the papal throne than in conflict over accession in a lay monarchy. The struggle between two contenders, who both maintained to be the rightful pope diminished the authority of the papacy. Each competitor excommunicated the other, declared the opponent a heretic,

---

1 Cf. Melville, 'Institutionen als geschichtswissenschaftliches Thema'.
2 For further explanation and conceptual criticism, see the following essays by Baumgartner, 'Institutionen und Krise'; Miethke, 'Politische Theorie in der Krise der Zeit'; and Schreiner, 'Dauer, Niedergang und Erneuerung klösterlicher Observanz'; all in *Institutionen und Geschichte*, ed. by Melville.
3 Schimmelpfennig, 'Das Papsttum im hohen Mittelalter'.
4 Schimmelpfennig, *Das Papsttum*, pp. 225 ff.
5 Tüchle, 'Abendländisches Schisma'; Heimann, 'Akzente und Aspekte', pp. 55 ff.
6 Rapp, *L'Église et la vie religieuse en Occident*, p. 208.

and led crusades against him. In order to keep their subjects and take followers from the adversary, they had to compete for support from secular rulers by granting them important concessions.

All of this applied particularly to the Great Schism of 1378.[7] It struck the Church unexpectedly, because the mechanism of papal elections had been perfected to such a degree that contested outcomes were deemed impossible.[8] The breach lasted longer, concerned a much greater number of people, and was seen as more dangerous than previous schisms, because in the intervening years the Church had become fundamentally dependent on the papacy both in terms of law and orthodoxy. The crisis was closely tied to ideas of reform, moreover. Contemporaries believed that reform was indispensable to overcome the Schism, which appeared to them as a symptom rather than the cause. Ironically, Pope Urban VI's desire for reform of the Roman Curia provoked the split in the first place, and once it had occurred, the same desire spread everywhere.[9] The reform debate — primarily understood as a 'reformation of the head and the Curia' — was institutionalized in 1417, when the implementation of its findings was delegated to the Council of Constance.[10] Convened to end the Schism, it threatened to undermine the monarchical governance of the Church from the papal perspective, aggravating the crisis even further.[11]

The scope and intensity of institutionalized reform discussions at the Councils attest to widespread consensus that the papacy and especially the papal Curia deserved much criticism and were in dire need of repair.[12] If we accept the above-mentioned typical progression from crisis to reform, or more specifically from crisis to criticism, to reform pressures, and the eventual implementation of change, several questions arise. Is the notion of something 'warranting criticism and reform' identical with the

---

7 For bibliography, see Schimmelpfennig, *Das Papsttum*, pp. 330 ff.

8 The last schism to occur previously was more than two centuries old at the time — discounting the one between Nicholas (V) and John XXII from 1328–1330. For a brief history of papal elections, see Fuhrmann, 'Die Wahl des Papstes'. On the origins of the Great Schism in detail, cf. *Genèse et débuts*, ed. by Favier. Technically speaking, schismatic elections were less than likely in 1378, because right before Gregory XI died and in view of hardened factionalism among the cardinals, the pope had changed the law in favour of a simple majority of voters; cf. Dykmans, 'La bulle de Grégoire XI'.

9 Emphasized by Pasztor, 'La Curia Romana', pp. 33 ff.; and Guillemain, 'Cardinaux et société curiale', p. 20.

10 *Conciliorum Oecumenicorum Decreta*, ed. by Alberigo and others, p. 444, line 6 (of 30 October 1417).

11 The popes of the Schism viewed the Council as a body of high clerics and universities, fundamentally at odds with the papal position; cf. Favier, 'Le Grand Schisme', pp. 7 ff. This was even more the case after the events at the Council of Basel.

12 On discussions about curial reform, see von Hofmann, *Forschungen zur Geschichte der kurialen Behörden*, I, pp. 5 ff.; and Haller, *Papsttum und Kirchenreform*, pp. 3–22, 154–63. For the fifteenth century, also Jedin, *Geschichte des Konzils von Trient*, I, pp. 93–102.

concept of 'being in crisis'? Are we confronted with a 'crisis of acceptance', anticipating actual manifestations of institutional dysfunction? What is the connection between reform proposals and the operational state of the institution in question? Did reformers aim at overcoming serious institutional defects or administrative incompetency? And to what extent were these eliminated in the end? It is difficult to answer these queries, not least because the term 'crisis' is very flexible. Apart from its classical, medical, legal, or military meanings, it permits nearly limitless application to difficult situations of any kind.[13]

Before I return to the issue in my conclusion, I would like to highlight important structural transformations that affected the papal Curia from the beginning of the Great Schism in 1378. The Curia was not just an 'administrative apparatus'.[14] It was the court of the supreme spiritual leader, the pope. The following treatment is guided by a socio-historical interest in life at the court. It does not offer an account of operations in the strict bureaucratic sense. To be sure, it is impossible here to present the social history of the late medieval Curia comprehensively.[15] Certain themes will not be addressed at any length.[16] They include the importance of the institution for matters of liturgy and ceremony.[17] The governance of the papal territories in central Italy is also omitted from view.[18] In addition, it must be noted that quite a few of my observations remain in need of further verification.

---

13 Cf. Baumgartner, 'Institutionen und Krise'.

14 While focusing on the Apostolic Chancery, the discussion of bureaucratic aspects from the time of the Schism by von Hofmann, *Forschungen zur Geschichte der kurialen Behörden*, is still unsurpassed; for the preceding centuries, Schimmelpfennig, *Das Papsttum*.

15 A social history of the Curia is lacking, although I have made a first attempt in Schwarz, 'Kurie, römische, im Mittelalter'. Schimmelpfennig, *Das Papsttum*, is of supplementary value. The fourteenth century has been covered by Guillemain, *La cour pontificale d'Avignon*. A socio-historical study reflecting the latest state of research and adjusting its focus to the limitations of what a single scholar can accomplish is Schuchard, *Die Deutschen an der päpstlichen Kurie*. For the thirteenth century, see the contributions by Antonio Paravicini Bagliani, for example, his article, 'Il personale della Curia romana'.

16 I am grateful to Kaspar Elm for calling my attention to three additional areas of competency, the late medieval Curia as a place of study, as a disciplinary authority for clerics, and as responsible for the reform of the religious orders.

17 On the liturgical and ceremonial aspects, Schimmelpfennig, *Das Papsttum*, with extensive bibliography; Schimmelpfennig, *Die Zeremonienbücher*, Index; Schimmelpfennig, 'Die Funktion des Papstpalastes'. After coming to a complete halt at Avignon, the Schism brought by necessity a return to itinerant papal rule, serving to promote claims to power in the propaganda wars with rival obediences. An example is the account of the Apostolic Chamberlain, François de Conzié, in *Rerum italicarum scriptores*, ed. by Muratori, III, cols 777–808, who also composed a ritual for the solemn entry of the pope into a city, cols 808–10; again ed. by Dykmans, 'D'Avignon à Rome', pp. 237–43.

18 On the administration of the papal territories, Partner, *The Lands of St Peter*.

The Schism had a great impact on the revenue of popes and officials at their respective Curia.[19] This in turn had significant effects on curial society. The members of the Curia earned income from various sources, which differed not only in amount but also in composition. To begin with, there were monetary transactions, payments made in kind, and residential accommodation provided by the Apostolic Chamber.[20] Very few curial residents had proceeds from all of them and not many relied on them alone.[21] Secondly, the papal household (*familia*), the cardinals and their entourage, the staff of the Chamber, and others received part of the pope's dues and charitable receipts.[22] There were also the fees officials charged for their services. I will say more about them below. Fourth, petitioners coming to the Curia gave tips, gifts, and pensions in hopes of facilitating the processing of their requests.[23] Fifth, curial staff held benefices far away from Rome (*in partibus*), typically in their place of origin, which formed the basis of their influence there and accrued profits necessitating transfer to the Curia. Some participated in speculative investments as well. They involved benefices or rights to them and promised future gain through brokerage deals.[24]

---

19 In general, Favier, *Les finances pontificales*; reviewed by Esch, in *Göttingische gelehrte Anzeigen*, 221 (1969), 133–59; also, Favier, 'La Chambre apostolique'.

20 Most payments in kind changed during the Avignonese period into monetary ones; cf. Schimmelpfennig, *Das Papsttum*, p. 229. Certain items marking special occasions were kept, including provisions of cloth for a restricted group of persons twice a year, which were increasingly monetized as well.

21 Rather than serving as pay, the assessment of dietary needs depended on one's status and its appropriate upkeep. Among the (impracticable!) reforms proposed at the Council of Constance, there was also the idea of a regular salary for curial officials.

22 The dues for promotions by the papal consistory (*servitia minuta*) were distributed among certain curial employees according to varying ratios, with four parts going to the household members and officials of the pope and one to the *familiares* of the cardinals; Clergeac, *La Curie et les bénéficiers consistoriaux*, pp. 157–87. New *servitia* were imposed by the pope in the fifteenth century. There were also the *iocalia*, or gifts for the admission of incorporated and other staff to papal service, which at times was purely honorary; see Baluzius, *Vitae paparum Avenionensium*, ed. by Mollat, IV, pp. 117–18; from the 1400s, there was also a contribution for the employees of the Apostolic Chamber, p. 164. Some took a share of the fees for the pallium, marking elevations to the rank of archbishop or bishop and taxed from the mid-fifteenth century, pp. 208–12; or for the *sacra*, payable upon consecration of a prelate at the Curia, pp. 188–207; Schimmelpfennig, *Die Zeremonienbücher*, p. 196. In addition, there was a string of differing disbursements for various recipients, depending on the occasion.

23 Reports by proctors furnish an interesting source in this regard, cf. Segrè, 'I dispacci di Cristoforo da Piacenza'. The payments indicate for historians the perceived or real importance of individuals; also p. 190 n. 88 below.

24 The greatest proportion of benefices in the *Repertorium Germanicum* (below, p. 194 n. 111) must be considered as assets of this type. This did not mean, however, that they could be bought and sold freely to the highest bidder, as their acquisition and possession was tightly regulated; cf. Schwarz, 'Klerikerkarrieren und Pfründenmarkt'; Meyer, 'Der deutsche Pfründenmarkt im Spätmittelalter'; and the fundamental study by Meyer, *Zürich und Rom*.

THE ROMAN CURIA (1378–1447)    181

The Schism caused a reduction of revenues for curial members, directly and indirectly. The popes, after all, received contributions only from those parts of the Western Church which fell under their control. Conversely, expenses went up due to demands arising from the conflict with papal rivals. The pope's diminishing income implied that payments by the Apostolic Chamber to curial clerics were no longer guaranteed. Simultaneously, their share in papal proceeds from taxation and tips became smaller, as popes during the Schism sought to preserve their prestige and claim to office by maintaining the size of the Curia whenever possible. Moreover, there were various ways in which the income of curial clergy was directly affected. Benefices located in territory loyal to the opposite camp, for example, were simply lost; even the transfer of money from regions within the respective pope's obedience often failed to go through.[25] The number of petitioners reaching the Curia decreased during the Schism as well, lowering fee revenue and with it the amount of gifts and pensions. Unwillingness to meet monetary obligations was also widespread because of the contentious situation.

These general tendencies, to be sure, did not affect all popes and areas (or 'obediences') adhering to one of them during the Schism. The Avignonese Pope Clement VI, for example, fared comparatively well, and so did Benedict (XIII) early in his pontificate (from 1394), until he lost part of his church provinces in 1398, 1408, and 1409. Both survived in fiscal terms, because they could count on the French church as their principal source of income.[26] The proceeds consisted of tributes they collected whenever there was papal involvement in the transfer of benefices from one holder to another, concerning, for example, so-called consistorial and certain lesser benefices which were not conferred by the local prelate known as the 'ordinary'.[27] If benefices were passed on or sold through 'resignation in favour or a third party', papal dispensation formed a prerequisite that also generated a steady monetary inflow.[28] In France, the circulation of benefices was intense, and the Curia served as the central marketplace for them.[29] The Roman obedience under Urban VI, on the

---

25 See below, pp. 191–92, with n. 96.

26 Favier, *Les finances pontificales*, pp. 579 ff., 587 ff.

27 *Servitia* and other income from consistorial benefices, annates from lesser ones. Against canonical norms, the Avignonese papacy exploited vacancies fiscally; cf. Favier, *Les finances pontificales*, pp. 586 ff.

28 Due to the defect of simony, only the pope was entitled to accept such resignations. He alone could dispose of benefices resigned in this way, see Gillmann, 'Die Resignation der Benefizien'. The papacy would reassign them upon receipt of an appropriate 'payment of recognition' (or *compositio*); cf. below, p. 187.

29 Favier, *Les finances pontificales*, p. 608. Already during the Avignonese period (1309–1378), the French church carried the burden of papal fiscal policies; for precise numbers, see *Die Einnahmen der apostolischen Kammer unter Innozenz VI.*, ed. by Hoberg, II, pp. 34*–35*.

182    CHAPTER 7

other hand, controlled regions with less profitable benefices and a lower frequency of exchange between tenants, which in some cases had not even been instituted as a practice. Moreover, Urban VI was compelled to restore revenue channels, as the Apostolic Chamber with its staff of collectors had altogether abandoned him for his rival.[30] The Roman popes had to cope with enduring financial difficulties.[31] Their Curia formed the core of the Pisan Curia, which in turn became the papal Curia in the period of the great Councils. The measures introduced under Urban VI and Boniface IX (1389–1404) to resolve the fiscal challenges remained in effect well beyond the end of the Schism (in 1415), which invites us to focus in the following on the Roman rather than Avignonese papacy.

Which options did the popes have when it came to untapping new revenue? Boniface IX proved to be inventive as the first to exploit systematically his powers of pardon in the judicial forum. He resorted to so-called 'compositions', a premium the pope would collect for granting special 'graces' exempting from canonical regulations.[32] He complemented papal offerings in this sector, soon meeting with considerable demand.[33] They extended, for instance, to incorporations, privileges, and 'mirroring' indulgences (ad instar), which secured for the receiving churches the spiritual favours of important pilgrimage sites.[34] Members of the Curia also benefitted from these transactions. They gained not so much because the Apostolic Chamber paid them a share, which would have been very small anyway. Instead, they took advantage of fees for the production of charters and procedural documentation, which were due to them, or rather to their guilds, and split evenly among associates.[35] These administrative charges

---

30  Pasztor, 'La Curia Romana', pp. 35 ff.; Guillemain, 'Cardinaux et société curiale', p. 27; Favier, *Les finances pontificales*, pp. 136 ff., 590 ff.; Esch, 'Simonie-Geschäft in Rom', pp. 443 ff.

31  Favier, *Les finances pontificales*, pp. 136 ff., has called the practice 'Roman improvisation'.

32  Cf. Reinhard, 'Ämterhandel in Rom', p. 43.

33  My collection of papal letters from Lower Saxony between 1198 and 1500 (below, p. 195 n. 117) confirms the findings of Favier, *Les finances pontificales*, pp. 591 ff., 609, in the records of the Apostolic Chamber. Boniface IX's fiscal ingeniousness was unparalleled. He is known as the first to have used indulgences for the jubilee as a source of income for the papacy, offering them also to those who could not, or preferred not to, come to Rome in person or during the year in question, and if they paid the pope their appropriate travel expenses. In addition, he repeated the indulgence for the jubilee of 1400. Without qualms, he granted dispensations and canonical exemptions, commuted vows, and sold licenses to trade with Muslim territories against general prohibition, while advertising his intervention for propaganda purposes.

34  Frankl, 'Papstschisma und Frömmigkeit'.

35  Such organizational form was characteristic of all curial staff participating in the older tributes and gifts mentioned above, p. 180 n. 22. Other residents of the Curia without bureaucratic function followed suit and formed rudimentary incorporations to manage their own fees, including the subdeacons, Protonotaries, and (from Nicholas V) the secretaries. For an example from the thirteenth century, see Gottlob, *Die Servitientaxe im 13. Jahrhundert*, pp. 158–61, concerning the *mappularii* and *addextratores*.

were very high. As elsewhere, they depended primarily on the value of the recorded matter, not just on the labour of putting it into writing.[36] Beginning with Boniface IX, there is evidence of additional charges petitioners had to disburse. Apart from the tax for scribal services, for instance, a smaller amount 'for the work' was introduced.[37] It is important to note that such quasi-fees were not imposed by papal decree, as the reform treatises critically observed. Nonetheless, the popes clearly tolerated them.[38]

Despite manifold measures to improve the income stream, however, the popes of the Schism, and particularly those on the Roman — and subsequently Pisan — side suffered from a persistent lack of funds that at times became very acute. To overcome shortfalls, it was possible to ask the curial residents for help.[39] The papacy began to exact large sums from applicants to offices under papal control at the Curia.[40] In this way, popes adopted the practice of lay rulers, while at Avignon before the Schism it had only been customary for candidates to offer an appropriate gift (*propina*).[41] In fiscal emergencies, the pontiff was not content to rely on vigorous assistance from relatives and 'friends' in his entourage.[42] He appealed for aid to all members of the Curia, whose oaths of loyalty obligated them to come to his rescue given the circumstances.[43] They were required to pay special taxes or provide mandatory credit with modalities of eventual repayment that must have seemed quite remote.[44] Refusal was nonetheless impossible, because the contributors could be forced with threats of incarceration.[45] Payable amounts depended in principle on the

---

36 Schwarz, *Die Organisation kurialer Schreiberkollegien*, pp. 29, 261–62.

37 See von Hofmann, *Forschungen zur Geschichte der kurialen Behörden*, I, p. 260; II, p. 207.

38 Cf. von Hofmann, *Forschungen zur Geschichte der kurialen Behörden*, II, pp. 246 ff.

39 This was common usage at contemporary courts; Favier, *Finance et fiscalité*, pp. 274 ff. It already occurred in the late Avignonese period under Gregory XI, who mobilized all his resources for the war with Florence; cf. Segrè, 'I dispacci di Cristoforo da Piacenza', pp. 44 ff. I have noted the same for the time after the Schism. The pope taxed the corporation of Scribes at the Chancery in 1445–1446 and demanded a tenth from curial employees in 1452. This differed from their customary obligation (especially in the Chamber) to fend off momentary insolvencies.

40 The popes did not appoint to all curial offices by any means, but often did so in competition with the heads of administrative units; see below, p. 188 n. 75.

41 Schwarz, *Die Organisation kurialer Schreiberkollegien*, pp. 177 ff.

42 Esch, 'Das Papsttum unter der Herrschaft der Neapolitaner', pp. 784 ff., on the creditors of the popes during the Schism, see Favier, *Les finances pontificales*, pp. 564 ff.

43 The Curia distinguished between oaths of loyalty and others promising only correct conduct in office; cf. Schwarz, *Die Organisation kurialer Schreiberkollegien*, pp. 72–73. Their wording (for the Chancery) is printed in *Die päpstlichen Kanzleiordnungen*, ed. by Tangl, pp. 33–52. A curial book of oaths does not survive before the time of Paul II (1464–1471).

44 Favier, *Les finances pontificales*, pp. 530–31, 564.

45 Favier, *Les finances pontificales*, p. 530, with n. 6.

extent of papal support someone had received in the past or could expect in the future.[46]

With regard to the collection and conditions of papal repayment, debtors without standing were disadvantaged, whether they were insignificant individuals or lacked the backing of a powerful person.[47] They were dependent on protection, which they found in a patron and possibly also in their guild.[48] At the Curia, office staff regularly associated in corporations to protect their administrative monopoly and privileges, to distribute fee income evenly among themselves, and, as in the present context, fight for the elimination or reduction of taxes while sharing, if needed, the burden among guild members.[49] The fiscal pressures arising during the Schism led to further proliferation of these formally constituted groups of curial administrators.[50] In view of the heavy expenses, the pope had to offer meaningful compensation to his staff. The fiscal emergency called for special feats of loyalty, service, and sacrifice. To reassure officials, he had to go along with efforts to exploit their administrative offices for maximum profit. Members of the Curia who provided services to third parties were in the best position to increase their income, as immediate contact with petitioners improved chances to charge extra fees, if not to extract bribes.[51]

Papal concessions in that regard took several specific forms. First, the rights of office-holders were strengthened. As early as during the Great Schism, a good number of administrative positions started to be conferred with permanent tenure. Others followed in the years of the papal break-up with the Council of Basel (from 1438), so that staff appointments came

---

46 Accordingly, we find among the creditors making high investments apart from relatives and friends especially the cardinals, members of the pope's inner circle like secretaries, chamberlains, and servants of the Apostolic Chamber and Chancery, who looked for advancement at the Curia; Favier, *Les finances pontificales*, pp. 566 ff.; Segrè, 'I dispacci di Cristoforo da Piacenza', pp. 44, 48.

47 For evidence, Favier, *Les finances pontificales*, pp. 537 ff., 555, 560, 562, 564–65.

48 Cristoforo da Piacenza reports that the Scribes (probably of the Chancery, because he speaks of one-hundred) each loaned one-hundred francs in 1373, thereby sharing the tax imposed on their guild among members; Segrè, 'I dispacci di Cristoforo da Piacenza', pp. 48, 44 (for a smaller sum). The total of 10,000 francs was considerable, but modest in comparison to the payments (of up to 60,000) by important individuals (a papal relative). Cf. Favier, *Les finances pontificales*, p. 568, for a loan from the guild of 1382; a few of the Scribes, probably belonging to the pope's friends, offered larger amounts.

49 On the corporate organisation of the guilds for staff, von Hofmann, *Forschungen zur Geschichte der kurialen Behörden*, I, pp. 109 ff.; Schwarz, *Die Organisation kurialer Schreiberkollegien*, pp. 151 ff.

50 See von Hofmann, *Forschungen zur Geschichte der kurialen Behörden*, I, pp. 109 ff.; Schwarz, 'Ämterkäuflichkeit, eine Institution des Absolutismus', p. 189 (English translation above, p. 174).

51 Emphasized by von Hofmann, *Forschungen zur Geschichte der kurialen Behörden*, I, pp. 257 ff., 301 ff.

THE ROMAN CURIA (1378–1447)  185

to be treated like those to a church benefice.[52] The move allowed officials to exchange or resign their position in favour of a third party, which effectively amounted to a sale.[53] Roland Mousnier has described this activity as 'the trafficking of offices'.[54] Through regular papal involvement, it transformed into a full-blown business.[55] Secondly, the privileges tied to office-holding were improved.[56] They sometimes brought preferment in the acquisition and possession of benefices, or afforded enhanced curial status as a papal household member (*familiaris*) or permanent table companion (*continuus commensalis pape*), two honourable titles carrying material benefits as well.[57]

Third, there was the possibility of papal dispensation from canonical restrictions and regulations such as the prohibition to accumulate offices.[58] Licenses allowed recipients to leave the exercise of their official duties to a substitute.[59] The pope also granted permissions to receive a stipend while

---

52 Schwarz, 'Ämterkäuflichkeit, eine Institution des Absolutismus', p. 185 (English translation above, p. 168). Until 1450, the (lower) curial positions, attaining corporate status gradually or through express conferral, included the Scribes of the Chancery and Penitentiary, the Scribes and clerics working at the registers of petitions and bulls, the staff of the *Audientia litterarum contradictarum*, the *bullarium*, the court of the Chamber, the Notaries, and toward the end of the period also the clerics there, the Couriers, and the Sergeants at arms. Subjective perpetuity was withheld from some of the household charges, which terminated with the pope's death and had to be reappointed by his successor, such as the various types of gatekeepers. Apart from the clerics of the Chamber, petitions for all these offices appear in the papal registers around 1440.

53 Resignations 'in favour of a third party' are initially found in the corporations of Scribes, before 1400 in the colleges of the Notaries at the Rota and the court of the Chamber as well. This is what the critics of the reform period had in mind when they complained about 'the sale of offices' around 1400. It rapidly spread thereafter to all positions mentioned above, p. 185 n. 52.

54 Cited after Mousnier, 'Le trafic des offices à Venise', p. 552; reprinted in Mousnier, *La plume, la faucille, et le marteau*, p. 387; cf. Schwarz, 'Ämterkäuflichkeit'.

55 I attempted a sketch of this in Schwarz, 'Die Ämterkäuflichkeit an der Römischen Kurie'.

56 For a survey of the curial privileges, cf. von Hofmann, *Forschungen zur Geschichte der kurialen Behörden*, I, pp. 289 ff.

57 In 1455, for example, the pope compensated the clerics of the Chamber, who had complained about his treatment of offices as a threat to their own rights, by appointing them as papal chaplains and as his continuous table companions.

58 Schwarz, *Die Organisation kurialer Schreiberkollegien*, pp. 58 ff. A typical manifestation of this was the prohibition to combine notarial positions at the courts of the Rota and the Chamber; cf. *Regulae cancellariae apostolicae*, ed. by von Ottenthal, p. 200 (§ 64). The norm was not motivated by concern about excessive workloads, but by the high income of the positions, capable of supporting two. Originally, there were rules against accumulation based on functional reasons, which by the fifteenth century had lost their meaning altogether; von Hofmann, *Forschungen zur Geschichte der kurialen Behörden*, I, pp. 197 ff.

59 The right to exercise an office through substitutes was sometimes conferred together with them, for example, the position of Scribe to certain secretaries, to the *taxatores* in the *bullarium*, to the higher charges in the register of papal bulls, and to the Notaries at the court of the Chamber and (later) the Rota.

being absent from the place that generated it.[60] In this way, he provided for curial officials already entitled to a salary from the Apostolic Chamber.[61] They collected a fee-based income as (inactive) members of a guild of administrative professionals at the Curia.[62] Fourth, the papacy developed a habit of tolerating excesses like the extortion of unwarranted payments. The practice was widespread, perhaps or in part because office-holders really depended on it and superiors took advantage of it as well.[63] It would be overly simplistic to assume that insatiable curial greed always acted as the main cause. Finally, the ever-increasing acceptance or confirmation of fees for administrative services that were previously free of charge also forms part of this context.[64] Their proliferation presupposed, of course, that the demand for curial intervention was not negatively affected.

The transformation of curial positions into quasi-benefices caused conflict over appointments and led to profound structural changes in the papal administration. Not only the pope, but also other leaders at the Curia including the Apostolic Chamberlain, the Vice-Chancellor, the Great Penitentiary, and the heads of individual compartments such as the judges at the courts of the Apostolic Chamber, the Audience, etc. could confer certain offices by themselves.[65] They all started to grant appointment to

---

60 These dispensations could undermine discipline, such as those placing the offices of a superior and his servant in one and the same hand; cf. von Hofmann, *Forschungen zur Geschichte der kurialen Behörden*, I, pp. 192–93.

61 See von Hofmann, *Forschungen zur Geschichte der kurialen Behörden*, I, pp. 190 ff.

62 Under Boniface IX, secretaries were secured financially through incorporation in the college of Scribes, together with dispensation from the exercise of their office; see Schwarz, *Die Organisation kurialer Schreiberkollegien*, pp. 57–58. Economically, this implied that administrative expenses were passed on to people not directly involved. The consolidation of positions and their income in guilds was another means to satisfy the demands of officials.

63 The judges of the Rota demanded from the Notaries a portion of their gains, aside from the price payable when a notarial position was sold. The *magistri* of the registers treated dependent officials in the same way.

64 See von Hofmann, *Forschungen zur Geschichte der kurialen Behörden*, I, p. 256. To illustrate the change, it is instructive to compare the functioning of the Penitentiary at Avignon (until 1378) with that under Eugene IV (1431–1447). The opportunities for officials to collect fees multiplied; Schwarz, *Die Organisation kurialer Schreiberkollegien*, pp. 115 ff., 124–25.

65 The pope held an uncontested right of nomination to very few offices, such as membership in the two scribal guilds or certain household positions. Concerning the latter, he had to reckon with competition from the Chamberlain and his *maiordomus* (thus prompting the reclamations of Eugene IV in 1437). The Chamberlain participated in the appointment of clerics in the Chamber, of its Notaries and court. He always sought to eliminate traditional and concomitant claims of the judge and the treasurer of the Chamber. He also named (next to the Vice-Chancellor) the *cursores* and perhaps the Sergeants at arms. The Vice Chancellor interfered with the Rota and the court of the Audience, while running into the resistance of the Auditors. The *magistri* of the registers did the same with office holders there, although the *bullatores* seem to have defended old prerogatives against them. From 1400, they all had to face papal interference. Only the Great Penitentiary maintained the autonomy of his administrative branch until 1473.

them against substantial payment, if not a share in future gains.[66] The pope had to go along with it because he was obligated to them and in need of their cooperation. Tension arose when rights of appointment were insufficiently defined.[67] One and the same 'institution' — anachronistically speaking — often had employees with diverging loyalties as clients or friends of a different patron.

The pope drew advantage from the transformation of curial offices into quasi-benefices insofar as his influence over official appointments increased at least in a formal sense. Two aspects of his mounting interference stand out. To begin with, the sale of curial offices did not fetch very high prices, unless it promised buyers a lucrative return on their initial investment, whether by way of resale, leasing, or as a security. Accordingly, the right to dispose freely of the position had to be guaranteed in the contract of acquisition, requiring intervention by the pope who alone was canonically authorized to grant permission, say, for the accumulation or multiple possession of offices.[68] As mentioned earlier, having a substitute take care of the official duties also necessitated apostolic approval.[69] The same applied to renunciations that were coupled with the binding presentation of a successor or continuing pension payments.[70] The papacy usually did not concede such favours except among the lower ranks, due to the risk of abandoning control over appointments largely to the holders. In addition, papal participation in the conferral was highly relevant for financial reasons, because dispensations were contingent on the payment of compositions to the pope.[71]

Moreover, an ever-growing number of positions became permanent, as we have seen.[72] They were exclusively reserved to papal appointment.

---

66 This was the case with the judges of the Rota and the *magistri* at the two registers (for bulls and petitions).

67 As curial charges transformed into quasi-benefices, the pope expanded his conferral 'by the law of prevention' at the expense of traditional rights pertaining to the heads of offices and lesser charges. The forms of appointment developed in perfect analogy with those for benefices. There was the papal provision, the instalment in office by the commissioned person who was typically the leader of the administrative unit, and the presentation to the guild (mimicking the introduction into a chapter of canons). On the nexus between these three components, see Meyer, *Zürich und Rom*, pp. 49 ff., 78 ff. A monopoly over the nomination of all curial officials was first claimed in principle by Pius II (1458–1464); cf. von Hofmann, *Forschungen zur Geschichte der kurialen Behörden*, I, p. 22 n. 5. The general trend unfolded quite differently depending on office, which I hope to explain in a monograph on the rise of venal positions at the Curia until 1463.

68 See above, p. 185 n. 58.

69 All curial offices presupposed personal exercise by the holder, which was also an express requirement in many of the reform constitutions.

70 Cf. above, p. 185, with n. 53.

71 Above, p. 182.

72 Some offices gradually attained this status, others received it through express conferral and confirmation, like the servants of the court of the Audience in 1435.

The change met with vigorous and (sometimes successful) resistance from other political leaders, whose own income and patronage was greatly affected.[73] Once an *officium perpetuum* fell vacant, the pope could reassign it at market value if the previous holder had not disposed of it otherwise, a rare occurrence. As a result, the papacy constantly sought to sell additional staff memberships in numbers above their fixed maximum through provision, mandatory incorporation, or the grant of claims to the next available opening. Guild members defended themselves against such papal nominations, which were bound to reduce their share of fee revenue.[74] They looked for support to their superiors, to the head of their administrative branch, or the Apostolic Chamberlain, who were very content to listen.[75] It strengthened their own political standing at the Curia when curial employees asked for their protection.

The developments described here meant for papal administration that the Avignonese levels of bureaucratic efficiency — according to contemporary and non-modern standards — were by and large lost. Three factors contributed to this above all. First, the formal hierarchy among officials was undermined by networks of personal dependency. Secondly, disciplinary oversight and spheres of competency suffered from the transformation of offices into quasi-benefices and their exploitation as material assets.[76] Third, the guilds of staff members gained considerable autonomy by appropriating the functions of their superiors. The transition toward the systematic sale of curial offices presupposed a change in the structure of these corporations. They increasingly served as associations of creditors with the power of 'vacabilists' to trade their positions at will.[77]

---

73 At the Rota, the struggle over rights of nomination continued beyond the establishment of the vacabilist college in 1477. They were split at last according to specific quota between the pope, the Chamberlain (who originally had no say in this), and the long-resisting judges of the Rota. The situation was similar in the court of the Audience and in the offices of registration.

74 The curial corporations used strategies for their defence that were akin to those adopted by the canons of ecclesiastical chapters. Definitions of membership were increasingly refined, distinguishing between those who held it only nominally (for the privileges) and others really serving as officials (the 'participants'), candidates without duties and income or with duties and partial pay, and so on.

75 Officials at the court of the Audience explicitly named their head, the Auditor, as 'defender' in 1435, the court of the Chamber may have acted analogously in 1455, and the guild of Notaries at the Rota turned for protection to the Vice-Chancellor in 1479. The protector of the *cursores* from 1451 onward has not been identified, although it was certainly not the Chamberlain acting as their principal adversary. The common goal was not only to fix the maximum number of corporate members and regulate the necessary reductions to reach it, but also to obtain assurances from the pope that he would abide by his commitments, an indispensable pre-requisite for the offices to be profitable.

76 See von Hofmann, *Forschungen zur Geschichte der kurialen Behörden*, I, pp. 119–20.

77 Schwarz, 'Ämterkäuflichkeit, eine Institution des Absolutismus', p. 189 (English version above, p. 174). Under Boniface IX, the two guilds of Scribes in the Chancery and in the

THE ROMAN CURIA (1378–1447)    189

The beginnings of the sale of offices were equally tied to the phenomenon of geographical diversity among the curial staff. Under the Pisan popes (from 1409) and especially under Martin V and Eugene IV (1417–1447), such diversity was more international in composition than it had ever been, including during the Avignonese period, or would be from after 1450 to the 1970s.[78] In the brief interlude between 1409 and 1450, the Curia was dominated by the French rather than the Italians, especially by clerics from France south of the Loire River, where they also held their benefices according to the thorough investigations of Bernard Guillemain.[79] The change was not due to conscious papal policies of recruitment, attempting to meet reform demands that local churches and regions be fully represented at the Curia, above all in the college of cardinals and certain other positions. While this has been assumed on occasion, it applied during the Schism only to a few instances, in which popes paid attention to the political expectations of churches in the periphery, or nodded in the direction of public opinion by staffing a handful of highly visible charges with foreigners of exceptional merit and qualification.[80] Such gestures, however, were restricted to moments in which the whole of Western Christianity was looking toward the papacy.[81]

Primarily, the international composition of the curial personnel derived from patchworks of 'obediences', made up of churches loyal to the pope and supplying his administrators.[82] This may come as a surprise, because the Curia was already fully staffed with employees who bitterly resisted the reduction of their incomes through the integration of newcomers.[83] Still, even the Councils had to acknowledge that staff members of all two or three papal courts had rightful claims to adequate compensation for their investments by the universal Church, once their pope had been deposed or resigned. Such claims obviously complicated eventual fusion of the schismatic administrations and related reform projects.[84]

---

Penitentiary held the status of 'vacabilists'. Under Eugene IV, it was apparently extended to the court of the Audience and the Chamber, the *bullarium* (though not to the *bullatores* themselves), the Scribes of the register of the bulls, the Notaries of the Chamber (1446), the Proctors of the Penitentiary, and the former household offices of the *cursores* and Sergeants at arms.

78 Cf. von Hofmann, *Forschungen zur Geschichte der kurialen Behörden*, I, pp. 238 ff.; Schuchard, *Die Deutschen an der päpstlichen Kurie*, pp. 41 ff.

79 Guillemain, *La cour pontificale d'Avignon*, pp. 454 ff., 477 ff., with Map 7 in the Appendix. Proportions were slightly different at the courts of the cardinals, pp. 258 ff., and Map 6 in the Appendix.

80 Schuchard, *Die Deutschen an der päpstlichen Kurie*, pp. 42–43.

81 Girgensohn, 'Wie wird man Kardinal?'.

82 Above, p. 189 n. 78.

83 This can be traced in *Le 'Liber officialium' de Martin V*, ed. by Uginet.

84 Plans to persuade schismatic popes to resign always entailed the repayment of their relatives; Esch, 'Das Papsttum unter der Herrschaft der Neapolitaner', p. 745, with n. 102. When

190    CHAPTER 7

Regardless, the two popes following the Council of Constance, Martin V and Eugene IV, did not eliminate every position becoming vacant to rein in the excess of curial offices. The contemporary books of the Apostolic Chamber are filled with notices of conflict, pitting the pope and his Chamberlain against corporations of staff, and concerning the admission of papal appointees to these guilds.[85] Despite many mandates to reduce the number of corporate memberships, the fixed caps proved to be too low. Tensions ran particularly high under Eugene IV, who in seeking to shore up his finances returned yet again and more thoroughly than before to the fiscal exploitation of offices. When the loyalty of his obedience started to waver, he had to give in to the existing holders.[86]

Simultaneously, there were two aspects restricting the international character of the Curia. First, the Curia of each pope only attracted clerics from areas within his obedience, who held benefices there or hoped to acquire them. If, secondly, the origin of curial office holders under the Neapolitan popes of the Schism is correlated with their respective positions in the hierarchy, it is noticeable that the most important charges (such as those in the Apostolic Chamber, the secretaries, Notaries, and personal papal servants) were dominated by Southern Italians. Christiane Schuchard primarily has shown this.[87]

In phases that were most critical for the preservation of obediences and again so under Eugene IV, all key positions were filled with members of the 'papal clan', that group of relatives, compatriots, and friends prepared to take risks for the cause of 'their' pope and whose fate was determined by the success of his faction.[88] Even a vehement opponent of nepotism

---

Gregory XII stepped down, the members of his Curia appointed a protector of their rights at the Council of Constance, 'to preserve and secure physical access to their offices, benefices, and prebends'; see Eubel, 'Die "Provisiones praelatorum" durch Gregor XII.', pp. 129–31.

85 The books in question consist of the *Diversa Cameralia*, the *Mandati*, and the *Libri Officiorum*, located in part in the Vatican and partly in the Roman State Archive. I have consulted the *Libri Officiorum* in Vatican, Apostolic Archive, Reg. Vat. 381–84, 432–35, 465–67, 516, 542–45, 697, 875; Vatican, Apostolic Archive, Arm. xxix: Diversa Cameralia 1–33; Vatican, Apostolic Archive, Introitus et Exitus 426, 449, 458, 464; the registers of oaths and the *Libri Officiorum* in Vatican, Apostolic Archive, Reg. Aven. 173, 198, 268, 288; Arm. xxxiv: Instrumenta Cameralia 4, 11 ff.; Reg. Vat. 500; also, Vatican, Apostolic Archive, Resignationes 1. See Boyle, *A Survey of the Vatican Archives*.

86 Resulting during his pontificate in the 'reform constitutions', which do not contain anything other than assurances to maintain the rights of incorporated staff. They are well-studied for the Scribes of the Chancery and the Penitentiary; less so for the Chamber, the *Camera collegii cardinalium*, the courts of the Audience, the Chamber, and the Rota (?), the register of the bulls, the Sergeants at arms, certain *janitores*, and the *cursores*.

87 Schuchard, *Die Deutschen an der päpstlichen Kurie*, pp. 76 ff., 80 ff., 150–52, 154. There is no reason to be misled by foreign names, who only held their office by honorary title, p. 349.

88 The relative importance of curial positions under a given pope is discernible in various ways. Pitz, *Supplikensignatur und Briefexpedition*, p. 77, has identified the circle of special papal friends through annotations (in the form of *recipe*) on the petitions. Other indicators

like Urban VI was utterly dependent on the commitment and funds of his nearest relations. Arnold Esch has demonstrated in several studies that the extreme nepotism of schismatic popes was wholly essential for their political survival.[89] This was true of Urban VI, Boniface IX, and Clement (VII).[90] It applied to Gregory XII.[91] In his conflict with the Council of Basel beginning in 1437, Eugene IV also had to rely on his personal connections.[92] Nepotistic practices were not remarkable in themselves, because they characterized contemporary ecclesiastical governance in general, but the extreme dependency of the papacy on these innermost networks was certainly a sign of crisis.[93]

Like the ties between protectors and protegees, nepotism figures among the personal relationships interfering with the 'substantive' ones of administrative organization. Both are part of the 'networks' that Wolfgang Reinhard has called to the historian's attention, whether they were based on blood, shared places of origin, patronage and clientele, or friendship, which did not have to constitute a sentimental bond, but could accommodate expectations of mutual utility or aid from the friends of friends as well.[94] Among clerics, similar connections also arose from membership in the same religious order or monastery, or attendance at a specific university. They were very important for the curial staff, at the Curia, and beyond it.[95]

Networks played a key role in managing benefices located in a curial official's home province.[96] Holders had to recruit capable and trustworthy representatives there, who did not have to be identical with the substitute personally performing the tasks associated with the benefice. Representatives were chosen to defend their superior's local right to tenure energetically, and to collect, transmit or possibly reinvest the income accruing from it. Their loyalty and commitment ensured in return that they knew someone who was obligated to promote their own interests at the Curia,

---

include the habit of personal audiences, or the conferral of recommendations, the presentation of gifts, letters, reports from envoys, or itemized expenses. The officials in question usually accumulated multiple functions to increase their power or income.

89  Esch, 'Das Papsttum unter der Herrschaft der Neapolitaner', p. 796 and elsewhere; Esch, 'Le clan des familles napolitaines'; Esch, 'Simonie-Geschäft in Rom'.

90  Binz, 'Le népotisme de Clément VII' (with additional literature).

91  Esch, 'Das Papsttum unter der Herrschaft der Neapolitaner', p. 770, and elsewhere.

92  The nepotism of Martin V belonged to a different category. He tried to promote his dynasty to the leading position in the Papal States, so that future popes had to reckon with it as well; Partner, *The Papal State under Martin V.*, pp. 194 ff.; Reinhard, 'Nepotismus. Der Funktionswandel', pp. 159–60.

93  Reinhard, 'Nepotismus. Der Funktionswandel'; and Reinhard, 'Nepotismus'.

94  Reinhard, *Freunde und Kreaturen*.

95  Schuchard, *Die Deutschen an der päpstlichen Kurie*, pp. 165 ff.

96  I have explored the significance of similar ties in Schwarz, 'Patronage und Klientel' (English translation above, pp. 49–66).

192 CHAPTER 7

through the sharing of information or by rendering curial services that either directly added to their portfolio of benefices, or indirectly enabled them to gain favours for others in their native environment.[97] Curial residents thus served as a conduit between the set of acquaintances back home and their friends and patron at the Curia, be it a cardinal or other leading prelate. There is no need to imagine that these networks furnished immediate access to the pope.[98]

In line with other princely courts, the Curia gave rise to conflict and rivalry between patrons and their clienteles, which both the pope and lay rulers endeavoured to contain.[99] When a single group like the Limousins of the late Avignonese period, or subsequently the Neapolitans under Urban VI, Boniface IX, and John (XXIII) gained the upper hand, papal rule was seriously threatened.[100] Curial networks were also important for the interaction between the papacy and the churches. Papal governance chiefly served to meet the general demand for legitimations, the settlement of disputes, and the granting of pardons and exemptions.[101] Because it was difficult to enforce the resulting decisions against competitors, particularly those concerned with benefices, apostolic intervention on behalf of someone in the provinces was unlikely to succeed, unless the interested person managed to have his network and its head at the Curia approach the pope. In this way, the papacy was constantly fed with news from all over the Western Church, which the pope could conveniently use to satisfy his own clientele as well. The pope also tapped into these networks for other purposes, for example, to deliver mail or conduct monetary transactions.[102] To some extent, the connections compensated for the lack of a supporting administrative structure at the Curia, apart from the collectors of the Apostolic Chamber.

How did the Schism affect the networks of curial patrons and provincial clienteles? The break-up of the Church into two or three obediences certainly interrupted the connection with areas rallying behind the other pope or remaining at a distance and undecided. It was the more important

---

97 Frequent favours from curial officials in the archival records include money deposits, the provision of credit and sureties; the performance of oaths; the presentation of claims and complaints in the Chamber or the Audience; assistance in the formulation of requests, representation in all official business, and the garnering of support from influential persons. The expertise and service of curial officials as informants were entirely indispensable.

98 The continuous presence of the curial oligarchy, as opposed to the rapid change of personnel in the pope's entourage, has been emphasized by Reinhard, *Freunde und Kreaturen* p. 45.

99 Paravicini, 'Administrateurs professionels et princes dilettantes', pp. 175 ff., with bibliography.

100 Esch, 'Das Papsttum unter der Herrschaft der Neapolitaner', p. 798; Guillemain, 'Cardinaux et société curiale', p. 27; Bresc, 'La genèse du Schisme', p. 46.

101 These constraints have been pointed out by Pitz, 'Die römische Kurie'.

102 The postal services of the *cursores* were much diminished at Avignon; Guillemain, *La cour pontificale d'Avignon*, p. 304.

to strengthen ties with regions that had not been in close contact with the papacy, a need especially felt on the Roman side.

The above-mentioned changes in the acquisition of curial offices had the effect that applicants required protection as well as money. Patrons were not just interested in compensation for the investments they had made while competing for control over administrative positions.[103] They also sought to gain in power by recruiting a clientele that was as influential as possible at the Curia and brought with it a maximum of ties to the outside world. In my view, the papal courts during the crisis of the Schism (from 1378) generally betray a higher degree of segmentation into groups and clienteles than in the preceding Avignonese period.[104]

A different type of network manifested itself in the appointment to offices with the help of so-called 'rope teams', formed by relatives, compatriots, and friends and extending from the Curia outward into a curial official's native region. They are found in the guilds of lesser staff operating with a high degree of autonomy.[105] The existence of similar networks depended above all on the interest of clerics in the periphery, who looked toward the Curia as their marketplace for benefices. After 1450, these ties were rapidly severed. The curial connections with the Western Church as a whole were increasingly disrupted, not least by a series of concordats between lay rulers and the ecclesiastical leadership from 1441, if not already following the Pragmatic Sanction of Bourges in 1438.[106] It was also affected by the definite turn of the papacy toward Italian politics, filling the papal personnel with Italians and isolating the Roman popes from developments outside the Peninsula.[107]

I speak about the networks at greater length because we know so little about them — for the time being — and because it is not easy to gather information about them. The clients who reveal their tie to a patron on certain occasions are the household members (or *familiares*) of eminent

---

103 They were no less affected by losses in the possession and exchange of benefices than other curial officials.

104 On the formation of clienteles in the Avignonese period, see Bresc, 'La genèse du Schisme', pp. 49 ff.; Guillemain, 'Cardinaux et société curiale', pp. 23–24.

105 As I have observed in connection with the corporations of Scribes and, successively, Abbreviators. For additional offices, see Schuchard, *Die Deutschen an der päpstlichen Kurie*. These extended to inferior charges at the Chamber, the register, and the servants of the papal palace. Apart from the social position, they seem to have required a certain level of professional qualification; Schuchard, *Die Deutschen an der päpstlichen Kurie*, pp. 76, 133–34, 149 (under Eugene IV).

106 Schwarz, 'Die Abbreviatoren unter Eugen IV.', with a list of the concordats, pp. 246 ff.

107 The convergence of several reasons for the collapse of the curial benefice market in the second half of the fifteenth century (which cannot be addressed here) has been discussed by Meyer, 'Das Wiener Konkordat'. Cf. also the literature above, p. 180 n. 24.

194    CHAPTER 7

persons at the Curia.[108] The *familiares* of cardinals enjoyed privileges as holders of benefices and made sure to mention this connection in their petitions related to the matter. The names of *familiares* were also kept in long lists, though none of them is known to have survived.[109] It is the more helpful to note that benefices were regularly passed on within one and the same clientele.[110] By exploring the history of benefice-holders, it is possible to trace such interpersonal relations. Much material is found in the *Repertorium Germanicum* and its Index of Places, which until recently was not available.[111] It can be complemented with data from the local archives featuring additional documentation, including, for example, acts of reverence (*pietas*) by clients toward their patron.[112]

What was the impact of these changes on the functioning of the Curia and its reputation in the wider world? And how did they relate to the programs of curial reform? For an answer, it is necessary to recognize that the papal court provided multiple services, that its operations could be compromised in several different ways, and that there were various mechanisms to address disruptions. To begin with, the Curia constituted the permanent environment of the head of the Church. If behaviour considered improper was spotted there, it undermined his acceptance or legitimacy, one of the conditions for the eventual success of the Reformation. The Curia was also the court of the pope as spiritual leader and hence a focal point of princely self-representation. In this regard, the curial break-up during the Schism triggered a crisis that was as acute as it was transitory. The courtly splendour quickly recovered after the Schism, matching Avignonese levels and surpassing them before long.[113]

---

108 True papal *familiares* are hard to track, because the titles of a *familiaris pape*, also known as *familiaris domesticus* or *continuus commensalis* and the like, had long become honorary even for persons far from the Curia. As a result, it is impossible to take them into account here.

109 They were kept by the chamberlain of each cardinal's suite; Mollat, 'Contribution à l'histoire du Sacré Collège', p. 50. The mention of *familiares* in the registers of petitions by a cardinal, requesting passports and the *status presentie* for his suite, is never complete and no more than momentary. The registers of petitions for expectancies contained such rolls for the *familia* and clientele of the political leadership (cardinals, princes, universities), but there are very few remnants; Diener, 'Zur Persönlichkeit des Johannes von Segovia', pp. 299–300.

110 As observed by Antonio Paravicini Bagliani for the fifteenth, and Wolfgang Reinhard for the sixteenth century. I have noted the phenomenon in my study on the benefices held by Cusanus, above, p. 191 n. 96.

111 *Repertorium Germanicum*, I–IX. Outside this series and encompassing petitioners other than German as well, see the *Repertorium concilii Basiliensis et Felicis V.*, ed. by Gilomen.

112 Restriction of the available data to the German Empire is perhaps acceptable, because the area was, as mentioned earlier, under greater papal influence during the crisis of the Schism than ever before or after. A second limitation is more substantial, given that Germans at the Roman Curia primarily held lesser and middling positions according to the investigations of Christiane Schuchard, which prevents insight into the truly important networks.

113 See Schimmelpfennig, *Das Papsttum*, pp. 266 ff.

THE ROMAN CURIA (1378–1447)    195

Simultaneously, the papal court had to manage the back and forth between the centre and the periphery of the Church. At the time, the court did not rely on the ecclesiastical hierarchy or on lower echelons of curial administration, as much as it involved the personal networks of curial residents. During the Schism, the Curia struggled to serve in this function. It operated perfectly under Martin V and in the early years of Eugene IV. From 1450, it increasingly led to almost complete failure.[114]

Most modern studies of the Curia focus on its 'administrative' aspects. They mainly investigate the offices and persons in charge of dealing with the requests of petitioners to the pope. As far as this role is concerned, curial efficiency suffered greatly under the above-mentioned structural changes that intensified over time. Before long, officials used their positions for economic ends rather than to fulfil their appointed tasks. Both they and their substitutes frequently lacked the necessary qualifications. Protracted procedures and the mounting monetary demands of curial staff made the execution of petitions for those requesting apostolic mandates more expensive. Rampant corruption conversely had its own way of facilitating speedy processing.[115]

From about 1350, the papacy introduced competing ways to expedite the execution of orders that were also made accessible to petitioners. The newly created offices, however, soon became available for sale, aligning them structurally with the old ones.[116] Despite these deficiencies in 'customer service' and although the benefice market contracted around 1450, there was no crisis in the demand for curial intervention. The nature of the requests changed, but the number of petitions did not suffer any notable reduction prior to the 1510s and the final few years before the Protestant Reformation, becoming more pronounced, of course, once it had started.[117] Until then, it was still considered necessary or at least advantageous to mobilize the pope for mandates that were based on his exclusive prerogatives of grace. Such requests included exemptions (from the prohibition to accumulate positions) in order to compete for high office, or for devout self-representation in the form of pious donations.

Numerous accounts written by contemporary visitors of the Curia undoubtedly spread criticism of the institution and contributed to calls for reform. On the other hand, detractors of the Curia had always existed,

---

114 Cf. the study by Andreas Meyer, above, p. 193 n. 107.

115 The analysis of these developments by Walter von Hofmann, above, p. 178 n. 12, remains unsurpassed.

116 First affected were the secretaries, then the *referendarii*, and lastly other officials from the pope's entourage; see von Hofmann, *Forschungen zur Geschichte der kurialen Behörden*, I, pp. 324 ff., and elsewhere.

117 This is the impression based on my materials, see Schwarz, *Die Originale von Papsturkunden*; and Schwarz, *Regesten*. Some of the causes have been identified by Meyer, *Zürich und Rom*, pp. 140 ff., warranting fuller investigation.

196    CHAPTER 7

spurred by the inherent contradiction in the concept of a 'spiritual ruler'. Objections were highly stereotypical so that it is impossible to take them simply at face value. Furthermore, they failed to capture some aspects drawing criticism from the modern perspective.[118] That the complaints mounted and were exacerbated during the Great Schism certainly implied the existence of added reason to voice them. The popes themselves as well as the cardinals began to launch their own attacks on the Curia, making reform proposals and using them as weapons against competitors.

It is impossible here to discuss the reform demands in comprehensive fashion.[119] Taken together, they form a canon of requests to overhaul the Curia and consisted of five principal points. First, taxes and fees were to be reduced to the levels of good old (namely, Avignonese) times, without collateral expenses. Maintenance of the tariffs was to be constantly controlled. To provide adequately for staff, benefices should complement their income. Next, the number of officials had to be brought down to traditional levels. Recourse to substitutes and the accumulation of positions were to be prohibited, not least to ensure that as many curial employees as possible were compensated in accordance with their status. 'Simony' (or the sale of spiritual rather than purely administrative positions) was to be shunned in the appointment process. Third, the prestige of the Curia had to be enhanced through the sole employment of personnel suited in terms of character and formal education, excluding laity.[120] Those unqualified were to be removed. Fourth, each region was to be represented appropriately at the Curia. And finally, official operations had to maintain or return to original standards marked by publicity and transparency.

To what extent were these demands put into practice? After prolonged debates, the Council of Constance did not pass any resolution, although it charged the pope with reform of the Church 'in both the head and the Roman Curia'.[121] A few points of the usual agenda were specifically named. Martin V issued a handful of constitutions.[122] Eugene IV did the same

---

118 Such as nepotism or the conferral of offices against payment. Both were deemed appropriate, provided the parties did not go against customary limitations; cf. Reinhard, 'Nepotismus. Der Funktionswandel', p. 162 n. 100.

119 See the studies above, p. 178 n. 12.

120 Here, the aspect of material maintenance was paramount, too; the demand came from the universities and the new group of 'intellectuals'.

121 *Decrees of the Ecumenical Councils*, ed. by Tanner, p. 444 line 6.

122 On the history of curial reform at the Council of Constance, cf. Schwarz, 'Die Abbreviatoren unter Eugen IV.', pp. 212 ff.; Meyer, 'Das Wiener Konkordat', p. 123. Martin V's constitutions were issued on 5 February 1418, ed. by von Hofmann, *Forschungen zur Geschichte der kurialen Behörden*, II, p. 5 (no. 20); and on 1 September 1418, in *Die päpstlichen Kanzleiordnungen*, ed. by Tangl, pp. 133–45. His two decrees of 13 April 1425 and 16 May 1425 were promulgated to prepare for the Council of Pavia and Siena, ed. by Döllinger, *Beiträge zur politischen und Cultur-Geschichte*, II, pp. 335–44; partly in *Die päpstlichen*

THE ROMAN CURIA (1378–1447)    197

before his breach with the Council of Basel.[123] The papal enactments were only partly enforced and had little impact.

During the Schism, popes appear to have created new cardinals with an eye on public opinion, actively by choosing candidates of special qualification, integrity, and prestige, and indirectly by avoiding overly contested individuals despite the need to accommodate the lay lords.[124] They pursued the same policy in appointments to other important positions, like those at the tribunal of the Rota or the Apostolic Court of Penance.[125] An internationally composed staff was obviously advantageous there.[126] Respect for public sentiment continued to characterize the pontificate of Martin V, who demonstrated good sense and versatility with his declarations and recourse to commissions of reform. Eugene IV's later elevations to the cardinalate, on the other hand, ignored general opinion altogether, once he felt unshackled by it upon turning against the Council of Basel.[127] He preferred to follow the wishes of the secular lords and his eventual success proved him right.

Although the international profile of the Curia under Marin V and Eugene IV was in line with the reform agenda, it was not introduced by design. As we have seen, it grew out of the need to combine multiple papal courts of the preceding Schism and attested to difficulties in reducing the number of staff. The same applied to the increasing proportion of clerics among the personnel of the Curia. Despite the concordats of Constance and especially after their expiration, the curial privileges regarding benefices were viewed as very enticing, at least until around 1450. In the following decades, cardinals gathered in reform commissions at regular intervals of approximately twenty years. Until the Council of Trent, a century afterwards, however, they did not issue a single constitution anymore.[128]

---

*Kanzleiordnungen*, ed. by Tangl, pp. 162–65; and in von Hofmann, *Forschungen zur Geschichte der kurialen Behörden*, I, p. 9 (no. 33).

123 Especially von Hofmann, *Forschungen zur Geschichte der kurialen Behörden*, II, no. 43; but cf. nos 46, 51.

124 As documented by Girgensohn, 'Wie wird man Kardinal?'.

125 The office of judge was particularly critical in the eyes of contemporaries; cf. Schwarz, 'Ämterkäuflichkeit. Eine Institution des Absolutismus', p. 180 (English version above, p. 162).

126 The two offices acted not only in response to requests from the periphery, they also had most of the direct contact with petitioners. See also Schuchard, *Die Deutschen an der päpstlichen Kurie*, pp. 114 ff., 121 ff.

127 This turning-point in the history of the cardinalate is clearly shown by Young, 'Fundamental Changes in the Nature of the Cardinalate', pp. 13 ff.

128 Cf. von Hofmann, *Forschungen zur Geschichte der kurialen Behörden*, I, pp. 325 ff. Even the much-quoted reform of the Curia at the Council of Trent (1545–1563) was largely cosmetic and ran into insurmountable structural problems; Reinhard, 'Ämterhandel in Rom', pp. 53–54; Reinhard, 'Reformpapsttum zwischen Renaissance und Barock', p. 793.

## CHAPTER 7

In sum, the curial reforms witnessing execution achieved very little in the way *reformatio curiae* was understood at the time. They also failed to accomplish reform in the modern sense, which has a different meaning. The principal goal of late medieval efforts was the transformation of the spirit, to be attained through growing persuasion that the Curia ought to be a community of clerics again, free of the vices of avarice, gluttony, and vainglory, and shunning all conduct contrary to the injunctions of clerical status.[129] Calls for institutional change proclaimed what was believed to be a return to the conditions of good old times, namely, the Avignonese era. Even though the reform programs demanded above all the restoration of proper conduct in the immediate environment of the head of the Church, there were also suggestions to improve communications between the ecclesiastical centre and periphery and to ensure greater administrative efficiency. The reformers did not recognize the difficulties of reinstituting the former status quo at Avignon. As a matter of fact, they could not be aware of them because the reform commissions were not staffed with experts.[130] They arguably did not wish to understand them either, because anything like a detached analysis of what prompted the criticized abuses was not part of the reform assignment as they saw it.

The popes and eventually the Council fathers at Constance had to acknowledge that regardless of intentions, they were unable to intervene decisively in favour of reforms against the resistance of the members of the Curia. How was it possible to reduce the number of curial officials without ignoring not only their legitimately acquired rights, but also those of their respective patron? How would both be compensated for their loss? Regarding lowering fees and eliminating collateral charges, where would the necessary capital come from to return the initial investment to holders, who viewed the administrative tariffs as interest they expected to earn on their position?[131] To defray their expenses plausibly with the help of benefices was not a strong option. Especially in the concordats of Constance, the nations turned against the idea of reserving benefices to curial officials.[132]

---

129 Rapp, *L'Église et la vie religieuse*, pp. 207 ff.; O'Malley, *Praise and Blame in Renaissance Rome*, pp. 195 ff.

130 When such experts were heard, reform programs were especially likely to run out of steam; see von Hofmann, *Forschungen zur Geschichte der kurialen Behörden*, I, p. 308.

131 And what was the point of spending rare funds on such a useless objective?

132 Schwarz, 'Die Abbreviatoren unter Eugen IV.', p. 214. The proposal of the Concordat with the English nation, in *Raccolta di concordati*, ed. by Mercati, p. 167 (§ 6), to have English clerics appropriately represented at the Curia despite their withdrawal from the curial exchange of benefices may not have been absurd. If the English had been admitted in larger numbers as curial officials, they probably would have been endowed with native church positions.

In similar vein, papal attempts to increase administrative efficiency by creating additional corporations of curial staff constituted less of a step toward reform than an illustration of its impossibility owing to the structural transformations mentioned earlier. These changes, moreover, represented an institutional adjustment of the Curia to novel circumstances requiring greater administrative effectiveness. In unprecedented fashion, the curial apparatus started to generate official positions, so that they would find buyers and alleviate the persistent financial shortfalls of the papacy. The sale of offices fulfilled this purpose. They were increasingly advertised as *vacabiles*, or permitting the exchange with third parties, and incorporated into 'colleges' capping their number and exercising a bureaucratic monopoly.

Organized in such a way, the curial officials were well-positioned to fend off occasional and uncoordinated papal interventions and initiatives of reform. The system of venality did not face a crisis until the seventeenth century, when the demand for apostolic mandates collapsed in the wake of the Tridentine Council.[133] In last analysis, the process of gradual adaptation during the period of the Schism pushed by curial officials and tolerated by the papacy cannot be defined as a reform, because it lacked planful execution and the essential component of change for the sake of improvement.

---

133 Reinhard, 'Reformpapsttum zwischen Renaissance und Barock', p. 795. This crisis also signified the end of systematic nepotism.

CHAPTER 8

# On Behalf of the Pope

*The Papal* cursores *from 1200 to about 1470*[1]

This essay treats the first few centuries in the long history of the papal *cursores*, whose office persisted until it was abolished by Pope Paul VI in 1968.[2] To a greater degree than might be expected, my inquiry highlights changes in the Couriers' functions, their recruitment, collegiate organization between corporate autonomy and regulation from above, and their ceremonial role. The position and corporation of the papal Couriers probably traces back to Innocent III (1198–1216), who thoroughly restructured the Curia.[3] Apart from greater efficiency and the elimination of criticised abuses, the pope made a push towards separation of the apostolic court from the city of Rome, which must have been a motivating factor as well.[4] However, actual documentation on the *cursores* only dates to the time of Honorius III (1216–1227) and continues to be intermittent throughout the thirteenth century. For other curial colleges, contemporary source material is similarly scarce. Borwin Rusch based his study on this small corpus of data.[5] Once the registers of expenses kept by the Apostolic Chamber commence under Boniface VIII (1294–1303), references to the Couriers multiply, albeit without providing a fuller account of their activities.

The situation changed altogether from the beginning of Clement V's pontificate. Known earlier as Bertrand de Got and archbishop of Bordeaux from the southwest of France, Clement V had no curial experience. Upon his election on 5 June 1305, which was preceded by almost a year of

---

1 In the following, the *cursores* are also referred to as the 'Couriers'.

2 The decision concerned the papal 'household' (*domus*) and was published in *Acta Apostolicae Sedis*, 60/6 (1968), 311 (II, 6 § 4).

3 Schwarz, 'The Roman Curia (until about 1300)'; cf. also Zutshi, 'Innocent and the Reform of the Papal Chancery'.

4 Given that the college of the *cursores* did not receive the Easter and Christmas 'gifts' (cf. p. 209 below), it cannot have existed in the early years of the Curia. It was not until the 1400s that the college invented for itself a long history reaching back to the twelfth century; see Moroni, 'Cursori apostolici o pontifici', p. 52b; also, p. 53, on the equal ranking of the *cursores*, judges, and *tabelliones* at the *Possesso*.

5 Rusch, *Die Behörden und Hofbeamten der päpstlichen Kurie*, p. 19. It is likely that additional references can be found in the papal registers, published by the *École française de Rome* for the thirteenth and (partly) fourteenth centuries and meanwhile available in CD-ROM as 'Ut per litteras apostolicas'. Paravicini Bagliani, *La cour des papes au XIIIᵉ siècle*, concentrates on life at the court and does not address the *cursores* and curial corporations. Only the study by Baumgarten, *Aus Kanzlei und Kammer*, pp. 216–47, covers the whole period treated here.

202    CHAPTER 8

discussions in the closed gathering (or conclave) of electing cardinals at Perugia, additional months went by before he had himself crowned in Lyon on 14 November 1305. Even thereafter, he was in no hurry to move to Italy to assume his (itinerant) rule of the Papal States, as the curial staff of his predecessor, Benedict XI (who died in Perugia on 7 July 1304), would have expected. Instead, Clement V travelled at a painfully slow pace through southern France toward his former bishopric. That this was his destination, the curial clergy in lesser positions accompanying him or witnessing events from Italy could not, or would not, have recognized in view of his confused itinerary in the spring of 1306.[6] The new pope showed in general little interest in the administrative habits of the Curia and preferred to rely on local networks or officials who had proven themselves during his time as archbishop of Bordeaux. They did not operate according to curial tradition, but applied norms that were familiar to them, which seems to have offended veteran members of the Curia, who gradually joined the pope and others who merely visited. Clement V appointed his successor in Bordeaux, Arnaldus de Canteloup, as the new Apostolic Chamberlain who, as head of the curial clergy and 'finance minister', occupied the most important position at the Curia.[7] He also raised Arnaldus to the cardinalate, departing from a tradition which assumed that the Chamberlain was not supposed to be a cardinal and continued into the mid-fifteenth century. Like Clement, Arnaldus was an upstart in curial matters.[8] After repeated and serious conflict with the established clergy, he commissioned an experienced member of the Curia to write a 'Report on the Rights and Duties of the Pope's Household (*familia*)' according to long-standing custom.[9] Referred to as the 'Report' in this essay, Frutaz has convincingly dated it to the year 1306.[10]

In the spring of 1306, the Statutes of the apostolic *cursores* were put in writing as well, and each member of the college (twenty names) took an oath on them on 25 April. Tilmann Schmidt has discovered a copy of the Statutes in the municipal archives of Lübeck. He has studied and

---

6 Presumably in response to widespread criticism, the Chamberlain did not oppose the view of the *cursores* that the stay in southwest France was merely temporary; see the Statutes, ed. by Schmidt, 'Das päpstliche Kursorenkollegium', pp. 597–601 (§ 9).

7 Arnaldus was Chamberlain from 1305 to 1307; Samaran and Mollat, *La fiscalité pontificale en France*, p. 167.

8 He was probably a relative of Clement V, who seems to have considered family ties to be the most important qualification for high curial positions; cf. Guillemain, *La cour pontificale d'Avignon*, pp. 67, 188 n., p. 192 n.

9 The text has long been known; it was treated in part by Haller, 'Zwei Aufzeichnungen über die Beamten der Curie'; and Mollat, 'Miscellanea Avenionensia'.

10 New and, this time, complete edition by Frutaz, 'La famiglia pontificia'; on the *cursores*, II, pp. 309–10. In the Appendix, II, pp. 320–23, there is also a new edition of the *Modus dividendi quinque minuta servitia camere et collegii* of 1307; see also, II, pp. 280–81, with reasons for the new date.

edited them while also consulting the 'Report' here and there.[11] Schmidt counted the Statutes among the ones 'collectively passed by curial officials', regardless of the fact that, in his view, the Couriers did not have any 'autonomous right to formulate statutes' at the time. He cited as proof 'the reservation of modifications in the final paragraph (§ 25), which gave the Apostolic Chamberlain the competency to make normative changes'. With or without this final restriction, however, Schmidt's interpretation seems to anticipate developments toward collegiate autonomy by several decades, if not a century. The first (known) compilation of statutes and customs by a curial corporation without authorization from the head official postdates the middle of the fourteenth century. It was put together by the college of Scribes in the Apostolic Penitentiary, whose corporate structure revealed a high degree of autonomy early on.[12] In my view, there is a simpler explanation, to the effect that it was the Chamberlain who convened the *cursores* present at the Curia, obliged them by his authority to pass the statutes 'unanimously and harmoniously' after having them redacted under his supervision, and threatened absent Couriers with the enormous fine of five gold ducats (§ 22), if they were unwilling to sign on. Recourse to the services of a public notary reflected the need of the Chamber to produce authenticated copies of the text, while the version containing the original signatures, now lost, was stored in the Chamber itself. The Chamberlain also determined the issues to be addressed, which explains without difficulty the lack, already noted by Schmidt, of regulations pertaining to the standard elements of statutes for curial colleges, comprising, for example, the 'mechanisms of admission to the college of the Couriers'. The contribution of the (physically present) *cursores* to the process of compilation was limited to answering specific questions about corporate customs. This is (according to Schmidt) the reason for 'the occasionally Italianizing and vernacular diction', which was not transformed into curial style because this was the language the recipients of the statutes could understand. The *cursores* held on to the text, which is still recognizable in the version of the late fifteenth century.

In my view, the text was crafted to eliminate serious abuses and maintain the traditional services of the *cursores* for the pope and his Chamber. The most important cause of the recent troubles can be inferred from stipulations in the Statutes themselves, especially when looking at the

---

11 Schmidt, 'Das päpstliche Kursorenkollegium'. Schmidt was able to identify the names of the Master and the remaining nineteen Couriers at the beginning of the document, pp. 588–90. Schmidt has also edited the registers of the Chamber under Boniface VIII; cf. p. 212 n. 51 below.

12 On the Statutes of the curial college of Scribes in the Penitentiary, see Schwarz, *Die Organisation kurialer Schreiberkollegien*, p. 221; the date of composition has been placed more narrowly between 1355 and 1363 or 1376 by Weiß, *Die Versorgung des päpstlichen Hofes in Avignon*, p. 275 n. 7.

sanctions. A group of Couriers arriving early at the Curia of the new pope had occupied the leading positions in the college and taken over the best assignments, while leaving the more onerous duties to the rest, presumably the latecomers, whose commitment and quality of administrative work had consequently suffered. As a result, it was necessary — from the perspective of the remaining *cursores* — to restore fairness and good custom. The preface, however, exclusively emphasizes the viewpoint of the Chamber, seeking, in Schmidt's words, 'greater effectiveness' in the rendering of services.

It is possible to offer more than 'speculation' (as stated by Schmidt) on what prompted the statutes to be put in writing. All Couriers, including those arriving early, must have been annoyed by the fact that the new pope had left the distribution of his letters of coronation to one of his household members (or *familiaris*) 'in recognition of his services'.[13] The announcement of papal elections and the expedition of coronation letters, however, had been an ancient privilege of the college of the *cursores*.[14] As conveyers of good news, they could collect lavish gifts not only from the final recipient, but at every station along the way.

Clement V's *familiaris* had left the letters for expedition to another cleric, who in turn used them 'in profitable fashion', receiving a lot of money and horses from his hosts on the journey. As proof of his identity, he simply presented the papal seals he carried, again in contravention of tradition. Since the coronation of Benedict XI had occurred barely three years earlier, one prelate probably recalled long-established modes of delivery and brought a complaint against the *familiaris*. Clement V arrested the dealer in letters. The *familiaris* was admonished and received a penalty, but 'refused to be corrected' and fled 'despairing of mercy from the Apostolic See'.[15] The pope reacted by declaring him deposed, took away the benefices he had recently bestowed on him, and re-ordered his imprisonment on 1 July 1306. This last mandate is our source of information.

It is easy to imagine the outrage among senior members of the college, who must have hurried to arrive in time for distribution of the coronation letters! The incident was probably not the only misstep by the new pope or his Chamberlain, undermining the traditional rights of the corporation. The Statutes of the Couriers yield, in my opinion, many additional clues about their tasks, organisation of services, and corporate structure. To this end, the text needs to be read systematically alongside

---

13 Vatican, Apostolic Archive, Reg. Vat. 52, fol. 179ᵛ; printed in *Regestum Clementis papae V*, no. 1052; *Tables des registres de Clement V*, ed. by Vogel and Lanhers, pp. 194–95; the summary by Baumgarten, *Aus Kanzlei und Kammer*, p. 228, is somewhat inexact.

14 Baumgarten, *Aus Kanzlei und Kammer*, pp. 225–29.

15 The printed version, in *Regestum Clementis papae V*, no. 1052, reads 'corrigi refugiens' rather than 'corrigi respuens' in the original.

the above-mentioned 'Report'. Moreover, special attention is due to the stipulated penalties.

According to the Statutes, the *cursores* had to send a daily detachment for service in the Apostolic Chamber. It had to provide the guard and deliver the summonses of the cameral court (§ 2).[16] Meanwhile, correspondence generated by the Chamber and subject to certain formal requirements had to be consigned to the 'Master Courier'. I refer to it as 'registered letters' in the following (§ 3).[17] The delivery of the mentioned citations to court, for which the Couriers were apparently paid by the litigants formed an important source of extra income for corporate members.[18] They only received food and a residence from the Chamber.[19] We are told in passing about the money they earned through this activity, because it had to be divided among the guardians at day's end. Behaviour undermining the solidarity of the group was countered with fines payable to the corporate cash register (in this case amounting to two *solidi*).[20] The 'Report' states that apart from the detachment in the Chamber, there was a

---

16 The fine for improper conduct during guard service was expressed in an unusual currency (one *Venetus de argento*), the same that also appears in the 'Report' for a *lecterium* of straw; ed. by Frutaz, 'La famiglia pontificia', §§ 56–57. Both passages are likely based on older regulations. On the *Veneti argentei parvi*, which in 1306 were calculated at one Florentine ducat for twenty-four *grossi* and figured in the Chamber until 1310, see the tables of conversion in *Die Ausgaben der Apostolischen Kammer unter Benedikt XII*, ed. by Schäfer, pp. 896 ff.

17 The Couriers were the only ones to receive them, as their guild was liable to deliver them promptly and safely; cf. p. 207 n. 22 below.

18 Regularly misunderstood by scholarship, the Chamber only provided food for the detachments. The relevant passage, ed. by Frutaz, 'La famiglia pontificia', p. 309, prescribing one *vivanda* per person and detailing exact kinds of nourishment, must refer alone to the members serving in person, as they were the ones whose punctual presence and correct conduct were rewarded in this way. The limitation of supplies at solemn occasions to seven *vivande* for all those present (*inter omnes*) — often supplemented during travel with five *prebende* of fodder and the allocation of two pack animals — was plausible, on the other hand, since the incentive to participate was stronger to begin with. The sole stipulation concerning all Couriers together rather than just the ones serving daily, the provision with cloth, does not speak of *omnes* but of each (*singuli*); cf. p. 211 n. 50 below. The holy events at which the Great Kitchen added a third course to the meal, both on the day of the feast and the following two, were Christmas, Easter, and (somewhat less opulent) Pentecost; otherwise, the exception was limited to the feast itself, namely, Circumcision, Epiphany, Christ's Ascension, Peter and Paul, John the Baptist, the Ascension of Mary, and All Saints; ed. by Frutaz, 'La famiglia pontificia', § 64.

19 See the 'Report', ed. by Frutaz, 'La famiglia pontificia', § 56; whenever the guards accompanied the pope on his travels, they obtained three *provisini* per night for a bed and straw to feed their horse (*pro lecto et stallatico*). If they spent the night in the immediate vicinity of the pope, they were given one *venetus* for a measure of straw (*pro lecteriis*); cf. § 57.

20 The low amount probably reflected the fact that summonses to the court of the Chamber were usually less lucrative than those to the other courts; see the Statutes, ed. by Schmidt, 'Das päpstliche Kursorenkollegium', § 6: 'Two Florentine gold ducats'; in addition, they were

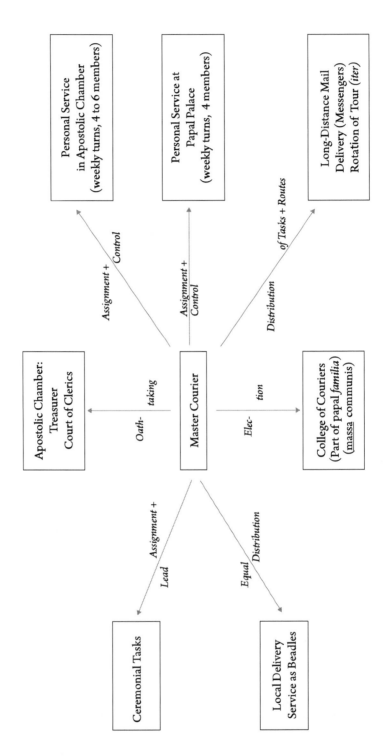

Figure 8.1. The Papal Couriers, c. 1306.

## ON BEHALF OF THE POPE   207

second one at the gate to the palace where the pope resided, which had to be at least four men strong.[21] The two units on duty were obliged to stand ready for any order the pope or Chamberlain might give them.[22]

Those not joining the two detachments dispatched to the pope and Chamber received their assignment from the Master Courier, among them the above-mentioned expedition of registered letters from the Chamber.[23] The Master also distributed summonses, which the litigating parties wanted to have handled by the *cursores* (§§ 4–5). In this instance, the appointed Courier could keep the payment for himself.[24] So-called commissions for cardinals and chaplains, consisting of orders by the pope or Chamberlain to investigate cases, had to be distributed as well.[25] Finally, there was 'additional documentation belonging to the *cursores*' (§ 12), again implying delivery against pay.[26] Both the commissions and the summonses pertained to a type of activity growing in importance over time, that is, the function of the Couriers as beadles.

Documents directed to the Curia and its immediate environment must be distinguished from letters to be sent abroad (§ 6), which also awaited distribution at the hands of the Master. Their fair assignment was usually not practicable, so that it was replaced by a rotation system the Master was

---

distributed by the guild, the ones to the Chamber only among the guards on duty. In both cases, the money was first deposited in the corporate register.

21 'Report', ed. by Frutaz, 'La famiglia pontificia': 'Quolibet die debent deputari quatuor ad custodiam palacii et plures, sicud videtur camerario'.

22 'Report', ed. by Frutaz, 'La famiglia pontificia': 'Debent esse solliciti ad faciendum servicia que imponuntur eis per dominum papam et camerarium'.

23 Apparently, they were meant by the words 'et portare litteras', ed. by Frutaz, 'La famiglia pontificia', starting the enumeration of specific tasks for the *cursores*. The list continues with the delivery of summonses and commissions.

24 Indicating that the Master's principal task was to see to the 'fair distribution' of assignments among the corporate members. He maintained a separate record of it. Opinions were divided, of course, as to what constituted fairness in every case, prompting the Master to decide definitively with the help of a chosen colleague. Because it was clearly improper to bypass the Master's choices and seek summonses directly from the sender, the penalty was draconian, amounting to two Florentine gold ducats and payment of the reward for the delivery to the one assigned for it according to the Master's book of distributions. On comparable arrangements in the colleges of curial Scribes, see Schwarz, *Die Organisation kurialer Schreiberkollegien*, pp. 32–39.

25 'Report', ed. by Frutaz, 'La famiglia pontificia': 'Portare commissiones auditoribus super causis audiendis'. In the rather poorly formulated text of the Statutes, the commissions are called 'petitiones'. Frequently, they were indeed petitions signed by the pope or Vice-Chancellor, although commissions also appear on the back of letters of accusation or appeal, for example, with the words: 'Audiat magister N. N. et iusticiam faciat'. On the commissions, cf. Dolezalek, 'Audientia sacri palatii'.

26 Statutes, ed. by Schmidt, 'Das päpstliche Kursorenkollegium', § 12: 'Vel aliqua res tangens cursores'.

expected to follow.[27] As long as he was head of the corporation, he had to renounce to his own turn. He was not permitted, for example, to have a servant deliver correspondence as his substitute.[28] Called 'messengers' in the following, the *cursores* far away from the Curia collected — besides their daily allowance payable by the Chamber — an additional portion (or *sors*) of the corporate income, which was credited to them at least for a certain period (§§ 9–11).[29] It is worth noticing that this share was owed to them even when they travelled on behalf of their own patron, or 'in their own service', as the formulation went (§ 11). Those, however, who expedited letters with positive news for the recipient did not obtain anything, because they could count on a handsome reward according to medieval usage (§ 10). This is what the Statutes address as the 'letters of grace', not to be confused with the gratial letters emanating from the Chamber.

The Statutes mention as duties the presence of everyone at daily morning Mass in the papal palace (§ 1) or outside for Mass and Vespers whenever the pope visited churches at his place of sojourn (§ 7). The latter regulation sanctioned absentees much more severely, especially when the Master was involved.[30] The reason is revealed to us by the 'Report', which states: 'When the lord rides on horseback, (the cursors) walk next to him so that nobody may approach him; when the lord appears in church or in the hall, they open a path for the lord so that he will not be pushed around'.

The Statutes of the *cursores* treat the structure of the corporation with great attention. In the following, I address their organization repeatedly as a guild, because the resemblance was close in contemporary Italy. The rights and duties of the corporate head, the Master Courier, were regulated extensively. He was elected for a term by his fellow members. Various rules were intended to guarantee that the election was truly free. To begin with, participation in the electoral assembly was mandatory (§§ 13 and 14).[31] Secondly, the master conducted the election at the end of his tenure

---

27 'Iter' does not signify 'area of delivery' as in other sources, but rather whose turn it was to deliver the letters. This is apparent from the rule that the Master was not permitted to prefer a friend by delaying a lucrative expedition with the help of a false date, which drew the high penalty of one Florentine gold ducat.

28 If he went against it, he not only had to pay the enormous fine of five gold ducats, but also was eliminated from the group taking turns on the *iter*.

29 'Report', ed. by Frutaz, 'La famiglia pontificia', § 56. There is a final clause concerning accommodation of the detachments accompanying the pope: 'Et quando mittuntur extra habet quilibet cursor a camerario duodecim provisinos'. According to *Les recettes et les dépenses*, ed. by Guillemain, nos 206, 495, 718, etc., to 1832, the Chamber regularly deposited the payments with the Master, 'pro (the number of) cursoribus missis extra'.

30 'Report', ed. by Frutaz, 'La famiglia pontificia', § 1: Four pennies; § 7: Twelve pennies; one *grossus Turonensis* of silver was the fine for the Master.

31 The penalty for absentees was twelve pennies, exactly as high as for those who did not attend the pope's Mass away from his palace.

and, thirdly, the decision was made by ballot. Any intentional delay in the process was penalized.[32] The same applied when a winning candidate refused to accept the outcome.[33] Subsequently, the new Master took his oath in the Apostolic Chamber (§ 15).

The primary task at the corporate level — as opposed to that of service — was the collection of money owed to the Couriers, its deposition in a shared cash register and regular distribution among the members.[34] Accounts were probably settled once a week (§§ 9–11), while payments were made at the latest when there was a change in office. Aside from the manifold penalties for statutory infractions flowing into the corporate coffers, other forms of collective income are only documented when the Couriers' demands were considered excessive or unjustified. During the three centuries discussed in the present essay, there were constant complaints about them for exploiting their position through various types of extortion. First of all, there were the 'spoils', that is, portions of the fabric and items used in the liturgy (§ 21), among them, according to the 'Report', the cloth for a precious baldachin.[35] It was held over the pope's head during his entry and exit from town.[36] There were also customary 'gifts' on the occasion of high feast days (§ 8).[37] Moreover, the guild

---

32 'Report', ed. by Frutaz, 'La famiglia Pontificia', § 14: After a deadline, each elector had to pay the high amount of six *grossi Turonenses*, to be collected by the Master in office who faced his own fine of twenty-four *grossi*.

33 'Report', ed. by Frutaz, 'La famiglia pontificia', § 23: Under pain of twenty *grossi Turonenses*.

34 Following the accounts of the Chamber, the Master routinely received from the Chamber payments for a specified number of Couriers — between sixteen and twenty-eight — either weekly or for shorter periods, such as when the messengers had left the Curia or returned to it; cf. *Les recettes et les dépenses*, ed. by Guillemain, nos 254, 360, 552, 670, etc. The Couriers were costlier than usual, then, because the Curia was constantly moving.

35 The Statutes of 1306 mention the embezzlement of wax reserved to the guild at papal, imperial, and royal funerals. It seems that only the Sergeants at arms obtained a share of the sacred items used during consecration of a bishop at the Curia; cf. Schimmelpfennig, *Die Zeremonienbücher*, pp. 197–98 (Ordo xxv).

36 'Report', ed. by Frutaz, 'La famiglia pontificia': 'Item consueverunt habere palia que portantur super capud domini quando intrat civitates'. This refers to the precious 'sky' carried above the pope on four poles. It was furnished by the hosting town. The item is not mentioned in the Statutes, it seems, because of the difficulty for individual Couriers to make it disappear; cf. p. 216 n. 74 below.

37 Provoked most likely by Couriers who had collected these gifts at their own initiative and kept them. They were requested from high-ranking personnel in the Chancery like the Vice-Chancellor, legal trainees, and notaries, as well as eminent people at the Curia such as prelates, proctors, and ambassadors, and may have derived from the *strena*, a donation at 'New Year's' reaching far back into the past and mentioned for the Couriers in later sources. The *strena* was probably meant when the representative of the Hamburg city council gave to the 'Masters' (in the plural, it seems, to denote the Master in the traditional company of two fellow Couriers) three *grossi papales* on Christmas Eve; cf. *Die Rechnungsbücher*, ed. by Schrader, p. 50. According to the Statutes of 1306, ed. by Schmidt, 'Das päpstliche Kursorenkollegium', §§ 8 and 19, the pope had issued a constitution to protect visitors to

## CHAPTER 8

had the right to be hosted by prelates during meals (§§ 19 and 20).[38] Explanation for this rule comes from the 'Report', which notes that the Couriers were entitled to deliver official invitations to higher clergy.[39] The Report further lists as income reserved to the corporation a share of the *servitia minuta*, fees that were due to the pope whenever he installed a bishop or other prelate.[40]

The Master punished misconduct and infractions by those on duty. Offensive language and physical attacks are treated at length in the Statutes (§§ 16–18). His competency even comprised bloodshed, which obliged him to restore peace between the parties upon exacting a high penalty (of ten pounds in this case) from the culprits. Only when reconciliation failed, the court of the Chamber stepped in to decide authoritatively.[41] According to the Statutes, the Master's coercive means were limited to the imposition of fines payable to the guild register. The text also introduces safeguards against the abuse of power by officials, such as brief periods of tenure (probably not lasting beyond a month).[42] Moreover, both the

---

the Curia from unjustified exactions by curial clergy, which cannot be found in the surviving registers. Schmidt does not address the matter.

38 'Report', ed. by Frutaz, 'La famiglia pontificia': 'Quicumque iret ad commedendum ad hospitium cardinalis, prelati seu ambassiatoris, vicecancellarii et helemosinariorum'.

39 'Report', ed. by Frutaz, 'La famiglia pontificia': 'To convene the prelates'; see also § 10, where an order for the *cubicularii* to this effect is mentioned. It probably functioned as a special reward. It is found in Michel de Montaigne, *Journal de Voyage en Italie*, ed. by Dédéyan, p. 207, that the Couriers still served in this role in the sixteenth century. Montaigne recounted a scene he did not understand, because he considered it to be a show of respect for his host, the French Cardinal Nicolas de Pellevé, archbishop of Sens, and indirectly for himself: 'Il y survint, deus homes d'Eglise, fort vetus, à tous je ne scay quels instrumans dans la mein, qui se mirent à genouil devant lui, et lui firent entendre je ne scay quel service qui se faisoit en quelque Église, il ne leur dit du tout rien: mais come ils se relevarent apres avoir parlé et s'en alloint, il leur tira un peu le bonnet'. Since he did not see it, Montaigne did not mention the opulent meal awaiting the two Couriers in the cardinal's residence; cf. Moroni, 'Cursori apostolici o pontifici', pp. 56–57, where the invitation by a cardinal like the one here is accurately described.

40 'Report', ed. by Frutaz, 'La famiglia pontificia', p. 319 (§ 68). The fee in question was the fourth *servitium* designated for the papal palace. It was divided (in very unequal amounts) between the *domicelli* (five parts) and *cursores* (one part) and, secondly, different categories of doormen. Of the first group, only the Couriers were paid during papal vacancies. Under Clement V, the *Modus dividendi quinque minuta servitia* (cf. above, p. 202 n. 10) made payment for services contingent on proper personal presence. Otherwise, the share was forfeited to the Chamber; see the 'Report', ed. by Frutaz, 'La famiglia pontificia', p. 322.

41 The stipulation in the Statutes, ed. by Schmidt, 'Das päpstliche Kursorenkollegium', § 24, that conflict among the *cursores* about gambling debts did not fall under the Master's jurisdiction was apparently based on a concrete incident, as previous office holders had claimed competency in this regard.

42 As is evident from the Statutes, ed. by Schmidt, 'Das päpstliche Kursorenkollegium', § 6 (exclusion from deliveries). When the Master attended the meals of high prelates several times a month, he always had to bring a different colleague and was free to choose him. This

consultation of colleagues in important decisions (§ 4 and, arguably, in §§ 16–18) and the distribution of assignments in writing were 'required' (§§ 4 and 5).[43] The Statutes are silent about the stipend of the Master, who was not permitted to operate as a Courier during his time in office.[44] It is likely that he was at least compensated for his loss of income. It was also his prerogative to deliver the above-mentioned invitations to higher prelates together with a collegiate 'friend' of his choice (§ 20). Following long-established custom, they were invited to a meal in the recipient's residence, a considerable reward given the difference in lifestyle.

Concerning the service and status of the *cursores*, both sources state that corporate members basically held their position for life.[45] They belonged to the papal household — as opposed to that of individual popes! — and were thus very close to the Chamberlain as their superior and judge.[46] This did not prevent them from joining the entourage of a leading figure at the Curia, while precluding the accumulation of additional offices.[47] Following the 'Report', the Chamber had to provide accommodation to all Couriers.[48] Each of them could also claim an annual share of cloth for their ordinary uniform.[49] Special fabric was owed to them on the occasion of a papal coronation.[50]

---

rule strongly suggests that another Master would give his friends the same opportunity the next month.

43 *Les recettes et les dépenses*, ed. by Guillemain, no. 140 (November 1308). The transfer of funds from the Chamber to the Master 'for the charters bought to renew the letters of the Couriers' implies that he had to provide the messengers with the necessary documents of identification and passports.

44 Following the Statutes of the late fifteenth century, ed. by Schmidt, 'Das päpstliche Kursorenkollegium', § 14, he received a share of all the commissions coming to distribution 'in the way it has been customary from old times', to offset the financial shortfall he incurred by being unable to deliver citations or announcements himself.

45 For evidence showing how the Chamber helped in the case of death or invalidity, see Schmidt, 'Das päpstliche Kursorenkollegium', p. 582; Hayez, 'Les courriers des papes d'Avignon', p. 54.

46 They did not lose their office when the pope died; cf. the receipt of *servitia* during vacancies on the papal throne, p. 209 n. 40 above.

47 See p. 207 above.

48 'Report', ed. by Frutaz, 'La famiglia pontificia', § 53, where the Couriers are mentioned among the guards and servants. The larger colleges only received a lump sum for the rent; it amounted to six monthly *solidi provisinorum* for the *cursores*, the Sergeants at arms obtained ten. If there was no bed, they were paid half a gold ducat *pro presepe* on top, § 44. In the mid-fourteenth century, the carriers were still given money to cover their rental expenses, see Hayez, 'Les courriers des papes d'Avignon', p. 53. The stipulations in the 'Report', ed. by Frutaz, 'La famiglia pontificia', § 56, refer to service in person; cf. p. 205 n. 18, p. 209 n. 40 above.

49 *Les recettes et les dépenses*, ed. by Guillemain, nos 1850 and 1952, concerning (a count of) 'vestments to be bought for the *cursores*' in October.

50 'Report', ed. by Frutaz, 'La famiglia pontificia': 'Each of them also used to have one arm of fabric during coronations and again on Holy Thursday'. When the pope was crowned, the

212    CHAPTER 8

Our two sources from the beginning of Clement V's pontificate attest to the state of development the college of the Couriers had reached over the course of the thirteenth century. Although there is more documentation for the Avignonese period (1309–1378), it would be difficult for us to benefit from it without the information of the Statutes and the 'Report'.[51] This is evident from the widely differing historiographical accounts.[52] They include the studies of Renouard,[53] Guillemain,[54] and Hayez,[55] who did not yet know of Schmidt's discovery.

The events of the Avignonese phase can be summarized as follows. First, there was change in the assignments, but most importantly a shift in focus. The detachment at the papal palace providing guards and serving as a task force was retained. The college had to send six members taking turns each week. It is clearly stated that they alone were paid by the Chamber, not all the *cursores* as scholarship has surmised.[56] The function of the former unit at the Chamber was absorbed by its own personnel. The

---

cloth distributed was especially precious, called 'rosati' in the sources. A register entry to this effect appears for seventeen Couriers in connection with the coronation of Nicholas V (1447); cf. Rome, State Archive, Fondo Camerale I, Mandati camerali 831, fol. 20ᵛ. On the other hand, they did not receive any textiles in the period of mourning for the dead pope. This is justified (around 1415) with the 'perpetuity' of their position; see Vatican Library, Vat. lat. 4736, fol. 4ᵛ. According to Rome, State Archive, Fondo Camerale I, Mandati camerali 830, fol. 258ᵛ, however, six Couriers were given black fabric for the funeral of Eugene IV (d. 1447), possibly because they belonged to the detachment at the papal palace; cf. p. 206 n. 21 above. The statutes from the late fifteenth century demand conferral of mourning attire to all members of the guild at the pope's death; ed. by Schmidt, 'Das päpstliche Kursorenkollegium', § 65: 'They each are to have three lengths of black fabric'.

51  From the time until 1417, there are only the registers of incoming and outgoing payments (*Introitus et exitus*) in the Chamber, beginning under Boniface VIII (1294–1303) and fragmentary at first, with their frequently cryptic entries. Unlike us, contemporaries knew who made these monetary transactions and why. In addition, there are the registers of expedited papal letters, and from Clement VI also those of petitions, plus a few records furnishing scattered data of difficult interpretation. For the registers of the Chamber, see *Libri rationum camerae Bonifatii papae VIII*, ed. by Schmidt; *Les recettes et les dépenses*, ed. by Guillemain; and *Die Ausgaben der Apostolischen Kammer*, ed. by Schäfer.

52  Highlighted by Hayez, 'Les courriers des papes d'Avignon', a methodological challenge inherent in the sources is that the term 'courier' is not used exclusively for guild members, but also for other messengers and professional deliverymen, similar to the less than specific reference to a 'custos' (guardian). Recourse to the identification of names does not help a great deal, because it often proves impossible to begin with; even where it succeeds, moreover, little insight is gained into the concrete circumstances of individuals.

53  Renouard, 'Comment les papes d'Avignon expédiaient leur courrier'; reprinted in Renouard, *Études d'histoire médiévale*, II, pp. 739–64.

54  Guillemain, *La cour pontificale d'Avignon*, pp. 301 ff.

55  Hayez, 'Les courriers des papes d'Avignon'.

56  This is made clear in a report of 1409, the *Avisamenta pro regimine et dispositione officiariorum*, composed to inform the newly elected Pope Alexander (V) about Avignonese customs. Its author was the long-serving Chamberlain, François de Conzié, in *Le cérémonial papale*, ed. by Dykmans, III, p. 442 (§§ 165–66): 'Ipsi ex se ipsis sex eligant qui alternatis

delivery of letters within the vicinity concentrated on commissions and summonses to the Rota, which began to emerge at the time. This led to change in the recruitment of Couriers, who increasingly needed legal skills that exceeded the elementary level. Among laity, the required knowledge was found only in Italy and the south of France, whereas other regions had to rely on growing contingents of clergy.

The expedition of correspondence to places farther away (called 'letters from the Curia' or 'secret letters') had never been a monopoly of the *cursores*. To lower expenses and improve efficiency, popes increasingly entrusted the task to banks and firms specializing in postal services for banks, which unlike the Couriers also accepted mail that was intended for third parties.[57] As a result, the guild remained solely responsible for those areas of Western Christendom that did not open to the Italian bankers, consisting of central-eastern and northern Europe. The same is true for the fifteenth century, when papal messengers chiefly appeared in those territories.[58] The selection of suitable corporate members there became ever more competitive, because close familiarity with the area in question was necessary apart from sophistication, leadership attributes, and a strong health.

The delivery of specific letters, both near and far, persisted as a monopoly of the guild. They included invitations and the like, imposing novel demands on the *cursores*, especially the ability to act 'honourably'. The same applied to the ceremonial functions, which certainly proliferated and gained in significance.[59] Adding to the obligations of the Couriers,

---

vicibus et septimanis in palatio apostolico serviant et ipsis sex de palatio provideatur de victu'. The Master was responsible for the selection of suitable colleagues.

57 Gasnault, 'La transmission des lettres pontificales'. Normal letters for third parties were taken along by 'travellers to Rome or other pilgrims'. The destruction of papal correspondence was apparently a frequent act of violence; cf. the powers of the Great Penitentiary in 1438, ed. by Göller, *Die päpstliche Pönitentiarie*, I/2, p. 39.

58 For reasons of space, an analysis of my prosopographical data on fifteenth-century *cursores* cannot be presented here.

59 Apart from participating in coronation processions (below, p. 214 n. 66), the Couriers were mobilized ceremonially as companions of the one honoured with the Golden Rose; see Schimmelpfennig, *Die Zeremonienbücher*, p. 261 (Ordo LII, § 7), receiving one *iocale* in recompense. During the pope's entry, they had various assignments according to an Ordo of *c.* 1418, ed. by Dykmans, 'D'Avignon à Rome', pp. 203–310. Some of them surrounded the horse carrying the consecrated bread with burning torches in hand, the rest walked between the cardinals and the pope (III, §§ 9 and 11). At Constance, the *cursores* and the Sergeants at arms competed for income at Jewish ceremonies, probably related to the maintenance of order and not documented elsewhere; cf. Vatican, Apostolic Archive, Arm. XXIX: Diversa Cameralia 3, fol. 42ʳ (7 December 1417). Moroni, 'Cursori apostolici o pontifici', lists additional obligations, such as the announcement of the *Possesso* (p. 53); the preservation of order at Corpus Christi and other processions (pp. 55, 58); broadcasting consistories and liturgical functions (p. 55); invitations to them (pp. 56–58); at the conclave (p. 57); and at funerals (p. 58). It remains to be investigated when exactly these rights were acquired.

214    CHAPTER 8

they had to buy the supplies of the papal Curia. The new task arose from the policy of the Avignonese popes to secure provisions for the court not on the general market, but rather internally or directly from the producer. The *cursores* operated in this regard either independently or as companions of the appointed buyer.[60] Prior to the research of Stefan Weiß, scholarship had only been aware of their mobilization for acquisitions at long-distance fairs.[61] Their widely recognized uniform allowed them and their company to travel toll-free and reside without charge at ecclesiastical institutions. To facilitate their identification everywhere, they also carried papal banners with them.[62] The payment of the Couriers was identical with what they received for deliveries abroad. Besides, they must have earned considerable sums by acting as buyers on behalf of persons with curial status, probably including their fellow guild members.[63] By the fifteenth century, the sole reminder of these activities was the acquisition of artfully plaited palms, which the pope distributed on Palm Sunday.[64]

As early as under Clement IV (1264–1268), the compensation of the Couriers was converted from naturals to cash. The payments steadily diminished from the mid-fourteenth century, due to the deteriorating papal finances.[65] Only the long-distance Couriers continued to receive their daily allowances during absence from the Curia and had their expenses refunded. Service fees (or 'taxes') as well as tips collected from customers became the principal source of income, apart from earnings made during ceremonies. The size of the college of *cursores* grew smaller. Its minimum was set by ceremonial necessities.[66] In addition, membership gradually changed depending on nationality. The leading role of the Italians was taken over by the French, who notably hailed from all Francophone

---

60  Weiß, *Die Versorgung des päpstlichen Hofes*.

61  Renouard, 'Achats et paiements de draps flamands'.

62  Weiß, *Die Versorgung des päpstlichen Hofes*, p. 427. At Beaune and other places, the Couriers bought on their own expensive Burgundian wine, already filled in barrels, and transported it all the way to the papal cellar. They accompanied the pope's almoner during his wholesale acquisitions, that is, to the harvest, packaging, and expedition; p. 345. When the wine production of entire villages had to be managed until its delivery to Avignon, the Apostolic Chamber preferred the use of papal *domicelli* who also wore uniforms with the papal coat of arms, most likely because they were better prepared to confront rural populations. For the same reason, the transfer of precious spices from Montpellier to Avignon may have been left to the *domicelli* rather than the *cursores*; p. 411.

63  Weiß, *Die Versorgung des päpstlichen Hofes*, p. 425.

64  Rodocanachi, 'Les courriers pontificaux', p. 399.

65  The relevant scholarship is surveyed by Schimmelpfennig, *Das Papsttum*, p. 229.

66  Because the Couriers had to surround the pope directly during his coronation and protect him with their silver staffs, their number could hardly drop below twenty; cf. Schimmelpfennig, *Die Zeremonienbücher*, p. 437 (Ordo CXXXVIII, § 43; from the time of Nicholas V). The remark in Vatican, Apostolic Archive, Schedario Garampi 110, Off. 2, fol. 5ᵃ, that the Couriers carried twelve banners during the coronation of 1335 (or rather, 20 December 1334) remains without confirmation in the original documentation.

regions. Neither the English nor the Germans were represented. I have already mentioned that the share of clerics went up. In the fifteenth century, there was another shift, as the portion of Couriers from the periphery began to increase and clergy became dominant.

Just as in 1306, conflict produced further information about the *cursores* in 1365, this time concerning their official dress. The dispute centred on details regarding the signs on the uniforms of corporate members in charge of protecting the pope and guarding his palace, in other words, the various classes of gatekeepers (*hostiarii*), the *domicelli* or Sergeants at arms, and the Couriers.[67] The quarrel erupted during preparations for Charles IV's imperial coronation in Avignon.[68] According to contemporary custom, it was preceded by his solemn entry into town on Ascension Day (22 May).[69] A week earlier, the pope resolved the matter authoritatively, mandating that the Couriers had to carry a long silver staff and ring as markers of their identity.[70] We are informed by other sources that they displayed the coat of arms of the reigning pope and that of the Roman Church on the front and back of their uniform. Later depictions especially in the statutes of the late fifteenth century show that it was purple with both emblems stitched onto it.[71] The Couriers covered it with a blue tunic and wore a biretta in carmine-red. They were meant to be very visible, not least for their own protection.

In anticipation of Charles IV's arrival, the pope and the Chamberlain also had to review the long-standing prerogatives of the college of Couriers. The corporation demanded two horses 'as proper spoils', probably the

---

67 See the constitution 'Etsi cunctorum Christifidelium' of 14 May 1365; Vatican, Apostolic Archive, Reg. Vat. 247, fols 263ᵛ–65ʳ; ed. by Mollat, 'Règlement d'Urbain V sur les insignes', p. 169.

68 On the preliminaries in the spring of 1365, cf. *Die Ausgaben der Apostolischen Kammer unter Urban V. und Gregor XI.*, ed. by Schäfer, pp. 98 ff.

69 Concerning this entry, see Hack, *Das Empfangszeremoniell*, pp. 549–62; and Weiß, *Die Versorgung des päpstlichen Hofes*, pp. 233 ff., with supplementary data.

70 The constitution of 14 May 1365 (p. 214 n. 68 above) allowed the Couriers to put on a decorated silver ring only when they served away from the Curia. While there, it had to be of less precious material, 'de ere vel electro seu letone'.

71 Rome, Biblioteca Casanatense, MS 4170, fol. 5ᵛ (see front cover image for this volume), shows the crucifixion and two figures situated below, one standing to the right, the other kneeling to the left. The latter has put down his biretta. The seated colleague is apparently a cleric, the one on his knees a layman, as lay *cursores* were permitted to wear the same head gear; cf. Moroni, 'Cursori apostolici o pontifici', pp. 55–56. The beginning of John's Gospel, on which new members of the corporation swore their oath, follows until fol. 6ʳ. The context, the posture of the two figures, and the way they hold their staff (*mazza*) suggests that the scene depicts the adoption ceremony of an entering Courier. I am grateful to Martin Bertram for the reference. Accordingly, the seated person shows the Master. The kneeling one reveals through slits in the overcoat, which like the garment underneath reaches to the floor, that he wears red stockings and gold-chipped shoes. The *mazza* has a ring around it at the top. For an incomplete description, cf. Lanconelli, 'Manoscritti statutari Romani', p. 320.

216 CHAPTER 8

splendid ones the emperor led in person at his entry.[72] For the Chamberlain, this was fraudulent.[73] The college may have insisted as well on one of the baldachins held above the pope and emperor and energetically made other claims the pope and his Chamberlain considered to be novel rights 'the Couriers sometimes pretended to have'.[74] The pope rejected them.

Due to the relative lack of documentation, it is nearly impossible to determine how the two and eventually three colleges of *cursores* persisted through the period of the Great Schism (1378–1415) and its countless improvisations. The evidence for the Avignonese Pope Clement (VII) is superior in comparison, although his pontificate was very exceptional.[75] Beginning in 1417, the sources improve significantly in conjunction with efforts to overcome and address the consequences of the Schism, as three papal courts had to be reconsolidated into one. Most of the material attests to conflict about corporate and membership rights between the guild of the Couriers on the one hand, and the popes and their Chamberlain on the other. References are found especially in the three series of records known as the *Diversa Cameralia*, the *Mandati*, and the *Libri officiorum*.[76] They

---

72 *Chronica Johannis de Reading*, ed. by Tait, pp. 165–66; on the emperor's baldachin, see Hack, *Das Empfangszeremoniell*, p. 554.

73 Vatican, Apostolic Archive, Reg. Aven. 198, fol. 506ʳ (27 May 1365), a mandate by the pope to the Chamberlain to hold the Couriers accountable for this; for an excerpt, see Baumgarten, *Aus Kanzlei und Kammer*, p. 233.

74 Vatican, Apostolic Archive, Reg. Aven. 198, fol. 506ʳ, ordering 'that his Couriers henceforth do not receive the *papalio* held above the pope or anyone else, nor ask for any other rights and gifts they sometimes claim to have'. In this case, it is not the *papalio* or liturgical umbrella, which rather than above was carried ahead of the pope — and certainly not of any other person — during procession. According to the Ordo of 1418, moreover, the *papalio* was held by a single person, the seneschal of the Sergeants at arms; cf. *D'Avignon à Rome*, ed. by Dykmans, p. 239 (§ 5). Instead, the reference on fol. 506ʳ is to the *pallium*, or baldachin, which the sources do not always distinguish clearly. The Couriers thus had transferred their traditional right to the pope's baldachin (above, p. 209 n. 36) 'by analogy' to the emperor's entry. On occasion of Urban V's arrival in Avignon on 27 September 1370, all *cursores* were suspended from office and not readmitted until 2 October; see Vatican, Apostolic Archive, Reg. Aven. 198, fol. 462ʳ. Unfortunately, the reason is not mentioned.

75 For an investigation especially of the development of the Roman and the conciliar Curia, see Schwarz, 'Die römische Kurie', p. 237 (English version, pp. 181–82 above). Under Clement (VII), the resignation of offices by the *cursores*, attested to in Vatican, Apostolic Archive, Collect. 457, fols 128ʳ–38ʳ, does not appear to have been 'in favour of a third party', which canonically speaking would have suggested that they could sell their offices. They rather seem to have transferred their positions to clients or relatives in the feudal sense. Likewise, the high entrance fee of two ounces in gold confirmed by the same pope, fol. 132ʳ (16 January 1389), to be divided equally between the Chamber and the college, was not immediately resumed by his successors after the Schism; cf. Genequand, 'Carrières immobiles à la cour de Clément VII'.

76 I have systematically examined the *Libri officiorum* in Vatican, Apostolic Archive, Reg. Vat. 348–51, 381–83, 432–34, 465–66, 515–17, 542–43; the *Libri officialium* (registers of oaths), Reg. Vat. 384, 435, 467, 545, 697, 875; the first volumes of the *Libri officialium* are not

inform, if in partial fashion, for the first time continuously and extensively about the college.[77] Additional and scattered data come from other types of registers, which I have tracked until around 1470.[78] The redaction of guild statutes from the end of the century (eighty paragraphs long!) is treated here only tangentially.[79] It features much material of older origin. Our Statutes of 1306, for example, are easily recognizable.

Given the limitations of space, I discuss next, without full citation of the evidence, and in condensed fashion — or cursorily as it were in view of the subject matter — the tensions which grew ever more pronounced from 1417 to *c.* 1470, while leaving aside the above-mentioned changes in composition and corporate duties of the college. The contest reveals a shift in attitude among popes and their Chamberlains toward the college, which transformed under permanent pressure to defend itself. Which were the main points of disagreement? Above all, there was the overcrowding of the college once the Council of Constance had decreed the reunification of the three previously existing papal governments.[80] The income, according to constant complaints, was insufficient to sustain members 'in accordance with their status'. Martin V (1417–1431) only conceded a reduction in

---

in the Apostolic Archive, but in Rome, State Archive, Fondo Camerale I, 1711: Ufficiali camerali (Martin V), 1712–13 (Eugene IV); the *Diversa cameralia* in Vatican, Apostolic Archive, Arm. XXIX, 1–33; also, Introitus et exitus 426, 44, 458, 464; Reg. Vat. 500; and Resignationes 1. For comparison with the Avignonese period and the Schism, I have used the registers of oaths and *Libri officiorum* in Vatican, Apostolic Archive, Reg. Aven. 173, 198, 268; Arm. XXXIV, 4; and Collect. 456–57. I have seen in Rome, State Archive, Fondo Camerale I, 830–32: Mandati camerali (and, in microfilm, a fragment from the pontificate of Boniface IX, now in Paris); Rome, State Archive, Fondo Camerale I, 1286–89: Tesoreria segreta; 1468–71: Spese minute di Palazzo; and Vatican, Apostolic Archive, Reg. Aven. 288. For a characterization of these series, cf. Schuchard, *Die päpstlichen Kollektoren*, pp. 3–8; for individual items, see the introductions to the *Repertorium Germanicum*, except vol. IV (on Martin IV).

77 The oath registers, see p. 216 n. 76 above, have their own rubric for the *cursores* under Martin V, in *Le 'liber officialium' de Martin V*, ed. by Uginet; cf. von Mitis, 'Zwei Amtsbücher aus der Kammer Martins V', which is still indispensable; also, under Eugene IV, in Rome, State Archive, Fondo Camerale I, 1712: Ufficiali camerali, fol. 111$^{rs}$, cf. fol. 116$^r$, with nine entries; Fondo Camerale I, 1713, fol. 68$^r$, has only one entry for the *cursores*. The so-called *Libri officialium* in Vatican, Apostolic Archive, Reg. Vat., contain occasional oaths not until Nicholas V (1447–1455).

78 I have placed the end of my study around 1470, because the organization of offices at the Curia changed fundamentally under Sixtus IV (1471–1484). I have only studied the origins of the venality of offices until that point, permitting me to offer comparative remarks on the development of other charges. It is possible that the surviving redaction of the statutes is also from that period, apart from later additions, unless it occurred around 1500, the date of the extant manuscript, Rome, Biblioteca Casanatense, MS 4170.

79 Closer examination of the conflict between the corporation and the pope and his Chamberlain based on detailed evidence, as well as an edition with commentary of the late fifteenth-century statutes must be left to a separate study.

80 See Schwarz, 'L'organizzazione curiale di Martino V'.

218   CHAPTER 8

general terms, but not the requested 'fixed number' of colleagues.[81] In claiming to constitute 'the' college of *cursores*, a group of attendees at the Council of Constance attempted to exclude latecomers, demanded from them an acceptance fee, rejected them on grounds of lacking qualification, and scrutinized the legitimacy of their right to join with full benefits.

In addition, there were office holders who sought to sell their position to third parties, if possible, by way of a papal dispensation known as a 'resignation in favour'. The first documented example dates to 1420. The new mechanism prevented the pope from leaving vacancies unfilled and undercut the reduction of guild memberships. Popes and Chamberlains even appointed new Couriers, while promises to diminish their number proved rather ineffective. The guild battled such 'impertinences' with litigation before the court of the Apostolic Chamber, but also by distinguishing between nominal status and actual exercise of the office, by conferring to new holders only the title of 'cursor', or by delaying their full admission against the Chamberlain's strict orders for years.

The Chamberlain tried to force compliance with tough measures like excommunication or suspension from office over extended periods, which were executed as well. The guild fought back in proceedings before the Chamber and other courts and scored partial successes. Among them was the concession that only the pope could appoint *cursores* (and not the Chamberlain), while the Chamber was limited to the ceremony of admission to office and to the administration of the official oath.[82] The college in turn went on to devise complicated procedures for acceptance into the guild (together with a rite of investiture), which remained incomplete without enrolment in the collegiate *pitaffium*. Not until then, the

---

81 In his bull, 'Apostolice sedis dignitas' (23 November 1420), in Vatican, Apostolic Archive, Reg. Lat. 219, fol. 177[vs]. It was preceded by a petition, Reg. Suppl. 148, fol. 23[rs].
Both references appear in Tübingen, Universitätsarchiv, Nachlaß Fink. The corporation complained that there had been nineteen members at the beginning of the pontificate, which had meanwhile ballooned to thirty-eight by mandate of the Chamberlain. The Couriers requested from the pope that those unqualified (whose description casts doubt on the decision-making of their immediate superior) be removed from office and the total reduced 'to a certain and reasonable amount', so that they could secure their sustenance from their occupation. Henceforth, candidates to be accepted had to show a petition signed by none other than the pope and pass an examination by the Chamber 'concerning their loyalty, conscience, knowledge, and good faith with suitable witnesses'. Martin V granted the request only in part, responding: 'So be it, that they shall not be admitted unless they have a petition that is signed by our hand'. The remaining grievances were to be investigated by a judge from the Rota, apparently without result. The bull was hardly effective, because in subsequent registers of petitions and in the *Libri officialium* (p. 216 n. 76 above), more admissions to the guild are found than before. One entrant of 1424 is called 'excess-numbered' (*supernumerarius*); see *Le 'liber officialium' de Martin V*, ed. by Uginet, p. 117.

82 As curial offices were increasingly set on a par with benefices, appointment by the pope alone implied that the guild could draw on the entire arsenal of arguments from the law of benefices; vgl. Schwarz, 'Die römische Kurie' (English version above, pp. 177–99).

new member was entitled to his full share of corporate income awaiting distribution, which was called *sors* in the Statutes of 1306 and *dividende* in those from the end of the fifteenth century.

The situation under Eugene IV was fundamentally different. After the loss of Rome, he had to move through northern Italy and was progressively deprived of followers and support, which reached its low point between 1439 and 1444.[83] The loyalty of his curial staff was important to him, but he was in no position to respect their traditional rights, because he needed offices to generate income. He no longer cared about the autonomy of the guild. The admissions fee for the college was waved or reduced by papal order, membership was mandated with instant access to full pay, and nominal colleagues were imposed to give them funding despite dramatically diminished revenues.[84] In case of refusal, the monies ready for distribution were confiscated, and the Master was threatened with the loss of his place among the *cursores*. The stipulated sanctions increased over time, including excommunication, removal of the Master from his office and benefice (!), a fine for the whole guild of one-hundred and, subsequently, 200 marks of silver (!) in 1435. Later still, the Master and the leading college representatives and, eventually, everyone involved was to face high penalties and imprisonment for being 'disobedient and rebellious'. Collegiate privileges to the contrary were abolished. In the end, however, Eugene IV was compelled to offer compensation to the corporation in 1439. He conceded — hardly a sacrifice for him — that the benefices of the Couriers (who meanwhile had become clerics for the most part) would fall under general reservation, thereby improving their status.[85] He confirmed their prerogatives and increased the admissions fee. Most importantly, though, Eugene IV finally established the maximum count of (nineteen) full members, the same that the old statutes of 1306 had (allegedly) proposed, and regulated by contract the mechanisms of reduction.[86] To attain it, standards were applied which had long been

---

83 Diener and Schwarz, 'Das Itinerar Eugens IV.', p. 200.

84 The Council of Basel had formed its own college of *cursores*, modelled after the Roman Curia; cf. Dephoff, *Zum Urkunden- und Kanzleiwesen des Konzils von Basel*, pp. 113–16, who counted them among the Chancery personnel. They must not be confused with the detachment of papal Couriers at the Council and previously that of Siena (cf. Vatican, Apostolic Archive, Arm. XXIX, 8, fol. 60$^r$; 17 December 1423), nor with the unit left in Rome during papal absences.

85 See the constitution of 29 December 1438, in Vatican, Apostolic Archive, Reg. Suppl. 360, fol. 40$^r$. From Nicholas V onward, the text became a firm component of the Chancery rules; cf. *Regulae cancellariae apostolicae*, ed. by von Ottenthal, p. 256 (§ 6). Already before that time, it was not infrequent for individual Couriers to rank among the *familiares*, or papal household members.

86 Moroni, 'Cursori apostolici o pontifici', p. 56, explains the difference between the original and successive counts (of twenty versus nineteen members) with the presence of one 'unfaithful' colleague who was not replaced.

developed in connection with venal offices and originated in the law of ecclesiastical benefices, with consequences for the Couriers' understanding of their position.[87] Eugene's successors confirmed both the fixed number and the statutes, providing the guild with a somewhat effective instrument to defend their customary liberties, as well as levels of sustenance in accordance with their status.

Soon after returning to Rome, Eugene IV and his Chamberlain showed their overall determination not to respect the customary monopolies of the Carriers any longer. The pope, for example, gave certain members license to offer commercial delivery services, while also permitting them to hire their corporate colleagues as employees. Upon litigation, the licenses were withdrawn, but the guild had to abandon various prerogatives as well. The current head of the corporation was named 'sole master' of the Couriers for life (!) — contrary to a tradition reaching back 250 years. Furthermore, some *cursores* were exclusively appointed as beadles at the Apostolic Rota, an innovation the guild successfully prevented from becoming permanent, although we do not know how. Meanwhile and with increasing frequency, the delivery of messages over long distances was entrusted to others. In fact, the Renaissance popes allowed commercial Couriers to wear the papal coat of arms on their clothing just as the *cursores* did, and extended to the former the privileges of exemption enjoyed by curial officials.[88]

The guild embarked in this period on a thorough search for old rights and long-standing sources of income, which the statutes from the end of the century extensively reclaim. The main reason for not permitting the office of the *cursores* to become a venal one was that the collection of income and enjoyment of the attending privileges remained tied to duties requiring personal administration. Nonetheless, the holders had to invest considerable amounts when acquiring their position in the first place. Only in 1586, the corporation was transformed into a so-called college of vacabilists, free to sell their membership to eligible successors.

The statutes of the late fifteenth century do not contain the following piece of information about the daily existence of the Couriers, which I provide to end my discussion rather than offering a conclusion in the proper sense. In 1461 or 1462, the guild was again involved in judicial proceedings, this time with the Roman *gabellarius*, or customs-collector. The point of contention was a public tavern operated by the Couriers and

---

87 I do not uphold my claim in Schwarz, 'Die römische Kurie', p. 245 n. 77 (English version above, p. 188–89 n. 77), that the Couriers transformed into a college of 'vacabilists' under Eugene IV. The fundamental study of vacabilists (whose curial office was for sale) remains von Hofmann, *Forschungen zur Geschichte der kurialen Behörden*.

88 Vatican, Apostolic Archive, Reg. Vat. 433, fol. 154^rs, where it is stated in the margin: 'Courier or messenger (*nuntius*)'.

ON BEHALF OF THE POPE    221

their Master. It did not have a fixed location, but opened wherever their traditional 'sign' was displayed. They claimed to possess an ancient right to dispense twenty barrels of toll-free wine each year. This echoes the number of twenty college members mentioned in 1306, which had become a myth, believed to predate human memory! At the time of the trial, the sign was posted at the 'Peacock's Bar'.[89]

Unfortunately, the exact address is not stated.[90] Perhaps, it was near San Michele and next to the church of San Celso and San Giuliano, in what now is the via Banchi Nuovi, 21–21c, where the fraternity of the *cursores* resided in the 1400s.[91]

---

89 Today, a *via del Pavone* crosses the *via dei Banchi Vecchi* and is situated close to the church of San Celso and San Giuliano.

90 The 'Peacock' does not appear among the guest-houses in the books of the Chamber for 1463, listing them as lodgings for the imperial entourage on occasion of Frederick III's second visit to Rome in 1468/1469; cf. *Repertorium Germanicum*, IX, ed. by Höing and others, no. 1334. Both, Romani, *Pellegrini e viaggiatori*; and Gnoli, *Alberghi e osterie di Roma nella Rinascenza*, are based on Cerasoli, 'Ricerche storiche intorno agli alberghi di Roma'. For corrections, see Esch, 'Preise, Kapazität und Lage römischer Hotels im Mittelalter', pp. 447–49; revised in Esch, *Wege nach Rom*, pp. 211–12. The volumes on the 'gabella vini ad minutum', also called 'gabella studii' in Rome, State Archive, Fondo Camerale I, Camera urbis 93–95, contain like the *Mandati camerali* references to Roman taverns. They only start in 1473, though. The new study by Sanfilippo, *La Roma dei Romani*, which treats hosts and taverners as well, pp. 375 ff., does not extend to the fifteenth century.

91 Sohn, *Deutsche Prokuratoren an der römischen Kurie*, pp. 274–75, has uncovered a contract (of 17 August 1472) between the chapter of San Celso and the guild, in which the chapter left to the use of the *cursores* the neighbouring chapel of San Michele, united with San Celso, renting and conceding it against payment 'to have therein Masses and other divine services celebrated for the salvation of their souls'. It is unknown where the fraternity had its seat before or after 1503, when the church building was modified. In the fifteenth century, San Michele served the papal *Audientia litterarum contradictarum* for a long time as its official residence. The chapter of the fraternity of the Proctors at the Rota was also located there. According to Moroni, 'Cursori apostolici o pontifici', p. 59, a 'street or quarter (*vicus*) of the *cursores*' had been in this area.

CHAPTER 9

# Leon Battista Alberti's Career in the Papal Chancery[1]

## An Unwelcome Incident in the Papal Chancery, 1432/1433

When Bartholomeus de Puteo (or, dal Pozzo) came to the Apostolic Chancery to retrieve the petitions as usual from the 'common box (*publica supplicationum capsula*)', he found among them an anonymous attack on his person.[2] It was written on several leaflets (*cartule*). As soon as he had looked at them, he concluded: 'This was my young friend, Battista Alberti'.[3] Deeply hurt, he told many of his colleagues about the discovery. He sought confirmation from them concerning his identification of the author, which he backed up with proof gathered along the way. The handwriting and style, he argued, were Alberti's, probably citing the young humanist's predilection for polemics, too.[4] Bartholomeus instantly spoke of other offenses Alberti was supposed to have committed. He threatened to bring them in a complaint against the Abbreviator to the Chamberlain's attention. Alberti soon heard about Bartolomeo's intentions, as interpretation of the affair depended on every informant's relationship with the two protagonists.

Fortunately for us, Alberti defended himself in a letter of his own. It is a well-crafted piece of rhetoric surviving in a collection of humanist correspondence at the National Library of Vienna.[5] The text yields insights that extend beyond Alberti's personality. It attests to his position in the papal Chancery, revealing some of its inner workings unlike our commonly consulted sources. According to the letter, Alberti was prompted to write

---

1 I am grateful to my friend, Katharina Colberg (Hanover), for her careful work as copy-editor.

2 Letter by Alberti, 'Si pacato animo', in *Opera inedita*, ed. by Mancini, pp. 272–77; newly edited by Vestri, in *Corpus epistolare*, ed. by Benigni and others, pp. 125–31 (no. 8); with references to classical passages (especially Cicero) in the commentary, pp. 131–33. I have consulted Vestri's text here.

3 In humanist fashion, he did not take on the name of Leon Battista Alberti until much later; it never appears in connection with the Chancery.

4 This can be inferred from Alberti, in his *Corpus epistolare*, ed. by Benigni and others, p. 129 line 15: 'Ut per capsulas amicos morderem'.

5 Vienna, Österreichische Nationalbibliothek, BPV Cod. 3420, fols 56ʳ–57ʳ.

at greater length after he waited a while for Bartolomeo to calm down. Hence the opening words: 'If, and once the mind has been appeased ...'. In the following, Alberti rejected Bartolomeo's accusation of him as author of the invective, stating towards the end that 'I have neither composed those leaflets of yours, nor seen them, nor do I know who is responsible for them'. Although he was unfamiliar with the pamphlet, Alberti wrote, he believed based on hearsay that it culminated in criticism against Bartholomeus de Puteo for acting 'with greed and harshness' against the 'order of Abbreviators'.[6] By artfully presenting the grievances against dal Pozzo (and himself) as the opinion and rumour of malignant voices, Alberti was able to package his own critique favourably. Many shared the impression that Bartolomeo dal Pozzo was overly quick to lose his temper and hurt people.[7] Alberti dismissed it as unsubstantiated and defamatory talk that dal Pozzo was using his office as reader (*lectionis officium*) for illicit gain through the invention of bureaucratic hurdles.[8] The same, Alberti remarked, applied as well to the hearsay that he, Battista Alberti, had illicitly tried to enrich himself while serving as reader in the Chancery: 'Only Battista is greedy in the Chancery, only he reads to claim for himself unjust profit'.[9] He argued that these views (perhaps shared by dal Pozzo) were untenable because he, as dal Pozzo knew, disposed of sufficient wealth 'honestly acquired elsewhere' to support his preferred lifestyle.[10]

Alberti went on to examine dal Pozzo's so-called evidence of authorship. He thought it was ridiculous for dal Pozzo to believe he had instantly recognized Alberti's handwriting on the leaflets. Dal Pozzo had seen samples of Alberti's hand only in annotations made occasionally of petitioners'

---

6 *Corpus epistolare*, ed. by Benigni and others, p. 126 lines 19–20. Alberti's formulation is elegant: 'They ask to prevent (*rogant caveri*) that anything be decreed to the future detriment of the order of Abbreviators'. Students of classical Latin recognized in the choice of words the request for a senatorial decree ordering the Roman consuls of Antiquity to proceed militarily, if needed, for the sake of the public good. See also p. 130 lines 22–23: 'Ego nec illas tuas cartulas scripsi neque vidi neque eorum autores novi'.

7 *Corpus epistolare*, ed. by Benigni and others, p. 127 line 5.

8 *Corpus epistolare*, ed. by Benigni and others, p. 128 lines 18–19: 'Ex obloquentium ratione ... qui et male et inepte dicunt'; p. 128 lines 24–25: 'Improborum rationes'. This is not a real refutation.

9 *Corpus epistolare*, ed. by Benigni and others, p. 128 lines 21–22: 'In Cancellaria solus Baptista est cupidus, legit solus Baptista, iniustum questum sibi vindicare studuit'. The manuscript contains numerous errors. The present passage has the words *legitur solus Bapista*, suggesting that Alberti made sure that especially his drafts passed examination, a difficult interpretation. I propose *legit* as a variant, which would be simpler and in line with the duties of a Chancery secretary. As Scribe, dal Pozzo did not have direct knowledge of internal Chancery operations, see pp. 228–32 below.

10 *Corpus epistolare*, ed. by Benigni and others, p. 126 lines 23–24: 'Nosti michi fortunam esse aliunde satis opulentam et honestam'. He referred to his benefice at San Martino a Gangalandi as well as his family possessions; cf. Schwarz, 'Die Bemühungen Leon Battista Albertis', p. 263.

names.[11] Despite dal Pozzo's assertions to the contrary, it was beyond his ability to judge the diction and caustic language supposedly so typical of Alberti.[12] But when those familiar with Alberti's works had objected that the leaflets were actually not written in his style, they merely faced dal Pozzo's wrath.[13] Dal Pozzo was now at his leisure to compare the mysterious leaflets with Alberti's letter.[14] Assuming that Alberti had wished to write anonymously, moreover, he could have changed his handwriting or asked one of his friends to do it for him.[15] And this was precisely the point. The decision to hide in anonymity was a clear sign that it could not have been him, for such behaviour was out of line with his notion of honour (as an Alberti!) and with his conduct consciously aspiring to humanist ideals. Although dal Pozzo seriously believed in the young colleague's authorship, Alberti did not elaborate on his style as a writer, probably because he thought that Bartolomeo, his senior by a generation, was unprepared to assess the matter anyway.[16]

Alberti emphasized throughout the letter that dal Pozzo was and remained his friend, far superior in age, experience, and judgment.[17] Dal Pozzo belonged to the leading group of Scribes and served among them as a *primarius*.[18] Alberti, calling himself a 'newcomer' (*homo novus*), had always shown him due respect, even when dal Pozzo was absent. Alberti, however, saw the importance of having the orders of Abbreviators and Scribes cooperate in traditional harmony and was acting accordingly, apparently in opposition to dal Pozzo.[19] With the Regent of the Chancery,

---

11 *Corpus epistolare*, ed. by Benigni and others, p. 129 lines 11–12: 'Pene divini ingenii illum esse oportet qui quatuor aut altera quatuor supplicantium nomina viderit scripta, inde omnem meam scriptionem tenuerit'.

12 *Corpus epistolare*, ed. by Benigni and others, p. 129 lines 13–17: 'Enimvero quantas et quam sepe meas litteras tractasti? Ubi didicisti nobis eam animi inscitiam et ignaviam esse, ut per capsulas amicos morderem ut non palam arguere, vituperare apertaque acie odisse consueverim? Tamen te ita compertum habere asseris'.

13 *Corpus epistolare*, ed. by Benigni and others, p. 129 lines 17–19.

14 *Corpus epistolare*, ed. by Benigni and others, p. 130 line 9.

15 Apparently, dal Pozzo had also claimed that Alberti was secretly plotting against him with the Regent of the Chancery; *Corpus epistolare*, ed. by Benigni and others, p. 130 lines 14–15.

16 Cf. *Corpus epistolare*, ed. by Benigni and others, p. 130 lines 16–17.

17 *Corpus epistolare*, ed. by Benigni and others, p. 126 lines 9–11: 'Viris exercitatissimis ac primariis ... ex quorum numero te sane unum esse iudicavi'; p. 126 lines 12–14: 'Tu rerum usu peritior ... callere astu, prestare doctrina, maturitate ... admirabili egregie sapere gestiebas'. The importance of *prudentia* provides a leitmotif in the description of the 'learned man (*vir doctus*)', for instance, p. 125 line 24; p. 126 line 29.

18 *Corpus epistolare*, ed. by Benigni and others, p. 126 lines 6–7: 'Cuius opera usque adeo familiarissime utebar, ut in nostro scriptorum ordine nemo fuerit cum quo coniunctius vixerim'. It seems that Bartholomeus de Puteo had composed manuals which were useful for Abbreviators and Scribes.

19 *Corpus epistolare*, ed. by Benigni and others, p. 128 lines 5–6: 'Me cum universo abbreviatorum et scriptorum ordine vivere ut nemo sit cui propemodum non sim

226 CHAPTER 9

the patriarch Blasius de Molino, dal Pozzo surely had a good relationship, but his own, Alberti's, was much better.[20] After all, Battista Alberti was a reader and interpreter in the Chancery, which dal Pozzo had to know since he, Alberti, had repeatedly and successfully intervened on dal Pozzo's behalf there.[21] This had to suffice about friendship, decency, and the obligations arising from them, for elders as well.[22] Alberti passed over the claim in the leaflets that Bartolomeo dal Pozzo had curtailed the Abbreviators' income and used tradition 'with greed and harshness' to their sole detriment.

Our focus here is on the actors and the stage. The scenario unfolded in the Apostolic Chancery. At the time of the episode, it did not constitute a fixed building with Chancery officials working simultaneously on specific days and hours, as the enormous *Palazzo della Cancellaria* in Rome (of 1495) would suggest.[23] Around 1432/1433, the Chancery was instead in a smaller and rented building, where Blasius de Molino resided momentarily. The exact place has not been identified yet.[24] The patriarch lived there with the core of his 'familia' in a shared household.[25] It included his four or five secretaries, among them Leon Battista Alberti.[26]

The Chancery was the destination of nearly all petitions (or supplications) submitted to the Curia. They were sorted and distributed there, unless the Chamberlain decided he had to treat a specific matter in person.

---

carrissimus?'; for similar principles, cf. Alberti, *I libri della famiglia*, ed. by Romano and Tenenti; newly ed. by Furlan. See also *Corpus epistolare*, ed. by Benigni and others, p. 126 line 10.

20 *Corpus epistolare*, ed. by Benigni and others, p. 127 lines 10–11: 'Si apud patriarcham cui est carus Baptista interprete non utendum esse videt'.

21 *Corpus epistolare*, ed. by Benigni and others, p. 128 lines 8–11: 'Optime nosti quotiens pro te pro tuo honore apud dominum Cancellarie causam egerim'.

22 To understand Alberti's stance on his relationship with the adversary, there is the important statement that in the present conflict, the weight of arguments and proper conduct leaned in his favour; *Corpus epistolare*, ed. by Benigni and others, p. 130 lines 21: 'Nam sumus te quavis in re non longe inferiores'.

23 Frommel, 'Il Palazzo della Cancellaria'; cf. Frommel, *Der römische Palastbau der Hochrenaissance*, I, p. 141.

24 In the spring of 1431, the Chancery was in the palazzo next to San Marco, apparently a temporary arrangement (see Vatican, Apostolic Archive, Arm. xxxiv: Diversa Cameralia 16, fols 29ᵛ–30ʳ). On the development of the Chancery as the official residence of the current head official, the Vice-Chancellor, or, between 1431 and 1436, the Regent Blasius de Molino, cf. Schwarz, *Kurienuniversität und stadtrömische Universität*, p. 222 n. 181; Schwarz, 'Leon Battista Alberti in der *familia* des Regens'. The Curia did not settle for good in Rome until the second half of the fifteenth century; Diener and Schwarz, 'Das Itinerar Eugens IV.', p. 194. Even thereafter, it took long before the papal offices attained fixed locations.

25 In the oath for household members of the Chancery head, the office is called 'the residence or guesthouse of the Chancery'; *Die päpstlichen Kanzleiordnungen*, ed. by Tangl, p. 35 (no. ii). In addition to the *familiares*, it accommodated the custodian (also known as the seneschal), a guardian, and various service personnel; on the custodian, also p. 231 below.

26 Schwarz, 'Leon Battista Alberti in der familia des Regens'.

Some of the granted requests were recorded in the registers of petitions and returned thereafter to the Chancery.[27] Those signed by the pope were handled in the same way.[28] Back in the Chancery, the signed petitions from everywhere were again sorted, along with other documents depending on the papal response they had solicited.[29] Aside from the 'common box for supplications', there must have been other boxes, among them one for the collection of so-called commissions, or mandates for judges at the Curia to investigate particular cases.[30] The custodian or seneschal of the Chancery was responsible for the receipt, channelling, and assembly of this documentation.[31]

The bulk of petitions was handed over to the Abbreviators, who generated draft responses or at least short annotations for subsequent elaboration.[32] Officials appointed by the corporation of Scribes would come to fetch these drafts and supplications from the Abbreviators for further handling in accordance with Chancery regulations. Supplications soliciting replies based on a very simple format were not annotated by the Abbreviators, but by the Proctors of the *Audientia litterarum contradictarum*. A smaller part of the completed papal letters would return to the Chancery for final verification. It was undertaken by chosen Abbreviators, who gathered at certain times to 'hold Chancery' together with the Regent and release the so-called Chancery letters.[33] Other types of correspondence

---

27 Characterized as the registers of petitions 'by way of concession', because of the Vice-Chancellor's annotated approval; see Christiane Schuchard, in *Repertorium Germanicum*, v.1/1, ed. by Diener and others, pp. LXIII–CXXX, with a survey of the surviving and lost registers, pp. XCIX–CI. The faculties popes defined at the beginning of their pontificate are found from John XXII (1316–1334) in *Regulae, ordinationes et constitutiones*, ed. by Meyer (online), Martin V – OT 65–87, ME 3–4; Eugene IV – OT 85–102.

28 They appear in the registers of petitions as signed *per fiat*. For Eugene IV, only conferrals of benefices are preserved in either category, so that the other two types of miscellaneous petitions (*de diversis formis*) and expectancies (*de vacaturis*) are lacking. A short version of them was displayed in public, as we know through an incident of 1418, in which someone excised names from the posting (Vatican, Apostolic Archive, Arm. XXIX: Diversa Cameralia 4, fol. 136ʳ). Petitions for expectancies *in forma pauperum* and those concerning the so-called 'minor justice' were only recorded in fascicles; cf. below, p. 242 n. 143; also, Müller and Schwarz, 'Zwei Originalsuppliken', pp. 289–90.

29 Including the *cedole consistoriales*, decisions by the consistory which mostly regarded appointments to a prelature known as 'charters of prefecture'; cf. pp. 240, 242 below.

30 Those were frequently petitions signed by the pope or the Vice-Chancellor; but there were also commissions on the back of accusations or appeals, worded as 'Master N. shall hear and do justice'. On the commissions, see Dolezalek, 'Audientia sacri palatii'. They were fetched from the Chancery by the Master of the Couriers (or *cursores*). He distributed them among the corporate members, who brought them to the judges named in the *commissio*; cf. Schwarz, 'Im Auftrag des Papstes', p. 56 (English version above, p. 207).

31 See below, pp. 231–232.

32 Other petitions went to the secretaries; cf. below, p. 240.

33 This was done in the fenced-off area of a room, whence the word 'park' (*parcus*) was used; Schwarz, '*Abbreviature officium*', pp. 794–95.

were controlled and dispatched in locations elsewhere.[34] Put differently, the Chancery operated primarily as a central distribution facility.[35] Apart from the regular sessions held by the 'lords of the Chancery' to expedite letters, very few administrative activities took place there.[36] The composition of drafts or clean copies did not occur in the Chancery.[37]

Returning to our letter, Leon Battista Alberti's duties as the Regent's reader or interpreter resembled those of the papal clerks known as *referendarii*.[38] They selected the supplications calling for the pope's signature and prepared his decision by presenting the case.[39] They provided commentary and notes on the resulting mandate and sorted it for eventual expedition.[40] In the process, it was possible, of course, to manipulate outcomes.[41] In his capacity as Blasius de Molino's secretary, Alberti was able to speak in Bartolomeo dal Pozzo's favour with his patron both in- and outside the Chancery, which he did more than once according to the letter.[42] At the time, the Regent represented the best opportunity in this regard, because he was the most influential cleric around Pope Eugene IV.[43]

In the letter, Leon Battista Alberti is clearly associated with the 'order' of Abbreviators. Bartolomeo dal Pozzo, on the other hand, belongs just as unambiguously to the 'order' of Scribes. Who was Bartolomeo dal Pozzo and what, above all, was his role? It is often assumed that we know nothing about him.[44] The letter tells us something about his position

---

34 Details below, pp. 241–42.

35 Cf. below, p. 242.

36 For example, the reading of constitutions and rules concerning the Chancery; see *Regulae, ordinationes et constitutiones*, ed. by Meyer (online), Eugen IV – OT 1, 93, 103, 105–08, 111. In other cases, it is only noted that they were entered into the *Liber cancellarie*.

37 For the Scribes, see Schwarz, *Die Organisation kurialer Schreiberkollegien*, pp. 67–71; for the Abbreviators, p. 143, with n. 108.

38 Katterbach, *Referendarii utriusque signaturae*; Fink, 'Zur Geschichte des päpstlichen Referendariats'.

39 A reference of 1456 speaks of the Vice-Chancellor's 'major secretary and *referendarius* for the commissions on justice'; Pitz, *Supplikensignatur und Briefexpedition*, pp. 55–56, 127, 168.

40 Cf. *Corpus epistolare*, ed. by Benigni and others, p. 129 line 11, which seems to indicate that Bartolomeo dal Pozzo had inferred Leon Battista Alberti's handwriting from 'four, or another four names of petitioners' in his script. Mockingly, Alberti commented on such acuity. Although dal Pozzo was 'of the sharpest and most analytical intelligence', here 'a nearly God-like mind of greatest depth' would have been necessary; cf. p. 225 n. 11 above.

41 Above, p. 224.

42 On Alberti's appointment as secretary to Blasius de Molino in the spring of 1431, cf. Schwarz, 'Die Bemühungen Leon Battista Albertis', p. 249.

43 Schwarz, 'Die Bemühungen Leon Battista Albertis', p. 264.

44 Vestri, in *Corpus epistolare*, ed. by Benigni and others, p. 132, speaks of 'the total absence of information about Bartolomeo dal Pozzo'; Vestri also mentions the 'signature of dal Pozzo in his role as Abbreviator', as well as his 'signature on the back' of an original papal letter, which shows him in the first position next to the fee (under the text, in front and to the left) as *rescribendarius*; see Schwarz, 'Die Bemühungen Leon Battista Albertis', pp. 246–47.

in the Chancery, which is not mentioned in other sources. There is archival evidence proving that he was a *primarius* among the Scribes of the Chancery.[45] He is documented as such from 1419.[46] His signature is found on letters requiring much skill from the Scribe.[47] He repeatedly held offices in the corporation of Scribes, for example, as *rescribendarius*, that is, distributor and taxator, or fee assessor, of the letters of grace.[48] In this function, he signed the well-known letter for Leon Battista Alberti of 7 October 1432.[49] Bartolomeo was also Abbreviator, appearing under Martin V among the *abbreviatores assistentes*.[50] The text of our letter contains indications about the position in which Bartolomeo administered the 'common box of petitions', was responsible for the 'office of reading', and acted not least as a person of authority in the Chancery. All these clues point to his role as custodian there.[51] Archival proof of it comes from an unexpected place. On 5 July 1431, Bartholomeus de Puteo, 'Scribe, Abbreviator, and custodian of the Chancery', was commissioned with a legal affair at the Curia alongside Ludovicus de Garsiis, a judge of the Apostolic Chamber.[52] Perhaps, it was Molino who conferred the custodianship to Bartolomeo, because he spoke, according to Alberti, of his good relationship with the

---

45 *Repertorium officiorum Romanae curiae*, ed. by Frenz (online). In Eugene IV's Vatican Registers, Bartolomeo consistently signed as 'B. de Puteo', both as Scribe and functionary; see *Repertorium Germanicum*, v, ed. by Diener and others, nos 367, 370–73, 375; cf. Schuchard, in *Repertorium Germanicum*, v.1/1, ed. by Diener and others, pp. CXVIII–CXXV. This would warrant careful inquiry.

46 According to the *Repertorium officiorum Romanae curiae*, ed. by Frenz (online), Bartolomeo is recorded as Chancery Scribe from 1419 to 1457, without interruption between 1419 and 1435 and again from 1438 to 1442. The evidence in Frenz postdating 1442 seems to confuse Bartolomeo with Gregorius Matheus Bartholomei de Puteo, Chancery Scribe from 1443 until 1474; see also Frenz, *Die Kanzlei der Päpste*, no. 965. Gregorius must have received the office from his uncle or father. In the Vatican Registers, he signed with 'G. de Puteo'. Under Paul II, he served as custodian of the Chancery as well.

47 See below, pp. 251–52, on the work of the Scribes. Leon Battista Alberti later became one of them.

48 For these offices, see Schwarz, *Die Organisation kurialer Schreiberkollegien*, pp. 100–02; Frenz, *Die Kanzlei der Päpste*, pp. 122–24, 205; also below.

49 On the fee annotation to the letter of 7 October 1432, see Schwarz, *Die Organisation kurialer Schreiberkollegien*, pp. 246–47.

50 *Repertorium officiorum Romanae curiae*, ed. by Frenz (online), cites as proof 'jul. 1428, nach Annate 3, fol. 162ᵛ'. Ciampini, *De abbreviatorum de parco maiori*, p. 22, has Bartolomeo as assistant Abbreviator on 6 March 1425. As custodian, he could no longer serve in that function; cf. p. 244 n. 158 below.

51 He is absent from the list compiled by von Hofmann, *Forschungen zur Geschichte der kurialen Behörden*, II, pp. 78–79. I have written (unpublished) short biographies for the custodians of the Chancery.

52 Piana, *Nuovi documenti sull'università di Bologna*, II, p. 754.

230    CHAPTER 9

Regent.[53] Alberti's letter also informs us that dal Pozzo composed manuals for Abbreviators and Scribes.

Bartholomeus de Puteo was born into a patrician family of Alessandria.[54] He probably studied at Bologna.[55] On 11 August 1432, he ranked in a list (*pitaphium*) of Chancery Scribes among the 'true and permanent table companions' of the pope (including those of Martin V), whose offices Eugene IV reserved to himself for reappointment.[56] On 18 April 1433, dal Pozzo had Emperor Sigismund accept him as one of his household members at Siena.[57] He already may have been married at the time.[58] We do not know how long he kept the custodianship.[59] As a result, Alberti clearly dealt with an eminent figure.

---

53 See above, p. 226. Following von Hofmann, *Forschungen zur Geschichte der kurialen Behörden*, II, p. 78 (no. 3), Johannes Montani (de Montanya) was dal Pozzo's predecessor. Johannes was a household member of the previous Vice-Chancellor. He is documented in his position as custodian from 1425. Given that he appears as Scribe and Abbreviator of the Chancery until 1446, he must have resigned his custodianship; *Repertorium officiorum Romanae curiae*, ed. by Frenz (online); and p. 236 n. 98 below.

54 The dal Pozzo family from Alessandria had supplied several of the bishops there; a studied jurist, Giacomo, who died around 1464, also belonged to it; cf. di Renzo Villata, 'Giacomo dal Pozzo'. On Alessandria as the native place, p. 230 n. 57 below.

55 As can be inferred from the commission of 5 July 1431, p. 229 n. 52 above. The connection between the petitioner (a priest from the Bolognese countryside) and the two curial clerics seems to have been their shared student experience. For Ludovicus de Garsiis, a native from Bologna, it is certain that he studied there; see Meuthen, 'Ein "deutscher" Freundeskreis an der römischen Kurie', pp. 492–94.

56 In the constitution 'Eterni patris familias' of 11 August 1432, in *Regulae cancellariae apostolicae*, ed. by von Ottenthal, p. 167; for a better version of the text, see Vatican, Apostolic Archive, Reg. Lat. 317, fols 225$^v$–27$^v$; also, von Hofmann, *Forschungen zur Geschichte der kurialen Behörden*, II, p. 11 (no. 40). Other names on the list include Ludovicus de Orto (Chancery Scribe from 1410 and reader of the *Audientia* from 1432); Ludovicus (Trivisanus) de Venetiis (Chancery Scribe, Abbreviator, and *cubicularius* from 1431, later cardinal); B. de Capranica (not found in the *Repertorium officiorum Romanae curiae*, ed. by Frenz); Antonius de Nepe (Chancery Scribe and Abbreviator from 1431 to 1451; not found in Frenz, either).

57 *Regesta Imperii*, ed. by Altmann, XI/2, p. 233 (no. 9411), where he is called Bartolomeo dal Pozzo 'de Alexandria'.

58 This is suggested by the rarity of mentions in the lists of Hermann Diener (below, p. 236 n. 98); see Vatican, Apostolic Archive, Reg. Lat. 383, fol. 46$^v$ (18 May 1441); Annatae 8, fol. 23$^v$ (13 March 1443); Rome, State Archive, Fondo Camerale I, 1120, fol. 88$^v$ (5 June 1439). As a married cleric, he could not apply for benefices (any longer). His documentation at the Curia ends in 1443.

59 Before 6 December 1439, the office was held by the papal physician, Andreas de Palazago; von Hofmann, *Forschungen zur Geschichte der kurialen Behörden*, II, pp. 78 (no. 4), 194; cf. Marini, *Degli archiatri pontifici*, I, pp. 136–37 (no. 17); *Repertorium officiorum Romanae curiae*, ed. Frenz (online). Perhaps, the new Regent (from the beginning of 1436), Jean Lejeune, insisted on a different custodian.

The head of the Chancery assigned the custodianship for life.[60] Holders swore an oath of fidelity which had to be repeated annually.[61] The office had long been granted only to respected and senior Scribes and Abbreviators. The college of Scribes counted the *custos* among its officials and had him share part of its corporate income.[62] His duties called for prudence, discretion, and knowledge of the Chancery traditions.[63] The charge was considered lucrative not just because of the fees.[64] As custodian, dal Pozzo was clearly capable of introducing many forms of bureaucratic harassment. They could be removed with adequate bribes, to cite the accusation in Alberti's letter.[65] But how, supposedly, had Bartolomeo dal Pozzo taken advantage of the 'order of Abbreviators' and curtailed their prospects of gain 'with greed and harshness'? In his position, he was able to downgrade letters to a 'simpler' category, which warranted lower fees per draft, or he could exclude them altogether from the Abbreviators' competency.[66] In the judicial sphere that he also managed and supervised, he could interpret rules stringently, or less so, to the disadvantage of the *abbreviatores assistentes*. As official in the college of Scribes who occupied the function of *rescribendarius*, distributor or assessor, he had to calculate the fees for individual services, including those the Abbreviators received for drafts,

---

60 For an overview and interpretation of the scarce information on the office, see von Hofmann, *Forschungen zur Geschichte der kurialen Behörden*, I, pp. 48–50; cf. Schwarz, *Zur Organisation der kurialen Schreiberkollegien*, p. 109 and elsewhere.

61 Schwarz, *Zur Organisation der kurialen Schreiberkollegien*, p. 72. The text of the oath, in *Regulae cancellariae apostolicae*, ed. by von Ottenthal, pp. 422–23 (of 1418), deals mainly with the custodian's duties in arranging the adjudication of gratial letters, with his income, and with opportunities for him to increase it through chicanery; cf. pp. 136–37 (§§ 10–11). A belated insertion treats his right to produce and correct charters of prefecture. His remaining tasks are barely outlined: 'And I will exercise ... my said office as seneschal otherwise according to the customs and laudable statutes of the said Chancery, passed and published in this regard'. On the oath for household members of the Vice-Chancellor, p. 226 n. 25 above.

62 His share in the *iocalia* was with two gold ducats as high as that of the *rescribendarius*, the top charge in the corporation; *Schwarz, Zur Organisation der kurialen Schreiberkollegien*, p. 113. The two readers of the *Audientia litterarum contradictarum* each received half the amount; below, p. 259.

63 *Regulae cancellariae apostolicae*, ed. by von Ottenthal, p. 168 (§ 1): 'So that through his prudence and discretion given to him by God, the weightier and more difficult matters ... be assigned'.

64 This is confirmed by the practice of appointments from 1439, when the office was viewed above all as securely profitable; von Hofmann, *Forschungen zur Geschichte der kurialen Behörden*, II, p. 78.

65 Above, p. 224. The reference to 'this office of reading', in *Corpus epistolare*, ed. by Benigni and others, p. 128 line 19, can mean many things, such as the various lists the custodian had to maintain; or the documents he stored prior to final release of the letters; or thereafter. He kept the official books of the Chancery and those of other administrative branches in his 'office'.

66 See below, p. 241.

or the different stages of correction.[67] With regard to the sums owed, this easily led to conflict over the portion, amount, or mode of payment.[68] The *ordines* of Abbreviators and Scribes each had their own customs, rights, and ceremonial rank, despite the fact that many of the Abbreviators were also Scribes. We are told by Leon Battista Alberti that Chancery leaders sought to maintain good relations between the two groups.

Alberti's letter has largely been ignored by scholarship. Veronica Vestri has reedited the text while struggling to distil meaning from it. She has considered its contents to be beyond verification and viewed it as testimony to 'the usual climate at the Curia, filled with greed, suspicion, envy, defamation, and hence a source of conspiracies involving Alberti, too'.[69] Vestri did not pay attention to the artful rhetoric that is key to a proper understanding. Neither Vestri, nor Paola Benigni, the editor of the above-mentioned papal letter for Alberti of 7 October 1432, bothered to consult special works on the Apostolic Chancery.[70] They are also available in Italian.[71] As a result, Vestri was unable to find ways to date Alberti's letter. She changed Mancini's previous attempt (that is, around 1433) without additional arguments to 'after 1433'.[72] To arrive at a more precise chronology, there are Alberti's remarks describing him as a novice who closely studied the guidelines crafted by his opponent, suggesting a timeframe within one or two years after his nomination as secretary and Abbreviator, or about 1431. Dal Pozzo took his office as custodian before 5 July 1431 and is documented as *rescribendarius* for the last quarter of 1432.

---

67 Schwarz, '*Abbreviature officium*', pp. 811–12; the fee for the expedition, as opposed to that for the draft, was not collected by the Abbreviators, because proctors paying on behalf of the petitioners did not have access to the Chancery at that point.

68 Cf. *Regulae, ordinationes et constitutiones*, ed. Meyer (online), Martin V – OT 157; Schwarz, '*Abbreviature officium*', p. 805 n. 97. The relationship between the *abbreviatores assistentes* and the secretaries was tense as well, because Martin V had assigned to the latter part of the fees for the 'letters of the Chancery', which traditionally had been claimed by the Abbreviators; Blasius de Molino preferred a restrictive interpretation of Martin V's rule in favour of the Abbreviators. According to an entry in Vatican, Apostolic Archive, Reg. Suppl. 267, fol. 125$^r$, the secretaries obtained a papal mandate to the Regent regarding this Chancery regulation in 1431. It had ordered 'that he receive from them, expedite, and send to the Bull, as before, all letters of which they have been deprived and which the secretaries have signed until now'.

69 Vestri, in *Corpus epistolare*, ed. by Benigni and others, p. 131: 'A tutt'oggi non verificabile nella veridicità'.

70 For the letter of 1432, see *Corpus epistolare*, ed. by Benigni and others, pp. 117–19 (no. 7); along with a diplomatic description, transcription, and commentary, pp. 119–23.

71 Frenz, *I documenti pontifici*, ed. by Pagano; Rabikauskas, *Diplomatica Pontificia*; Rabikauskas, 'Chancellerie pontificale'.

72 *Corpus epistolare*, ed. by Benigni and others, p. 124.

I thus place our letter by way of hypothesis between the spring of 1432 and that of 1433.[73] The letter provides precious testimony to Leon Battista Alberti's career in the papal Chancery, which is our main topic.

## State of Research and Sources

Alberti's curial offices are discussed subsequently. The pertinent scholarship is hard to comprehend for non-specialists.[74] On the one hand, there are studies largely reliant on a model of nineteenth-century administration. They discuss the function and competency of officials and identify the purpose of their position in the overall organisation of the Apostolic Chancery. Their principal sources are constitutions and mandates, which are treated as bureaucratic regulations. A classic example of this approach is the manual by del Re on the Roman Curia.[75] Next to them are inquiries with an interest in the format (or diplomatic) of papal documents, which seek to reconstruct the operations of the Chancery as the production site of innumerable papal charters. Works of this kind are based on observations deriving directly from the documentation or examine late medieval visitor guides to the Curia. A leading representative is Bresslau's *Handbook of Diplomatic* (1912).[76] There is also, and especially, Frenz (1986).[77] Like the manuals on the Curia, they pay insufficient attention to change over time.[78] Finally, there are socio-historical studies looking diachronically at specific groups of employees, such as the Scribes of the Chancery and Penitentiary or, for a limited period, the Abbreviators, the Correctors, and the Proctors, while pursuing particular research questions as well.[79] They are based above all on prosopography, a method employed since the 1970s. A useful survey of positions in the Chancery from the socio-historical

---

73 For a fuller chronology of dal Pozzo's career as *rescribendarius*, distributor, and assessor (of fees), I hope for the discovery of further annotations to original papal letters, in addition to my references from the Vatican registers; cf. above, p. 229 n. 45.

74 Schwarz, 'Die Erforschung der mittelalterlichen römischen Kurie'.

75 Cf. del Re, *La Curia romana*, which departs from the new Curia as reformed by Pope Paul VI (1963–1978), with extensive information about the history of institutions, including those meanwhile abolished. From the socio-historical perspective, Schwarz, 'Die römische Kurie' (English version above, pp. 177–99).

76 Bresslau, *Handbuch der Urkundenlehre*, I; Italian version, *Manuale di diplomatica*, trans. by Voci-Roth, with the original pagination.

77 Frenz, *Die Kanzlei der Päpste*; his socio-historical part on 'Structures and Personnel' follows the general bibliography, pp. 181–257; Frenz, *Papsturkunden*.

78 Which has been the primary interest of my diachronic studies, listed p. 222 n. 1 above (Abbreviators, Scribes); p. 242 n. 141 below (correctors).

79 See the previous note; and, on the Proctors, p. 258 n. 243 below. The Rota and the Couriers belonged to the Chancery in a broader sense; Schuchard, 'Zu den Rotanotaren'; Schwarz, 'Im Auftrag des Papstes' (English version above, pp. 201–22).

234   CHAPTER 9

perspective is offered by Schuchard (1987) for the years from 1378 to 1447.[80] Covering the following period and the curial 'system' from 1378 to the Reformation in general, the best study remains Walther von Hofmann's *Forschungen* (1914).[81]

To recapture Alberti's working conditions, identify his colleagues, and understand the hierarchical relationships and administrative rules around him, it is necessary to accumulate as much information as possible about the people holding office there at the time and insert it into an appropriate classification scheme. For works of prosopography, it proves most helpful to list various categories of employees. They are available in von Hofmann's *Forschungen* for a few higher offices at the Curia and the immediate entourage of the pope.[82] Pitz (1972) has furnished them for the Chancery broadly speaking, but only between 1455 and 1458.[83] From 1471, Frenz (1986) has offered extensive inventories.[84] They can be supplemented with repertories for the Scribes (beginning in 1417) and Abbreviators (from 1463/1464).[85] Curial charges of middle or lower rank have met with special interest if they were active in the fields of art, culture, or learning, as singers, librarians, or creative artists.[86] They have been spotted above all in the registers and in the lists of the Apostolic Chamber.[87]

The mass of petitions and letters registered at the Apostolic Chancery as the largest corpus of contemporary documentation in the Vatican has rarely been utilized for research in the curial offices.[88] These registers preserve data concerning the benefice market at the Curia to the exclusion of

---

80  Schuchard, *Die Deutschen an der päpstlichen Kurie*, pp. 92–114.

81  See von Hofmann, *Forschungen zur Geschichte der kurialen Behörden*, especially Lists I to VI, of Vice-Chancellors, their Regents, the Auditors of Contradictory Letters (each supplemented by Herde, *Audientia litterarum contradictarum*), the correctors, the custodians, and the Notaries. The following Lists (VII–IX) with the heads of various registers and the *bullatores* were part of the Chancery only in a wider sense.

82  See p. 234 n. 81 above. For the *referendarii*, another list has been provided by Katterbach, *Referendarii utriusque signaturae*.

83  Pitz, *Supplikensignatur und Briefexpedition*.

84  Frenz, *Die Kanzlei der Päpste*, pp. 261–455, with 'short biographies of individual clerics at the Curia'.

85  Frenz, 'Zum Problem der Reduzierung'; Frenz, 'Die Gründung des Abbreviatorenkollegs'; and below, p. 247 n. 180.

86  More recently in two volumes, *Offices et papauté*, and *Offices, écrits, et papauté*, both edited by Jamme and Poncet.

87  A complete survey and brief analysis of source material in the Vatican for Eugene IV's pontificate is offered by Christiane Schuchard, in *Repertorium Germanicum*, v.1/1, ed. by Diener and others, pp. LXIII–CXXX. In the volumes of the *Repertorium*, the initial description of archival materials for other popes is nowhere comparable to Schuchard's and altogether absent from vol. IV; on Nicholas V, cf. p. 250 n. 195 below.

88  For the specific holdings, see p. 234 n. 87 above.

almost everything else.[89] The obvious reason is that petitioners mentioned their curial offices in the written request (and again in the response) when they expected them to facilitate papal approval of the matter. The Abbreviators, for instance, were generally entitled (by so-called prerogative) to preferential treatment in the acquisition and control of benefices, along with certain other curial clerics, university graduates, and nobles.[90] As a result, they turned to the papacy over and over again.[91] In my collection of biographies counting more than 650 Abbreviators from Eugene IV's pontificate, the great majority has more than ten register entries.[92] Ninety per cent of the mentions for curial clergy occur among the petitions. Unfortunately, though, the Abbreviators did not call themselves such, unless they knew of no better way to win the pope's favour. If they held a different position, for example, as Chancery Scribe or an even higher one, they referred to their function as Abbreviator only on occasion and for reasons we cannot discern.[93] They preferred to stress the role of Scribe, because it accorded them higher legal status.[94] Besides, it secured them, similar to membership in the Regent's household, free delivery of their letters, which is traceable in certain Chancery annotations.[95] In the registers, Abbreviators are therefore underrepresented or altogether absent, except when they belonged to the category of highest privilege, the *Parcus maior*.[96]

How are the relevant references to be found? If the register in question has an Index, which most do not, it simply states that someone (x)

---

89 The work of Meyer, *Zürich und Rom*, has been pathbreaking in understanding the rules of the late medieval benefice market in the German Empire, for which the Curia was the trade floor (not partner). The same approach has been continued by Meyer, 'Der deutsche Pfründenmarkt'; and Schwarz, 'Klerikerkarrieren und Pfründenmarkt'. It has been pursued with great success and certain modifications even outside the Empire, such as for the great baronial families of Rome (Andreas Rehberg) and the Duchy of Milan (Giorgio Chittolini).

90 *Regulae, ordinationes et constitutiones*, ed. by Meyer (online), Martin V – OT 75: 'Also, he (the pope) can freely rule and mandate as he sees fit that everyone among the Scribes and Abbreviators is admitted as equal to university graduates in terms of prerogatives, upon consideration of sufficient merit and personal status; and the same for nobles born from one or two knightly parents'; OT 76 regulates for both offices the receipt of income during absences.

91 Cf. Schwarz, 'Dispense der Kanzlei Eugens IV.', p. 139, where petitioners specify their academic degrees, merit, and protectors.

92 The number of 600, in Schwarz, 'Die Abbreviatoren unter Eugen IV.', p. 219, refers to a shorter timeframe and is slightly outdated, of course.

93 Alberti did the same while he was a Scribe, see pp. 248–49 below; likewise, Bartolomeo dal Pozzo, his opponent of 1432.

94 Cf. below, p. 249.

95 Below, pp. 239 and 248.

96 Schwarz, 'Die Abbreviatoren unter Eugen IV.', p. 220 n. 9. Alberti was never part of the *Parcus maior*; below, p. 244. Once he obtained the position of Scribe, references to his office as Abbreviator were no longer automatic. Accordingly, we can at least infer that he was not yet Chancery Scribe in 1432.

obtained a benefice (y). Whereas the full text identifies offices, they are rarely mentioned in finding aids like the *Schedario Garampi* and so on.[97] For Eugene IV's pontificate, on the other hand, there is a wonderful instrument at our disposal, Hermann Diener's compilation of names extending to curial staff in the broadest sense and comprising the household members of cardinals and Chamberlains as well.[98] I examined this collection searching for Alberti in particular, but without discovering anything for reasons I have discussed elsewhere.[99] For the Scribes and higher classes of Abbreviators, moreover, another type of source known as the Chancery annotations is available.[100] They appear on the original papal letters sent out to recipients all over Europe. A small portion of these notes was also copied into the Vatican registers. The *Censimento Bartoloni*, a collection of outgoing apostolic correspondence concentrating on the annotations ends as early as in 1417.[101] The diplomatic of original letters from 1431 to 1447 has seldom been analysed.[102] The notes on them and in the *Registra Vaticana* form the core of the collections undertaken by Thomas Frenz.[103] However, their focus is on the period after 1471.[104] The passages in question furnish (often heavily abbreviated) names and, depending on their placement on the letter, the function presently held.

Aside from the Abbreviators, I have compiled personal data for the period from 1431 to 1471 for curial offices at the middling level, which over the course of the fifteenth century became venal like membership

---

97 Working mainly with Florentine material, Boschetto, *Società e cultura a Firenze*, p. XII, has noted that when going through 'the list of sources on Eugene IV's pontificate examined in the volumes of the *Repertorium Germanicum*', he realized 'with regret' what masses of hitherto unused data are contained in them. If Boschetto had studied the entire 'Introduction' (cf. above, p. 227 n. 27), he would have encountered my presentation of Diener's compilation. As usual, however, 'texts in German are not read'!

98 Now in Rome, German Historical Institute, N11: Hermann Diener, wissenschaftlicher Nachlaß, Teilbestand Eugen IV: Sammlung von Quellenbelegen zu Kurialen in 36 Heften. The names there have partly been transferred into alphabetical lists. The thirty-six fascicles were continuously compiled alongside the entries of *Repertorium Germanicum*, v, while not being as detailed and comprehensive. I have completed the list after Diener's death.

99 Schwarz, 'Die Bemühungen Leon Battista Albertis', pp. 239–40.

100 Including also the *referendarii* and the secretaries.

101 The *Censimento* is an international project to collect all original papal letters from 1198 and 1417. For a survey of the publications until 2009, see Schwarz, 'Die Erforschung der mittelalterlichen römischen Kurie', p. 423 n. 28.

102 *Schedario Baumgarten*, III, ends in 1431; vol. IV extends until 1862, without much coverage for the fifteenth century.

103 Frenz, *Die Kanzlei der Päpste*. The brief biographies in the *Repertorium officiorum Romanae Curiae*, ed. by Frenz (online), extend further in time, but rest on a narrow base of originals and select Vatican registers.

104 *Repertorium officiorum Romanae curiae*, ed. by Frenz (online), has the following: 'Albertis (de), Baptista (I) 1448–1464, Baptista (II) 1494'.

in the *Audientia contradictarum*.[105] For them, the registers and lists of the Apostolic Chamber are my principal informants in the years that Diener's collection does not cover. The following treatment concentrates on the period from about 1430 to 1450. Alberti's offices are discussed in the order in which he acquired them as far as we know. My chief concern is the day-to-day of operations, dependencies, and the association of officials with external groupings, such as the households of leaders at the Curia. In addition, I am interested in the corporate existence of office holders, the inner life of their fraternities, the ceremonies and public display of their colleges, and their institutional dimension. After all, the Curia did not resemble a modern bureaucracy, but rather Max Weber's ideal-type of a 'feudal lordship'.[106]

## Leon Battista Alberti as Secretary of the Regent in the Chancery, Blasius de Molino

As early as in April 1431, Alberti likely became secretary and household member of the new Regent of the Chancery, Blasius de Molino.[107] Molino was appointed to the position on 4 March 1431, that is, before Eugene IV's coronation.[108] He headed the Chancery until 26 September 1431, when a new Vice-Chancellor was installed with Jean de Rochetaillée.[109] Jean was absent from the Curia between 1433 (at the latest) and the end of 1435. In the beginning of 1436, a different Regent had been instituted by the

---

105 I have repeatedly reported on this enterprise; see Schwarz, 'Die römische Kurie' (English version above, pp. 177–99); Schwarz, 'Im Auftrag des Papstes' (English version pp. 201–22 above); Schwarz, 'Les courriers pontificaux'.

106 Weber, *Wirtschaft und Gesellschaft*, ch. VII.a.3; cf. ch. II (§ 19).

107 Ceccon, 'Molino, Blasio da'. Ceccon's article is based on Venetian material. Her account of Molino's ecclesiastical career is imprecise and deficient on the curial side. I thank Dieter Girgensohn for additional information about the Venetian context. Regarding Molino's role at the Curia, cf. von Hofmann, *Forschungen zur Geschichte der kurialen Behörden*, II, pp. 12, 72, 131; Katterbach, *Referendarii utriusque signaturae*, p. 16 (no. 1); *Hierarchia Catholica Medii Aevi*, ed. by Eubel, I, pp. 266, 281, 404; II, p. 164. For his biography, see Schwarz, 'Leon Battista Alberti in der *familia* des Regens'. Another vita was composed by Vespasiano da Bisticci (d. 1498), *Le vite*, ed. by Greco, I, p. 273. Molino appears there in stereotypical fashion as a pious man (like Alberti). Da Bisticci seems to have had no special biographical knowledge of him.

108 *Regulae, ordinationes et constitutiones*, ed. by Meyer (online), Eugene IV – OT 1.

109 For a short biography on him, see Schwarz, *Kurienuniversität und stadtrömische Universität*, p. 615 (Liste II/191). It includes his career at the Curia, which began with his nomination as corrector by Alexander (V) in 1409 and continued as *referendarius* under Martin V, when Jean also served for a time (1421) as the Vice-Chancellor's substitute, or Regens. On other facets of Jean's career, cf. Müller, 'Une carrière ecclésiastique'.

238    CHAPTER 9

Vice-Chancellor.[110] Elevated to the dignity of Latin Patriarch of Jerusalem on 20 October 1434, Blasius de Molino remained at the Curia until he died in October 1447.

We must ask now for how long Alberti was part of Molino's *familia*.[111] With one exception, the other members of Molino's household left it at the end of his regency, suggesting the same for Alberti.[112] Nonetheless, the above-mentioned close relationship between Alberti and his former patron persisted, as is evident from the invitation to write the biography of Ambrogio Traversari, which Alberti probably received at Molino's prompting in 1440. As secretary, Alberti had been unable to compose a series of saint's lives for him.[113] Molino had not found Alberti's first product, the *vita* of Saint Potitus, to his liking.[114] Before 4 June 1434, Alberti finished the first three books of his 'Libri della famiglia', indicating that his obligations as secretary and Abbreviator left him with time to spare.[115] The household of the Chancery Regent consisted of his 'domestics' and other members of the *familia*. They all took an oath at the time of entry.[116] As secretary, Alberti was one of the chaplains accompanying Molino in public. Perhaps, he wore his patron's uniform during ceremonies.[117]

---

110 Jean Lejeune. On him, Schwarz, *Kurienuniversität und stadtrömische Universität*, pp. 532–33 (Liste I/161). It is unclear whether Blasius de Molino had limited functions from the time of the Vice-Chancellor's appointment to his departure for Basel. Molino remained at any rate Eugene IV's most trusted *referendarius* until the pope's flight from Rome on 4 June 1434.

111 To limit the length of the present essay, I have treated Alberti's service for Molino and his colleagues in Molino's household separately; see next note below.

112 Schwarz, 'Leon Battista Alberti in der *familia* des Blasius'. Apparently, attempts to join the household of the papal nephew and Apostolic Chamberlain, Francesco Condulmer, did not negatively affect Alberti's relationship with Molino; cf. the letter of recommendation sent by the lordship of Florence to Condulmer on 5 December 1433, in *Corpus epistolare*, ed. by Benigni and others, pp. 134–36 (no. 9).

113 *Opuscoli inediti*, ed. by Grayson, pp. 27, 31–32, 63–64; 'Potito, santo, martire', cols 1072–74. On Molino's request and Alberti's problems with it, see Knowles Frazier, *Possible Lives*, pp. 67–70, 337–38.

114 Alberti sought to complete the assignment by writing a praise of the saint instead of a life. Its new date is between spring 1431 and 20 October 1434, because the dedication refers to Molino as patriarch of Grado.

115 He wrote it in just ninety days in Rome and hence before his patron's and the pope's flight from the city; cf. 'L'autobiografia di Leon Battista Alberti', ed. by Fubini and Menci Gallorini, p. 70 lines 13–23.

116 The oath is printed, in *Regulae cancellariae apostolicae*, ed. by von Ottenthal, p. 34 (no. 11). In a manuscript at the Vatican, Apostolic Archive, Arm. XXXI, 82, fols 232ᵛ–33ʳ, it has the title of 'Oath, which His Domestics and Other *familiares* Will Swear Our Lord'. Apart from loyalty, the promise of officials was to maintain secrecy and shun bribery.

117 The *familia* of Molino as Chancery Regent competed with that of contemporary cardinals; see Dendorfer and Märtl, 'Papst und Kardinalskolleg im Bannkreis der Konzilien', pp. 386–88; *Le cérémonial papal*, ed. by Dykmans, III, pp. 446–61, describes the ideal-typical arrangement toward the end of the Council and itemizes various service functions.

The letter by Alberti discussed above shows that household members of the Chancery Regent were mobilized for several types of business, which in a more bureaucratic age would have been kept neatly separate.[118] We do not know whether Molino's other secretaries were employed in similar ways, namely, Furseus de Bruille from Peronne, a veteran Abbreviator of the *Parcus maior* and already a secretary under Molino's predecessors; the two Romans, Cornelius de Blanca, doctor of both laws, and Johannes Baptista de Mellinis; the Frenchman, Johannes de Angeroles; and Jacobus Bigneti from Normandy.[119] They all served as Abbreviators, of course, forming the pool from which the Regent took his secretaries. Holding the right of appointment, he was able to offer his favourites lucrative prospects in return. The Regent's household members were entitled to the expedition of Chancery letters free of charge.[120] From the perspective of clerics seeking sustenance and career opportunities at the Curia, association with the Regent's *familia* provided, besides prerogatives akin to those of a cardinal's *familiaris*, the advantage of unimpeded access to the Chancery.

## As Abbreviator

Most likely, Molino appointed Battista Alberti as Abbreviator soon after his reception into the Regent's household, because the right to do so went from 26 September 1431 to the new Vice-Chancellor, Jean de Rochetaillée. Alberti is expressly named as Abbreviator (and secretary of the Regent) on 7 October 1432.[121] In the letter discussed earlier, he appears as the 'exponent' of the Abbreviators. Other testimony to Alberti's self-identification as Scribe and Abbreviator is found in 1447 in his instalment as proctor overseeing the conferral of a canonry at the dome of Florence and in the provision of 7 December 1449 to be examined below.[122] Without justification, the historiography often has cited the bull of Pope Pius II establishing the Abbreviators as a corporate group or college as additional proof of Alberti's presence among them.

The Abbreviators' primary (and in accordance with their name, original) assignment was the composition of papal letters, either in outline or

---

118 Cf. *Regulae, ordinationes et constitutiones*, ed. by Meyer (online), Martin V – TA 7.

119 Bigneti is not documented as member of Molino's *familia* until 1435.

120 This is also borne out by the Chancery annotations on Alberti's letter of 7 October 1432, both in the Scribe's signature on the fold to the right and in the fee assessment; Schwarz, 'Die Bemühungen des Leon Battista Alberti', pp. 247–48.

121 Schwarz, 'Die Bemühungen des Leon Battista Alberti', pp. 247–48.

122 *Corpus epistolare*, ed. by Benigni and others, pp. 202–03 (no. 18). In the provision with the benefice at the dome of Florence, he is only called a Scribe; Boschetto erroneously speaks of Alberti as 'Abbreviator of apostolic letters', pp. 210–11; cf. Schwarz, 'Die Bemühungen des Leon Battista Alberti', p. 253.

240    CHAPTER 9

draft format (called 'minutes').[123] The Scribes of the Chancery consulted with them in a second step to produce clean copies.[124] In the case of gratial letters like the dispensation for Alberti of 7 October 1432, the Abbreviator had to transform the original petition into a papal mandate based on the pope's decision (or signature) added to it.[125] The final version had to abide by the rules, written regulations, and orally transmitted style of the Chancery. For one thing, this was a challenging task in juristic terms, so that all Abbreviators had at least practical legal training and most of them law degrees, including Battista Alberti. The task also required a keen sense of rhetorical nuances and an appreciation for the beauty of the diction, or so-called *cursus*, of papal documents.[126] The function of the Abbreviator did not call for the stylistic artistry of a humanist, which was rather the resort of the secretaries composing political correspondence (primarily in the form of briefs) and often appearing as independent authors, too.[127] Around 1432, some of them were literary celebrities.[128] In addition, the secretaries were responsible for letters falling outside Chancery regulations.[129]

The initial annotations merely outlined core concerns and alluded to formulaic passages, which an experienced Scribe could easily supply. The composition of gratial letters, also called 'letters from the Chancery', was left to those Abbreviators who stood and worked directly under the Vice-Chancellor. As a result, they were known as Chancery Abbreviators, and Alberti was one of them between 1431 and 1435. It was easier to produce the so-called 'minor letters of justice', which consisted of gratial matters and mandates and followed a fixed format. A few words scribbled on a scrap of paper or on the petition itself offered sufficient guidance. There was again little demand for the Abbreviator's expertise when it came to the major letters of justice, because the main content had to be crafted by the curial courts, while the rest was once again strictly formulaic. The charters of prefecture for the appointment of prelates belonged to that group as well. Until the time of Martin V (1417–1431), this simpler and

---

123 Frenz, 'Abbreviator'; Frenz, *Papsturkunden*, p. 94; Frenz, *Die Kanzlei der Päpste*, pp. 104–08, 121–24, 208–10.

124 I have attempted to classify the letters not as they were registered, but as they were requested locally, in *Regesten*, ed. by Schwarz, pp. XVII–XXI.

125 Schwarz, 'Die Bemühungen des Leon Battista Alberti', p. 245.

126 The dispensation of 7 October 1432 is a perfect example of this.

127 Frenz, *L'introduzione della scrittura umanistica*; Gualdo, 'Umanesimo e segretari apostolici'.

128 Studt, '*Tamquam organum nostre mentis*'. For a list of the secretaries, cf. von Hofmann, *Forschungen zur Geschichte der kurialen Behörden*, II, pp. 110–22 (from Martin V); cf. Kraus, 'Die Sekretäre Pius' II.'.

129 On secretarial expedition 'by the Chamber', which can be tracked in the Vatican Registers, see Frenz, *Papsturkunden*, §§ 133–34. Signed *per fiat* in the registers of petitions, there are annotations of conferral (*Recipe*), which the Chancery Regent directed at individual secretaries or Abbreviators.

less demanding task was relegated to another category of Abbreviators preparing documentation for the Protonotaries.[130] Under Eugene IV, it turned into the assignment of specific Abbreviators in the Chancery, who were delegated by the Protonotaries. The Protonotaries themselves had ceased to be part of the Chancery for a while.[131]

The Regent of the Chancery assigned the drafting of gratial letters to Abbreviators he considered suited for the task.[132] The responsibility for the composition of letters of justice rested with the Abbreviators themselves, who distributed them according to a scheme ideally securing each of them the same income.[133] The Abbreviator could charge a fee (or tax) for every draft he produced. Once completed, the rough version or *notula* had to be signed by the Abbreviator, usually with his initials.[134] Before papal letters were rendered in clean copy, the college of Scribes checked their external form and subjected them to various additional controls.[135] Gratial letters were inspected by experienced Abbreviators to make sure that the wording was accurate as envisioned in the draft version. This opening round of verification was also known as the 'first revision'. It was in the hands of the 'assistant Abbreviators', a restricted circle among those working at the Chancery.[136] To join them required passing an exam, which was conducted by the corrector and two Abbreviators from the *Parcus maior*.[137] The *assistentes* formed their own group. Under Eugene IV, it came to be known as the *Parcus minor*. It did not necessarily conduct gatherings in the way of the *Parcus maior*.

By 1430, the verification of letters of justice occupied the Abbreviators only insofar as one of them was chosen to deal with the matter every fifteen days.[138] His sole task was to sign the major letters.[139] Normally, the

---

130 For the Abbreviators working with the notaries, see also Zutshi, 'The Office of Notary in the Papal Chancery', pp. 670–71. The drafts for the minor letters of justice were written by the Proctors of the Audience of Contradictory Letters; Frenz, *Die Kanzlei der Päpste*, p. 62.

131 Schuchard, *Die Deutschen an der römischen Kurie*, pp. 93–95; Haubst, 'Der Reformentwurf Pius' des Zweiten', p. 188.

132 *Regulae, ordinationes et constitutiones*, ed. by Meyer (online), Martin V – OT 122, 157.

133 Schwarz, *Die Organisation der Schreiberkollegien*, pp. 142–43. After the college of Abbreviators was established, it was the distributor of the petitions who assigned them without distinction between those granted *per concessum* and *per fiat* to members of the *Parcus minor*.

134 The original draft versions have perished almost without exception.

135 Schwarz, *Die Organisation der Schreiberkollegien*, p. 145.

136 Schwarz, 'Abbreviature officium', pp. 793–96; Frenz, *Papsturkunden*, § 127 (position 30 on the original letters).

137 Schwarz, 'Abbreviature officium', pp. 794, 796–97.

138 Schwarz, 'Abbreviature officium', p. 790 n. 6. *Regulae, ordinationes et constitutiones*, ed. by Meyer (online), Martin V – DL 22 (Reform constitution).

139 The Chancery annotations to this effect appear on the back; cf. Frenz, *Papsturkunden*, § 136 (position 21). In the *Repertorium officiorum Romanae curiae*, ed. by Frenz (online), the functionary is found under the key word of *substitutus protonotariorum*. The letters of

242    CHAPTER 9

Protonotaries were responsible for the letters, with fees that were often quite high.[140] The examination was a plain formality. The minor letters of justice including, as mentioned, routine gratial mandates, were checked by the 'corrector of apostolic letters'.[141] The corrector released both types of correspondence, except for the simple 'rescripts of delegation', which fell under the competency of the 'corrector of minor justice', who was also called *corrector conquestum*.[142] The technical term was 'expedition by the office of correction'.[143] Before the letters of justice were examined, some had to go through the *Audientia litterarum contradictarum*.

The final control of the gratial letters occurred in the Chancery. The clean copies were compared with all prior documentation and especially the petitions, to make sure that the meaning of the signature below was rendered with accuracy. In addition, the wording was scrutinized for the possibility of legal pitfalls, and each formulation was pondered for adverse effects. This process was entrusted to the 'lords of the Chancery', a group consisting of the most experienced 'assistant Abbreviators', who identified as those 'from the *Parcus maior*'.[144] It was frequently complemented with persons of special expertise and always comprised the 'Corrector of apostolic letters'.[145] The assembly met formally like a court and was headed by the Vice-Chancellor or Chancery Regent, who cleared the documents for expedition.[146]

---

justice included the charters of prefecture, which were drafted in part by the custodian who was also responsible for their verification. He collected fees for both, as well as for the registration of mandates from the consistory; above, p. 231 n. 61.

140 *Regulae, ordinationes et constitutiones*, ed. by Meyer (online), Martin V – TA 16 and 36. The rules of Martin V (TA 4 and 9), which speak of one weekly meeting by the 'Chancery of justice' (or up to three, depending on the workload) are merely nostalgic references to the Avignonese period. This 'Chancery' really consisted of one Abbreviator taking his turn from another.

141 Schwarz, 'Der *corrector litterarum apostolicarum*'; Schwarz, 'Corrector litterarum apostolicarum'. For the period treated here, cf. also von Hofmann, 'Über den *corrector litterarum apostolicarum*'; von Hofmann, *Forschungen zur Geschichte der kurialen Behörden*, I, pp. 45–46, 62–63.

142 From 1471, these texts were no longer drafted by the Abbreviators, but by the Proctors of the *Audientia litterarum contradictarum*; Frenz, *Die Kanzlei der Päpste*, pp. 62, 145; the Scribes had their own assessor of fees for the letters of minor justice; Schwarz, *Die Organisation der Schreiberkollegien*, p. 113.

143 Frenz, *Papsturkunden*, §§ 136–39. A 'scribe, registrar, and custodian' served at the office of correction on 14 April 1442; see Vatican, Apostolic Archive, Reg. Lat. 388, fol. 134[r–v]; it was the Abbreviator Thomas Hilde, who died before 22 June 1442. This implies that the release of the letters of justice was recorded, most likely in fascicles.

144 See above, p. 227 n. 33.

145 Schwarz, 'Anselmus Fabri (Smit) aus Breda', p. 181.

146 The 'Chancery' usually met three times a week. It was convened by the custodian, who posted the announcement at the Chancery gates. He had to partake in the meetings and maintain order during the proceedings; cf. *Regulae cancellariae apostolicae*, ed. by von Ottenthal, p. 423. The reporting Abbreviator from the *Parcus maior* signed on the back, next

In 1430, the total of assistant Abbreviators was around twenty-five.[147] We do not know how many Abbreviators existed overall, as no numerical limit was set for them.[148] Their appointment, pertaining in principle to the Regent and the Protonotaries, is not recorded in the surviving source material.[149] Beginning in 1431, I have encountered occasional nominations by the pope, which figure in the registers as papal mandates.[150] Those who asked for them pursued insertion into the list of twenty-five Abbreviators kept at the Chancery, which secured certain prerogatives concerning the law of benefices. According to the concordats of Constance, general reservation had been restricted to the benefices of twenty-five Abbreviators, which meant that, from 1418, they alone could not be filled by ordinary collators in the interested territories. The limit was put arbitrarily. When Eugene IV raised it in his concordats after 1442 to one-hundred Abbreviators whose positions were generally reserved to papal appointment, he suddenly faced a surge of applicants for them.[151] As a result, the number of Abbreviators rose considerably, with some of them joining only in a nominal sense. Their geographical origin also shifted, because they increasingly came from areas governed by the concordats, an aspect worthwhile considering when investigating individual careers.[152] Probably unintended, a side-effect was that the papal appointment of Abbreviators started to undermine the right of Chancery leaders to do the same, as many did not wish to receive the position unless they were placed on the list of those enjoying general reservation. When the college of Abbreviators was founded by Pius II (1458–1464), the competency of the Chancery was abolished at first, but then restored.

It is unclear whether the assistants participated in the appointment of new Abbreviators. They were without enforceable right to do so.[153]

---

to the cords of the seal (Frenz, *Papsturkunden*, position 29a); the Vice-Chancellor or Regent signed on the front, in the two upper corners (positions 1 and 4a).

147 Schwarz, 'Die Abbreviatoren unter Eugen IV.', pp. 219–24. Pius II wrongly claimed that Benedict XII (1334–1342) had established a fixed number of twenty-four Abbreviators; his assertion is still repeated by many.

148 Schwarz, 'Die Abbreviatoren unter Eugen IV.', p. 221; cf. *Regulae, ordinationes et constitutiones*, ed. by Meyer (online), Martin V – TA 10. By 1340, the count was already well above one-hundred; Schwarz, 'Die Abbreviatoren unter Eugen IV.', pp. 224–27.

149 Schwarz, 'Die Abbreviatoren unter Eugen IV.', p. 227.

150 Schwarz, 'Die Abbreviatoren unter Eugen IV.', pp. 200, 222–23. Subsequently, I discovered another three petitions, see Vatican, Apostolic Archive, Reg. Suppl. 268, fol. 200$^v$ (13 April 1431); Reg. Suppl. 286, fol. 27$^v$ (1433, before September); Reg. Suppl. 365, fol. 13$^{r-v}$ (11 March 1440).

151 Schwarz, 'Die Abbreviatoren unter Eugen IV.', pp. 224–27.

152 Schwarz, 'Die Abbreviatoren unter Eugen IV.'.

153 Much litigation was brought before the court of the Apostolic Chamber, in which curial colleges defended themselves against newcomers, especially by limiting the number of colleagues so that each member could collect a proper income; cf. Schwarz, 'Die römische

244    CHAPTER 9

They were sworn in by taking a general oath as officials.[154] The administrative activities of the Abbreviators are most easily traceable among the assistants.[155] This is because their annotations in a particular place on the original letters were directly copied into the Lateran registers.[156] It is found in the upper corner to the right of each entry.[157] For Eugene IV's pontificate, I have collected from there the monograms of assistant Abbreviators and used them to construct brief biographies. The data are nonetheless incomplete![158] Alberti is not among them.[159] Apparently, he never belonged to the Abbreviators of the *Parus maior*. The sources do not suggest his association with it, regardless of their deficiencies.[160] Moreover, membership presupposed decades of service in the office, interest in the intricacies of Chancery style, and a constant personal presence. I do not think that Alberti was the right type for that. I have described the career of someone with the proper characteristics in my vita of Anselmus Fabri de Breda (d. 1449), who in his role as assistant Abbreviator, corrector, and *referendarius* was Battista Alberti's colleague and superior.[161]

Once installed, the Abbreviator kept the title and privileges of his position for life, even when he left office or the Curia.[162] The holder enjoyed many advantages, above all when he (like Alberti) was also a cleric. Concerning the law, the benefices of an Abbreviator fell, to begin with, under general reservation except in the territories governed by concordat.[163] In the latter, only the above-mentioned twenty-five (and subsequently one-hundred) Abbreviators listed at the Chancery were privileged in such

---

Kurie', pp. 240–42 (English version pp. 184–86 above); and the articles above, p. 227 n. 30; pp. 240–42 n. 105.

154 *Regulae cancellariae apostolicae*, ed. by von Ottenthal, p. 44 (no. IX b); cf. Schwarz, 'Abbreviature officium', pp. 791–92.

155 Schwarz, 'Die Abbreviatoren unter Eugen IV.', p. 231.

156 Frenz, *Papsturkunden*, p. 96 (§ 127), p. 105 (§ 141); position 30 is on the back, in the upper right corner and upside-down. On the annotations of substitutes signing for the Protonotaries (position 21), see p. 241 n. 139 above.

157 Frenz, *Papsturkunden*, p. 65 (§ 75); together with the secretary's signature, if the letter was checked by him.

158 Schwarz, 'Abbreviature officium', p. 807 n. 111. Since I focused especially on the volumes for the year 1431/1432, I expected to find Alberti, presuming that he assisted at least on occasion, pp. 814–15 n. 160. Dal Pozzo's absence from them is due to the fact that he was custodian at the time.

159 Schwarz, 'Abbreviature officium', pp. 816–23.

160 Otherwise, he would have been named at the new foundation of 1463, when Abbreviators of the *Parcus maior* did not have to pay for membership in the college.

161 On Anselmus Fabri (Smit), see p. 242 n. 145 above.

162 Schwarz, 'Die Abbreviatoren unter Eugen IV.', pp. 229–30.

163 Schwarz, 'Die Abbreviatoren unter Eugen IV.', pp. 212–19. On the concordats of Constance 1418, Genezzano 1426, and relevant Chancery rules, pp. 216–17. Nicholas V again put the benefices of Abbreviators under general reservation; Vatican, Apostolic Archive, Reg. Vat. 433, fol. 106ᵛ.

a way.[164] With the 'Italian nation', however, no comparable agreement was reached at Constance in 1418, nor did one exist after 1442 with Florence, the place Alberti was longing for. Therefore, the restriction did not affect him, unless he sought benefices in France or the Empire. A great benefit of generally reserved positions lay in the possibility for holders to sell them profitably with the help of papal dispensations and licenses, which is documented twice in connection with Alberti. The ordinary collator of the benefice, typically the local bishop, could not interfere in the matter. Secondly, they received along with other curial clergy more favourable responses and treatment when petitioning for expectancies, although it was relatively uncommon in Italy to secure benefices in such a way.[165] Prerogatives in the handling of expectancies that involved concurrent claims were only given to the assistant Abbreviators.[166] Simultaneously, Abbreviators belonged to the class of officials at the Curia who automatically enjoyed the status of 'papal household members'.[167] Contrary to the Scribes of the Chancery, though, they were not exempt from outside jurisdictions.[168] But as household member of the Regent, Blasius de Molino, Battista Alberti enjoyed judicial immunity anyway. Finally, and apart from the fees for various administrative steps, like the drafting and, on the part of the assistant Abbreviators, control and adjudication, there were also tips paid by the petitioners or their proctors in order to expedite the process.[169] Unlike the Chancery Scribes, Abbreviators were not entitled to the free delivery of papal letters.

Abbreviators had much time for other activities, if they did not belong to one of the two *Parci* where the workload remained tolerable, too. As a rule, they held additional offices at the Curia, most commonly that of Chancery Scribe.[170] Abbreviators were ideally placed to offer advice to petitioners and their proctors about the best way to write petitions and helped steer them through the complex administrative stages.[171] An

---

164 Schwarz, 'Die Abbreviatoren unter Eugen IV.', p. 219.

165 When requesting the parish of San Michele, Alberti had to deal with a competitor, whose claim rested on an expectancy; cf. Schwarz, 'Die Bemühungen Leon Battista Albertis', pp. 257–58; Ansani, 'La provvista dei benefici'.

166 Schwarz, 'Die Abbreviatoren unter Eugen IV.', p. 223.

167 Schwarz, 'Die Abbreviatoren unter Eugen IV.', p. 233, with n. 145; Schuchard, *Die Deutschen an der Kurie*, p. 129, with nn. 676–77.

168 1 July 1349, remaining in force despite the revocation of 31 January 1357, see *Regulae cancellariae apostolicae*, ed. by von Ottenthal, pp. 125–26; cf. p. 145. Repeatedly claimed by the Abbreviators in the fifteenth century.

169 Schwarz, 'Die Abbreviatoren unter Eugen IV.', pp. 230–31; a reform of the fee structure did not occur until the creation of the college of vacabilists under Pius II in 1460; cf. p. 206.

170 See above, pp. 232, 235.

171 The mechanism was not automatic, involving constant reminders and prodding with the help of favours.

assistant Abbreviator could do even more.[172] All Abbreviators had access to the Chancery depending on their specific duties. Alberti for his part was under no restrictions as the Regent's *familiaris* from 1431 to 1435.

Alberti's letter informs us that the Abbreviators formed an 'order'. They maintained some form of collegiate structure, which was necessary to distribute the 'letters of justice' for processing and to supervise the charging of fees. Held in high esteem, the Abbreviators of the *Parcus maior* were more thoroughly organized.[173] Their number was usually around a dozen. The *Parcus maior* admitted new members through co-optation. Within the college, the principle of seniority prevailed. The group constituted an elite and competed in ceremonies with similar circles at the Curia, including the secretaries, the clerics of the Chamber, the advocates of the Consistory court, and so on.[174]

The moment has come to address the assumption, apparently hard to eradicate among art historians, that Alberti was one of the founding members of the college of Abbreviators.[175] Pius II granted them a new corporate constitution as vacabilists in 1463 or 1464, imitating the model of the Chancery Scribes.[176] In so doing, the pope wished to sell the fifty-six positions of the *Parcus minor* in hopes of financing his crusade. The Abbreviators of the *Parcus maior*, fourteen in total, were merely obliged to pay an extraordinary tax, whereas the *Parcus minor*, excessively large as it was, was an unprecedented creation intended to raise funds. Abbreviators unwilling to buy their way in lost their office, or rather the right to serve actively and derive earnings from the accruing fees. Apart from specific prerogatives, they were not deprived of their status.[177]

The names of the joining members are preserved in the papal bull originally establishing the college. Battista Alberti was not among them,

---

172 Schwarz, 'Anselmus Fabri (Smit) aus Breda', p. 179; cf. p. 173.

173 Schwarz, 'Die Abbreviatoren unter Eugen IV.', p. 221.

174 Cf. von Hofmann, *Forschungen zur Geschichte der kurialen Behörden*, II, p. 31 (no. 132; of 1472).

175 Accordingly, Grayson, 'Alberti, Leon Battista', who does not know about the two other positions Alberti held in the Chancery from 1449.

176 See the bulls of 15 November 1463, in Vatican, Apostolic Archive, Reg. Vat. 516, fols 201ʳ–03ᵛ; printed in *Regulae cancellariae apostolicae*, ed. by von Ottenthal, pp. 179–83; and of 30 May 1464, in Reg. Vat. 496, fols 155ᵛ–58ʳ; *Regulae cancellariae apostolicae*, ed. by von Ottenthal, pp. 183–88. Summarized in von Hofmann, *Forschungen zur Geschichte der kurialen Behörden*, II, p. 27 (nos 108, 112). Die blueprint offered by the Chancery Scribes is repeatedly acknowledged in the *Regulae cancellariae apostolicae*, ed. by von Ottenthal, p. 180 § 2; cf. Schwarz, 'Die Abbreviatoren unter Eugen IV.', pp. 205–07.

177 *Regulae cancellariae apostolicae*, ed. by von Ottenthal, p. 180 §§ 2 and 7; cf. Schwarz, 'Die Abbreviatoren unter Eugen IV.', pp. 205–06, with nn. 30–31. The fees were newly assessed as a result. The status and privileges of the existing Abbreviators were not addressed!

although close inspection is required to discover that.[178] The relevant list contains in the twenty-first position one 'Baptista Alberto'. A second hand supplied above the line a 'de' between the baptismal and family name, which does not appear in the old printed editions.[179] Frenz, on the other hand, has provided the reading of 'Baptista de Albertis'.[180] The identification was based on his consultation of the *Registrum Vaticanum* 515 in addition to *Registrum Vaticanum* 496, which induced him to spot our B(attista) de Albertis (without indication of the page) among the 'annotations of Chancery Scribes'.[181] The variant is from the former source, which Frenz silently used to 'correct' the reference in the latter by omitting the 'de'. Moreover, he checked this against the *Libri officiorum* for letters of appointment to the position of Abbreviator in the *Parcus minor*, albeit without success for our Alberti. He did not consult the books of the Apostolic Chamber containing in volume 30 of the *Diversa cameralia* several obligations to pay the sales price. One concerned 'Baptista Gasparis de Alberto'.[182] An account book for the crusade includes an entry on the partial payment of 150 guilds by 'Battista da Oliveto'.[183] Given that the twenty-first Abbreviator from the *Parcus minor* of the Chancery is called 'Baptista de Alberto' in the bull papal of 1463/1464, in the official registers of the Apostolic Chamber 'Baptista Gasparis de Alberto', and 'Battista da Oliveto' in a fascicle written for internal use, he was hardly identical with our Battista Alberti, a familiar figure in the Chancery. At the time, he had occupied two functions in the college of Chancery Scribes for decades! At least formally, he was also an Abbreviator and had held the position from 1431. Everyone at the Curia knew that this most famous man was from the Florentine family of the Alberti and always signed as 'de Albertis' (or 'degli

---

178 Vatican, Apostolic Archive, Reg. Vat. 496, fol. 156ʳ; the text also appears as an insert into Paul II's bull in manuscripts from the Chancery; see Vatican, Biblioteca Apostolica, Barb. lat. 2825; Vat. lat. 6343, fols 188ᵛ–90ᵛ; Paris, Bibliothèque nationale, lat. 4172.

179 *Regulae cancellariae apostolicae*, ed. by von Ottenthal, p. 184, has 'Battista de Albeto' misspelled, which von Hofmann, *Forschungen zur Geschichte der kurialen Behörden*, ɪɪ, p. 27 (no. 112), does not correct.

180 Frenz, 'Die Gründung des Abbreviatorenkollegs', p. 305. In his attempt to identify the names on the list, Frenz consulted with Hermann Diener, the editor of the *Repertorium Germanicum* for Eugene IV's pontificate. Diener did not find any contemporary documentation on 'Baptista de Albertis', despite his purported appearance in the twenty-first position. In investigating the matter, neither Diener, nor Frenz suspected that the name might refer to the famous humanist; instead, Claudia Märtl, below p. 247 n. 183, was the first to notice it.

181 Pavón Ramírez, 'Leon Batista Alberti', p. 430; and *Corpus epistolare*, ed. by Benigni and others, pp. 263–65 (no. 31), each cite from this register four documents dated between January and April 1459; Vatican, Apostolic Archive, Reg. Vat. 515, fols 152ᵛ, 155ᵛ, 163ʳ, 170ʳ. The signature there ('B. de Albertis') is that of the *taxator* at the time; cf. below, p. 253.

182 Vatican, Apostolic Archive, Arm. xxɪx: Diversa Cameralia 30, fols 127ʳ–33ᵛ at 128ʳ.

183 18 June 1464; discovered by Märtl, 'Der Papst und das Geld', pp. 200–03, especially n. 83.

248    CHAPTER 9

Alberti' in Italian). His relatives in Florence had long acknowledged him as such by 1463/1464.

Those sharing the belief that Battista Alberti belonged to the *Parcus minor* when the college was founded in 1463/1464, view him by consequence as a victim of Paul II's decision to disband the vacabilist corporation on 3 December 1464, in continuation of a myth created by the notorious polemicist Platina.[184] Frenz has shown to the contrary that Paul II merely restored the Vice-Chancellor's old right of appointment, returned the payments, and established the previous status quo. The Abbreviators retained their office as before Pius II's foundation.[185] On 11 January 1479, it became available for sale again, and this time for good.[186] Furnishing indirect proof that Alberti was an Abbreviator unable to market his position, a report circulated at the Curia after his death about the reassignment of his offices and benefices. His positions as Chancery Scribe and Reader (*lector*) in the *Audientia litterarum contradictarum* were instantly filled, that is, sold. The same did not apply to his function as Abbreviator, which could not be put up for money.[187]

## As Chancery Scribe (and Papal Household Member)

From 21 December 1439 at the latest, Battista Alberti was also a 'Scribe of apostolic letters'.[188] Subsequent documentation of curial and non-curial origin refers to him in this capacity, occasionally adding the words 'and Abbreviator'. He identified himself accordingly in his will, and Sixtus IV's bull, which cites it, does so as well. He retained the scribal office until

---

184 Accordingly, Grayson, 'Alberti, Leon Battista', and others.

185 To provide a final argument, why would a man, who in medieval terms was already old and held two additional offices in the Chancery, including his very lucrative one in the Audience of Contradictory Letters, make the costly investment of buying a position in the *Parcus minor*, and especially when there was no guarantee that the pope's fiscally very audacious move would be successful? A particular tie to Pius II obliging others (see Märtl) is not discernible here. Moreover, Alberti's ambitions were no longer directed toward the Curia, but rather the clan of the Alberti in Florence, whose head he had become in the meantime.

186 See von Hofmann, *Forschungen zur Geschichte der kurialen Behörden*, I, pp. 124–28.

187 Böninger, 'Antonino e Leon Battista Alberti', p. 75, with n. 103; letter from the Curia of 24 April 1472: 'Alberti went to paradise, and the scribal office was given to Platina and the Contradictory one (the readership at the *Audientia litterarum contradictarum*) to Master Valerio, and Ghangalandi to Master Giuliano Davanzati, and (Borgo) San Lorenzo to Master Lorenzo (Malegonelle) of San Piero in Palcho'. I am grateful to Lorenz Böninger for sharing his typescript with me.

188 Böninger, 'Da "commentatore" ad arbitro della sua famiglia', p. 416, reproduces a proctorship issued by 'the eminent doctor of the decrees, Lord Baptista of the late Laurentius de Albertis, and Scribe of apostolic letters'. It was written after the bull of 7 October 1432, in which Alberti is identified as Abbreviator and secretary of the Regent.

his death.[189] His successor was Platina, the papal librarian.[190] The position of Chancery Scribe was held in high regard, and holders were addressed with the title of 'master'.[191] The status of papal household member had long been tied to it, with considerable prerogatives on the benefice market and the right to have papal letters processed for free. The office became available for sale well before 1440. As a matter of fact, the college of Chancery Scribes formed the prototypical corporation of vacabilists at the Curia, marked by a fixed number of members (101), objective perpetuity or conferral for life in the way of a real benefice, and subjective perpetuity or freedom on the part of the official to dispose of his position as foreseen by the canonical rules for benefices. Other prerequisites comprised the admissibility of proxies or substitutes. Primarily, though, the organisation served to collect all fee income in a central place, administering and distributing it evenly. Following protracted conflict with the pope and the Apostolic Chamberlain especially about the admission of additional members, the college of Chancery Scribes obtained a fundamental constitution in 1445. Known by its opening words as 'Sicut prudens', the corporation went on to defend it as sacrosanct.[192] The college furnished a model for the restructuring of existing and founding of new vacabilist enterprises, including that of the Abbreviators in 1463/1464.

Pending permission of the whole group, the position in question could be vacated (as *vacabilis*) and sold by the holder. When the pope could dispose of it by way of exception, through forfeit, or because someone had failed to transfer it in timely fashion, it was possible to ask for the market price. Otherwise, the succeeding official had to pay compensation for papal authorization to keep the office. The payment was viewed as a kind of tax, reaching about ten per cent of what the vacancy would have been worth in full.[193] This leads to the question of the precise moment when Alberti was nominated Chancery Scribe by Eugene IV. Unfortunately,

---

189 *Il testamento di Leon Battista Alberti*, ed. by Bentivoglio and others, pp. 9–48 (facsimile); pp. 49–70 (transcription).

190 For his biography, see Bauer, 'Platina, Bartolomeo'.

191 The address in the letter to Alberti of 24 December 1449, printed in Schwarz, 'Die Bemühungen Leon Battista Albertis', pp. 264–66, is in line with Chancery style: 'To the beloved son, Master Battista Alberti, parish priest of San Lorenzo at Borgo San Lorenzo, doctor of the decrees, Scribe, and our household member'. As Chancery Scribe, Alberti had to be addressed as master and papal *familiaris*. Due to the prestige of his doctorate in church law (*in decretis*), it was mentioned prior to his scribal office. The text is accompanied by the note: 'Free of charge for the colleague'.

192 A poor and faulty version was printed by von Ottenthal, 'Die Bullenregister Martins V. und Eugens IV.'. I plan to provide a new edition, plus commentary.

193 Under Eugene IV, the papal compensation (or composition) following resale stood at one-hundred ducats; Rome, State Archive, Fondo Camerale I, 1468: Spese minute di Palazzo, fols 2$^r$–3$^r$. Just as under Pius II, a vacant position was probable worth 1100 ducats; see Schwarz, 'Die Ämterkäuflichkeit an der römischen Kurie'.

Alberti's petition and eventual appointment letter, which had to mention the previous holder and cause of the vacancy, have not been found yet.[194] As a result, we do not know if he bought his office from another Scribe or the pope.

From the end of 1438, the differences between Eugene IV and the Council of Basel became irreconcilable, making it easier to obtain one of the coveted positions, because many Scribes could not or did not wish to return from Basel to the Curia.[195] Those who did not sell in time had their positions declared forfeited, to the effect that the pope enjoyed exceptional freedom in reassigning several of them. They were not very valuable, however, as demand for papal mandates had dramatically diminished. It was not until Nicholas V (1447–1455) that it attained the level of 1436 again.[196] In financial terms, the businesses of the Alberti family suffered greatly between 1436 and 1439, too.[197]

Normally, petitions for the office of Scribe in the Chancery or in the Penitentiary are easy to track in the registers, because the right of appointment belonged to the pope, which was not the case with the Abbreviators. The entries are conveniently highlighted in the left margin by a reference, say, to the (officium) script(orie).[198] For the period from Martin V (1417– 1431), though, scholarship has not yet attempted to find Alberti's request. Chancery Scribes can be spotted in the registers more easily than Abbreviators, since petitions mention the former with regularity.[199] In this way, we can trace many of them — especially clerics and those active on the benefice market — whether they wrote in person or merely collected fees from their position.[200] Just as for assistant Abbreviators, additional evidence is furnished by the Chancery annotations. First, they consist of the signature on the right of the folded portion, or *plica*, which is provided

---

194 There is hardly any hope to come across them, even when the registers of petitions are scanned digitally; cf. p. 236 above, with n. 98.

195 On the defection of curial clergy in general, Schwarz, *Kurienuniversität und stadtrömische Universität*, pp. 159–61.

196 For the Empire, see the evaluation of petitions by Christoph Schöner, in *Repertorium Germanicum*, v; I have repeatedly commented on it; see, for example, Schwarz, 'Vom Nutzen des vatikanischen Archivs', pp. 215–23 (English version above, pp. 132–36). On France, Tewes, *Die römische Kurie*, pp. 117–20.

197 Boschetto, 'I libri della famiglia'.

198 Other mandates in connection with the scribal office are marked in the same way; for instance, dispensations to keep the position despite getting married, or while being absent from the Curia (!), and permissions to resign. If the date is known, acts of appointment are readily found in the registers of outgoing letters.

199 The holders of higher dignities are an exception. They saw their scribal office primarily as a steady source of income.

200 Until 1447, they must be sought in Diener's fascicles; see p. 236 n. 98 above.

in stylized fashion by the Scribe responsible for the clean copy.[201] If he acted as a substitute, the name of the colleague he represented appears in the line below, preceded by the words 'instead of'. Other officials signed in specifically reserved parts of the papal letter as well. Particularly important in our context are the notes below the *plica* on the left. They show the fee (or tax) assessment.[202] It is most helpful that scribal signatures were frequently repeated in the registers of outgoing letters, at times together with the tax.[203]

A collection of data like to the one I have compiled for the Abbreviators does not exist for the Chancery Scribes of the period. The few repertories of annotations mentioned contain almost nothing on Alberti.[204] In line with my discussion of the Abbreviators, I summarize here the function and significance of the scribal office in the Chancery. The Scribes there were the artisans of the Chancery. According to complicated rules, they crafted the documentation, which was admired and imitated all over Europe in its external appearance and formulations.[205] Based on the draft version which the Abbreviators and secretaries had sent them, the Scribes had to extend the formulaic notes properly and generate a full text in correct fashion. Under recourse to the formularies, petitions containing standard requests had to be turned from the Abbreviators' notes directly into clean copies. The omission of a clause or even a single word had to be avoided at all cost! Special attention had to be paid to the proper use of titles for addressees and the adequate spelling of individual names and places, as errors could be exploited to challenge the entire letter.[206] This was most difficult when petitioners came from regions of Latin Christianity the average curial cleric had barely heard about.

Visually, the perfect distribution of words on the parchment was paramount.[207] It called for complicated calculations, especially when the text was long, because the distance between lines and the script had

---

201 Like modern signatures, they were unique to the person, but much more stylized, in the way of notarial monograms; Frenz, *Papsturkunden* (position 8).

202 Frenz, *Papsturkunden*, § 125 (position 11).

203 The study by Frenz, 'Zum Problem der Reduzierung', does not extend beyond Martin V (1431); on the *Repertorium officiorum Romanae Curiae*, ed. by Frenz (online), see p. 247 above.

204 See pp. 253–54 below.

205 *Papsturkunde und europäisches Urkundenwesen*, ed. by Herde.

206 Bishops and archbishops were addressed as 'venerable brother', unlike other Christians ('beloved son'); women differently than men as 'beloved daughter in Christ'; excommunicates different from those in good standing, etc. Office holders were not called by name, but blank space in the form of two dots was left to indicate that the mandate continued to apply after the current official died.

207 Frenz, *Papsturkunden*, §§ 27–29. The scribal art in the papal Chancery of the thirteenth century is clearly and amusingly described by Graber, 'Ein Spurium auf Papst Gregor X.'; with references to relevant studies in diplomatic.

252    CHAPTER 9

to be equal throughout.[208] Next, the vertical and horizonal lining was carved into the writing material. The peculiar curial cursive had to be used consistently. Certain words needed to be highlighted in their initial.[209] This was determined by age-old habits kept secret for the most part.[210] When looking at the opening line, it was already clear whether the mandate was a gratial one, or belonged to the so-called 'letters of justice'.[211]

Taken together, the Scribes were not plain copyists of preformulated texts. Counting 101 colleagues overall, however, at best one-half was active around 1440.[212] I call them the master artisans. The rest had substitutes write for them and paid those among the master artisans the proper share, which appears in the annotation as one of them writing for (*pro*) another. Alternatively, they hired a replacement, offering an allowance.[213] The Scribes did not work close to the Chancery. Instead, the production of letters took place in each master artisan's private residence.[214] The steps of expedition to follow occurred in a specific location, or 'bank', which the scribal college had reserved and where the appointed charges served in person at given times. It was there that the petitioner or his proctor paid for the release of his mandate, carrying a final note to this effect.

The Chancery Scribes were traditionally organized like a guild. Because I have treated this aspect on several occasions, the briefest of summaries can suffice here.[215] Officials chosen by the college distributed the petitions, in draft form or notes, as equally as possible in view of the prospective fee income. They appointed substitutes from among their colleagues

---

208 If very few words occupied the last line, they had to be spread out to present the text in a block.

209 The address, the first character of the narrative, and the two clauses containing the sanction, 'Nulli ergo' or 'Si quis' in mandates with seals on a silk cord, had to be highlighted along with the names of persons and places, also the offices and dignities (except for the 'bishop' in the opening line), and the year of the pontificate. This involved capitalisation or special forms of small letters with elongated ends; cf. Graber, 'Ein Spurium auf Papst Gregor X.', pp. 100–01.

210 For example, where and how abbreviations or erasures had to be made; where they were not allowed at all (especially in the dating clause). For more information on the mysteries of the curial minuscule, which changed into a bastarda during the fourteenth century, see Graber, 'Ein Spurium auf Papst Gregor X.'.

211 The pope's name was emphasized in the latter through large and illuminated initials, while the remainder appeared in elongated script. If letters of justice were of the simple kind, only the first character was capitalised and blackened, the rest did not differ from the whole text. Most visible was the attachment of the lead seal which, depending on the class of letter, was affixed to the fold either by yellow and red silk cords (*cum serico*), or by one made of hemp (*cum filo canapis*).

212 Schwarz, *Die Organisation der kurialen Schreiberkollegien*, p. 51.

213 Many seeking a position as Scribe supported themselves as substitutes for a long time and waited for their opportunity.

214 Schwarz, *Die Organisation kurialer Schreiberkollegien*, pp. 69–70.

215 For details, Schwarz, *Die Organisation kurialer Schreiberkollegien*; and more recently, Schwarz, 'Die Korporationen der Schreiberkollegien an der päpstlichen Kurie'.

or determined whether such replacements were admissible. Others controlled the clean copies executed on parchment, ordered corrections, or had the text rewritten, if necessary. Then, the letters were taxed by a different charge known as the *rescribendarius*, or distributor and calculator, who before signing placed the fee along with the date of release below the fold on the left side of the document.[216] Dues were collected when the letter was handed over for further delivery. The payment was credited to the Scribe, except for the amount he owed to his substitute, typically one-fifth. The calculator recorded the sums.[217] The scribal *taxa* formed the base of all fees including those of the Abbreviators.[218] The guild had long appropriated much of the disciplinary oversight formerly pertaining to the Vice-Chancellor and other superiors.

The Scribes staged many corporate events.[219] They gathered at least once a month to settle and give each member his portion of the shared revenue. Those in charge rendered account and were confirmed or replaced, providing ample opportunity for gossip. Elections or the admission of new members called for extraordinary meetings. The guild commemorated their dead and supported colleagues during illness. They jointly celebrated specific feasts and held memorial services, for which they maintained their own chapel as well as for daily mass. Many among the higher curial staff were members of the scribal corporation. In von Hofmann's work, lists of officials such as those for the secretaries, *referendarii, cubicularii*, heads of the registers, and so on, read like an index of people belonging to the college of Chancery Scribes. They obviously did not write or no longer composed letters themselves. But they would still show up at collegiate meetings, not least because of the fees distributed there.

Chancery annotations indicate two periods in which Alberti held the office of calculator in the corporation, once in the first quarter of 1448.[220] He appeared a second time from January to April 1459.[221] The editors of Battista Alberti's *Corpus epistulare* were only interested in his autograph

---

216 Concerning the Chancery Scribe and the fee annotation on the bull of 7 October 1432, Schwarz, 'Die Bemühungen Leon Battista Albertis', pp. 246–47.

217 Schwarz, *Die Organisation kurialer Schreiberkollegien*, pp. 33–34, 99–100, 107–08, 113–14, 146–47, 156.

218 See above, p. 232.

219 Schwarz, *Die Organisation kurialer Schreiberkollegien*, pp. 151–66.

220 See the Chancery note on an outgoing letter (from Darmstadt) of 19 March 1447, signed in January 1448, in *Repertorium officiorum Romanae curiae*, ed. by Frenz (online); and of 18 March 1448, in Mantua, Archivio Gonzaga 3302 c. 11; printed in *Corpus epistolare*, ed. by Benigni and others, p. 216 (no. 20); in photocopy, p. 473. The *taxa* was noted in March, explaining the 'Mar' before the names of the two officials.

221 There are four notes by Alberti in this function, see Vatican, Apostolic Archive, Reg. Vat. 515, fols 152ᵛ (13 January 1459), 155ᵛ (17 February 1459), 163ʳ (5 April 1459), 170ʳ (10 April 1459); cited after Pavón Ramírez, 'Leon Battista Alberti', who followed a remark by Frenz, see p. 247 n. 180 above. The *Repertorium officiorum Romanae curiae*, ed. by Frenz (online),

254 CHAPTER 9

and did not consider its form or function.[222] It is likely that researchers will find more instances of Alberti's handwriting in the archival material. The evidence shows that like dal Pozzo before him, Alberti had risen to top rank in the college. From there, the Regent recruited his higher charges, who received from the guild something like a salary for their services. To improve the chance of other members to attain these positions, corporate statutes stipulated that someone was to occupy such a 'lucrative post' only every two years.[223]

## As Reader in the *Audientia litterarum contradictarum*

In 2005, Marta Pavón Ramírez searched the papal registers of petitions for Alberti's request of provision with the parish church of San Lorenzo in Borgo San Lorenzo al Mugello. Known through local sources, she found it with relative ease because of the date (7 December 1449).[224] She was rather surprised to see, however, that his petition mentioned the provision with San Lorenzo (and additional favours related to it) only in the second part.[225] The benefice had become vacant due to the death of the previous holder, Carlo di messer Palla di Nofri Strozzi. The opening portion asked for something entirely different. I have analysed the outgoing version of the provision as well as the odd format of the petition elsewhere, after finding it in a Lateran register.[226]

Alberti's request was not primarily concerned with the benefice at San Lorenzo, but rather with the office of Reader (*lector*) in the *Audientia litterarum contradictarum*, which Strozzi also held before dying at the Curia.[227] The text contains the fully extended phrases of such an appointment,

---

offers another reference of April 1459, in Munich, Bayerisches Hauptstaatsarchiv, Passau DU.1946. On the form of the note added by the calculator, see Schwarz, *Die Organisation kurialer Schreiberkollegien*, pp. 146–47; Frenz, *Papsturkunden*, § 125.

222 Unlike the scribal monogram put on the right of the fold, the *rescribendarius* and the *taxator* signed in their usual hand below the *plica* to the left.

223 Schwarz, *Die Organisation kurialer Schreiberkollegien*, pp. 157–58.

224 Vatican, Apostolic Archive, Reg. Suppl. 437, fol. 277ᵛ; printed in Ramírez, 'Leon Battista Alberti', pp. 439–40, with misleading summary; *Corpus epistolare*, ed. by Benigni and others, pp. 221–24 (no. 22), which is the text used here; see also the reproduction, pp. 483–84, permitting correction and a diplomatic description. For my critique of Benigni's edition, see Schwarz, 'Die Bemühungen Leon Battista Albertis', pp. 258–59.

225 As a result, Pavón Ramírez consulted with me in 2005. My extensive responses to her queries are cited in her essay.

226 Schwarz, 'Die Bemühungen Leon Battista Albertis', p. 259.

227 Luca Boschetto has examined the relationship between Alberti and Strozzi. The two were relatives at multiple levels and in-laws; *Corpus epistolare*, ed. by Benigni and others, pp. 228–29; Boschetto, 'Società e cultura a Firenze', p. 384. For Strozzi's vita, see Schwarz, 'Die Lektoren in der Audientia litterarum contradictarum'; to appear.

although the extent of formulaic passages is quite modest, asking for provision with the 'office of readership in the Audience of Contradictory Letters at the Roman Curia', which was to be bestowed 'by apostolic authority'.[228] The position was given so that 'we', the pope, 'receive and admit and order to be received and admitted to this office and its free exercise and all accustomed payments, etc.' the provided person, who for both parts of the petition is identified as 'Baptista de Albertis, cleric from Florence, Scribe and papal household member'.[229] The pope granted the two requests by signing with 'so be it by my own will (*motu proprio*) regarding either', which was apparently enough for the petition to secure access to the office of Reader and to be sworn in.[230] Perhaps, it was supplemented with a mandate from the Chamberlain. At last, we have a firm date for Alberti's admission to this office.

The 'Audience of Contradictory Letters' was one of the ordinary courts at the Curia.[231] Originally, it had been a subdivision of the Public Audience, where a large but continuously diminishing number of papal documents was read in public before they could be released. The reading served to preserve the interests of those at risk of suffering a disadvantage from the favour a curial 'office' was about to concede which, after all, was based solely on the petitioner's description of the case and constituted, technically speaking, merely a 'rescript'. The Curia itself did not consider it essential, nor did it have the means, to acquire the necessary informa-

---

228 Suggesting that the deal had already been concluded. An express petition for one of the two readerships of 9 December 1445 has been edited by Schwarz, *Die Organisation kurialer Schreiberkollegien*, p. 102 n. 86.

229 It does not matter that his function as Abbreviator was not mentioned, because the scribal office formed the sole prerequisite for Readers. It has not surprised anyone except myself that Alberti is called a 'Florentine cleric', here as elsewhere; see Schwarz, 'Die Bemühungen Leon Battista Albertis', p. 240.

230 The *motu proprio* probably served to convey to the recipient of the favour prerogatives against competitors, which is why it must have referred to the benefice (of San Lorenzo) in this context. It did not have any significance for the readership; cf. Frenz, 'Motu proprio'.

231 Herde, *Audientia litterarum contradictarum*; Herde, 'Audientia litterarum contradictarum', cols 1192–93; and Frenz, *Die Kanzlei der Päpste*, pp. 150–51; Frenz, *Papsturkunden*, § 139. Both Herde and Frenz claim that they also cover the period from 1300 to 1471. However, Herde approaches the topic from thirteenth-century diplomatic and the formularies, which do not extend in their recent versions and extant manuscripts beyond the pontificate of John XXII (1316–1334). Frenz for his part relies apart from the Chancery annotations on the normative texts, especially the constitutions, and on two procedural tracts of the late fifteenth and early sixteenth centuries. The latter only treat gratial letters and cannot be used as sources in the present context. Frenz, *Papsturkunden*, p. 46, rightly finds the constitutions after 1470 difficult to understand. They must be consulted with caution, moreover, because they frequently seek to restore older standards or contain rules addressing the venality of offices rather than Chancery routine at the time. They reveal little about the situation prior to 1470; cf. pp. 233–34 above.

tion independently.[232] Other documents were published in the *Audientia*, too. Traditionally, the 'Auditor of Contradictory Letters' presided over its sessions, while the Proctors accredited at the *Audientia* safeguarded their clients' interests during the 'readings'. They objected when needed, and the Auditor determined the validity of their complaint.[233] There was still a great hall for the 'Public Audience' in the papal palace at Avignon. From the Great Schism (1378–1415), the *Audientia litterarum contradictarum* absorbed as the former sub-unit the functions of the Public Audience, causing confusion to the present day. The term of 'Audience' without further qualification is rare in the sources, despite the fact that the great sessions persisted into the fifteenth century.

From the perspective of the Chancery, the Audience of Contradictory Letters constituted in some sense one of its branches. Therefore, and not just for historical reasons, the Vice-Chancellor was the head of the Audience, wielding disciplinary authority over it, whereas the 'correctory' or *correctoria*, which checked the letters initially for formal mistakes, formed its smaller pendant also during ceremonies. According to Chancery annotations on the original papal mandates, the *Audientia litterarum contradictarum* received in clean copy not even all letters of justice anymore, but only the ones called 'of major justice', and half of those concerning 'minor justice', which were to be released by the *correctoria*.[234] These pieces of correspondence alone continued to carry a Proctor's note in the classical position on the back, where papal documents requested by petitioners had once featured them as a matter of course. The name of the proctor commissioned by the party appeared there previously. Now, it was a Proctor from the *Audientia* who formed with his colleagues a college of thirteen members.[235] There is no study of the causes behind the dramatic decline in demand for such letters from the mid-fourteenth century onward.[236]

---

232 Cf. Hageneder, 'Päpstliche Reskripttechnik'; Schwarz, 'Supplik'.

233 We owe several constitutions to their misconduct, (futile) attempts to discipline them and secure the proper functioning of the *Audientia*. The texts inform us about institutional conditions, mostly before the Schism of 1378. Contested documents were set aside by the Notary of the *Audientia*.

234 Frenz, *Papsturkunden*, § 139. A formulary for letters of major justice from the mid-fifteenth century was once located at the State Archive of Hanover; Meinardus, 'Formelsammlungen und Handbücher', pp. 58–59.

235 Frenz, *Die Kanzlei der Päpste*, p. 94.

236 I have observed this decline in my catalogue of papal documents preserved in Lower Saxony and Bremen, p. 240 n. 124 above. Frenz, *Die Kanzlei der Päpste*, pp. 2–9, provides at the beginning a survey of the original letters he has examined. Mandates of minor justice are rare among them, counting twenty-one of 161 items from the pontificate of Sixtus IV (1471– 1484). Of these, notes from the *Audientia* (or in *valvis*; p. 257 n. 239 below) are only found on those (fifteen) with the incipits *Conquestus* or *Conquesti*, *Sua nobis*, and *Ad audientiam*. Two of them were rewritten (nos 80, 132) perhaps owing to contradictory challenges. Notes from the *Audientia* also appear on two letters of major justice (nos 11, 150).

One of the reasons may have been the legal resolution of many issues.[237] The Chancery reacted by simplifying the process of expedition and by streamlining the individual steps. The Proctors did so by becoming more professional and creating one of the typical curial colleges. On the positive side, contradictory challenges grew rare and with it the need for re-writing, which was time-consuming and expensive for the petitioners.

It is likely that the so-called 'reading' implied for simple letters of justice the straightforward signing of documents by those involved in their production, namely, the Proctors of the Audience and the Readers. By 1450, Chancery annotations reflecting this stage in the expedition process had changed into a receipt for the proper fee.[238] It had to be paid at the site of the *Audientia litterarum contradictarum*. As a result, the letters do not contain any mention to the effect that they had been read out in public. The few letters of major justice carrying a note confirming that they 'had been read in the Audience', must have been publicized accordingly.[239] Traditionally, the Auditor of Contradictory Letters determined complaints reaching the Public Audience. The contentious documents or passages were treated before him in separate session and at a different location, where the conflict was settled as needed through modification of the wording. The resulting changes were added to the original or on a supplementary piece of writing.[240] The Advocates also acted in that phase. Around 1450, this process of contradiction was rarely recorded. We do not know how it was handled.

The most important task of the Audience at the time was probably the publication of documentation other than Chancery output. It consisted of summonses and sentences passed by the curial courts.[241] It also comprised

---

237 Due to the development and differentiation of forms, on which fundamental research is lacking, and because of the spread of pertinent expertise in the regions away from the Curia. Schmugge, 'Kanonistik und Pönitentiarie', pp. 103–08, has shown the immense dissemination of basic canonistic knowledge. Herde, 'Die "Registra contradictarum"', p. 411, refers to the 'decentralisation of ecclesiastical adjudication' as the main factor for the 'decline in mandates of justice'.

238 Annotations on the reading in the *Audientia* appear in the upper right margin on letters of minor justice, otherwise in the right margin, usually in position 4 and taking the form of a 'q' crossed twice in the lower shaft. It is possible that the note on the letter of 1459 in Würzburg, Staatsarchiv, Historischer Verein, Urk. 1459 V 23 (N. 1895), which under 'Alberti', in *Repertorium officiorum Romanae curiae*, ed. by Frenz (online), is characterized as 'another unspecified office', refers to this activity of Alberti.

239 Frenz, *Die Kanzlei der Päpste*, pp. 124–25. During summer vacations, the reading in the *Audientia* could be replaced by a public posting at Saint Peter's (*in valvis*); see p. 6 (no. 101).

240 Frenz, *Die Kanzlei der Päpste*, § 139; cf. Stelzer, 'Über Vermerke der beiden *Audientiae*'. There is no scholarship on contradictory procedure in late medieval papal documents.

241 The *Audientia* issued summonses to its own court as well, if no other judicial path was available; one case is from heretical Bohemia, see Vatican, Apostolic Archive, Reg. Suppl. 404, fol. 4$^{r-v}$ (11 March 1445); *Repertorium Germanicum*, v, ed. by Diener and others, no. 2511. A second case is from the area controlled by the Council of Basel, cf. Vatican,

258   CHAPTER 9

resignations of benefices or offices and the launch of proceedings over benefices subject to papal provision, in particular the validity of expectancies.[242] Official declarations of various sorts were published there as well, including the dates of court holidays, a move of the Curia, papal constitutions, new Chancery rules, etc. In this regard, the *Audientia* worked in the way of an official bulletin. Like the Chancery, the fifteenth-century Audience did not have a fixed residence. Under Eugene IV and long thereafter, the corporation of Proctors at the Audience gathered at San Michele next to San Celso and San Giuliano, where the Audience must have been located, too. The collegiate church of San Celso and San Giuliano was still quite large. It probably accommodated major sessions of the Audience, given that announcements had to be posted there.[243]

The staff of the Audience included the Auditor from early on.[244] In addition, there were the accredited Proctors, two Readers, two Notaries from the mid-fourteenth century instead of one, and a few servants.[245] By 1450, they had a corporate structure in which all officials held their position in perpetuity, including the Readers. In 1435, this form of organization was conceded to them in a fundamental constitution, known by its opening words as 'Gerentes in terris'.[246] A focal point was the Proctors' guild. Their offices were already for sale. In the present context, though, only the Readers are of interest.

The office of the two Readers in the Audience can be traced back to the thirteenth century.[247] Like the Abbreviators in the Chancery, they

---

Apostolic Archive, Reg. Suppl. 368, fol. 69ᵛ (15 September 1440); *Repertorium Germanicum*, v, ed. by Diener and others, no. 8633.

242 Beginning under Eugene IV, resignations in favour and pensions required the holder's prior consent; *Regulae, ordinationes et constitutiones*, ed. by Meyer (online), Eugene IV – OT 72, Nicholas V – OT 87; von Hofmann, *Forschungen zur Geschichte der kurialen Behörden*, I, p. 54. The declaration of Calixt III for the Notary of the Audience, who was also notary of the Auditor and the Vice-Chancellor, touched on the function of the Audience as well; Vatican Archives, Reg. Vat. 453, fols 253ᵛ–54ᵛ (8 July 1458).

243 Sohn, *Deutsche Prokuratoren an der römischen Kurie*, pp. 271–72, 277–78, 286–87; Schwarz, *Kurienuniversität und stadtrömische Universität*, p. 222.

244 For the office-holders, see Herde, *Audientia litterarum contradictarum*, I, pp. 74–78; from 1400, von Hofmann, *Forschungen zur Geschichte der kurialen Behörden*, II, p. 76 (List III). Their position and status are discussed by Schwarz, 'Der *corrector litterarum apostolicarum*', pp. 175–76.

245 The Proctors have been treated by Sohn, *Deutsche Prokuratoren*; Sohn, 'Procuratori tedeschi alla curia Romana'; Schuchard, *Die Deutschen an der römischen Kurie*, pp. 191–94; Schuchard, 'Lübecker und Hamburger Interessenvertreter'; Zutshi, 'Proctors Acting for English Petitioners'.

246 Inadequately published by Teige, *Beiträge*, pp. LI–LXXXII. I am planning a new edition of this text, too.

247 Schwarz, *Die Organisation kurialer Schreiberkollegien*, pp. 100–02; Schwarz, 'Der *corrector litterarum apostolicarum*', pp. 178–79. Also relevant are the constitutions of 1331, in *Regulae*

swore a simple oath as officials.[248] They always served in a pair and had long been recruited from the most experienced Chancery Scribes.[249] According to the constitution for the Scribes of 1445, 'Sicut prudens', the Readers counted among the corporate officials.[250] It remains unclear to what extent the Readers were responsible for other announcements and how they were rewarded for them. They were the ones, however, who published the Chancery rules in the Audience, which is documented for Alberti and Strozzi, his predecessor.[251] Entries in the Chancery regulations of Nicholas V have been preserved for Carlo Strozzi.[252] Alberti himself features in them as well.[253]

The Readers had a regular and considerable additional income, because they received a fee for the reading of Chancery documents directly from the petitioners, whatever the amount may have been in 1450.[254] The above-mentioned constitution of 8 February 1435, 'Gerentes in terris', informs us that the readership had been viewed as a lucrative position for some time. Later, it became venal.[255] The offices of Scribe and Reader

---

*cancellariae apostolicae*, ed. by von Ottenthal, p. 111 (§§ 1–3); and of 1435, ed. by Teige, *Beiträge*, §§ 20–24, 44.

248 Into the fifteenth century, they were called *lectores in audientia* or 'those Scribes who read in the Audience' according to older copies containing their oath; newly ed. by Schwarz, *Die Organisation kurialer Schreiberkollegien*, p. 257; on the manuscripts, p. 245. This replaces the previous version in print, in *Regulae cancellariae apostolicae*, ed. by von Ottenthal, p. 43 (no. VIII).

249 Schwarz, *Die Organisation kurialer Schreiberkollegien*, pp. 100–01. The rule in the constitution of 1435 has been printed by Teige, *Beiträge*, § 20.

250 'Sicut prudens', ed. by von Ottenthal, 'Die Bullenregister Martins V', § 6. They received a portion of the *iocalia*, although the scribal corporation did not compensate them like other charges. On their rank within the corporate hierarchy, see Schwarz, *Die Organisation kurialer Schreiberkollegien*, p. 113 n. 126.

251 See the next two notes below.

252 Strozzi appears as Reader in the *Regulae, ordinationes et constitutiones*, ed. by Meyer (online), Nicholas V – OT 13 (20 March 1447); another Strozzi, Antonio, later as a substitute Reader; Nicholas V – HO 32 (5 December 1452).

253 *Regulae, ordinationes et constitutiones*, ed. by Meyer (online), Nicholas V – HO 33 (7 February 1453).

254 Constitution of 1435, ed. by Teige, *Beiträge*, § 44. §§ 20, 21, and the rules governing absences, § 24, show that the right to confer the position belonged alternatingly to the pope and to the Vice-Chancellor. The Auditor of the *Audientia* was invited to conduct the admission, perhaps a sign that he also wanted to be part of the process.

255 See von Hofmann, *Forschungen zur Geschichte der kurialen Behörden*, II, p. 172, referring to the letter by Petrus de Noxeto of 18 November 1443, in *Der Briefwechsel des Eneas Silvius Piccolomini*, ed. by Wolkan, I/1, pp. 351–69 (nos 95, 97). On the secretary Petrus de Noxeto, cf. von Hofmann, *Forschungen zur Geschichte der kurialen Behörden*, II, p. 112 (no. 77); and the list of Readers in Schwarz, 'Die Lektoren in der Audientia', to appear. About the development of the sales price for readerships, cf. Frenz, *Die Kanzlei der Päpste*, pp. 211–12, 216–17.

were coupled.[256] The nexus was customary to such a degree that exceptions from it called for special permission.[257] The readership was granted for life. The collation, or right to confer the position when it became vacant was maintained by the pope and the Vice-Chancellor, apparently against the Auditor's claims.[258] Both seem to have exercised it according to the principle of alternation, which also applied to the Notaries of the *Audientia*.[259] In the registers of petitions, therefore, pertinent requests are only found when the pope was in charge of the appointment because of a vacancy, or when the current holder wished to sell his office by 'resignation in favour' of a third party, which necessitated a papal licence.[260]

When Alberti took office on 7 December 1449, it must have been the pope's turn and not that of the Vice-Chancellor to make the collation following Carlo Strozzi's death.[261] The Vice-Chancellor at the time was the foremost papal confidant (or 'nephew'), Francesco Condulmer, whereas the position of Regent remained unfilled.[262] We do not know if death had surprised Strozzi, given that the plague decimated curial ranks in the summer of 1449. Alternatively, he may have resigned his post in favour of Alberti, who took over as his relative, inheriting, so to speak, Strozzi's benefice as well. In that case, the pope would have agreed to the resignation and obtained a payment of composition for it. If death put the coveted

---

256 Constitution of 1435, ed. by Teige, *Beiträge*, § 20 (at the end).

257 The appointment of a new Reader following the death of his predecessor (20 April 1455), in Vatican, Apostolic Archive, Reg. Vat. 436, fols 241ᵛ–42ʳ: 'Now that the mentioned readership is vacant, which customarily has been held by one of the Chancery Scribes, we depart from that tradition for this time, notwithstanding that you are not from among the Chancery Scribes'; catalogued by Rius Serra, 'Catalanes y aragoneses', p. 329 (no. 71).

258 The Auditor in question was Marinus Orsini, Bishop Elect of Tarantaise, appointed on 8 November 1445, in Vatican, Apostolic Archive, Reg. Vat. 282, fol. 31ʳ; still documented in 1470, Reg. Vat. 543, fol. 82ʳ; he died in 1472 according to *Hierarchia Catholica*, ed. by Eubel. He hardly served in person; apart from his two substitutes noted by von Hofmann, *Forschungen zur Geschichte der kurialen Behörden*, II, p. 76, there are another four listed in the *Regulae, ordinationes et constitutiones*, ed. by Meyer (online).

259 Constitution of 1435, ed. by Teige, *Beiträge*, § 20: 'The conferral pertains to the pope or his Chamberlain'.

260 Vatican, Apostolic Archive, Reg. Vat. 381, fol. 138ᵛ (5 May 1432); Reg. Suppl. 408, fol. 248ʳ (9 December 1445); the same position was addressed in either entry.

261 The situation may not have been all that clear. Perhaps, it involved a show of strength between the pope and the Vice-Chancellor, resembling the conferral of the custodianship in the Chancery, which at the time also alternated between the two. This would call for further research.

262 Cf. von Hofmann, *Forschungen zur Geschichte der kurialen Behörden*, II, p. 72 (nos 6–8). From 1439, Chancery Regents only appeared when Condulmer was absent; for example, Honofrius Francisci de Sancto Severino (1444/1445; May 1449); or temporarily like the judge of the Rota under Nicholas V, Berardus Eroli de Narnia, who became head *referendarius* in the last year of the pontificate. Berardus was only named Regens on 2 December 1453, after Condulmer's death on 30 October 1453. On Berardus, see Schwarz, *Kurienuniversität und stadtrömische Universität*, p. 545 (List 1/193).

office at the pope's free disposal, on the other hand, he would have been able to pass it on to his friend as a generous gift. The college of Chancery Scribes was unlikely to object to the appointment, because Alberti was a long-standing and highly esteemed member of the guild and a relative of Strozzi's.[263] Battista Alberti held the position until he died. His successor was 'messer Valerio', to be identified with the physician, Valerius Iacobi de Viterbio.[264] Alberti and his colleagues may have had substitutes work for them repeatedly.[265]

Insofar as other office holders have been found until now for the time from 1417 onward, a comparison with them can help assess the value of the favour, which Nicholas V conceded to Alberti on 7 December 1449. Unfortunately, von Hofmann's study does not provide a list of Readers next to that of equally lucrative positions like the calculator of fees in the *bullaria* or the custodian of the Chancery. As a result, I have collected the names of office holders from 1417 to 1471 by myself, putting together short biographies for each of them.[266] A look at these biographical sketches reveals that they are scanty for the most part and do not add up to a coherent picture. We do not even know who among the Readers was nominated by the pope and who by the Vice-Chancellor.[267] It is difficult to infer whether the office was granted to reward faithful service, for example, as private physician or personal secretary, for exceptional merit, or at least to provide sustenance in line with status requirements.[268] Perhaps, funding for an artist as the probable cause of Alberti's appointment was a novelty. From 1441 to 1467, Strozzi's and then Alberti's fellow Reader was the well-known personal secretary, Petrus de Noxeto, himself a friend of Nicholas V, who on 25 June 1449 gave to him the lucrative post of Chancery custodian along with permission not to exercise it in person.[269]

---

263  Schwarz, *Die Organisation kurialer Schreiberkollegien*, pp. 176–77.

264  Böninger, 'Antonio e Leon Battista Alberti'. Böninger agrees with my identification.

265  As confirmed for a relative of Carlo Strozzi, who served as his substitute Reader; cf. p. 259 n. 252 above.

266  Schwarz, 'Die Lektoren in der *Audientia litterarum contradictarum*', to appear.

267  The question proved irrelevant between 1437 and 1447, when Francesco Condulmer, a nephew of Pope Eugene IV, was Vice-Chancellor.

268  The appointment of the two Florentines, Rosellus de Hugonibus (nominated in December 1445; deceased before 1449) and Carlo Strozzi, was probably tied to the sojourn of the Curia in the city. Otherwise, the pope or his Vice-Chancellor may have been indebted to them, offering repayment in this way.

269  The difference is indicative. The custodian had to be present according to regulations, which prompted the papal dispensation.

## Final Considerations

Access to the Chancery came with many advantages. The information flows converging there were vital for optimal management of the benefice market. Alberti's personal ambitions were limited in this regard.[270] Still, he was able to act quickly when needed, take care of his 'friends', or accommodate the friends of friends.[271] Access was given to the household members of head officials, the Abbreviators in the Chancery, the custodian, and auxiliary personnel. Molino was Regent in the Chancery until the end of 1435. It is unclear if and how much longer Alberti remained active as Abbreviator there. Regardless, he must have accumulated enough valuable Chancery contacts at the time to have benefitted from them later. Additional insight could be obtained in the Audience of Contradictory Letters, which topped the Chancery as far as insider knowledge was concerned.

Alberti's key office was that of Scribe. Apart from the associated advantages I have mentioned earlier, the impact of social relationships must not be underestimated. When the guild invited to gatherings on a regular basis, Alberti met with the cultural and academic elites around the pope and the administrative hierarchy. His readership, moreover, afforded immaterial opportunities apart from the considerable income it generated. Its holder ranked among the officials of the scribal corporation, who otherwise changed constantly. He caught the eye of many during ceremonial and liturgical events, where the whole college of Scribes was present in person.[272] Alberti's careful choice of benefices shows that prestigious positions were just as important to him as to many of his contemporaries. His goal was the dignity of prior at a collegiate church, even though he just functioned as a parish priest.[273]

The offices Alberti held in the Chancery from 1431 left him sufficient freedom of time and mobility to advance his artistic projects. The more he gained recognition, the easier it must have been for him to arrange for a substitute. It would be a worthwhile research topic to investigate the curial positions of Alberti's correspondents and friends and place them in a socio-historical context!

---

270 Schwarz, 'Die Bemühungen Leon Battista Albertis', pp. 262–63.
271 Schwarz, 'Die Abbreviatoren unter Eugen IV.', pp. 232–33.
272 Schwarz, *Die Organisation kurialer Schreiberkollegien*, p. 180 n. 76.
273 Schwarz, 'Die Bemühungen Leon Battista Albertis', p. 263.

CHAPTER 10

# Position and Rank of the (Vice-)Chancellor at the Curia

In the middle of illustrious experts in papal diplomatic especially of the high medieval period, I am a rare bird. First, because I am a scholar of the late Middle Ages, once called 'dark' by Friedrich Kempf; and secondly, because I have not studied diplomatic. I say this at the beginning not only to appeal to the benevolence of my audience, which I do considering that I left academic employment so long ago; but I also speak in such terms to describe the scope of my present argument. To begin with, the Chancellor at the centre of my presentation was always the Vice-Chancellor, except for his appearance in official ceremonies, which have prompted me to address earlier times as well. For the rest, my chronology starts with the pontificate of Honorius III in 1216, when the Vice-Chancellor replaced the Chancellor for good. It ends with the death of Paul II in 1471. Thereafter, the venality of offices transformed the whole organisation of the Curia.

There is an abundance of late medieval documentation on the Vice-Chancellor. Contrary to the High Middle Ages, it is found to a small extent in original papal letters. Instead, I go far beyond the thematic limitations that the sources of diplomatic strictly speaking impose on me.[1] I extend my reach to other evidence of curial origin, which multiplied enormously through the period and offers unprecedented insight into the Vice-Chancellor's position and rank.[2] I cannot discuss in detail which primary materials I have in mind here.[3] My goal is to address the administrative functions and competencies of the Vice-Chancellor, his

---

1 The text largely preserves the original, oral form of presentation. I have added notes and the concluding remarks below, pp. 276–78. I am grateful to my friend, Dr Katharina Colberg (Hanover), for her copyediting. For a concise survey on the development of the papal Chancery in the Middle Ages, see Meyer, 'Die päpstliche Kanzlei im Mittelalter'; and, for a much shorter, English version, Meyer, 'The Curia: The Apostolic Chancery'. I thank Mr Meyer for allowing me to access his typescript prior to publication.

2 Meyer, 'Die päpstliche Kanzlei', pp. 327–30, on the registers. Until his death in February 2017, Andreas Meyer kept working on his *Regulae, ordinationes et constitutiones*, ed. by Meyer (online), a revised edition of *Regulae cancellariae apostolicae*, ed. by von Ottenthal; and, for Meyer's 'Extravagantes', most of *Die päpstlichen Kanzleiordnungen*, ed. by Tangl. On the *Liber cancellariae*, cf. Meyer, 'Die päpstliche Kanzlei', p. 334. Information about staff appears in other sources of the Vatican Archives as well; see Boyle, *A Survey of the Vatican Archives*.

3 For the following, I refer to my article, Schwarz, 'The Roman Curia (until about 1300)'.

position at the Curia, his sources of income, and his ceremonial role.[4] I will look from a bird's eye view at developments, which lead from his modest position as head of household at the Chancery in 1216 to that of one of the foremost figures at the papal court. In line with the original theme of the conference from which this essay has emerged, I hope to offer a contribution to the field of European cultural history.

It is well known that Innocent III greatly transformed the Apostolic Chancery. He re-created the office as a collegiate enterprise with seven Notaries under the leadership of a Vice-Chancellor, whose household consisted of the Auditor of Contradictory Letters, the corrector, and the keepers of the seal (*bullatores*).[5] Already by the mid-thirteenth century, the Auditor had left to establish his own household.[6] Before 1300, the corrector and the *bullatores* went their separate ways as well.[7] By then, the Notaries had long abandoned the Vice-Chancellor's entourage, who in turn began to fill his Vice-Chancery with his own servants, above all with his Abbreviators and the custodian, in charge of expediting the largest and most important share of papal letters.[8] A smaller rest remained with the Notaries, especially because of the fees from letter-writing, similar to developments in the Consistory court.

Concerning the status of the leading officials in the Chancery as opposed to their ceremonial rank to be discussed below, both the Vice-Chancellor and the Auditor stayed on from the mid-thirteenth century during the rather frequent vacancies on the papal throne, continuing their administrative tasks at reduced levels.[9] It became customary for the new pope to confirm the Vice-Chancellor in his position.[10] He would continue in his function until a suitable papal candidate and an honourable solution

---

4 From a seventeenth-century standpoint, Ciampini, *De abbreviatorum de parco maiori*, primarily treats ceremonial aspects and in marvellous detail.

5 Other innovations included the service status of the Scribes and Proctors; Schwarz, 'The Roman Curia (until about 1300)', pp. 209, 212–13.

6 Henceforth, the Vice-Chancellor shared his disciplinary authority over the staff and judicial personnel of the Audience with the *Auditor litterarum contradictarum*.

7 In the court statute of 1278, the Apostolic Chamber calculates the *vadia* of the Vice-Chancellor's household with twelve units, apart from those of the Auditor and the corrector with two units each, and four or six units for the *bullatores*; Baethgen, 'Quellen und Untersuchungen', pp. 195–206. In the treaty with the town of Viterbo from the same year, the *bullatores* are listed among the small monastic communities; Paravicini Bagliani, 'La mobilità della Curia romana', pp. 271–75; cf. pp. 275–78.

8 Schwarz, *Die Organisation kurialer Schreiberkollegien*, pp. 68–69, 139–40, 146–47.

9 For the evidence, see Fischer, 'Kontinuität und Institutionalisierung'.

10 I rely here on the list of Vice-Chancellors in Bresslau, *Handbuch der Urkundenlehre*, I, pp. 223 ff., 241–42. The Vice-Chancellor took his oath (of 1405) into the pope's hands, with several cardinals, the Apostolic Chamberlain, and Chamber clerics being present; cf. *Regulae, ordinationes et constitutiones*, ed. by Meyer (online) – Innocent VII, § 20; printed in Baumgarten, *Von der apostolischen Kanzlei*, p. 116; cf. also, p. 146. The text of the oath is found in *Die päpstlichen Kanzleiordnungen*, ed. by Tangl, pp. 33–34.

for the one still in office was found. The leading Chancery personnel was recruited from the papal chapel. Apparently, their selection also depended on proof of skill in matters of written correspondence (*dictamen*) and on juristic expertise. Many Vice-Chancellors of the thirteenth century were eminent lawyers, who had served in part as Auditor of Contradictory Letters. The Notaries, on the other hand, were often sent on diplomatic missions due to their elevated ceremonial rank. Because they were frequently appointed from among favourites, their distance to bureaucratic activities increased over time.[11] Eventually, they only worked on simple assignments not calling for special qualifications.[12]

In the fourteenth and fifteenth centuries, nearly all Vice-Chancellors had high academic degrees, although many of them did not accumulate their merits in the Chancery. Under Boniface VIII (1294–1303), it first occurred that a Vice-Chancellor continued in office after being raised to the cardinalate. Those succeeding him became cardinals as soon as new ones were created following their appointment as Chancery leaders. From 1325, they held both dignities right from their nomination. Beginning with John XXII (1316–1334), we encounter 'Great Vice-Chancellors' who kept their position for decades until they died. They included Pierre des Prés from 1325 to 1361, and regardless of the manifold divisions caused by the Schism, both Pierre de Monteruc from 1361 to 1385 and Jean de Brogny between 1391 and 1426. Next, there were Francesco Condulmer (1437–1453) and Rodrigo Borgia (1457–1492), foremost papal nepotists proving immune to replacement.[13] In the fourteenth and fifteenth centuries, the administrative operations ran so smoothly that the Vice-Chancellors, their title on full display, could be sent for years on diplomatic missions abroad.

The jurisdictional competency of the Vice-Chancellor arose from his high-medieval function as something like a gatekeeper controlling access to the pope.[14] He was fundamentally the one who accepted accusations and decided about their treatment.[15] He advised the pope in legal matters concerning the handling of petitions (in accordance with curial style) or in the Consistory court, where more important requests and complaints were

---

11 Cf. Paravicini Bagliani, *La vita quotidiana*, pp. 81–85.

12 The office of Protonotary became increasingly honorary; those 'participating' in it, that is, receiving a share of the income from the Chancery, formed a special group among them; see also Zutshi, 'The Office of Notary in the Papal Chancery'.

13 I refrain from providing biographical references here.

14 Hirschmann, *Die päpstliche Kanzlei und ihre Urkundenproduktion*, p. 82.

15 For specific studies, see Schwarz, 'The Roman Curia (until about 1300)'. In 1458, Enea Silvio Piccolomini, in *Aeneas Silvius, 'Germania'*, ed. by Schmidt, pp. 108–09 (III, 39), first itemized the Vice-Chancellor's judicial responsibilities before turning to the Chancery in the proper sense.

presented.[16] At first, this always occurred together with the Notaries.[17] In the consistory, the Vice-Chancellor was supposed to propose solutions to problems, write reports, and pronounce sentences. Into the fourteenth century, the Notaries were in charge of record keeping; then, the Chamber clerics took over until the fifteenth century, when the task was apparently given to the Vice-Chancellor's household members, or *familiares*.[18] He executed specific resolutions of the consistory, noting the papal decision at the bottom of submitted petitions.[19] He formulated the *contracedula*, which replaced the petitioner's request to form the basis of consistorial provisions.[20] In addition, he issued procedural mandates for curial judges, ordered the release of charters, and determined their mode of expedition.

Based on his jurisdictional authority, the Vice-Chancellor supervised and controlled the staff of the Consistory during legal proceedings, including the Advocates and Proctors who had to be accredited in the Vice-Chancery and present their commissions there. The Vice-Chancellor also wielded disciplinary powers over representatives of the parties in the Audience of the Sacred Palace (subsequently turning into the Rota) and, to a lesser extent, its judges, scribal personnel, and beadles, who delivered his mandates to the judges of the Rota, announced court dates and the like, and eventually published the sentences through posting. Through the fourteenth and fifteenth centuries, the significance of the Rota grew even further.

The two Audiences, the Public one and the one for Contradictory Letters, constituted courts in a certain sense as well. Both belonged in principle to the Chancery.[21] The Vice-Chancellor's supervision and control

---

16 No study exists on the daily routine in the public consistories. Hack, 'Zeremoniell und Inszenierung', has focused on the grand receptions, primarily consulting ceremonial sources.

17 Who started to take turns; Rusch, *Die Behörden und Hofbeamten*, p. 9. From the mid-fourteenth century onward, they were increasingly replaced by the *referendarii*.

18 The Apostolic Chamberlain seems to have been a permanent presence at the Consistory in the Avignonese period. On his appropriation of responsibilities formerly belonging to the Chancery and concerning, for example, the staff of the register or the expedition of certain letters, cf. p. 269 n. 39 below. An overview of the Apostolic Chamber in the Middle Ages (omitting the fifteenth century) has been furnished for the first time by Weiß, 'The Curia: Camera'; I thank Stefan Weiß for sharing his typescript with me.

19 *L'oeuvre de Patrizi Piccolomini*, ed. by Dykmans, I, p. 167 §§ 451–54 (of 1485/1488), also informing about the assisting *familiaris*. Contrary to this passage, another one, II, p. 494 § 1552, insists that record-keeping was the prerogative of the Protonotaries, if the *procurator fiscalis* invited them to exercise it, which seems to have been a historical reminiscence without significance at the time.

20 Consistorial provisions formed a special category of Chancery letters. The right to compose them was very lucrative; von Hofmann, *Forschungen zur Geschichte der kurialen Behörden*, II, p. 209.

21 The Audience ceased to operate when the Vice-Chancellor died; Baumgarten, *Von der apostolischen Kanzlei*, pp. 90–91. Only the 'letters of justice' could be expedited, not those already approved by the cardinals, p. 103.

POSITION AND RANK OF THE (VICE-)CHANCELLOR AT THE CURIA 267

also extended to legal representatives and personnel admitted to the Audience. All documentation affecting the rights of third parties was read in the Public Audience.[22] The same applied to curial announcements of general interest.[23] In the fourteenth century, the importance of the two Audiences diminished. They seem to have been combined into one during the Great Schism (1378–1415).[24] Finally, the Vice-Chancellor's right to appoint notaries 'by apostolic authority' also derived from his judicial competency. The act consisted of a letter required of all scribes serving at curial courts and chanceries. It was necessary to administer at other ecclesiastical tribunals and scribal offices, too.[25]

The core competency of the Vice-Chancellor was the Apostolic Chancery, where he was in charge of expediting papal letters, from the incoming petitions, which the pope or the Vice-Chancellor had signed depending on the faculties conceded to him, to the final imposition of the seal.[26] Already for the thirteenth century, Andreas Meyer has recently assumed a monthly documentary output of 2000 to 3000 items.[27] Accordingly, the Chancery as their site of production expanded in our period not unlike a modern bureaucracy, which it did not resemble in any other respect, though. From Innocent III (1198–1216), operations were for the most part conducted in private residences, caused not only by the growing volume of business, but also in order to secure income supporting the apparatus through fees and tips. Rationalization hardly benefited the petitioners, who still had to invest much money and effort. At the heart of the Chancery, the secretaries arose as competitors from the mid-fourteenth century onward. They began to appropriate the old function of

---

22 For annotations on papal letters by the Audience, see *Die Originale von Papsturkunden*, ed. by Schwarz, p. xxv.

23 The Vice-Chancellor announced the summer vacations of the curial courts, the pope's travel plans given that the Curia was itinerant into the Avignonese period (and again later).
From Alexander (V) (1409–1410), Chancery regulations and important constitutions were published in the *Audientia*, as Andreas Meyer has kindly informed me.

24 Schwarz, 'Die Karriere Leon Battista Albertis', pp. 93–101 (English version above, pp. 255–61).

25 Revealing its profitability, the same right was often granted to legates to help finance their mission.

26 On the development of the Vice-Chancellor's right to sign, von Hofmann, *Forschungen zur Geschichte der kurialen Behörden*, I, pp. 25–28; Meyer, 'Regieren mit Urkunden', pp. 80–82. His pertinent prerogatives were identified one by one from the time of Benedict (XIII) (1394–1417) and John (XXIII) (1409–1410) under the rubric, 'On the Powers of the Lord Vice-Chancellor', in *Regulae cancellariae apostolicae*, ed. by von Ottenthal. Spontaneous additions were usually made at his own request. Contents varied under Martin V (1417–1431), before being standardized under Eugene IV (1431–1447).

27 Meyer, 'Regieren mit Urkunden', p. 76, has estimated an annual 19000 items even prior to 1250. To arrive at the correct monthly figures, calculations must consider the summer vacations of the Chancery (from mid-July to mid-September at least) and the frequent breaks for liturgical reasons.

the Chancery as advisory board and executor of the papal will.[28] Moreover, they assumed responsibility for the expedition ('through the Apostolic Chamber') of all letters by the Chancery that risked rejection because of the Chancery's continuously perfected formulaic standards, or style. The processing was accelerated in this way, and prospects of winning grew along with the associated costs. The change led to a major shortfall of profits for the people around the Vice-Chancellor, but not for the Chancery Scribes.

Table 10.1(a). The Apostolic Vice-Chancellor in the Later Middle Ages. His Residence.

| 1210: Household of the Vice-Chancellor and notaries, with Auditor, corrector, and others. Notaries, Audience, and the correctory became separate before long. | Around 1300: Vice-Chancery centre for the expedition of papal documents, with Abbreviators, *familiares*, Chancery secretaries, custodian. | From *c.* 1330: Residence of the cardinal Vice-Chancellor and his household, still serving as Vice-Chancery. |
|---|---|---|
| The Chancery register and Office of the Seal (*bullaria*) became separate, too. | The 'Common Date' turned into the point of arrival for all petitions. | Consolidation of tasks tied to other functions of the Vice-Chancellor. |

Let us briefly return to the aspect of administrative operations.[29] The signed petitions were typically submitted to the Vice-Chancery after they were recorded in various registers or fascicles of registration.[30] Either in person or through his Chancery Regent, the Vice-Chancellor had to exercise key functions at the beginning and end of the expedition process properly speaking. He distributed the petitions granted by the pope among the Abbreviators he considered suitable, so that they would formulate draft versions of the outgoing papal letters. A large part of this assignment was left to the Abbreviators themselves, or to the Scribes in charge of producing clean copies.[31] Before they were sent off, the Vice-Chancellor presided

---

28 Meyer, 'Regieren mit Urkunden', pp. 82–83.

29 Described by Schwarz, *Die Organisation kurialer Schreiberkollegien*, pp. 141–49. The inscription of petitions was posted in public to inform proctors about their success or failure; Schwarz, 'Die Karriere Leon Battista Albertis', p. 55 (English version above, p. 227).

30 The registration of petitions for special graces went back to John XXII (1316–1334); Zutshi, 'The Origins of the Registration of Petitions', pp. 185–88. On the pivotal function of the custodian, cf. Schwarz, 'Die Karriere Leon Battista Albertis', pp. 54–56 (English version above, p. 227).

31 Meyer, 'Regieren mit Urkunden', pp. 77–79, has emphasized the decentralization of services here.

## POSITION AND RANK OF THE (VICE-)CHANCELLOR AT THE CURIA

over the final controls, in a session known as 'holding Chancery', where he was joined by the assistant Abbreviators under the leadership of the corrector.[32] Papal mandates crafted from other petitions went for release to the correctory, sometimes after going through the Public Audience or Audience of Contradictory Letters. Then, they were ready for entry into the Chancery registers, if petitioners were willing to pay for it, which most of them were not. Lastly, the letters were sealed.[33] The Vice-Chancellor also dealt with forged papal correspondence (Table 10.1(b), pp. 280–81).[34]

By the second third of the fourteenth century, the contents of the petitions had shifted dramatically. The benefice market, which centred on the Curia, had begun to dominate nearly everything, including the Rota.[35] Henceforth, the Vice-Chancellor had to examine all candidates who had obtained papal provisions and were present at the Curia for their suitability to assume the requested church position.[36] At the beginning of a new pontificate, clerics appeared in such masses to secure expectancies 'in the form of the poor', that he left their approval and formal verification to commissioned officials.[37] The impact of the letters on papal finances was significant, generating in case of success the payment of so-called annates.[38] As a result, the Vice-Chancellor was increasingly compelled to share supervision of the registers with the Apostolic Chamber.[39] Beginning with Boniface VIII (1294–1303), one task concerning the benefice market was willingly performed by the Vice-Chancellor, though not exclusively.[40]

---

32 The Vice-Chancellor did not sign in person, however, leaving the task to an Abbreviator; Schwarz, 'Die Karriere Leon Battista Albertis', pp. 75–76 (English version above, pp. 241–42).

33 The individual steps of expedition are treated by Frenz, *Papsturkunden*, pp. 87–107.

34 *Die päpstlichen Kanzleiordnungen*, ed. by Tangl, p. 67 (no. VII § 20); Herde, *Beiträge zum päpstlichen Kanzlei- und Urkundenwesen*, pp. 129–30; Göller, 'Zur Geschichte der Kriminaljustiz', pp. 190–93.

35 Schwarz, 'Römische Kurie und Pfründenmarkt' (English version above, pp. 177–99). For an overview of the state of research, cf. Schwarz, 'Die Erforschung der mittelalterlichen römischen Kurie', pp. 433–35.

36 For the thirteenth century, see Rusch, *Die Behörden und Hofbeamten*, p. 9; on fourteenth-century practice, Hotz, *Päpstliche Stellenvergabe am Konstanzer Domkapitel*, pp. 49–56, 131–32.

37 I have described the mechanism using two examples; see Müller and Schwarz, 'Zwei Originalsuppliken'. Also, Meyer, *Arme Kleriker auf Pfründensuche*. The registers in question were rather fascicles, kept unlike those of the other outgoing letters by the custodian of the Chancery; Müller and Schwarz, 'Zwei Originalsuppliken', p. 298.

38 Diener and Schuchard, 'Über den Zusammenhang von Thesaurarie und Kollektoren'. The collectors received extracts from the registers. At the end of the fourteenth century, they were preserved in the papal palace, together with the registers of outgoing letters.

39 See von Hofmann, *Forschungen zur Geschichte der kurialen Behörden*, I, pp. 24, 103 ff.; Enea Silvio Piccolomini, in *Aeneas Silvius, 'Germania'*, ed. by Schmidt, pp. 108–09 (III, 59), associated them and the officials of the seal without question with the Chancery.

40 Baumgarten, *Von der apostolischen Kanzlei*, p. 147.

It was the handling of resignations 'in the pope's hands', as the legal formula ran, which chiefly involved the exchange of benefices.[41]

Incidentally, the Vice-Chancellor sometimes sent letters under his own seal.[42] This was done by one of his secretaries in residence. Like all curial leaders, the Vice-Chancellor lived in his own palace, which he shared with household members including several scribes.[43] The higher he rose in the administration, the greater and more prestigious became his entourage. Well into the Avignonese period, he obtained from the Apostolic Chamber provisions and food (*vadia*) for his personnel and *familia*.[44] As usual, no distinction was made between services strictly speaking, other curial obligations, and those of a private nature. The residence was consequently the site where the Vice-Chancellor pursued his administrative activities and where his *familiares*, including his abbreviators, gave assistance in handling petitions and judicial business next to Chancery staff not belonging to his household. The petitions arrived there as well, mandates were issued, and so forth. His auditor was present to investigate forgeries among other things, as the residence also housed a prison.[45] The Vice-Chancellor's gatekeeper was a key figure in the whole process of expedition.[46] He controlled public access. The clerics among the Vice-Chancellor's *familiares* enjoyed along with the higher Chancery officials and 'old' ranks like the Scribes free processing of papal letters, marked by the words: 'No charge for the household member of the Vice-Chancellor' or 'Regent'.

Next, we turn to the Vice-Chancellor's sources of income. From Innocent III, the Chancery was always entitled to its share of the *servitia minuta*, which had to be distributed among superior officials according to a fixed formula.[47] The arrangement persisted beyond the thirteenth-century

---

41 He could grant such petitions independently; Meyer, 'Regieren mit Urkunden', p. 80. According to the *Regulae, ordinationes et constitutiones*, ed. by Meyer (online) – Benedict XIII (§ 117), identical with – John XXIII (§ 46), he was authorized to issue provisions for benefices resigned in this way.

42 Baumgarten, *Von der apostolischen Kanzlei*, p. 97. Mandates with the Vice-Chancellor's seal appeared especially during vacancies on the papal throne, when the pope's *bulla* was unavailable; Fischer, 'Kontinuität und Institutionalisierung'.

43 Schwarz, 'Leon Battista Alberti in der *familia* des Regens', pp. 172–74, 188–89.

44 Described in marvellous detail by Frutaz, 'La famiglia pontificia', where other payments and provisions are mentioned as well. A comparison with the Apostolic Chamber is instructive. Monetary support for the Vice-Chancellor continued, in *Les recettes et les dépenses*, ed. by Guillemain; *Die Ausgaben der apostolischen Kammer*, ed. by Schäfer; and even under Martin V (1417–1431), see Baumgarten, *Von der apostolischen Kanzlei*, p. 122.

45 His principal assignment was the investigation of major and very lucrative cases given directly to the Vice-Chancellor.

46 Schwarz, 'Die Karriere Leon Battista Albertis', pp. 54–56 (English version above, p. 227).

47 The 'services', both 'common' and 'minor', were payments due at the conferral of prelacies. The Chancery obtained a full *servitium minutum*. In the court order of 1306 (cf. Frutaz, 'La famiglia pontificia'), it was left to the Chancery to distribute the monies among staff. In addition, gifts were not infrequent; Lunt, *Financial Relations of the Papacy with England*, I,

break-up of the Vice-Chancellor's household and his subsequent rise. He lost part of the fees for the register and the seal to the Chamber, just as his disciplinary oversight of the personnel was reduced in favour of the latter.[48] Nobody has calculated yet to what extent the Vice-Chancellor participated in fee revenue from the exercise of his official functions.[49] Payment was also collected for the right to nominate staff and the administration of oaths, as the 'honouring' of the person bestowing the office was generally acknowledged by custom.[50] The so-called *iocalia* for admission to the oath were regulated by tradition and amounted to a considerable sum. The appointment of *tabelliones* was increasingly viewed from this perspective alone. The long-standing rule according to which the Vice-Chancellor was entitled to accept resignations 'in the hands of the pope' proved profitable as well.

The right to nominate personnel, or office patronage, was primarily an expression of power and prestige. Baumgarten considered the Vice-Chancellor to be the 'first and most honourable', though not 'the most influential and powerful official'.[51] The attribute of 'first' applied without doubt. Because the Curia greatly depended on demand for services (in the form of documentation and decisions), the Vice-Chancellor looked dominant from the outside.[52] In ceremonies, the development of the Vice-Chancery was either not reflected or merely with great delay. The high medieval regard for the Chancery was preserved. The old liturgical handbooks from the pre-Avignonese period maintain the state-of-affairs under Innocent III, except for the seating arrangements at general councils. The order for the two Councils of Lyon (1245 and 1274) and that of Vienne (1311) still commemorates the elevated rank of the ancient Chancery at papal synods.[53] On the three-tiered pulpit with the papal throne under a

---

p. 475. Of course, the Vice-Chancellor secured his share of the 'common services' alongside his income as cardinal.

48 Cf. von Hofmann, *Forschungen zur Geschichte der kurialen Behörden*, I, pp. 28–29, mentioning income from the registers (one-half); the sale of offices, mainly beginning under Sixtus IV (1471–1484); the examination of notaries; *iocalia* at the admission of staff; and from certain acts in the *Audientia* of Contradictory Letters; cf. II, p. 209 (XIX, 21).

49 They comprised the fees for examination of the notaries; *Die päpstlichen Kanzleiordnungen*, ed. by Tangl, p. 368 (§ 10). On the lists of expenses kept by proctors, there is among those at the Curia they had to 'bribe' constant reference to the simple personnel of the Vice-Chancery, Audience, and Rota; higher charges are noted only in case of personal intervention. The acceptance of 'gifts' indirectly lowered the costs of the patron's household, of course.

50 Schwarz, *Die Organisation kurialer Schreiberkollegien*, pp. 180–81.

51 Baumgarten, *Von der apostolischen Kanzlei*, p. 143.

52 Meyer, 'Regieren mit Urkunden'.

53 Roberg, 'Zur Überlieferung'; Roberg, *Das zweite Konzil von Lyon (1274)*, pp. 5–15; *Il Concilio II di Lione (1274)*, ed. by Franchi. The *ordines* for Vienne are also printed in Schimmelpfennig, *Die Zeremonienbücher*, pp. 153–58, see especially p. 154 (no. V § 5), p. 158

272    CHAPTER 10

baldachin, the Vice-Chancellor, the Notaries, the Auditor of Contradictory Letters, and the corrector are seated one step below the pope, flanked by the cardinal deacons on the right and left. Supplementary notes for Vienne in 1311 mention the Vice-Chancellor for the last time and by way of hypothesis, given that the current holder was a cardinal and thus placed among them.[54] Since he was always part of the cardinalate going forward, his title disappeared from ceremonial instructions.[55]

In the first column of Table 10.3 below, I have compiled the oldest Chancery data informing about its traditional rights and revenues. I have read them against statements from the ceremonial handbooks in the second and third columns. The overall picture that emerges can be summarized as follows. In terms of precedence during public appearances, the Chancery members walked behind the pope. The depiction in the first column still reflects ideas of the twelfth century, when he figured in processions as the lord of Rome, with his court following in his wake. Beginning with Innocent III (1198–1216), however, a new conception of papal authority arose, which placed him at the head of Christendom, to the effect that processional arrangements were reversed to lead toward him, with clergy preceding him in ascending order and rank.[56] The early origin of the Chancery notice is also suggested by the absence of any reference to the Auditor and corrector. Among the processional handbooks, the closest equivalent is the version in the third column. It dates to the Great Schism (1378–1415) and describes the proper entry and departure from town of the Curia, which remained itinerant for a long time.[57] The core of the Chancery with the Auditor and corrector preserves its traditional positioning between the cardinals and the prelates, albeit with some change, as

---

(no. VIII § 10). The seating at the Councils of Constance and Basel was again adopted at the Council of Ferrara and Florence; cf. *The General Councils of Latin Christendom*, ed. by Garcia y Garcia and Lauritzen.

54 In 1245, the Vice-Chancellor Marino da Eboli was named next to the cardinal deacons, along with the Notaries, the Auditor, the corrector, the chaplains, 'subdeacons, and certain others'; Roberg, 'Zur Überlieferung', pp. 39–40. Already in 1274, the number of assistants seems to have been reduced. In 1311, the Vice-Chancellor was replaced by the Apostolic Chamberlain; Schimmelpfennig, *Die Zeremonienbücher*, p. 158 (no. v § 10). The question of the patriarch was contested from 1245, when the patriarch of Aquileia made his appearance; it was resolved in 1311 in the sense that the Latin ones were placed behind the cardinals; pp. 153–54 (no. v § 8); cf. p. 158 (§ 11).

55 He re-emerged on a single occasion toward the end of the fifteenth century, at the emperor's (and probably king's) reception outside the city gates. This is when the Chancery Regent, or the currently highest charge of the Chancery, preceded 'the ranks of the Curia'; *L'oeuvre de Patrizi Piccolomini*, ed. by Dykmans, I, p. 96 § 209 (coronation); p. 191, lines 11–13 (pilgrimage, 1468).

56 Schimmelpfennig, 'Die Krönung des Papstes im Mittelalter'. The coronation of 1458 cannot serve as a model, however, because it was staged with overly learned and archaizing intent.

57 Schimmelpfennig, *Die Zeremonienbücher*, p. 336 (§ 2); cf. Diener and Schwarz, 'Das Itinerar Eugens IV', pp. 212–22.

## POSITION AND RANK OF THE (VICE-)CHANCELLOR AT THE CURIA    273

Table 10.2. Synopsis of the Seating at General Councils (Thirteenth Century).

In the presbytery, there is a large construction in the form of a tent* on a podium where the pope sits on an elevated folding-chair with his feet resting on a stool. In the same tent, the emperor and kings, if present, are placed on (lower) folding-chairs to his left and right**. A few papal chaplains and one subdeacon stand around the pope. To his feet, on sacks of wool, the cardinal deacons are resting in their Dalmatic robes, in their midst also the officiating cardinal or cardinals wearing the *pluviale*. The Chancery appears next to them on both sides, with the Vice-Chancellor, Notaries, Auditor, and corrector. The assisting chaplains and subdeacon in the tent are in white overcoats.

In the choir, the crossing, and the transept, seats are arranged in three tiers of elevation. On the highest in the choir, the cardinal bishops sit to the right of the pope, with the cardinal priests to his left placed slightly lower according to their seniority in office. After the cardinals, the hierarchy follows, beginning with the archbishops who also serve as primates, the bishops, etc., also abbots, all wearing a mitre like the pope. Behind or below the prelates, the envoys of the princes are seated, etc. and other high-ranking individuals like the masters of the military orders and the generals of the mendicants. The (Latin) patriarchs*** are put on elevated chairs (in the crossing?), facing the pope. Everyone else stands in the nave.

*The tent can also accommodate other guests of honour, seated or standing.

**Always to the left and (higher-ranked) right from the pope's perspective. Proximity is another measure of preferment.

***There was still conflict about the Latin 'patriarchs' in 1245. They were placed in the nave in 1245 (?), 1274, and 1311.

the Master of the Sacred Palace has inserted himself between them and the archbishops.[58] Unlike the clerics surrounding them, the Chancery staff does not wear liturgical vestments but those of the court, even though a few of them could be of high ecclesiastical rank, as the handbook explains.[59] Another modification concerns the Protonotaries, who have lost their former place and appear behind the pope in a white linen dress, again not a liturgical one.[60]

The old order claimed in the Chancery notes (and reflecting the situation around 1216) has no parallel in the processional handbooks when it comes to the placement of the Chancery in the presbytery of a church during celebrations conducted by the pope himself. The same applies to

---

58  About this office, see Schwarz, *Kurienuniversität und stadtrömische Universität*, pp. 253–63.

59  Schimmelpfennig, *Die Zeremonienbücher*, p. 336 (§ 2).

60  On the dress of the Protonotaries at the end of the fifteenth century, see Märtl, 'Zwischen Habitus und Repräsentation', pp. 293–94. By 1500, the Auditor and the corrector appeared in association with the Protonotaries; *L'oeuvre de Patrizi Piccolomini*, ed. by Dykmans, I, p. 80 (§ 154).

274    CHAPTER 10

Table 10.3. The Chancery in the Ceremonial Handbooks.

| Chancery Memorandum Regarding Customary Ceremonial Privileges (c. 1270) | Liturgical Processions in the Papal Chapel (towards the altar; late Avignonese period) | Processions of the Roman Church when Entering Town |
|---|---|---|
| At processions through town or places nearby, the Vice-Chancellor and Notaries* follow the pope directly as his 'special family'; when the Curia travels, he is followed by the youngest Notary.<br><br>If the pope celebrates in person, the cardinals sit on both sides (in the presbytery). The Vice-Chancellor, Notaries, Auditor, and corrector are placed immediately behind the cardinal priests, followed by the prelates.<br><br>On the high holidays of Christmas and Easter, the Chancery receives communion from the hands of the pope right after the cardinal deacons. Subsequently, they all visit the pope and share the meal with him. On this occasion, the pope offers them special 'gifts' (likewise on Holy Thursday and the day of his coronation). | If the pope celebrates at the altar, he is assisted (in descending order) by the:<br><br>+ Cardinals according to their rank and seniority<br>+ Curial prelates<br>+ Chamberlain<br>+ Patriarchs<br>+ <u>Protonotaries</u>**<br>+ <u>*Auditor litterarum contradictarum*</u><br>+ <u>Corrector</u><br>+ Archbishops<br>+ Bishops<br>+ Abbots, etc.<br>The Chancery wears the same festive clothes as the other papal household members, to distinguish them from the participants in liturgical garments. | In ascending order:<br><br>+ Mendicant monks (four orders)<br>+ Clergy at collegiate churches<br>+ Cathedral canons<br>+ The processional cross, carried by members of the papal chapel<br>+ Honorary chaplains<br>+ Secretaries<br>+ *Referendarii*<br>+ Minor penitentiaries<br>+ Judges of the Apostolic Chamber<br>+ Judges of the Rota<br>+ Papal house chaplains<br>+ Abbots<br>+ Generals of the monastic orders<br>+ Bishops<br>+ Archbishops<br>+ Master of the Sacred Palace<br>+ <u>Corrector</u><br>+ <u>Auditor litterarum contradictarum</u><br>+ Cardinal deacons<br>+ Cardinal bishops<br>+ Patriarchs<br>+ Pope<br>+ Chamberlain with the church treasury<br>+ <u>Protonotaries</u>, in white robes<br>+ Chamber clergy<br>+ *Cubicularii* |

*The Auditor and the corrector are not mentioned, probably reflecting older arrangements.

**<u>Underscored</u> charges were part of the Apostolic Chancery; cf. Table 10.4 below.

Table 10.4. Table Arrangements at Receptions, *c.* 1378–1415.

| |
|---|
| + Pope (with assistants), at table on the highest pulpit |
| + Cardinal bishops and patriarchs to the right*, at tables on a pulpit |
| + Cardinal priests and deacons to the left, at tables on a pulpit, probably toward the front |
| + Apostolic Chamberlain, separate table |
| + Prelates of the papal household, separate table |
| + <u>Protonotaries</u>, <u>Auditor</u>, <u>corrector</u>, separate table |
| + Master of the Sacred Palace, archbishops, bishops, generals of the orders, abbots, at a long table lining the wall to the right |
| + The appointed preacher, papal chaplains, then alternating one judge, one chamber cleric, one acolyte, etc., according to seniority, at a long table lining the wall to the left |
| + Minor penitentiaries, (simple) *referendarii*, secretaries, honorary chaplains, at a long table next to the entrance |

\*Left and (in higher regard) right, always seen from the viewpoint of the pope; proximity to him was another measure of rank. The spatial distribution here is hypothetical.

the positioning of participants in the liturgies of Christmas and Easter.[61] The handbook passages in the second column on processions in the papal chapel — an Avignonese innovation — held on Mary's Purification, Ash Wednesday, and other feasts before select gatherings, reserves to the Chancery a rank of comparable eminence.[62] Again, its members wear non-liturgical dresses.

Only the processional handbooks contain seating arrangements for grand receptions (Table 10.4), again from the period of the Schism.[63] Tradition was not as decisive for them as it was in connection with liturgical and ceremonial events. Accordingly, the Apostolic Chamberlain occupies the highest position in the curial hierarchy and even sits at his own table. His actual rank is also highlighted by the order for large public processions in the third column of Table 10.3. It shows him during the Schism as head of the Curia and the Papal States immediately behind the pope. The Chamberlain held without doubt the politically most influential office at the Curia, another reason why he was not a cardinal until the 1430s. Whenever he became one thereafter, he was substituted in ceremonies by the Vice-Chamberlain, an indication of how 'the Chamberlain was

---

61 For the *presbyteria*, see Paravicini Bagliani, *La vita quotidiana*, pp. 104–05.

62 Schimmelpfennig, *Die Zeremonienbücher*, pp. 258, 299. The various versions of handbooks published by Marc Dykmans, especially in *Le cérémonial papal*, i–iv, do not contain anything relevant here.

63 Schimmelpfennig, *Die Zeremonienbücher*, pp. 336–37 (§ 7).

of paramount importance, not the (Vice-)Chancellor'![64] Meanwhile, the above-mentioned Great Vice-Chancellors carried so much weight due to their influence on many administrative positions, their patronage, and their wealth, that they were in second place among the curial prelates in terms of power.

## Remarks on the Contribution of Studies in Diplomatic to the Cultural History of Europe

Labelled among scholars as the 'Censimento Bartoloni', the plan to provide an 'Index of Acts by the Roman Popes from Innocent III to the Elect Martin V' for original papal letters between 1198 and 1417 was launched under the leadership of the *Commission Internationale de Diplomatique* in the 1950s.[65] Until now, the series inaugurated on the occasion has only produced eight volumes.[66] A few can be added by including those not arranged according to the prescribed (and repeatedly modified) format, appearing in other venues, selecting different chronological limits, or featuring copies together with first-hand documentation.[67] Meanwhile, production continues.[68] In all, though, the current yield is meagre. In geographic terms, alone England and most recently Portugal have been covered altogether by Linehan and Sailler. For France, only the holdings of the National Archives have been catalogued by Barbiche; from the Empire, a handful of areas like Austria, Switzerland, southwest, east, and northern Germany, offering little of interest specifically from the curial point of view. In addition, there are editions of sources, which to the best of their editors' abilities also take note of the Chancery annotations on papal letters.[69]

The restriction of the *Censimento Bartoloni* to documentation from the Apostolic Chancery seems hardly justified for the later Middle Ages, even less than the time limit of 1417. The expanding recourse to writing in other curial offices, such as the Apostolic Chamber, the Penitentiary,

---

64 Incidentally, the rise of all-powerful Chamberlains from Eugene IV onward caused many problems, whence Paul II (1464–1471) rather employed his nephew as an unofficial equivalent; cf. Schwarz, *Kurienuniversität und stadtrömische Universität*, pp. 196, 222 n. 182.

65 See most recently, Sailler, 'Papsturkunden in Portugal von 1198 bis 1394'.

66 For the latest, see *Documenti originali pontifici in Puglia e Basilicata*, ed. by Aurora.

67 Cf. p. 276 n. 65 above. A survey of relevant volumes up to 2009 is offered by Schwarz, 'Die Erforschung der mittelalterlichen römischen Kurie', p. 423 n. 28. For an exemplary analysis, see Kobayashi, 'Original und kopial überlieferte Urkunden'; also available online.

68 *Portugalia Pontificia*, ed. by Linehan; Sailler, 'Papsturkunden in Portugal von 1198 bis 1304', also online; Hrubon and Psik, *Kanceláéské poznámky na papežkých listinách*, with English summary; *Butllari de Catalunya*, ed. by Schmidt and Sabanés i Fernández.

69 *Die Papsturkunden des Hauptstaatsarchivs Dresden*, ed. by Graber, p. VIII n. 8, provides an exhaustive list of pertinent editions and catalogues including smaller collections; and, pp. XV–LIV, full titles comprising works on Chancery annotations as well.

among the cardinals, in the General Councils, and by papal legates is ignored in this way. For the time from 1198, I have made the sole attempt to encompass all of the above-mentioned material for Lower Saxony and Bremen, extending it until 1503.[70] In response, Frenz has grouped the same sources in the second edition of his handbook systematically under the 'Non-Papal Documents of the Papacy'.[71] In the catalogue for Bremen and Lower Saxony, however, I went further and compiled in the spirit of the *Europa Pontificia*-Project everything attesting to contacts between the Curia and the periphery.[72] The preparation and orchestration of activities at the Curia and the reaction to papal documents in the provinces are far more interesting from the viewpoint of cultural history than the increasingly formalized documentary output of the later Middle Ages itself.[73]

By calling for the coverage of entire territories, the parameters set for contributors to the *Censimento* are fundamentally different from those for the *Papsturkunden* project of the Pius-Stiftung in Göttingen. The late medieval material is far more differentiated, often reflecting minute administrative steps. The locations preserving it are also more widely scattered.[74] Because modern depositories are frequently uninformed about papal letters, they are neglected. Unlike the oldest pieces of correspondence, they do not enjoy the prestige of 'antiquities'. The state of preservation is frequently precarious as a result. Descriptions are superficial and misleading where they exist, inviting the intervention of true detectives to track things down, just as Kehr has written about research in the *Italia Pontificia*. These investigators will be grateful for digital assistance as well. It is under development for the earliest papal documentation, promising better legibility especially for damaged items.

---

70 *Regesten*, ed. by Schwarz, pp. VIII–IX (justifying the chronological boundaries); for additions and corrections, see Schwarz, in *Niedersächsisches Jahrbuch*, 75 (2003), 333–45.

71 Frenz, *Papsturkunden*, pp. 110–17; cf. also his online version with supplementary illustrations, in *Repertorium officiorum Romanae curiae*, ed. by Frenz, including lists of curial officials, 1378–1550; and *Lexikon der Papstdiplomatik*, ed. by Frenz (online).

72 Schwarz, *Regesten*, pp. IX–X; *Portugalia Pontificia*, ed. by Linehan, has meanwhile followed a similar path.

73 Schwarz, *Regesten*, pp. XXVII–XXVIII. To be sure, Lower Saxony with its poor literacy does not provide a very suitable area of investigation in this regard. Hitzbleck, '*Veri et legitimi vicarii et procuratores*', has shown how the communication with curial proctors alone was far more sustained and extensive elsewhere.

74 Solemn privileges, for example, which in the High Middle Ages held a lion's share of the documentary output, were so rare by the fourteenth century that the Avignonese Chancery kept a summary of the relevant papal rules for the Rota from the time of Clement IV (1264–1268), in case petitioners would ask for something as old-fashioned; *Die päpstlichen Kanzleiordnungen*, ed. by Tangl, pp. 305–06. Consistorial bulls originating under Eugene IV mimicked the old privileges, albeit without the date 'by the hands' (*per manus*). They remained rare; cf. Krüger, 'Konsistorialurkunden'; Frenz, *Papsturkunden*, p. 29 (§ 25: 'Consistorial Bulls').

278 CHAPTER 10

The interest of diplomatic in late medieval papal letters is of a different kind. Their layout and format had been rendered so generic at the time that contemporaries were able to recognize the type of writing at once, akin to the way we instantly discern the various specimens of paper money. The main objects of the field are therefore the ever more numerous and elaborate Chancery notes on original mandates. They afford deeper insight into administrative routines both in theory and practice. Obviously, they also serve to verify the authenticity of a given piece of evidence. The individual annotations and their purpose are clearly presented by Frenz.

The Vice-Chancellors have left many traces, not only on the final Chancery output but also on preparatory documents, the petitions and minutes surviving in considerable quantity from the later Middle Ages.[75] These written notes were mandatory and (should have) appeared in a specific position and format (like monograms), depending on letter category.[76] Alternatively, they were situational, arising from concrete needs like the instruction of servants.[77] Among them were especially the so-called 'acknowledgments of receipt', insofar as they were signed by the Vice-Chancellor.[78] It is hard to gather clues concerning his functions and competencies from the clean copies, which merely attest to the release of certain 'common letters' and consistorial provisions, while omitting that of the much more important 'special' correspondence.[79] Information obtained from the internal mandates remains problematic whenever the official responsible for them cannot be identified conclusively. Excellent electronic scans and a data-base will be necessary to arrive at good results. The monogram of 'vic', or sometimes the initial followed by 'vic' right after the recipient's address, must be compared to its equivalent in other letters, and even more so where the monogram is lacking. The assembly of Chancery notes is the principal focus of the digital *Registrum officiorum*

---

75 See the bibliography by Frenz (online); p. 277 n. 71 above.

76 Cf. *Die Originale von Papsturkunden*, ed. by Schwarz, pp. XXIV–XXV; *Original Papal Letters from England*, ed. by Zutshi, pp. LXXV–LXXVII. For parallel references from the Avignonese papacy during the Schism, see *Les actes pontificaux*, ed. by Barbiche. In expectancies written 'in the form of the poor', the Vice-Chancellor's monogram granting their release appears under the fold to the right; Meyer, *Arme Kleriker auf Pfründensuche*, p. 23 n. 65.

77 As in Baumgarten, *Von der apostolischen Kanzlei*, pp. 76, 78–80, etc., where 'Michael de T.' is very active, for instance. Numerous also in the volumes of the *Censimento*, p. 276 n. 66 above.

78 For a survey of recent scholarship, see Linehan and Zutshi, 'The Earliest Known Roll of Petitions'. Petitions carrying the Vice-Chancellor's release (*concessum*) and his signature in the original are rare, unlike those approved by the pope along with the Vice-Chancellor's acknowledgement of receipt.

79 The category of 'common letters' constantly widened, from simple letters of justice to simple graces, etc., including those 'in the form of the poor'; Zutshi, 'Petitions to the Pope'; Meyer, 'Regieren mit Urkunden', pp. 80–82. When the Vice-Chancellor's mark is missing in the original letter, the lack is noted in the register; Baumgarten, *Von der apostolischen Kanzlei*, p. 102 and elsewhere. Other departures from the norm are noted as well.

*Romanae curiae* compiled by Thomas Frenz, which concentrates on the period after 1450.[80] It rests on material that has been collected over decades, transcribed letter by letter according to the technical standards of the time. The annotations, to be sure, offer a lot on aspects other than the workings of the Chancery. The names and tasks of curial employees, for example, can serve as building blocks toward their biography, reveal the composition of personnel at the Curia, and not least the existence of networks reaching through officials into the periphery.[81] Clearly a treat for cultural historians!

---

80 *Repertorium officiorum Romanae curiae*, ed. by Frenz (online). Based primarily on papal documentation in the German archives and specific registers of original letters from the Apostolic Chancery in the Vatican; cf. p. 277 n. 71 above.

81 Schwarz, 'Die Erforschung der mittelalterlichen römischen Kurie', pp. 431–33.

Table 10.1(b). The Apostolic Vice-Chancellor in the Later Middle Ages. His Competencies.

| Additional Functions | Core Competencies of the Chancery from c. 1320 | | Judicial Functions |
| --- | --- | --- | --- |
| | *Gratial Chancery* | *Judicial Chancery* | |
| Examination and nomination of notaries 'by apostolic authority'. | *Assistance at the signing of petitions (later done by the <u>referendarii</u>\* as well).* | *Signing of 'small petitions'.* | Organisation of general sessions in the consistory; consistorial provisions; and proceedings in 'major cases'. |
| Examination of candidates for benefices present at the Curia, especially 'poor clerics'. | *Supervision and control of the register of petitions.* | *Control of the 'small register of petitions'.* | Supervision of the consistorial Advocates; admission and substitution of the Proctors; verification of proctorial commissions. |
| Acceptance of resignations and control of benefice exchanges (lucrative!). | *Supervision and control of draft letters written by Chancery Abbreviators, later also by the <u>secretaries</u>.* | *Supervision of draft letters produced by the Notaries and their abbreviators.* | Formulation and assignment of commissions for judges to proceed in a case. |
| Competency in cases of forgery; Vice-Chancellor's prison. | *Supervision and control of clean copies furnished by Chancery Scribes.* | *'Minor office' of the Scribes.* | Supervision of the beadles or Couriers. |

| | | | |
|---|---|---|---|
| | *Various controls of letters written in the Vice-Chancery by the Abbreviators, with the final 'Chancery' being presided over by the Vice-Chancellor.* | *Control by the correctory; release partly from there.* | The Audience of the Sacred Palace (Rota) with general supervision; cooperating in the appointment of judges; control of Advocates; admission and disciplinary oversight of Proctors. |
| | *Convocation and conduct of the (Great) Audience; see consistory.* | *Supervision and control of the Audience of Contradictory Letters; cf. consistory.* | Issuance of summonses and sentences; draft versions of 'letters of major justice'. |
| | *Control of Chancery registers; increasingly assumed by the Apostolic Chamberlain.* | | |
| | *Supervision and control of Office of the Seal.* | | |

*'Offices' outside the Chancery are <u>underscored</u>.

# Bibliography

## Manuscripts and Archival Sources

Dresden, Sächsisches Hauptstaatsarchiv
    OU 6942, 7009, 7047
Mantua, Archivio Gonzaga
    3302 c. 11
Munich, Bayerisches Hauptstaatsarchiv
    Passau DU.1946
Paris, Bibliothèque nationale de France
    MS fonds latin 4172
Rome, Biblioteca Casanatense
    MS 4170
Rome, Deutsches Historisches Institut
    N11: Hermann Diener, wissenschaftlicher Nachlaß, Teilbestand
Eugen IV: Sammlung von Quellenbelegen zu Kurialen
Rome, Archivio di Stato
    Fondo Camerale I,
        830–32: Mandati camerali
        1120: Quietanze
        1286–89: Tesoreria segreta
        1468–71: Spese minute di Palazzo
        1711–13: Ufficiali camerali
        Camera urbis 93–95
Tübingen, Universitätsarchiv
    Nachlaß Fink
Vatican, Apostolic Archive (Archivio Apostolico)
    Annatae 8
    Armarium XXIX: Diversa Cameralia 1–33
        XXXI: 82
        XXXIV: Instrumenta Cameralia 4, 11 ff.
    Collectoriae 456–57
    Introitus et Exitus 421, 426, 449, 458, 464
    Registra Avenionensia 173, 198, 268, 288
    Registra Lateranensia 82, 219, 317, 383, 388, 460, 467
    Registra Supplicationum 148, 267, 268, 286, 360, 365, 368, 404, 408,
421, 427, 437, 440, 442, 452

Registra Vaticana 52, 247, 282, 348–51, 381–84, 386–87, 432–36, 453, 465–67, 496, 500, 515–17, 542–45, 697, 875

Resignationes et Consensus 1

Schedario Garampi 110, Officiali 2

Taxae 7

Vatican, Biblioteca Apostolica

MS Barb. lat. 2825

MS Vat. lat. 6343

Vienna, Österreichische Nationalbibliothek

BPV Cod. 3420

Würzburg, Staatsarchiv

Historischer Verein, Urk. 1459 V 23 (N. 1895)

## Primary Sources

*Acta Camerae Apostolicae, I: 1207–1344*, ed. by Jan Ptaśnik (Kraków: Akademia Umietejętności, 1913)

*Acta concilii Constantiensis*, I–IV, ed. by Heinrich Finke, Johannes Hollnsteiner, and Hermann Heimpel (Münster/W.: Regensberg, 1896–1928)

*Acta Cusana. Quellen zur Lebensgeschichte des Nikolaus von Kues*

———, I/1–4 (to March 1452), ed. by Erich Meuthen and Hermann Hallauer (Hamburg: Meiner, 1976–2000)

———, II/1–7 (to 30 May 1458), ed. by Johannes Helmrath and Thomas Wölki (Hamburg: Meiner, 2012–2020)

———, III/1 (to 31 December 1459), ed. by Johannes Helmrath and Thomas Wölki (Hamburg: Meiner, 2022)

*Acta Martini V. pontificis Romani. 1417–1431*, ed. by Jaroslav Eršil, 3 vols (Prague: Academia, 1996–2001)

*Acta nationis Germanicae universitatis Bononiensis ex archetypis tabularii Malvezziani*, ed. by Ernst Friedländer and Carlo Malagola (Berlin: Reimer, 1887)

*Aeneas Silvius, 'Germania', und Jakob Wimpfeling, 'Responsa et replicae ad Eneam Silvium'*, ed. by Adolf Schmidt (Cologne: Böhlau, 1962)

Alberti, Leon Battista. *I libri della famiglia*, ed. by Ruggiero Romano and Alberto Tenenti (Turin: Einaudi, 1969); newly ed. by Francesco Furlan (Turin: Einaudi, 1999)

*Analecta Vaticana, 1202–1366*, ed. by Jan Ptaśnik (Kraków: Akademia Umietejętności, 1914)

*Antiquissimae constitutiones synodales provinciae Gneznensis, maxima ex parte nunc primum e codicibus manu scriptis typis mandatae*, ed. by Romuald Hube (Saint Petersburg: Cancellaria imperatoris, 1856)

*Baldi Perusini tomus primus in Digestum vetus* (Lyon: Nicolaus Baccaneus, 1551)

Baluzius, Stephanus, *Vitae paparum Avenionensium, hoc est Historia pontificum Romanorum qui in Gallia sederunt ab anno MCCCV usque ad annum MCCCXCIV*, ed. by Guillaume Mollat, 4 vols (Paris: Letouzey, 1914–1928)

*Benoit XII (1334–1342). Lettres communes analysées d'après les registres dits d'Avignon et du Vatican*, ed. by Jean-Marie Vidal, 3 vols (Paris: Fontemoing, 1903–1911)

*Briefwechsel des Nikolaus von Cues*, I, ed. by Josef Koch (Heidelberg: Winter, 1944)

*Bullarium Poloniae. Litteras apostolicas aliaque monumenta Poloniae Vaticana continens*, I–II: *1000–1378*, ed. by Irena Sułkowska-Kuraś and Stanisław Kuraś (Lublin: Polski Akademia Nauk, 1982–1985)

*Butllari de Catalunya: documents pontificis originals conservats als arxius de Catalunya (1198–1417)*, ed. by Tilmann Schmidt and Roser Sabanés i Fernández, 3 vols (Barcelona: Pagès, 2016)

*Calendar of Entries in the Papal Registers Relating to Great Britain and Ireland: Papal Letters*, A.D. *1198–1503*, ed. by William Bliss, Jessie Tremlow, Michael Haren, and Anne Fuller, 17 vols (London: HM Stationary Office, 1893–1998)

*Chronica Johannis de Reading et Anonymi Cantuarensis, 1346–1367*, ed. by James Tait (Manchester: Manchester University Press, 1914)

'Chronica principum Poloniae', in *Monumenta Poloniae Historica*, III, ed. by Zygmunt Węclewski (Lwów: Gubrynowicz i Schmidt, 1878), pp. 423–578

*Codex diplomaticus Saxoniae regiae*, II/1–3: *Urkundenbuch des Hochstifts Meißen*, ed. by Ernst Gersdorf (Leipzig: Giesicke, 1864–1867)

*Conciliorum Oecumenicorum Decreta*, ed. by Giuseppe Alberigo, Giuseppe Dossetti, Perikle Joannou, Claudio Leonardi, and Paolo Prodi (Bologna: Istituto per le scienze religiose, 1973³)

*Conciliorum oecumenicorum generaliumque decreta*, II/1–2: *869–1517*, ed. by Giuseppe Alberigo, Antonio Garcia y Garcia, and Frederick Lauritzen, 2 vols (Turnhout: Brepols, 2013)

*Corpus epistolare e documentario di Leon Battista Alberti*, ed. by Paola Benigni, Roberto Cardini, and Mariangela Regoliosi (Florence: Polistampa, 2007)

*Corpus iuris canonici*, I–II, ed. by Emil Friedberg (Leipzig: Richter, 1879–1881)

*Cyni Pistoriensis iurisconsulti praestantissimi in Codicem et aliquot titulos primi Pandectorum tomi id est Digesti veteris doctissima commentaria* (Frankfurt/M.: Feyerabendt, 1578; reprint, Turin: Bottega d'Erasmo, 1964)

*Das Erzbistum Trier*, II: *Die Stifte St. Severus in Boppard, St. Goar in St. Goar, Liebfrauen in Oberwesel, St. Martin in Oberwesel*, ed. by Ferdinand Pauly (Berlin: De Gruyter, 1980)

*Das Formelbuch des Domherrn Arnold von Protzan*, ed. by Wilhelm Wattenbach (Breslau: Max, 1862)

*Decrees of the Ecumenical Councils*, I: *Nicaea I to Lateran V*, trans. by Norman Tanner (London: Sheed & Ward, 1990)

*Der Briefwechsel des Eneas Silvius Piccolomini*, I, ed. by Rudolf Wolkan (Vienna: Hölder, 1909)

*Deutsche Reichstagsakten, Ältere Reihe*, I–III: *Deutsche Reichstagsakten unter König Wenzel (1376–1400)*, ed. by Julius Weizsäcker, 3 vols (Munich: Cotta, 1868–1877)

*Deutsche Reichstagsakten. Ältere Reihe*, XIII–XIV: *Deutsche Reichstagsakten unter König Albrecht II. (1438–1439)*, ed. by Gustav Beckmann and Helmut Weigel, 2 vols (Stuttgart: Perthes, 1925–1935; Göttingen: Vandenhoeck & Ruprecht, 1957²)

*Die Ausgaben der Apostolischen Kammer unter den Päpsten Urban V. und Gregor XI., 1362–1378*, ed. by Karl Schäfer (Paderborn: Schöningh, 1937)

*Die Ausgaben der Apostolischen Kammer unter Benedikt XII, Clemens VI. und Innozenz VI., 1335–1362*, ed. by Karl Schäfer (Paderborn: Schöningh, 1914)

*Die Ausgaben der apostolischen Kammer unter Johann XXII. Nebst den Jahresbilanzen von 1316–1375*, ed. by Karl Schäfer (Paderborn: Schöningh, 1911)

*Die Berichte der Generalprokuratoren des Deutschen Ordens an der Kurie*, II–IV, ed. by Kurt Forstreuther and Hans Koeppen, 3 vols (Cologne: Böhlau, 1960–1973)

*Die Einnahmen der apostolischen Kammer unter Benedikt XII.*, ed. by Emil Göller (Paderborn: Schöningh, 1920)

*Die Einnahmen der apostolischen Kammer unter Innozenz VI.*, ed. by Hermann Hoberg, 2 vols (Paderborn: Schöningh, 1955–1972)

*Die Einnahmen der apostolischen Kammer unter Johann XXII.*, ed. by Emil Göller (Paderborn: Schöningh, 1910)

*Die Originale der Papsturkunden in Niedersachsen 1199–1417*, ed. by Brigide Schwarz (Città del Vaticano: Biblioteca Apostolica Vaticana, 1988)

*Die päpstlichen Kanzleiordnungen von 1200–1500*, ed. by Michael Tangl (Innsbruck: Wagner, 1894; reprint, Aalen: Scientia, 1959)

*Die Papsturkunden des Hauptstaatsarchivs Dresden*, I: *Originale Überlieferung*, 1: *1104–1303*, ed. by Tom Graber (Hanover: Hahn, 2009)

*Die Rechnungsbücher der hamburgischen Gesandten in Avignon (1338–1355)*, ed. by Theodor Schrader (Hamburg: Voß, 1907)

*Die Rota-Manualien des Basler Konzils. Verzeichnis der in den Handschriften der Basler Universitätsbibliothek behandelten Rechtsfälle*, ed. by Hans-Jörg Gilomen (Tübingen: Niemeyer, 1998)

*Documenti originali pontifici in Puglia e Basilicata 1199–1415*, ed. by Isabella Aurora (Città del Vaticano: Biblioteca Apostolica Vaticana, 2016)

*Henrici de Segusio cardinalis Ostiensis in quinque libros decretalium commentaria* (Venice: Giunti, 1581; reprint, Turin: Bottega d'Erasmo, 1965)

*Hierarchia catholica Medii Aevi sive summorum Pontificum, Sanctae Romanae cardinalium, ecclesiarum antistites series e documentis tabularii praesertim Vaticani*, I–II: *1198–1503*, ed. by Konrad Eubel, 2 vols (Münster/W.: Regensberg, 1913–1914)

*Il testamento di Leon Battista Alberti. I tempi, i luoghi, i protagonisti. Il manoscritto Statuti Mss. 87 della Biblioteca del Senato della Repubblica 'Giovanni Spadolini'*, ed. by Enzo Bentivoglio, Giuliana Crevatin, and Marcello Ciccuto (Rome: Gangemi, 2005)

*Joannis Dlugossi Annales seu Chronicae incliti Regni Polonorum*, IX, ed. by Danuta Turkowska (Warsaw: Państwowe Wydawnictwo Naukowe, 1978)

'Katalogi biskupów krakowskich', in *Monumenta Poloniae Historica. Series nova*, X/2, ed. by Józef Szymański (Warsaw: Państwowe Wydawnictwo Naukowe, 1974)

*Kodeks dyplomatyczny katedry krakowskiej ś. Wacława*, I, ed. by Franciszek Piekosiński (Kraków: Paszkowski, 1874)

*Kodeks dyplomatyczny Małopolski*, III: *1333–1386*, ed. by Franciszek Piekosiński (Kraków: Anczyc, 1887)

*Kodeks dyplomatyczny Wiekopolski*, I–II: *984–1349*, ed. by Franciszek Piekosiński, 2 vols (Poznań: Biblioteka Kórnicka, 1877–1878)

'L'autobiografia di Leon Battista Alberti: Studio e edizione', ed. by Riccardo Fubini and Anna Menci Gallorini, in *Rinascimento*, 12 (1972), 21–78

*L'oeuvre de Patrizi Piccolomini ou le cérémonial papal de la première Renaissance*, ed. by Marc Dykmans, 2 vols (Città del Vaticano: Biblioteca Apostolica Vaticana, 1980–1982)

*Le 'Liber officialium' de Martin V*, ed. by François-Charles Uginet (Rome: Ministero per i beni culturali e ambientali, 1975)

*Les recettes et les dépenses de la Chambre apostolique pour la quatrième année du pontificat de Clément V (1308–1309)*, ed. by Bernard Guillemain (Rome: École française de Rome, 1978)

*Les registres de Boniface VIII. Recueil des bulles de ce pape publiées ou analysées d'après les manuscrits originaux des Archives du Vatican*, IV, ed. by Antoine Thomas, Maurice Faucon, Georges Digard, and Robert Fawtier (Paris: Boccard, 1939)

*Lettres communes de Jean XXII*, ed. by Guillaume Mollat, 17 vols (Paris: Boccard, 1904–1959)

*Lexikon der Papstdiplomatik*, ed. by Thomas Frenz, online (University of Passau, 2019) https://www.phil.uni-passau.de/histhw/forschung/lexikon-der-papstdiplomatik/

*Libri rationum camerae Bonifatii papae VIII*, ed. by Tilmann Schmidt (Città del Vaticano: Scuola Vaticana di Paleografia, Diplomatica, e Archivistica, 1984)

*Lites ac res gestae inter Polonos Ordinemque Cruciferorum*, I, ed. by Helenę Chłopocką (Wrocław: Ossolineum, 1970)

*Liv-, Est- und Kurländisches Urkundenbuch nebst Regesten*, I, ed. by Friedrich von Bunge, Hermann Hildebrand, Philipp Schwartz, and August von Bulmerincq, 12 vols (Reval: Kluge and Ströhm, 1853–1910; reprint, Aalen: Scientia, 1967–1981)

Loyseau, Charles, *Cinq livres du droict des offices, avec le livre des seigneuries et celuy des ordres* (Paris: l'Angelier, 1613²)

BIBLIOGRAPHY

Michel de Montaigne, *Journal de Voyage en Italie par la Suisse et l'Allemagne en 1580 et 1581*, ed. by Charles Dédéyan (Paris: Les belles lettres, 1946)

*Najstarsze statuty synodalne krakowskie biskupa Nankera*, ed. by Jan Fijałek (Kraków: Nakładem Akadęmii uniejętności, 1915)

*Opera inedita et pauca separatim impressa di Leon Battista Alberti*, ed. by Girolamo Mancini (Florence: Sansoni, 1890)

*Opuscoli inediti di L. B. Alberti: 'Musca', 'Vita S. Potiti'*, ed. by Cecil Grayson (Florence: Olschki, 1954)

*Original Papal Letters in England, 1305–1415*, ed. by Patrick Zutshi (Città del Vaticano: Biblioteca Apostolica Vaticana, 1990)

*Ordonnances des rois de France de la troisième race, recueillis par ordre chronologique*, 21 vols (Paris: Imprimerie royale, 1723–1790, 1814; Paris: Imprimerie imperiale, 1811; Paris: Bertrand, 1820–1849)

*Portugalia Pontificia. Materials for the History of Portugal and the Papacy, 1198–1417*, ed. by Peter Linehan, 2 vols (Lisbon: Fundação Calouste Gulbenkian, 2013)

*Quellen zur Verfassungsgeschichte des Römisch-Deutschen Reiches im Spätmittelalter (1250–1500)*, ed. and trans. by Lorenz Weinrich (Darmstadt: Wissenschaftliche Buchgesellschaft, 1983)

*Raccolta di concordati su materie ecclesiastiche tra la Santa Sede e le autorità civili*, I: *1098–1914*, ed. by Angelo Mercati (Rome: Tipografia Poliglotta Vaticana, 1954²)

*Recueil général des anciennes lois françaises depuis l'an 420 jusqu'à la revolution de 1789*, ed. by Athanase Jourdan, François Isambert, Nicolas Decrusy, and Alphonse Taillandier (29 vols; Paris: Belin-Le-Prieur and Verdière, 1821–1833; reprint, Ridgewood/NJ: Gregg, 1964–1966)

*Regesta Imperii*, XI: *Die Urkunden Kaiser Sigismunds 1410–1437*, ed. by Wilhelm Altmann, 2 vols (Innsbruck: Wagner, 1896–1900)

*Regesten der in Niedersachsen und Bremen überlieferten Papsturkunden 1198–1503*, ed. by Brigide Schwarz (Hanover: Hahn, 1993)

*Regesten zur schlesischen Geschichte*, V: *1316–1326*, ed. by Colmar Grünhagen and Konrad Wutke (Breslau: Max, 1898)

*Regestum Clementis papae V*, 9 vols and 1 appendix (Rome: Typographia Vaticana, 1885–1892)

*Regulae, ordinationes et constitutiones cancellariae apostolicae*, ed. by Andreas Meyer, online (University of Marburg) https://www.uni-marburg.de/de/fb06/mag/institut/prof-dr-andreas-meyer/kanzleiregeln

*Regulae cancellariae apostolicae. Die päpstlichen Kanzleiregelungen von Johannes XXII. bis Nikolaus V.*, ed. by Emil von Ottenthal (Innsbruck: Wagner, 1888; reprint, Aalen: Scientia, 1968)

*Repertorium Fontium Historiae Medii Aevi*, II: *Fontes A-B* (Rome: Istituto storico italiano per il Medio Evo, 1967)

*Repertorium Germanicum. Verzeichnis der in den Registern und Kameralakten vorkommenden Personen, Kirchen und Orte des Deutschen Reiches, seiner Diözesen und Territorien*

——, I: *Clemens VII. von Avignon (1378–1394)*, ed. by Emil Göller (Berlin: Weidmann, 1916)

——, II/1–2 (Calendar, Index of Places): *Urban VI., Bonifaz IX., Innocenz VII. und Gregor XII. (1378–1415)*, ed. by Gerd Tellenbach (Berlin: Weidmann, 1933–1938); vol. II/3 (Index of Persons), ed. by Hermann Diener (Berlin: Weidmann, 1961)

——, III: *Alexander V., Johann XXIII., Konstanzer Konzil (1409–1417)*, ed. by Ulrich Kühne (Berlin: Weidmann, 1935)

——, IV/1–3 (Calendar): *Martin V. (1417–1431)*, ed. by Karl August Fink (Berlin: Weidmann, 1943–1958); vol. IV/4 (Index of Persons), ed. by Sabine Weiss (Tübingen: Niemeyer, 1979)

——, V/1 (Calendar): *Eugen IV. (1431–1447)*, ed. by Hermann Diener, Brigide Schwarz, and Christoph Schöner, 3 vols (Tübingen: Niemeyer, 2004); vol. V/2 (Indices), ed. by Christoph Schöner, 3 vols (Tübingen: Niemeyer, 2004)

——, VI/1 (Calendar): *Nikolaus V. (1447–1455)*, ed. by Josef Abert und Walter Deeters (Tübingen: Niemeyer, 1985); VI/2 (Indices), ed. by Michael Reimann (Tübingen: Niemeyer, 1989)

——, VII/1–2 (Calendar, Indices): *Calixt III. (1455–1458)*, ed. by Ernst Pitz, 2 vols (Tübingen: Niemeyer, 1989)

——, VIII/1 (Calendar): *Pius II. (1458–1464)*, ed. by Dieter Brosius und Ulrich Scheschkewitz (Tübingen: Niemeyer, 1993); vol. VIII/2 (Indices), ed. by Karl Borchardt (Tübingen: Niemeyer, 1993)

——, IX/1–2 (Calendar, Indices): *Paul II. (1464–1471)*, ed. by Hubert Höing, Heiko Leerhoff, and Michael Reimann (Tübingen: Niemeyer, 2000)

*Repertorium officiorum Romanae curiae*, ed. by Thomas Frenz (online; University of Passau) https://www.phil.uni-passau.de/histhw/forschung/rorc

*Repertorium Poenitentiariae Germanicum. Verzeichnis der in den Supplikenregistern der Pönitentiarie vorkommenden Personen, Kirchen und Orte des Deutschen Reiches*

——, I: *Eugen IV. 1431–1447*, ed. by Ludwig Schmugge, Paolo Ostinelli, Hans Braun, and Hildegard Schneider-Schmugge (Tübingen: Niemeyer, 1998)

——, II: *Nikolaus V. 1447–1455*, ed. by Ludwig Schmugge, Krystina Bukowska, Alexandra Mosciatti, and Hildegard Schneider-Schmugge (Tübingen: Niemeyer, 1999)

——, III: *Calixt III. 1455–1458*, ed. by Ludwig Schmugge, Wolfgang Müller, and Hildegard Schneider-Schmugge (Tübingen: Niemeyer, 2001)

——, IV: *Pius II. 1458–1464*, ed. by Ludwig Schmugge, Patrick Hersberger, Béatrice Wiggenhauser, and Hildegard Schneider-Schmugge (Tübingen: Niemeyer, 1996)

——, V: *Paul II. 1464–1471*, ed. by Ludwig Schmugge, Peter Clarke, Alessandra Mosciatti, and Wolfgang Müller (Tübingen: Niemeyer, 2002)

*Schedario Baumgarten. Descrizione diplomatica di bolle e brevi originali da Innocenzo III a Pio IX*, vol. III: *Bolle e brevi da Clemente V a Martino V (anni 1305–1431)*, ed. by Sergio Pagano (Città del Vaticano: Archivio Segreto Vaticano, 1983)

*Sanctorum conciliorum nova et amplissima collectio*, vol. XXIX, ed. by Giovanni-Domenico Mansi (Venice: Zatta, 1788)

*Summa domini Henrici cardinalis Hostiensis* (Lyon: Portonari, 1537; reprint, Aalen: Scientia, 1962)

*Tables des registres de Clement V publiés par les Bénédictines*, ed. by Cyrille Vogel and Yvonne Lanhers (Paris: Broccard, 1957)

Thomas de Aquino, *De regimine principum et de regimine Judaeorum ad ducissam Brabantiae politica opuscula duo*, ed. by Joseph Mathis (Turin: Marietti, 1948[2])

*Übersicht über die Bestände des Niedersächsischen Staatsarchivs in Hannover*, I, ed. by Carl Haase and Walter Deeters (Göttingen: Vandenhoeck & Ruprecht, 1965)

*Urkundenbuch des Bistums Lübeck*, II–IV: *1220–1530*, ed. by Wilhelm Leverkus, Wolfgang Prange, Kurt Hector, and Hans Hennings, 3 vols (Neumünster: Wacholtz, 1994–1996)

*Urkundenbuch des Hochstifts Hildesheim und seiner Bischöfe*, VI: *1370–1398*, ed. by Hermann Hoogeweg (Hanover: Hahn, 1911)

'*Ut per litteras apostolicas* .... Les lettres des papes des XIIIe et XIVe siècles', CD-ROM (Turnhout: Brepols, 2002)

Vespasiano da Bisticci, *Le vite*, ed. by Aulo Greco, 2 vols (Florence: Olschki, 1970–1976)

*Vetera monumenta Poloniae et Lithuaniae gentiumque finitimarum historiam illustrantia*, I: *1217–1409*, ed. by Augustin Theiner (Città del Vaticano: Typographia Vaticana, 1860)

*Vindemiae litterariae, hoc est veterum monumentorum ad Germaniam sacram precipue spectantium*, II, ed. by Johann Schannat (Fulda: Weidmann, 1724)

*Zbiór dokumentów katedry i diecezji krakowskiej*, I: *(1063–1415)*, ed. by Stanisław Kuraś (Lublin: Uniwersytet, 1965)


## Secondary Works

*A Companion to the Medieval Papacy: Growth of an Ideology and Institution*, ed. by Atria Larson and Keith Sisson (Leiden: Brill, 2016)

*Ämterhandel im Spätmittelalter und im 16. Jahrhundert*, ed. by Ilja Mieck (Berlin: Colloqium, 1984)

*Ämterkäuflichkeit. Aspekte sozialer Mobilität im europäischen Vergleich (17. und 18. Jahrhundert)*, ed. by Klaus Malettke (Berlin: Colloqium, 1980)

Angermeier, Heinz, *Die Reichsreform 1410–1555. Die Staatsproblematik in Deutschland zwischen Mittelalter und Gegenwart* (Munich: Beck, 1984)

Ansani, Michele, 'La provvista dei benefici. Strumenti e limiti dell'intervento ducale (1450–1466)', in *Gli Sforza, la chiesa lombarda, la corte di Roma. Strutture e pratiche beneficiarie nel ducato di Milano (1450–1535)*, ed. by Giorgio Chittolini (Naples: Liguori, 1989), pp. 1–113

Ascheri, Mario, 'Giuristi, umanisti e istituzioni del Tre-Quattrocento: qualche problema', *Annali dell'Istituto storico italo-germanico in Trento*, 3 (1977), 43–73

Autrand, Françoise, 'Offices et officiers royaux en France sous Charles VI', *Revue historique*, 242 (1969), 285–338

Baethgen, Friedrich, 'Quellen und Untersuchungen zur Geschichte der päpstlichen Hof- und Finanzverwaltung unter Bonifaz VIII.', *Quellen und Forschungen aus italienischen Archiven und Bibliotheken*, 20 (1928/1929), 114–237

Baier, Hermann, *Päpstliche Provisionen für niedere Pfründen bis zum Jahre 1304* (Münster/W.: Aschendorff, 1911)

Baix, François, 'Notes sur les clercs de la Chambre apostolique (XIII$^e$–XIV$^e$ siècles)', *Bulletin de l'Institut belge de Rome*, 27 (1952), 17–52

Barbiche, Bernard, 'Les "scriptores" de la Chancellerie apostolique sous le pontificat de Boniface VIII (1295–1303)', *Bibliothèque de l'École des chartes*, 128 (1970), 115–87

Barraclough, Geoffrey, *Papal Provisions: Aspects of Church History, Constitutional, Legal, and Administrative in the Later Middle Ages* (Oxford: Clarendon, 1935)

Bauer, Clemens, 'Der Wucherbegriff der *Reformatio Sigismundi*', in *Aus Stadt- und Wirtschaftsgeschichte Südwestdeutschlands. Festschrift für Erich Maschke zum 75. Geburtstag*, ed. by Friedrich Facius and Jürgen Sydow (Stuttgart: Kohlhammer, 1975), pp. 110–17

——, 'Die Epochen der Papstfinanz', *Historische Zeitschrift*, 138 (1928), 457–503; reprint, in Bauer, *Gesammelte Aufsätze*, pp. 112–47

——, *Gesammelte Aufsätze zur Wirtschafts- und Sozialgeschichte* (Freiburg/Br.: Herder, 1965)

——, 'Mittelalterliche Staatsfinanz und internationale Staatsfinanz', in Bauer, *Gesammelte Aufsätze*, pp. 88–111

Bauer, Stefan, 'Platina, Bartolomeo', in *Biographisch-Bibliographisches Kirchenlexikon*, vol. 22, ed. by Traugott Bautz (Nordhausen: Bautz, 2003), cols 1098–1103

Baumgartner, Hans, 'Institutionen und Krise', in *Institutionen und Geschichte. Theoretische Aspekte und mittelalterliche Befunde*, ed. by Gerd Melville (Cologne: Böhlau, 1992), pp. 97–114

Becker, Richard, 'Ein Beitrag zur Geschichte des Streites über die exemte Stellung des Bistums Meißen', *Neues Archiv für sächsische Geschichte*, 18 (1897), 273–84

Belloni, Annalisa, *Professori giuristi a Padova nel secolo XV. Profili bio-bibliografici e cattedre* (Frankfurt/M.: Klostermann, 1986)

*Bericht über die 38. Versammlung deutscher Historiker in Bochum, 26. bis 29. September 1990*, ed. by Wolfgang Schmale (Stuttgart: Klett, 1991)

Binz, Louis, 'Le népotisme de Clément VII et le diocèse de Genève', in *Genèse et débuts du Grand Schisme d'Occident (1362–1394)*, ed. by Jean Favier (Paris: Centre Nationale des Recherches Scientifiques, 1980), pp. 107–24

Böninger, Lorenz, 'Antonino e Leon Battista Alberti', *Memorie domenicane*, 43 (2012), 55–77

——, 'Da "commentatore" ad arbitro della sua famiglia. Nuovi episodi albertiani', in *La vita e il mondo di Leon Battista Alberti*, 2 vols (Florence: Olschki, 2008), pp. 397–424

Böse, Kuno, 'Die Ämterkäuflichkeit in Frankreich vom 14. bis 16. Jahrhundert', in *Ämterhandel im Spätmittelalter und im 16. Jahrhundert*, ed. by Ilja Mieck (Berlin: Colloquium, 1984), pp. 83–111

Boockmann, Hartmut, *Laurentius Blumenau. Fürstlicher Rat, Jurist und Humanist, ca. 1415–1484* (Göttingen: Vandenhoeck & Ruprecht, 1965)

Borchardt, Knut, 'Die römische Kurie und die Pfründenbesetzung in den Diözesen Würzburg, Bamberg und Eichstätt im späteren Mittelalter', *Jahrbuch für fränkische Landesforschung*, 57 (1997), 71–96

Boschetto, Luca, 'I libri della famiglia e la crisi delle compagnie degli Alberti negli anni trenta del Quattrocento', in *Leon Battista Alberti. Actes du congrès international de Paris (Sorbonne, Institut de France, Institut culturel italien, Collège de France), 10–15 avril 1995*, ed. by Francesco Furlan, Pierre Laurens, and Sylvain Matton (Paris: Urin, 2000), pp. 87–131

——, *Società e cultura a Firenze al tempo del Concilio. Eugenio IV tra curiali, mercanti e umanisti (1434–1443)* (Rome: Edizioni di storia e letteratura, 2012)

Boyle, Leonard, *A Survey of the Vatican Archives and of Its Medieval Holdings* (Toronto: Pontifical Institute of Mediaeval Studies, 1972)

Brentano, Robert, *York Metropolitan Jurisdiction and Papal Judges Delegate, 1279–1296* (Berkeley, CA: University of California Press, 1959)

Bresc, Henri, 'La genèse du Schisme: les partis cardinalices et leurs ambitions dynastiques', in *Genèse et débuts du Grand Schisme d'Occident (1362–1394)*, ed. by Jean Favier (Paris: Centre Nationale des Recherches Scientifiques, 1980), pp. 45–57

Bresslau, Harry, *Handbuch der Urkundenlehre für Deutschland und Italien*, 1 (Leipzig: Veit, 1912²)

——, *Manuale di diplomatica per la Germania e per l'Italia*, trans. by Anna Maria Voci-Roth (Rome: Ministero per i beni culturali e ambientali, 1998)

Brosius, Dieter, 'Das Repertorium Germanicum', in *Das Deutsche Historische Institut in Rom 1888–1988*, ed. by Elze and Esch, pp. 123–65

——, 'Die Pfründen des Enea Silvio Piccolomini', *Quellen und Forschungen aus italienischen Archiven und Bibliotheken*, 54 (1974), 271–327

——, 'Päpstlicher Einfluß auf die Besetzung von Bistümern um die Mitte des 15. Jahrhunderts', *Quellen und Forschungen aus italienischen Archiven und Bibliotheken*, 55/56 (1976), 200–28

Caillet, Louis, *La papauté d'Avignon et l'église de France. La politique bénéficiale du Pape Jean XXII en France* (Paris: Presses universitaires de France, 1975)

Ceccon, Silvio, 'Molino, Blasio da', in *Dizionario biografico degli italiani*, vol. 75 (Rome: Istituto dell'enciclopedia italiana, 2011), pp. 417–20

Cerasoli, Franscesco, 'Ricerche storiche intorno agli alberghi di Roma dal secolo XIV al XV', *Studi e documenti di storia e diritto*, 14 (1893), 383–409

Chabod, Federico, 'Stipendi nominali e busta paga effettiva dei funzionari dell'amministrazione milanese alla fine del Cinquecento', in *Miscellanea in onore di Roberto Cessi*, 2 vols (Rome: Edizioni di storia e letteratura, 1958), II, pp. 187–363

Clergeac, Adrien, *La Curie et les bénéficiers consistoriaux. Étude sur les communs et menus services, 1300–1600* (Paris: Picard, 1911)

Ciampini, Giovanni, *De abbreviatorum de parco maiori, sive assistentium Sanctae Romanae Ecclesiae vicecancellario in literarum Apostolicarum expeditionibus antiquo statu illorumve in collegium erectione, munere, dignitate, prerogativis ac privilegiis dissertatio historica* (Rome: Typographia Reverendae Camerae Apostolicae, 1691)

Como, Franz, *Das kaiserliche Kollegiatstift St. Martin in Worms. Ein Beitrag zu seiner 900jährigen Geschichte* (Koblenz: Selbstverlag, 1962)

Contamine, Philippe, *La guerre au Moyen Âge* (Paris: Presses universitaires de France, 1980)

*Das Repertorium Germanicum. EDV-gestützte Auswertung vatikanischer Quellen: Neue Forschungsperspektiven*, ed. by Arnold Esch (Tübingen: Niemeyer, 1992)

d'Avray, David, 'Germany and the Papacy in the Late Middle Ages', *The Journal of Ecclesiastical History*, 71 (2020), 362–67

de Luca, Giovanni, *Tractatus de officiis vacabilibus Romanae Curiae* (Rome: Typographia Reverendae Camerae Apostolicae, 1682)

de Roover, Raymond, *The Rise and Decline of the Medici Bank, 1397–1494* (Cambridge, MA: Harvard University Press, 1963)

del Re, Niccolò, *La curia Romana. Lineamenti storico-giuridici* (Rome: Edizioni di storia e letteratura, 1970³)

Demurger, Alain, 'Guerre civile et changement du personnel administratif dans le royaume de France de 1400 à 1418: l'exemple des baillies et sénéchaux', *Francia*, 6 (1978), 151–298

Dendorfer, Jürgen, and Claudia Märtl, 'Papst und Kardinalskolleg im Bannkreis der Konzilien – von der Wahl Martins V. bis zum Tod Pauls II. (1417–1471)', in *Geschichte des Kardinalats im Mittelalter*, ed. by Jürgen Dendorfer and Ralf Lützelschwab (Stuttgart: Hiersemann, 2011), pp. 335–98

Denzel, Markus, 'Kleriker und Kaufleute. Polen und der Peterspfennig im kurialen Zahlungsverkehr des 14. Jahrhunderts', *Vierteljahrschrift für Sozial- und Wirtschaftsgeschichte*, 82 (1995), 305–31

Dephoff, Joseph, *Zum Urkunden- und Kanzleiwesen des Konzils von Basel* (Hildesheim: Borgmeyer, 1930)

di Renzo Villata, Giliola, 'Giacomo dal Pozzo', in *Dizionario biografico degli italiani*, vol. 32 (Rome: Istituto della Enciclopedia italiana, 1986), pp. 219–24

Diederich, Anton, *Das Stift St. Florin zu Koblenz* (Göttingen: Vandenhoeck & Ruprecht, 1967)

Diener, Hermann, 'Materialien aus dem vatikanischen Archiv. Die Registerserien des Spätmittelalters als Quelle', in *Bericht über den 16. Österreichischen Historikertag in Krems/Donau 1984* (Vienna: Verband Österreichischer Geschichtsvereine, 1985), pp. 387–97

——, 'Zur Persönlichkeit des Johannes von Segovia. Ein Beitrag zur Methode der Auswertung päpstlicher Register des späten Mittelalters', *Quellen und Forschungen aus italienischen Archiven und Bibliotheken*, 44 (1964), 289–365

——, and Brigide Schwarz, 'Das Itinerar Eugens IV.', *Quellen und Forschungen aus italienischen Archiven und Bibliotheken*, 82 (2002), 193–230

——, and Christiane Schuchard, 'Über den Zusammenhang von Thesaurarie und Kollektoren zur Zeit Clemens VI. (1342–1352)', *Quellen und Forschungen aus italienischen Archiven und Bibliotheken*, 79 (1990), 234–347

Döllinger, Johann, *Beiträge zur politischen und Cultur-Geschichte der letzten sechs Jahrhunderte*, 3 vols (Regensburg: Manz, 1862–1882)

Dolezalek, Gero, 'Audientia sacri palatii', in *Lexikon des Mittelalters*, vol. 1 (Munich: Artemis, 1980), cols 1193–94

Domínguez Ortíz, Antonio, 'La venta de cargos y oficios públicos en Castilla y sus consecuencias económicas y sociales', *Anuario de historia económica y social*, 3 (1970), 105–37

Dykmans, Marc, 'D'Avignon à Rome. Martin V et le cortège apostolique', *Bulletin de l'Institut historique belge de Rome*, 39 (1968), 203–310

——, 'La bulle du Grégoire XI à la vieille du Grand Schisme', *Mélanges de l'École française de Rome – temps moderns*, 89 (1977), 485–95

——, 'La maison cardinalice', in *Le cérémonial papal de la fin du Moyen Age à la Renaissance*, ed. by Marc Dykmans, 4 vols (Rome: Institut historique belge de Rome, 1977–1985), III, pp. 446–61

Esch, Arnold, 'Bankiers der Kirche im Großen Schisma', *Quellen und Forschungen aus italienischen Archiven und Bibliotheken*, 46 (1966), 277–398

——, 'Das Papsttum unter der Herrschaft der Neapolitaner. Die führende Gruppe Neapolitaner Familien an der Kurie während des Schismas 1378–1415', in *Festschrift für Hermann Heimpel zum 70. Geburtstag am 19. September 1971*, 2 vols (Göttingen: Vandenhoeck & Ruprecht, 1972), II, pp. 713–800

——, 'Le clan des familles napolitaines au sein du Sacré Collège d'Urbain VI et de ses successeurs, et les Brancacci de Rome et d'Avignon', in *Genèse et débuts du Grand Schisme d'Occident (1362–1394)*, ed. by Jean Favier (Paris: Centre Nationale des Recherches Scientifiques, 1980), pp. 493–506

——, 'Preise, Kapazität und Lage römischer Hotels im Mittelalter. Mit Kaiser Friedrich in Rom', in *Regionen und Europa in Mittelalter und Neuzeit. Festschrift für Peter Moraw*, ed. by Barbara Krauß (Berlin: Duncker & Humblot, 2000), pp. 443–57; revised in Arnold Esch, *Wege nach Rom. Annäherungen aus zehn Jahrhunderten* (Munich: Beck, 2003), pp. 30–43, 211–12

——, Review of 'Jean Favier, "Le finances pontificales"', in *Göttingische gelehrte Anzeigen*, 221 (1969), 133–59

——, 'Simonie-Geschäft in Rom 1400: "Kein Papst wird das tun, was dieser tut"', *Vierteljahrschrift für Sozial- und Wirtschaftsgeschichte*, 61 (1974), 433–57

——, 'Überweisungen der Apostolischen Kammer aus den Diözesen des Reiches unter Einschaltung italienischer und deutscher Kaufleute und Bankiers. Regesten der vatikanischen Archivalien 1431–1475', *Quellen und Forschungen aus italienischen Archiven und Bibliotheken*, 78 (1998), 262–387

Eubel, Konrad, 'Die "Provisiones praelatorum" durch Gregor XII. Nach Mitte Mai 1408', *Römische Quartalschrift*, 10 (1896), 99–131

Favier, Jean, *Finance et fiscalité au bas Moyen Âge* (Paris: Sedes, 1971)

——, 'La Chambre apostolique aux lendemain du Concile de Pise', *Annali della Fondazione italiana per la storia amministrativa*, 4 (1967), 99–116

——, 'Le Grand Schisme dans l'histoire de France', in *Genèse et débuts du Grand Schisme d'Occident (1362–1394)*, ed. by Jean Favier (Paris: Centre Nationale des Recherches Scientifiques, 1980), pp. 7–16

——, *Les finances pontificales à l'epoque du Grand Schisme d'Occident* (Paris: Boccard, 1966)

Feine, Hans-Erich, *Kirchliche Rechtsgeschichte*, I: *Die katholische Kirche* (Weimar: Böhlau, 1955³)

*Festschrift für Hermann Heimpel zum 70. Geburtstag am 19. September 1971*, 2 vols (Göttingen: Vandenhoeck & Ruprecht, 1972)

Fijałek, Jan, 'Przełość Nankera, biskupa krakowskiego (1320–1.X.1326), następnie wrocławskiego († 10.IV.1341)', in *Z księgi pamiątkowej ku czci Bolesława Orzechowicza*, I (Lwów: Popierania Nauki Polskiej, 1916), pp. 257–81

Fischer, Andreas, 'Kontinuität und Institutionalisierung im 13. Jahrhundert. Zum Fortbestand der Ämter an der Kurie und im Kirchenstaat nach dem Tod des Papstes', *Mitteilungen des Österreichischen Instituts für Geschichtsforschung*, 124 (2016), 322–49

Folz, Robert, 'Le Concordat germanique et l'élection des évêques de Metz', *Annuaire de la Société d'histoire et d'archéologie de la Lorraine*, 40 (1931), 157–305

Fouquet, Gerhard, *Das Speyrer Domkapitel im späten Mittelalter (ca. 1350–1540). Adelige Freundschaft, fürstliche Patronage und päpstliche Klientel* (Mainz: Gesellschaft für Mittelrheinische Kirchengeschichte, 1987)

—, 'Ein Italiener in Lübeck: der Florentiner Gherardo Bueri (gestorben 1449)', *Zeitschrift des Vereins für lübeckische Geschichte und Altertumskunde*, 98 (1998), 187–220

—, 'Reichskirche und Adel. Ursachen und Mechanismen des Aufstiegs der Kraichgauer Niederadelsfamilie von Helmstatt im Speyrer Domkapitel zu Beginn des 15. Jahrhunderts', *Zeitschrift für Geschichte des Oberrheins*, 129 (1981), 189–233

Fraga Iribarne, Manuel, and Juan Beneyto Pérez, 'La enajenación de oficios públicos en su perspectiva histórica y sociológica', in *Centenario de la ley del notariado*, I: *Estudios históricos* (Madrid: Colegios Notariales de España, 1964), pp. 393–472

Frankl, Karl-Heinz, 'Papstschisma und Frömmigkeit. Die "ad instar"-Ablässe', *Römische Quartalshefte*, 72 (1977), 5–124, 184–247

Frenz, Thomas, 'Abbreviator', in *Lexikon des Mittelalters*, vol. 1 (Munich: Artemis, 1980), cols 15–16

—, 'Die Gründung des Abbreviatorenkollegs durch Pius II. und Sixtus IV.', in *Miscellanea in onore di Monsignor Martino Giusti, Prefetto dell'Archivio Segreto Vaticano*, 2 vols (Città del Vaticano: Archivio Segreto Vaticano, 1978), I, pp. 297–329

—, *Die Kanzlei der Päpste der Hochrenaissance (1471–1527)* (Tübingen: Niemeyer, 1986)

—, *I documenti pontifici nel medioevo e nell'età moderna*, ed. by Sergio Pagano (Città del Vaticano: Scuola Vaticana di Paleografia, 1989)

—, *L'introduzione della scrittura umanistica nei documenti e negli atti della curia pontificia del secolo XV* (Città del Vaticano: Scuola Vaticana di Paleografia, 2005)

—, 'Motu proprio', in *Lexikon des Mittelalters*, vol. 6 (Munich: Artemis, 1993), cols 874–75

—, *Papsturkunden des Mittelalters und der Neuzeit* (Stuttgart: Steiner, 2000[2])

—, 'Zum Problem der Reduzierung der Zahl der päpstlichen Kanzleischreiber nach dem Konzil von Konstanz', in *Grundwissenschaften und Geschichte. Festschrift für Peter Acht*, ed. by Waldemar Schlögl and Peter Herde (Kallmünz: Lassleben, 1976), pp. 256–75

Frommel, Christoph, *Der römische Palastbau der Hochrenaissance*, 3 vols (Tübingen: Wasmuth, 1973)

—, 'Il Palazzo della Cancellaria', in *Il palazzo dal Rinascimento a oggi in Italia, nel Regno di Napoli, in Calabria. Storia e attualitá*, ed. by Simonetta Valtieri (Rome: Gangemi, 1989), pp. 29–54

Frutaz, Amato, 'La famiglia pontificia in un documento dell'inizio del secolo XIV', in *Paleografica, diplomatica et archivistica. Studi in onore di Giulio Battelli*, 2 vols (Rome: Edizioni di storia e letteratura, 1979), II, pp. 277–323

Fuhrmann, Horst, 'Die Wahl des Papstes. Ein historischer Überblick', *Geschichte in Wissenschaft und Unterricht*, 9 (1958), pp. 762–80

García Marín, José, *El oficio público en Castilla durante la baja Edad Media* (Seville: Universitad, 1974)

Gasnault, Pierre, 'La transmission des lettres pontificales au XIII$^e$ et au XIV$^e$ siècle', in *Histoire comparé de l'administration*, ed. by Werner Paravicini and Karl Werner (Munich: Artemis, 1980), pp. 79–87

Gawlas, Sławomir, 'Die spätmittelalterliche Nationenbildung am Beispiel Polens', in *Mittelalterliche Nationes – neuzeitliche Nationen. Probleme der Nationenbildung in Europa*, ed. by Almut Bues and Rex Rexheuser (Wiesbaden: Harassowitz, 1995), pp. 121–44

——, 'Wladyslaw I. Lokietek', in *Lexikon des Mittelalters*, vol. 9 (Munich: Artemis, 1998), cols 285–86

*Gelehrte im Reich. Zur Sozial- und Wirkungsgeschichte akademischer Eliten des 14. bis 16. Jahrhunderts*, ed. by Rainer Schwinges (Berlin: Duncker & Humblot, 1996)

Genequand, Philippe, 'Carrières immobiles à la cour de Clément VII d'Avignon (1378–1394)', in *Offices et papauté (XIV$^e$–XVII$^e$ siècle). Charges, hommes, destins*, ed. by Armand Jamme and Olivier Poncet (Rome: École française de Rome, 2005), pp. 761–82

*Genèse et débuts du Grand Schisme d'Occident (1362–1394)*, ed. by Jean Favier (Paris: Centre Nationale des Recherches Scientifiques, 1980)

Gillmann, Franz, 'Die Resignation der Benefizien', pt I, *Archiv für katholisches Kirchenrecht*, 80 (1900), 50–79, 346–78, 523–69, 665–708; pt II, vol. 81 (1901), 223–42, 433–60; also printed separately (Mainz: Kirchheim, 1901)

Girgensohn, Dieter, 'Wie wird man Kardinal? Kuriale und außerkuriale Karrieren an der Wende des 14. zum 15. Jahrhundert', *Quellen und Forschungen aus italienischen Archiven und Bibliotheken*, 57 (1977), 138–62

Gnoli, Umberto, *Alberghi e osterie di Roma nella Rinascenza* (Rome: Moneta, 1942)

Göhring, Martin, *Die Ämterkäuflichkeit im Ancien Régime* (Berlin: Ebering, 1938)

Göller, Emil, 'Zur Geschichte der Kriminaljustiz und des Gefängniswesens am päpstlichen Hof in Avignon', *Römische Quartalschrift*, 19 (1905), 190–93

——, 'Hadrian VI. und der Ämterkauf an der päpstlichen Kurie', in *Abhandlungen aus dem Gebiete der mittleren und neueren Geschichte und ihrer Hilfswissenschaften. Eine Festgabe zum siebzigsten Geburtstag Geheimem Rat Prof. Dr. Heinrich Finke gewidmet* (Münster/W.: Aschendorff, 1925), pp. 377–83

Goldfriedrich, Rolf, *Die Geschäftsbücher der kursächsischen Kanzlei im 15. Jahrhundert* (Leipzig: Schwarzenberg, 1930)

Gottlob, Adolf, *Die Servitientaxe im 13. Jahrhundert. Eine Studie zur Geschichte des päpstlichen Gebührenwesens* (Stuttgart: Enke, 1903)

Gottschalk, Joseph, 'Nanker († 1341)', in *Lexikon für Theologie und Kirche*, vol. 7 (Freiburg/Br.: Herder, 1962), col. 786

# BIBLIOGRAPHY

Graber, Tom, 'Ein Spurium auf Papst Gregor X. für das Zisterzienserinnenkloster zu Leipzig (1274 Juni 22)', in *Diplomatische Forschungen in Mitteldeutschland*, ed. by Tom Graber (Leipzig: Universitätsverlag, 2005), pp. 89–143

Gramsch, Robert, 'Erfurter Juristen im Spätmittelalter' (unpublished doctoral thesis, University of Jena, 2001)

———, *Erfurter Juristen im Spätmittelalter. Die Karrieremuster und Tätigkeitsfelder einer gelehrten Elite des 14. und 15. Jahrhunderts* (Leiden: Brill, 2003)

———, 'Kurientätigkeit als "Berufsbild" gelehrter Juristen. Der Beitrag Roms zur Akademisierung Deutschlands im Spätmittelalter. Eine personengeschichtliche Betrachtung', *Quellen und Forschungen aus italienischen Archiven und Bibliotheken*, 80 (2000), 117–63

Grayson, Cecil, 'Alberti, Leon Battista', in *Dizionario biografico degli italiani*, vol. 1 (Rome: Istituto della Enciclopedia italiana, 1960), pp. 702–09

Grünhagen, Colmar, 'König Johann von Böhmen und Bischof Nanker von Breslau. Zur Geschichte des Kampfes mit dem Slaventhum im deutschen Osten', in *Sitzungsberichte der kaiserlichen Akademie der Wissenschaften in Wien, philosophisch-historische Classe*, vol. 47 (Vienna: Gerold, 1864), pp. 4–102

Gualdo, Germano, 'Umanesimo e segretari apostolici all'inizio del Quattrocento: Alcuni casi esemplari', in *Cancellaria e cultura nel medioevo*, ed. by Germano Gualdo (Città del Vaticano: Archivio Segreto Vaticano, 1988), pp. 307–18

Guenée, Bernard, *Tribunaux et gens de justice dans le baillage de Senlis à la fin du Moyen Âge (vers 1380–vers 1550)* (Paris: Gap, 1962)

Guillemain, Bernard, 'Cardinaux et société curiale aux origins de la double élection de 1378', in *Genèse et débuts du Grand Schisme d'Occident (1362–1394)*, ed. by Jean Favier (Paris: Centre Nationale des Recherches Scientifiques, 1980), pp. 19–44

———, *La cour pontificale d'Avignon 1309–1376. Étude d'une société* (Paris: Boccard, 1962)

Gustaw, Romuald, 'Nanker', in *Hagiografia polska. Słownik bio-bibliograficzny*, 2 vols (Poznań: Księgarnia świętego Wojciecha, 1971–1972), II, pp. 149–60

Hack, Achim, *Das Empfangszeremoniell bei mittelalterlichen Papst-Kaiser-Treffen* (Cologne: Böhlau, 1999)

———, 'Zeremoniell und Inszenierung der öffentlichen Konsistorien im Spätmittelalter', in *Versammlungen. Ritualisierung und zeichenhafte Darstellung politischer Willensbildung im Vergleich*, ed. by Jörg Pelzer, Gerald Schwedler, and Paul Töbelmann (Heidelberg: Winter, 2009), pp. 55–92

Hageneder, Othmar, 'Päpstliche Reskripttechnik: Kanonistische Lehre und kuriale Praxis', in *Stagnation oder Fortbildung? Aspekte des allgemeinen Kirchenrechts im 14. und 15. Jahrhundert*, ed. by Martin Bertram (Tübingen: Niemeyer, 2005), pp. 181–96

Haller, Johannes, *Papsttum und Kirchenreform*, I: *Vier Kapitel zur Geschichte des ausgehenden Mittelalters* (Berlin: Weidmann, 1903)

————, 'Zwei Aufzeichnungen über die Beamten der Curie im 13. und 14. Jahrhundert', *Quellen und Forschungen aus italienischen Archiven und Bibliotheken*, 1 (1898), 1–38

Haubst, Rudolf, 'Der Reformentwurf Pius' des Zweiten', *Römische Quartalschrift*, 49 (1954), 188–242

Hayez, Anne-Marie, 'Les courriers des papes d'Avignon sous Innocent VI et Urbain V (1352–1370)', in *La circulation des nouvelles au Moyen Âge* (Rome: École française de Rome, 1994), pp. 49–62

————, 'Les rotuli presentés au pape Urbain V durant la première année de son pontificat', *Mélanges de l'École française de Rome – Temps moderns*, 96 (1984), 327–94

Heimpel, Hermann, *Die Vener von Gmünd und Strassburg 1162–1447. Studien und Texte zur Geschichte einer Familie sowie des gelehrten Beamtentums in der Zeit der abendländischen Kirchenspaltung und der Konzilien von Pisa, Konstanz und Basel*, 3 vols (Göttingen: Vandenhoeck & Ruprecht, 1982)

Heinig, Paul-Joachim, 'Gelehrte Juristen im Dienst der römisch-deutschen Könige', in *Recht und Verfassung im Übergang vom Mittelalter zur Neuzeit*, I: *Bericht über Kolloquien zur Erforschung der Kultur des Spätmittelalters 1994 bis 1995*, ed. by Hartmut Boockmann, Ludger Grenzmann, Bernd Moeller, and Martin Staehelin (Göttingen: Vandenhoeck & Ruprecht, 1998), pp. 167–84

Helbig, Herbert, *Der wettinische Ständestaat. Untersuchungen zur Geschichte des Ständewesens und der landständischen Verfassung in Mitteldeutschland bis 1485* (Cologne: Böhlau, 1955)

Helmrath, Johannes, *Das Basler Konzil 1431–1449. Forschungsstand und Probleme* (Cologne: Böhlau, 1987)

Heimann, Heinz-Dieter, 'Akzente und Aspekte in der deutschen Forschungsdiskussion zu spätmittelalterlichen Krisenerscheinungen, insbesondere im Bereich des geistigen Lebens', in *Europa 1400. Die Krise des Spätmittelalters*, ed. by Ferdinand Seibt and Winfried Eberhard (Stuttgart: Klett, 1984), pp. 53–64

Heintschel, Donald, *The Medieval Concept of an Ecclesiastical Office. An Analytical Study of the Concept of an Ecclesiastical Office in the Major Sources and Printed Commentaries from 1140–1300* (Washington, DC: Catholic University of America Press, 1956)

Hennig, Bruno, *Die Kirchenpolitik der älteren Hohenzollern in der Mark Brandenburg und die päpstlichen Privilegien des Jahres 1447* (Leipzig: Duncker & Humblot, 1906)

Herde, Peter, 'Audientia litterarum contradictarum', in *Lexikon des Mittelalters*, vol. 1 (Munich: Artemis, 1977), cols 1192–93

————, *Audientia litterarum contradictarum. Untersuchungen über die päpstlichen Justizbriefe vom 13. bis zum Beginn des 16. Jahrhunderts*, 2 vols (Tübingen: De Gruyter, 1970)

—, *Beiträge zum päpstlichen Kanzlei- und Urkundenwesen im 13. Jahrhundert* (Kallmünz: Lassleben, 1967[2])

—, 'Die "Registra contradictarum" des vatikanischen Archivs (1575–1799)', in *Paleografica, diplomatica et archivistica. Studi in onore di Giulio Battelli*, 2 vols (Rome: Edizioni di storia e letteratura, 1979), II, pp. 407–44

Hesse, Christian, *St. Mauritius in Zofingen. Verfassungs- und sozialgeschichtliche Aspekte eines mittelalterlichen Chorherrenstiftes* (Aarau: Sauerländer, 1992)

Hilderscheid, Heinz, 'Die päpstlichen Reservationsrechte auf die Besetzung der niederen Kirchenämter im Gebiete des Deutschen Reichs' (unpublished doctoral thesis, University of Cologne, 1934)

Hinschius, Paul, *System des katholischen Kirchenrechts mit besonderer Rücksicht auf Deutschland*, 6 vols (Berlin: Guttentag, 1869–1897)

Hirschmann, Stefan, *Die päpstliche Kanzlei und ihre Urkundenproduktion (1141–1159)* (Frankfurt/M.: Lang, 2001)

*Histoire comparé de l'administration (IVe–XVIIIe siècles)*, ed. by Werner Paravicini and Karl Werner (Ostfildern: Thorbecke, 1980)

Hitzbleck, Kerstin, '*Veri et legitimi vicarii et procuratores*. Beobachtungen zu Provisionswesen und Stellvertretung an der päpstlichen Kurie von Avignon', *Quellen und Forschungen aus italienischen Archiven und Bibliotheken*, 86 (2006), 208–51

Höing, Hubert, 'Die Erschließung des Repertorium Germanicum durch EDV-gestützte Indices. Technische Voraussetzungen und Möglichkeiten', *Quellen und Forschungen aus italienischen Archiven und Bibliotheken*, 71 (1991), 310–24

Holbach, Rudolf, 'Die Besetzung des Trierer Erzbischofsstuhls im späten Mittelalter. Konstellationen und Konflikte', *Archiv für mittelrheinische Kirchengeschichte*, 35 (1983), 11–48

—, '*Disz ist dy ansprache dy wir do wydder unssen heren ....* Bemerkungen zur Regierungszeit des Erzbischofs Otto von Ziegenhain 1418–1430', *Kurtrierisches Jahrbuch*, 23 (1983), 17–35

—, *Stiftsgeistlichkeit im Spannungsfeld zwischen Kirche und Welt. Studien zur Geschichte des Trierer Domkapitels und Domklerus' im Spätmittelalter*, 2 vols (Trier: Trierer Historische Forschungen, 1982)

Hollister, Warren, and John Baldwin, 'The Rise of Administrative Kingship: Henry II and Philipp Augustus', *American Historical Review*, 83 (1978), 867–905

Hotz, Brigitte, *Päpstliche Stellenvergabe am Konstanzer Domkapitel während der avignonesischen Periode (1316–1378) und die Domherrengemeinschaft beim Übergang zum Schisma (1378)* (Ostfildern: Thorbecke, 2005)

Hruboň, Pavel, and Richard Psík, *Kancelářské poznámky na papežkých listinách v odobí 1389–1417 na příkladu listin dochovaných v moravských archivech* (Ostrava: Univerzity, 2013)

*Il Concilio II di Lione (1274) secondo la Ordinatio concilii generalis Lugdunensis*, ed. by Antonino Franchi (Rome: Edizioni Francescane, 1965)

*Institutionen und Geschichte. Theoretische Aspekte und mittelalterliche Befunde*, ed. by Gerd Melville (Cologne: Böhlau, 1992)

Jackowski, Leo, 'Die päpstlichen Kanzleiregeln und ihre Bedeutung für Deutschland', *Archiv für katholisches Kirchenrecht*, 90 (1910), 3–47, 197–235, 432–63

Jedin, Hubert, *Geschichte des Konzils von Trient. Der Kampf um das Konzil*, I (Freiburg/Br.: Herder, 1949)

——, 'Kann der Papst Simonie begehen?', in *Kirche des Glaubens, Kirche der Geschichte*, ed. by Hubert Jedin, 2 vols (Freiburg/Br.: Herder, 1966), II, pp. 264–84

Katterbach, Bruno, *Referendarii utriusque signaturae a Martino V ad Clementem IX et praelati signaturae supplicationum a Martino V ad Leonem XIII* (Città del Vaticano: Biblioteca Apostolica Vaticana, 1931)

Kersken, Norbert, *Geschichtsschreibung im Europa der 'nationes'. Nationalgeschichtliche Gesamtdarstellungen im Mittelalter* (Cologne: Böhlau, 1995)

Kienast, Walter, *Deutschland und Frankreich in der Kaiserzeit (900–1270). Weltkaiser und Einzelkönige*, 3 vols (Stuttgart: Hiersemann, 1974–1975)

Kisky, Wilhelm, *Die Domkapitel der geistlichen Kurfürsten in ihrer persönlichen Zusammensetzung im 14. und 15. Jahrhundert* (Weimar: Böhlau, 1906)

Knossalla, Josef, '*Acta synodalia decanatus Bythomiensis*. Ein Beitrag zur Kirchengeschichte Oberschlesiens', *Mitteilungen des Beuthener Geschichtsvereins*, 3 (1913), 16–28

Knowles-Frazier, Alison, *Possible Lives: Authors and Saints in Renaissance Italy* (New York: Columbia University Press, 2005)

Kobayashi, Asami, 'Original und kopial überlieferte Urkunden der Zeit 1378–1417 in mährischen Archiven' (unpublished doctoral thesis, University of Marburg, 2014)

Koch, Bettina, *Räte auf deutschen Reichsversammlungen. Zur Entwicklung der politischen Funktionselite im 15. Jahrhundert* (Frankfurt/M.: Lang, 1999)

Koch, Josef, *Der deutsche Kardinal in deutschen Landen. Die Legationsreise des Nikolaus von Kues (1451/1452)* (Trier: Paulinus, 1964); reprint, in Josef Koch, *Kleine Schriften*, 2 vols (Rome: Edizioni di storia e letteratura, 1973), I, pp. 495–530

——, *Nikolaus von Kues und seine Umwelt* (Heidelberg: Winter, 1948)

Konetzke, Richard, 'Territoriale Grundherrschaft und Landesherrschaft im spanischen Spätmittelalter. Ein Forschungsbeitrag zum spanischen Partikularismus', in *Mélanges en honneur de Fernand Braudel*, 2 vols (Toulouse: Privat, 1973), II, pp. 299–310

Kowalski, Marek, *Prałaci i kanonicy krakowskiej kapituły katedralnej od pontyfikatu biskupa Nankera do śmierci biskupa Zawiszy z Kurozwęk 1320–1382* (Kraków: Towarzystwa Miłosników Historii i Zabytków Krakowa, 1996)

Kozłowska-Budkowa, Zofia, 'Johannes Grotonis', in *Polski Słownik Biograficzny*, vol. 7 (Kraków: Polska Akademia Umiejętności, 1948–1958), p. 77

——, 'Nanker', in *Polski Słownik Biograficzny*, vol. 22 (Kraków: Polska Akademia Umiejętności, 1977), pp. 514–17

Kraus, Andreas, 'Die Sekretäre Pius II.', *Römische Quartalschrift*, 53 (1958), 25–80

Kreidte, Peter, *Die Herrschaft der Bischöfe von Włocławek in Pomerellen, von den Anfängen bis zum Jahr 1409* (Göttingen: Vandenhoeck & Ruprecht, 1974)

Krüger, Thomas, 'Konsistorialurkunden in der päpstlichen Herrschaftspraxis. Kontinuität und Wandel nach dem Basler Konzil', in *Nach dem Basler Konzil. Die Neuordnung der Kirche zwischen Konziliarismus und monarchischem Papat (ca. 1450–1475)*, ed. by Jürgen Dendorfer and Claudia Märtl (Berlin: Duncker & Humblot, 2008), pp. 357–83

Küchler, Winfried, 'Ämterkäuflichkeit in den Ländern der Krone Aragons', *Spanische Forschungen der Görres-Gesellschaft*, I: *Gesammelte Aufsätze zur Kulturgeschichte Spaniens*, vol. 27 (Münster/W.: Aschendorff, 1973), pp. 311–36

Kubler, Jacques, *L'origine de la perpétuité des offices royaux* (Nancy: Société impressions typographiques, 1958)

Kürbis, Brygida, 'Johannes Dlugosz als Geschichtsschreiber', in *Geschichtsschreibung und Geschichtsbewußtsein im späten Mittelalter*, ed. by Heinz Patze (Sigmaringen: Thorbecke, 1987), pp. 483–96

*Kurie und Region. Festschrift für Brigide Schwarz zum 65. Geburtstag*, ed. by Brigitte Flug, Michael Matheus, and Andreas Rehberg (Stuttgart: Steiner, 2005)

Kurze, Dietrich, *Pfarrerwahlen im Mittelalter. Ein Beitrag zur Geschichte der Gemeinde und des Niederkirchenwesens* (Cologne: Böhlau, 1966)

*La vita e il mondo di Leon Battista Alberti*, 2 vols (Florence: Olschki, 2008)

Labuda, Gerard, 'Dlugosz', in *Lexikon des Mittelalters*, vol. 3 (Munich: Artemis, 1986), cols 1139–40

Lager, Johann, 'Raban von Helmstadt und Ulrich von Manderscheid – ihr Kampf um das Erzbistum Trier', *Historisches Jahrbuch*, 15 (1894), 712–70

Lanconelli, Angela, 'Manoscritti statutari romani. Contributo per una bibliografia delle fonti statutarie dell'età medioevale', in *Scrittura, biblioteche e stampe a Roma nel Quattrocento*, ed. by Massimo Miglio, Paola Farenga, and Anna Modigliani (Città del Vaticano: Scuola Vaticana di Paleografia, 1983), pp. 305–21

Laufner, Richard, 'Die Manderscheidsche Fehde. Eine Wende in der Geschichte Triers', pt I, *Trierisches Jahrbuch* (1953), 48–60; pt II, (1954), 52–59

*Le cérémonial papal de la fin du Moyen Age à la Renaissance*, ed. by Marc Dykmans, 4 vols (Rome: Institut historique belge de Rome, 1977–1985)

Lefebvre, Christian, 'Les juristes du Moyen Âge et la venalité des charges', in *Miscellanea historica in honorem Leonis van Essen – Universitatis Catholicae in oppido Lovaniensi iam annos XXXV professoris*, I (Louvain: Editions universitaires, 1947), pp. 273–85

Lieberich, Heinz, 'Die gelehrten Räte. Staat und Juristen in Baiern in der Frühzeit der Rezeption', *Zeitschrift für bayerische Landesgeschichte*, 27 (1964), 120–89

Liebs, Detlev, 'Ämterkauf und Ämterpatronage in der Spätantike. Propaganda und Sachzwang bei Julian dem Abtrünnigen', *Savigny-Zeitschrift für Rechtsgeschichte, Romanistische Abteilung*, 95 (1978), pp. 158–86

Linden, Peter, *Der Tod des Benefiziaten in Rom. Eine Studie zu Geschichte und Recht der päpstlichen Reservationen* (Bonn: Grüner, 1938)

Lindner, Theodor, 'Beiträge zu dem Leben und den Schriften Dietrichs von Niem', *Forschungen zur deutschen Geschichte*, 21 (1881), 67–92

Linehan, Peter, and Patrick Zutshi, 'The Earliest Known Roll of Petitions Signed by the Pope (1307)', *The English Historical Review*, 222 (2007), 998–1015

Louis-Lucas, Paul, *Étude sur la venalité des charges et fonctions publiques et sur celle des offices ministériels depuis l'Antiquité romaine jusqu'à nos jours*, 2 vols (Paris: Challamel, 1883)

Lunt, William, *Accounts Rendered by Papal Collectors in England, 1317–1378*, ed. by William Lunt and Edgar Graves (Philadelphia: American Philosophical Society, 1968)

——, *Financial Relations of the Papacy with England*, 2 vols (Cambridge, MA: Medieval Academy of America, 1939–1962)

——, *Papal Revenues in the Middle Ages*, 2 vols (New York: Columbia University Press, 1934)

Lutz, Georg, 'Zur Papstfinanz von Klemens IX. bis Alexander VIII. (1667–1691)', *Römische Quartalschrift*, 74 (1979), 32–90

Machatschek, Eduard, *Geschichte der Bischöfe des Hochstifts Meißen in chronologischer Reihenfolge. Zugleich ein Beitrag zur Culturgeschichte der Mark Meißen und des Herzog- und Kurfürstenthums Sachsen* (Dresden: Meinhold, 1884)

Männl, Ingrid, 'Die gelehrten Juristen im Dienst der deutschen Territorialherrren 1250 bis 1440' (unpublished doctoral thesis, University of Giessen, 1987)

——, 'Die gelehrten Juristen im Dienst der Territorialherren im Norden und Nordosten des Reiches von 1250–1440', in *Gelehrte im Reich. Zur Sozial- und Wirkungsgeschichte akademischer Eliten des 14. bis 16. Jahrhunderts*, ed. by Rainer Schwinges (Berlin: Duncker & Humblot, 1996), pp. 269–90

Märtl, Claudia, 'Der Papst und das Geld. Zum kurialen Rechnungswesen unter Pius II. (1458–1464)', in *Kurie und Region. Festschrift für Brigide Schwarz zum 65. Geburtstag*, ed. by Brigitte Flug, Michael Matheus, and Andreas Rehberg (Stuttgart: Steiner, 2005), pp. 175–95

——, 'Zwischen Habitus und Repräsentation. Der kardinalizische Ornat am Ende des Mittelalters', in *Die Kardinäle des Mittelalters und der frühen Renaissance*, ed. by Jessika Nowak, Jürgen Dendorfer, and Ralf Lützelschwab (Florence: Sismel, 2013), pp. 265–300

Maleczek, Werner, 'Deutsche Studenten in Italien', in *Kommunikation und Mobilität im Mittelalter. Begegnungen zwischen dem Süden und der Mitte Europas (11.–14. Jahrhundert)*, ed. by Siegfried de Rachewiltz and Josef Riedmann (Sigmaringen: Thorbecke, 1995), pp. 77–96

Maleczyński, Karol, 'Dominik', in *Polski Słownik Biograficzny*, vol. 5 (Kraków: Polska Akademia Umiejętności, 1939–1946), pp. 318–19

Mantese, Giovanni, 'Ein notarielles Inventar von Büchern und Wertgegenständen aus dem Nachlass des Nikolaus von Kues', *Mitteilungen und Forschungsbeiträge der Cusanus-Gesellschaft*, 2 (1962), 85–116

Marini, Gaetano, *Degli archiatri pontifici* (Rome: Pagliarini, 1784)

Marquis, Bettina, *Meißnische Geschichtsschreibung im späten Mittelalter (ca. 1215–1420)* (Munich: Hupe, 1998)

Marx, Jakob, *Geschichte des Armen-Hospitals zum heiligen Nikolaus zu Cues* (Trier: Cusanus Gesellschaft, 1907)

Maschke, Erich, *Der Peterspfennig in Polen und dem deutschen Osten* (Sigmaringen: Thorbecke, 1979²)

Mathies, Christiane, *Kurfürstenbund und Königtum in der Zeit der Hussitenkriege. Die kurfürstliche Reichspolitik gegen Sigmund im Kraftzentrum Mittelrhein* (Mainz: Gesellschaft für Mittelrheinische Kirchengeschichte, 1978)

Matuszek, Antoni, 'Jan Grotowicz h. Rawa', in *Polski Słownik Biograficzny*, vol. 9 (Wrocław: Polska Akademia Umiejętności, 1960–1961), pp. 15–18

McCurry, Charles, '*Utilia Metensia*: Local Benefices for the Papal Curia, 1212–ca. 1370', in *Law, Church, and Society: Essays Presented to Stephan Kuttner*, ed. by Paul Horwitz and Kenneth Pennington (Philadelphia: University of Pennsylvania Press, 1977), pp. 311–23

Meinardus, Otto, 'Formelsammlungen und Handbücher aus dem Bureaux der päpstlichen Verwaltung des 15. Jahrhunderts in Hannover', *Neues Archiv*, 10 (1885), 35–79

Melville, Gerd, 'Institutionen als geschichtswissenschaftliches Thema. Eine Einleitung', in *Institutionen und Geschichte. Theoretische Aspekte und mittelalterliche Befunde*, ed. by Gerd Melville (Cologne: Böhlau, 1992), pp. 1–24

Meuthen, Erich, 'Auskünfte des Repertorium Germanicum zur Struktur des deutschen Klerus im 15. Jahrhundert', *Quellen und Forschungen aus italienischen Archiven und Bibliotheken*, 71 (1991), 280–309

——, *Das Trierer Schisma von 1430 auf dem Basler Konzil. Zur Lebensgeschichte des Nikolaus von Cues* (Münster/W.: Aschendorff, 1964)

——, *Die letzten Jahre des Nikolaus Cusanus. Biographische Untersuchungen nach neuen Quellen* (Cologne: Westdeutscher Verlag, 1958)

——, 'Die Pfründen des Cusanus', *Mitteilungen und Forschungsberichte der Cusanus-Gesellschaft*, 2 (1962), 15–66

——, 'Ein "deutscher" Freundeskreis an der römischen Kurie in der Mitte des 15. Jahrhunderts: Von Cesarini bis zu den Piccolomini', *Annuarium historiae conciliorum*, 27/28 (1995/1996), 487–542

——, *Nikolaus von Kues, 1401–1464, Skizze einer Biographie* (Münster/W.: Aschendorff, 1982⁵)

———, 'Nikolaus von Kues auf dem Regensburger Reichstag 1454', in *Festschrift für Hermann Heimpel zum 70. Geburtstag am 19. September 1971*, 2 vols (Göttingen: Vandenhoeck & Ruprecht, 1972), II, pp. 482–99

———, 'Nikolaus von Kues in Aachen', *Zeitschrift des Aachener Geschichtsvereins*, 73 (1961), 5–23

———, 'Obödienz- und Absolutionslisten aus dem Trierer Bistumsstreit', *Quellen und Forschungen aus italienischen Archiven und Bibliotheken*, 40 (1960), 43–64

———, 'Peter von Erkelenz (ca. 1430–1494)', *Zeitschrift des Aachener Geschichtsvereins*, 84–85 (1977–1978), 701–44

———, 'Reich, Kirche und Kurie im späten Mittelalter', *Historische Zeitschrift*, 265 (1997), 597–637

Meyer, Andreas, *Arme Kleriker auf Pfründensuche. Eine Studie über das in forma pauperum-Register Gregors XII. von 1407 und über päpstliche Anwartschaften im Spätmittelalter* (Cologne: Böhlau, 1990)

———, 'Das Wiener Konkordat von 1448 – eine erfolgreiche Reform des Spätmittelalters', *Quellen und Forschungen aus italienischen Archiven und Bibliotheken*, 66 (1986), 108–52

———, 'Der deutsche Pfründenmarkt im Spätmittelalter', *Quellen und Forschungen aus italienischen Archiven und Bibliotheken*, 71 (1991), 266–79

———, 'Die päpstliche Kanzlei im Mittelalter – ein Versuch', *Archiv für Diplomatik*, 61 (2015), 287–337

———, 'Regieren mit Urkunden im Spätmittelalter. Päpstliche Kanzlei und weltliche Kanzleien im Vergleich', in *Urkunden und ihre Erforschung. Zum Gedenken an Heinrich Appelt*, ed. by Werner Maleczek (Vienna: Böhlau, 2014), pp. 71–91

———, 'Spätmittelalterliches Benefizialrecht im Spannungsfeld zwischen päpstlicher Kurie und ordentlicher Kollatur', in *Proceedings of the Eighth International Congress of Medieval Canon Law. San Diego, University of California at La Jolla, 21–27 August 1988*, ed. by Stanley Chodorow (Città del Vaticano: Bibliotheca Apostolica Vaticana, 1992), pp. 247–62

———, 'The Curia: The Apostolic Chancery', in *A Companion to the Medieval Papacy: Growth of an Ideology and Institution*, ed. by Atria Larson and Keith Sisson (Leiden: Brill, 2016), pp. 239–58

———, *Zürich und Rom. Ordentliche Kollatur und päpstliche Provisionen am Frau- und Grossmünster 1316–1523* (Tübingen: Niemeyer, 1986)

Miethke, Jürgen, 'Politische Theorie in der Krise der Zeit', in *Institutionen und Geschichte. Theoretische Aspekte und mittelalterliche Befunde*, ed. by Gerd Melville (Cologne: Böhlau, 1992), pp. 157–86

Militzer, Klaus, 'Geldüberweisungen des Deutschen Ordens an die Kurie', in *Der hansische Sonderweg? Beiträge zur Sozial- und Witschaftsgeschichte der Hanse*, ed. by Stuart Jenks and Michael North (Cologne: Böhlau, 1993), pp. 30–48

Miller, Ignaz, *Jakob von Sierck 1398/1399–1456* (Mainz: Gesellschaft für Mittelrheinische Kirchengeschichte, 1983)

——, 'Kurtrier und die Übernahme des Herzogtums Luxemburg durch Philipp den Guten von Burgund', *Hemecht. Zeitschrift für Luxemburger Geschichte*, 36 (1984), 489–514

Mollat, Guillaume, 'Contribution à l'histoire du Sacré College de Clement V à Eugène IV', *Revue d'histoire ecclésiastique*, 46 (1951), 22–112, 566–94

——, 'Gentile da Montefiore', in *Dictonnaire d'histoire et de géographie ecclésiastiques*, vol. 20 (Paris: Letouzey, 1984), pp. 506–07

——, 'Les graces expectatives du XII$^e$ au XIV$^e$ siècle', *Revue d'histoire ecclésiastique*, 47 (1942), 81–102

——, 'Miscellanea Avenionensia', *Mélanges d'archéologie et d'histoire de l'École française de Rome*, 44 (1927), 1–5

——, 'Règlement d'Urbain V sur les insignes des sergents d'armes, des portiers et des courriers de la Cour pontificale', in *Mélanges Eugène Tisserant*, 7 vols (Città del Vaticano: Biblioteca Apostolica Vaticana, 1964), V, pp. 165–69

Moraw, Peter, 'Aspekte und Dimensionen älterer deutscher Universitätsgeschichte', in *Academia Gissensis. Beiträge zur älteren Gießener Universitätsgeschichte*, ed. by Peter Moraw and Volker Press (Marburg: Historische Kommission für Hessen, 1982), pp. 1–43

——, 'Beamtentum und Rat König Ruprechts', *Zeitschrift für Geschichte des Oberrheins*, 77 (1968), 59–126

——, 'Brandenburg im späten Mittelalter. Entwicklungsgeschichtliche Überlegungen und europäischer Vergleich', in *Im Dienste von Verwaltung, Archivwissenschaft und brandenburgischer Landesgeschichte. 50 Jahre Brandenburgisches Landeshauptarchiv*, ed. by Klaus Neumann (Frankfurt/M.: Lang, 2000), pp. 83–99

——, 'Der Lebensweg der Studenten', in *Geschichte der Universität in Europa*, I, ed. by Walter Ruegg (Munich: Beck 1993), pp. 227–54

——, 'Die gelehrten Juristen der deutschen Könige im späten Mittelalter (1273–1493)', in *Die Rolle der Juristen bei der Entstehung des modernen Staates*, ed. by Roman Schnur (Berlin: Duncker & Humblot, 1986), pp. 77–147

——, 'Die Juristenuniversität in Prag (1372–1419), verfassungs- und sozialgeschichtlich betrachtet', in *Schulen und Studium im sozialen Wandel des hohen und späten Mittelalters*, ed. by Johannes Fried (Sigmaringen: Thorbecke, 1986), pp. 439–86

——, 'Improvisation und Ausgleich. Der deutsche Professor tritt ans Licht', in *Gelehrte im Reich. Zur Sozial- und Wirkungsgeschichte akademischer Eliten des 14. bis 16. Jahrhunderts*, ed. by Rainer Schwinges (Berlin: Duncker & Humblot, 1996), pp. 309–26

————, 'Stiftspfründen als Elemente des Bildungswesens im spätmittelalterlichen Reich', in *Studien zum weltlichen Kollegiatsstift in Deutschland*, ed. by Irene Crusius (Göttingen: Vandenhoeck & Ruprecht, 1995), pp. 270–97

————, 'Über Patrone und Klienten im Heiligen Römischen Reich des späten Mittelalters und der frühen Neuzeit', in *Klientelsysteme im Europa der frühen Neuzeit*, ed. by Antoni Maczak (Munich: De Gruyter, 1988), pp. 1–18

————, 'Über Typologie, Chronologie und Geographie der Stiftskirche im deutschen Mittelalter', in *Untersuchungen zu Kloster und Stift* (Göttingen: Vandenhoeck & Ruprecht, 1980), pp. 9–37

————, 'Zur Sozialgeschichte der deutschen Universitäten im späten Mittelalter', *Gießener Universitätsblätter*, 8/2 (1975), 44–60

Moroni, Gaetano, 'Cursori apostolici o pontifici', in *Dizionario di erudizione storico-ecclesiastico*, ed. by Gaetano Moroni, vol. 19 (Venice: Tipografia emiliana, 1843), pp. 49–62

Mousnier, Roland, 'Le trafic des offices à Venise', *Revue d'histoire du droit français et étranger*, 30 (1952), 552–65; reprint, in Roland Mousnier, *La plume, la faucille et le marteau. Institutions et société en France du Moyen Âge à la Révolution* (Paris: Presses universitaires de France, 1970), pp. 387–401

————, *La venalité des offices sous Henri IV et Louis XIII* (Paris: Presses universitaires de France, 1971$^2$)

Müller, Harald, and Brigide Schwarz, 'Zwei Originalsuppliken *in communi forma pauperum* des 14. Jahrhunderts', *Archiv für Diplomatik*, 51 (2005), 285–304

Müller, Heribert, 'Une carrière ecclésiastique dans l'Europe du xv$^e$ siècle: le cardinal Jean de Rochetaillée (m. 1437)', in *Relations, échanges et transferts en Europe dans les derniers siècles du Moyen Âge*, ed. by Bernard Guenée and Jean-Marie Moeglin (Paris: Académie des Inscriptions et Belles-Lettres, 2010), pp. 87–113

Müller, Wolfgang, 'The Price of Papal Pardon. New Fifteenth-Century Evidence', in *Päpste, Pilger, Pönitentiarie. Festschrift für Ludwig Schmugge zum 65. Geburtstag*, ed. by Andreas Meyer, Constanze Rendtel, and Maria Widmer-Butsch (Tübingen: Niemeyer, 2004), pp. 457–81

Neal, Fred, 'The Papacy and the Nations. A Study of Concordats (1418–1516)' (unpublished doctoral thesis, University of Chicago Press, 1946)

Neu, Peter, 'Geschichte und Struktur der Eifelterritorien des Hauses Manderscheid vornehmlich im 15. und 16. Jahrhundert' (unpublished doctoral thesis, University of Bonn, 1972)

Niwiński, Mieczysław, 'Bodzęta z Wrześni', in *Polski Słownik Biograficzny*, vol. 2 (Kraków: Polska Akademia Umiejętności, 1936), pp. 181–82

Nowak, Zenon, 'Die Rolle der Gelehrten in der Gesellschaft des Ordenslandes Preußen', in *Gelehrte im Reich. Zur Sozial- und Wirkungsgeschichte akademischer Eliten des 14. bis 16. Jahrhunderts*, ed. by Rainer Schwinges (Berlin: Duncker & Humblot, 1996), pp. 211–23

Nowakowski, Tomasz, 'Krakowska kapituła katedralna wobec panowania Przemyślidów w Małopolsce w latach 1292–1306', *Przegląd Historyczny*, 82 (1991), 3–20

Nüske, Gerd, 'Untersuchungen über das Personal der päpstlichen Kanzlei 1254–1304', pt I, *Archiv für Diplomatik*, 20 (1974), 39–240; pt II, vol. 21 (1975), 249–431

O'Malley, John, *Praise and Blame in Renaissance Rome: Rhetoric, Doctrine, and Reform in the Sacred Orators of the Papal Court, c. 1450–1521* (Durham, NC: Duke University Press, 1979)

*Offices, écrits, et papauté (XIIIᵉ–XVIIᵉ siècle)*, ed. by Armand Jamme and Olivier Poncet (Rome: École française de Rome, 2007)

*Offices et papauté (XIVᵉ–XVIIᵉ siècle). Charges, hommes, destins*, ed. by Armand Jamme and Olivier Poncet (Rome: École française de Rome, 2005)

Olivier-Martin, François, 'La nomination aux offices royaux au XIVᵉ siècle d'après les pratiques de la Chancellerie', in *Mélanges Paul Fournier* (Paris: Sirey, 1929), pp. 487–501

Ourliac, Paul, 'Souveraineté et lois fondamentales dans le droit canonique du XVᵉ siècle', in *Herrschaftsverträge, Wahlkapitulationen, Fundamentalgesetze*, ed. by Rudolf Vierhaus (Göttingen: Vandenhoeck & Ruprecht, 1977), pp. 22–33

Ożóg, Krzysztof, *Kultura umysłowa w Krakowie w XIV wieku: środowisko duchowieństwa świeckiego* (Wrocław: Ossolineum, 1987)

——, 'Reinbold', *Polski Słownik Biograficzny*, vol. 31 (Wrocław: Polska Akademia Umiejętności 1988–1989), pp. 22–23

Pagès, Georges, 'La venalité des offices dans l'ancienne France', *Revue historique*, 169 (1932), 477–95

*Paleografica, diplomatica et archivistica. Studi in onore di Giulio Battelli*, 2 vols (Rome: Edizioni di storia e letteratura, 1979)

*Päpste, Pilger, Pönitentiarie. Festschrift für Ludwig Schmugge zum 65. Geburtstag*, ed. by Andreas Meyer, Constanze Rendtel, and Maria Widmer-Butsch (Tübingen: Niemeyer, 2004)

Paravicini, Werner, 'Administrateurs professionels et princes dilettantes. Remarques sur un problème de sociologie administrative à la fin du Moyen Âge', in *Histoire comparé de l'administration (IVᵉ–XVIIIᵉ siècles)*, ed. by Werner Paravicini and Karl Werner (Ostfildern: Thorbecke, 1980), pp. 168–81

Paravicini Bagliani, Antonio, *Cardinali di Curia e 'familiae' cardinalizie dal 1227 al 1254*, 2 vols (Padua: Antenore, 1972)

——, *I testamenti dei cardinali romani del Duecento* (Rome: Società romana storia patria, 1980)

——, 'Il personale della Curia romana pre-avignonese. Bilancio e prospettive di ricerca', in *Proceedings of the Sixth International Congress of Medieval Canon Law: Berkeley, California, 28 July–2 August 1980*, ed. by Stephan Kuttner and Kenneth Pennington (Città del Vaticano: Biblioteca Apostolica Vaticana, 1980), pp. 391–410

———, *La cour des papes au XIII<sup>e</sup> siècle* (Paris: Hachette, 1995)

———, 'La mobilità della Curia romana nel secolo XIII. Riflessi locali', in *Società e istituzioni dell'Italia communale: L'esempio di Perugia (secoli XII–XIV)* (Perugia: Società storia patria per l'Umbria, 1988), pp. 155–278

———, *La vita quotidiana alla corte dei papi nel Duecento* (Bari: Laterza, 1996)

Partner, Peter, 'The "Budget" of the Roman Church in the Renaissance Period', in *Italian Renaissance Studies*, ed. by Ernest Jacob (London: Faber, 1960), pp. 256–78

———, *The Lands of St Peter: The Papal State in the Middle Ages and the Early Renaissance* (London: Methuen, 1972)

———, *The Papal State under Martin V: The Administration and Government of the Temporal Power in the Early Fifteenth Century* (London: The British School at Rome, 1958)

*Papsturkunde und europäisches Urkundenwesen. Studien zu ihrer formalen und rechtlichen Kohärenz vom 11. bis 15. Jahrhundert*, ed. by Peter Herde and Hermann Jakobs (Cologne: Böhlau, 1999)

Pavón Ramírez, Marta, 'Leon Batista Alberti, official de la cancillería pontificia: nuevos documentos del archivo secreto vaticano', in *La vita e il mondo di Leon Battista Alberti*, 2 vols (Florence: Olschki, 2008), pp. 425–40

Pasztor, Edith, 'Funzione politica-culturale di una struttura della Chiesa: il cardinalato', in *Aspetti culturali della società italiana nel periodo del papato avignonese* (Todi: Accademia Tudertina, 1981), pp. 197–226

Pfotenhauer, Paul, 'Schlesier auf der Universität Bologna', pt I, *Zeitschrift des Vereins für Geschichte und Altertumskunde Schlesiens*, 28 (1894), 433–46; pt II, vol. 29 (1895), 268–78

Piana, Celestino, *Nuovi documenti sull'università di Bologna e sul Collegio di Spagna*, 2 vols (Bologna: Real Colegio de España, 1976)

Pilvousek, Josef, *Die Prälaten des Kollegiatstiftes St. Marien in Erfurt von 1400–1555* (Leipzig: St. Benno, 1988)

Pitz, Ernst, 'Die römische Kurie als Thema der vergleichenden Sozialgeschichte', *Quellen und Forschungen aus italienischen Archiven und Bibliotheken*, 58 (1978), 216–359

———, *Supplikensignatur und Briefexpedition an der römischen Kurie im Pontifikat Papst Calixts III.* (Tübingen: Niemeyer, 1972)

Pleyer, Kleo, *Die Politik Nikolaus' V.* (Stuttgart: Kohlhammer, 1927)

Plöchl, Willibald, *Geschichte des Kirchenrechts*, II (Vienna: Herold, 1962²)

Porschnew, Boris, *Die Volksaufstände in Frankreich vor der Fronde 1623–1648* (Leipzig: Bibliographisches Institut, 1954)

Raab, Heribert, 'Aschaffenburg und das Wiener Konkordat', *Aschaffenburger Jahrbuch*, 4 (1957), 463–70

Rabikauskas, Paul, 'Cancellerie pontificale', in *Dictionnaire historique de la papauté* (Paris: Fayard, 2006), pp. 331–36

———, *Diplomatica Pontificia* (Rome: Universitas Gregoriana, 1998⁶)

## BIBLIOGRAPHY

Rapp, Francis, *L'Église et la vie religieuse en Occident à la fin du Moyen Âge* (Paris: Presses universitaires de France, 1971; 1980[2])

*Recht und Verfassung im Übergang vom Mittelalter zur Neuzeit*, I: *Bericht über Kolloquien zur Erforschung der Kultur des Spätmittelalters 1994 bis 1995*, ed. by Hartmut Boockmann, Ludger Grenzmann, Bernd Moeller, and Martin Staehelin (Göttingen: Vandenhoeck & Ruprecht, 1998)

Reinhard, Wolfgang, 'Ämterhandel in Rom zwischen 1534 and 1621', in *Ämterhandel im Spätmittelalter und im 16. Jahrhundert*, ed. by Ilja Mieck (Berlin: Colloqium, 1984), pp. 42–60

——, *Freunde und Kreaturen. 'Verflechtung' als Konzept zur Erforschung historischer Führungsgruppen. Römische Oligarchie um 1600* (Munich: Vögel, 1979); reprint, in Wolfgang Reinhard, *Ausgewählte Abhandlungen* (Berlin: Duncker & Humblot, 1997), pp. 289–310

——, 'Nepotismus', in *Handwörterbuch der Rechtsgeschichte*, vol. 3 (Berlin: Schmidt, 1984), pp. 947–51

——, 'Nepotismus. Der Funktionswandel einer papstgeschichtlichen Konstante', *Zeitschrift für Kirchengeschichte*, 86 (1975), 145–85

——, 'Papa Pius. Prolegomena zu einer Sozialgeschichte des Papsttums', in *Von Konstanz nach Trient. Beiträge zur Geschichte der Kirche von den Reformkonzilien bis zum Tridentinum. Festgabe für August Franzen*, ed. by Remigius Bäumer (Munich: Schöningh, 1972), pp. 261–99

——, 'Reformpapsttum zwischen Renaissance und Barock', in *Reformatio Ecclesiae. Beiträge zu kirchlichen Reformbemühungen von der Alten Kirche bis zur Neuzeit. Festgabe für Erwin Iserloh*, ed. by Remigius Bäumer (Paderborn: Schöningh, 1980), pp. 779–96

——, 'Staatsmacht als Kreditproblem. Zur Struktur und Funktion des frühneuzeitlichen Ämterhandels', *Vierteljahrschrift für Sozial- und Wirtschaftsgeschichte*, 61 (1974), 289–319

Renouard, Yves, 'Achats et paiements de draps flamands par les premiers papes d'Avignon de 1301 à 1346', *Mélanges d'archéologie et d'histoire de l'École française de Rome*, 52 (1935), 273–313; reprint, in Renouard, *Études d'histoire médiévale*, II, pp. 765–92

——, 'Comment les papes d'Avignon expédiaient leur courrier', *Revue historique*, 180 (1937), 1–29; reprint, in Renouard, *Études d'histoire médiévale*, II, pp. 739–64

——, *Études d'histoire médiévale*, 2 vols (Paris: École des Hautes Études en Sciences Sociales, 1968)

Rey-Courtel, Anne-Lise, 'L'entourage d'Anglic Grimoard, cardinal d'Albano (1366–1388)', in *Genèse et débuts du Grand Schisme d'Occident (1362–1394)*, ed. by Jean Favier (Paris: Centre Nationale des Recherches Scientifiques, 1980), pp. 59–64

——, 'Les clientèles des cardinaux limousins en 1378', *Mélanges de l'École française de Rome*, 89 (1977), pp. 889–944

Riesenberg, Peter, *Inalienability of Sovereignty in Medieval Political Thought* (New York: Columbia University Press, 1956)

Rittenbach, Willi, and Siegfried Seifert, *Geschichte der Bischöfe von Meißen 968–1581* (Leipzig: St. Benno, 1965)

Rius Serra, José, 'Catalanes y aragoneses en la corte de Calixto III', *Analecta Sacra Tarraconensia*, 3 (1927), 193–330

Roberg, Burkhard, *Das zweite Konzil von Lyon (1274)* (Paderborn: Schöningh, 1990)

——, 'Zur Überlieferung und Interpretation der Hauptquelle des Lugdunense I von 1245', *Annuarium Historiae Conciliorum*, 22 (1990), 31–67

Rodes, Robert, *Ecclesiastical Administration in Medieval England. The Anglo-Saxons to the Reformation* (Notre Dame/IN: Notre Dame University Press, 1977)

Rodocanachi, Emmanuel, 'Les courriers pontificaux du XIVᵉ au XVIIᵉ siècle', *Revue d'histoire diplomatique*, 26 (1912), 392–428

——, *Les institutions communales de Rome sous la papauté* (Paris: Picard, 1901)

Rogge, Jörg, 'Zum Verhältnis von Bischof und Domkapitel des Hochstifts Meißen im 14. und 15. Jahrhundert (1376–1518)', *Römische Quartalschrift*, 91 (1996), 182–206

Rollo-Koster, Joëlle, *Avignon and Its Papacy, 1309–1417: Popes, Institutions, and Society* (New York: Rowman & Littlefield, 2015)

Romani, Mario, *Pellegrini e viaggiatori nell'economia di Roma dal XIV al XVII secolo* (Milan: Vita e pensiero, 1948)

Rueß, Karl, *Die rechtliche Stellung der päpstlichen Legaten bis Bonifaz VIII.* (Paderborn: Schöningh, 1912)

Rusch, Borwin, *Die Behörden und Hofbeamten der päpstlichen Kurie des 13. Jahrhunderts* (Königsberg: Ost-Europa Verlag, 1936)

Rybicka-Adamska, Anna, 'Zbigniew ze Szczyrzyca, kanclerz Władysława Łokietka i Kazimierza Wielkiego', *Nasza Przeszłość*, 78 (1992), 151–66

Sägmüller, Johann, *Lehrbuch des katholischen Kirchenrechts* (Freiburg/Br.: Herder, 1904)

Sailler, Gerhard, 'Papsturkunden in Portugal von 1198 bis 1304', in *Das begrenzte Papsttum. Spielräume päpstlichen Handelns. Legaten – delegierte Richter – Grenzen*, ed. by Klaus Herbers and Frank Engel (Berlin: De Gruyter, 2014), pp. 83–104

——, 'Papsturkunden in Portugal von 1198 bis 1304. Ein Beitrag zum Censimento' (unpublished doctoral thesis, University of Vienna, 2008)

Salmon, John, 'Venality of Office and Popular Sedition in Seventeenth-Century France: A Review of the Controversy', *Past and Present*, 37 (1967), 21–43

Salonen, Kirsi, and Ludwig Schmugge, *A Sip from the 'Well of Grace': Medieval Texts from the Apostolic Penitentiary* (Washington, DC: Catholic University of America Press, 2009)

—, *Papal Justice in the Late Middle Ages: The Sacra Romana Rota* (London: Routledge, 2016)

Samaran, Charles, and Guillaume Mollat, *La fiscalité pontificale en France au XIV^e siècle. Période d'Avignon et Grand Schisme d'Occident* (Paris: Fontemoing, 1905)

Samulski, Robert, *Untersuchungen über die persönliche Zusammensetzung des Breslauer Domkapitels im Mittelalter bis zum Tode des Bischofs Nanker (1341)* (Weimar: Böhlau, 1940)

Sanfilippo, Isa, *La Roma dei romani. Arti, mestieri e professioni nella Roma del Trecento* (Rome: Istituto storico italiano per il Medio Evo, 2001)

Sawicki, Jakub, 'Ze studiów nad konstytucjami wrocławskimi biskupa Nankera (1327–1331)', *Sobótka*, 16 (1961), 567–97, 636

Scheyhing, Rudolf, *Amtsgewalt und Bannleihe. Eine Untersuchung zur Bannleihe im hohen und späten Mittelalter* (Cologne: Böhlau, 1960)

Schimmelpfennig, Bernhard, *Das Papsttum. Grundzüge seiner Geschichte von der Antike bis zur Renaissance* (Darmstadt: Wissenschaftliche Buchgesellschaft, 1984; 1996[5]); English version in *The Papacy*, trans. by James Sievert (New York: Columbia University Press, 1992)

—, 'Das Papsttum im hohen Mittelalter: Eine Institution?', in *Institutionen und Geschichte. Theoretische Aspekte und mittelalterliche Befunde*, ed. by Gerd Melville (Cologne: Böhlau, 1992), pp. 209–30

—, 'Der Ämterkauf an der römischen Kurie von Pius II. bis zum Sacco di Roma (1458–1527)', in *Ämterhandel im Spätmittelalter und im 16. Jahrhundert*, ed. by Ilja Mieck (Berlin: Colloquium, 1984), pp. 3–41

—, 'Die Funktion des Papstpalastes und der kurialen Gesellschaft im päpstlichen Zeremoniell vor und während des Schismas', in *Genèse et débuts du Grand Schisme d'Occident (1362–1394)*, ed. by Jean Favier (Paris: Centre Nationale des Recherches Scientifiques, 1980), pp. 317–28

—, 'Die Krönung des Papstes im Mittelalter, dargestellt am Beispiel der Krönung Pius' II. (5.IX.1458)', *Quellen und Forschungen aus italienischen Archiven und Bibliotheken*, 54 (1974), 192–270

—, *Die Zeremonienbücher der römischen Kirche im Mittelalter* (Tübingen: Niemeyer, 1973)

Schmidt, Tillmann, 'Das *factum Bonifatianum* auf dem Konzil von Vienne (1311/1312)', in *Forschungen zur Rechts-, Papst- und Landesgeschichte. Peter Herde zum 65. Geburtstag dargebracht*, ed. by Knut Borchardt and Enno Bünz (Stuttgart: Hiersemann, 1998), pp. 623–33

—, 'Das päpstliche Kursorenkollegium und seine Statuten von 1306', *Deutsches Archiv für die Erforschung des Mittelalters*, 50 (1994), 581–601

—, *Der Bonifaz-Prozess. Verfahren der Papstanklage in der Zeit Bonifaz' VIII. und Clemens' V.* (Cologne: Böhlau, 1989)

Schmitz, Marianne, *Lebens- und Arbeitsweise zweier südfranzösischer Kollektoren in der ersten Hälfte des 14. Jahrhunderts in England* (Frankfurt/M.: Lang, 1993)

Schmugge, Ludwig, 'Kanonistik und Pönitentiarie', in *Stagnation oder Fortbildung? Aspekte des allgemeinen Kirchenrechts im 14. und 15. Jahrhundert*, ed. by Martin Bertram (Tübingen: Niemeyer, 2005), pp. 93–116

Schreiner, Peter, 'Dauer, Niedergang und Erneuerung klösterlicher Observanz im hoch- und spätmittelalterlichen Mönchtum', in *Institutionen und Geschichte. Theoretische Aspekte und mittelalterliche Befunde*, ed. by Gerd Melville (Cologne: Böhlau, 1992), pp. 295–342

Schuchard, Christiane, 'Brigide Schwarz (1940–2019)', *Blätter für deutsche Landesgeschichte*, 155 (2019), 739–46

——, *Die Deutschen an der päpstlichen Kurie im späten Mittlelalter (1378–1447)* (Tübingen: Niemeyer, 1987)

——, *Die päpstlichen Kollektoren im späten Mittelalter* (Tübingen: Niemeyer, 2000)

——, 'Zu den Rotanotaren im 15. und frühen 16. Jahrhundert', in *Offices et papauté (XIVᵉ–XVIIᵉ siècle). Charges, hommes, destins*, ed. by Armand Jamme and Olivier Poncet (Rome: École française de Rome, 2005), pp. 805–25

——, 'Lübecker und Hamburger Interessenvertreter an der päpstlichen Kurie im 14. und 15. Jahrhundert', in *Der Kaufmann und der liebe Gott. Zu Kommerz und Kirche in Mittelalter und Früher Neuzeit*, ed. by Antjekathrin Graßmann (Trier: Porta Alba, 2009), pp. 89–111

Schuller, Wolfgang, 'Ämterkauf im Römischen Reich', *Der Staat*, 19 (1980), 57–71

——, 'Probleme historischer Korruptionsforschung', *Der Staat*, 16 (1977), 373–92

Schulte, Wilhelm, *Die politische Tendenz der 'Chronica principum Polonie'* (Breslau: Wolfarth, 1906)

Schwarz, Brigide, '*Abbreviature officium est assistere vicecancellario in expeditione litterarum apostolicarum*. Zur Entwicklung des Abbreviatorenamtes vom Großen Schisma bis zur Gründung des Vakabilistenkollegs der Abbreviatoren durch Pius II.', in *Römische Kurie. Kirchliche Finanzen. Vatikanisches Archiv. Studien zu Ehren von Hermann Hoberg* (Rome: Universitas Gregoriana, 1979), pp. 789–823

——, *Alle Wege führen über Rom. Beziehungsgeflecht und Karrieren von Klerikern aus Hannover im Spätmittelalter* (Göttingen: Wallstein, 2021)

——, 'Alle Wege führen über Rom. Eine "Seilschaft" von Klerikern aus Hannover im späten Mittelalter', *Hannoversche Geschichtsblätter*, 52 (1998), 5–87

——, 'Ämterkäuflichkeit', in *Lexikon des Mittelalters*, vol. 1 (Munich: Artemis, 1978), cols 561–62

——, 'Ämterkäuflichkeit, eine Institution des Absolutismus und ihre mittelalterlichen Wurzeln', in *Staat und Gesellschaft in Mittelalter und Früher Neuzeit. Gedenkschrift für Joachim Leuschner* (Göttingen: Vandenhoeck & Ruprecht, 1983), pp. 176–96 (English version above, pp. 000–000)

—, 'Anselmus Fabri (Smit) aus Breda in Brabant (1379–1449), Abbreviator, Referendar, Protonotar und – beinahe – Kardinal. Skizze einer Biographie', *Quellen und Forschungen aus italienischen Archiven und Bibliotheken*, 88 (2008), 161–219

—, 'Corrector litterarum apostolicarum', in *Lexikon des Mittelalters*, vol. 3 (Munich: Artemis, 1984), cols 278–79

—, 'Das Bistum Verden und die römische Kurie im Spätmittelalter', in *Immunität und Landesherrschaft. Beiträge zur Geschichte des Bistums Verden im Mittelalter*, ed. by Bernd Kappelhoff and Thomas Vogtherr (Stade: Landschaftsverband, 2002), pp. 107–74

—, 'Das Repertorium Germanicum. Eine Einführung', *Vierteljahrschrift für Sozial- und Wirtschaftsgeschichte*, 90 (2003), 429–40

—, 'Der *corrector litterarum apostolicarum*. Entwicklung des Korrektorenamtes der päpstlichen Kanzlei von Innozenz III. bis Martin V.', *Quellen und Forschungen aus italienischen Archiven und Bibliotheken*, 54 (1974), 122–91

—, 'Die Abbreviatoren unter Eugen IV. Päpstliches Reservationsrecht, Konkordatspolitik und kuriale Ämterorganisationen (mit 2 Anhängen: Konkordate Eugens IV.; Aufstellung der Bewerber)', *Quellen und Forschungen aus italienischen Archiven und Bibliotheken*, 60 (1980), 200–74

—, 'Die Bemühungen Leon Battista Albertis, einen standesgemäßen Pfründenbesitz aufzubauen: Die kurialen Quellen', in *Trier-Mainz-Rom. Stationen, Wirkungsfelder, Netzwerke. Festschrift für Michael Matheus*, ed. by Anna Esposito, Heidrun Ochs, Elmar Rettinger, and Kai-Michael Sprenger (Regensburg: Schnell & Steiner, 2013), pp. 237–66

—, 'Die Erforschung der mittelalterlichen römischen Kurie von Ludwig Quidde bis heute', in *Friedensnobelpreis und Grundlagenforschung. Ludwig Quidde und die Erschließung der kurialen Registerüberlieferung*, ed. by Michael Matheus (Berlin: De Gruyter, 2011), pp. 415–39

—, 'Die Exemtion des Bistums Meißen, 1399', *Savigny-Zeitschrift für Rechtsgeschichte – Kanonistische Abteilung*, 86 (2001), 294–361

—, 'Die Karriere Leon Battista Albertis in der päpstlichen Kanzlei', *Quellen und Forschungen aus italienischen Archiven und Bibliotheken*, 93 (2013), 49–103 (English version above, pp. 000–000)

—, 'Die Korporationen der Schreiberkollegien an der päpstlichen Kurie', in *'Eure Namen sind im Buch des Lebens geschrieben'. Antike und mittelalterliche Quellen als Grundlage prosopographischer Forschung*, ed. by Rainer Berndt (Münster/W.: Aschendorff, 2014), pp. 307–18

—, *Die Organisation kurialer Schreiberkollegien von ihrer Entstehung bis zur Mitte des 15. Jahrhunderts* (Tübingen: Niemeyer, 1972)

———, 'Die römische Kurie im Zeitalter des Schismas und der Reformkonzilien', in *Institutionen und Geschichte. Theoretische Aspekte und mittelalterliche Befunde*, ed. by Gerd Melville (Cologne: Böhlau, 1992), pp. 231–58 (English translation above, pp. 000–000)

———, 'Die Stiftskirche St. Galli in Hannover. Eine bürgerliche Stiftung des Spätmittelalters', pt I, *Niedersächsisches Jahrbuch*, 68 (1996), 107–35; pt II, vol. 69 (1997), 185–227

———, 'Dispense der Kanzlei Eugens IV. (1431–1447)', in *Illegitimität im Spätmittelalter*, ed. by Ludwig Schmugge (Munich: Oldenbourg, 1994), pp. 133–47

———, 'Ein Freund italienischer Kaufleute im Norden? Berthold Rike, Dompropst von Lübeck und Domkustos von Breslau (gestorben 1436). Zugleich ein Beispiel für die Nutzung des Repertorium Germanicum für eine Biographie', in *Italia et Germania. Liber amicorum Arnold Esch*, ed. by Hagen Keller, Werner Paravicini, and Wolfgang Schieder (Tübingen: Niemeyer, 2001), pp. 447–67

———, 'Ein "Schülerulk" mit Folgen. Über die Beziehungen zwischen der Stadt und der Domkirche Hildesheim zu Ende des 13. Jahrhunderts', *Die Diözese Hildesheim in Vergangenheit und Gegenwart*, 66 (1998), 1–35

———, 'Eine "Seilschaft" von Klerikern aus Hannover im Spätmittelalter', *Quellen und Forschungen aus italienischen Archiven und Bibliotheken*, 81 (2001), 256–77 (English version above, pp. 000–000)

———, 'Ergänzungen und Berichtigungen zu meinen Regesten der Papsturkunden in Niedersachsen', *Niedersächsisches Jahrbuch*, 75 (2003), 333–46

———, 'Hannoveraner in Braunschweig. Die Karrieren von Johann Ember (gestorben 1423) und Hermann Pentel (gestorben 1463)', *Braunschweigisches Jahrbuch*, 80 (1999), 9–54

———, 'Hannoversche Bürgersöhne im adeligen Domkapitel von Hildesheim. Das Beispiel des Arnold von Hesede (gestorben nach 1476)', *Die Diözese Hildesheim in Vergangenheit und Gegenwart*, 67 (1999), 77–109

———, 'Im Auftrag des Papstes. Die päpstlichen Kursoren von ca. 1200 bis 1470', in *Päpste, Pilger, Pönitentiarie. Festschrift für Ludwig Schmugge zum 65. Geburtstag*, ed. by Andreas Meyer, Constanze Rendtel, and Maria Widmer-Butsch (Tübingen: Niemeyer, 2004), pp. 49–71 (English version above, pp. 000–000)

———, 'Karrieren von Klerikern aus Hannover im nordwestdeutschen Raum in der 1. Hälfte des 15. Jahrhunderts', *Niedersächsisches Jahrbuch*, 73 (2001), 235–70

———, 'Klerikerkarrieren und Pfründenmarkt. Perspektiven einer sozialgeschichtlichen Auswertung des Repertorium Germanicum', *Quellen und Forschungen aus italienischen Archiven und Bibliotheken*, 71 (1991), 243–65

——, 'Kurie, römische, im Mittelalter', in *Theologische Real-Enzyklopädie*, vol. 20 (Berlin: De Gruyter, 1990), pp. 343–47

——, *Kurienuniversität und stadtrömische Universität von ca. 1300 bis 1471* (Leiden: Brill, 2013)

——, 'Leon Battista Alberti in der *familia* des Regens der päpstlichen Kanzlei, Blasius de Molino (April 1431 bis Ende 1435)', *Zeitschrift für Kirchengeschichte*, 125 (2015), 169–97

——, 'Les courriers pontificaux du XIII$^e$ au XV$^e$ siècle (vers 1200–vers 1470)', in *Offices et papauté (XIV$^e$–XVII$^e$ siècle). Charges, hommes, destins*, ed. by Armand Jamme and Olivier Poncet (Rome: École française de Rome, 2005), pp. 647–50

——, 'L'organizzazione curiale di Martino V ed i problemi derivanti dallo Schisma', in *Alle origini della Nuova Roma: Martino V (1417–1431)*, ed. by Maria Chiabò, Giusi d'Alessandro, Paola Piacentini, and Concetta Ranieri (Rome: Istituto storico italiano per il Medio Evo, 1992), pp. 329–45

——, 'Norddeutschland und die römische Kurie im späten Mittelalter (1200–1450): Probleme der Kommunikation', in *The Penitentiary, the Curia and the Local Context in the Later Middle Ages*, ed. by Christian Krötzl and Kirsi Salonen (Rome: Institutum Romanum Finlandiae, 2003), pp. 3–22

——, 'Nutzungsmöglichkeiten des Repertorium Germanicum für die Kanonistik', in *Stagnation oder Fortbildung? Aspekte des allgemeinen Kirchenrechts im 14. und 15. Jahrhundert*, ed. by Martin Bertram (Tübingen: Niemeyer, 2005), pp. 65–91

——, 'Patronage und Klientel in der spätmittelalterlichen Kirche', *Quellen und Forschungen aus italienischen Archiven und Bibliotheken*, 68 (1988), 284–310 (English version above, pp. 000–000)

——, 'Prälaten aus Hannover im spätmittelalterlichen Livland: Dietrich Nagel, Dompropst von Riga (gestorben Ende 1468/Anfang 1469), Ludolf Nagel, Domdekan von Ösel, Verweser von Reval (gestorben nach 1477)', *Zeitschrift für Ostmitteleuropa-Forschung*, 49 (2000), 495–532

——, 'Rolle und Rang des (Vize)-Kanzlers an der Kurie', in *Papstgeschichte im digitalen Zeitalter*, ed. by Klaus Herbers and Viktoria Trenkle (Cologne: Böhlau, 2018), pp. 171–90 (English version above, pp. 000–000)

——, 'Römische Kurie und Pfründenmarkt im Spätmittelalter', *Zeitschrift für historische Forschung*, 20 (1993), 129–52 (English version above, pp. 000–000)

——, 'Supplik', in *Lexikon für Theologie und Kirche*, vol. 9 (Freiburg/Br.: Herder, 2000³), cols 1136–37

——, 'The Roman Curia (until about 1300)', in *The History of Courts and Procedure in Medieval Canon Law*, ed. by Winfried Hartmann and Kenneth Pennington (Washington, DC: Catholic University of America Press, 2016), pp. 160–228

————, 'Volkmar von Anderten, (Mit-)Begründer der Ratsbibliothek Hannover, Domherr und Offizial von Lübeck (gestorben 1481)', *Wolfenbütteler Notizen zur Buchgeschichte*, 24/2 (1999), 117–31

————, 'Vom Nutzen des vatikanischen Archivmaterials für die Landesgeschichte, dargestellt an sächsischen Beispielen', in *Diplomatische Forschungen in Mitteldeutschland*, ed. by Tom Graber (Leipzig: Universitätsverlag, 2005), pp. 197–235 (English version above, pp. 000–000)

————, 'Who Studied (and Taught) at the University of the Roman Curia and Why? A Prosopographic Approach', in *L'università in tempo di crisi. Revisioni e novità dei saperi e delle istituzioni nel Trecento, da Bologna all'Europa*, ed. by Berardo Pio and Riccardo Parmeggiani (Bologna: Clueb, 2016), pp. 103–24

————, 'Zwei Lüner Pröpste aus Hannover im 15. Jahrhundert: Konrad von Sarstedt (gestorben 1400) und Dietrich Schaper (gestorben 1466)', *Jahrbuch der Gesellschaft für niedersächsische Kirchengeschichte*, 97 (1999), 7–53

Schwarz, Ulrich, 'Ludolf Quirre (gestorben 1436). Eine Karriere zwischen Hannover, Braunschweig und Halberstadt', *Braunschweigisches Jahrbuch*, 75 (1994), 29–72

————, 'Petenten, Pfründen und die Kurie. Norddeutsche Beispiele aus dem Repertorium Germanicum', *Blätter für deutsche Landesgeschichte*, 133 (1997), 1–21

Schwinges, Rainer, 'Europäische Studenten des späten Mittelalters', in *Die Universität in Alteuropa*, ed. by Alexander Patschovsky and Horst Rabe (Constance: Universitätsverlag, 1994), pp. 129–64

Sciuti Russi, Vittorio, 'Aspetti della venalità degli uffici in Sicilia (secoli XVII–XVIII)', *Rivista storica italiana*, 88 (1976), 342–55

Segrè, Arturo, 'I dispacci di Cristoforo da Piacenza, procuratore mantovano alla corte pontificia (1371–1383)', pt I, *Archivio storico italiano*, 43 (1909), 27–95; pt II, vol. 44 (1909), 253–326

Sellert, Wolfgang, 'Zur Rezeption des römischen und kanonischen Rechts in Deutschland von den Anfängen bis zum Beginn der frühen Neuzeit. Überblick, Diskussionsstand und Ergebnisse', in *Recht und Verfassung im Übergang vom Mittelalter zur Neuzeit*, I: *Bericht über Kolloquien zur Erforschung der Kultur des Spätmittelalters 1994 bis 1995*, ed. by Hartmut Boockmann, Ludger Grenzmann, Bernd Moeller, and Martin Staehelin (Göttingen: Vandenhoeck & Ruprecht, 1998), pp. 115–66

Silnicki, Tadeusz, *Biskup Nanker* (Warsaw: Pax, 1953)

Sohn, Andreas, *Deutsche Prokuratoren an der römischen Kurie in der Frührenaissance (1431–1474)* (Cologne: Böhlau, 1997)

————, 'Procuratori tedeschi alla Curia romana intorno alla metà del Quattrocento', in *Roma capitale (1447–1527)*, ed. by Sergio Gensini (Rome: Ministero per i beni culturali, 1994), pp. 493–504

*Stagnation oder Fortbildung? Aspekte des allgemeinen Kirchenrechts im 14. und 15. Jahrhundert*, ed. by Martin Bertram (Tübingen: Niemeyer, 2005)

Steffen, Walter, *Die studentische Autonomie im mittelalterlichen Bologna. Eine Untersuchung über die Stellung der Studenten und ihrer Universitas gegenüber Professoren und Stadtregierung im 13./14. Jahrhundert* (Berne: Lang, 1981)

Stelzer, Winfried, 'Über Vermerke der beiden *Audientiae* auf Papsturkunden in der zweiten Hälfte des 13. Jahrhunderts', *Mitteilungen der Österreichischen Gesellschaft für Geschichtsforschung*, 78 (1970), 308–22

Stieber, Joachim, *Pope Eugenius, the Council of Basel and the Secular and Ecclesiastical Authorities in the Empire: The Conflict over Supreme Authority and Power in the Church* (Leiden: Brill, 1978)

Stocker, Christopher, 'Office as Maintenance in Renaissance France', *Canadian Journal of History*, 6 (1971), 21–44

Strandberg, Carl, *Zur Frage des Veräußerungsverbotes im kirchlichen und weltlichen Recht des Mittelalters* (Stockholm: Nordiska, 1967)

Streich, Brigitte, 'Die Bistümer Merseburg, Naumburg, Meißen zwischen Reichsstandschaft und Landsässigkeit', in *Mitteldeutsche Bistümer im Spätmittelalter*, ed. by Roderich Schmidt (Lüneburg: Nordostdeutsches Kulturwerk, 1988), pp. 53–72

——, *Zwischen Reiseherrschaft und Residenzbildung. Der wettinische Hof im späten Mittelalter* (Cologne: Böhlau, 1989)

Strzelczyk, Jerzy, 'Auf der Suche nach der nationalen Identität im Mittelalter. Der Fall Polen', in *Das europäische Mittelalter im Spannungsbogen des Vergleichs. Zwanzig internationale Beiträge zu Praxis, Problemen und Perspektiven der historischen Komparatistik*, ed. by Michael Borgolte (Berlin: Akademie, 2001), pp. 359–69

Strnad, Alfred, '*In grossem Irsail* .... Streit um das Bistum Trient, 1419–1423', *Tiroler Heimat*, 57 (1993), 57–78

Studt, Birgit, '*Tamquam organum nostre mentis*. Das Sekretariat als publizistisches Zentrum der päpstlichen Außenwirkung', in *Kurie und Region. Festschrift für Brigide Schwarz zum 65. Geburtstag*, ed. by Brigitte Flug, Michael Matheus, and Andreas Rehberg (Stuttgart: Steiner, 2005), pp. 73–92

Stump, Phillip, *The Reforms of the Council of Constance (1414–1418)* (Leiden: Brill, 1994)

Suhle, Arthur, 'Die Besetzung der deutschen Bistümer unter Papst Johann XXII. (1316–1334)' (unpublished doctoral thesis, Humboldt-University of Berlin, 1921)

Sułkowska-Kuraś, Irena, and Stanisław Kuraś, 'La Pologne et la papauté d'Avignon', in *Le fonctionnement administrative de la papauté d'Avignon. Aux origines de l'état moderne* (Rome: École française de Rome, 1990), pp. 113–33

Sullivan, Donald, 'Nicholas of Cusa as Reformer: The Papal Legation to the Germanies', *Mediaeval Studies*, 26 (1974), 382–428

Swart, Koenraad, *Sale of Offices in the Eighteenth Century* (The Hague: Nijhoff, 1949)

Szczur, Stanisław, 'Dyplomaci Kazimierza Wielkiego w Awinionie', *Nasza Przeszłość*, 66 (1986), 43–107

Szewczyk, Wilhelm, and Jan Malicki, *Nanker: dialogi wrocławskie z roku 1339 w trzech odsłonach* (Katowice: Biblioteka Śląska, 1996)

Teige, Josef, 'Beiträge zum päpstlichen Kanzleiwesen des 13. und 14. Jahrhunderts', *Mitteilungen des Österreichischen Instituts für Geschichtsforschung*, 17 (1896), 408–40

Tewes, Götz-Rüdiger, *Die römische Kurie und die europäischen Länder am Vorabend der Reformation* (Tübingen: Niemeyer, 2001)

Thomson, John, *Popes and Princes, 1417–1517: Politics and Polity in the Late Medieval Church* (London: Allen & Unwin, 1980)

Tihon, Camille, 'Les expectatives *in forma pauperum* particulierement au XIVe siècle', *Bulletin de l'Institut historique belge de Rome*, 5 (1925), 51–118

Tomás y Valiente, Francisco, 'Origen bajo medieval de la patrimonialización y la enajenación de oficios públicos en Castilla', in *Actas del I Symposium de historia de la administración* (Madrid: Instituto de Estudios Administrativos, 1970), pp. 123–59

Tüchle, Hermann, 'Abendländisches Schisma', in *Lexikon des Mittelalters*, vol. 1 (Munich: Artemis, 1980), cols 19–22

Ulbrich, Tobias, *Päpstliche Provision oder patronatsherrliche Präsentation? Der Pfründenerwerb Bamberger Weltgeistlicher im 15. Jahrhundert* (Husum: Matthiesen, 1998)

Ullmann, Walter, *Principles of Government and Politics in the Middle Ages* (London: Methuen, 1978[4])

Urban, Wincenty, 'De testimoniis vitam Nankeri episcopi Wratislaviensis illustrantibus', *Collectanea theologicae societatis theologorum Poloniae cura edita*, 26 (1955), 250–86

van den Hoven van Genderen, Bram, *De Heren van de Kerk. De kanunniken van Oudmunster te Utrecht in de late middeleeuwen* (Zutphen: Pers, 1997)

Vansteenberghe, Edmond, *Le cardinal Nicolas de Cues (1401–1464). L'action – la pensée* (Paris: Champion, 1920; reprint, Frankfurt/M.: Minerva, 1963; reprint, Geneva: Slatkine, 1974)

Verger, Jean, 'L'entourage du cardinal Pierre de Monteruc (1354–1385)', *Mélanges de l'École française de Rome*, 85 (1973), 515–46

Vogtherr, Thomas, 'Die Kanzler der Wettiner (um 1350–1485). Bemerkungen zu ihrer Auswahl, ihrer Tätigkeit und ihren Karrieren', in *Diplomatische Forschungen in Mitteldeutschland*, ed. by Tom Graber (Leipzig: Universitätsverlag, 2005), pp. 185–95

von Brunn, genannt von Kaufungen, Kunz, 'Das Domkapitel von Meißen im Mittelalter', *Mitteilungen des Vereins für Geschichte der Stadt Meißen*, 6 (1907), 121–53

von Hofmann, Walther, 'Über den *corrector litterarum apostolicarum*', *Römische Quartalschrift*, 20 (1906), 91–96

———, *Forschungen zur Geschichte der kurialen Behörden vom Schisma bis zur Reformation*, 2 vols (Rome: Loescher, 1914)

von Mitis, Oskar, 'Zwei Amtsbücher aus der Kammer Martins V.', *Mitteilungen des Österreichischen Instituts für Geschichtsforschung*, 6 (1901), 413–48

von Ottenthal, Emil, 'Die Bullenregister Martins V. und Eugens IV.', in *Mitteilungen des Österreichischen Instituts für Geschichtsforschung – Ergänzungsband*, 1 (1885), 401–589

von Stromer, Wolfgang, *Oberdeutsche Hochfinanz 1350–1450* (Wiesbaden: Steiner, 1970)

Watanabe, Morimichi, 'The Episcopal Election of 1430 in Trier and Nicholas of Cusa', *Church History*, 39 (1970), 299–316

Weber, Christoph, *Familienkanonikate und Patronatsbistümer. Ein Beitrag zur Geschichte von Adel und Klerus im neuzeitlichen Italien* (Berlin: Duncker & Humblot, 1988)

Weber, Max, *Wirtschaft und Gesellschaft. Grundriß der verstehenden Soziologie* (Frankfurt/M.: Zweitausendeins, 2010)

———, *Wirtschaft und Gesellschaft. Grundriß der verstehenden Soziologie*, ed. by Johannes Winckelmann (Tübingen: Mohr, 1976)

Weiss, Sabine 'Kurie, Konzil und Kirchenreform. Salzburg und seine Eigenbistümer im Bannkreis von Papalismus und Konziliarismus' (unpublished thesis of *Habilitation*, University of Innsbruck, 1987)

———, *Kurie und Ortskirche. Die Beziehungen zwischen Salzburg und dem päpstlichen Hof unter Martin V. (1417–1431)* (Tübingen: Niemeyer, 1994)

Weiß, Stefan, *Die Versorgung des päpstlichen Hofes in Avignon mit Lebensmitteln (1316–1378). Studien zur Sozial- und Wirtschaftsgeschichte eines mittelalterlichen Hofes* (Berlin: Duncker & Humblot, 2002)

———, 'The Curia: Camera', in *A Companion to the Medieval Papacy: Growth of an Ideology and Institution*, ed. by Atria Larson and Keith Sisson (Leiden: Brill, 2016), pp. 220–38

Wendehorst, Alfred, *Das Würzburger Landkapitel Coburg zur Zeit der Reformation* (Göttingen: Vandenhoeck & Ruprecht, 1964)

———, 'Gregor von Heimburg', in *Fränkische Lebensbilder*, IV, ed. by Gerhard Pfeiffer (Würzburg: Gesellschaft für fränkische Geschichte, 1971), pp. 112–29

———, 'Zum Itinerar des Kardinals Nikolaus Cusanus 1451', in *Festschrift Friedrich Hausmann*, ed. by Herwig Ebner (Graz: Akademische Druck- und Verlagsanstalt, 1977), pp. 553–58

Werner, Matthias, 'Johannes Kapistran in Jena', in *Studien zum 15. Jahrhundert. Festschrift für Erich Meuthen*, ed. by Heribert Müller and Johannes Helmrath, 2 vols (Munich: Oldenbourg, 1994), I, pp. 505–20

Wiggenhauser, Béatrice, *Klerikale Karrieren. Das ländliche Chorherrenstift Embrach und seine Mitglieder im Mittelalter* (Zurich: Chronos, 1997)

Willich, Thomas, 'Wege zur Pfründe. Die Besetzung Magdeburger Domkanonikate zwischen ordentlicher Kollatur und päpstlicher Provision (1295–1464)' (unpublished doctoral thesis, University of Innsbruck, 2001)

————, *Wege zur Pfründe. Die Besetzung Magdeburger Domdekanate zwischen ordentlicher Kollatur und päpstlicher Provision (1295–1464)* (Tübingen: Niemeyer, 2005)

Willoweit, Dietmar, 'Die Entstehung exemter Bistümer im deutschen Reichsverband unter rechtsvergleichender Berücksichtigung ausländischer Parallelen', *Savigny-Zeitschrift für Rechtsgeschichte – Kanonistische Abteilung*, 52 (1966), pp. 176–298

Young, Francis, 'Fundamental Changes in the Nature of the Cardinalate in the Fifteenth Century and Their Reflection in the Election of Pope Alexander VI' (unpublished doctoral thesis, University of Maryland, 1983)

Zacour, Norman, 'Papal Regulations of Cardinal's Households in the Fourteenth Century', *Speculum*, 50 (1975), 434–55

Zani, Karl, 'Neues zu Predigten des Kardinals Cusanus, "ettlich zu teutsch"', *Der Schlern*, 59 (1985), 111–15, 620–21

Zieschang, Rudolf, 'Die Anfänge eines landesherrlichen Kirchenregiments in Sachsen am Ausgang des Mittelalters', *Beiträge zur sächsischen Kirchengeschichte*, 23 (1910), 1–156

Zutshi, Patrick, 'Innocent and the Reform of the Papal Chancery', in *Innocenzo III. Urbs et Orbis*, ed. by Andrea Sommerlechner, 2 vols (Rome: Istituto storico italiano per il Medio Evo, 2003), I, pp. 84–101

————, 'Petitions to the Pope in the Fourteenth Century', in *Medieval Petitions, Grace, and Grievance*, ed. by William Ormrod, Gwilym Dodd, and Anthony Musson (Woodbridge: York Medieval Press, 2008), pp. 82–98

————, 'Proctors Acting for English Petitioners in the Chancery of the Avignonese Popes (1305–1378)', *The Journal of Ecclesiastical History*, 35 (1984), 15–29

————, *The Avignon Popes and Their Chancery: Collected Essays* (Florence: Sismel, 2021)

————, 'The Office of Notary in the Papal Chancery in the Mid-Fourteenth Century', in *Forschungen zur Rechts-, Papst- und Landesgeschichte. Peter Herde zum 65. Geburtstag dargebracht*, ed. by Knut Borchardt and Enno Bünz (Stuttgart: Hiersemann, 1998), II, pp. 665–83

————, 'The Origins of the Registration of Petitions in the Papal Chancery in the First Half of the Fourteenth Century', in *Suppliques et requêtes. Le gouvernement par la grace en Occident (XII<sup>e</sup>–XV<sup>e</sup> siècle)*, ed. by Hélène Millet (Rome: École française de Rome, 2003), pp. 177–91

————, 'The Papal Chancery: Avignon and Beyond', in Zutshi, *The Avignon Popes*, pp. 3–24

# General Index

Aachen: 46 n. 93, 56 n. 39, 58 n. 53
abbreviators: 20, 32, 38–39, 68, 95,
    111, 130 n. 57, 168 n. 76, 193 n.
    105, 223–36, 238–51, 253, 255,
    258, 262, 264, 268–70, 280–81
absenteeism: 17, 41, 208
absolutions: 44 n. 83, 55 n. 33, 90, 99,
    146
Absolutism: 157–58, 161, 167
Alberti, Leon Battista: 233–62
Albrecht Achilles of Hohenzollern:
    137 n. 75
Alessandria: 230
Alexander (V), pope (1409–10): 213
    n. 55, 237 n. 108, 267 n. 23
Alexander of Masowia: 141
alienations: 89 n. 38, 92 n. 52, 99,
    164, 169
altars, portable: 43, 62, 135, 139
Altenburg: 138, 143–44
Altrich: 52, 58 n. 53
Altzelle: 123
Andreas
    Colonus: 140 n. 85
    de Palazago: 231 n. 59
    Tinacius de Verulis: 88 n. 31, 93
        n. 57, 95–97, 102 n. 94, 114
annates: 21, 34–35, 39 n. 61, 63 n. 80,
    97–98, 129–30, 132, 138 n. 77,
    181 n. 27, 269
Annibaldo de Ceccano: 114
Anselmus Fabri de Breda: 244
Antonius de Nepe: 230 n. 56
appeals, judicial: 54 n. 30, 165, 207 n.
    25
Aquileia: 140 n. 85, 272 n. 54

Aragon: 160, 167
archbishops: 41, 46 n. 93, 49–54, 56–
    57, 85–86, 88–92, 100–01, 107 n.
    112, 113, 131, 141 n. 85, 143–45,
    147–48, 180 n. 22, 201–02, 210
    n. 39
*arenga*: 142
Arnaldus de Canteloup: 202
Arnaud d'Aux: 97
Arnold
    of Hesede: 67, 72, 78
    of Zwrócona (Protzan): 106,
        111–12
Arnošt of Pardubice: 113
Audience (*Audientia*): 186–90, 192,
    241 n. 130, 248 n. 185, 255–59,
    262, 264 n. 6, 266–69, 271 n. 49,
    281
    of Contradictory Letters
        (*Audientia litterarum
        contradictarum*): 185 n. 52,
        221 n. 91, 227, 231 n. 62, 234
        n. 81, 237, 242, 248, 254–58,
        261 n. 266, 264 n. 6, 274
    *see also* Rota
Augsburg: 63, 141 n. 85
Austria: 148, 276
Avignon: 17, 88, 91–92, 95–98, 108,
    110, 113, 177, 179 n. 17, 183, 186
    n. 64, 192 n. 102, 198, 214–16,
    256
    St Agricola: 113 n. 148

B. de Capranica: 230 n. 56
Baest, Nicolaus: 58 n. 54
Balduinus of Dijck: 39 n. 64

## GENERAL INDEX

Baldus de Ubaldis: 163
Bamberg: 142, 145
banks: 69, 74, 213
   *see also* Medici
Bartholomeus de Puteo
   *see* dal Pozzo, Bartolomeo
Bartholomeus of Bibra: 128, 140
Basel, Council of: 17, 40, 44–46, 49
   n. 4, 54–57, 70–73, 76–78, 124 n.
   29, 132–34, 136, 179 n. 11, 184,
   191, 197, 219 n. 84, 238 n. 110,
   250, 257 n. 241, 272 n. 53
Bautzen: 122, 138 n. 78, 140–41, 150,
   152,
Bavaria: 148
Bazmer: 108 n. 112
Beaune: 214 n. 62
Benedict XI, pope (1303–04): 202,
   204
Benedict XII, pope (1334–42): 106
   n. 110, 241 n. 147
Benedict (XIII), pope (1394–1417):
   181, 267 n. 26, 270 n. 41
benefices: 18–22, 27–48, 50–66, 68–
   78, 84, 87, 97 n. 70, 118, 123–41,
   230 n. 58, 270
   *see also* expectancies, apostolic;
      dispensations, apostolic;
      permutations; provisions,
      apostolic; reservations
   accumulation of: 31, 41 n. 73, 44,
      72, 130, 185 n. 58
   consistorial: 19, 181, 266
   devolution of: 172
   minor, lesser: 19, 28, 181
Benigni, Paola: 232, 254 n. 224
Berardus Ercoli de Narnia: 260 n.
   262
Berlin: 24 n. 35
Bernkastel: 49, 58
Bertholdus: 107 n. 111
   Herwici de Cruceborg: 128 n. 43
   Institoris de Satzungen: 128 n. 44

Bertrand de Got
   *see* Clement V, pope
Bertrandus Bertrandi de Maletanis:
   113 n. 152
Bibra: 126, 128
Bindo de Senis: 113 n. 153
bishops: 19, 29 n. 114, 46, 59, 102,
   131–32, 137 n. 72, 171, 251 n.
   206, 273–75
Blasius de Molino: 226, 228, 232 n.
   68, 237–38, 245
Blondus, Gasparus: 63 n. 81
Blumenau, Laurentius: 50 n. 10
Bocksdorf, Dietrich: 147 n. 111
Bodzęta de Wreśna: 87, 93, 103
Böninger, Lorenz: 248 n. 187, 261 n.
   264
Bogufalus de Couale: 93
Bohemia: 58 n. 55, 90, 100–01, 113,
   121, 140, 145, 151–53, 257 n.
   241
Bolesław of Toszek: 90 n. 41
Bolko of Ziębice: 100 n. 81
Bologna: 68, 72–73, 77, 85, 98, 103,
   105, 107, 137 n. 71, 150, 230
Boniface VIII, pope (1294–1303):
   17, 110–13, 201, 203 n. 11, 212 n.
   51, 265, 269
Boniface IX, pope (1389–1404):
   141–42, 144–45, 182–83, 186 n.
   62, 188 n. 77, 191–92, 217 n. 76
Boppard: 40–41
Borchardt, Karl: 124 n. 30
Bordeaux: 201–02
Borgia, Rodrigo: 265
   *see also* Alexander VI, pope
Borgo San Lorenzo al Mugello: 248–
   49, 254
Borislaus of Gniezno: 90 n. 40
Bossinger, Konrad: 63 n. 82
Bourges, Pragmatic Sanction of: 45
   n. 85, 193
Branda da Castiglione: 39 n. 62

Brandenburg: 121
Bremen: 80, 125, 128, 277
Brentano, Robert: 75
Breslau: 69–70
    see also Wrocław
Brieg
    see Brzeg
Brixen: 58 n. 53, 62–64
brokage: 165
Bruille, Furseus de: 239
Brunswick: 67, 70, 72–73, 80
    and Lüneburg, duchy: 68, 72
Brzeg: 83
Bulach, Gebhard: 63 nn. 80 and 82
*Bullaria, bullatores*: 130 n. 58, 186 n.
    65, 189 n. 77, 234 n. 81, 261, 264,
    268
Burgundy: 58 n. 55, 133 n. 64, 173,
    214 n. 62
Bussi, Giovanni Andrea: 61 n. 70,
    63–64
Bytom: 84

Calabria: 114 n. 162
Calixt III, pope (1455–58): 258 n.
    242
canon law
    see law, canon (church)
canonries: 28–29, 37 n. 51, 44, 46, 55
    n. 38, 75, 118, 157
canons: 19, 27, 29–30, 41, 54–55, 63
    n. 82, 67, 69–73, 85, 88, 91–92,
    100, 120, 152, 187–88, 274
cardinals: 19–20, 32, 39, 52 n. 20,
    59–62, 98, 109 n. 116, 178 n. 8,
    180, 184 n. 146, 189, 194, 196–
    97, 202, 207, 213 n. 59, 236, 238
    n. 117, 264–66, 272–74, 277
Carinthia: 140–41
Carniola: 141 n. 85
Carvajal, Juan: 58 n. 55, 128 n. 46
Capua: 111 n. 129
Casimir the Great: 102 n. 91

Castile: 160, 171 nn. 95 and 99, 173
celibacy: 19
*Censimento Bartoloni*: 236, 276–78
ceremonies: 60, 99, 213–14, 237–38,
    246, 256, 263–64, 271–76
    see also coronations
Cervantes, Juan, see John of Segovia
Chamber, Apostolic: 34, 38–39, 86–
    87, 91–92, 96–97, 102 n. 94, 110,
    114 n. 157, 130 n. 58, 144, 180–
    86, 188–90, 192–93, 201, 203–
    05, 207–12, 214, 216, 218, 221 n.
    90, 234, 237, 240 n. 129, 243 n.
    153, 266 n. 18, 268–71
Chamberlain, Apostolic: 20, 59 n. 56,
    97, 179 n. 17, 186, 188, 190, 202–
    04, 207, 215–18, 227, 249, 266 n.
    18, 272 n. 54, 274–76, 281
Chancery, Apostolic: 19–20, 32, 34,
    38–40, 42, 89 n. 34, 94 n. 57, 99,
    102 n. 94, 144, 179 n. 14, 184–85,
    223–62
    see also abbreviators; Vice-
        Chancellor, Apostolic;
        correctory; proctors, curial;
        scribes, curial
chaplainries: 29 n. 13, 47, 68
chapters: 19, 46–47, 166, 188
    at cathedrals: 50, 72, 78, 131, 140
    at domes: 19, 28 n. 11, 42, 122
    rural: 124 n. 30
Charlemagne: 161
Charles IV, emperor: 107 n. 114,
    150–51, 215
Charles of Hungary: 114 n. 161
Chelmno: 86, 106 n. 109
Chersones: 151
China: 157
Chittolini, Giorgio: 235 n. 89
Christianus, *magister*: 107 n. 111
Christopherus de Sancto Marcello:
    39 n. 62

Clement IV, pope (1264–68): 214, 277 n. 74

Clement V, pope (1305–14): 109, 201–02, 204, 210 n. 40, 212

Clement VI, pope (1342–52): 181

Clement (VII), pope (1378–94): 191, 216

clergy: 22, 32, 46–47, 56, 60, 68, 74–76, 78, 80, 138, 181, 202, 210, 213, 215, 272
*see also* monks

Coburg: 124 n. 30

Colberg, Katharina: 223 n. 1, 263 n. 1

collators: 21, 28–29, 31, 34–36, 42, 44–47, 169, 171, 243, 245

collectors, papal: 37, 66, 69, 102, 146–47

colleges
*see also* cardinals; guilds, as professional corporations
of curial officials: 20–21, 175, 185 n. 53, 199, 203–04, 217–21, 249, 252–54
of royal officials: 159 n. 20, 165–66

Cologne: 39 n. 64, 50, 55, 125

Colonus, Andreas: 140 n. 85

compositions: 34–35, 97, 182, 187, 249 n. 193

conclave: 202, 213 n. 59

concordat(s): 17, 45, 47 n. 50, 135, 173, 193, 198 n. 132, 243–44
of Constance: 45 nn. 86–87, 197–98, 243–44
of Genezzano: 244 n. 163
of Vienna: 28, 45–48, 77, 129–30, 137–38, 147

Condulmer, Francesco: 39 n. 62, 238 n. 112, 260–61, 265

confiscation: 55 n. 35, 57 n. 48

Constance: 121, 153, 213
*see also* concordat(s), of Constance

Council of: 17, 44–45, 59 n. 56, 70, 76, 131–32, 145, 178, 180 n. 21, 189–90, 196–98, 217–18, 245, 272 n. 53

Constantinople: 40 n. 68, 49 n. 4, 168

Cornelius de Blanca: 239

coronations: 84 n. 6, 86, 88, 90–92, 96, 204, 211–15, 237, 272 nn. 55–56, 274

correctory: 39 n. 62, 256, 268–69, 281

Cossa
*see* John (XXIII), pope

Cossebaude: 139

counsellors
*see* jurists

Couriers: 20, 185 n. 52, 201–21, 227 n. 30, 234 n. 79, 280

crusades: 168, 178, 246–47

Cunow: 89 n. 36

Curia, Apostolic: 17–18

*cursores*
*see* Couriers

Cusa
*see* Kues

Cusanus
*see* Nicholas of Cusa

dal Pozzo
Bartolomeo: 223–26, 228–32, 254
Giacomo: 230 n. 54
Toscanelli, Paolo: 39 n. 62

Daniel, Friedrich: 126

Datary, Apostolic: 34, 173 n. 117

d'Avray, David: 24 n. 36

de Aleis, Petrus Bartholomei: 63 n. 81

de' Baglioni, Lodovico: 69 n. 10

Derneburg: 44 n. 83

Desiderius of Bistorff: 63 n. 81

Deutsch-Brod: 141 n. 85

Diener, Hermann: 23, 28 n. 5, 236–37, 247 n. 180

Dietrich
    Lamberti of Goch: 152
    of Nieheim: 68
    of Xanten: 63–65

dignities, ecclesiastical: 19, 28, 45 n. 88, 77, 90, 129, 250 n. 199

diplomatic, papal: 24, 117, 233, 236, 251 n. 206, 255 n. 231, 263, 278

disability, physical: 31

disclaimers (*non obstante*): 18 n. 9, 33 n. 32, 36, 94, 97 n. 67

dispensations, apostolic: 22, 33 n. 33, 43, 62, 97, 110 n. 123, 166, 182, 185–86, 250 n. 198
    *see also* requirements, canonical
    for incompatible benefices: 32, 39–40, 95, 98 n. 70, 129–30
    from minimum age: 31, 153, 159
    from pastoral duties: 28 n. 11, 123–24, 127 n. 40

dispensations, royal: 159, 165, 167, 172

Długosz, Jan: 83, 87

doctorates: 49, 68, 72, 108, 249 n. 191

Dörrig, Joachim: 62 n. 75

Dominicans: 83 n. 5, 91 n. 47, 151
    *see also* mendicants

Dominicus, *episcopus Methelinensis*: 91

Dorolf, Simon: 40

Dorpat: 67, 69–71

Dortmund: 39 n. 64

ducats: 41 n. 73, 130, 203, 205 nn. 16 and 20, 207–08, 211 n. 48, 214 n. 62, 249 n. 193

Ebersdorf: 139 n. 81

Eckard, Johann: 141 n. 85

Egg: 141 n. 85

Eifel: 55 n. 38

Eisfeld: 124 n. 30, 127

Elbe, River: 121

Elm, Kaspar: 179 n. 16

Ember, Johann: 67, 70, 72

Empire: 23, 27–28, 74, 77, 87 n. 27, 118–19, 121–22, 124, 130 n. 57, 132–38, 142, 144, 165 n. 61, 194 n. 112, 235 n. 89, 245, 250 n. 196
    *see also* Frederick III; Charles IV; Germany; Sigismund; towns; Wettin
    electoral princes: 49, 124–29, 138–40
    imperial diets: 38 n. 60, 58 n. 55

Enea Silvio Piccolomini: 30 n. 22, 38 n. 46, 42 nn. 74 and 77, 64
    *see also* Pius II, pope

England: 30 n. 21, 47 n. 95, 56 n. 38, 58 n. 55, 157–58, 165, 198 n. 132, 215, 276

Erfurt: 72, 124 n. 29, 126, 128, 152

Estonia: 67, 71, 80

Esztergom: 90 n. 41, 107 n. 112

Eugene IV, pope (1431–47): 17, 40, 46 n. 92, 55–59, 118–19, 121–24, 132, 134–38, 184 n. 65, 189–91, 195–97, 212 n. 50, 219–20, 235–38, 243–44, 250, 258,

Excommunication: 55 n. 35, 107, 177, 218–19, 251 n. 206

execution, mandates of: 32, 36, 39, 94, 119, 144

exemptions: 15 n. 1, 141–48

expectancies, apostolic: 21, 30–31, 33–34, 44, 47, 99, 101, 124–26, 133 n. 55, 139, 258
    for poor clerics: 29 n. 12, 227 n. 28, 269, 278 n. 76
    for public offices: 166, 171

expectancies, royal: 167, 172

## GENERAL INDEX

*familia, familiares*: 32, 42–43, 45 n. 86, 58–63, 68, 101, 180, 202, 238–39, 270

fees: 19–20, 46, 132, 160, 165–66, 168, 171, 182–84, 186, 188, 210 n. 40, 219, 229 n. 44, 249, 251–53, 271

*see also* annates; *servitia*; compositions

Feldbach: 141 n. 85

Felix (V), pope (1439–49): 28 n. 7. 124 n. 29, 138 n. 76

Fermo: 113 n. 151

Ferrara and Florence, Council of: 272

Fieschi, Lucas: 114

Fijalek, Jan: 105–06

Florence: 137 n. 71, 183 n. 39, 238–39, 245, 248, 255

formularies: 106, 147, 251, 255–56

France: 30 n. 21, 157–58, 161, 163, 165–68, 170, 174, 181, 189, 201–02, 213–14, 276

Franciscus, *magister*: 86, 89–92, 103, 107

François de Conzié: 179 n. 17, 212 n. 56

Franconia: 128

Franken, Konrad: 126 n. 37

Frankfurt: 15, 41 n. 69

Fredericus, *magister*: 107 n. 111

Frederick III, emperor: 139, 154, 221 n. 90

Frederick the Gentle: 123, 125, 128, 137, 139, 154

Friedrich of Bibra: 127–28

friendships: 37–42, 57–60, 64–65, 68–69, 71, 190–93, 262

Frenz, Thomas: 247–48, 255 n. 231, 277–79

Frosinone: 109, 114 n. 162

funerals: 209 n. 35, 212–13

Furnes: 94–96

*gabella*: 221 n. 90

Galhardus de Carceribus: 107 n. 110, 114 n. 161

Gandersheim: 44

Garsitz: 138

Genezzano

*see* concordat(s), of Genezzano

Gentilis de Montefiore: 89 n. 38, 92

Gerardus de Randen: 58 n. 51

Germany: 13, 23, 30, 43, 45, 50, 56 n. 38, 58 n. 55, 67, 69, 74–75, 77–79, 121–23, 134–35, 144, 157, 194 n. 112, 276

Gerward of Włocławek: 87, 91–94, 96–97, 103, 112

Girgensohn, Dieter: 237 n. 107

Głogów: 102, 106

Golden Rose: 213 n. 59

Gordon, Sally: 16

Gniezno: 92, 99, 104, 107–08

Görlitz, Johann: 140 n. 84

Goslar: 67–69, 70

Graber, Tom: 117

Grado: 238 n. 134

Gratian, *Decretum*: 162

Great Britain: 22

Great Penitentiary: 44 n. 83, 118, 186, 213

Great Schism: 17–18, 28, 30 n. 21, 45, 144–45, 148, 173, 177–79, 181–84, 189–90, 192–94, 196–97, 199, 216–17, 256, 267

Greek Church, church fathers: 57

Greffe, Otto: 128

Gregorius Matheus Bartholomei de Puteo: 229 n. 46

Gregory XI, pope (1370–78): 178 n. 8, 187 n. 39

Gregory XII, pope (1406–15): 68, 190–91

Gregory of Heimburg: 50–51

Grossenhain: 129, 154

## GENERAL INDEX   329

*grossi*: 127, 205 n. 16, 209 nn. 32–33
   and 35
Grotowicz, Jan
   *see* Johannes Grotonis
Grove, Ludolf: 67, 70–72, 77–78
Guelfs: 72–73
guilds
   as monetary currency: 92, 98–99,
      114 n. 162, 127, 132, 153–54,
      247
   as professional corporations:
      159, 166, 168, 172, 182, 184
      n. 48, 186 nn. 62 and 65, 188,
      190, 193
Guilelmus
   de Sanguineto: 90 n. 41
   Testa: 92 n. 50
Guillemain, Bernard: 189
Gundolt, Georg: 126 n. 37

Haberlant, Nikolaus: 140 n. 84
Habotey, Geoffrey: 58 n. 55
Haiger, Ernst: 16
Halberstadt: 67, 72
Hamburg: 157, 209 n. 37
Hanover: 15, 24, 49 n. 1, 67–82, 157,
   256 n. 254
Hanseatic League: 69
Hartning, Johann: 141 n. 85
Hartungus Molitoris de Cappel
   junior: 141 n. 85
Haugwitz, Georg: 123–24, 129, 137–
   38
Heidelberg: 49
Heimerus de Campo: 58 n. 54
Heinrich
   Engelhard of Salza: 124, 141 n.
      80
   Stoube of Goch: 137 n. 71
Helmstatt, Rhaban of: 54 n. 31
Helwig of Boppard: 41 n. 69
Henry of Wrocław: 85 n. 16
heresy: 110, 162, 177, 257 n. 241

Herde, Peter: 255 n. 231
Herzberg, Johann: 140 n. 83
Hilde, Thomas: 242 n. 143
Hildebrand de Gusenicz: 129
Hildesheim: 15 n. 1, 67–68, 72–73
Hoffmann, Johann: 127, 154
Honofrius Francisci de Sancto
   Severino: 260 n. 262
Honorius III, pope (1216–27): 201,
   263
Hostiensis: 162–63
Hotz, Brigitte: 120
household, *see familia, familiares*
Hugonis, Christian: 140 n. 83
Hundred Years War: 173
Hungary: 92, 100 n. 81, 107 n. 112,
   114
Hussites: 141, 146–47

Idensen: 44 n. 83
illegitimacy: 31
immunity: 100, 160, 167
   fiscal: 99, 113 n. 148
   judicial: 58, 60, 245
Imram: 84
Incus, Damarus: 62 n. 79
indulgences, apostolic: 43, 135, 139,
   173, 182
Innocent III, pope (1198–1216): 22,
   165, 201, 264, 267, 270–72, 276
Innocent VI, pope (1352–62): 60 n.
   63
Innocent VII, pope (1404–06): 145
Investiture Contest: 169
*iocalia*: 188 n. 22, 213 n. 59, 231 n.
   62, 259 n. 250, 271
Irdning: 140 n. 85
Ireland: 22
Italy: 17, 22 n. 28, 30 n. 21, 50, 69,
   73–74, 157, 168, 173, 179, 193,
   202, 208, 213, 219, 245

## GENERAL INDEX

Jacob of Sierck: 41, 46 nn. 92–93, 54
n. 30, 56 n. 39, 58 n. 53
Jacobus:
Bigneti: 239
Blasii de Verulis: 113
de Oratoribus: 58 n. 55
Jakob Baruth: 140 n. 85
Jakub of Gniezno: 85 n. 16
Jarostius: 89 n. 38
Jean de Brogny: 265
Jerusalem: 238
Jews: 213 n. 59
Johann
Bulkenhagen: 139
of Echte: 126 n. 36
of Eisenberg: 149
of Jentzenstein: 151
of Kittlitz: 152
of Magdeburg: 139
Rodenberg: 126 n. 36
Schak de Schuneburg: 140 n. 84
Tylich: 142
Johannes
Baptista de Mellinis: 239
Boccamazza: 109 n. 118
de Angeroles: 239
de Regio: 113 n. 153
de Verulis: 88, 90–91, 93–97,
109–13
Grotonis: 87–89, 91, 98, 103,
106–07, 112
Laurentii de Pontecurvo: 111 n.
131
Montani (de Montanya): 230 n.
53
of Raesfeld: 63 n. 78
of Stetenberg: 63 n. 78
John XXII, pope (1316–34): 29 n.
15, 44 n. 83, 59 n. 60, 85–90, 92,
95, 98–02, 108–09, 111 n. 131,
113–14, 178 n. 8, 255 n. 231, 265
John (XXIII), pope (1410–15): 68–
69, 77, 192, 267 n. 26
John: 215 n. 71

of Bohemia: 101 n. 91, 107
of Capistrano: 139
of Segovia: 38 n. 56, 42–43
Jubilee: 17, 182 n. 33
Judenburg: 140 n. 85
Julich (and Berg), duchy: 46 n. 93
Julius II, pope (1503–13): 28 n. 5,
175 n. 23
jurists: 18 n. 10, 45 n. 90, 50 nn. 7
and 10, 74, 76, 120, 123, 130, 137
n. 71, 175

Kalocsa: 114
Kamień: 84, 142, 145
Koblenz: 53 n. 26, 55 n. 38, 64 n. 92
Konrad
of Kirchberg: 150
of Sarstedt: 67
Kraków: 83–115
St Mary's: 87, 96
Krebs:
see also Nicholas of Cusa; Römer,
Katharina
Dietrich: 55 n. 37
Henne (Johannes): 49, 55
Johannes: 52, 55 n. 37, 58 n. 53
Matthias: 52
Kruszwica: 87 n. 29, 92 n. 50, 104
Kues: 49, 52, 55, 58 n. 53, 64 n. 90
Kule, Johann: 140 n. 84
Kuyavia: 85

Latvia: 80
Laudun: 111 n. 129
Laurentius
de Albertis: 248 n. 188
de Wratislavia: 111 n. 131
Laval, Gasbart: 97
law: 58 n. 55a
canon (church): 18–21, 74, 105–
08, 119, 127, 143–44, 164–
78
Roman: 162–63, 165

GENERAL INDEX    331

Lebus: 152

legates, apostolic: 58, 61–63, 105,
    143, 147, 267 n. 25

Leiden: 50

Leipzig: 72, 124 n. 29
    St Georg: 139 n. 83

Lejeune, Jean: 231 n. 59

Lello de Mevanca: 92 n. 50

Lenczyce: 86

Leonardus Melioris de Verulis: 115

Leubing, Heinrich: 124 n. 28a, 137 n.
    71

Leuschner, Joachim: 157 n.

licenses, papal: 22 n. 25, 52 n. 16,
    135, 182 n. 33, 185, 220

Liege: 57 n. 50, 111 n. 129, 133 n. 64

Limoges: 60 n. 61, 192

Livonia: 67, 69–71, 73, 77–78, 80,
    121 n. 22

Loire, River: 189

Lorraine: 121 n. 22

Louis XII, king: 168

Louis of Bavaria, emperor: 99

Louvain: 58 n. 54

Lower Saxony: 28, 68, 80, 182 n. 33,
    256 n. 236, 277

Ludovicus
    de Garsiis: 230
    de Orto: 230 n. 56
    (Trivisano) de Venetiis: 230 n.
        56

Ludwig, duke: 83

Lübeck: 67, 69–73, 77–78, 151, 202

Lüne: 67, 73, 76

Lüneburg: 67–68, 70, 72–73

Lusatia: 141, 145

Luther, Martin: 170

Lutkehus, Hermann: 130

Luxemburg: 131

Lyon, Councils of: 271


Maesheim, Heinrich: 38–39, 41

Magdeburg: 121–24, 125, 131–32,
    139, 143–47, 150–54

Mainz: 38 n. 61, 50 n. 8, 58 n. 53,
    125, 128, 141 n. 85
    Acceptation of: 133–34

Mair, Martin: 50 n. 10

Manderscheid: 54–55
    Ulrich of: 54–56, 63 n. 80

Marino da Eboli: 272 n. 54

marriage: 30, 62

Martin V, pope (1417–31): 17, 34,
    70, 132, 189–91, 195–97, 217–
    18, 232 n. 68

Mathias de Paluca: 111 n. 132

Mecklenburg: 121

Medici: 69–70, 154
    see also banks

Meissen: 15 n. 1, 117 n., 121, 127–32,
    137–54
    margraves of: 131, 142–45, 147,
        149, 151–53
    St Magdalen: 125, 127

mendicants: 72

Mengeler, Wigand: 63–64

*mensa*: 19, 88–90, 92, 98–99, 132

Merseburg: 121, 132, 138, 144 n. 99

metropolitans: 143, 145, 147

Metz: 43, 46 n. 93

Meuthen, Erich: 121

Meyer, Andreas: 34, 36, 263 n. 2, 267
    n .23,

Milan: 157 n. 6, 160, 235 n. 89

military orders: 273
    *see also* Teutonic Order

Minden: 44 n. 83, 67, 72–74

monasteries: 30, 53, 99, 191

monetization: 180 n. 20

Mongiano, Elisa: 28 n. 7

monks: 19, 71

Montaigne, Michel de: 210 n. 39

Montpellier: 214 n. 62

Moravia: 140

GENERAL INDEX

Moraw, Peter: 56 n. 38, 74 n. 21, 120–21
Mordek, Hubert: 83 n.
Mos, Johannes: 140 n. 85
Moselle, River: 49
Mousnier, Roland: 35 n. 43, 158 n. 14, 161, 167
Mrozowicz, Wojciech: 83 n. 1
Münstermaifeld: 40 n. 68
Münzmeister, Paul: 127
Mundel, Paulus: 128
Muskata, Jan: 85–87, 89–90, 92, 103, 105 n. 96
Muslims: 173, 182 n. 33

Nagel, Ludolf: 67, 71, 77
Nanker Ingrami: 83–115
Naples: 60 n. 61, 190, 192
nations (*nationes*): 45, 84, 105, 107, 198 n. 132, 245
Naumburg: 121, 126, 129, 132, 138–39, 151–53
nepotism: 53, 65, 76, 190–91, 196 n. 118, 199 n. 133
Netherlands: 24 n. 35, 38 n. 61, 57–58, 165 n. 61
Neustadt: 141 n. 85
Nicholas (V), antipope (1328–30): 178 n. 8
Nicholas V, pope (1447–55): 17, 46 n. 92, 63, 124 n. 31, 139, 250, 261
Nicholas of Cusa: 37–42, 46 n. 93, 49–56, 147
Nicolas de Pellevé: 210 n. 39
Nicolaus de Verulis: 109 n. 116
Nikolaus of Elstraw: 141 n. 54
Nisan: 150
nobility: 27, 32, 42, 50, 54–56, 73–75, 78, 101, 107, 120, 131, 160, 171, 235
*non obstante*
    *see* disclaimers

notaries, curial: 185–86, 188–90, 234 n. 81, 258, 260, 264–68, 271–74, 280
nuns: 44 n. 83
Nuremberg: 52 n. 61

oaths: 94–95, 147, 154, 183, 190 n. 85, 202, 209, 215 n. 71, 217–18, 226 n. 25, 231, 238, 244, 259, 264 n. 10, 271
obediences: 17–18, 55 n. 38, 179, 181, 189–90, 192
Ösel: 67, 70–71, 79
offices, public: 158, 160, 163–65, 167–68, 170, 173
    *see also* venality of offices
officials: 45, 158–60, 164 n. 50, 168, 171–75
    curial: 15–16, 18–21, 58, 180 n. 21, 186–87, 192–93, 198–99
Oksza: 86
Oldenzaal: 58 n. 53
Oleśnicki, Zbigniew: 83 n. 4
Olomouc: 100–01, 140 nn. 84–85
Ones, Nikolaus: 140 n. 85
Opole: 100–02
Ordinations, clerical: 19, 49 n. 4, 119, 123
Orsini
    Giordano: 38–39
    Marinus: 260 n. 258
Ottomans: 157, 168

Pacoslaus: 89 n. 37
Padua: 49–50, 57
Palatinate: 40–41
Papal States: 90, 109 n. 116, 157, 161, 171 n. 101, 191 n. 92, 202, 275
*parlements*: 159 n. 18, 164 n. 54, 172
Parliament: 157–58
Pasco: 100 n. 80
Passau: 148
patriarchs: 238, 266, 272 n. 54

patronage: 51, 56, 63–65
    lay: 29, 46, 54 n. 27, 68, 72–73,
      76–79, 81
Paul II, pope (1464–71): 248, 276 n.
    64
Paul VI, pope (1963–78): 201, 233 n.
    75
Paulus Andree: 100 n. 80
Pavia and Siena, council of: 196 n.
    122
Pavón Ramírez, Marta: 254
penance: 139
penitentiaries, minor: 106 n. 109
Penitentiary, Apostolic: 185–86,
    189–90, 197, 203, 233, 250, 277
    *see also* Great Penitentiary;
      penitentiaries, minor
pennies: 105 n. 100, 20 nn. 209
Pentel, Hermann: 67, 73, 78
Percivallus de Verulis: 109 n. 116
permutations: 21, 29, 44, 94–95, 127
    n. 39, 159, 169 n. 86
Peter
    of Byczyna (Bitschen): 83
    of Erkelenz: 63–64
    of Schaumburg: 63
Peter's Pence: 86
petitions: 21–22, 24, 118, 121–23,
    132–36, 167, 227, 234–35, 242,
    245, 250–52, 269
    see also *rotuli*
Petrus: 114 n. 157
    Bertrandi: 109 n. 116
    Bertrandi junior: 109 n. 116
    de Alvernia: 112
    de Mera: 38–41, 58 n. 54
    de Molendino: 58 n. 54
    de Noxeto: 259 n. 255, 261
    de Sancto Laurentio: 114 n. 157
    de Verulis: 109, 113–14
    Iacobi militis de Verulis: 113
Philip
    of Burgundy: 57 n. 50

    of Fermo: 105 n. 103
Pierre
    de Monteruc: 265
    des Prés: 265
Pinnenberch, Johannes: 128
Pisa, Council of: 153, 182
Pitz, Ernst: 35
Platina, Bartolomeo: 248–49
plenitude of power: 17, 21, 169–71
Pofi: 114 n. 162
Poland: 24 n. 35, 70, 83–115, 157
Pomerelia: 86, 91
Pomert, Heinrich: 64 n. 91
Pomezania: 106 n. 109
Porchnev, Boris: 161
Portigal, Johann: 140 n. 83
Portugal: 276
possession: 31, 35–37, 129 n. 50
Potitus, St: 238
Poznań: 49 n. 1, 91 n. 47, 101 n. 88,
    104, 108
Prague: 113, 140–41, 143, 145, 149,
    151–52
prebends: 28, 35
Prechen, Christian: 62 n. 79
Przecław of Pogorzela: 105 n. 96
procedure, romano-canonical: 146
proctors: 68, 70, 73, 91–92, 140 n.
    85, 256
*propina*: 59 n. 59, 167 n. 71, 183
protonotaries: 32 n. 26, 182 n. 35,
    241–44, 266 n. 19, 273–75
*provinciale*: 144 n. 100
provisions, apostolic: 27–30, 33–36,
    42, 44–48, 99, 132, 135–36, 166,
    266, 269–70
    *see also* expectancies; offices,
      public
    dating clauses: 31 n. 25, 33, 36–
      37, 125–26
    *fiat ut petitur*: 33 n. 33
    *motu proprio*: 38–39, 125–26,
      129, 255

*perinde valere*: 33, 39 n. 63
*si neutri*: 31, 128 n. 48
provisions, by lay rulers: 171–72
provisions, in kind: 214, 270
Prussia: 58 n. 55, 70, 121 n. 20
Puntel, Mathias: 140 n. 85

Quirre, Ludolf: 67, 72, 78

Rad, Nikolaus: 141 n. 85
Ranboldus: 89–91
Rapp, Francis: 177
Raskop, Heinrich: 58 n. 54
*referendarii*: 32 n. 26, 195 n. 116, 228,
    234 n. 82, 253, 266 n. 17, 274–75,
    280
Reform: 44, 177–79, 185 n. 53, 187
    n. 69, 189–90, 194–200
Reformation: 17, 80, 147, 194–95
*regalia*: 163
*Regulae cancellariae apostolicae*
    *see* Chancery, Apostolic;
        rescripts; style, curial
Rehberg, Andreas: 235 n. 89
Reinhard, Wolfgang: 37, 57, 99
Reichenau: 27 n. 1
Reichenbach, Christian: 139
*Repertorium Germanicum*: 23, 28 n. 5,
    79, 119, 121–30
requirements, canonical
    *see also* dispensations, apostolic
    holy orders: 30 n. 22, 49 n. 4, 52
        n. 16
    residency: 28 n. 12, 31, 95 n. 62,
        159
rescripts: 35, 99 n. 77, 255
Reseler, Dietrich: 67–71, 79
reservations, apostolic: 21, 29–30, 33
    n. 43, 38, 45, 94, 131, 133, 138,
    169 n. 85, 243–44
resignations: 21, 31, 44, 46, 97, 159,
    165, 167–70, 218, 260
    *simonia iuris*: 52 n. 17

Reval: 71
Rhine, River: 24 n. 35, 58 nn. 54–55
Richardi, Heinrich: 141 n. 85
Riga: 67, 70–71
Rike, Berthold: 67, 70–71, 77–79
Robertus de Ponte: 112 n. 141
Rochetaillée, Jean de: 237, 239
Rodestock, Sigismund: 63 n. 81
Römer, Katharina: 49
Rome: 15, 22–23, 40 n. 68, 50, 67 n.,
    73, 80, 83 n., 138, 146, 157 n. 6,
    201, 219–21, 235 n. 89, 238, 272
    Anima, confraternity: 124 n. 29
    *Palazzo della Cancellaria*: 226
    San Celso: 221, 258
    San Giuliano: 221, 258
    San Marco: 226 n. 24
    San Pietro in Vincoli: 61 n. 70, 64
        n. 92
    St Peter: 111
    via Banchi Nuovi: 221
    via del Pavone: 221 n. 89
Rosellus de Hugonibus: 261 n. 268
Rostock: 71–72
Rota: 18 n. 4, 68, 128 n. 43, 185–86,
    213, 221 n. 91, 233 n. 79, 266,
    274, 281
    *see also* Audience (*Audientia*), of
        Contradictory Letters
        (*Audientia literarum
        contradictarum*)
*rotuli*: 61, 126 n. 32, 194 n. 109
Rudolf of Planitz: 140 n. 85, 154

Saalfeld: 139
Saarema, *see* Ösel
sacraments: 19
sale of offices
    *see* venality of offices
Salzburg: 140 n. 85, 148
San Genesio: 92 n. 150
Sandomierz: 85, 87 n. 28, 104, 108
Santiago de Compostela: 111 n. 129

Savoy: 121 n. 20
Saxony: 120–48
Scarampo, Luigi: 39 n. 62
Scarbimir: 104
Schaper,
  Dietrich: 67, 73
  Johann: 73
Scheitler, Heinrich: 140 n. 83
Schele, Johann: 67–68, 70
schism: 178 n. 8
  *see also* Great Schism
Schlick
  Kaspar: 139
  Matthias: 139
Schmidt, Tilmann: 202–04
Schönberg
  Dietrich: 128, 139 n. 79, 150, 154
  Kaspar: 128–30, 139, 154
Schöner, Christoph: 23, 78–79, 118–
  20, 122 n. 21
Schuchard, Christiane: 47 n. 98, 66 n.
  97, 179 n. 15, 190, 194 n. 112
Schwarz, Brigide: 9, 15–16, 20, 23–
  24
scribes, curial: 19–20, 22, 165–67,
  185–86, 188–89, 203, 233–36,
  240–42, 249, 251–53
Sens: 210 n. 39
Sergeants at arms: 185–86, 189–90,
  209 n. 35, 211 n. 48, 213 n. 59,
  215–16
*servitia*: 21 n. 23, 59 n. 69, 86–87, 98,
  132, 149–54, 180–81, 202, 210–
  11, 270
Seuberlich, Johann: 140 n. 85
Sicily: 160
Siena: 68, 219 n. 84, 230
Sieradz: 85–86, 103
Sigismund, emperor: 137–39, 153–
  54, 230
Silesia: 69, 83–84, 86–87, 95, 107 n.
  112, 110, 140
Simon

de Marsow: 92
of Wehlen: 61 n. 70
simony: 19–20, 34–35, 94, 126–27,
  162–63, 169, 196
sinecure: 19, 28 n. 12, 127 n. 40
Sixtus IV, pope (1471–84): 46, 144
  n. 99, 217 n. 78, 248, 271 n. 48
Spain: 22 n. 28
Speyer: 54 n. 31, 120
Spisz: 107 n. 112
Spitko: 89 n. 37
Sponheim: 55 n. 38
Stam, Johannes: 63–64
statutes
  corporate: 20, 105, 202–05, 207–
    12, 215, 217–20, 231 n. 61,
    254, 264 n. 7
  diocesan: 106, 108
  papal: 105
Stephanus de Pelagio: 113
Strozzi:
  Antonio: 259 n. 252
  Carlo di messer Palla di Nofri:
    254, 259–61
style, curial: 32–34, 240, 244, 249 n.
  191, 251–52, 268
  *see also* rescripts
Styria: 141 n. 85
Stzrelczyk, Jerzy: 84 n. 7
suite: 52 n. 20, 58–61, 194 nn. 108–
  09
  see also *familia, familiares*
Sulejów: 86, 88
Swartze, Heinrich: 140 n. 84
Switzerland: 276

Tallinn, *see* Reval
Tancred of Bologna: 162–63
Tannenberg: 69
Tarantaise: 260 n. 258
Tartu, *see* Dorpat
*taxae*
  *see* fees

## GENERAL INDEX

Tetenborn, Heinrich: 126 n. 38
Teutonic Order: 69–71, 76–78, 80, 87 n. 28, 91
theology: 83, 151–52
Therouanne: 94
Thomas: 90
Titel: 114
tithes: 40, 99, 102 n. 93
Topór: 89 n. 36
towns: 27, 41–42, 45 n. 90, 50 n. 10, 68, 72–74, 78–80, 140 n. 85, 157, 173, 209, 215, 264 n. 7, 273–74
Trani: 113
translations
    *see also* permutations
    episcopal: 99, 101 n. 89, 131, 151–52
Traversari, Ambrogio: 238
Trent, Council of: 141, 197
Trier: 41, 46, 49–51, 53–58, 62–63, 125
    St Simeon: 52, 58 n. 53
Tropea: 114 n. 162

universities: 18–19, 27, 31–32, 43–45, 47, 49–50, 72–75, 77–78, 123, 178 n. 11, 196 n. 120
Uniejów: 98 n. 73
Urban V, pope (1362–70): 131, 216 n. 74
Urban VI, pope (1378–89): 151, 178, 181–82, 192
usury: 162–63
Utrecht: 122 n. 21, 133 n. 64

vacabilists: 20, 188–89, 220, 245–46, 248–49
vacancies, papal: 210–11, 264, 270 n. 42
Valerius Iacobi de Viterbio: 261
Veldenz: 55 n. 38
venality of offices: 20 n. 18, 157–75, 199, 220, 237, 255 n. 231, 259, 263

Venice: 160, 165 n. 64, 167–68, 171 n. 96
Verden: 130 n. 60
Veroli: 90, 109, 111 n. 129, 113–14
Vespasiano da Bisticci: 237 n. 107
Vestri, Veronica: 232
Vice-Chancellor, Apostolic: 20, 33–34, 186, 188 n. 75, 226–28, 230–31, 234 n. 81, 237–40, 248, 253, 256, 259–61, 263–81
    *see also* Chancery, Apostolic
Vienna
    *see* concordat(s), of Vienna
Vienne, Council of: 110, 113 n. 53, 271–72
Villach: 140 n. 85
Virneburg: 54–56
    Rudolf of: 55 n. 38
Viterbo: 110, 264 n. 7
Vitus of Wrocław: 102 n. 94, 112 n. 135
Volkmar of Anderten: 67, 72–73, 78
von Hofmann, Walther: 179 n. 14, 195 n. 115, 220 n. 87

Wall Street: 18
Walter of Gouda: 38 n. 60, 58 n. 54
Weber, Max: 170, 237
Weiß, Stefan: 214, 266 n. 18
Wenzel, king: 144, 151–53
Wettin: 121, 124, 131, 137–42, 144–46
    *see also* William
Wetzlar: 151
William, duke: 139
    Monoculus: 142
    the Younger: 144
Willich, Thomas: 122
Windisch-Gräz: 140 n. 85
Wiślica: 104
Wittego of Colditz: 149
Wittlich: 55 n. 32

GENERAL INDEX 337

Władysław Łokietek, king: 84–93,
95–96, 101, 103–04, 107–08, 111
Wolfenbüttel: 80
Wolfsberg: 140 n. 85
Worms
chapter: 38–41
St Martin: 38
Wrocław: 69, 83, 85, 89, 92–93, 95–
96, 152, 98–109, 111–13, 140 n.
85
*see also* Breslau

Würzburg: 124 n. 30, 127, 138
Wurzen: 123, 138

Zbigniew ze Szczyrzyca: 86 nn. 21–
22, 90 n. 42, 103
Zeitz: 122, 129–30, 138
Ziegenbock, Nikolaus: 151
Ziegenhain, Otto of: 53–54
Zoppot, Konrad: 63 n. 82
Zurich: 27–28, 36–37, 42–44